Ritchie
Mined

Ritchie's Perfect Press • Seattle

Ritchie Mined - Voume I
1969 - 2009
by Bill H. Ritchie

Assisted by Nellie Sunderland

Ritchie's Perfect Press
Division of Emeralda Works
500 Aloha #105
Seattle WA 98109

ISBN: 978-1-387-78923-8

Preface

Ritchie Mined is designed after the Time Life series, "everything worth knowing." However, that was a series of picture books. People subscribed and a book arrived in the mail every month. Wikipedia describes the example, *Time Life Photography*:

> "For example, the series Library of Photography of the early-1970s featured very high-quality duo-tone printing for its black-and-white reproductions in its original edition, and was of course able to draw on *Life* magazine's vast archive of journalistic and art photographs from virtually every major photographer; *Foods Of The World* featured contributions by Julia Child and many others. . . . The content of these series was more or less encyclopedic, providing the basics of the subjects in the way it might be done in a lecture aimed at the general public."

Paraphrasing, or copy-writing, explains *Ritchie Mined*:

The series in *Ritchie Mined* is able to draw on Bill Ritchie's archive of journals dating from the 1960s from virtually every year of his career. Samples from the Ritchie Family Art Collection and art by others are included in the Kindle e-book version published in 2010. Text entries in this paperback version give fleeting glimpses of Ritchie's ideas over the years, sometimes drawing on the Ritchie Video Archives. Summaries of essay subjects are the main content of *Ritchie Mined*, an encyclopedic accounting as it might have been presented in a 20th Century slide show lecture to a college class.

As a digital monograph giving a comprehensive catalogue of musings by an artist— Ritchie Mined has the essential elements of a catalogue raisonné: (a) it purports to be an complete list of works for (b) a defined subject matter (c) describing the works in a way so that they may be reliably identified by third parties. However, no pictures.

When one of our daughters, Nellie, and I published the first *Ritchie Mined* series in 2010 as an e-book, I thought there might someday be a paper version, with all 11 volumes under one cover. It would have been too costly then. This is no longer a problem since just-in-time publishing is here and so a paperback version is now ready.

However, considering that one of the *Time Life* series—*Time-Life Music*—is still viable, attests to successes of electronic publishing. Something like this applies to *Ritchie Mined*. Digital publishing was part of my plan to augment higher education channels by making professors' minds available online in an electronic publishing form. Our first e-book series was designed for Kindle, amazon.com's e-book reader. It's still there, in color, for a nominal fee.

Of hundreds of thousands of art professors still working and retired, I am but one; but I am one to whom anyone—student or not—is now able to go to one of my virtual, imaginary place - *Emeralda Region* and visit one of my islands-of-domains-of-expertise. In this book or online one may read over three thousand of my abstracts.

The ebook Kindle also has hundreds of images, digitized, compiled and edited. Some the electronic version's pages are decorated with handwritten journal excerpts, collectible *Artist Trading Cards* and *Artists Stamps*.

As shown later, I can also go to the full text of the essay with a few keystrokes using the index numbers that go with each abstract.

Why? One may wonder. I think that, within this work, the answer is self-evident.

In April, 2018 I counted the number of 'Zine essays - articles I wrote whose abstracts I created up to the end of 2009 - and the total was 3,026 nested in roughly 700 Mb of space on the computer hard drive.

Purpose

My original purpose in creating Ritchie Mined was to give future art students and interested scholars an online opportunity to "pick a professor's brain."

In a perfect, old-fashioned world, a student might get insights by this kind of picking, in effect looking into the professor's knowledge base by raising a hand and asking questions in a classroom setting.

Or they may gain knowledge from the professor at a chance encounter at a store or a coffee shop. Opportunities increase for the student if they are in a small class or a seminar, even more so if they are working one-on-one with the professor. Graduate students usually have these better chances.

Opportunities for "picking the professor's brain" is one of the advantages of higher education. Students in high school seldom, if ever, have the chance to learn from their teachers on deeper levels. Teachers at all levels posess wellsprings of knowledge that they could share with their students, but the opportunities to share this knowledge in detail are rare.

Today, thanks to the Internet, students can read their teachers' blogs - something like picking their brains. Ideally, professors could publish their work online so students don't have to buy their books, or they can keep a blog anyone can access.

Students can use the Internet this way or they can get a proessor's database like buying this one as an online ebook - a Kindle Book or other platform, and read them on their PCs, Macs, or mobile devices.

There are many opportunities today, not like the old days when it was hardly possible to know any more about a teacher's knowledge and experience than what the professor taught in class. For their part, the professors had to shoehorn their knowledge into one-hour sessions, giving only what was required for students to pass the course.

Game-changer

When I was teaching on a campus I had an eye-opening experience that proved to me the value of my knowledge. I was reading many books on a range of topics and many of them were about things outside the courses I was teaching. My reading notes are on three-by-five cards. By the fourth year of teaching, I had several boxes containing hundreds of reading-note cards.

One day I showed these cards to students in one of my printmaking classes. To my surprise, a student asked if she could borrow all of the boxes! She assured me that she would take good care of them. She was a college teacher, too, taking courses to advance her degree. As a teacher, she knew the personal value that these cards meant to me

and understood my reluctance. I said okay.

When she brought them back, my boxes were bristling with little pieces of paper with comments. Some were suggestions for further reading; others were short exclamatory remarks like "Wow!" and, "This is so TRUE!" It was like chatting over coffee, something she and I would seldom have opportunities for nor within the limits of class time.

From that experience, I learned some students are interested in learning more about my knowledge than what is being given in the classroom. They wanted to learn more than the outline of the curriculum. Some students wanted deeper insights from me as their professor, and, possibly, from their other professors. They wanted to "pick their professors' brains."

Years later, when I was learning information technology, computer databases and thinking about artificial intelligence, I found the term *mining* information. Picking someone's brain means "mining" someone's database of knowledge.

There are mountains of knowledge in a human mind, deep wellsprings of experiences and wisdom. Looking for gold or diamonds, a person mines for them in a mountain. Seeking nuggets of wisdom or bits of glittering knowledge, a student may now mine a teacher's mind. These nuggets or threads are waiting to be found and used by anyone who is interested.

Students want and deserve mining equipment and maps to mine their teacher's knowledge base. The tools are there in laptops and mobile devices.

In this my *Ritchie Mined* project, my purpose is to provide opportunities for students (or anybody who is interested) to "mine" my knowledge and experience without needing to ask me directly.

My ideas, concerns and hopes (and, sometimes, anguish) is in journals I wrote in almost daily for four decades. No longer on reading notes on three-by-five cards like the ones I lent my student years ago, what is in *Ritchie Mined* are the subject lines and searchable abstracts of my essays (unpublished articles). Some I wrote in my journals, others on computer, and some were transcribed from videos by one of our daughters, Nellie Sunderland.

While it may be my purpose in offering my mind to students and scholars will turn out to be futile, but I have already been rewarded personally. At 76 and living in my golden years, I find a small pleasure in opening up my Kindle versions on my smart phone and breezing through the musings of a younger me - mining my own mind.

Scanning started when teaching

I had a lot to say, and I all the means at my disposal to say it. My UW career peaked in the 1970s. I could describe a typical day in my printmaking classroom as exciting. I recall day in particular. It was the middle of the morning in an etching class, a work period for everyone; across the hall students were working on lithograph stones.

One of the etching students brought me a zinc etching plate she was working on, evidently to ask a question. But she had to wait while I explained to someone from across the hall why her lithograph was too light.

In the corner three students were fiddling with a TV camera and one called to me from the video setup: "Mr. Ritchie, is this tape cued?" He was referring to the kind of open, reel-to-reel videotape recorder we used to tape my demonstrations.

Now it was the girl with the etching plate's turn; she asked me, "How do you do it? How do you keep track of all this?" Amid these print productions, experiments in video art, how did I manage solving myriad technical problems?

"I pretend it's like a radio dial. I tune in to something—teaching, research, practice, or service—and focus on it. Like changing channels," I said, and I took her plate and put a magnifier on it. "Your plate is etched enough, yes."

It was wonderment: in one room people were experiencing teaching, research, and practice. If, as it did happen on occasion, a visitor wandered in for a look, also service. These four were happening at the same time, or concurrently. I was calm, because I loved it; here were the four cornerstones of university life: Teaching, Research, Practice and Service I came to call the TRPS Principle.

Across the campus was the UW Hospital—a teaching hospital. I'd read about the concurrent approach to medicine that started in Scotland in the 1700's. The same approach—teaching, research, practice and service—could be taken in art. I called the idea my "Perfect Studios."

My concurrent notion took shape slowly, as I had no idea where this path would lead. Maybe, if I had known it would mean the end of my career at the UW Art School, I would not have taken this path. It may have worked in medical schools and teaching companies, but could it work in art school?

A working study experience abroad, in 1969, had ignited a change in me. Like an explosion in slow motion, foment of the '70s in America rippled through everything And there was Viet Nam. The times were changing, and I wanted to change with them. My great notion, *Perfect Studios*, was the right idea, the right time and right here, on the job at the UW School Of Art was the only place.

Or, so I thought.

Architecting Perfect Studios

To design my Perfect Studios, I went inside myself and examined my career. I thought about my successes so far, and those of my students. I hypothesized these successes owed to diverse kinds of expertise.

I counted ten skills ranging from the newest digital technologies to the oldest printmaking methods and artistic practices, public speaking, teaching, computer graphics, and more, all connected, overlapping and complementing one another. Ten would serve as a convenient numeric base for a new curriculum. The eleventh was the entry level I call Interval.

Were I to actualize this idea at the college level and not in a corporation, then I would need to change the existing UW printmaking curriculum. To justify this I needed proof of my hypothesis that print is the ancestor of technologies and that there was evidence of a global trend in this direction. In 1982 an opportunity arose to make a tour of printmaking and electronic studios around the world, and I took it.

After the travel and study in fifteen countries I was certain of the ancestral connection of old and new technologies—video and computer graphics with printmaking. My mission was then to convince the faculty and administration of the UW School Of Art that a progressive curriculum would be advantages for current and future students - and former students, too.

Nineteen eighty-four was a decisive year for my "Perfect Studios." The art faculty rejected the notion of blending printmaking with new media. I resigned the next year. Unlike the medical school across campus, the university's School Of Art was not the environment, not the time or place where I could actualize a model of a concurrent teaching, research, practice and service.

Therefor I left university teaching in 1985 to search for my "Perfect Studios," an educational environment suitable for art students who would practice in the 21st Century. They'd need something similar to a teaching hospital (or teaching company) where the four pillars of higher education in art would support one roof, as today what are called *incubators* and *accelerators*.

The four activities would be concurrent in this environment. Electronic arts were central to this idea, connected in some way to traditional printmaking.

Influence of my college professor, Sarah

I was a college student in 1962 and I lived in my professor's two-story rental house in Ellensburg, Washington. My painting professor, Sarah Spurgeon, had a modern rambler on the other side of the fence she shared with another professor, Amanda Hebeler.

Between them, their book collection was so big that Ms. Spurgeon had to keep most of hers on the second story of her rental. While I lived in it, he said I had the run of the several rows of shelved books and that I could use them any time.

Sarah Spurgeon, named her rental *Purser Place* after one of her favorite students, Bob Purser star student who was a year ahead of me in class. We both lived there, in successive years, while getting our degrees at Central Washington State College.

When it was my turn, Sarah (she insisted her students call her Sarah) approved my choice of house-mate and I shared rent with a psych major, Bob Biersner, who had the upstairs bedroom next to the library. We both loved Purser Place.

The house was a skinny, two-story structure that was originally a barn built around the turn of the century, or so I I was told.

Since I was raised on farms in the Yakima Valley - fifty miles from Ellensburg - out there in the boon docks we didn't have access to private libraries like that at Purser Place. I made it my goal to have a library like Sarah's someday.

After graduation from Central, I went on to get a Masters of Arts degree and then a position at the University of Washington. By 1985, I had it all - like Sarah - a professor's title and a home with a growing library.

My dreams of being a professor, and having all the accoutrements of the profession – like a library and a studio – were coming true. But in another twenty years I downsized and kept only a few choice books.

Looking back, I wonder what became of Sarah's library. She died in 1985. Purser Place was still sitting on the alley behind the rambler the last time I stopped. In fact, once I entertained a concept to save Purser Place as a historic landmark and use it to start a Leadership Training School for senior citizens. So I went to check on it.

On that visit I walked along old familiar alley that goes past Purser Place. The door was wide open, so I stuck my head in and called out "Hello."

A woman who was packing boxes and moving out answered my call. She let me look around the old place. It was the same as I remembered it. No doubt Sarah's library was long gone. I wondered what became of her collection.

What happens to professors' libraries when they retire and pass on? I had seen many libraries in professors' homes during my career, but as for me, I never needed a whole room to keep all my books. Those I read were from libraries; many I bought I gave away or sold - but I kept my reading notes on computer media after 1979. Those that pre-dated my computers I eventually keyed in or dictated with voice-recognition software.

Today, thanks to computers, there is no need for a room-sized library. There is also no need to give special permission to your students to use one's personal library. Bob Purser and I had privileged access to our professor's wealth of reading material, but today, there is no need for preferential treatment.

But, is a professor's library really all that special? Speaking personally, it is for their students as it satisfies curiosity. What kinds of books does a professor read? Can a student get insight into the professor's teaching by seeing what books they keep on their bookshelves? I believe a private library is a reflection of the owner's character.

For example, finding a compendium of children's stories alongside a biography of Dylan Thomas, makes a person wonder, *How do those subjects connect?* If the books are arranged in neat, alphabetical order, it reflects something about the nature of the owner.

The traits that can be discerned in a professor's library, might be the traits a student needs to pursue to become a professor. No doubt that, at my impressionable age during those days in 1962, that this notion crossed my mind while looking at Sarah's library at old Purser Place.

Now, although nothing remains of Sarah's library, her memory remains in the name of the art school's gallery a mile away from Purser Place. There, in real life and, in virtual reality, in several places on my computer (like right here, for example).

My memory of her library is special. It became a model, the groundwork for a metaphor for a new and better kind of professor's private library where, not only his or her books are stored and wehre titles and authors are listed but also where more insight into the professor's mind is can be tapped, their brains picked, and even their methods and character.

Still, people might wonder, *Who Cares*? After all, if I had *not* been privileged to have access to Sarah's library, would it have occurred to me that I was *not* so privileged? Out of all the art majors, as far as I knew, Bob and I were the only ones who had access to Sarah's private library. What effect did her library have on our education? We both succeeded in becoming art professors, too.

How much better (as students) were Bob and I, actually? We may have had a little more skill, hand-eye coordination and patience. We may have had whatever it took to get A's and advanced degrees in art. Were we distinguished or gifted in any special way? Or was it being in the right place at the right time that gave Bob and me access to Sarah's library, a glimpse of her inner sanctum.

Dumb luck?

Whatever, I think the incident of a college professor giving her students access to her library is rare and a privilege. It's one more reason I created this compendium of my musings and essays - a kind of bound blog on paper.

My way, the Information Highway

The age of digital reproduction changed this for every student in any professor's course - or for people who are not the professor's students, or people who are not even students! Anyone can enter a professor's inner sanctum if the professor puts his or her library into digital form.

This system is in place so everything that a professor wrote and said in their teaching career is in a cyber library. Their mass-produced publications would be listed along with their unique, unpublished articles, private journals, diaries, manuscripts, screenplays and miscellany. These are things that have disappeared in the age of mechanical printing due to the professor retiring, losing their mental faculties or dying.

Dead Professors keep on Teaching

Well into my college teaching career, I experienced another awakening in 1983. My family and I were on our way across the country and we stopped in Montana. Our older daughter, Billie Jane, had a friend who lived near Flathead Lake. She is related to my old college mentor, Reino Randall. He had a brother, Arnie, who was also a college art professor. They were also both chairmen of their art departments.

We were invited to visit Arnie's widow at home, really their dream home on a tiny island on Flathead Lake. He was working on it when, tragically, he died. His daughter gave us a tour of the house—an unusual work of architecture (as you might expect of an art guy). As she opened the door she said words that were branded on my brain:

"This is where Dad kept his things. We don't know what they are." I stuck my head in the door to see what she was talking about. I recognized What it was, instantly. Boxes of slides, portfolios and sketchbooks, files burgeoning with notes and articles spanning forty years of college teaching, research, practice and service to his community. All resigned to a room on a rock in Montana, imprisoned in a sense. Like Alcatraz.

A chilling thought came over me: I had a room just like it!

Techno-teaching

It wouldn't have to be that way for me, not this art professor. My contact with older artists in their sixties, seventies and eighties—people like Sarah Spurgeon, Rolf Nesch, Stanley Hayter, Maria Guaita—helped me to see the value of a teaching artist's life work. Since 1968 I had logged my thoughts in journals. In 1979 I started using a computer, an Apple II+. I digitized my reading notes. After thirty years they reside on my computer - upgraded with each technical improvement.

Even as I write now, it's possible that someone might be reading the notes I wrote in my Blog, the popular web log since the Internet went with the World Wide Web. All my notes could be found online by students – or anyone – curious enough to read them. They can be found by people who are curious to know what I have read and of what I took note.

Finally it has come to pass that any teacher can keep his or her brain alive with the aid of a computer. That is what my 'Zine database is about. In the '90s, when electronic publishing was the way of the future, I extended my reading notes to notes on my own thoughts. No longer were my ideas confined to private journals and diaries. Nor were my current reading notes kept in little boxes on three-by-five cards. Now everyone has access to what has been on my mind at different times in my life.

For a small fee.

Mapping *Ritchie Mined*

After I left the UW, I missed campus life, especially the students. Briefly I worked at The Evergreen State College—a more experimental college; a short stay at the University of Oregon came next. They proved better, but I couldn't stay.

That meant there was no place for me to try again to re-conceive printmaking education to fit the times. I was out of luck; I was, at best, an itinerate professor with no campus to call home. So I made up *Emeralda Communiversity*, a kind of haven for printmaking education located in an imaginary region I named *Emeralda*.

Through the next decade, building on the basis of TRPS and my hypothesis of ten domains of a printmaker's education, I architected and built *virtually* my imaginary school on a gigantic lake dotted with ten island domains-of-expertise. Listed alphabetically, That is why the eleven sections have titles like ArtsPort, Electronic Studios and Art Galleries (or E'Studios) and so on. The eleventh is called Interval, an interim five-day orientation session set in Emeralda City.

The Emeralda Region has four cities bordering a huge lake, is like a huge artist's retreat or colony. Ten "islands-of-domains-of-expertise" dot the lake. I call the region a *communiversity*.

In this fantasy region, a reader might imagine being on one of the islands and coming upon a teacher's cottage and studio. Like in *Goldilocks and the Three Bears*, and finding no one home. Instead is a professor's studio. The professor is absent, and instead of hot porridge on the table, there's a workbench, an etching press, a sleeping computer workstation and a library of books in a corner.

Browsing through the teacher's journals and computer files, you would find something like what this volume contains - my ideas, an old professor's musings, written and indexed in my eleven-domain-based system, supposedly on this secluded island on days when I resided here. I call these collections on these ten islands, 'Zines.

The Boss of Emeralda

There was a period at the turn of the century when distance-learning was being developed and I thought about teaching printmaking online. Many experiments in distance learning failed because the media have a language of their own and unless the language is mastered by the teachers, then the teacher's content cannot be communicated. The failed examples are the boring, poorly conceived efforts by teachers accustomed to the old ways and mores.

I may not escape my times, but in a region like Seattle where video games are made, I pursue my dream of making a college-level printmaking course for online with a game-like interface made out of my great notion of TRPS and *Emeralda*.

My virtual land - Emeralda - is already in place, an alternate universe already mapped. It is a paradise but, like a too-long vacation, it can be boring. Reading how-to books on digital storytelling, I learned that I needed a conflict to liven it up.

Also I needed permission to go there to kickstart the story, such as a prize. I'd been reading about a 19th Century genius named Elmer Gates, and that gave me the idea of the *Gates Prize*, the way you win entry to Emeralda. You have to be really good to go!

In many computer games there's a *boss*, a significant computer entity to be defeated. I had to be really good to win and, once in Emeralda, I had to defeat the boss. Strangely, in my treatment of the plot line, the boss turns out to be Elmer Gates.

Not the real Elmer Gates, of course, because the real Elmer Gates was a good guy in my opinion. In my legend of him, he's not evil. Besides, he died in 1923.

However, these things were happening when I was wondering how artists could respond to the *Union of Concerned Scientists' Warning to Humanity* I read in 1992 - the same year I named Emeralda. I zeroed in on carbon dioxide as a main problem we face. This connected with the boss, a significant computer entity to be defeated because he (or she) is part of the problem of carbon dioxide and other gases contributing to environment problems.

Thus, to gain entry to Emeralda Region I had to win the Gates Prize, and to win I had to teach, research, produce and give service to the community.

Like the Emeralda Region itself, the Gates Prize for Great World Teaching is a fantastic idea, an imaginary award for an imaginary world. I created the imaginary place and then I created the imaginary award to get me there.

So it was in 1996 that I first won the Gates Prize. Yes, as the reader might have guessed, I awarded it to myself! I believe others can win; but to win, they must first learn about Elmer Gates.

Here's a quick tutorial: Elmer Gates' name appears in a book by Napoleon Hill titled *Think and Grow Rich*. That's where I found it. Hill explains the value of concentration and a focused mind, and the kinds of discipline and vision that go with invention, creativity and discovery. Elmer Gates is an example.

Elmer Gates (1859-1923) was a pioneering neuroscientist. A child prodigy, he was home-schooled and self-taught in many disciplines. By 1900 he had achieved wide notice and was sought out for his theories of "mind-growing," i.e., the idea that a person could develop more brains by self-discipline and meditation.

He proved his theory not only by empirical experimentation but by inventing numerous practical devices himself. The US Patent Office awarded him about 200 patents for his inventions. He knew a number of other leading innovators in his day such as Edison, Ford, and others.

Elmer Gates became more interested in education in his later years since he determined that learning was the core of his mission in life. He called his discipline *The Art of Mind-Using*.

He envisioned a world school and a cadre of world teachers. Sadly, his mission was doomed to fail in part because he was not a business man and there was no partner to help him carry on his life work - except for one. His works would have been lost except for the aid of a loyal, dutiful sister-in-law who saw to it that his records were organized and saved.

In the sad ending of his life he was alone and bankrupt. He died with only his loyal help mate, Pearlie, beside him. Years later, one of his sons wrote his biography.

Late in the 20th Century (now a hundred years after Elmer Gates envisioned his new school) I had been thinking there should be a prize for great teachers who may have shared his vision - something on the order of the *Pulitzer* or *Nobel Prize*.

This idea imprinted itself on my mind. I gave a name to this imaginary prize: *The Gates Prize*, but actually it was before I'd heard of Elmer Gates. I was thinking locally of the Gates family living in my own part of the country, the Bill Gates of Microsoft fame.

But of course it would be embarrassing (or worse, people warned me) to use the Gates' name without the family's knowledge. So when I happened to find the older Gates in Napoleon Hill's book, I adopted Elmer Gates' name.

With amazement I read Elmer Gates' biography titled, *Elmer Gates and the Art of Mind-Using*, written by Donald Gates. Gates' pioneering work pointed more clearly to education than even that of our local hero, Bill Gates. Of course his family founded the *Bill and Melinda Gates Foundation*, which is the world's largest endowment for education, among other things.

The *Gates Prize* is part of my Emeralda Suite of games I'm inventing. I call these *Games for the Gifts of Life*, a key element in the background story for my wishful dreaming where teachers, learners, researchers, practitioners and community servants would be invited to live and work for 360 days in a paradisaical land with like-minded people.

Years of Living Copiously

Three-hundred sixty days - nearly a year - living and working in Emeralda Region are divided among the ten islands-of-domains-of-expertise. The year begins on December 15, but there are four or five days of orientation called *Interval*.

These days consist of learning the rules and etiquette of practice and research on the islands. The Emeralda year has 360 days divided into cycles commensurate with the ten islands. Thus, a combined total of thirty-six days are devoted to the islands where the winners, known as *Residents-in-Stay*, carry out their teaching, research, practice and service.

Because of the richness of the year living in Emeralda Region, it's called a *Year of Living Copiously*. *Copious* refers to *Copia*, the sense of plenitude. In my quest for a meaningful, productive life, these are my days of freedom to pursue my passions for teaching, productivity, research and service. Here I'm enjoying freedom to blend the art and craft of printmaking with art philosophy, history, technology, economics and social sciences.

One of the experiences I completed was to document my days on a hand-held, mobile device that came on the market in 1989. It fit in my pocket and opened like a clamshell to reveal a small screen and a tiny Qwerty keyboard and stylus. I used it for ten years, noting every minute, every waking hour of the days - my "days of living copinously."

With an alphanumeric indexing system I devised, and because this device included a connecting cable it could transfer my notes to my desktop computer. Using this routine, I compiled my notes into ten volumes I titled *Years of Living Copiously*. When self-publishing via online services came along twenty years later, I made these electronic notes into paperbacks averaging around 200 pages each and made them available on lulu.com, the service I employed to make them.

Definition of Emeralda Region

Every year winners of the Gates Prize are given 360 days to spend in Emeralda Region, plus five days' orientation sessions - Interval - in Emeralda City, gateway to the ten islands-of-domains-of-expertise on the Great Lake of Emeralda Region. This book contains ten years' Zine essays and journal notes by Bill Ritchie collected and configured as part of all winners' tasks. This section will help the reader understand the context of these Zine entries.

Discovery legend

Emeralda Region was discovered on a computer sometime between 1985 and 1993. The discovery was gradual, coming about through fragmentary notes collectively titled *Women Who Fell to Earth* by a mid-twentieth century self-made ITinerate art professor. He claims that bits and bytes of the narratives were leaked to him via silicon-based chipsets found in his outmoded digital computer and a palmtop—an Apple II+ and Casio B.O.S.S.

In a distracted and meditative state, (this professor's meditative state was achieved by studying Elmer Gates' methods he called "mentation.") he described typing out his discovery of Emeralda "as if the words, the letters phosphorescent green on a black ground, were already there on my vintage Apple's dark screen. My keystrokes were merely uncovered them, as though they'd been buried in the guts of my new machine." They were dictated by "ghosts in those new machines," he said, and he took notes in those devices, transcribing, as best he could, the messages and wondering, "Are these from the past, present or future?"

Geography

Emeralda Regions are located in six places on Earth. For the purposes of this definition the locations of only two are discussed.

The first is in the area of the Mediterranean Sea off the coast of France. The site is not far from Cosquer, on the southern coast of France. The second is between the United States and Canada—and is the center of focus here.

The exact locations of these two landing sites have never been charted. They compare to the Land of Oz, Middle Earth or Mount Analogue. (See See Manguel, Alberto& Gianni Guadalupi. *The Dictionary of Imaginary Places*. Harcourt Brace Jovanovitch. NY. 1980-87.) The obscurity is likely due to a high concentration of the mineral beryl, (Beryl is sought in semiprecious gemstones Morganite, Aquamarine, Yellow Beryl and Emerald) creating an invisible force shield that confounds all methods of ordinal measurement.

The most notable and, for the purpose of explaining the games of Emeralda, most important feature of the Emeralda Region is its great bottomless lake. Surrounding this are three mountain peaks, unique for their symmetry and equal distances from each other. Seen from above, they form the points of an equilateral triangle.

The peaks are called *The Three Sisters*, and individually their names are *Techne, Media* and *Aurel* named after three of the four Women Who Fell to Earth. A fourth peak is hypotheical, and likened to an inverted peak at the deepest point of the lake. It is named for the fourth sister, *Tetra*. The professor speculated that here was the tip of the huge spacecraft plunged deep into the heart of the Earth, like thte tip of a spear, forming the lake's deep center. These four apexes form a tetrahedron, the outlines of the aliens' spacecraft. There are no islands in the lake's center owing to its depth.

The lake is in part spring-fed (giving rise to the expression, *deep well of knowledge*) and partly by melt-off from the Three Sisters' peaks, giving the water magical qualities. Remarkably pure water swells to the surface from the source of Tetra. Some believe that if you drink this water you will benefit from Tetra's deep well of knowledge, and the same can be said of the other sisters' runoff.

Ten islands ring the edge of the Great Lake of Emeralda Region. Their characteristics are described later in this text as Islands of Emeralda Region or *Islands-of-domains-of-expertise*.

History

In ancient times, according to the professor, a sextuplet—four women and two men from a place known as *Flower Planet* AKA *Fleura*—landed on or fell to Earth about 30,000 years ago. This astronaut family of was on a mission, the professor thinks, to conserve Earth's human biological and intellectual sustainability.

He fears, however, that their main goal was to save Earth's trees and flora, and that human life sustainability was at best a side effect to be tolerated, and, at worst, an obstacle. It is useful to note the aliens' morphology is based on silica instead of carbon, as human biology is, which accounts for their immortality and ability to infect silica-based computer chips.

Our focus, the Emeralda Region of the Pacific Northwest, is the site of the landing of one of the spacecraft. The four immortal sisters on such craft are the heroes in Emeralda folklore based in this particular area and most familiar to those who reside here. Another craft is thought to have landed in the Mediterranean—as mentioned above.

In modern times, hints of Emeralda's existence come as evidence of shared creative experiences among humans who explore imaginary places. The professor himself describes his discovery as being like returning home after being institutionalized for nineteen years.

After his escape from the institution, and with his nucleus accumbens undamaged, his story covers a recursive, creative life on Emeralda's ten fantastic islands that reflect the characteristics of his notion of a perfect studio. His residence on each island domain-of-expertise threw his desired self into relief and clarified his self-image.

Today, Emeralda players (mostly artists, writers, musicians, poets, and other civilized, humanistic people) use both old and new technologies to add to the Emeralda Archives, logging stories, songs and poems in these using digital systems creatively. The authors call these activities games, or *Emeralda Play*.

Plays of kinds that seem to have similar qualities are collected into suites or collections. The game structures are ineffable, not unlike the *Glass Bead Game* of Hermann Hesse in his novel, *Magister Ludi*, published in 1969 - the same year as the professor's epiphanous, first study abroad trip to Europe, visiting Rolf Nesch, S. W. Hayter and other creative printmaking pioneers.

City States of Emeralda Region

Four city-states are situated around the lake at the cardinal points, each having its own capital. On the North is *Emeralda City*. To the East is *Centri City* and, opposite it across the lake, *Eccentri City*. At the southern edge is *Toxi City*, the polar opposites culturally, structurally and functionally of Emeralda City. The cities to the east and west sides of the lake have mixed cultures blending characteristics of Emeralda City and Toxi City.

Emeralda City is the point of departure for certain players who receive the *Elmer Gates Prize*. This award is from a secret society devoted to the ideals of a 19th Century brain scientist, a person of high creative powers and moral virtues who envisioned a corps of World Teachers. The Elmer Gates Foundation owns the Emeralda Region and selects winners of the Gates Prize based on creative promise and service to Earth Human Life Sustainability.

Islands of Emeralda Region

There are ten islands in Emeralda Region, referred to as *Domains-of-Expertise*. They are homes to Communities-of-Practice in ten skill areas. The following listing is alphabetic, and the list is also the sequence which visitors follow in the islands' circuit of the Great Lake of Emeralda. The ferry's traffic flow is fixed so that a regulated, continual circuit of the islands is ongoing.

Ways to explore Emeralda

(Or, "How to have fun with this book"))

Do you know Bill Ritchie? He may know you, and he may have mentioned you in an essay - or several essays among the thousands listed in this enclopedia of Bill's musings between the late 1960's until, in first volume, the year 2009.

If you have a CD/DVD drive on your device, insert the CD/ROM if one is included in this book and peform a search with your name. Try it. If you're not in this book, it's no wonder as few peoples names are to be found in this volume.

If Bill hasn't mentioned you, then try another kind of search: enter a date using the format of YYMMDD. In other words, the last two digits of the year - only numbers between 69 and 09 (1969-2009) followed by two-digit months (01,02, etc) and the days, again using two digits - 09,10, 11 - etc. A search may look like this: 020205.

If you get no meaningful result or garbage, try again by replacing the last digit or two digits (the DD) with the next larger or lesser number. If it ended with a 5, as in this example, change it to 6 and try again. Keep doing that until you get what reads like an essay.

I tried it myself in writing these instructions, and was pleasantly surprised when I found a six-page essay titled, "Memo to a former art student" with index number *sp980401*.

One might wonder, "That's not the same as the search term! The search term was 020205." You would be correct, but the search engine will bring up *anything* with a six-digit string, and in this instance the string happened to be the essay's character count, not the date. Surprise!

Incidentally, I was so taken by this chance occurrence that I printed out the essay - a long one - and mailed it to two former students with whom I had been communicating by email and social media. Additionally, these two individuals were quite opposite in character, like polar opposites among the levels I ascribe to student performance.

Try it yourself using the index number - or any of the index numbers you see listed among the approximately three-thousand essays listed in this book.

Additionally, note that the six-digit date number string is preceded by, or has a prefix of, two alphabetic characters. AP, for example, or ES and on through MR, OS, PP, PS, RI, SP, VI and VP. These indicate the Islands-of-domains-of-expertise in Emeralda: ArtsPort, E'Studios, MacRitchie's, O'Studios, Perfect Press, Perfect Studios, RIISMA, SPEACON, Video and Video 'N Print.

Sample Essay

In my search for an informative and entertaining method to find links, I went back to the 3,000-title 'Zine database. From the beginning of my writing, I knew that if I ever want to integrate the my content with digital reproduction of my visual arts and multimedia, then locations would have to be in a systematic, machine-readable format.

"Searching" seems to be a main feature of exploring the digital universe, so I set limits to my writing to meet this requirement; the SUBJECT field in the database had to be searchable; a paragraph summarizing the 'Zine article had to contain no more than 255 characters and spaces.

Combining this searchable feature with this publication let me locate one essay to use as an example to include in this section. So I put in the search word, "education," and 26 examples came up. The search term I used - education - showed many references to my teaching journey that came to a fork in the road, one might say, in the 1980s. Thankfully, I took the fork in the road that landed me in the position to teach in a new world via distance learning.

Looking at titles from my search, I found one that seemed appropriate to give the reader of this volume of *Ritchie Mined* as an example of my writing and I cut and pasted it here.

My choice, *es030912 Diary of the Absent Professor: Forty years and one week to get ready*, sounded appropriate. The word *absent* refers to my being gone from the 20th Century campus and a tongue-in-cheek insinuation, the oft-heard, *absent-minded professor*. Written in 2003, I was re-entering campus life in my own way - by accident. That Is, I was at Shoreline Community College as a guest and then I was offered an adjunct's job.

(Note: when I typed this sentence in rough draft, I mis-typed it and it read absent-mined professor; there's an interesting typo for you!)

Diary of the Absent Professor

(Subtitled)

Forty years and one week to get ready

Subject: The "absent professor" he calls himself because it's the theme of one concept in his online art education iteration, part of his life-long game, Emeralda. Given a week to prepare to re-enter a studio/classroom to teach fine art drawing, he's introspective.

Statistics: 1261 Words. 5677 Characters. 63 Pages. es030912 Diary of the Absent Professor. Copyright 2003 Bill H. Ritchie.

"Hey, I'm special!" That's what I'd like to say to the students who fill the room a week from now—their first day of college perhaps—and my 40th year! For them it's just another class at their community college, and I'm just another teacher. But I feel special. I feel like a very unusual teacher. In fact, it may be they'll wish they hadn't hired me because I'm so different.

I've been hanging around the college for a month and a half. It all started when one of the Summer School students sent me an email asking if I could contribute some moving video image time to her Web site project. We got together, and she introduced me to her faculty man who, it turned out, was an acquaintance of mine from 25 years ago. It was a very pleasant surprise; in fact, it seemed like we had just met a little while back and we were both, still, interested in art and technology.

I proposed my project I call "art education online" and he said the facilities of the college, during the break, might be used and that he'd help me. He did help me, too, and my research on using games as interfaces for hybrid online teaching of art went along very well. Then, out of the blue, the Visual Communications Technology Program manager invited me to teach a drawing class. Someone had suddenly decided they didn't want to teach that class and I was hired.

"Hey, I'm filling in for Mr. _____, but I'm special so that's okay!"

The question should come back, "What makes you think you're special?" That's a good question, and a fair one. Shall I tell my story? Or, shall I, to prove how special I am, apply what I've learned in the last 40 years? Shall I, for example, launch my game theory in this drawing class? There's evidence that I should, and here it is:

This is the age of digital reproduction. The Visual Communications Technology (VCT) program at this community college is mainly business and industry driven. Otherwise, you wouldn't see all the technology that they have. It's a joint-venture, sort of, between the faculty and the students. The faculty masterminded the program and, to pay for the hardware and software, the students pay a fee on top of their tuition and textbooks.

Okay, my time is running out, so I'll cut to the chase. Or, I'll cut to one of the chases. The VCT is business and industry driven, as I said, but everyone seems to agree that the element that makes people successful in this field is creativity and productivity. The combination of creativity and productivity comes down to an element that's hard to find in business and industry outside the campus—except in rare cases where there is a lot of money to buy the best creative person's time and ability.

While people are on campus, they can be more creative and original, perhaps, then they will be allowed after they leave. Or, if they plan to go on to another college, institute or professional school, they'll need to show evidence that they have what it takes. Therefore, in the mix of teachers they'll have, they need a few "special" people. And, I think I'm special.

It's hard being special. It's almost painful, and it's a little scary. For example, a day or two after I accepted the job of teaching basic drawing, I woke up feeling I'd made a big mistake. The more I learned about how things are done in basic drawing classes, the more like déjà-vu it became. Here I might insert that I taught basic—and advanced— drawing classes many times. Some say I was good at it, too.

But it was 18 years ago that I taught my last drawing class! The really odd thing I see, now, is that nothing seems to have changed. I was in a seminar a few years ago, about using new technologies in education. Someone remarked, "If a retired business person went into a business today—like a bank or a retail store—they'd be awestruck by the changes that have been made in the way things get done. There's a lot of technology! But if the same person went into a school or college classroom, they'd see a lot of familiar things going on."

That was ten years ago, and a lot has changed in those ten years. But when I think back to 1966, when I taught my first basic drawing class at the University of Washington, and I compare it to what I see at this college, very little has changed. It's like déjà-vu. Why, in 37 years, are beginning drawing students still doing the same thing, using the same tools?

Is it that some things never change, such as the visual arts and performing arts? I don't think so. When, after three years of teaching at the UW, I began to wonder if I had reached the end of the road in art (that my uphill climb from undergraduate to graduate school and into teaching college had leveled out) I got a ladder.

To keep that sense of climbing, I got an imaginary ladder and leaned it on an imaginary wall called "technology". I thought if I climbed up there and looked over that wall I'd see a whole new vista, new worlds to explore and maybe achievements I could make. I thought it was fun to achieve, to explore and—as a bonus—socialize with other people who felt that art was all about creativity and production.

That made me special. I was almost the only one in the art school who could manage to bring technology into the classroom/studios and, not only live to tell about it, but also go back for more. But my specialty was too much, and both the UW art school faculty and I got tired of each other and we parted ways.

I don't regret being "special." It's costly, yes, but it feels to me like something people should aspire to. The next challenge is to figure out how to engineer a drawing class so I can balance my "special" qualities with the expectations of the students. They're not expecting a "special" faculty person; it wasn't in the catalog nor does the course description include ideas like I have, e.g., the work of fine art drawing in the age of digital reproduction.

But if these students are to come out of school with above-average portfolios, I'd like to try to be one of the faculty team who helped.

••••

Ritchie Mined:
3,026 searchable essays if
a CD/ROM is included

If the reader has the CD/ROM database of the full text, then the essays listed here can be accessed on a computer. Choose the alphanumeric string on the essay wanted, for example, or keywords from the title.

Or, enter keywords of choice. These will bring random articles to choose from.

Another random search method is to use numbers only in the format of YYMMDD. In other words, the last two digits of the year - only numbers between 69 and 09 (1969-2009) followed by two-digit months (01,02, etc) and the days, again using two digits - 09,10, 11 - etc. A search may look like this: 020205.

If no meaningful result or garbage comes, try again by replacing the last digit or two digits (the DD) with the next larger or lesser number. If it ended with a 5, as in this example, change it to 6 and try again. Keep doing that until you get what reads like an essay.

I tried it myself in writing these instructions, and was pleasantly surprised when I found a six-page essay titled, "Memo to a former art student" with index number *sp980401*.

One might wonder, "That's not the same as the search term! The search term was 020205." You would be correct, but the search engine will bring up *anything* with a six-digit string, and in this instance the string happened to be the essay's character count, not the date.

ArtsPort (AKA as *AP*)

Artsport seen in the late afternoon, showing the eastern side. ArtsPort is populated with self-proclaimed experts in cybernetics.

This island is proximate to Emeralda City and connected by a daily ferry boat, but only from Emeralda City to ArtsPort. Once departing Emeralda City for ArtsPort, one cannot return to Emeralda City for 360 days—the duration of the Elmer Gates Prize Year-of-Living-Copiously.

ap780114
Journal Entry
Video Class Significance
The author writes about a "printing marathon" to make the Munch Posters. His class was shut-out and he missed his video class which he feels is his most significant teaching. Without teaching video classes, his job felt like a pointless comfort station. 270 Words. 1978.

ap791215
Journal Entry
The Dangers of Lundin
The author writes about the dangers of Norman Lundin, an enemy that returned and he represented the worst of academia. 352 Words. 1979.

ap850124
Journal Entry
Port Townsend
The author spends time at Port Townsend, a small town northwest of Seattle. He reflects on how Seattle is changing, wondering if artists are getting bored. Also reflects on his opportunities other than working at the U. 508 Words. 1985.

ap850315
Journal Entry
Deciding the End at the U.W.
The author decides that the end of his U.W. teaching career was over. Teaching basic art classes doesn't give him the fulfillment he needed. He wanted to teach graduate students. He hoped to set the record straight with a letter to the faculty. 276 Words. 1985.

ap871129
Journal Entry
Family History Repeating Itself

The author is comparing his own attitude towards his father when he was a teen ager and the attitude his oldest teen age daughter is showing towards himself. What is the same and what is lacking, but later will result in wisdom. 987 Words. 1987.

ap871215
Journal Entry
Hump-Day
The author is reviewing his half way marker through the 5 year evaluation after leaving the college art teaching and becoming a successful individual. He writes his thoughts about the art industry of the day. 457 Words. 1987.

ap880124
Journal Entry
A Reading in Rifkin's "Time Wars"
This is from the author's GoalBook1. The author writes notes of Jeremy Rifkin's notion of "simulation" brought about by increasing use of cybernetics in western culture. He includes a quote from Eric Jantsch describing a leader as a "manager-priest." 278 Words. 1988.

ap890615
Art Forum Proposal to CompuServe
Overview of proposal for online arts channel
A restored article from the proposal to CompuServe to have an art forum on line with specialties in Northwest arts and crafts suppliers. The author based his suggestions for online shopping on two arts and craft companies that originated in his community. 870 Words. 1989.

ap901107
Defining Art, Craft and Design
An Itinerate Professor holds forth
An anecdote about the definition of art and craft when the author was a visiting professor of art, newly defined as an itinerate professor, at The Evergreen State College in Olympia, Washington. He gives his students' the difference between art and craft. 393 Words. 1990.

ap900104
Journal Entry
The Rising of the Age of "Menipulation"
The author writes about menipulation. He considers the 50/50 split of people using computers and those who aren't. He also looks at economics and the foreign buyers of U.S. products. He writes his thoughts about the joining of dreams with fellow artists. 1344 Words. 1990.

ap901130
ToolBook Diary
Experiment with hypermedia
The artist who keeps journals and diaries will do well in his or her studio work, and also in relations with other people. New technologies, such as computers and word processors, provide an exciting new way to "hyper-journalize" and stimulate creativity. 1756 Words. 1990.

ap910307
A Proposal for A Radio Talk Show
Visualize a grove of seedling trees
Proposing to launch a radio show may seem like a departure from the Perfect Studios. This author developed this idea to bring a new kind of focus on process and he provides some guidelines for planning and the philosophy of the radio show, "Art Business". 1767 Words. 1991.

ap911107
Arts Wire's Funny Money Smell of Fasces
Art goes up in flames
The author is formatting an issue of Arts Wire, received over an online information service. As he works, many thoughts come to mind, reflections on the tone, or feel, of this electronic newsletter. The feeling grows that this is a political newsletter. 635 Words. 1991.

ap911206
C. T. Chew on Perfect U
Electric conversation between two artists
Bill Ritchie and C. T. Chew talked about reviving an artist's co-op from the 80s called "Triangle Studios." A Perfect Studio, in Bill's definition, is one where production, teaching and research go on at the same time. Triangle Studios was like that. 1457 Words. 1991.

ap910429
From Paper to Interface
Converting to multimedia navigation
Management by Goals is a paper-and-pencil process taking in long term, middle and short-term organization. Converting this to a hyper media software program, the author notes environmental issues come from the hold on press-and-paper values. 1115 Words. 1991.

ap911231
Print's Minor Elitism
Lament of the rejected writer:
This writer believes printing is a dying communication form, and a newspaper on crafts should, if it is to maintain its role in the crafts community, change with the times. The author was to write a technology column for a locally produced craft magazine. 636 Words. 1991.

ap911203
Publishing Pains
Train to change
Growing pains will visit the publisher who waits for the bell to ring before he or she goes to digital publishing. Learning how to remain a publisher for long will also involve pains of change, financial risk, plain difficult work and concentrated vision. 1556 Words. 1991.

ap911114
Three Artists Reinvent School
Perfect U
Following are notes prepared in advance of a proposed memo of understanding among C. T.

Chew, Bill Ritchie, and Norie Sato. The exchange shown is specific to the research, development and licensing of their distance learning concept they call "Perfect U." 918 Words. 1991.

ap911117
Wired Food?
Metaphors of the Information Technology era
The author saw perfectly good peaches lying on the ground in the orchard. He thought about the people miles away who would pay for those peaches. If only the peach could be turned into electronic data! Then it could be sent via telephone or TV. 1871 Words. 1991.

ap920520
ArtsPort Magalog Defined for the reinvented arts studio
One of ten magalogs of Ritchie's, Inc.
From Ritchie's, Inc. Business Plan, creative Words. such as Magalog are defined in terms of markets, audience, format and value. Magalogs are part of Perfect Studios and each division-like ArtsPorT--of the Perfect Studios has a representation in a Magalog. 329 Words. 1992.

ap920530
ArtsPort Magalogs Defined
From caves to computers
Each of Ritchie's Magalogs represents a business division and reflects the nature of the business of the division. The ArtsPort Magalog content relates to information services for media arts via telecommunications, covering subjects for on-line education. 611 Words. 1992.

ap920430
ArtWire News Opinion
My view
The origins of art-by-wire are the same that inspired Ritchie's ArtsPort and that of other pioneers in electronic media such as ArtWire. This is a comparison of their histories. The author gives the background for his ideas about online news for the arts. 704 Words. 1992.

ap920104
Confessions of A Computer Nut
Reinventing the crafts studio
The author of this article is an artist who uses a palm-top computer and enters thoughts about virtual museums and marketing strategies. He is a computer nut, and in this article, which he wrote for his own contemplation, explains why this was inevitable. 1012 Words. 1992.

ap920607
Distance Post Graduate Education in Art
Back-to-school via information highways
Copy-written article about a networked information resource intensive institution for distance graduate education for adults. The author found the original article to be an almost exact parallel with what he envisions for art education in the

near future. 1156 Words. 1992.

ap920130
Finding Plato's Cave
Introduction to Living Prints
Suppose while searching for values you found Plato's cave. Would you shout, "Here's Plato's Cave! I found it!" How would you know it was his famous cave? Would it have a plaque? Who put it there? What would it look like? This is a proposal for an article. 217 Words. 1992.

ap920308
Forecasts Coming True
Arts nearer to multimedia
Originator of Perfect Studios sees the formation of private museum enterprises as a signal of change in art. He forecasts that art collections will be more highly valued for the content that can be re-purposed for electronic publishing. He plans to do it. 371 Words. 1992.

ap920516
Making It Interactive
Special Newsletter for the Virtual Realist
An electronic newsletter inspired by one CompuServe by the Edwards', illustrating an electronic newsletter. The text has been copy-written. I am grateful to the Edwards' for their inspiring development of home-based businesses. 3583 Words. 1992.

ap920617
Marketing articles and the Glass Bead Game
Advantages of electronic publishing
This article, when completed, will describe the mechanics and benefits of writing and publishing using a computer as the Perfect Studio environment. The ideas in it are inspired by the famous book by Herman Hesse titled Magister Ludi: The Glass Bead Game. 300 Words. 1992.

ap920120
News is No News
ING means Interactive News Gathering
It's not news if it's not interactive. News tradition goes back before the printing press, this article, when completed, would suggest the printing press has reigned supreme too long. Now people say, No News is Good News, meaning printed news is junk. 265 Words. 1992.

ap920627
Scripting Art Business Consultant (A-B-C)
Proposal for art business on the radio
ArtsPort proposal by the author to produce a series of twenty seven one-minute radio infomercials to sell copies of his book, "The Art of Selling Art." The following are script, production and technical considerations in producing this first A-B-C series. 451 Words. 1992.

ap920318
Signals from ArtsPort Control
A yarn

Some lines from the imagination of a computer-using artist/writer as he notices increasing communications coming and going in his new device. He's writing for ArtsPort, the island the domains-of-expertise in online communications, and these are the parts. 340 Words. 1992.

ap920404
Touring A Logic Tree
Drive C of Ritchie's hard-drive
Describing the way the artist's "reinvented studio" is created on the computer hard-drive, using the traditional "tree" that has been his principle motif all his life, this artist sets the stage for his online, virtual art studio. He describes his theory. 861 Words. 1992.

ap930426
E-mail and SafeTNet:
Understanding email and electronic arts
The Student Alliance for Edutainment Technology Network (SAFETNET) is part of a plan to teach, research and produce within the arts, crafts and design communities. This essay is a broad, big picture view and assesses how telecommunications makes new jobs. 2168 Words. 1993.

ap930518
Pon-e Express
The Olde Dayes of the SuperHighways
Script idea for video for Seattle Vocational Institute & Academic Resources Network and Part of the EarthSafe 2022 project. If you don't have a job, or if you're thinking about having your own business, this article will be useful because it's futuristic. 341 Words. 1993.

ap930524
Student Alert to SafeTNet:
Sign up to cruise first class
SafeTNet, Students Alliance for Edutainment Technology Network, is one way to separate fact from fiction in a new and interesting - possibly artistic - way. Yesterday there was no way to "sign up" to SafeTNet but today there is thanks to new technologies. 355 Words. 1993.

ap930324
Understanding Email - A Course Proposal
Littlebook, dynaset and textbook versions
Perfect Studios requires perfect textbooks which are "dynasets," that is, textbooks defined by the user's quest for experience. A better name will come for these textbooks such as dynabooks. For now, the LittleBook design will be sufficient. SVI proposal. 773 Words. 1993.

ap940507
ArtsPort Magalogs reviewed
Seeding the information superhighways
The electronic campus system is in its embryonic stages. The seeds are articles that are written and stored on electronic databases maintained by the professors themselves and formatted in Magalogs - magazine and catalog combined. 1590 Words.

1994

ap940523
Living Prints on-line
Hyperliterate entrepreneurship
In the latest example of concurrent hyperliterate entrepreneurial art business, the author logs a thread based on print making and computer art. The thread's name is Art of Selling Art On-line. (Progressing as on-line communication continues). 4752 Words. 1994

ap950315
Designing a Server with me in mind
The Perfect Studios On-line
The author, 53, is inspired by an article about how to set up a server for a nursery school and Junior High. He is older in years but he is a young art student at heart. The article may serve communities of creative and artistic and technical people. 1843 Words. 1995.

ap951225
Journal Entry
Birthday Report and Re-discovery of a Video Art Work
Notes recorded from the author's "palmtop" B.O.S.S. computer. The author writes about his 54th birthday with his family, making a video and was rewarded by re-discovering one of his video art works. He valued it as a museum piece and put it on the net. 237 Words. 1995.

ap950604
The World's first Dial-An-Artist
Early experiments in telecommunications and arts
History of a conceptual artwork consisting of a shallow wooden box of stones with a telephone nested in them. 662 Words. 1995.

ap951021
Welcome to Washington, Mike
This isn't Kansas, but sort of like It
An old resident of Washington State addresses a friend who recently "retired" from Microsoft with advice on how to live off-campus. 1708 Words. 1995.

ap960929
A day in the life of a webmaster
PortMaster's secrets revealed
A webmaster is the nameless, faceless caretaker of websites on the World Wide Web. A PortMaster handles similar technical things at ArtsPort. Use your imagination and visit a one-hour lecture by a pioneering PortMaster. 2139 Words. 1996.

ap960411
ArtsPort Opens
A new kind of property developer
Traditional publishing brings mail to the founding father of ArtsPort on the same day he is surveying the virtual landscape for the new "Port for Art World Navigators." He concludes that a new kind of capital is the key to developing property on the

Web. 1277 Words. 1996.

ap960308
Fine art telecards
Some scenarios
Slightly ahead of her time, a shopper is startled to find a new art form emerging. The best is yet to come as technology and art go on-line. 856 Words. 1996.

ap960903
Free Home Page at ArtsPort
A New Use for an Old Idea
Printmaking artists have allies--business people, collectors, galleries and museums that have co-operated in the production of artworks. Experiments, too, are possible when they cooperate. A new idea, a studio accessible on the Internet, is envisioned. 137 Words. 1996.

ap960114
Journal Entry
An Elevator Ride
Notes recorded from the author's "palmtop" B.O.S.S. computer. The author writes about a ride in his building's elevator with his neighbor. He saw a possibility of meeting their need for a webmaster for them. He writes of the E&SRB meeting as successful.
181 Words. 1996.

ap960104
Journal Entry
Improving Home Page
Notes recorded from the author's "palmtop" B.O.S.S. computer. The author writes of an improved philosophy and strategy regarding his home page, more localized and breaks from the traditional "book by its cover."
169 Words. 1996.

ap961019
Perfect day at ArtsPort
Handling the challenge of TCWA
The Gruddite Apprentice User tells how telecommunications (the main business of ArtsPort) is the site where TCWA is conceived, studied and presented to advocates of the principle of giving back to the community for what they took a long time to create. 1566 Words. 1996.

ap960321
Tour of ArtsPort
First stop on the Great Lake of the Domain of Expertise
Chapter one from the experimental workbook for "Reinventing Arts Studios"--a manuscript that has been in progress since the completion of the first in the Perfect Studios trilogy. Ten islands await the visitor to an imaginary lake community. 2382 Words. 1996.

ap970417
A Flash of Long Duration
Insuring Artists' Assets

Laughing all the way to the bank cures depression. Artists who plan to live on the sales of their works may enjoy success if rich people, corporations and governments want them. Insurance companies may proffer a better idea: Life Assurance for artists. 2098 Words. 1997.

ap971120
ArtGuild
The Co-op that Flopped
ArtGuild, an online co-op, flopped. How did it happen? This is a never-told story of a '95 co-op idea that has been filed with Bill Ritchie's persistent efforts to realize a lifelong dream of an artists' co-op online. Events in this story really happened. 5518 Words. 1997.

ap970306
Departing on a dream scheme
By cruise ship or kayak?
A volunteer, doing his time in for USTC, was invited to join a group for a brainstorming session for raising funds for a school. He conjures an image of a vapor-ware cruise ship and kayak fleet that are destined for one goal: Improved education in the US. 2822 Words. 1997.

ap970214
How big a battleship is to wash
ArtsPort's ship washer
Approaching today's educational issues in the US is like approaching the task of washing a battleship - a very large job and not something for which to volunteer. That's true unless you live in Washington State. The author has a proposition to offer USTC. 1848 Words. 1997.

ap970114
Journal Entry
Teaching, Reinvented Studio and Toymaker
The author writes his long range goal of being an effective teacher through today's communication technologies. He writes about reinventing studio, museum and school through a HSIC model. He ends by describing himself as a toymaker for educated adults. 278 Words. 1997.

ap971215
Meni for Many
Your choice, their choice
Without fanfare or speeches, day one of the second year of living copiously begins at ArtsPort. The Master finds himself back at the beginning, seeing the place for the first time. The day begins appropriately, with a toss of the peak and a deal of cards. 941 Words. 1997.

ap971001
Metrics and HSIC
Quantum management of artists' assets
The first time I saw the word quantum used outside physics and math it struck me as being an interesting combination. Science and the arts of human interaction in an business context had not seemed so closely connected since when I discov-

ered hyper media. 1321 Words. 1997.

ap970319
Planning to celebrate
TCWA and the mid-Year of Living Copiously
Midway in A Year of Living Copiously, Bill talks to himself as if he is ten avatars. They are a board of vice presidents he visualizes as sitting around a table, discussing a ten-day clinic for Tech Corps Washington, on the winning of the Gates Prize. 1293 Words. 1997.

ap971011
Registering Emeralda
Technicalities of Protecting the Game for the Gifts of Life
The inventor of Emeralda outlines the methods he must follow to register the name as a trademark with the USPO. He supports his description with illustrations and focuses on Telecard Maker and the Pacific Digital Fine Arts Festival.. 844 Words. 1997.

ap970819
The Zines at InfoHaus
Planning a ten-part Zine
InfoHaus, the virtual shopping mall of at First Virtual, has Bill's shop, "Artists Business Consultant." It's part of a plan to put artists' business education on-line. He thinks it will help creative people improve their managing, marketing and selling. 805 Words. 1997.

ap980114
Announcing HSICICA
Artist be aware--you could be an investor
Here is the background of a Corporate Press Release we will see in the future. This essay explains a new kind of investment for exceptional people who want to invest in a new kind of fund, based on the value of their human structural intellectual capital. 531 Words. 1998.

ap980325
ArtsPort, E'Studios and ATMs
Case Based Reasoning meets the artists and Dentist in cyberspace
Someone (in the beginning there was only one) in a game of Emeralda has collectible cards. This assumption must be examined. The root of this assumption traces back to the Emeralda Master, who invented ten decks of cards in this, the collectible card ..
2714 Words. 1998.

ap980812
ArtsPort's greatest visitor
SS United States
In an imaginary place for higher learning and teaching, research and practice he's expecting a ship to come in-the SS United States. People have their favorite sections in the paper; this artist/writer visualizes a cybernetic news columnist in "ArtsPort". 1243 Words. 1998.

ap981218
Book of fools
Future tension
The fourth day of ArtsPort Residency Stay is for turning one's attention to the future, the world of imperfect information. Three days open up to re-mediation. 1480 Words. 1998.

ap980713
Cartoon strips
From caves to e-mail
From e-mail lists to the cave paintings, the author shows analogies with the old media and the new and examines ways of predicting the success or failure of virtual communities. 1649 Words. 1998.

ap981217
Fatal Error
Why art schools fail
Perfect Information is that which has happened and can not be changed. The author reflects on the failure of the art schools--like the one he taught in--and how he narrowly escaped death as an art-ist, craftsman and designer in today's promising art world. 751 Words. 1998.

ap980223
Flash! in the Pan
And the Fire
This article is one of those written at a much lat-er date--October 21, 1998--and comes from one of those inspirations I call a Flash! It was on my mind, I believe, because I completed 20 days of videotape interviews yesterday, and the prospects of . . .. 622 Words. 1998.

ap980822
Going on-line
What it's like in Emeralda Play
A few seconds before going on line to register a day's Score sheet, the inventor of Emeralda stops and notes some of the skills needed by Emeralda players. He exemplifies Emeralda Play itself--the ways of creating, inventing, discovering and imag-ineering. 961 Words. 1998.

ap980213
Here Comes the Judge
What's a mailing list worth, really?
Two kinds of lists are described as it is necessary to identify, control, evaluate and disseminate them. The bottom line is, Is it worth it? How much is it worth? Who is the judge?
372 Words. 1998.

ap980911
I want my Emeralda
Emeralda for Dummies--Part III
In Part III of Emeralda for Dummies, the inventor explains that before Emeralda was released, ev-ery Score sheet was hand made in a spreadsheet environment. Now the spreadsheets have been replaced by real relationships and experiences for living copiously. 863 Words. 1998.

ap980921
ICED A, T and C
The shapes of skills
The comparisons of T-shaped skills, A-shaped skills and C-shaped skills as are helpful in the invention and the playing of Emeralda. Part X of Emeralda for Dummies--the basics for under-standing the values of debts in human structural intellectual capital. 639 Words. 1998.

ap980315
Journal Entry
Numbers and Emeralda
The author writes about opening the index page of Emeralda and checking to see what was chosen ten days before. He describes the process of sup-plying contents for a blank field; an image, or text, or a song. He reports on the peaks of the sister's cards.
342 Words. 1998.

ap981001
Joys of Scoring
Only Real Boomers play Emeralda
Emeralda Score keeping is not a game for little ba-bies, nor children. Even adults have a hard time even starting. Only Real Boom-timers have pa-tience for the first step--Scoring. Without a Score sheet, though, there's no accounting for what hap-pens to us. 965 Words. 1998.

ap980901
Legacy Transfer
My domain for a smile on her face
Legacy transfer is borrowed from industry, which means both the useful and not useful are moved up from the past to the present and positioned for the future. In an individual, it means a similar thing but its values are in the sovereignty of indi-viduals. 650 Words. 1998.

ap980802
Memories of advisers
Future search for art youth
Art Youth (a provisional title) in Estonia respond to the receipt of a physical gift tape from the au-thor made in 1981. They ask questions, and he an-swers via e-mail. He also responds to their request for more text. 2095 Words. 1998.

ap981215
My first day at ArtsPort
Third Year of Living Copiously
The author, formerly with a university teaching art courses, compares one manager of a mutual fund in securities with college class management. He wonders whether the comparison of students to customers has validity when he encounters his former students. 1405 Words. 1998.

ap980603
Passed Away or Pissed away
Demonstration in Capturing your Wealth
Have you ever felt like your life is being pissed away? Do you worry, or, to use a less stressful word

are you concerned that much of what you value will be squandered by other people when you have passed away? I think it does not need to happen this way. 412 Words. 1998.

ap981130
Perfect Knowledge
Prisoner of a perfect past
Emeralda, the inventor calls games for the gifts of life, is in a class called games of perfect information. The outcome of these games is determined by a chosen strategy. The author, an artist/teacher, chose prints, the ancestral root of multimedia arts. 1516 Words. 1998.

ap980623
Picture Martians Monitoring Earth Artists
A Demonstration in Emeralda Play
Picture Martians. They cluster around their viewing screens, taking notes on the data coming in from Earth. They can't tell, with their low-resolution listening devices, whether the messages are localized or if they are coming from . . .. 2392 Words. 1998.

ap980723
Picturing Emeralda
First time visitors welcome
The visual effects, the social contacts, the challenges of Emeralda Games Work will make it a destination worth the trip and the investment. The main thing people will like is the experiences and relationships that seem to spring from the visits. 591 Words. 1998.

ap980105
Prisoners and lunatics
HandMade Dogs reborn
Like prisoners in the game, "Prisoner's dilemma," an artist and a poet get back together, take a quick tour of a game center and printery, and decide to re-start their ten-year old project. There is a new wrinkle, though, that might ensure success. 1523 Words. 1998.

ap981011
Q&A from ArtsPort Agents
Emeralda Inventor Interviews
The inventor of Emeralda prepares for a videotape interview. These are some questions asked and, in its final iteration, the answers he provided visitors from ArtsPort when the inventor was investing time on the Isle of Information and Telecommunications. 5368 Words. 1998.

ap980613
The Concentration Camp
Using your talent to escape with Living Prints
To some, conflict is a kind of war, of fears realized. Serving conflicts is amusing, as a talented person might, instead of fearing the gods of war, would rather serve the good agent that empowers the muse within creative, inventive, discovering people. 2706 Words. 1998.

ap980504
Vice Regent of Egotism and Hierarchical Mania
It's Not your Usual Game Instruction Book
The inventor of Emeralda: Games for the Gifts of Life, is trying to write down the method of play while he's playing it. It's what is called by one writer (in a book that will be published in three years) reflexivity . . .. 1817 Words. 1998.

ap980703
Welcome to ArtsPort
A Visitor's Day
On the holiday, "Interdependence Day" (which offsets the stress created by the illusions of independence) the author of the novel, "Women who fell to earth" consider the art and science of interdependent creativity, invention, discovery and imagination. 995 Words. 1998.

ap980514
Your Demonstrator is the Printer
Demonstration 11 in ArtsPort Cells
Her name is Hannah. She's a printer. A whole new cycle begins as we return to ArtsPort, and here we'll receive demonstration 11. What would happen, though, if we pressed both buttons (row or column) at the same time? Please don't do it . . .. 1278 Words. 1998.

ap990613
A Ghost in the New Machine
N. C. Cornish, pizza and the BAM
The author of the unpublished manuscript, Ghosts in the New Machine, draws a picture of the ghost of Nellie C. Cornish as a primary agent in the funding of a proposed online publishing project. The story is for a creative woman who performs her own plays. 1537 Words. 1999.

ap990617
Conversion, Convergence and Concurrence
Chicken-and-egg
On the first of three days of looking in his rear view mirror in Emeralda Play (Days of Perfect Information) its inventor re-reads Videospace by a pioneer in experiments in television, Brice Howard. And he gets more depth in his defining of a convergence. 1075 Words. 1999.

ap990616
Copublish Calendar for Convergencies
A Proposal
With his neo-use(age) of electronic resource locators (intelligent agents), the author brings his desk calendar concept closer to reality. Rising like emergencies from past mornings' epiphanies from his electronic instruments and toy box, it crystallizes. 731 Words. 1999.

ap990415
Death, Taxes and Public Speaking
Hit parade of the mythical
Twain was a pioneer cybernetic artist. In the tangible arts and the performance arts, different

schools prevail but the age of digital reproduction is creating a perspective to re-examine the myth of certainty, as in death, taxes and public speaking fear. 917 Words. 1999.

ap990216
Football Field Mentor
Recollection of the SS United States
Three paragraphs from the ArtsPort Resident-In-Stay's diary, a journal that RIS' are required to keep. It is in the form of fiction, as he pictures himself on the football field on the island of ArtsPort, in mid-February, perhaps on an early morning walk. 438 Words. 1999.

ap990614
Ghosts in the New Machine
A Letter to A Former Student Not Sent
Digging in his digital archives of Good Ideas Not Acted Upon, the author finds a letter that is over a year old containing the kernel of his concept of a futuristic online interactive arts festival. At the time he wrote it he had no address to send it to. 1437 Words. 1999.

ap990217
Intrepid Trio
Founders of DISCO-OP unite
Triple entry bookkeeping and single entry bookkeeping are virtually unknown. They cannot be reconciled where double entry bookkeeping dominates. Common sense says you can teach neither art nor dentistry online but what if triple entry bookkeeping is used?
1031 Words. 1999.

ap990214
Joy of Emeralda
Reasons for play
Copy-writing Alfie Kohn, an Emeralda player at ArtsPort dreams of a movie that he says develops the non-competitive theme, prevailing over the industrialization of education, creativity, invention, discovery and imagination. Interviews follow the premier. 925 Words. 1999.

ap990612
My talk at SKCDAS
Getting specific
Anticipating his lecture to dental assistants, the author considers how he will answer the imminent question: What Next? and he thinks everything must begin within their organization's five year plan. Past performance seems to indicate future performance. 720 Words. 1999.

ap990215
Old Growth, New Growth
From the dead eaters to cyber disk keepers
Mid-February, time to prune the fruit trees. They grow from a central core, form branches and on the branches-twigs. On the twigs, flowers and fruit. An old man began to tell his story: "Heard of the dead-eaters?" Then he talked about moving of Web sites. 932 Words. 1999.

ap990413
Principles and Interests in Cooperation
Writing the business plan for DISCO-OP
Founders of some software companies start businesses without business plans or conventional capital investors. The Mondragon Co-operative stock basis for their business plan was equilibrio, or balance. The writer offers these as metaphors for a new co-op. 994 Words. 1999.

ap990417
Reviewing Personal Financial Management
The inventor's private concerns
At ArtsPort the days of Imperfect Information--days when we consider how we do not know the future. In states of Perfect Information, we knew the past. Now we must learn the arts of balancing perfect information, imperfect information and strategic faith. 784 Words. 1999.

ap990416
Space, time and DISCO-OP
Sci-fi for the soul
The author created a game based on the movie, The Man Who Fell to Earth in a sequel, The Women Who Fell to Earth. Dental Internet Services Co-Operative, DISCO-OP, is an enterprise between two worlds. His game, Emeralda, is a way of playing his space/time. 1456 Words. 1999.

ap990615
Where in the World is Dentalisco?
Getting there from here
A nascent question, "Where is this city of dental dreamers, anyway?" occurs to him while ArtsPort's DeedHolder views the calendar of events at Dentalisco--his fantasy on the edge of Emeralda's Great Lake. He writes his accounting of the birth of the city. 1660 Words. 1999.

ap990218
Your Web Site Is Your Work of Art
Old names, old ideas and the age of digital reproduction
Rauschenberg, famous artist, said, "You have to understand the language of a work of art, and to understand the language, you have to experience it." Who is Rauschenberg? Is he a Web site artist? The name's familiar. The author role-plays his way in time. 638 Words. 1999.

ap000224
A Gentleman, A Scholar, A Sales Person-An Artist
Which Are You?
An online mentor-teacher writes out the first of four tutorials for his online course, Art of Selling Art2, and introduces an opinion of the difference between what the art of selling art used to be and what it is today. He uses role-play as introduction. 1338 Words. 2000.

ap000705
All My Databases
Making the Rounds

A database by any name is worth something if it is worth creating at all, and in the process of re-inventing arts' studios, a database may be the difference between success and failure. The author imagines the update of databases being as a ride on a lake. 1792 Words. 2000.

ap000302
Creating Washington's Arts Base with Craft and Design Knowbot
WABCDK to the Rescue!
A knowbot is a clever computer, blending the Words. robot and knowledge-an all-knowing robot. A WABCDK that this writer describes resulted from his research of a proprietary search engine needed for his home state arts commission's Year 2000. Strategy Plan. 1457 Words. 2000.

ap000315
DWERP Debuts in Washington State
Interesting Invitation to Invest In
Data Warehousing of Enterprise Resource Planning is the locus of the Arts Business Craft and Design E-Commerce. Information can be Web-enabled, making arts business-to-business, practitioners and consumer-oriented electronic commerce and much easier. 1713 Words. 2000.

ap000410
F2F with Brian
Memories of the Ancestors
The Emeralda inventor met face-to-face with Brian Davis and recalled what they talked about. He describes it in counsel with Dr. Stephen R. Covey, who begins, "Did you listen to Brian? Can you repeat what you heard?" The author tests his own memory of it. 1003 Words. 2000.

ap000526
Fantasy Tourism
Beer, wine and a PDA
The author prefaces a business proposal to a publisher to create an Arts Navigation System. He shares a vision of the future with similar dreams. Citing his past, his art and patronage experiences he sees the future of arts as business-to-business online. 2679 Words. 2000.

ap000313
Getting There, Getting In
Action on the Cultural Back Roads
Get there, get in-this is the theme of a copy-written article about a third gateway for users of the arts' Web site for Washington State. The ITinerate Professor wants to introduce potential partners to fill an empty space on a virtual, virtuous Web site. 526 Words. 2000.

ap000420
I Love Essay Contests!
Living Prints the Writer's Way
When his attorney sent him a reminder to update his registration for his trademark, Living Prints, the printmaker (the Emeralda Inventor) was inspired to offer something he wanted to for a long time: An online essay contest. Here's how the contest starts. 323 Words. 2000.

ap001209
Journal Entry
Experience and Relationships in Printmaking
The author writes a theme for the day: The purpose is to have experience and relationships in printmaking by hand. He writes about creating a DVD for his asset management and legacy transfer. He discusses interface and specifying. 313 Words. 2000.

ap001030
Journal Entry
A Dream of a Successful Class
The first time in 15 years the author dreamed of being a highly successful teacher. The students were smiling and attentive. He said, "3 things about printmaking, the parent of all media arts, a process, not a product and it's nothing if it isn't fun."
321 Words. 2000.

ap001005
The Artist's Way of Getting On the Web
Day One
The artist/teacher considers a curriculum plan for an intensive class in Web work. This is his first draft of the outline. He includes factors that influenced his lifelong commitments to art and the conservation of human appreciation for human creativity. 340 Words. 2000.

ap000427
The Dental Arts' Problem with High Tech
The Artful Science in the Digital Age
Not everyone is an artist. Not everyone can be a dentist. Not everyone can be a concert pianist. No one can do any one of these things well and believe that it's a solo-practitioner art. This artist-writer examines the issue in connection with technology. 986 Words. 2000.

ap000312
Ticket to Ride
Hitching on the ITinerate Professor's Hike
What does it mean to be an ITinerate Professor? How do you get to be an ITinerate Professor? What is the Ticket? Where, when and why would one want to be it? Who says? An ITinerate Professor answers these six FAQs as his way of examining his own progress. 972 Words. 2000.

ap000402
What Is Art Worth, Mr. Gates?
Going On About the WSAC
He saw art education going online. In a few years, he wants the state of Washington to zoom from 48th to first position in its commitment to arts in schools. Not by a traditional path, changing from the inside, but from the outside, from him and his kind. 693 Words. 2000.

ap000612

While Downloading My First ISP Protocol
Launching for a five-year journey into the future
of Media Arts
Developing a portfolio of Human Structural Intellectual Capital includes a review of the pathway
that brought the Emeralda Inventor to the Net.
This essay, made from the original notes I took
while downloading the Seanet protocols, establishes my purpose. 394 Words. 2000.

ap001205
Why I Make Money
The Wealthy Artist1
His busy schedule does not stop him from sharing some of the secrets of his success as this artist
writes some of the reasons for his financial success
and for his success at being free. He owes his success to what he calls the power of his "imagivision".
1851 Words. 2000.

ap000208
Wisdom of A Pineapple
Leap off your desktop
The author writes, What does it mean when your
desktop computer crashes toward the end of the
Third Year of Living Copiously (The Gates Prize)?
This is what I asked myself this morning. Then,
again, at the end of that year, when it goes into a
slow death?
1840 Words. 2000.

ap000101
Yes, Debra, You Can Play Emeralda
Let me think of ways
The Emeralda Works proprietor (also known as
the Emeralda Inventor) considers the question;
I want to play Emeralda, so how do I begin Emeralda Play? He enumerates the ways a person
can start. A person named Debra asked, and he
answers in an Emeralda Way. 1383 Words. 2000.

ap011215
A New Angle on Art Education Reform
A wicked idea from grumpy old art teachers
On his first day at ArtsPort, in his sixth year playing Emeralda, its inventor muses about a plan to
put art schools out of business. He'll offer shares in
a company that provides free art ed on the Internet that also pays art resources or teachers money.
1081 Words. 2001.

ap010524
A Real Feeling of Community
Emeralda co-housing concept an antidote to society's isolation
This article is being copy-written over an article in
the Seattle Times, so most of the names are those
of real people. The idea that Emeralda is an intentional community is still fiction several years after
this news focused on co-housing in Puget Sound.
1305 Words. 2001.

ap010822
About the NWPC Web site
Questions you should ask and answers you should

get
Here's a golden opportunity to educate, stated the
woman on the other end of the master's telephone
line. As a teacher, the Words. golden opportunity
stuck in his mind. He began copying the conversation as it might have happened to himself as Dusty
Cann. 1282 Words. 2001.

ap010514
Art Teachers Beware
What you don't know CAN hurt you
The author is both chilled-out and a fired-up as he
carves on a wooden table top while, at his elbow,
an old VCR pours his how-to video into a desktop computer. It is a microcosm of a world he left
behind 15 years before, and a vision coming into
reality. 2295 Words. 2001.

ap010213
Artsport Revisited
Reorientation Movie
Recalling how his story of his fantasyland all started over thirty years ago it seems like he's been
writing an autobiography without knowing; worse
yet, much of what wrote was like a self-fulfilling
prophecy. If he'd known what he was doing, he
wouldn't. 927 Words. 2001.

ap010424
AUREL Main Interface
Finding the Emeralda Channel
Earth Day comes again and an artist asks himself,
What did I do for it? An inventory ensued-not in
writing but in actions that may be summed up in
four Words.: Artists Education Information Technology. Partway through the day's routine, a channel opens up. 1253 Words. 2001.

ap010223
Best One for the Job
Four Promises of the Emeralda Warrior
At the gateways to ArtsPort, first of the ten Is-
lands of the Domains-of-Expertise of the multi-
media artist, the author meditates on freedom. Dr.
David Viscott, his Words. trapped in ink on paper,
provides him the Words. that he needs to win the
Gates Prize. 2935 Words. 2001.

ap010104
Dead Artist's League Job Opening
Social Worker Wanted On-line
Writing business plans is tricky business, what
with so much changing. Thanks to the Internet
World Wide Web new relationships and experiences are opening up. This story, about an artist's
assistant seeking a job, entails a business plan for
fantasy work. 606 Words. 2001.

ap010603
Dry Ingredients for A Screenplay
Try Rendering This Down
He imagines a great lake as green as emerald, and
he travels there in his imagination with his desktop computer. This author/artist thinks this is the
beginning of a story like those in the magical fan-

tasies of C. S. Lewis' Narnia, and he's the professor. 896 Words. 2001.

ap011120
Hello, Mr. Chips
A perfect match for an old dream
His DVD project (he creates a passport-style book and puts stamps on its pages to show where he has been) is a way of building on an old dream. This professor of art planned to be up to speed as a re-newable teacher when a new age of art education arrived. 1140 Words. 2001.

ap011021
Hey Buddy, Got Time?
Value-adding to artists' assets
It takes him away from real printmaking, but he plans to keep making DVDs as if they are prints themselves says this author. Prints are the forerun-ners of socializing effects of the arts, and DVDs are similar with the added value of thrifty dissem-ination. 1899 Words. 2001.

ap010414
Introduction to Art Education On-line
A Proposal to A Parent Teacher Association Artist
This teacher has a new perspective that reduces six fears listed in old books. All six fears come from not-understanding. A course on Art Education On-line gets criticism from quarters dominated by not understanding, neither on-line technology nor art ed. 1810 Words. 2001.

ap010203
Navigators and Naughty Games
Among the Islands of Hawaii I found True Ro-mance
Using the role-playing game, Emeralda, the inven-tor tests the laptop he chose for the toolkit to teach online interactive gaming on a ship. Using visual-ization, he actuates the image of cruising among the islands of Hawaii on a United States Cruise Liner. 812 Words. 2001.

ap010305
Need for An Online Art Ed Philosopher
People Run into Burning Houses
Imagining an on-line art auction to raise funds for a non-profit, the author reflects on the climb that brought him to this idea. Things that are seldom done-like heroes who run into burning houses-re-quire a philosopher or a fool to see them done. 2073 Words. 2001.

ap011031
Note from the Emeralda Inventor's Journal
What you do when you've finished a DVD
The daily routine of the Emeralda Inventor in-cludes making DVDs and advertising their com-pletion to his Web e-store where people can order them. There's also the job of moving megabytes of data to make room for the next one. These give pause for thoughts. 778 Words. 2001.

ap010124

On each island there is a tree
Arborescence at ArtsPort
Beginning the fifth volume of his fifth year, the Emeralda Player writes an essay about an Island, a Domain-of-Expertise named ArtsPort, how it was treeless when he first visited, and how it has changed since that first year he won that great Gates Prize. 1826 Words. 2001.

ap010713
Something More About A Closet
Virtual Assistant ITinerant Professor Takes Notes
For days the artist/scholar has been playing his role in a closet game, The Professor's Closet which is based on a paragraph that summed up C. S. Lewis' story, Bed Knobs and Broomsticks as being a tale of passage to a land that was accessed via a closet. 1012 Words. 2001.

ap010325
The Amazing Mr. Giedion
Talking Dolls and DVD
The author was a "boy wonder" among older pro-fessors. Twenty-something, hired by a major re-search university to teach art, and set to bridge the worlds of art education, technology and eco-nom-ics, then given a book that set him up for a lifetime of labor. 467 Words. 2001.

ap010802
The Missing Mysterious Professor
Moving the Professor out of the Closet
The first step in making a DVD portal leading stu-dents to their former missing and hidden profes-sor. This is a story about a family that gets caught in a fantasy stamp collecting game. The professor's expertise in game critique and analysis saves the day. 785 Words. 2001.

ap010315
What We Will Do Is Play
A Proposal to Art Ed Leaders
Proposed brochure to explain the ITinerant Pro-fessor Plan for art department chairs. The author will teach, learn, research and practice on-line education at its best, and invites school leaders to share exploration at the Perfect Studios closest to home. 751 Words. 2001.

ap010613
Your Mine to Keep
Data Mining in the Artists' Communities
The author passed through customs when he traveled around the world, but he was no regular tourist, so he paid no duty or tax. But when he returned to his home, he carried valuable infor-mation in his head and on videotape so today he writes on data mines. 1431 Words. 2001.

ap020223
A Search for An E-stamp and Validity
ArtsPort Stamp 1 for My Sacred Cows of Print-making
Reviewing his electronic passport-the core of his strategy for art education on-line-recaptures a

memory from the artist/scholar's 5th grade introduction to the joys of the stamp arts. His quest leads to amazing discoveries, and still another editing job. 1199 Words. 2002.

ap020901
Another Day, Another Story
Moving Toward New Paradigms in Publishing
In this age of digital reproduction the writer, the artist, the scholar and community activist are required to try new ways of communication. Start by thinking globally, says this artist/scholar, then-if you're not too depressed-act locally and digitally. 982 Words. 2002.

ap020504
Art Education and Addiction
Knowing the difference
An art addict for almost his whole life explains the difference between what is an addiction to his arts education and how it is the difference between having power and being powerless, concluding with a description of Emeralda, his idea of a home remedy. 1545 Words. 2002.

ap020713
Artistamps As Neighborhood Profit Centers
Visualizing Trees at East Uptown Seattle.
Can artists make millions on artistamps? This artist thinks so, based on his experience of the distant and near past. Why isn't someone already doing it? Possibly someone is but what isn't clear is the channel effect and how it works for the neighborhood. 816 Words. 2002.

ap020514
Artists, Crafts People and Designers of Hybrid Green Galleries
Qualifiers for a Virtual Real Gallery
What would a perfect gallery be like? Mine would be to me like my reflection in mirrors-what is called a virtual image. It's partial, naturally, but a mirror image will serve until my real person from my insides out is known. That's what it would be like. 745 Words. 2002.

ap020104
Between the Paragraphs – Part 1
An imaginary dialog between two professors
An artist/teacher began to read the essay by Mark C. Taylor and then Taylor's ideas gave him the feeling of déjà vu. It was like meeting a classmate he never knew, on the old campus, yet they'd had the same course. He began writing between the paragraphs. 1750 Words. 2002.

ap021001
Building My E-Portfolio As I Travel
Help from An Alaskan Traveler
Surprised and pleased by a special piece of e-mail, the artist/scholar sees an unexpected assist by an expert in e-folios in the form of ten questions she posed for a third e-correspondent in distant Singapore. The list is a pop quiz in the author's mind. 732 Words. 2002.

ap020822
Certified Money Making Artistamps
Reviewing
There are two kinds of money, that which chases the past and that which chases the future. Invest in the latter, says this artist and scholar. People who spend their lives pursuing the dead past are crazy; the future is where the action is-and real money. 476 Words. 2002.

ap020315
Dear Former Professor
Fantasy Postcard from A Virtual, Virtous Former Student
An inveterate role-player in his own fantasy, role-playing-game called Emeralda, the artist/scholar, alone in his study, imagines what a former student or present-day on-line student might ask him about personal Web sites, and what answer he will provide. 1165 Words. 2002.

ap021130
Dirge Music Please
Visualizing your funeral
Recalling the best-selling audiotape by Dr. Steven Covey, in which he asked his listener to imagine their own eulogy, this artist/scholar imagines his family's dilemma after he dies. He thinks his legacy is his art, his teachings, and his overall example. 1757 Words. 2002.

ap020802
Emeralda City Comfort Zone
Early Morning Mind Stretches
He takes twenty-one days to form his habits, and then those habits form him awhile-until he deconstructs those habits. This community artist/scholar practices building habits and deconstructing them as one way for keeping his body, mind, and spirit alive. 778 Words. 2002.

ap020114
Fantasy Role Playing Gamer Mates Fun, Skill-building
Adapting from a news story
Adapting text from a story that appeared in the Seattle Times November 06, 2002, the inventor of Emeralda plans to use his on-line game to fit the needs of art teachers. He links printmaking and on-line technologies the way chess players employ metaphors. 959 Words. 2002.

ap020203
Future of Printmaking
Another angle
After a vision of the future of printmaking was shared freely via an e-mail message to printmakers, a vision of free fine art prints free for viewing on-line (but for which printmakers will be paid using e-commercial printing), the author presents a plan. 482 Words. 2002.

ap020305
Getting Into the Role Play Thing

First Act Writing for A Screen Play
Taking Words. of Rob Tobin-a screenwriter-and then turning them into an instrument to describe a First Act for an Emeralda play, the author gets some surprising results. The game is played in order to make DVDs, and there's no end in this suspenseful game. 1106 Words. 2002.

ap020213
Introducing Emeralda
From the horse's mouth, as it were
The inventor of Emeralda, a fantasy role-playing game characterized by non-competition and art, wants to invite other artists-especially printmakers-to join him. The trouble is, he is the only one who knows how to play, so he's trying to tell how to play. 2177 Words. 2002.

ap020921
Islands Lost
Restoring Your Islands of Expertise
He's been so close to his domains-of-expertise he says he lost, for a while, his appreciation and exploration of his knowledge base. The game he plays is to support his knowledge base and help others learn to manage theirs, too, but play has its pitfalls. 1496 Words. 2002.

ap020812
Let Us Play Emeralda
Symbolizing the Games for the Gifts of Life
There's another woman who's interested in Emeralda. At this time there seems to be no way across the chasm that separates this writer from people who are interested in his game, but he says people must imagine a bridge before one can be built. Here's how. 1417 Words. 2002.

ap020623
New Game in Town-Hybrid Green Gallery
Want to Play?
How about a new co-op art gallery in Uptown Seattle? The stakes are high and the time is right this man says. He is an artist/writer/scholar and wants opinions from like-minded people and those who can make a game out of it. His brochure accompanies this. 1511 Words. 2002.

ap021021
PDA-based Art Ed On-line
Mobility and fine art in the age of digital reproduction
The author accepts an invitation to show wall-based digital fine art and considers what it means. This is part of his re-entry into a mobile, PDA-based artistry in the age of digital reproduction. He questions its validity, however, and starts a critique. 461 Words. 2002.

ap020424
Playing with the Game Chip of Steve Rock
Three events in the routine activities of an Emeralda Defender
The author gets a stamp-sized, pretty paper chip from a friend, sending him wandering along a mental pathway like being on a mystery or quest for the answer to a riddle. He's engaged in several Web events that connect with his puzzlement and recites them. 1514 Words. 2002.

ap020524
Real Yanks Don't Do IT the Same Way
US American artists' contribution to the history of fine art printmaking
In defense of a philosophy of a fine art printmaker, this artist claims that US Americans added several dimensions to the art and craft of print. A major one is their disavowal of the mechanical reproduction as the benchmark of success, saying it's music. 591 Words. 2002.

ap021031
Remember the Metaphors
Problem solving as a lost art
Facing an opportunity to invest in a public retail space he must apply his skill at reaching the right decision fast. An Einstein homely about solving problems, on one hand, guides him and also his vision of what is the problem that a retail space solves. 872 Words. 2002.

ap020911
Screen Savers to the Rescue
Another Iteration of the Artist's Last Love Letter
Islands of domain-of-expertise have stamp collections, souvenirs, as it were, the residents-in-stay produced based on their life story, their art, and works in their collections of art by others, memorabilia and stories about them. They are screen savers. 867 Words. 2002.

ap020325
Stamps and A Good Life
Debugging failures and flaws
The age of digital reproduction gives US education a special mission, beyond its past 300 year history. In the arts, it is especially true because it is here where creativity is the key to success, freedom and a good life; and the key to solving problems. 734 Words. 2002.

ap020613
The Biggest, Boldest Picture
Where is NODO, anyway?
He is making a bold picture, so he proposes a make-believe city district he calls NODO, short for North of Downtown. His community is really called Uptown, but since his alliance with the natives in this neighborhood is friendly, he seeks out more advice. 597 Words. 2002.

ap020723
The First of 12 Steps Making DVD/PC Art
Got A Goal?
Thinking of Goals Planning for A Multimedia Center at Uptown Seattle, one who aspires to the title of public artist scholar is ready to debut as the neighborhood guru of DVD/PC arts. The question that's puzzling him is the place of the local art

festival. 1136 Words. 2002.

ap020124
The Village of My Dream
The Little Brick Studio School at Ward Springs Park
He's digging in the dirt. Snow is starting to fall. Amid the clutter and mud he's planting ornamentals with a group of neighbors who volunteered to help put a tiny city park in order. Spring is just around the corner and his artist/scholar's mind wanders. 768 Words. 2002.

ap020703
Underexposing the Arts
Reflections on community arts event planning
The author, after attending community meetings, reflects on hearing artists asking why they should be put in the streets of the community on one particular Saturday in the autumn. Business people respond that it's to attract more business traffic to them. 932 Words. 2002.

ap021011
What Fun is Emeralda?
A Little Boy, A Little Thrill
When he's in the frame of mind of a 5-year old, he can see why Emeralda play gives him a little thrill sometimes. From the viewpoint of a 60 year old he knows few would agree with him that one wrong keystroke is anything to be excited about-and no wonder!
2091 Words. 2002.

ap030613
A Story Only A Cyber Artist Could Love
Taking your images all the way to the outer limits
He taps commands with his fingers and files change to other types, arranged in a new composite, tuned to different contrasts and tones and given new formats. His mind is full of visions; describing a new kind of artistic work, he's in this cybernetic age. 1379 Words. 2003.

ap030812
Concurrent Marketing, Sales, Design and Production
Concept development in the arts in the age of digital reproduction
One professor asks another, "How do you teach concept development in students?" and the other professor-after sleeping on it-cites a principle that he heard they used in designing the Boeing 777 he calls Concurrent Marketing, Sales, Design and Production. 444 Words. 2003.

ap030822
Confessions of A Cowboy Professor
Lessons I learned in college
The author is a professor-or was-who's studying computer game development the way an academic would study lessons to be learned from two industry insiders. He describes the similarity between cowboy programming and his story, and realizes he was a cowboy. 1245 Words. 2003.

ap030911
Drawing Sickness
Waking George
As he read the current syllabi created by his colleagues in teaching drawing, the author gets a queasy feeling in his stomach something like feeling afraid. He's always been so analytical, like "George," a drawing student in a story he wrote 31 years ago. 521 Words. 2003.

ap030802
Dreaming of ArtsPort
A Better, Bigger Game
Looking over a pile of colorful postcards he created for his imaginary place called Emeralda, the author thinks about what other artists would do if they were invited to create postcards like this place. His is a better game than any other games he tries. 1412 Words. 2003.

ap030104
Emeralda Publishing Club
Notes from an inspiration
The author carries a PDA with him wherever he goes, and one day in early January he wrote these notes in it about a publishing club based on a digital print he created. The club is an entry into his game, Emeralda, and could provide the games player-base. 485 Words. 2003.

ap031215
E-Stamps and Essays
The deep reader's payoff
While he is designing his own Essay CD, this writer puzzles over the combination of electronic stamps to accompany his thousands of articles-something to make the search for useful ideas more rewarding. Is there a connection between e-stamps and articles?
739 Words. 2003.

ap030603
I Had A Friend Who Made Tests
Musings on digital game based learning
Making a digital-game based learning package feels at times like a student feels getting ready for an examination, preparing a performance, and writing cheat sheets as he goes. It is all in a day's work, plus the benefits of reflection. He remembers Fred. 1025 Words. 2003.

ap031129
Journal Entry
Charlie Drafft's Toxi City
The author writes about an artwork made by Charlie Drafft called "Toxi City." It's a place that celebrates the imperfect world. He also writes that he read theories by a paleontologist of human life sustainability. He considers art becoming political. 254 Words. 2003.

ap030211
My Talk at the Rotary Club
Notes before the event

After he was invited to talk to a Rotary Club luncheon, the author was then asked to write some autobiographical and thematic notes his sponsor could use for his introduction. The following is what he wrote, soon after he met with the Rotarian in January. 725 Words. 2003.

ap030524
Omission Impossible-How Iteration 30524 Was Played
Continuing Omission Impossible-A Case of A Missing Professor
When he's designing for EDGBL (Experience Digital Game-Based Learning, pronounced "Edgeable") he's like the elusive character in the movie, Catch Me If You Can. A phony professor is on the run, island-hopping in a paradisiacal art colony called Emeralda. 1076 Words. 2003.

ap031130
Quest for Emeralda Maps
Today's search at ArtsPort
A quest in a video game is the imaginary travail that a player undertakes to survive the perils of a "dangerous mission". Emeralda quests are partly imaginary and real. A search for digital maps he made years ago is destined to lead to a real world print. 873 Words. 2003.

ap031110
The Itinerate Professor Logs On
Creating a college drawing journal
An art teacher who calls himself an Itinerate Professor is taking a drawing class with a plan to teach it in the context of the times of digital reproduction technologies. Hand-drawn art works have no equivalent in computers-or do they? He logs on to see. 563 Words. 2003.

ap031120
There's A Game in Seattle's Artists
Searching for the Perfect Studios
He resigned the UW in '85 to search for the perfect studios, where teaching and learning, research and development, practice and production and community service all happen at the same time, under one roof. He found this fantasyland and named it Emeralda. 1264 Words. 2003.

ap030514
Visualize The Gates Game
A Study Plan for the Life and Work of Elmer Gates
He's doing a study on digital games, which will revolutionize the way art education is approached in this the "age of digital reproduction." For an example that he thinks might become an on-line mentorship project he describes how a real game might begin. 755 Words. 2003.

ap030921
Why Online Art Ed Now?
Seizing the Day
From a press release about distance learning trends titled Online Learning is as Good as Being There, an art professor makes a case for starting an online art studio course. He says it's an opportunity not to be missed and it's more than it appears to be. 2055 Words. 2003.

ap040124
A Project to Like
Vision of an online archive
With an eye to releasing an archive of unique videotapes he has saved for thirty years, the onetime professor considers a project to share with the university where the videos were made and a regional museum. He thinks they must result in the form of DVD. 1018 Words. 2004.

ap040712
ArtsPort and the Mini Halfwood Press
A portal for learning printmaking
ArtsPort is a key to success of the Mini Halfwood Press because here there is an emphasis on using the new information and telecommunications technologies to find and develop the market for this press and the information people need to use it effectively. 695 Words. 2004.

ap040702
ArtsPort Mentor
Seeking the identity of mentor/teacher online
Years ago this author faked his way into a conference called Learning Any Time, Any Where where he found himself among groups calling themselves mentor/teachers. They meant they intended to be the teachers of teachers. The idea had a strong appeal to him. 249 Words. 2004.

ap040801
Clearing My Head at ArtsPort
Reflecting on an Art Rally at Guemes Island
The Itinerate Professor has been away for a day, testing the idea of working on an island far from the city, a quest for his imaginary place, Emeralda. Upon return, he ponders the question: Is he really stopping doing what he's been doing? Is this better?
334 Words. 2004.

ap040114
Getting Started Setting up Emeralda
Notes on method
He invented a game he bases on a fantasy land he calls Emeralda, and when he has to set up his new computer for the game, he uses the opportunity to answer the question, "How do you play Emeralda?" It's not an automatic program; so he starts from scratch. 943 Words. 2004.

ap041030
It Started with A Stamp
Steps toward a new angle in the art of selling art
His friend told him about software that was good for listing numerous items from a database to put in an e-store. Trying it out, he realized he could not go it alone, so he conjured a scheme to help himself and others learn the software and put it to use. 730 Words. 2004.

ap040223
Journal Entry
Level Designer for a Video Game
The author writes about the future artists; the video game and virtual world creators. He writes the difference of the generational arts; from individual artists to team membership artists. He considers the future of printmaking pupils at Cornish College. 673 Words. 2004.

ap040811
Magic ArtsPort
Moving toward a CD/ROM and mini press for online education
His thinking since the last ten days has been influenced by more computer work than printmaking because his vision is to accompany a mini press with a complementary disc in CD/ROM that can carry a great deal of information about the press and printmaking. 397 Words. 2004.

ap040403
Make It Happen
The magic of applied media arts
He has written something down on paper, and in digital media, and he believes "it" will happen. What is it, you ask? A digital art village, a blend of school and art studios linked with various media arts ranging from antiquity to today's high technology. 363 Words. 2004.

ap040213
Make Something Worth Money
A game for communities
There was a time when artists did not have to turn their vision and skill into money, but we may have to go back to the cave dwelling days to find it. Magic was a stronger force then. A new possibility has emerged. IT can affect the arts in the same ways. 1230 Words. 2004.

ap040821
Pick A Path to Adventure
Life in a community of practice
His endless quest is to be a teacher, to learn, to research and produce for his lifetime and beyond. He's grateful to have been able to remain in the art community, he feels as though he's practicing for a performance but that he may never get to perform. 1368 Words. 2004.

ap040910
Renewable Resource
Human creativity as the solution
There's an analogy between renewable resources of energy and renewable resources of human creativity. As the Earth's capacity to support human life is under examination and limitations are disclosed, human creativity may be the resource to solve problems. 385 Words. 2004.

ap040831
System Shock
Awakening from a cyber-slumber
A routine search and destroy session turns up a cryptic account of a video game written by an educator named Gee. The game has a familiar sound to it, so this art professor rewrites the account, forcing it into a line of thought he's had for a generation. 1479 Words. 2004.

ap040722
The Science of Art
Towards a new higher education paradigm
Education in his field is waning, he thinks, and his opinion is that higher education needs to be reformed along the lines of the new millennium. He wants to help reform the institutions. Students have gone ahead, though unconscious of what they're doing. 384 Words. 2004.

ap040930
The Video Dig Reloaded Payoff
Outcomes elaborated
He is role-playing as a professor in the hot seat of a video art seminar that has not yet been formed, based on a proposal to the city's museum of art. After creating a database of videos that would be useful to study, he begins the tasks of going online. 663 Words. 2004.

ap040104
What REALLY started Emeralda?
Reflections of an estranged professor
It is a time for reflection and renewal for this former professor, as he looks forward to another twenty-year career as meaningful as was his career in teaching. Anticipating it will be his game, Emeralda, that sets the stage for his future, he tells why. 1118 Words. 2004.

ap040830
When Worlds Collide
Persistence of Vision
An evening with people of the old art world shows the contrast of a fresh look at the arts and the old views held dear their hearts. Ample hindsight and immediate experience makes foresight and change too challenging. He thinks about two worlds colliding. 1037 Words. 2004.

ap050901
A Grant from TIAA
Not that is a Good Idea
The Teacher's Insurance and Annuity Association is the worlds oldest and largest teacher pension program that has, for almost a century, meant financial security for professors. Now it is time to account for their real wealth—that of intellectual capital. 956 Words. 2005.

ap051110
A Great Epiphany
Searching for a Reason to Believe
In an email from a man he met 37 years ago, when he was an art student, he said they could expect a "Great Epiphany". In the lives of artists, epiphanies can be like stock in trade. The old professor wonders what it might be, and how it will come to pass. 1105 Words. 2005.

ap050723
A Journey Down Video Memory Lane
It All Begin with a Photo
He was searching for a photograph to make an etching, and one thing led to another until he was experiencing a kind of mental voyage back to the 'seventies. The photo was of C. T. Chew, an artist who shared some amazing experiences during the Video Years. 910 Words. 2005.

ap050911
A New Industry
Basis for Continuous Learning and Earning
Constantly on the lookout for changes in the economy and the aging wave, this artist and former professor suggests that a new kind of industry is on the horizon, thanks to new communications technology. He presents an idea that appeals to him, especially. 1485 Words. 2005.

ap051031
A New Wrinkle
The Payoff of the Month
He's discovered a potential new wrinkle in the Calendar game of Emeralda, his fantasy role playing game based on stamps, cards and other ephemeral art forms. He's creating a collection of stamps that he made over the years and applying it to October 2005.. 559 Words. 2005.

ap050524
A Park About Time
A Visionary Considers a City Park Plan
This artist is also a scholar and he studies time. "Time has form," he heard a student say in one of her performances. How can you study an amorphous thing such as time is, and give it form? And, as in this instance, how can such pursuits apply to a park?
1403 Words. 2005.

ap050921
An ArtsPort Job Description
Making Little Books
Inspired by reading his wife's job description, this artist—with a bent toward entrepreneurship—composes a job description based on one of his routine activities, that of creating miniature instructional manuals that go along with his occasional teaching. 459 Words. 2005.

ap051225
Contents of a Halfwood CD
A Plan for a Learner's Instrument
In coming months he must produce a CD to go with his design of a tiny etching press he calls the Mini Halfwood Press. What should the CD contain? He thinks CDs have advantages over printed User's Manuals, but what are they and how will they work together?
589 Words. 2005.

ap050305
Emeralda Dollars

Artist Trading Cards that you Make with Photo Etching
Ever on the trail of the Missing Professor, this Emeralda Player submits a proposal to combine the Artist Trading Card with the currency of Emeralda Region, the Emeralda Dollar. It features copper printing plates with backward writing and a story to tell. 520 Words. 2005.

ap050822
Fantastic Connections
Restoring the Aura of Authenticity
Inner dialog, it is said, may be an untapped resource of innovation and creativity if the one who's talking to him or her self would just write down the ideas they're having at the moment they enter the conscious mind. Making the connections is the trick. 783 Words. 2005.

ap051215
Great Wave
From the Tool Trade to Instruments of Art
He's beginning the tenth Year of Living Copiously, and finds himself with a slightly different assignment: Bury the Professor and say goodbye to academia. It means this is the year to put more importance on fiction and less on valorizing his college days. 601 Words. 2005.

ap051001
How Was the Bellevue Demonstration?
Recalling a Printing Session at Daniel Smith Inc.
Just before leaving for his demonstration at Bellevue's Daniel Smith Inc., the artist/teacher considers his plan: teaching etching, engraving and dry point all in an hour and printing the plate. He wonders if this is the payoff, the privilege of teaching. 923 Words. 2005.

ap050613
I Want My Wiki
Learning a New Language in the Age of Digital Reproduction
A wiki is a kind of communication format that people use on the Internet to carry on discussions. Through Words. and hypertext, they tell "what I know is", an acronym of which phrase is one way of naming the wiki form. This artist and scholar wants a wiki. 722 Words. 2005.

ap050223
It's Your Asset
Defining Emeralda
While reviewing his essay database he discovers that, seven years ago, he was closer to explaining Emeralda play than today. Then he thinks again: Perhaps not! At the forefront of his thoughts are his newest interests, trading cards and a miniature press. 527 Words. 2005.

ap051120
Learning the Ritchie Method of Media Arts
Toward the Ritchie Institute of Media Arts
Staring at a sheet of stamps by C. T. Chew, the inventor of a method for learning media arts reaches

the conclusion that his example points to the possibility of a new way of teaching print making and other media arts the same way the Suzuki method works. 1028 Words. 2005.

ap050514
Playing and Growing Old
Regarding an Interview with Bill Ritchie
The author wrote himself into an interview, making this essay partly fiction and partly real. It's based on an interview titled Seniors Gaming: Regarding an interview with Mihai Nadin by a columnist for Digital Games Research Association, an online forum. 3756 Words. 2005.

ap051011
Printing A Master's Plate
First 10 Days of EtchingKit Owner Lessons
The Etching Kit came with a plate ready to print. The Master of the Etching Kit created the plate, from his photograph, for the student who purchased the kit. The boy sent his snapshot the day his mother ordered the Etching Kit and the plate came with it. 798 Words. 2005.

ap051130
Secret Challenge
Secret World of the Printmaker
A comment from a retail store performance programmer sets the artist's creative mind working, considering what it means to speak of a printmaker's secret world. Is it formulas and methods? Or is it a great deal more, an entire fantasy world only he knows. 677 Words. 2005.

ap050802
The E Word in Appreciative Systems
Searching for Meaning in Children's Games
He's in his 'sixties—the age when you might picture him playing chess with his old cronies—and he's thinking about children's games like Dungeons and Dragons. There's something to be learned here, as one author put it, "What video games have to teach us."
1239 Words. 2005.

ap050812
The Perfect Thing
Altering the Course of Emeralda
His persistent goal in a persistent world is to become the professor he started out to become. Like a cabin boy on an old time galleon who is aspiring to be captain of the ship, this artist-teacher—in his sixties—wants to reach the level of Great Teacher. 1145 Words. 2005.

ap050404
Using Mihai
My Story Through that of Mihai Nadin
This writer sometimes finds reading someone else' story to be so much like his own life story that he cannot help but "copy-write" over it, putting his Words. over the others. Here he uses an interview of Mihai Nadin, and learns a lesson from the exercise. 2576 Words. 2005.

ap050315
Which Is Your Island of Success?
Playing Emeralda by the Disc
Beginning his day today on the island of ArtsPort, his mind—and his disc drive directory—is directed to another island called Perfect Press. This is the home of the Mini Halfwood Press, and he thinks of a new rule in Emeralda: Games for the Gifts of Life. 469 Words. 2005.

ap050424
Whittling Bill
Reflecting on the Older Set
On a sunny, warm day in Seattle, this printmaker saw himself as one of the "spittin' and whittlin'" set he read about, referring to the oldsters who sometimes sit in front of small town stores chatting. But there's more to this picture than meets the eye. 549 Words. 2005.

ap050713
Why Emeralda Won't Work in School
Reflections Inspired by James Gee
While reviewing a book by James Gee that is about what we can learn from video games, the would-be inventor of a game he calls Emeralda comes across a paragraph that perfectly describes his own experience. He adapts it to this essay. 474 Words. 2005.

ap050623
Wiki 101
Turning Over a New Leaf on the Web
The artist/scholar turns his attention to a new kind of communication form that uses the Internet Web Page as a forum for discussion of What I Know Is. He can begin a community but the question arises, "On what topic?" Here he lists his options and ideas. 810 Words. 2005.

ap050213
Wondering About Emeralda Trading Cards
What are the Rules of the Game?
The inventor of Emeralda: Games for the Gifts of Life, ponders the question of the way Artist Trading Cards fit into the game. He has the International ATC rules in mind, but he's looking for a link between this convention and his own goals. 1074 Words. 2005.

ap060812
A Class that Pays for Itself
Making Productivity a Part of Art
A former professor printmaking reflects on his short happy career on a campus where a shortage of money drove him and his students to explore new ways of balancing productivity and livelihood. Now he is preparing to take on the changes of the digital age. 906 Words. 2006.

ap060822
Assignment
Invent A Game

An assignment to invent a game that serves as an interface to a digital game based learning experience for making intaglio prints. A personal reflection of how the author is driven. 2647 Words. 2006.

ap061001
Author
At the Start of the Play
This artist, practiced with the word visual in front of his title, is trying his hand at writing a screenplay. He wants to base this on his experience and he wants it to convey his philosophy or lessons. He wonders, Is he is more a teacher than an artist? 932 Words. 2006.

ap060713
Before I Go
Vision and Values
Before he leaves his studio on a day in July, this artist—who is dreaming of a different kind of future than most people of his 64 years—hurriedly writes a description of the features he imagines that comprises his vision of an Advanced Leadership School. 970 Words. 2006.

ap060723
Dead Man's Tale
It's in the Cards
A dead man's tale, told by his six children and written here by one who is on a search for a lost emerald known as La Emeralda, an ostrich-egg sized stone said to have been taken from Peru to the region we now call the Pacific Northwest. 237 Words. 2006.

ap061110
Dustin and MAD
A Disappointing Story for A Little Boy
A boy, Dustin, is disappointed by the story he read from the MAD comic book. Too bad about the story. Nothing happened, and it would be another month before his favorite artist would bring another story. Dustin would give him another chance. 519 Words. 2006.

ap061031
Example of A Conflict
In of all Places An Art School
Premise – power struggles and ideological opposition can topple the best of them. Tim is an art student and he likes it. His dad is the department chairman. Among the 800 students in this art school, he's got an inside track. 876 Words. 2006.

ap060114
First Day at the Seattle Print Fair
A Forecast
He's anticipating being part of the 6th Seattle Print Fair on this the first of two days that the fair runs. He plans it to be an enjoyable part as he plans to print for those two days from a plate he made for the occasion—an enlarged commemorative stamp. 713 Words. 2006.

ap061111
Imagine A Sheet Like This
Art Stamps
Then you learn about the INCHPRINT exhibition, where all prints are 1 inch or less on their longer dimension. It is geared toward artist's stamps, of course, and themes are determined by the American Print Dealers Association. 164 Words. 2006.

ap060921
Investing in Life Time
Volunteerism
But why did the author volunteer? Is it not a full time job to be doing what he really wants to do, which is to do something great in the arts and maintain an education-based lifetime career? Yes, it's more than a fulltime job. 290 Words. 2006.

ap061130
My Advice
Spreadsheets and Printmaking
It begins with an ArtGrid that charts the course of your experience with images and Words.. 351 is the number of an artwork in a list of over 450 works the author considers the Ritchie Family Collection. This is a listing of artworks dating back to 1960. 253 Words. 2006.

ap060104
Navigable Thinking
Brain Food for Thinking
The challenge of designing games lies partly in taking oneself back in time to before the game existed. This is like taking oneself back to childhood naiveté, for imagining the game completed would be to imagine the game as commonplace. 531 Words. 2006.

ap060911
Teacher-Student Owned Schools
An Unconscious Sense of Ownership
The root of the public schools' problems is the lack of a sense of ownership. The opposite is true, that the teachers, students and staff feel pride and love for their school, this is because of an unconscious sense of ownership. 674 Words. 2006.

ap060622
Values and Art in the Digital Age
Towards a New Kind of Fundraiser
He thinks he is sitting on a goldmine in artworks, but, in the age of digital reproduction, the visual arts are undergoing a devaluation period. Some new thing must be done if artist's legacies are to be identified, controlled, evaluated and disseminated. 1443 Words. 2006.

ap071130
Another Day, Another Card
The Thrill of the Search
At a moment when he has placed a digital image of a playing card—one that exists also as a piece of paper on the desktop at his side—he gets a fleeting sense of reward—the kind of reward he feels when placing a piece in a puzzle, a mild kind of discov-

ery. 550 Words. 2007.

ap070603
ArtsPort – 5th Day
Emeralda's Alphabet
Listed alphabetically, ArtsPort is the first imaginary island you come to on Bill's computer directory. However, ArtsPort was not the first of the ten domains Bill dreamed up when he envisioned his game, Emeralda. Perfect Studios was. 2171 Words. 2007.

ap071031
Certificate Cards
A New Kind of Stock
Studying to decide whether it would be a good investment of time and money to incorporate, this artist—who is inventing a digital based learning game—makes a connection between the collectible trading cards he's created and corporation stock certificates. 423 Words. 2007.

ap070901
Day One of 12th Year
Emeralda: Games for the Gifts of Life
Game pieces for Emeralda. 649 Words. 2007.

ap071021
Getting Set
Ready to Play Emeralda?
Things have changed slightly since the inventor of Emeralda met with and showed a fellow artist (and art dealer) the basics of the game and he said, "Next time we meet, let's play!" Now, as the self-appointed Master works on cards, he's getting set. 68 Words. 2007.

ap071001
On GAS
Envisioning a Session Back at the U
GAS—Games and Simulation—a loose knit, informal group that meets periodically at the University of Washington. 828 Words. 2007.

ap070114
Second Day at the 7th Print Fair
My Purpose at the Print Fair
The author can reflect on the events of yesterday and make a few notes of things that happened that might have importance to both purposes of his being at the Print Fair. 365 Words. 2007.

ap071225
Template
A Template for One Card
You have received the template for one card from the domain of Perfect Studios. 270 Words. 2007.

ap070921
The Farmer in the Bill
A Plot for Cultivating an Artist's Intellectual Capital
Reading a book by Robert Kiyosaki, the artist is inspired to reconsider the value of his intellectual capital, an asset that Kiyosaki says is qualified

to turn into financial wealth. He's spotted a small space for sell that would serve as gallery for him. 531 Words. 2007.

ap071215
Welcome to ArtsPort – Again
First Day of the 12th Year of Living Copiously
It is December 15, 2007., and it is on the 15th of December for the past 11 years that the author has given himself the Gates Prize: A Year of Living Copiously. It's a day to look ahead and ponder the possibilities and opportunities while playing Emeralda. 379 Words. 2007.

ap080314
Alumni Loveletter
Pathways and Shoes to Walk Them
He has occasion to think about his Alma Mater when someone from the university's development office calls to pay a visit. Usually such calls mean that they hope for a gift of his legacy, but his definition of legacy is different from conventional thought. 852 Words. 2008.

ap081215
Auspicious Beginning A YOLC
Change in the Wind at ArtsPort
It seems there is something new in the air as the winner of the Gates Prize begins his 13th year in Emeralda Region. His studio on ArtsPort seems cleaner, the work space more organized. Situations in the real world may be making change in Emeralda Region. 1223 Words. 2008.

ap080921
Come-On
Art Ed Online
The title of this essay implies a promotional bait to bring members of the community together. It would be both entertaining and business. The author would begin with the vivid image of an undiscovered source of money for all members: Art Ed Online. 559 Words. 2008.

ap080114
Comic Professor
News from Lake Emeralda
Affecting the style of the renowned radio show, Prairie Home Companion, and yarns that Garrison Keillor features each episode, the Emeralda Inventor writes what it would be like to describe himself as an eccentric character in the News from Lake Emeralda. 1111 Words. 2008.

ap081129
Finding A Black Book One Day
A Black Ring Binder
How can the author write a book explaining how artists can take care of their legacy. In ways that when they pass on, their work doesn't end up in a landfill or, at best, auctioned off for a fraction of their value. 423 Words. 2008.

ap080124
Leaving Mind

A Clue from J. S. Bach
Somebody once said J. S. Bach left us his mind in the composition, Well Tempered Clavier—an instance of a beautiful and instructional work of art. It is possible that today an artist can achieve the equivalent—combining instrumentation with digital media. 608 Words. 2008.

ap080223
Matriz Temporal
Un Projecto in the Making
After nine years of sporadic email communications with an artist in Chile (referring to herself as designer and art educator), the artist/entrepreneur has an actual proposal for his first international exchange since the 1980s. He recalls his old desires. 993 Words. 2008.

ap080324
Next Stage
Designing the Cards for Emeralda
After many months the artist, designing a collectible card game version of his game that he calls Emeralda, has been using Excel spreadsheets to organize his legacy data, paralleling Access. Next, he will probably carry over the content to Adobe InDesign. 631 Words. 2008.

ap080901
Outline for the Baker University Lecture
A Presentation in Four Parts
Experience Print Making is an idea thought up a few blocks from Seattle's EMP—the Experience Music Project, and the Science Fiction Museum. Somehow music and sci-fi are linked to the history of printmaking, as this speaker would explain in a lecture-demo. 427 Words. 2008.

ap081120
Reviewing Zines
An Overview of Nellie Sunderland's Project – Part 1
As a student in a small college town where he enjoyed extensive student/teacher interchange, the author rented a house from one of his professors. She gave him run of her library that she kept in that rental, and this was a precursor to his Zine database. 1837 Words. 2008.

ap081010
Show Me Xbox
A Digital Immigrant Contemplates XNA
Calling himself a "digital immigrant," the 66-year old author contemplates changing his mind. He wonders about a console-based game delivery as a viable way to build his notion of a digital game-based approach to teaching the art and craft of printmaking. 1186 Words. 2008.

ap080403
Teaching Materials
Needs for Learning Printmaking Online
The inventor of the world's first online, hybrid course in the art and craft of printmaking that incorporates video game elements in its syllabus describes reasons the course is needed, what is in the box for it, and explains the reasons for taking it on. 1694 Words. 2008.

ap081020
Test Plate
Participant/Student
He will soon have to leave ArtsPort—a matter of a day, and he must have a "stamp of approval" from his mentor. But where is he? Or she? All he has for instructions is a cryptic note: "The test plate must be a card."
295 Words. 2008.

ap080821
The Work of Art in the Age of Digital Reproduction
Towards A Book
In prior years this artist wrote manuscripts and self-published books. He has yet another idea for a book that explains what he plans to do for art education. He will create an online, hybrid art course in the art of fine printmaking. He has four reasons. 802 Words. 2008.

ap080911
Visual Language and Me
Art in the 21st Century
Planning notes for talks to three college classes titled Visual Language gives the 20th C professor pause to think about where he has been, where he is now and where he plans to be. Point-of-view seems to be the key to thinking about art in the 21st. C. 617 Words. 2008.

ap080104
We Build Our Rhythm as We Live It
Emeralda Rhythm Compared to the Circadian in Us
The rhythm we automatically respond to with the rising and setting of the sun. It's a natural rhythm, a biological level. By playing Emeralda, we learn to follow rhythms of the creative life within the age of digital reproduction. 582 Words. 2008.

ap080902
We Write the Rules and We Play
Steps to Validating Stamps
The player needs to perfect his image from the Missing Professor's archive and make a validating stamp for the passport inspectors. 238 Words. 2008.

ap080203
Why Play?
Keeping Memory Alive
Keeping his brain alive is as important to this author as good nutrition is to most people. As he is in his sixties he must guard against memory loss so he is inventing a game that exercises his memory, and he uses computers and the Internet to help play. 1059 Words. 2008.

ap090514
Clearing

A Parting in the Clouds over Emeralda Region
Writing the bible of ELPO (the author's brainchild
for teaching printmaking online) he has the task
of organizing his thoughts into an understandable
document. Outlining this for what is like the hun-
dredth time, visions of clearing, parting clouds
appear. 666 Words. 2009.

ap090603
Coop Art
When Artists Share their World
This artist thinks the time is right for realizing a
global artist's co-operative that has been in existence for a hundred years, but—like people who
live on a mountain so they cannot see the mountain—few artists have known about it. It is a
shared world. 1475 Words. 2009.

ap090203
ELPO Narrative and Gaming Elements
Describing the Fun and Games of Learning Print-
making Online
Questions about Narrative and Gaming. 148
Words. 2009.

ap090124
ELPO Setting, Worlds, and Characters
Describing the Virtual, Virtuous World where
Printmaking is King
Author Carol Miller presents a checklist for developing digital games. This is the 5th in the list,
commented on by the wannabe professor/inven-
tor of Emeralda: Learn Printmaking Online—a
plan for a digital-game based, blended distance
learning experience. 890 Words. 2009.

ap091001
Emeralda ATC
Two Kinds, Two Reasons for Artist Trading Cards
An offer to make a Flash! electronic card (e-card)
brings up the question, "What for?" Is it an opportunity to make the e-ATC, or electronic Emeralda
Artist Trading Card? Or is it a distraction to the
work at hand? His database of art and essays is
ready. 456 Words. 2009.

ap090315
Emeralda Was Created in Five or Six Days
Depending on if your Year of Living Copiously is
a Leap Year or Not
The inventor of Emeralda: Learn Printmaking
Online is responsible for writing the bible of the
game-like user interface for the course. He bases
the bible on ten years of previous efforts to create
an intelligible description of the game and its benefits. 360 Words. 2009.

ap090623
Gage Model
Impressions of Gage Academy
Impressions of Gage Academy; their forthright,
business-like way of conducting an art school,
starting with the competition between the University of Washington and the Cornish College of Art
for students who wanted to become artists. 2880

Words. 2009.

ap090220
Games as Autobiography
Inspired by the Movie "The Class"
The author attempts, on a daily basis, to create a
digital-game based story intended to be a user interface for teaching a fine art as a blended learning
experience. Reading about the French film The
Class, he's struck by the autobiographic in his effort. 533 Words. 2009.

ap090223
Gaming Autobiography
Can Autobiography be a Video Game?
A student, Mark, was unusually early to class
bringing with him a whole sheaf of targets and
pinned them to some firewood. He took out a gun
from his coat and fired at the targets. "Here's my
editioned print," he said. 1622 Words. 2009.

ap090104
Genre in ELPO
If Emeralda Learn Printmaking Online can be for
Kids too, then What is the Genre?
This Emeralda inventor is challenged in reading
that, in the games for children industry, his idea
for "Emeralda: Learn Printmaking Online" must
make the choice of genre from a list of dozens of
possibilities. Printmaking itself may answer this
challenge. 721 Words. 2009.

ap090504
Introduction to ELPO Development 4
Introducing the Changes in the Fourth Version of
Emeralda – Learn Printmaking Online
A year after following the advice he got in a book
about designing video games and adapting these
for an online learning course, this art professor introduces the significant change that has occurred,
which is mainly the miniature, toy-like etching
press. 1144 Words. 2009.

ap091215
Opening Day
First Day at ArtsPort 2009.-2010
He pretends like a little kid who is at his first day
in camp. ArtsPort is the name of an island he
made up, placing it in a great lake in an imaginary
place called Emeralda Region—a mysterious place
haunted by ghosts in his new "machines," his computers. 1053 Words. 2009.

ap090325
Planes and Games
Reminiscences of a Senior Gamer
He had a short and interesting conversation with
a software developer about their childhood hobbies that might, today, be related to today's new
and complex world of video game development.
They agree model airplane toys may help creative
problem-solving. 780 Words. 2009.

ap091021
Problem One

Thoughts of a Dying Diehard Printmaker
Winding his way through a problem on his computer one morning he hits on an understanding of the first problem to set before online printmaking users—a kind of jigsaw puzzle of why to learn old-time printmaking in a time of digital reproduction of prints. 1287 Words. 2009.

ap090404
Scott Turow Profile
The Protagonist of ArtsPort Chapter in "Hunt for the Emeralda Treasure"
Imaginary islands serve as places to situate main characters for the manuscript for "Hunt for the Emeralda Treasure." According the author, each protagonist's story follows one of ten genres. The genre for Scott Turow, protagonist of ArtsPort, is mystery. 499 Words. 2009.

ap090213
Teacher Unbound
Blended Learning in Virtual Worlds
The morning after his sixth session in a new certificate program on Virtual Worlds, the Itinerate Professor blends a lifetime college professor experience being inside and outside ivory towers. As the finals week approaches, he takes note of a book topic. 2053 Words. 2009.

ap090114
Ultimate Emeralda
Inventing "Emeralda: Games for the Gifts of Life" takes Reflection on One's Lifetime
Structuring Emeralda: Games for the Gifts of Life sometimes requires the game's inventor to pause and to reflect on his original mission. Details are important to note because it is a team effort. Communication is decisive. He thinks about the end game. 1011 Words. 2009.

ap091011
Underserved Markets
What I Learned in the Back Room Yesterday
Ever alert to opportunities to serve communities of interest in printmaking, the author gives an account of what he learned at an art supply retail store while demonstrating printmaking. He believes a market for learning printmaking online is underserved. 1832 Words. 2009.

Electronic Studios and Hospitality (AKA E'Studios, ES)

The ferry takes Residents-in-Stay to E'Studios, short to experience real and virtual spaces where artists make and display their art, craft and design.

With its roots in printmaking history, arts' reproductions are electronic (usually digital, but sometimes analog) as opposed to mechanical. Performance arts, too, are produced in combination of TV, computer and mobile devices.

A 20th Century art historian named Miriam Levin is said to have established the E'Studios culture when she proclaimed: "In a pluralistic society, where much of our work involves analyzing visual information transmitted on video screens, art might have the most profound effect on our lives by providing designs for the organization and sequencing of information."

In the domain of E'Studios, electronics serve— and are served by—artists in creative arts, learning and teaching, doing research and production, practicing and serving their community with multimedia aid.

es760115
Journal, Thu. Jan. 15, 1976
New York, Barbara Myers and Electronic Arts Intermix
The author spent time in New York meeting people in the art world and video world. Barbara Myers encouraged him to show and sell his prints. He talked to people at Electronic Arts Intermix, their rejection was discouraging and he shortened his trip. 800 Words. 1976.

es770326
Journal, Wed. March 26, 1977
Thoughts on Video Classes
The author writes about his thoughts about past video students who worked at Channel 9 (the local public television station). He also writes his thoughts about next year's video class and scheduling time to plan. The video classes broaden con-

sciousnesses. 562 Words. 1977.

es800415
Journal, Mon. April, 15, 1980
School Administration Trivia
The author writes about his continual struggle with the art school's administration. He was moved into a different office in the art history wing. He planned to teach and make art, and to leave the office trivia that clutters educational scene behind him. 650 Words. 1980.

es840214
Journal, Tues. February 14, 1984
Experience and Repetition
What is basic to experience, and basic to art experience too is the repetition of the events. They become real; media makes experience repeatable on one or several levels. 413 Words. 1984.

es860515
Journal, Thu. May 15, 1986
Dressing for Success
The author is adding another book to his collection; "Dress for Success." He shares his struggles with lack of proper attire. He also focuses on the objective of the day which was a meeting with Sandy Kroupa about a videodisc. 426 Words. 1986.

es891011
Computer Art is A Dead Mike
Only the front row knows IT
An entrepreneur in a desktop publishing company hosts an art show and asked the author to write something for it. He likens it to a dead mike: In the front they know what computer art is but those who are way in the back are saying, "What's IT all about?" 689 Words. 1989.

es900606
Why Rugs?
Artist's statement on rugs and computer art
The digital artist works in the back room of a rug dealer and wonders why he is there. His conclusion is that computer graphics have their roots in weaving. The evolution of graphics by mechanization in printing, and in fine art prints, is relatively new. 610 Words. 1990.

es911011
A True Story Art in Public Places
One artist's experience (1962 - 1991)
Starting from the author's first phone call and continuing to the last encounter for an art in public places programs, he tells it to its sad ending at the library of Spokane Community College. He concludes that this experience offered short-term rewards. 2558 Words. 1991.

es920926
Goethe's Mistake
Interfere, always interfere
Goethe wrote, Connect, always connect, but to understand the changes going on around the university and in the city as a whole, look at the obverse: Interfere, always interfere. (Outlined proposal) 276 Words. 1992.

es920111
IICS Asks, Ritchie Answers
IICS Art forum review
Based on the International Interactive Communications Society board's questions, three artists show their work and speak in a panel discussion. 5488 Words. 1992.

es920825
Silica No, Silicon Yes
Dialog of the sand-masters
The author recounts his inner dialog with a glass artist who argues that glass art is great. Silica--the stuff computer chips are made of--is the greater art, he says. 1238 Words. 1992.

es920908
About StoryBored
Visualizing the reinvented studio directories
A digital artist describes process and history of a computer art work, the structure of which is intended to be an animated version of a fly-through of his vision of Perfect Studios. 2746 Words. 1992.

es930613
Give Me Product
Moving toward the game
Creative people cringe at product demands; creativity is not a consumer commodity. At its worst, product demand invites mechanization to take command. At best, product demand lets artists, crafts people and designers restore cultural values. 683 Words. 1993..

es931206
What does E'Studio Look Like?
A concept for kiosks
An electric studio looks like an ordinary art gallery except it has artist's kiosks instead of worktables and walls. (Concept) 83 Words. 1993.

es940104
Early the 11th Day
Meeting a ghost in the new machine
Opening files about electronic studios, the author met a ghost in his new machine. Full-circle, from when he saw he needed software to make writing more accessible on the disk-top, to now, when even he himself would be in for a pleasant surprise. 420 Words. 1994.

es940105
She Carries the Prints
The story of Living Prints(r)
From the Personal Digital Assistant (PDA) notes are gleaned, in text form, that will explain what is meant by Living Prints(r). Part game, part history, and partly an old dream, the author begins his version. 884 Words. 1994.

es940507
E'Studio 'Zines Reviewed

What is an artist's estate really worth?
The seeds of essays about art and technology that are written for electronic databases maintained by the professors' own digital craft and design. Periodically the professor reviews his or her own databases. With each review, the essays get better. 1652 Words. 1994.

es940728
To Be Effective, Artist
Soul of a new work
The backmatter text proposed for the operating manual for EarthSafe 2022. The author's database includes Arthur C. Clark and Novalis, whose words help to understand the engineer's demands. 376 Words. 1994.

es951226
Journal, Tues. December 26, 1995.
Restore Family Relations and a Talk with John Thomas
Notes recorded from the author's "palmtop" B.O.S.S. computer. This entry includes wins of helping restore family relations in Yakima, talking to John Thomas, PE, Spanish and Mega Memory. Also mentions developing income-earning activity for the next year. 180 Words. 1995.

es951229
The Cyber Legionnaire's Story:
A Senior at PATCWA
What would it be like if Washington technology industries trained a legion of volunteers to be assistants to the state's schools? The author is an artist is going through a phase in life when he believes old ties can be restored and communities re-formed. 2314 Words. 1995.

es960919
An Artist's Self-Portrait in the Age of Digital Communication
New screens for an old idea
Having electronic studios for artists today means that the time-honored practice of making self-portraits can be pursued in a new, digital way--but what does the new way look like? 2018 Words. 1996.

es961020
Perfect Day at E'Studios
Center and node of attraction
A Gruddite Apprentice-user sums up what, in his view, would be a perfect day spent at a gallery where all the art is connected to digital and video media. A blend of cafe and art gallery, a center for as well as a node in cybernetic games. 1433 Words. 1996.

es960105
Journal, Fri. January 5, 1996.
Woodcutting and Other Interesting Things
Notes recorded from the author's "palmtop" B.O.S.S. computer. The author is happy to find the book, "The Game of Life and How to Play it" and he was doing a lot of woodcutting. His daughter, Jane, found his home page and an email from Dana Lemieux. 233 Words. 1996.

es960125
Journal, Thu. January 25, 1996.
Wonderful Message from Emanuel Pimenta
Notes recorded from the author's "palmtop" B.O.S.S. computer. The author writes about his wins from a couple of days prior to 960125. He received a wonderful message from Emanuel Pimenta. He was proud of his writing "Finding it Out – Part I." 181 Words. 1996.

es960314
Tour of E'Studios
Second Isle in the Domain of Expertise
Excerpted from the draft of the workbook for Reinventing Arts Studios, a fictional account of a tourist's view of the ten islands in the domain of Emeralda. E'Studios is a showcase for cybernetic arts. 2353 Words. 1996.

es960531
The Web Curator wants to Know
Entries for an electronic curator log
Hasty notes taken on a hand-held device by a fictional electronic curator while he/she observes the making of a digital file for an image destined to go on-line. 418 Words. 1996.

es960929
Hold it Right There, PortMaster
What are you doing with those keys?
An imaginary lecturer in an imaginary lecture hall, spurred by an imaginary questioner in the front row who wants to know, "How do you spend your time in your electronic studio?" 1546 Words. 1996.

es960410
Plumbing Creativity
Billy builds home pages with running money
There's more to building a home page on the World Wide Web than software alone. It is money spent, time, and connections to fountains of creativity. An idea to fulfill the artists' dream: Running money in artists' electronic studios. 754 Words. 1996.

es970405
TCWA Review
In 30 seconds or less!
Over a year lapsed since the author filed an intent to charter Tech Corps Washington. Now, he's asked to update someone on the development. How to summarize 18 months? This topic of education reform goes back much longer, as this article describes. 1963 Words. 1997.

es971111
The Mysterious History of Emeralda
Imaginary lost land and gained again
Initial paragraphs of an essay to recount the history of Bill Ritchie's "Games for the Gifts of Life" he calls "Emeralda." How the name came about is still a mystery to many, but not the author; it is a

game about becoming an artist in the cybernetic age. 596 Words. 1997.

es971129
Journal, Sat. November 29, 1997.
360 Emeralda Postcards, 360 Images
The author writes his time log of the day, the activities and projects he did that day. He writes a vision of a box-set of 360 Emeralda Postcards, 36 each of the ten Isles and a total of 360 images. He writes a cascade of intellectual capital as treasure. 431 Words. 1997.

es971130
Emeralda Detailed
Notes from the Inventors Journal
The inventor of Emeralda Games for the Gifts of Life struggles to find the words that describe his method of play before he really knows how to play, or why he wants to play that he's inventing. Conventional, competitive games no longer guide or help him. 735 Words. 1997.

es971222
Searching for Emeralda
The Labor Game
What does "invest in labor" mean? This has haunted the author for years. He says he believes he has found the reference point he needs to leverage a new kind of financial asset management game all creative, inventive and discovering people can play. 1058 Words. 1997.

es970110
Journal, Fri. January 10, 1997.
Trip to Yakima, E-mails and GoalBook3
The author writes his time log of the day, the activities and projects he did that day. He records emailing Guys@Gazelle and C.T. Chew. He writes about visiting his granddaughter in Yakima and writes some of his ideas for future generation's safety. 552 Words. 1997.

es970307
Cyber Scouts
Youth in the Electronic Studios
Cyber comes from the Greek word Kybor. Cybernetics may be the best science to describe a communications age scout movement. Educators may find a structured human communications approach to be a way values can take over school-based computer clubs. 2327 Words. 1997.

es981002
What is it Worth to Move
Zooming in on routine activities
The invention of Emeralda, which is a game for the gifts of life and therefore a dynamic game, the act of zooming in on details in a player's Routine Activities is one of the main features of successful play. Converting this into numbers is the challenge. 1414 Words. 1998.

es980823
Beyond What Than the Eye Can See

Luca Pacioli's gift
On occasion the creative, inventive, discovering and imaginative individual crosses the two-way bridge between mathematics and art--a crossing portrayed in some films, songs and multimedia. These arts make a lot of money for those who crossed the bridge." 751 Words. 1998.

es980922
Pretend You are Me
The Dummy looks for money
Part XI of Emeralda for Dummies. When you contrive to get the support of certain, powerful others to achieve your goals, how Emeralda shines! This is an account of how the Game for the Gifts of Life is the secret weapon in the artist's arsenal of ideas." 926 Words. 1998.

es981012
Q&A from Electronic Studios and Galleries Agents
Emeralda Inventor Interviews
Interviews of the Inventor of Emeralda by himself, for him self, as his striving continues and he asks the questions that build the bridges across the chasm between the world before Emeralda and the world that is becoming one--concurrently--with Emeralda. 5994 Words. 1998.

es981022
Browsing and Mining
What's the difference?
The difference between the haves and have-nots is equal to the difference between browsing and mining. An old dilemma tale, thousands of variations come to mind, from the story of Cain and Able to the gap between ones who know how to do a Web site or not. 443 Words. 1998.

es981221
Moment of Entry
Date stamping your life away
Life's like a passenger terminal on a transportation line; you go through the Gates, you're date-stamped. Later you pass again through that Gates and get yet one more date-stamp. Entry to E'Studios Isle of Domain-of-Expertise is similar, but much shorter. 819 Words. 1998.

es981222
Managing Equity
Tales from Four Insights
An order for a book, "Art of Selling Art" arrived. The author's wife told him that a woman who took his advice on stock investing made $10,000 on it. How these two small events relate to managing equity as a many-sided story-a tale from four perspectives? 1080 Words. 1998.

es981224
Placholder 5 of 18
Brain Surgery and Rocket Science
Innovator's dilemma
A dreamer writes on his 58th birthday: "Day one of my 59th year on Earth. I will turn sixty during

the Year of the Millennium. If I knew more about that pseudo-science called numerology, then perhaps I could make something out of this Perfect Information." 707 Words. 1998.

es980813
Tax Reform for Electronic Studios and Galleries
Uncertainty of death and taxes
Death and taxes are a certainty in conventional thinking, but both are uncertainties and should remain as uncertainties in the minds and hearts of artists. The IRS, in the United States, is not to control the freedom of individuals--unless they let them." 1113 Words. 1998.

es980912
Emeralda Keepsake
Emeralda for Dummies--Part IV
Keepsakes of Emeralda are the software application specific integrated algorithms (ASIA) possessed by each of the Four Women Who Fell to Earth. In the original version of Emeralda (AD 1985-2000.) all the applications were designed for Microsoft Windows." 262 Words. 1998.

es980604
Never Write It Down
Tempting the Self-fulfilling Prophecy
Confessions of a self-exiled art professor who sometimes feels like he's living in a prison of his own making. At worst, he's right; at best, he's right also, but the payoff for his risk is the invention of a better "art education game" he calls Emeralda. 1693 Words. 1998.

es980803
Automating Emeralda
Continuity, permutation and permeation
Seamless, automated operations are akin to the notion of continuity, which is a dream and an illusion toward which creative, inventive, discovering and imaginative people often feel attracted. Routine activities, however, seem to work against these goals. 555 Words. 1998.

es980724
Hold that Keystroke
The monitor halts all
An inventor's dilemma, like that of prisoners' in their dilemmas, is that he must write about what is happening at the same time that he is escaping doing it. Few things require both sides of the brain and all aspects of a personality in quite this way." 984 Words. 1998.

es980714
Through the One-Way Mirror
Signs of life, signs of death
Striving to understand Emeralda himself even though he created it, the inventor tests it for life using a mirror, a way one tries to see if an inert person is breathing by holding a mirror to their face. You will be surprised at what you see in a mirror! 1567 Words. 1998.

es980902
Marketing Cascades
Introducing the soap opera of the future
Introduction to the opera, Emeralda, in the form of a dynamic on-line "Soap" that people can get themselves into by playing this Game for the Gifts of Life on-line. Part of one's daily routine is included--which is the first entry to garage.com as a game. 1676 Words. 1998.

es980614
Setting the Stage
A background for Emeralda
Set in the year 2028, the scene is of a dying Earth and the character who was frozen a half-century before and is now walking around on a campus for those people who are in need of learning a new life. Based on the author's semi-autobiographical allegory. 1054 Words. 1998.

es980525
Role of the Goal
Taking no chances
In his fantasy role playing game he invented for his own delight (he calls it Emeralda) the artist/professor ponders the state of the art of using the Internet World Wide Web and how he can communicate the meaning of his game to people networked anywhere. 1365 Words. 1998.

es980515
Not One-To-Many Anymore
Reversing the picture
First in a two part demonstration in which the author explains how the old model of one teacher speaking to many students will change, and in the future it will be several teachers who address a single student, like the service you have on a luxury liner. 968 Words. 1998.

es980224
Who's in Charge Here?
The asset manager is playing games
A flash of insight brings about the next step in the invention of Emeralda. The author (the inventor of Emeralda) decides it is time to divide the labor of asset management, despite the warnings from a doubtful intelligent agent. 893 Words. 1998.

es980107
Me and Cardano
A striking resemblance
Continuation of writing that began as a cyber-signal intended to contact a fellow player of Emeralda on the Web. Nested in "Stranded on an island," this essay is developed on Bernstein's story of Girolamo Cardano, introducing a cooperative game's history." 1574 Words. 1998.

es971221
Stickers on Your Luggage
Where have you been? Where are you going? Where are you now?
Written almost a year later, the author looks back at souvenir stickers on his old videotape carry-

ing case collected on his trip around the world in search of the perfect studios. Those were from the days before E'Studios existed, but still pertain today. 1483 Words. 1998.

es980624
Teaching at a Distance
Emeralda's Side Benefits
Looking into his past, the author recounts his first ideas about distance learning. He then demonstrates the current state of this idea--teaching art on-line--and sums up with an outline to take the idea to the next step: Investment. 1400 Words. 1998.

es990225
Where Do You Get Time?
Observations of an Emeralda Player
Emeralda is a story or a fabled fantasy land that is like beauty: in the mind of its inventor and beholder. He follows his locus of beauty and writes about the comparison of this self-delusion with the delusion that one can get time or make it for things. 546 Words. 1999.

es990622
Departing Emeralda's E'Studios
A Preface to Printing the Emeralda Inventor Interviews
Be Your Own Pet was a slogan made up years ago for a T-shirt art project between this author and the poet Stevan Worley. This essay serves as a Preface for a transcript of a ten hour videotaped series of mock auto-interviews of the author with himself(s). 1818 Words. 1999.

es990623
Mute and Lonely in Its Possessor's Heart
Grudin on Bloom
Chance occurrences always fit in Emeralda Play so long as the player is engaged both in producing while practicing. The essay starts with a coincidence as reader/writer finds one plus one equals four--two writers plus him equals an interesting experience. 1350 Words. 1999.

es990621
The Calendar and the Wheel
Reinventing goes around
Aware as he is of the need to reinvent himself as he reinvents his studio, the artist of yesterday, today and tomorrow discovers a hidden electronic intelligent agent in the silicon of computers. Comparisons to reinventing the wheel are not absurdity now. 1385 Words. 1999.

es990620
Reinventing Arts' Studios
Foreword to Workbook II
Time lines tend to create the illusion of calculation and distort the natural way things happen. Lines are mechanical, connecting, always connecting. Life does not follow linear patterns and such simple order. These are selections from the brief Foreword. 347 Words. 1999.

es990619
Reinventing Arts' Studios
Preface to Workbook II
The reader is asked to use powers of imagination, looking at the light side of technology. At times we learn things better if we see education or training in a playful way, finding pleasure in changing our minds. To learn, one has to be willing to change. 1254 Words. 1999.

es990618
A Living Calendar
Wandering and wondering
Defining and specifying are two different routine activities for a writing Emeralda Player. The former is science and perfect knowledge, the latter is art and imperfect knowledge. It's like the difference between what happened and what you want to happen. 937 Words. 1999.

es990423
How Proverbs Help Me Play Emeralda
A place for rituals, rites and rights
There are many rituals, or routine activities, associated with playing Emeralda. In his third year, this Emeralda Defender is copying Proverbs from the Bible, using a PDA. He says he learns things this way, not only fathoming the meanings of the Proverbs. 610 Words. 1999.

es990424
Corner of A Big Picture Puzzle
Putting pieces together in an organization
If a jigsaw puzzle is in a tetrahedron shape--a four sided pyramid--then it will be a witty invention whose four sides are made to interlock in some clever way. The author saw spherical puzzles in a toy catalog and posits this idea for his game, Emeralda. 2234 Words. 1999.

es990421
A Simple Twist of Faith
From lecture to Web
The economics of this fact are interesting: The writer claims he went to a lecture and, thanks to the Internet, was able to tell many more people about it than were in the lecture hall (who paid a lot to attend). He Netcast it for pennies, in a few hours. 1224 Words. 1999.

es990419
Real Dental Tour Project
What is it?
Dentists are sought to commit resources for their assistants' training for critical review and practices in the Real Dental Tour project. The project is based on cooperation-based videos giving patients close up, private tours featuring their oral health. 1331 Words. 1999.

es990224
On Using the Internet for Dentistry
Five tips
Inspired by a general information article he read in a computer news tabloid, the author tailors the ideas to fit the dental practice office. He is finding

ways to help accelerate using the Internet for benefits to the oral medicine community of practice. 2278 Words. 1999.

es990223
Where in the Real World has the Professor Been?
Breakfast at E'Studios Isle for world travelers
In a make believe breakfast speech, real author Lydia Bronte introduces the author's character as a world traveler who is about to show scenes from his sabbaticals. Taken during his stay on the Real Campus, he contradicts the writer's opinion of his type. 870 Words. 1999.

es990221
BOSS of Mine
Caption for a candid snapshot
To illustrate how a professor writes--and sometimes reads and writes concurrently--the author provides a snapshot of him. And among his paraphernalia surrounding the professor in his cell is a Personal Digital Assistant (PDA), which this article explains. 240 Words. 1999.

es990220
Electronic Portfolio
Presenting your digital case
On a computer screen--moving data from one area of a hard drive to another, or from Internet server to desktop--seems like moving artworks from one folder to another. Instead of paper shuffling, it happens in digital forms. Cyber art and portfolios blend. 652 Words. 1999.

es990420
Ten by Ten
100 Testimonials for Real Dental Tour
A man appeared on a path of the locus of beauty, walking with four women--two on each side of him. He appeared to be under their escort as if he were an important figure. Or, it appeared he is under their guard, like a criminal. Which is he? Who can tell? 747 Words. 1999.

es990422
The Truth about Dentistry
Manipulation in a teaching practice
Admitted failures resulted from a dentist's ignorance of the principles of communication forced him to learn more than what they'd taught him in dental school said a speaker. Has more to learn while he practices: his part in the economics of this society. 2628 Words. 1999.

es000717
Glimpsed
A wine label
A typographical error results in a flash of insight and the author thinks of a wine label for his growing list of ideas for projects he'd love to be involved in. The creative, inventive, discovering and imaginative sovereign individual works strange ways. 409 Words. 2000.

es000110
The Problem with George

The artist's trust and the artist's thrust
The Emeralda Player begins a game by taking up a broken strand that was part of the founding of Artist Trust-family dental care-and reconnects it to fundamental laws of art, economics and life science. Online Dental and Studio Practice Simulation results. 404 Words. 2000.

es001021
New Words in Art Education
Backable assets
A curriculum for on-line arts education takes on forms that are unrecognized by 20th-Century art educators. It is because new technologes0 effect economic values of art. What used to be important were bankable assets. In Y2K, legacy transfer is important. 1683 Words. 2000.

es000822
Journal, Tues. August 22, 2000.
Awakening from a dream
The author dreamed he would create an installation for one of his works that closely resembled the art he created in his computer. He envisioned it as "built-in" the wall, requiring a sculpted cavity with acoustic controls. It was to be temporary. 209 Words. 2000.

es000604
Ghost Students
Conversation with a metaphor
The author, as an art student, was impressed by his teacher's creativity, private library, and interesting surroundings. In a make-believe scene, he shows how teachers and students are changed, how perception of students is changed and they become ghosts. 2060 Words. 2000.

es000222
As a Tub Runs Over
Art Ed Online Proprietary Search Engine-Part II
Envisioning an online art education channel for Washington, an ITinerate Professor looks at a voluminous, ordered database growing on a public Web site at the start of Y2K. Then he suggests how to use this example of human structural intellectual capital. 1520 Words. 2000.

es000221
Another Day in the Life of Emeralda Inventor
Early one morning
The Emeralda Inventor is interviewed, a "self-talk dialog" exercise he uses to look back at Perfect Information comprising that that has happened and cannot be changed. He offers the essay to two other individuals he thinks share his interest in networks. 775 Words. 2000.

es000123
Driving Son of HAL Crazy
If Doug Lenat made moves
Turning points are features of a written script for a movie or plays that carry the audience from one event to another. The sequence is a combination gives us Acts I, II, and III. An Internet company, Cycorp, likewise develops dramatically along a

course. 1928 Words. 2000.

es000116
Emeralda Works for Dummies
Baby crawls, toddles, walks, runs
A linear process is necessary to communicate interrelated, complicated ideas that confront this Emeralda Inventor. He must begin at a certain measurable point and then go stepwise to a conclusion if he truly wants and needs an audience's help and support. 1246 Words. 2000.

es000113
Top Ten Most Complex Information
Hits of the Y2K
The author returned to an old interest-State support for the arts-by attending conventions of the Washington State Arts Commission. This article resulted from the first convention, held on the campus of his alma mater, CWSU. His notes comprise this essay. 745 Words. 2000.

es000228
What I Learned at School Today
At my professors trees
The ITinerate Professor grapples with his tired old ethics as he considers his pathway into the strange world of cybernetics that he was born into. He finds himself among many teachers like himself--tired of the old ways, but unsure how to take new paths. 410 Words. 2000.

es000929
Farmers and Framers
Everything I needed to know about Emeralda I learned on my father's farm
A farmer's son reflects on a life faith-based and expressed in a game he named Emeralda. Compared to his father's life as a potato farmer, the values of a framer of artworks, he concludes, are dimmer; the sun has not risen to illuminate his game's values. 1534 Words. 2000.

es011201
Complete this DVD Passport She Said
A Complete idiot's guided in Emeralda
It is by no means possible to guide you through the method of playing Emeralda in this essay, but you may come along with me while I solve my problem. Maybe this experience will enlighten you, sharing, as it were, a flame of a candle as we go in the dark. 382 Words. 2001.

es010614
My Mission
Why I Need amazon.com
There's only one way to be practical about selling art on the Internet World Wide Web, and that's the on-line auction. The art is linked to a video or DVD listed in amazon.com's video store and books the artist has written. Visitors see art in many views. 1053 Words. 2001.

es010624
Re-inventing the PTSA
Licenses and certificates now possible

In this re-invented PTSA, the teacher, agent, estate or survivors issues a fee-based license to a student. Written letters of intent establish plans to develop multimedia additions to the Living Prints database, benefiting all who share in on-line art ed. 337 Words. 2001.

es010714
About this DVD
Prithwish and me
Inserted with the DVD, Prithwish and Me, this is the text that helps the recipients of the trial versions of the author's innovative approach to the use of on-line and disc-based arts education. An accounting of what's on the DVD and definitions is given. 873 Words. 2001.

es010803
Your Move
Another day, another play
Second installment of the Missing Mysterious Professor, created for the satisfaction of the requirement to enter E'Studios, the Domain of Expertise in Electronic Studios and Arts Galleries. This essay includes a brief review and theory for DVD art design. 1123 Words. 2001.

es010912
What Comes after your DVD?
Cleaning up your mess
Making DVDs is easy compared to when he started nine months ago. He's got his fifth Gates Prize, and the artist/scholar is readying himself for a new phase, identified as somewhere between a virtual college professor, game inventor, artist and technician. 450 Words. 2001.

es011022
Now you have your Dream Press
How will you keep it busy?
His sequel to his first trade paperback, Art of Selling Art will include financial planning. His focus is on the free fine art of printmaking, and how a printmaker can approach the eternal questions of buying, maintaining and selling their intaglio press. 1664 Words. 2001.

es011102
Finding Reprieve by Examination on DVD
Inspiration of Father O'Grady and Professor Lovett
The solitude of the artist/scholar is unrelenting, it seems, but this author finds solace in reading about people from the past whose lives were devoted to unpopular ideas. They eventually got reprieve after having been scorned and banned by the skeptics. 1162 Words. 2001.

es011121
Glad you Asked
Ten questions about Emeralda answered
His game Emeralda is his answer to the question, "What next?" in printmaking, but raises more questions. His is a revolutionary idea: An online, interactive, cooperative strategy that turns art education on its head. New print technologies start-

ed it all. 2245 Words. 2001.

es011216
Implicit Importance of Passports
Your daily routine
The Emeralda Passport daily routine is going to the imaginary services area of each domain of expertise in Emeralda region, enter the library, go to the DVD directory and select the passport waiting there. Opening it is like entering a four-way mini-film. 1200 Words. 2001.

es010125
Artists Equity in the Age of Digital Reproduction
Straight pathways from root to twigtip
Money flows in channels that non-artists create so this artist sees them as extrinsic to the creative, inventive, discovering and imaginative soul. Their intrinsic values cannot easily be converted and thus suffer the conversion of their gifts into money. 1336 Words. 2001.

es010604
Sammy's Stamp
A digital art educator's wish
Fifteen years ago she gave me my first exposure to laser video disc, and put my art on it. Then she gave me her laser disc player. Last week she gave me an idea, a practical way of providing free fine art education on line, directed to "Sammy". Who is it? 310 Words. 2001.

es011111
Invisible Armor and An Emeralda PassPort
Looking at my E'Studios PassPort
The Emeralda Inventor reviews his PassPort and senses that it affords him passage from the restraints and concerns of the past. The role-playing game, based on a make-believe region he named Emeralda, is one way of an asset management and legacy transfer. 1147 Words. 2001.

es010214
How DVD Helps Me Dream and Think Creatively
The Evans Stair Climb
A Digital Versatile Disk, in the author's dream, showed the artwork of artist Dennis Evans in made-for-TV segments. The video bit he saw was part of a DVD that included the artist's cooking. Awakening, he bridged the insight into his current DVD practice. 1337 Words. 2001.

es010115
Artist's Last Postcards
Something from the heart of I'Estudios
DVD plays as heart of this artist's vision of a new fine art school based on multimedia. His example is the "Blue Book" of a "visionarian" school. He starts with a picture postcard and works his way toward a new real online school as artist legacies rule. 344 Words. 2001.

es010105
Planning Emeralda Cruises
From the Provisionary's Mouth
Specifying the curriculum for the Emeralda Cruises comes easily once the creative person realizes he cannot do it alone and he does not need to try. He focuses on the high points of the cruises, calling it "Creating your on-line art gallery and e-studio." 774 Words. 2001.

es010525
Properly Developing PrintmakingLibrary.com
Bill Goes Public in Seattle Print Arts Channel
A bill arrives in the mail telling him he owes another two years lease on the name Printmaking-Library.com so the artist/netpreneur contemplates forming a development team. He chooses a list-serve to announce his readiness and describes how he got the idea. 1401 Words. 2001.

es010204
No Place to Hide
E'Studios' Refugee
Where can an ITinerate professor go when there is no place for him or her on a traditional campus? Perhaps imaginary Electronic Studios and Galleries are the venues for teaching that is open. Popular films on DVD, however, may be a way for the time being. 1633 Words. 2001.

es010224
Emeralda Defender
Think big and small is beautiful
Tired old ethics from the last one hundred years will not fit in with all the needs we face this century. Artists, crafts people and designers must think big now that the numbers are coming in regarding Earth's life-sustainability. There is no denying IT. 1138 Words. 2001.

es010306
Problem of Leadership
Obstacle to new schools
The author wants to meet other artists, crafts people and designers who are interested in a new school of multimedia arts, but prescience has command. He sees the ironic fact that leadership in forming the school contains the seeds of its own destruction. 1780 Words. 2001.

es010405
What did you do for Earth today, Grandpa?
Earth Day 2021 recalled
A singer once sang, "What did you do in school today, child?" and this is the same as what this artist/writer is thinking on Earth Day 2021. He tries to see himself through his granddaughter's eyes and wonders if his actions count toward saving the Earth. 1239 Words. 2001.

es010415
Building the April DVD
Acting in A Property of the Month Club Game
Despite apparently necessary obstacles and interferences, the Emeralda Player makes progress toward the goal of Emeralda Play-that is, happiness with the achievement of a successful EarthSafe 2022 mission. This involves monthly measurement in making DVDs. 1073 Words. 2001.

es010425
Small Suite Journal
Owner's Guide for This Suite of Drawings
The artist/author made a series of drawings, starting in the alleyway outside the Triangle Studios-a Seattle co-op studio. He wanted to journalize the process, so he kept notes. Many years later he collected the notes into what he calls an owner's manual. 1186 Words. 2001.

es010515
So you want to go Back to School?
There's only one place to go now -- Home School
The author, a former college professor, proposes a home school for adult, mature and senior members of US American society. In this essay he compares graduation from schools and colleges to being exiled from education, and grown ups as living as refugees. 2403 Words. 2001.

es010316
Widows and Orphans
I got art, you got frames
The artist with a thousand artworks going on line needs a thousand frames for their owners. The framer with dozens orphaned frames can go online with this orphanage, finding matches among the art, the frames, and the future "parents." Who will take them? 840 Words. 2001.

es010505
My Notion
At my own expense
A lot of work goes into maintaining college curricula, the big picture, the long haul for those who wanted preparation for themselves and their children for life's journey. Changing maps and crossing borders is also part of crossing continents and oceans. 1018 Words. 2001.

es020912
How to Write High Impact Highly Structured Arts Ed On-line Curricula
A modest proposal for 21st Century arts students. To help faculty and arts students prepare for their next two decades of teaching, an on-line course, lived and learned, is what colleges need. This artist/scholar offers his game-like, highly-structured interactive, three-colleges development-and himself. 643 Words. 2002.

es020704
Searching for the Upside of Fear Marketing
A paradigm for cooperation
A marketing paper explained how to market to the aging population, using a hand grenade to stir up fears and thus sell annuities to reluctant seniors. At first horrified, and then the author realized fears have always been with us and could be a positive. 1491 Words. 2002.

es020714
Tipping-in Artistamps
Little things mean a lot to art education on-line
The root of the Perfect Studios Trilogy is EarthSafe 2022, but that movement, being of global proportions, has a microscopically small but significant element in the artistamp movement. Stamps are going electronic digitally on the Net in the Emeralda Way. 6224 Words. 2002.

es020724
Good Morning from E'Studios
Reflections on yesterday
Access, I said, when she asked me what I want. Accessibility. Access-ability. As the Inventor of Emeralda I write about the meaning of accessibility in the age of digital reproduction. I begin this day reading a tri-fold and comparing it to E'Studios. 1106 Words. 2002.

es020803
Developmental Assets-What are they?
A new course in game design
There comes a time in the life of the Emeralda Inventor when he must design his solitary games for other people so they, too, can play to win. Beginning with the end in mind-EarthSafe 2022-he sets out to define terms: asset management and legacy transfer. 805 Words. 2002.

es020813
Accounting in Human Structural Intellectual Capital
Measuring progress in community service efforts
There come times in the search for a Perfect Studios when the Emeralda Defender, playing for keeps, measures what might be progress, yet not progress in the common sense of the word. For progress is a continuum, concurrent teaching, research and practice. 560 Words. 2002.

es021002
The Visiting Adjudicator
E-portfolio inspector at large
Adjudicators are the checkers in inspection lines. They represent standards, given to them by best-practices advocates from somewhere, sometime that-over generations-proved correct and the right way. They can come from the future, too as well as the past. 678 Words. 2002.

es020902
Rising in Love at Caffe Vita
E-books come into the picture, and vice versa
What goes up must come down, but falling in love defied the rule when the author learns to make love a beginning and end for life, his wife and his art. In the age of digital reproduction it's especially important to learn how this becomes a lifelong job. 679 Words. 2002.

es020615
Journal, Fri. June 14, 2002
How the ITinerant professor got his job
The author is answering the question "How the ITinerant Professor get his job and how does he get paid. There is nothing to compare the profession with in the US. The answer about getting paid is through e'stamps. 265 Words. 2002.

es020922
What Moves you to Emeralda?
Reflections on motivational theories behind distance learning
His dream is becoming a reality as more institutional educators look for ways to maintain their classes as the economy turns from one universe to a different one. Rather than laissez-faire, they're pro-active, and more open today to his ideas than before. 1446 Words. 2002.

es021022
Habits, Health, and Effectiveness
Introducing Emeralda to a new region
We think of our effectiveness and how habits determine this, but what about meta habits of such kinds as art teacher have? If the knowledge base one habitually connects one's routine activities is in fact part of an ineffective one, then what does one do? 1478 Words. 2002.

es021101
First Day at The Professor's Cabinet
Next chapter in the Artist's Last Love Letter
The author is about to enter the third an final year of his self-made 40-year retrospective and decides to rent space in a storefront. His design is likened to an absent professor's cabinet, a place where the public can view his achievements-and buy them. 422 Words. 2002.

es020823
Reinventing Arts Studios Again
For the Age of Digital Reproduction
New times require new books. The author started a book in the 20th C. that he thought would merely bridge art and technology but, in addition, it spanned the old century and the new century. Reinvention, to him, is a continuous process, not an end result. 476 Words. 2002.

es020224
Printmaking, Music, Books and DVD
Roots of the Gates Prize
His vision of a print in front of him in the form of trial proofs, two woodblocks and, beside these, a powerful desktop computer makes the author want to fit them with musical form. He scans a book defining a canon, and recalls the sources of his imagery. 532 Words. 2002.

es020614
Artist's Last Love Letter
About the title
Part fiction, part technology and part autobiography, this is the author's first attempt at writing an e-book in the medium of e-book, using the concurrent marketing, sales, design and production method he learned about from The Boeing Company's 777 saga. 329 Words. 2002.

es021012
The Portable Professor
The lightness of uninflatable, indefatigable undevaluable being

No more inflatable grades, the inflatable college degrees and the inflatable dollar--the age of digital reproduction brings with it harder, substantial value exceeding certificate face value. It's the interface value that matters, a mediate gratification. 1254 Words. 2002.

es020105
Writing Between the Paragraphs - Part 2
An imaginary dialog between two professors
A continent apart and over vast reaches of time two professors can, in the mind of one, have a dialog. Of course it's a fantasy, but this one is using a fantasy role-playing game as one method of understanding and using new technologies for art education. 2088 Words. 2002.

es020115
Fantasy Role Playing Gamer Mates Fun, Skill-building
Adapting from a news story
Adapting text from a story that appeared in the Seattle Times November 06, 2001., the inventor of Emeralda plans to use his on-line game to fit the needs of art teachers. He links printmaking and on-line technologies the way chess players employ metaphors. 1020 Words. 2002.

es020306
My Objective Is No Teacher Left Behind
Reconciling the retirement myth
Close examination of the long range goal of real teachers shows it is a lifetime of learning, meaning retirement from teaching is a myth. Examination of educational institutional infrastructures shows it is led by retirement. Do you reconcile the paradox? 430 Words. 2002.

es020316
Goals and Roles of an ITinerant Professor of Art
Revisiting the Perfect Studios in the Age of Digital Reproduction
The future offers a role in higher education unlike that which he played in the past-an art professor at a research institution. To prepare for this career he must role-play backward into the future, conserving his creative gifts while building new paths. 924 Words. 2002.

es020326
It's your Links, Not What or Who you Know
Art E-portfolios and the Age of Digital Reproduction
Henry Ford admitted his ignorance but said if he didn't have the answers, he knew someone who did. Great teachers and artists, too, have benefited society not by virtue of their own knowledge but because they could cite knowledge by linkages and pathways. 891 Words. 2002.

es020415
The Future Art Professor
Letters to a 10th Grader from an ITinerant professor of art
A high school student sends e-mail asking about

a course of study for higher education. The author uses it as an opportunity to express his future vision of what professors will need to know around the years 2012-22, and envisions a better college system. 1256 Words. 2002.

es020425
Raising and Exceeding the Art Bar
Passing the art ed on-line test
You know you've learned something when they stamp "Passed" on your paper version of the page of stamps, on one of the twelve positions of the encrypted stamps in your E'Studios Stamp Collection. This is like taking a forty-minute walk in downtown Seattle. 253 Words. 2002.

es020604
Rules, Rules, Rules
So many rules, so few players
Emeralda, the Games for the Gifts of Life, has rules to play by but only when other people say they want to play too. One goes dumb when people ask how they can play, because it's a game of building the road as one travels. Rules come, then, as signposts. 482 Words. 2002.

es020505
Crisis and Opportunity
The sow's ear and silk purse
Hit by a computer virus, this artist/writer lost almost two years of his research and development on a new computer game. From the ashes, like Phoenix rising, came a new idea for an event that may not only restore but grow his idea for his game, Emeralda. 1498 Words. 2002.

es020515
E'Studios Listing in Dictionary of Imaginary Places
Electronic Studios and Art Galleries
The third in a series of suggested additions to The Dictionary of Imaginary Places. E'Studios is the second, alphabetically, island in the chain of ten Islands-of-Domains-of-Expertise in the great lake of Emeralda Region. Look under E in a future edition. 245 Words. 2002.

es020405
If I Had Some Good Students
ITinerant professor on learning backward and living forward
The author examines a worn-out, first edition copy of a book by H. G. Wells and wonders what he'd do with it if he were in a teaching position. He gets the idea of deconstructing the book both physically and intellectually by teaching students DVD making. 860 Words. 2002.

es020525
Chair Thief's Redemption
Bored chair man reveals his secret
He's grateful for having nearby parks where he can walk, contemplate natural resources living in the midst of busy Seattle. Concerned about the fu-

ture and pressing need of acting to balance management and transfer of these benefits, he thinks about deeds. 2389 Words. 2002.

es020114
Ready to Teach Art On-line
Certified, registered and getting over the bar
Is art education barred from the Internet World Wide Web? It's a high jump from a traditional art form such as painting, or a theatrical performance to the Internet. How can a hands-on, live performance be simulated on computer screens or home DVD player? 1272 Words. 2002.

es031226
Hire Education
Reviving an old practice for a new education
A chance encounter at a holiday party sets this Itinerate professor on a new quest. He's searching for an intentional community and he uses a form of game play to reach his goal. His archives contain clues, and as he follows these he thinks of a strategy. 1263 Words. 2003.

es030912
Diary of the Absent Professor
Forty years and one week to get ready
The "absent professor" he calls himself because it's the theme of one concept in his online art education iteration, part of his lifelong game, Emeralda. Given a week to prepare to re-enter a studio/classroom to teach fine art drawing, he's introspective. 1261 Words. 2003.

es031101
There is a World
Last day at Iron Springs
On vacation 150 miles from an urban center, where he's used to a world of arts and teaching, this "Itinerate" professor meditates on the past forty years he invested in his dual profession-and the past forty days he re-invested in it after a long absence. 1934 Words. 2003.

es031111
Learning about Teaching
A reality check in a virtual world construction project
After two months of experiencing life on a community college as both a student and a teacher, this Itinerate Professor (one who wanders around teaching, learning, researching and practicing) writes his impressions. Things are not what they appeared to be. 944 Words. 2003.

es031216
Ulises' Ghost
Waking an old dream
A request for a videotape arrives from a college somewhere out in academe land, and revives this artist's memories of a dead book artist named Ulises. He celebrated the idea of imagination in the art of books, and encouraged the creation of fantasylands. 523 Words. 2003.

es030823
Doing Two Things At Once
Dilemma tale of a DGBL designer
Each practice session playing the game he's designing, the author begins to realize that he's writing about game design and old printmaking lessons he learned a long time ago. Which is the right thing to be doing? He wonders: Digital arts or print making? 618 Words. 2003.

es030902
How to Jump Start Art Ed Online
An idea whose time has come
Given a temp job teaching three levels of beginning drawing, a veteran art professor says he could launch a 21st Century art education experience based on the work of fine art drawing in the age of digital reproduction. It's an embryonic idea he can grow. 446 Words. 2003.

es031201
Games and Printmaking
Finding the context for hands on printmaking
A newspaper article in his local paper excites this artist because he has been forecasting the making of a new kind of video game-one that educates and stimulates the players. The article says it is women over 50 who are the most likely to play this game. 667 Words. 2003.

es030803
Power Games and Art Games
Differences like night and day
The author, a former professor of art in a university, reflects on the difference between competitive violent video games and the game he's inventing. His game, Emeralda, is noncompetitive and nonviolent so he wonders what kind of future it holds for him. 1896 Words. 2003.

es030704
Visualizing the Tacoma Connection
An exercise in focusing on the long range goal
In a week the Emeralda inventor, an Itinerate Professor, will have his opportunity to discuss future projects with the Tacoma Art Museum curators in education and art. Alongside his daily routine - working on his model game - he imagines what will happen. 799 Words. 2003.

es030624
What Did You Learn in School Today?
A professor inventing his next university
To learn digital game-based learning project design and development, I needed to start a school, a digital game-based learning example that teaches people how digital mediums fit in artists' studios. The personal e-folio shows how I study multimedia arts. 1044 Words. 2003.

es030604
Learning the Game's Big Payoff
Payoff versus patience-who wins?
When, as a young artist, I played the art game for the big payoff-to me it must have meant fame and good money for my artwork. As a professor I played hard to win keeping my professor career going. Now, going for the big one, I'm inventing a new art game. 1278 Words. 2003.

es030504
Steal this Game!
Fantasy news release not sent
A flash of inspiration sometimes sends this author into a fantasy news release-writing binge. He has a wild idea to make a community club out of the inventing of an online game. This is stuff only a fiction writer could love; game developers deplore this. 400 Words. 2003.

es030224
SIM-ulated Interview
Stimulating alternative futures
He's a visionary looking for entrepreneurs who have similar intentions and who share ideals about interdependence, and community development. After trying at the Seattle Independent Mall 4 months, he reflects on this phase by pretending to be interviewed. 1963 Words. 2003.

es031002
If I were a Drawing Teacher
Observations of a visiting artist
His reading is a strange combination for a traditional fine artist, consisting of books on video game design, traditional fine art drawing, and papers on higher education. His college years were spent in the liberal arts, preparing him for changing times. 1028 Words. 2003.

es030813
Reading Backwards between the Lines
Surprises in a text on online game development
He finds guidance in the strangest places. When he's searching for a meta-view for the design of art education on-line he borrows a book about MMG design. Key phrases stand out, reminding him of his career mistakes, and how to start his career over again. 1366 Words. 2003.

es040224
How You Play Emeralda Online
Choose the right response
He's trying to put his game online, placing his project Stamps 'N Stories on the web in some fashion similar to the CD-based version he made the year before. In this essay he explains to himself laying the game out in outline form before taking it online. 612 Words. 2004.

es040812
Proposal to SAM
The problem and the solution for media arts
Since 1985 there has been little measurable progress in the study of the work of art in the age of digital reproduction. University students do not have extensive opportunities to study. The larger community has no access to study materials like archives. 398 Words. 2004.

es040802
A Business Opportunity
Restarting an old dream with a new press
His mode of operation has turned from writing long essays lately to short flashes of inspirations focused on making a tiny press for a tiny market-yet he thinks it's a market that could grow to be something substantial. He takes a minute to write it down. 346 Words. 2004.

es040724
Ships and Artist's Stamps
A note of nautical concerns
There is something about ship preservation that interests this author-ever since he began to follow the sagas of the SS United States in 1992.. The Big U became a symbol of legacy restoration-and this is the theme of Emeralda. Here he meets a kindred soul. 199 Words. 2004.

es040714
The Mini Halfwood Press at E'Studios
Looking through the glass at a press
At times as the author travels in his mind to E'Studios located in his imaginary place Emeralda Region he writes and wonders, "How does my work on the Halfwood Presses-the Mini Halfwood Press in particular-look in the perspective of the E'Studios island?" 665 Words. 2004.

es040822
A Guide to the Northwest Pioneers Video Artist's Archive
Getting ready for a visit to the archive
He keeps a treasure stashed down in the basement of his condo, filled with videos he made in the last century. It was before the art department dismantled the video art course and set out to shut down the printmaking division. He writes about his archive. 753 Words. 2004.

es040404
Death of Art and Rebirth
Lessons of art from the bygone era
I feel like the art world of the past fifty years is dying, or dead, and I'm feeling the conception of a new one that will be born. Perhaps those artists in New York's SOHO district in the fifties felt the same way as they looked around at their painting. 327 Words. 2004.

es041021
Considering a New Career
Taking my own advice
Having been designing and building an etching press-ostensibly to make prints-the artist/author finds himself at a juncture where some signs point to a different job than what he has long hoped for: A press-maker. It may be a new career, using his skills. 626 Words. 2004.

es040214
Art, Games and Education
The convergence for the new millennium
Artistic growth demands evolution. As older practices pose risks to artistic development, artists must adopt new methodologies. They must also develop new ways to engage their audience. Audience expectations are raised as technologies change the language. 403 Words. 2004.

es040603
What's the Big Idea?
Notes on the conclusion of the Halfwood Press
The Big Idea-that is what some artists are thinking about. If one is a painter, one thinks about the painting that is going to be the centerpiece of a life's work. There are many precedent paintings to look at, judging from art history and fine art books. 936 Words. 2004.

es040901
Simple Screensavers
An introduction to woodcut in the age of digital reproduction
The Itinerate Professor of Art imagines how it would be to meet a thirty-something Mom and her 12-year old son on a tourist walk through the history of the woodcut, and along the way they try out the processes. Their journey takes them on a future search. 1131 Words. 2004.

es040911
Placemat in an Archive Visitors Free E-book
Prelude to a dinner
As a plan to raise funds for an electronic publishing project, the keeper of a video tape archive from the early days of multimedia creates an overview of new ways to access the work of pioneering artists in the Northwest. He's thinking of a dinner party. 733 Words. 2004.

es041011
Autobiography Fragment
2001.-2003.
Partway through the updating of his E'Studios article archives, the author gets the feeling he ought to be writing his autobiography in order to keep his memory of the past from falling into disarray. This may be the start of something big-or forgettable. 934 Words. 2004.

es041031
Restoring the Emeralda Dictionary
Towards the new
He gets email on listserves from printmakers and papermakers, and one of the messages referred to an imaginary place called Arazonia, created by Betty Pulver. In an exchange off-line, he discovered he'd lost his definition of Emeralda, and so restored it. 1418 Words. 2004.

es040125
Imagine A Circle
A conversation café for the arts
Imagine a circle based on a form of the meetings called "Conversation Café" that started a few years ago. The idea is to restore a sense of community that comes from artists and students meeting in casual settings, discussing topics such as arts in

depth. 459 Words. 2004.

es040115
Why I Play Games
Exercising your skills in the digital age
His wife asked him why he plays Emeralda and he recounts a routine activity that seems to keep his brain alive and functional in the age of digital reproduction. It seems like a trivial thing, but considering the stakes over the long term, it isn't trite. 272 Words. 2004.

es040105
What Can I Offer a Museum?
Thinking about a video art archive in the museum
With the rumor of Emeralda in the back of his mind, he has a proposal to museums in his region to resuscitate the video archive from the 1970s. His suggestion is that it be a digital game-based learning experience and not a boring account of days gone by. 1152 Words. 2004.

es040204
It was One of those Pivotal Times
Reflections on a golden era
Inspired by reading the book "Dungeons and Dreamers", this has-been art professor compares his own story to that of a leading video game creator. The gamer's teenage experience at a computer summer camp is similar to the art professor's early bygone days. 1061 Words. 2004.

es040921
What was I Thinking about SAM?
Contemplating a visit by two important museum people
It is the day he plans to receive two guests from the major museum in his home city of Seattle. He's been preparing for this visit-which will last only about 15 minutes-since, a month ago, he met one of them at a dinner party at his former student's home. 1179 Words. 2004.

es051226
Why Learn Computers?
Taking the Contrarion Viewpoint
As if it never occurred to ask, the artist who uses computers daily in his routine stops to take a different point of view, putting himself in the shoes of one who is asking where they can learn how to use computers in their art and craft. Why should she? 1077 Words. 2005.

es050724
Critical Learning in Art and Games
Reflections on things that made Emeralda Works
One of his favorite authors, James Gee, gives this artist—who would like to design a game—ideas that apply not only to Gee's field (interactive learning) but also to the arts. A key concept is appreciative systems, which is like art appreciation theories. 843 Words. 2005.

es050105
My Secret Garden of Words

Reflections of an essay writer
Messages from a distant office elicit thoughts by an old college professor, sending him on a search of his database of musings and bibliography that he has maintained for over thirty years. The messages portend a proof of his theories of asset management. 698 Words. 2005.

es051201
EtchingIT Kit and Home Schooling
A bigger splash than Tamarind
Home schooling may be the form of education that restores the values of an earlier age. Those values underlay the original idea of the Mini Halfwood Press, the brainchild of two older artist/craftsmen. Connect it with the Internet and then it is powerful. 667 Words. 2005.

es051216
Thinking CVD
A nesting concept
After an absence from making DVDs the author plans to restart the process of converting what he does in his art studio to contents of DVDs. He's planning to include discs with his EtchingIT Kit, a chest of printmaker's instruments he's building this year. 578 Words. 2005.

es051111
E-writers Unite!
The what's next of America's wise artists
As more artists respond to the need for arts in education and gravitate toward electronic media to help make this happen, this artist—a onetime professor of art who used technology to help him teach—calls for a league of artist/teachers to share ideas. 921 Words. 2005.

es051101
I thought you were Someone
What's in a name?
A movie about a girl living in the shadow of her successful father suggests that we sometimes choose to acquaint ourselves with youth whose parentage we know, and we see them through their parents' image. We miss the importance of the individual's effort. 1043 Words. 2005.

es051012
About EtchingIT
Toward a product description
He is planning a business. It will be an online art education service provider producing the things that home schoolteachers need for teaching the basics of intaglio printmaking. He knows that such a package must relate to the age of digital reproduction. 1208 Words. 2005.

es051002
Calendar Game
A game to teach the sequence of ten studios
Always interested in games, but seldom playing them, this artist searches for a way to combine printmaking and computer graphics in a playful fashion. A calendar is a perfect format for a game

because it requires daily play and stamps are a possible part. 861 Words. 2005.

es050922
Little Prints
A new business plan
An aging artist and professor must look out for his future, and he envisions a shop on a main street of Seattle where he can spend the rest of his days. It is an art gallery rooted in the past and reaching for the future, celebrating "small is beautiful." 1109 Words. 2005.

es050912
Behind an Artist's Clock
Story telling time
Invited to make an artist's clock, he thinks about words he can put on the back of his creation that the buyer of the clock would enjoy reading. Of course there's the biographical matter, but for his subject—his artist's stamps—something more is in order. 1085 Words. 2005.

es050902
Visualize a Burgeoning Business
Pressures of an economic kind
He's a dreamer and therefore he has left aside the matters of money and economic success in favor of his long-term vision of being a great teacher. But now he's sensing it may be time to pay close attention to making a business work for his teaching goal. 690 Words. 2005.

es050823
Urge of Reality
The desire for the real thing
Daily routine for this artist is to write and make images on metal and paper, coming full circle as it were from theory to practice and back again. To have the facility and faculties to do this is like having one's own studio/school in his head and hands. 464 Words. 2005.

es050803
Appreciative, Evaluation and Anticipatory Systems in Game Design
Coming full circle
From reading books by Prensky and Gee, and an interview with Nadin, this artist—who wants to create an intellectual game for mature adults—is coming closer to a foundation for his game theory. From each author he gets clues, making this search reflective. 1274 Words. 2005.

es050714
Imagine Yourself a Designer
Visualizing art student – again
This artist devoted himself to printmaking, sees a need to educate his art market. Reflecting on his earlier career as an art professor, he saw how his courses prepared people to appreciate the value of prints. As school is ending, a new course is needed. 1346 Words. 2005.

es050704

Emeralda Constitution
Tracing his story
A paragraph taken from Robert Grudin's book On Dialogue describes the evolution of the constitution of Emeralda, an imaginary place in this artist's mind where ten islands form a colony of creative states of mind for him. It's all about environmentalism. 785 Words. 2005.

es050405
How Can I Teach in the Age of Digital Reproduction?
The game of art
There will be a class in printmaking and this artist/teacher will be the "Pied Piper" teaching it. It is the first time he has been asked to teach in the Age of Digital Reproduction. His students are middle-aged or older—like himself. How will he teach it? 826 Words. 2005.

es050115
Emeralda's Seven Habits for Highly Effective Media Artists
Converting Covey's 7
This artist read the book by Stephen Covey, Seven Habits of Highly Effective People. It is a very good guide, and the mindful artist might reword those seven habits' terms and make them apply to daily routines in the studio, at home, and in the community. 271 Words. 2005.

es050125
Keeping Your Brain and Your Blog Alive
Essays in the age of digital memory
Comparing the invention and development of today's communications technologies to those of writing, printing, and double-entry bookkeeping, this writer takes a look at a particular form of essays called blogging. He thinks it helps keep one's brain alive. 781 Words. 2005.

es050224
Mini Halfwood Press and ETC
Connecting the dots
What is the shape of his future? the artist/essayist wonders as he contemplates the miniature etching press he designed and uses to print Artist Trading Cards. He changes the words to Emeralda Trading Cards, hoping to illuminate his path to his tomorrows. 750 Words. 2005.

es050813
Card Payoff
Playing Emeralda with Artists Trading Cards
Emeralda is a game about resource management. Assets are stored in a computer in various forms, and access to the player's resources is collectible Artists Trading Cards that advance knowledge. You interact with other artists, crafts people and designers. 908 Words. 2005.

es050326
The S-Word
Adding a fourth dimension to art, craft and design
As a college professor in his younger formative

years, the author settled on a triumvirate set to guide his thinking about the endowments most artists possess. As the 21st century unfolds and its differences from the past become clear, a new word adds on. 759 Words. 2005.

es050624
Wiki Your Way to the Perfect Condo
A new experience opening up for Condopoly
This artist lives in a condo but he keeps a studio and gallery one block away. The blend of condo living and having a creative workspace—plus using computers at the same time he's making traditional artworks—has given him an idea about a condominium game. 1010 Words. 2005.

es050415
The Successful Company
Reading the signs
Scanning the morning e-mail on his computer, he reads about Seattle being the "digital Hollywood" because of the gaming and music software businesses here. His plan is to win in a business in hardware and software for printmaking, so he sees a connection. 845 Words. 2005.

es050425
Sensing a Game Idea
Estate planning and art
Twice this writer has seen his name in journals about estate planning and personal assets, on his claim that intangibles have value too and should be included in a professional's list of valuables. What's missing is an interface, something to prove value. 833 Words. 2005.

es050505
What I want to have Happen
Treating myself as though I already am what I'm capable of becoming
He'd been told that to develop the most in other people, treat them as though they already are what they're capable of becoming. Thinking this could work also when one is determined to get the most from the gifts with which one has been endowed, he tries. 1195 Words. 2005.

es050515
Funding Emeralda
Gleaning ideas from Mihai Nadin
The writer thinks he's on the threshold of a major funding project that will eventually put Emeralda on the Web as an open system (instead of the solitaire he's been playing for thirteen years). He found a similar project in an interview with Mihai Nadin. 1128 Words. 2005.

es050525
Perfect Anticipation
A game player gets boxed
For several years now this Emeralda Player has been interested in public parks, finding them to be a kind of mental playground for participation in his community. He feels like it's a game within Emeralda, and he's just suffered a defeat. He

bounces back. 961 Words. 2005.

es050604
Blog or Zine-Which is it?
Time and the Art of Games
A generation or more before now, this artist hit upon the way he would use his own "'Zine"— those quirky alternative magazines made by creative people. He created his electronic 'Zines for each of his imaginary islands in his game. Now, a new form appears. 634 Words. 2005.

es050614
The Perfect Condo Prize
Winners in a cooperative learning game
Partway into the design of an interactive learning game for condominium dwellers, this former art professor reviews his long-term goal of living in an intentional community. It is his lifelong dream of being a part of a community-of-practice for the arts. 695 Words. 2005.

es050316
Grantaphor
What and who a grant is for
Advised to get a grant to develop Emeralda, the inventor asks himself what proposal is the most likely to win and why? Playing with the word metaphor, he invents the word grantaphor—referring to the composite answer to who, what, when, why, how and where. 410 Words. 2005.

es060902
Emeralda Group
The characters of Emeralda and their roles
In the book edited by Chris Bateman, Andrew Walsh explains the various ways that video game writers can create characters. In the age of digital reproduction the "reader" or the game player controls the characters. 714 Words. 2006.

es061101
Why a Story
Learning printmaking from video games
Distance learning printmaking entails making up by means of literature and other art forms what is lost in translation from real, face-to-face experience in a printmaking studio. We learn from video games. 900 Words. 2006.

es061111
Genres of Hunt for the Emeralda Treasure
How can you use the power of the limits of genre? In Robert McKee's book, Story, he asked what is your story's plot or genre? Then he provided what the author needed to know: Socio-educational. The social part is educational reform. 819 Words. 2006.

es061004
Subject Line Writer
Waiting in the wings
The Subject Line Writer has to wait in the wings while the author takes his time and writes the piece. It even has to wait while the Assistant to the

Asset Manager gets her act together. 285 Words. 2006.

es061003
Newsworthy
Financing of a course
A professor in Washington State resurrected artworks from his earliest days of teaching, sold them, and used the proceeds to finance a new art course. 382 Words. 2006.

es061002
Bateman Says
Or Maas or whatever
A student in a certificate program called Popular Fiction II agonizes over the truths he's discovering because of the textbooks he's required to read. The author tell him things he hates to hear—things like why his protagonist is a mirror of his failures. 2268 Words. 2006.

es060912
Stranger than Popular Fiction
Video game backstory
"I'm writing the Backstory for a videogame," he had started. "But to be more exact it's really a textbook for an online certificate course in art. Printmaking." 175 Words. 2006.

es060724
Estate Insurance and Other
Things we study at CWALS
Taking his cue from a book that was published a decade ago titled The Digital Estate, this former art professor contemplates a community living project, which is centered on a method for intellectual property management and legacy transfer he named CWALS. 746 Words. 2006.

es060714
If Castaway
What do you want to have with you?
What computer files would the author want most to have with him, saved on a USB Memory stick? 485 Words. 2006.

es060704
Skunkworks Stamp Work Study
Auction/Play stamps
Imagine a Work Study program where students spent several hours a week creating artist's stamps based on the art of the CWU faculty and alumni. The stamps become part of the Auction/Play series. 301 Words. 2006.

es060525
GPS Caching, Proximates and Printmaker's Treasure
Object of the game
A description of the objective of the game, collecting prints and other things from the GPS Caches site. 115 Words. 2006.

es060405
Textbook for an Online Printmaking

Theory
Each page of a book is illustrated with a picture and a quote, aphorism, saying, parable or whatever the author happens to dream up. They are shown in a box, separate from the body text of the story. 615 Words. 2006.

es060115
Second Day and Next Year at the Seattle Print Fair
Reflections on the first day
He has spent the first of two days at the Seattle Print Fair and he's now beginning to think about the 7th Fair in 2007.. While there's no guarantee that the sponsors will let him come again he hopes they will and thinks about what he might do differently. 960 Words. 2006.

es060105
Calendar Art
Puzzling over art in the age of digital production
Can a calendar be an artwork? The author thinks perhaps the Mayan calendar is art. Considering the calendar as "art with content". The advent of the digital online calendar, with massive numbers of Internet calendar users, makes an artwork possible. 649 Words. 2006.

es061226
Method of Play is Simple
Filling in the parts
The parts are writing essays or stories (or both), making things that are real, making things that are virtual, selling things from both categories that complement one another, and walking. 172 Words. 2006.

es060813
Writing in the Age of Digital Reproduction
An Emeralda method-of-play
Creating a calendar stamp from the Emeralda Year of Living Copiously schedule. 426 Words. 2006.

es071002
A Community of Practice for What?
Walking the talking
A community of practice that is partly virtual, i.e., Web-based communities, and partly real, or people working face to face. In the arts, there are many examples in the performing side, but few in the visual arts. 974 Words. 2007.

es071226
Silent Auction and Artists Trading Cards
A daughter's idea
His daughter and the artist shared a brainstorming session to connect the artists trading cards he made, based on their family art collection, to an ultimate art auction. This essay documents the idea they came up with—virtual cards become license to bid. 584 Words. 2007.

es071216
Post Grad
Reflections on Machiavelli
Many times the author has a thought about the fall

and aftermath of Machiavelli that he reads about in an account by Professor Christian Gauss. 895 Words. 2007.

es071201
Press Pieces
Current happenings in my studio
The press maker calls himself a maker of instruments of art. The etching presses he designs and builds are for making works of art, therefore they are instruments analogous to musical instruments. One day he saw the pieces of the presses as game elements. 426 Words. 2007.

es071012
Why Emeralda is a Creative Game
Aha
When the author creates the cards for Emeralda, he is setting up for an "Aha!" Example, he just created number 20, with the painting by Geoffrey Bowman on it, and an essay, "The Biggest RPG Ever." How does the painting relate to the essay? 437 Words. 2007.

es070912
Game Engrossed
Warning of a death in a tenured position
Increasingly the author is learning what his game, Emeralda, is about. That's because his computers are brimming with stories, images, outlines and plans he has written over the past 22 years. 324 Words. 2007.

es070604
Chapter Six from "Halfwood Press: The Story"
Electronic studios and art galleries
This is chapter six from the press maker's book about his Halfwood Press as set on E'Studios Island. Here it is held that, in today's media-heavy world, when people's eyes are opened to art it is most often they are looking at a digital electronic image. 2130 Words. 2007.

es070115
The IFPDA Portal
Considering an alliance
Printing an etching for forty people who came to the Seattle Print Fair is great fun for the author. He loves the response he gets when people see "how it's done." That includes the kids that come with their families. 1141 Words. 2007.

es071121
Making the CD/ROM for Emeralda Play
Saving family collection's property value
ArtGrid evolved as a combination of Excel and Access listing about 400 artworks and other kinds of tangible property in the Ritchie collection. The purpose was to establish the intellectual property value of these to insure they would not be wasted. 501 Words. 2007.

es080325
College Formula
Institute Emeralda at CWU

The best thing that can come from further communication with my Alma Mater is to institute Emeralda at CWU. Next best is to create a pathway for our granddaughter, Matilda, into the university when—and if—she is ready to go there ten years from now. 530 Words. 2008.

es080524
Logical Data Model
Square three in the functioning enterprise framework
The man extolled the virtues of learning and teaching Chess to children. The Zachman Framework is before him now, and with its grid of 42 squares resembles a board game like Chess (Chess, however, has 64) the author is reminded of Chess Mates. 860 Words. 2008.

es080515
Introducing Online Infrastructure
Autosummary
Last year—2006.—the author saw the first online printmaking course, originating in England. A better infrastructure for Learning Printmaking Online, as he sees it, depends on acceptance of a reinvented printmaking. 386 Words. 2008.

es080514
Introducing Infrastructure
Online
The author watches for online art education infrastructure started in earnest around the turn of the century in Seattle. He asked his former students who are active in public school art programs how their computer artwork was coming along. 1441 Words. 2008.

es080504
Lesson One
Introduction to learning printmaking online
He may be teaching printmaking in a new way soon, and the professor, entering the final phase of his lifelong career as a teacher, considers ways he will approach the vital first lessons of his plan to teach printmaking in the age of digital reproduction. 1124 Words. 2008.

es080404
Any Day
Nicolaides, then and now
Can an imaginary 21st Century Freshman, an art major in the essay, planning to graduate and use her education in 2012, learn what she needs from a faculty which was educated in the 20th Century? She faces choices that are between tradition and technology. 572 Words. 2008.

es080305
Tangible Art
Data driven art and production
In the age of digital reproduction, there is a new art experience opening up, thanks to computers, software, and the Internet. It seems to this artist that human creativity has a new dimension in which to develop—something between tangible

and intangible. 1336 Words. 2008.

es080224
Journal Game
Page play with an artist's diary
On one of these busy days when he is balancing new projects, ongoing projects and old projects all at the same time, he imagines a dialog between two players who are engaged in a kind of game. It's one that they play with entries in old artist's journals. 687 Words. 2008.

es080214
Studio Bound
Note from a studio of anticipatory studies
What would it be like, he asks, if he spent his entire day bound to his studio, like being housebound? Surrounding him are unfinished projects that he knows are part of the anticipatory world of Emeralda, his imaginary, perfect world of arts and artistry. 1179 Words. 2008.

es080125
Holding Labor
I choose Emeralda
Ideas are the commerce of artists. Not only their productions in the form of paint, paper and other matter, but the impulse or notions—musings—behind them, their hands owe the brain of the artist. In economics, artists labor in the precarious professions. 743 Words. 2008.

es080115
Card 40
Getting to the right language of art in the age of digital reproduction
The 14th collaboration session established the idea that XML would be the language for Emeralda Artist Trading Cards. Not Excel not Access, as had been the dilemma. So the inventor turns his attention to the designing of card number forty for testing. 812 Words. 2008.

es080424
Draw Me
Modern day draw me matchbook
Writing a syllabus for an online printmaking class reminds the author of the old days when matchbooks carried invitations to take art courses by correspondence. 471 Words. 2008.

es080315
Next Gorilla
Hard times for a CEO
Overhearing a remark about the difficulties that his friend's employer, a CEO of a company that the man recently bought, the author compares the 500-pound gorilla metaphor to a business owner who has not learnt to navigate the age of digital reproduction. 651 Words. 2008.

es090912
Millionaire Printmaker
When I opened my eyes to prints I was looking at time

He liked to say, "When I opened my eyes to art, I was looking at prints." This was his mantra for over 40 years. The author may have thought prints were the carriers for fine art, art's time-and-space vehicles, but printmaking is in fact a time-based art. 1145 Words. 2009.

es090505
Stamp Scan
Towards a tool for art education online
Two animated players—a dog and cat—take part in the art education plan this author is making. One of them tests the student by scanning the artists stamp that he or she creates as one of the tasks of learning printmaking on the Web. It's one of ten tests. 1092 Words. 2009.

es090525
Selling Sequel
The art of selling prints
Twenty years ago he wrote "The Art of Selling Art," based on his experience selling his own creations. It was an education, and his textbooks were many, their advice skewed toward commercial gain. His book was personalized. Now he wants to write a sequel. 1860 Words. 2009.

es090604
Meta Soap
A soap opera for the age of digital reproduction
There's an essay he would like to write to enter for today during his day stay on the island of Electronic Studios and Art Galleries—but his time is up, used up in a review of Chapter 7 of his novel, "Hunt for the Emeralda Treasure," a meta-daytime drama. 1111 Words. 2009.

es090415
Staring at the Gates Prize Calendar
A calendar is art stuff
If it is true what they say about time, that it has form, that it is the other side of space, that space does not exist alone, and space has faded like a shadow as the sun goes behind a cloud to be replaced by a form of time, then a calendar is art stuff. 1055 Words. 2009.

es090714
Erica Williams
After all that she did for me
A telephone call inspires an artist, who had his heyday in the '80s, recalls some things that the caller did for him as an art dealer back then. He recalls highlights of his short, happy career, and how her help brought about creative acts and made money. 1017 Words. 2009.

es090224
Characters in ELPO
Players and non player characters in Emeralda: learn printmaking online
Sixth of a ten-part development process recommended by the author of Digital Storytelling, 2nd edition. The focus in this section is on the charac-

ters in the game—the player and nonplayers (or NPCs). Parts from the first version of this list are included. 705 Words. 2009.

es091201
Fourth Place
Meeting up in a changed world
The "third place" was popular in the last century to describe a place between work and home, like a stop at the tavern or coffee shop to see friends, gossip or maybe do a little business. There is a fourth place today in cyberspace, as artists go virtual. 1231 Words. 2009.

es090614
Intern Task
Ideas for a web design intern
With an opportunity to gain the assistance of an intern, the taskmaster notes some ideas to serve as guidelines for the intern period of 12 weeks. His goal is to use the Internet as part of an online course that bridges art history and new technologies. 611 Words. 2009.

es090406
Laura Durflinger Profile
Character description of Dr. Durflinger, retired dentist
Hers is a tragic story; now she lives with the illusion she is being punished for an indecent act committed as a teen. Her career was ended by a brutal attack. Her husband was killed in the attack, but she was able to save herself by killing her attacker. 446 Words. 2009.

es090405
Dear Former Students
A professor asks his former students to be his board of advisers
For years I have watched people who used to be art students at the UW as they became good citizens as well as fine artists, craftspeople, designers, teachers and professionals in various important functions in our communities. I need their advice on ELPO. 1229 Words. 2009.

es090316
Red Dots in the Morning
Six-fifty-four in the morning at E'Studios
In the art gallery show, a sure sign of success used to be red dots—lots of red dots. A red dot on the label by an artwork meant it was sold. The artist would get money—half the art's indicated value. Today, when games are art, a red dot might be similar. 940 Words. 2009.

es090214
He Wants to Teach Teachers
The mad professor returns to campus from a virtual world
Taking a moment from his work on the development checklist for ELPO (Emeralda: Learn Printmaking Online), the Itinerate Professor reflects on his primary motivation, which is an outreach across the boundaries of all campuses with his of-

fer of experiences. 625 Words. 2009.

es090204
Co-ops in Game Land
Is anyone using the co-operative model in making serious video games?
There are many examples of digital-game based learning and training games; the video game industry calls them "serious games." This former professor of art thinks there should be a game for learning art online, and he thinks about cooperative game making. 1252 Words. 2009.

es090125
ELPO User's Role
The individual in the user community and what they do
Inventing a user interface for a distance learning course putting more emphasis on the users involves focusing on entertainment. This is one of the ten must-do points in C. H. Miller's book, Digital Storytelling, a checklist for developing a digital game. 1002 Words. 2009.

es090115
Practical Realities of ELPO
Emeralda: learn printmaking online is not only an imaginative creation
Forty-five years of experience—including experiments and follow-up reviews spanning generations—makes a good foundation for the launching of a blended online course in college-level printmaking. He looks back upon his college teaching career he built upon. 379 Words. 2009.

es090105
On Quest
His quest is to make an online interactive game for printmaking
With a lifelong quest to make printmaking understood by children and adults, this professor takes up the study of the state of the art of digital games. Reading a book by Carolyn Miller a paragraph jumps out at him as it contains three secrets of success. 958 Words. 2009.

es090326
Printmaker Playwright
Considering the power of play writing in the age of digital reproduction
When David Lotz asked him, "Have you considered a one-act play to get your message across?" the author—a printmaker making etching presses and selling them—considered the potential of David Lotz' question. Is there more power in play writing than prints? 1000 Words. 2009.

MacRitchie's Fast Free Fine Art (AKA MacFast, MacRitchie's, or, MR)

MacRitchie's Fast Free Fine Arts, or McFast, seen in this photo at dawn from the bow of the ferry from E'Studios.

MacFast, short for MacRitchie's Fast Free Fine Arts, is the favorite of people using rapid prototyping and creation of arts, crafts and design for education, research, practice and service by using computer graphics and multimedia systems. Here, training and education assists artists economically as it facilitates marketing and selling in this segment of the overall knowledge, skills and attitudes of artists, crafts people and designers.

The name is credited to a speaker named MacRitchie who, in 1972, announced to an audience at the Seattle Art Museum that print making, as a fine art, was at the point of entering a revolution. He used an analogy between art and food to illustrate that what brought about the fast food phenomenon was about to happen in art because of information technology.

mr770615
Journal Entry, Wed. Jun. 15, 1977
Possibilities of a Small Enrollment Summer
The author writes about the possibilities of the upcoming summer quarter. He had a small enrollment of 20 students. He looked for opportunity, rather than depression over last Autumn. Small classes can go outside the classroom on trips in his car. 347 Words. 1977.

mr780225
Journal Entry, Sat. Feb. 25, 1978
A Business Idea
The author writes about sharing his idea with his wife, Lynda, about creating a business. It would be for her. He would provide the basics and she would carry it out. 209 Words. 1978.

mr830615
Journal Entry, Wed. Jun. 15, 1983

Observation Notes
The author writes his observations about a printmaking studio in Edinburgh, Scotland. He didn't approve of the leisure and privileged atmosphere in the studio. He expresses a loss of opportunity for exploration. 158 Words. 1983.

mr850506
Journal Entry, Mon. May 6, 1985
Frustration about the U.
The author writes his frustration about his teaching career at the U. He felt there wasn't a future there. He demanded a fair evaluation before his work was thrown out as unimportant at the huge institution. 230 Words. 1985.

mr901211
MacRitchie's Fast Art
A visionary metaphor
The author, in 1972, thought he saw an idea of a kind of art that was going fast and cheap, an almost totally mechanized art for everybody. Fast, colorful, fun and temporary, it was to be to the art world what fast food is to haute cuisine. 1761 Words. 1990.

mr910408
Fantasy Printmaking
MacRitchie's Fast Art
In a city where art and sports are not friends, fantasy sports might bridge art and sports, or fantasy sports may produce forms of virtual reality arts. The author dreams of an institute for the study of multimedia arts in Washington state. 6023 Words. 1991.

mr910414
Obituary
He took IT seriously
An adaptation of the obituary of Dr. Orville Vogel. The author has a secret, like his admiration for the wheat cultural researcher. Like an earlier article about Dr. Roman, these inspired the author's lecture, Peas, Corn and MacRitchie's Fast Art. 786 Words. 1991.

mr910419
Video Wall for a Port City
Background to a proposal
Bill Ritchie has a plan for video walls, sometimes known as vidiwalls, for the city of Seattle. He paints in the background for a three-way partnership plan for his Perfect Studio's, the Seattle Art Museum and Port of Seattle. 1254 Words. 1991.

mr911201
Mac'd From Ten to Fifty
Old Masters flipping fast art
'Zines are multimedia publications aimed at education, practice and research markets. A forerunner to arts, crafts and design 'Zines is the Videozine, made for multimedia. This essay is a proposal for an electronic art magazine. 2135 Words. 1991.

mr920213
Art that pleases
And make it fast!
Speed is the essence of .intangible property evaluation. Property, such as electronic art, is identified, controlled, evaluated, and disseminated. In the age of the electronic reproduction, this is by high-speed electronic data exchange. 337 Words. 1992.

mr920214
McDonald's Metaphor
The next step
This author compares Perfect Studios for artists to fast food phenomena. The computer graphics movement is propelled, first of all, by the fact that art is necessary, and secondly, is available for affordable price to numbers of people and fast. 599 Words. 1992.

mr930408
Craig Rosenberg at NSPI
When Professors go virtual
Notes from a live presentation by Craig Rosenberg, part human factors engineer and part artist. The notes are almost raw, with side remarks by the author. 713 Words. 1993.

mr930420
Skate to the future
Graphics on the fly
How skate boards meet postcards. How business and the sport of skate boarding interconnect. 1000 Words. 1993.

mr930425
Engineering EarthSafe 2022
No quick fix
To create the right griddle for the fast food, food for the eye, the hand, the heart takes engineering, plus a philosophy of ergonomics that takes people into account. The whole-person with a sense of the power of limits on a calculus. 647 Words. 1993.

mr930503
Win/Win Again
Apprentices and interns in reinvented art studios
The old guild system was a win/win situation for master and apprentice alike. Maybe, changes made by the information age mean it is time to borrow some ideas from the age before machines took command. 917 Words. 1993.

mr930709
MacRitchie's ToolBooks
How many on the hard drive?
It is not how many ToolBooks (hypermedia creations using IBM compatible desktop computers) Bill MacRitchie has made, but their theme and style that matters. Artists' electronic books belong in art galleries as well as libraries and book shops. 1274 Words. 1993.

mr940623
Closure economics and intellectual property

Artists' future game plans
Artistic insights, strokes-of-genius and inventions are kinds of intellectual property you won't find at the shopping mall or in ordinary art galleries. Only by expert assistance can save money and make wise investments in arts, crafts and design. 455 Words. 1994.

mr950824
Paradigm shift
Workbook
Slowly, imperceptibly at first, then, more noticeably, the economics of arts, crafts and design begin to move as the force of ecological economics grows. 180 Words. 1995.

mr960106
Journal Entry, Jan. 6, 1996
A Dream Realized
Notes recorded from the author's "palmtop" B.O.S.S. computer. The author realizes that he never failed at the UW and he wanted to move on to spread his campus, teaching of art to the world at large. He lists some contacts, Brett Weathers and Norie Sato. 290 Words. 1996.

mr960113
Bill Gates' Mistake
Bottled art without the fizz
Bill Gates' mistake is when he set out to deliver bottled art and failed to plan its owner's manual, plus he failed to address the boomers' acquired taste for champagne on a beer budget. 1542 Words. 1996.

mr960116
Journal Entry, Tue. Jan. 16, 1996
Perfect Pay and MIT, Wisdom of Arts – Integration
Notes recorded from the author's "palmtop" B.O.S.S. computer. Things are improving financially for Perfect Studios. The author is excited about EarthSafe. He notes a broadcast on NPR about MIT and the wisdom of arts – integration. 235 Words. 1996.

mr960121
Heritage calls
Memories of your ancestors
Dated for next year--1997--this is a copy-written article from Jan. 21, 1996 to help guide the development of MacRitchie's Heritage Calling Cards, also known as heirloom telecards. 676 Words. 1996.

mr960124
Finding it out
MacRitchie's Prepaid calling cards
Seeking the Next Step in MacRitchie's Fast Art evolution of the Heritage Calling Cards online, a new twist on an old business. 2468 Words. 1996.

mr960126
Journal Entry, Fri. Jan. 26, 1996
Mystical Helper and Mystical Great Grand-

mother's Art
Notes recorded from the author's "palmtop" B.O.S.S. computer. The author records his activities of finishing inputting his mysterious helper F.S. Shinn's book and delivering his mysterious Great Grandmother's art to the printers. 165 Words. 1996.

mr960202
Sweet, sweeter and sweetest
Cookies, candy and calling cards
Artistry and entrepreneurship can beat the sweets sold by young people who want to earn money for their cause. The kids who want a laptop in every backpack may hit the streets one summer selling prepaid telephone cards for the Tech Corps initiative. 1940 Words. 1996.

mr960215
TeleCard Maker
An introduction
Creative arts on collectible telecards is limited by legal restrictions from two sources. The Telecard Maker software is designed to reduce these limits, opening new channels for artists' reinvented studios, on-line games and digital fine arts festivals. 802 Words. 1996.

mr960216
MacRitchie's Fast Art
Defined or defied by the competition?
Comparing the effect photography had on painting a hundred years ago in Europe (Impressionism and cubism), prepaid long distance cards, also known as telecards, will be the "holy griddle" of MacRitchie's dream. 1057 Words. 1996.

mr960219
Billy's Mistake
A farm boy's bad adventure
Sometimes an artist's creativity goes awry, and then spelling errors and illogical things can happen. These may put the creative person at odds with the rules, and he loses the game! 965 Words. 1996.

mr960225
Running money
An idea for supporting artists' home pages
Excerpt from the business plan of MacRitchie's Fast Art, explaining the way to get support for the EarthSafe 2022 theme via homepage appliance design. 3314 Words. 1996.

mr960301
Seeing the future
MacRitchie's Fine Art Telecards
Introducing MacRitchie's FAT-an Issuer of Prepaid Long Distance Telephone Cards for the Arts, Crafts and Design Professionals and Organizations. 3394 Words. 1996.

mr960304
Telecard FAQs
Telecards as fine art

People will want to know, "What is a fine art telecard?" These will be the most frequently asked questions, or FAQs. 113 Words. 1996.

mr960316
Visit to MacRitchie's Fast Art
An island in the lake of the Domains of Expertise
A virtual tourist continues a week at the Lake of Domain of Expertise with a visit to the island where artists are trained for art of the 21st Century--professional practice that resembles in some ways those of healthcare, accounting and engineering. 1821 Words. 1996.

mr960404
Crisis and opportunity
TQM in the free fine arts
Not since the heyday of so-called "new art forms" that popped up everywhere in America in the 1960s and '70s has anything happened like the fine art telecard. Current development is traced to roots in those decades, however. 744 Words. 1996.

mr960409
New art in the reinvented arts studios
MacRitchie's Fine Art Telecard Defined
Outline for an article to define a new art form based on the communications technologies and the tradition of fine art printmaking. 77 Words. 1996.

mr960427
Telecard Market Segments
Who cares about telecards?
For every thousand customers who want to buy telecards, there is a name. 198 Words. 1996.

mr960504
WaHi Calling
Reunioneer Telecards
Article for Emerging Seniors Network Newsletter, a formative group of pre-boomers, with an originial idea for fund-raising and do-gooding. 384 Words. 1996.

mr960512
Calling artists' telecards
Proposal for an unusual print show
What is it like to enter the International Fine Art Telecard Show? Apparently not like anything else we've seen yet. 384 Words. 1996.

mr960930
A perfect day in a perfect studio
Hanging out at MacRitchie's Fast Art
An author-mentor advises, "Describe a perfect day" as a way of sharpening one's sense of time, so a day in the life of a MacRitchie's apprentice-user is recorded. 1485 Words. 1996.

mr970106
Journal Entry, Jan. 6, 1997
Gates Prize, MAEA, and Nightingale-Conant People
The author writes about winning the Gates Prize as

a great mystery and conflict. He also writes about the possible new meaning of Master's of Arts and Education and Art (MAEA). He ends with a quote describing service as a possible fundamental part to art. 292 Words. 1997.

mr970308
How fast is fast?
Depends on your altitude and attitude
Speaking of "fast art" raises questions, sometimes. Answers come by considering a point of view, relationships between the artist, the work of art and the audience for the art. This article explains how attitude shapes the definition of fast art. 2437 Words. 1997.

mr970320
Going my way?
Cyber teacher proposal
How to teach 500 teachers some ways to use a laptop computer effectively in schools, communities and families in one hour. Achieving this is as easy as a cooking lesson. You must have the right stuff. 866 Words. 1997.

mr970407
The cybernetic telecard
Fun and fundraising proposal
The visionary of TCWA, as proposed in 1995, has a proposal to get money for the people who pursue technology in education. It is a telecard. Ritchie illustrates his first sketch and example of one that has the inventors of cybernetics. 744 Words. 1997.

mr970427
To play Emeralda
The right stuff
Artists' Stamps, old postcards and new, handmade postcards-these are some of the supplies you need to play one version of Emeralda. As an apprentice-user, you must be teachable. Finally, it is compulsive that you are creative and productive. 1008 Words. 1997.

mr970903
Interview with a check artist
Pioneer in HSIC Bank
A fictional interview with an artist who began putting miniature artworks on his checks, using a computer and hand-painting designs on each blank check before using it to make purchases. 1251 Words. 1997.

mr971023
Recalling all art students
Flaws in early art education
An art professor sends a Recall Notice to all the students who were in classes at the U of W. He explains why in this article, stressing the fact that we need their wisdom now and they can make good on their earlier dreams. 1349 Words. 1997.

mr971102
Journal Entry, Sun. Nov. 2, 1997
Updating GoalBook3 and Reading Stewart's, Gar-

field's Patent
The author writes his time log of the day, the activities and projects he did that day. He writes his cascade, "The evolution of resolution." He records his reading Stewart's, Garfield's patent and hearing R. G. Allen's story about Disney's Licensing. 610 Words. 1997.

mr971105
About Ritchie's logos
MacRitchie's Fast Art
MacRitchie's logo consists of a triangle, a belt and a cat. The snake-like belt weaves through the triangle. These three elements have sources in the story of my life. 477 Words. 1997.

mr971121
Journal Entry, Mon. Nov. 21, 1997
What InterDev is All About
The author writes his time log of the day, the activities and projects he did that day. He writes about the moment on his website was alive, linked to the element in the database of images resident on the server, so this is what InterDev is all about! 475 Words. 1997.

mr971227
The Master Sets Up A Game
Emeralda Inventor at Work and Play
On the first day at MacRitchie's the Emeralda Inventor's address to Newbies on the subject of putting images on the Score sheet, and how this is one of the first steps toward opening the gates to ones gifts, as they come from a database of digital images. 1143 Words. 1997.

mr971228
The screen in between
Two worlds of the Emeralda Player
The Emeralda Master imagines a traditional classroom setting where a student prompts him to explain the first step of an Emeralda session. The screen of the antique desktop computer is the focus of the 90s-style iteration of Emeralda, with icons and maps. 312 Words. 1997.

mr971229
Conversing with a Dolphin:
Basics of fast art
A day at MacFast and a one-act play is the order of the day. The author, daydreaming, finds for himself a message from an imaginary dolphin, breaking in on a radio talk show about old-age retirement planning. All due to a motion picture from over the Web. 737 Words. 1997.

mr980101
Don't Touch That Mouse!
Voices in the Webmaster's head
Confronted by an imaginary command not to go further without thinking about the task, the author entertains a stream of conscious-raising points about maintaining links between his Emeralda Website and Amazon.com. 660 Words. 1998.

mr980506
Leveraging Debt
Key to the debit column in triple-entry bookkeeping
While a call for information about a videotape may be a distraction, it also gives apprentice-users the opportunity to learn more about the debit column of Emeralda's Score Sheets. Start in debt, and you have something to leverage into understanding HSIC. 651 Words. 1998.

mr980516
Audit day!
End of a morality play
This is devoted to the dictum, "What you can do to help others get what they want" and this, of course, is the bottom line. To some people, that day is like an audit. If Emeralda is being played out of fear then the word "audit" can be a fearful prospect. 767 Words. 1998.

mr980526
Journal Entry, Tue. May 26, 1998
Parable on Intro
The author describes a professor's dream of having a yacht. He watched the yachts, schooners and runabouts crossing the Seattle locks for four decades. He records his thoughts while watching these boats during the 60s, 80s and 90s. 356 Words. 1998.

mr980605
Model Shifting and Model Building
Q and A and more on getting started
Curious how, within one hour, he receives a call on his telephone from a seller of on-line data financial services and, via e-mail, a request for "anything on ArtStudent and Perfect Studios", the author considers the commercial value of his essays. 1856 Words. 1998.

mr980615
Mythical Master Month
On closing books briefly
A few words on the end-of-the month ritual, or routine activity, of the Master Emeralda Player. In defense of his or her assets and their capacity to be shared and disseminated, it involves several interoperable digital systems and also traditional media. 428 Words. 1998.

mr980705
Market analysis
Who Cares about printmakinglibrary.com
Market analysis in global languages of peace is a tool, like tools of a crafts person, artist or designer with few limits on creativity. It's possible today to do a market analysis on a small Pocket PC, with some simple-to-use software, as described here. 1311 Words. 1998.

mr980715
True Emeralda
World messages form databases
MacFast receives deposits to a bank of data about

old media arts (such as woodcut printmaking). Also, there are new technologies coming in. This article is part of a "Demonstration" series, in which the reader uses his or her imagination to follow a tour. 1228 Words. 1998.

mr980725
Getting Started at MacFast
Demonstration at the Isle of fast, free fine art
You picture yourself as if being in a class or a tour group on your first visit to MacRitchie's, and a guide is speaking to you, explaining the origins of the concept. It's written in the words of Emeralda's inventor, therefore there's autobiography here. 1750 Words. 1998.

mr980804
Automata MacFast
Paying the cyber-piper
As the time approaches when MacRitchie's is to be woven into a cybernetic campus curriculum for the media arts the author confronts the timeworn issue of paying the artist. Even if the ideal is to give away the art for free, economic balance is desirable. 811 Words. 1998.

mr980814
Making millions asleep
The artist's dream
The plan is for artists, crafts people and designers to grow their personal revenue while they sleep by use of the features of the Internet that are designed for on-line commerce. An example is the making of graphics that people can get for a nominal fee. 913 Words. 1998.

mr980824
Breakfast with Emeralda Champions
Cereal box school and power breakfasts
From his childhood the Inventor of Emeralda remembers "breakfast school" as the cereal box lessons in bite-sized amounts that inspired his imagination. The equivalent in tomorrow-land is virtual power breakfasts, and they begin with HSIC education. 1239 Words. 1998.

mr980903
The trouble with concurrent engineering, marketing
It's hard to explain
A work of media art carries its original state wherever it is, whenever it occurs. The art of Emeralda is being created in a medium that carries all while being disseminated. To experience it or talk about it is a variation on the same form that makes it. 1001 Words. 1998.

mr980913
What's a Metaphor
Comparing Amazon.com with Emeralda
Part IV of Emeralda for Dummies. Big on-line bookstores provide enough mass-produced information to satisfy virtually everyone, but there's another site available on-line satisfying the changing needs and values of virtuous people, changing

every moment. 806 Words. 1998.

mr980923
Ecolonomics Technology On-line Curriculum Development
Emeralda Games Work Offering
Emeralda for Dummies Part XV. One way to grow ecolonomics to maximum effectiveness is fast art to facilitate and sustain players' participation. Emeralda, the Game for the Gifts of Life, offers a fund of perfect solutions to the Institute of Ecolonomics. 1585 Words. 1998.

mr981003
Moving and copying
Rites of Score sheets
Routine activities happen in both intrinsic and extrinsic realms when one plays Emeralda. Invention, too--like creativity and discovery--go on inside and outside a person's self. Awareness of explicit and implicit knowledge seem most alive when in motion. 825 Words. 1998.

mr981013
Q&A at MacRitchie's
The Emeralda Inventor Interviewed
Third of thirty interviews of the inventor of Emeralda, this one taking place on the Isle of Mac-Ritchie's Fast Art, a training and education center for electronic media fine arts. The series was started ten days before, and continues for a total of three. 4248 Words. 1998.

mr981102
A dozen moments in a half-hour
Reflections of an Emeralda Master
An art professor who used to be viewed by some as a loose cannon considers his routine activity of a half hour from a place he calls his "Cell of the Velvet Prisons of Emeralda." It's a fantasy region where he is inventing the on-line canon of the region. 1607 Words. 1998.

mr981122
The Basics
Getting there from here
The basic of Emeralda Play is the same as in Spanish lessons. No other word in the English language, applied to the method of playing Emeralda, is more basic than the word Cell. It is the game's fundamental unit or block. (You may complete this article). 337 Words. 1998.

mr981202
Looking to Montana
Background of a proposal
The Canon seems to be the perfect counterpart of this author/artist's idea is of what multimedia arts means. Montana educators wanted proposals for a strategy for a statewide media education program once, and he applied. Is there a connection? He wonders. 914 Words. 1998.

mr981228
Writing on the walls

The master in doubt
"The Emeralda Master held our attention for only a few minutes. Then we began to doubt that he knew what he was doing. The moment that he re-opened his attempt in a new format, things changed." The author describes fantasy scenes for a play he is writing. 690 Words. 1998.

mr981229
Walls crumbling down
Freedom and the prisoner's dilemma
The illusion of space on a two dimensional plane-the illusion of a third dimension-is relatively easy, especially by hand. A screen background may begin to look like a faceted glass prison-cell wall, an array of tetrahedrons. The author writes extreme-ly. 655 Words. 1998.

mr981230
Woodworker parable
Toward reverse compound interest
A parable about one who thinks that getting what one wants has two sides. One side says that what it is that appears to be what one wants is based on past events. The other side is that that appears to be what one wants is based on a future that's coming. 1212 Words. 1998.

mr981231
Emeralda Balance Sheet
Testing the Master
A vision in which the author-a prescient artist-forecasts that e-book reading devices would be expanded to have sound (for people who can't (or won't) read) and images, too. He's describing a textbook for understanding the score in his new game, Emeralda. 807 Words. 1998.

mr990101
A Pretty Morning
View on the last day at MacRitchie's Resident Stay
The age of digital reproduction is here and, to some, compared to gray shadow, darkening the view of all true artists. To others it is a place between darkness and light, all hopeful, virtuous and real, tradition and technology, production and livelihood. 819 Words. 1999.

mr990227
Mac'd on A Safe Earth
Alternatives in education
The author role plays in his practice and testing of his invention, a game he calls Emeralda-Games for the Gifts of Life. Experience and relationship are key words during this period when Alfie Kohn's book, No Contest, was contributing the method of play. 531 Words. 1999.

mr990228
Journals and diaries
Forward and backward in time
Communication is key to both artistry and health-care. Education is the bridge. People talk about it but ignore the changes that cybernetics has caused; hardly anyone stops and paints the big

picture. The old systems, reliant on papers, don't work anymore. 621 Words. 1999.

mr990301
Last day at MacRitchies
Reflections on slow times
An Apprentice User gets ready to embark on the next stage of his circuit of the Emeralda Region, and takes time to comment on the tools one uses while at MacRitchie's Fast Art. 374 Words. 1999.

mr990425
Something New and Valuable
Offering Into A Cash Stream
Looking forward to a lunch meeting with a leader of a growing local community that serves the dental assisting profession, the inventor of Emeralda speculates on the nature and quality of what it is he offers to a community in the dental practices domain. 945 Words. 1999.

mr990426
Investing in A Co-operative with Dental Assistants
Some Thoughts for Dentalisco
The artist spent two years at the chair side of a practicing dentist, assisting the actual dental assistant, and also the dentist's office manager. He is pioneering ways that artists, craftspeople and designers can become involved in continuing education. 838 Words. 1999.

mr990427
Getting Started Building Dental-Artist Teams
Intentions to Succeed
A dentist's editorial appeared and as this artist/author read it he envisioned standards issues that would lead to world-class practices. Patient centered oral health care and a kind of team leadership may involve creative artists' help to solve problems. 1205 Words. 1999.

mr990428
The Multifaceted Auxiliary
A New Paradigm for Arts Education
As he learns about dental practices he sees similarities with the art assistant. Dentistry is closer to science than art, and therefore the term dental assistant is a profession, whereas art assistant can mean almost anything in this artist/writer's view. 857 Words. 1999.

mr990429
A Most Imperfect Day at MacRitchie's Fast Art
Breakfast with Champions
A fragmented excerpt from a story or a screenplay, this essay focuses on the nature of imperfect information-that which has not yet happened-as partly dream, partly recall. The author uses stream-of-conscious, and notes from his PDA, in a salad of images. 724 Words. 1999.

mr990430
We Don't Need No Stinkin' Badges!
(However A Few Medals Will Do)

Entertainment provides images a cybernetic navigator needs to visualize where he or she is going in dentalisco, the virtual city being built on the shore of Great Lake of Emeralda. Preparation to depart from MacRitchie's Isle includes making a slide show. 637 Words. 1999.

mr990625
The Magic Moments Calendar
Threading Your Way On the Locus of Beauty
There is too much emphasis on being fast at MacRitchie's Fast Art. People are getting carried away, like white-water rafters, not in control of their craft. Yet they appear to enjoy it. They know one thing: they under natural law--nature is steering them. 701 Words. 1999.

mr990626
What's in Your Calendar for Me?
Ten Reasons to Buy a Page in Ritchie's Year of Living Copiously
The creator a The Calendar for the Year of Living Copiously lists reasons that fifty four people he knows will get their money's worth if they buy a calendar page for his project. A desk calendar is in progress, and he seeks to build interest in Emeralda. 2428 Words. 1999.

mr990627
Between Perfect and Imperfect Information
Jules Verne and ArtsEdge
What is the connection between the movie, 10,000 Leagues Under the Sea and ArtsEdge--the so-called bleeding edge art fairs held in Seattle? This essay may fill the order to answer this question, or it may be filler in the sense of dispensable and useless. 381 Words. 1999.

mr990628
Specifying the Calendar
Years ahead of the Game
The science of the illusion of calculation depends for its vitality on calendar specifications. To earn the Gates Prize, the Emeralda Player must specify (in both technical and artistic terms) the industrial standards of the calendar and keep it a secret. 346 Words. 1999.

mr990629
Good Morning, MacRitchie's!
Goodbye, Mcdonalds!
The nice thing about fast art is change. Even the basis for it changes, including the basis for the name of MacRitchie's Fast Art (which was of course fast food). The analogy of McDonald's was appropriate in its time, but time changes and we change in it. 924 Words. 1999.

mr000222
Why MacRitchie's
Fantasy and Reality in the Salon
Why is this short story in MacRitchie's 'Zine? The author scratches his head. Later he will return and solve this mystery, finding this article to be fiction and fact, and exemplifying what is meant by con-

current creativity, design, marketing and selling. 3844 Words. 2000.

mr000325
Eighth Round and Counting
The Boxing Match Metaphor
EarthSafe 2022 is compared to a thirty-round match between the insidious forces against Earth's life sustainability and the Emerald Works Missionary. After its eight round (each round is a year), the owner takes stock using an Intellectual Capital audit. 469 Words. 2000.

mr000507
Legacy Transfer Defined
The Artist's Check
His experience of losing everything taught the writer how, if he were to be given a second chance or a way to recover his loss, lead to the Artist's Check Works. This essay uses this peculiar notion of art as an example to define the term Legacy Transfer. 1290 Words. 2000.

mr000606
What's A Ritchie Stampworth
Introduction to Stamp Collecting
Analyzing an artist's Net Worth involves many steps, including the answers to the value of graphics that exist only on the Web and never touch paper or other depleted resources. The author compares this to the faith/fear dilemma of older economic systems. 1586 Words. 2000.

mr001105
Finding True Artists On-line
Benefits of the Retrospective
People fulminate when they see the phrase true artists, as it is judgment of artistic integrity. It is justifiable because art collectors are responsible for judging. It is not economics. But issues of morality and ethics as decided by artists themselves. 1354 Words. 2000.

mr001217
The End of Driveway.com Insight
Prescience Applied For
He receives word weeks in advance of the demise of the online storage system called Driveway.com and so he writes about the analogy of this passing utility with the ultimate demise of artists who rely on other people to take care of their assets for them. 1495 Words. 2000.

mr010126
When I went in I was an Art Student
And Then I came out a Professor
Waking from a dream at 3:00 AM, the author writes fast what it is he thinks the dream conveyed. Fast Art depends on, among other factors, his being able to respond quickly to intuition and dreams, and ArtStudent-an old idea-is a dream coming true for him. 1682 Words. 2001.

mr010205
Reds seeing Red

Can't Lives on Won't Street
A videotape on personality and color-typing played, and this author establishes that human structural intellectual capital is based on the ability to change, not false assumptions like people cannot change styles Like a child, he says, we can and we must. 1190 Words. 2001.

mr010215
Discovery
Another Brick in the Wall of Bill's Gate
Artist Bill pretends to be a ship's cook in order to get himself out of a jam. He learns of an ancient curse that will destroy all oxygen-breathing creatures on this planet. Discovery of his real identity forces him into a secret mission to stop the plot. 1297 Words. 2001.

mr010225
How Do You Eat an Elephant-sized Bag of Cookies?
One Cookie at A Time
Major finances are needed to shoot the Mac-Ritchie's concept, a moon shot idea, into orbit, so the author explains how he takes a bite-sized approach and nibbles a way into a general financial plan for his business plan. A window of opportunity is opening. 1989 Words. 2001.

mr010307
My Life as A Dog and an Astronaut
Corralling far out ideas for studio space-time
How does a person start a moon shot? How do you get something akin to equity for artists, crafts people and designers going? Is there a formula, a propellant of some kind, or is it magnetic in principle? The author is divided as to how to find the answer. 2267 Words. 2001.

mr010317
Dusty Hits the Road
Already a Wiener?
Years ago-it seems like a lifetime-a student handed this professor a cartoon: A hotdog opening his mail and reading, "You may already be a wiener," was the caption. The professor never knew whether to be angry or laugh. So he laughed. Today he's a winner! 1946 Words. 2001.

mr010406
IT's Alive!
Information Technology in Artist's Action
The author uses the acronym IT (Information Technology) to describe the feeling when he reviews the complexity of matters that are involved in making his art part of an auction. He uses computer software and the Internet to simplify the process. 1042 Words. 2001.

mr010416
Platform Books and Emerald Suites
Contemplation of Emeralda
The poet's work was bound by language, said one writer. Another writer follows literary tradition by writing one foundational, or platform, book and

then building on that achievement. Emeralda is a platform work, too, but I make it in and for a new world. 964 Words. 2001.

mr010426
How Emeralda Got its Rules
Interview with the Referee
Games must have rules in order to have the utility value we need and want in risk-taking. The inventor of Emeralda has a talk with himself and writes down an interview as he works up a proposal for a funding strategy to take computer games to a new level. 1791 Words. 2001.

mr010506
The Day I Read Morris Graves Died
Reflecting on an influential artists' legacy
His computer shows him two news articles via a headline downloading system, and the author, at a crossroads in his art and craft, thinks about his oldest encounters with art and his current work. He's making an art magazine on DVD, connecting old and new. 2157 Words. 2001.

mr010526
Funnest Part of Art Ed On-line
Getting there from here
How do you combine traditional printmaking with true digital arts? The answer is in the library gallery where hybrid, highbrow art is displayed on the World Wide Web. They are the results of TRP-Teaching, Research and Practice-a give-and-take celebration. 776 Words. 2001.

mr010605
What teachers need to develop the online art experience
A game no one plays
Like similar books published in the last forty years, Jerry Mander's critique of the media sells well and probably assists many educators in classifying problems in on-line education. Teachers beware! Games today or more influential than TV and books are. 512 Words. 2001.

mr010615
Foreword to my DVD Catalog
First draft
By June of 2001 I had created six digital versatile discs (DVD) when two organizations offered grants describing the specifics of which fit my DVD project. In the application I was forced to review and organize my work. That is how this DVD got its start. 1068 Words. 2001.

mr010625
A New Deal
A new art dealer in town
A blend of secret agent, e-store manager and art curator presents a new deal for a few people today, a new kind of art dealer made possible by information and telecommunications means. The author, fond of playing the role of a prescient artist, tells how. 1892 Words. 2001.

mr010804
Big Brother and Little Sister
Third Day in Resident Stay
As if he can write from the viewpoint of a fourth grader, the inventor of Emeralda tries his hand at role-playing "childe writer". A friend of C. T. Chew (who gave up his art career to go teach middle school) the author thinks about his class' adventures. 322 Words. 2001.

mr010924
Emeralda Passport Play
Filling your passport to Emeralda Region's Islands of Domains-of-Expertise
Seven Habits of Highly Effective Emeralda Players would be one title of a handbook for art education on-line. It'd be an orientation for new kinds of education for artists, crafts people, designers and teachers, and would be free on an Internet Web site. 1232 Words. 2001.

mr011003
Emeralda City Library DVD Section
Where you get the information you need and want
One of the earliest self-organized clusters of Free Intelligent Agents was Franklin's 1727 Junto. He created a subscription library for members. It became the first public library in America. It's a metaphor for the DVD Publishers Club this teacher wants. 2238 Words. 2001.

mr011013
DVD is the Backbone of My New School
Let me tell you how
I was at my Mother's Wake, talking to an 8-year-old relative. His name was Addison, and it turned out we have a lot in common. He listened to my problem, that I was stuck in the development of the backbone story behind my game, Emeralda. Then, I listened. 697 Words. 2001.

mr011023
Paying the Future Teachers
Making your debit card playable
A debit card can be used to utilize future teachers in on-line art education. There are many ways such as e-books, distance-learning tuition, and, according to the author, buying artworks or DVDs that are unique textbooks made by the Itinerant Professors. 1310 Words. 2001.

mr011102
Opening My Heart's Desire
DVD Library in the Ten Domains-of-Expertise in Emeralda Region
Serendipity rules the multimedia artist's way. The inventor of a non-competitive game he titled Emeralda works daily in sometimes a routine manner like a practicing musician, perfecting his method of play. Sometimes he gets surprises, as this essay shows. 1211 Words. 2001.

mr011112
Kpelle Passport Masks and Emeralda Passports
Remnants of bygone eras

His goal is to help students and teachers speak and act freely using new technologies. That having been said, how does a computer game method of play help him? As he makes his play on today's Passport, he describes parallels with a Liberian he read about. 1081 Words. 2001.

mr011122
Million Dollar Prizes for Printmaking Surprises
How the surprise of this century got started
The dreamer started dreaming of printmaking as a youngster, having become addicted to prints at a very young age. By middle age he had it all: presses, a studio and art galleries. Times changed, and a new world opened up complete with a pot of gold in it. 1895 Words. 2001.

mr011202
If Not for Corruption Where We'd Be Now
Public education's Achille's Heel
Petty and trivial instances of corruption in school begin early and run though the whole education system according to this writer. The result is degradation of the public education system that spreads also into private sectors and is ruinous to a nation. 1248 Words. 2001.

mr011217
Inside and Outside The Box
New era in art education
The author, dubbed an ITinerant Professor for a decade, wanders into his rented classroom and executes his routine activity. He's reminded of times past when his classroom would have been populated with students. Now empty, still feedback comes from afar. 1255 Words. 2001.

mr020106
Writing Between the Paragraphs - Part 3
An imaginary dialog between two professors
Cutting and pasting, revising and creating new e-stamps for his curriculum passport at MacRitchie's, the author adds his ideas to those of Mark C. Taylor. The e-stamps for art ed on-line are like the building blocks of a new curriculum suitable for today. 1111 Words. 2002.

mr020116
Secret of Emeralda
A paradigm for looking at art ed on-line
Twenty-five years ago this artist/writer and teacher discovered a book on anthropology on a new way of looking at technology in art education. He describes here how pathways are more important than goals, for it's in his creation of a path that he learns. 440 Words. 2002.

mr020205
Before Breakfast with A Champion
Confessions of an Art Nazi
What motivates artists in their quest for communities? The author reflects on his own past and thinks about the early events in his artist career and how these resemble what he's doing today, which is creating electronic stamps for an electronic passport. 1180 Words. 2002.

mr020215
Do As I Do, Will You?
Or, can artists lead?
Awakening with a memory of a well-regarded community leader named Sam Stroum, and he read that his motto was "Follow me." Was that associated with his military service? Leadership is important but can it be applied in art education? Can one follow in art? 1253 Words. 2002.

mr020225
Imagine A Better Art Game
Game of Life Becomes Emeralda
Wishing to convey a gift to arts education communities-of-practice, the inventor of Emeralda contemplates his greatest obstacle: No one has ever heard of this game. It is a co-operative game playing between a dying world and a new world trying to be born. 1051 Words. 2002.

mr020307
How e-Stamps Get An Artist Money in the Night
My stamp collection as a work of art in the age of digital reproduction
Like a flash of insight experienced by a stamp collector deep in studies of rare stamps, the creator of Emeralda, the Games for the Gifts of Life, flashes upon the idea that he can "sell" his stamps to students for e-cash for which they also get a lesson. 824 Words. 2002.

mr020317
Welcome Back, Mac!
The Importance of Names
Routine activities of the ITinerant Professor of art include real printmaking (tangibles) and virtual printmaking (digital productions) at about the same time, and researching and practicing game-playing. Routine activities are the beginning of expertise. 865 Words. 2002.

mr020327
Amazing Blows Alongside the Head
My morning at MacRitchies Free Fast Fine Art
This writer goes from one kind of work to another, ranging from old-fashioned, traditional woodcut to cutting edge, digital versatile disc-making. In the way of chaotic approach to his art and craft, he's following a vision of being a great world teacher. 1027 Words. 2002.

mr020416
Art Professors and Other Oddities in the Age of Digital Reproduction
Wizardry at Odds with Academe
Sixties' professors had it made, but good times were over. Starting art as a student, this author saw the joy of college art teaching could never be again. When he became an art professor himself, he had a fantastic vision of his future in arts education. 1425 Words. 2002.

mr020426

AUREL's Search for A Search Engine
Course Management Software for the Fine Arts
In order to get art education on-line, the motivation to do so must be strong. To get it one creates incentives for fine artists, crafts people and designers who want to have significant involvement in the economy of their communities as well as artistic. 445 Words. 2002.

mr020804
Starting Up A New Gallery in the Age of Digital Reproduction
Twelve Steps to Success
Art, like commerce, is both affected and effective by digital reproductions. This artist/scholar has made a lifetime study of media arts, beginning with traditional printmaking and, today, creating digital works. It's time to go public, he says, and acts. 866 Words. 2002.

mr020814
ArtistStamp of the Week Club
A Marketing Sketchbook
He is calculating how he can be of service to an after-school program, a community multimedia arts center, and still develop his artistic assets. The game he invented, Emeralda, will be the key to these projects. E-folios and e-stamps are the objectives. 615 Words. 2002.

mr020824
Full Circle
From a Hole in the Wall Printmaker
Thirty years ago he had a vision of printmaking at distances, actually an art class, taking place in his own future. Today he saw the eerie truth, that the teacher-working from a distance-was actually himself. He saw himself as a ghost in the new machine. 592 Words. 2002.

mr020825
Journal Entry, Sun, Aug, 25, 2002
File Structure for Stakeholders
The author describes the file structure for stakeholders. He describes how one is published annually and it is produced on a CD/Rom and a DVD. The chief value of the task is marketing in the spirit of "The Last Loveletter." 336 Words. 2002.

mr020903
I Write My Last Love Letter
What Keeps People Coming Back for More
It's the coffee that keeps me coming back to the Caffe Vita. It has a high replay value. How does an e-book writer match it? Answer: In the age of digital reproduction anything seems to be possible, virtually writing and virtually imaging stamp and story. 1073 Words. 2002.

mr020913
Am I Going to be Lonely for Rest of My Life?
The Navigator's Whine
As small an incident as window shopping can cause a disenfranchised artist to wonder if he made the wrong decision when he chose to follow a star that only he seems to be seeing. Art is a lonely, precarious profession, he knows, but how long will that be? 2187 Words. 2002.

mr020923
What Emeralda Teaches Art Students
And Your Benefits
It seems crazy to be playing a non-competitive game in a highly competitive, even combative, society like the US Americas, so the author, an artist/scholar who invented one, takes stock in the benefits of file management to ideal creative problem-solving. 1200 Words. 2002.

mr021003
Adjudicator at MacRitchie's
Why Fast Art?
The possibility that someone might actually arrive at his fantasy island for fast, free fine art and question the purpose of this outpost for hi-tech, low-touch art has this artist wondering, Who should set the standard? She asked that question of others. 1375 Words. 2002.

mr021023
MacRitchie's Metric
Measuring up in the age of digital reproduction
The age of digital reproduction is raising the measurement bar on arts institutions, resisted by arts educators. New demands are placed on the fine arts to prove their integrity and value of what art and poetry do for culture, society and the environment. 1348 Words. 2002.

mr021102
Professor's Cabinet at Seattle Independent Mall
A diary of an absent professor - 90-days
The author suddenly finds himself manning The Professor's Cabinet at a mini mall. He must assess what the cabinet is, and what are its goals, roles and purposes. The professor disappeared 17 years ago, and finds he has painted himself into a SIM's corner. 987 Words. 2002.

mr021122
We All Have Stories
Let me tell you mine
He is discovering his story as he lives it, and now he's experiencing life in a mall, in Seattle, in the year 2002. The author is looking back over a 40-year career in the arts. Once he was a professor, but he left campus life to find his Perfect Studios. 1317 Words. 2002.

mr021202
Contract Studies Strategies for Success
Putting the human before the hand
Asked to consider a contract for an independent study the Itinerate professor writes about the subject. The student is interested in the art of relief printmaking in the area of social justice. The professor sees in it both a challenge and an opportunity. 1950 Words. 2002.

mr030516

Plan for a New School
A School of Art in the Age of Digital Reproduction
Like a schoolboy drawing pictures in the margins of his notebook paper, an old art professor sketches a vision from his views on 40 years in art and teaching. In his mind he sees a new school taking shape, one that runs like a game he read about long ago. 1289 Words. 2003.

mr030526
Stamp Out Brain Damage:
Keeping Your Brain Alive with Artist's Stamps 'N Stories
If you want to know what Stamps 'N Stories is about, read this essay. Its author is a 60ish artist/mentor who loves to teach, do research, produce new works in old media, and find a way to serve his community at the same time. Stamps keep his brain alive! 1070 Words. 2003.

mr030605
What I Am Getting Ready For
Making artist stamps under pressure
He is recycling a small but rich collection of videotape that he thinks has a place in art education. By building a model for on-line education that links traditional art with new electronic art forms-using a video collection-he'll create a shell to sell. 705 Words. 2003.

mr030615
First in Digital Art Game Learning:
You don't have to be best if you're first
Reflecting on his 40-year career, the art professor (missing from campus for 18 years) determines he was the first to use non-competitive games in art education, analogous to the real world. Today's new game is for art in this age of digital reproduction. 1087 Words. 2003.

mr030625
Publish and Perish
Inspiration and desperation readings in higher ed
Every day, as a teacher getting ready for the burst that's coming soon in electronic publishing in the arts education field, I practice reading and writing electronically. My reading, for example, is a newspaper, The Chronicle of Higher Education On-line. 1592 Words. 2003.

mr030804
Loneliness of A DGBL Product Inventor:
Thinking a dream game can come true
Sometimes it happens that when I read a novel, I feel like it was written for me. In the story I'll find a message that helps me develop the next phase of a game I call Emeralda. This is an essay about a surprise I found in a novel, a feeling that fit me. 1368 Words. 2003.

mr030814
Who Invented Emeralda?
Or do games invent the players?
In forty years since he started art school a lot happened to change this author, an artist and teacher. He writes about a piece of Flash Fiction that he wrote in 1972 that set him on a pathway terminating at the gate of an imaginary place called Emeralda. 879 Words. 2003.

mr030903
Data Warehousing and Video Games:
A Marriage Made in Heaven
Urged on by what he sees as both a terrible waste of human creativity and resources and also by his own data warehouse, the author explains what a data warehouse is in the arts, crafts and design worlds, and how these worlds can be made into a video game. 1272 Words. 2003.

mr030923
Persistence of Emeralda:
Progressing toward online art education
The author's hunch is that some people with artistic interests will use some computers as tool kits for continuing education and also for working toward professional goals. A humanist, he says surprises will come from extraordinary uses of new technology. 1444 Words. 2003.

mr031102
A Graphic Learning Community:
Proposing an online hybrid humanities class with an arts focus
A short telephone call to his art student is not a momentous occurrence, but this teacher has his mind open to catch any small difference between the age in which he was educated and the present time, when most artistic graphics are digital reproductions. 802 Words. 2003.

mr031112
Collecting Students is Like Collecting Magic Cards
Assembling student drawings for an e-portfolio
As he was putting a few more students' images into a type of e-portfolio he calls Quarter Review (for a beginning drawing class) this author/teacher got a high like that which a game card collector might feel-it's a clue in a quest for his game interface. 364 Words. 2003.

mr031122
Getting Started in Graphics Communities
A Wizard looks back
Reflection is one of the benefits of using digital game based learning as a guide to wizard status in the multimedia arts. This essay is about looking back to how I got started on my path, and why I have taken the road less traveled-sometimes unwillingly. 828 Words. 2003.

mr031202
Emeralda Works for High Self Esteem:
A Game for the Gifts of Life
In an artist's middle stage of life he or she might face a variety of dilemmas. Looking back at one's history is one way of building self-esteem; looking forward and preparing for the future is anoth-

er. Playing a game like Emeralda is the ultimate method. 1502 Words. 2003.

mr031227
Proving Utility Value:
A wisdom boomer's offering
There is perhaps nothing more rewarding to a teacher in his or her senior years than to find that they are valuable to members of younger generations. A self-appointed Itinerate Professor offers his insights on one topic: a technology example to consider. 1212 Words. 2003.

mr040205
How My Computer Shapes My Art
Immedia arts and Loop-da-loo IV
For over thirty years he used electronic media, such as video and computer graphics, as adjuncts to his works in traditional art studio media and today he is aware what the media arts did to shape his daily routine. He calls it the effect of immedia arts. 867 Words. 2004.

mr040405
A Lifetime Achievement Waiting to Happen
A very old friend shows me the way
Having taught for 19 years at a University, and after 19 more years not doing much of any account, I wonder what I can call a lifetime of achievement and devotion to culture and the arts in the way Lisel Salzer can? Perhaps Media's Art Village is one way. 489 Words. 2004.

mr040415
Press Fantasies
Ideas for a new venture in printmaking
News that his old university is cutting back on printmaking-the domain of his expertise-seems at first to be a devaluation of his knowledge, skills and attitude. On second thought their attenuation of the program is an opening, a chance for a new venture. 473 Words. 2004.

mr040425
What To Do About Printmaking At The U?
The liberal arts' and printmaking
Reading a guest columnist piece that was especially poignant to this author having learned recently that the printmaking program at the University of Washington-a tiny by powerful piece of the liberal arts-is being discontinued. He asks what he should do. 5 Words. 2004.

mr040515
Big Dreams, Little Dreams
Hope in a printmaking gray area
His dreams as a boy came true-going from his father's farm to the big city, and a career in art and university teaching. But everything changed when he tapped the fresh new veins of technologies and printmaking outgrew its old self. Now he is coming back. 926 Words. 2004.

mr040615
A Business on A Roller Coaster Ride

Towards an intentional community and working
He sees the highest value of the arts as creating community, both intrinsic and extrinsic, as the forming of intentional communities. As commerce has always been a means to communing with other communities, this artist thinks about an arts-based business. 1149 Words. 2004.

mr040714
The Mini Halfwood Press at MacRitchies
Stranger things I've known
Fast art and etching presses don't go together, you would think. Therefore, the existence of the Mini Halfwood Press at MacRitchie's Fast Free Fine Art-the Emeralda Region's island of computer-assisted art systems of all kinds-seems weird. Yet here it is. 782 Words. 2004.

mr040724
Garden Party Printmaking
Sundays at Anne's
The wonder of the Mini Halfwood Press is that it's possible to go to a rooftop garden party and for the entertainment of all, print an intaglio print right there by the barbecue grill. This is free, fast fine art at its best! The inventor/author explains. 521 Words. 2004.

mr040803
A Sense of Closure
His dream goes on the rocks
At the end of the past six months an event across town impinged itself on his conscience: The University of Washington would be cutting back its printmaking division. What he feared the most is happening-the replacements there put his dreams on the rocks. 692 Words. 2004.

mr040804
Topping the Logic Tree
Growing at the extreme
He learned in biology that plants and trees have a "growth tip" at the outer, or uppermost extreme tip of their stems and branches. That image stuck like an analogy to human cultures. Learning is the "growth tip" of a human being, and likewise to society. 718 Words. 2004.

mr040813
Laminating the Past and Present
Collage and the age of digital arts
Artists like Braque and Picasso introduced collage in the 20th Century. Maybe that was the first time that ready-made images were permitted to mix with handmade artistic gesture and original graphic form. Today's equivalent would be to mix games and arts. 993 Words. 2004

mr040823
I Never Got to Finish School
The impossibility and possibility of teaching art
Someone said, "My secret dream is to be head of an art school, 'cause I believe art schools are impossible," like, "You can't teach art." You can set up situations and environments where learning,

teaching, research and practice can happen simultaneously. 1109 Words. 2004.

mr040912
Start Your Own Art School for Fun and Profit
Raising ephemera
While creating a CD/ROM based e-book, the author has a vision of himself starting his own school, the purpose of which is to restore ephemeral video artifacts from a regional art history period dating back a generation. This vision has the quality of Aha! 751 Words. 2004.

mr040922
Imagine A Student Today:
Doing what comes naturally
He enjoys imagining what a college senior or graduate student would be doing currently if the natural course of events in his domain of expertise had not been stopped twenty years ago. Today a student in multimedia arts would be taking a seminar from him. 907 Words. 2004.

mr041002
A Hidden Treasure
The Little-known Artist Stephen Hazel
He is struck by the fact that we are seeing the end of offset lithography now as the age of digital reproduction reaches its maturity. Closure of a nearby offset shop sparks his imagination; he thinks of the artist Stephen Hazel, whose studio is a museum. 613 Words. 2004.

mr041003
Vision of A Puzzle
Where in the world can you learn?
While fitting the exact specifications of articles into the database for the year 2000, I had a vision that showed how fitting these numbers-clipped from their meaning-was like fitting the pieces of a puzzle together. I wondered then Is this another game? 789 Words. 2004.

mr041012
Autobiography on MacRitchie's
Getting the facts straight
It occurred to the author when he was updating his database of essays that sometime it might be a useful project to write a simple autobiography—something like an expanded resume—to give an accounting of his lifework. The MacRitchie essays are a big help. 675 Words. 2004

mr050126
Artists Trading Cards in the Age of Digital Reproduction
One Maker's Point of Departure
Ever since he learned that there's a category of art called ATC, or Artists Trading Cards, this writer has been thinking of a card that exists in both the real and the virtual worlds. He's considering changing his tiny gallery/studio for this proposition. 929 Words. 2005.

mr050205

Anatomy of An Artist Trading Card
Planning the Scope of Fiction
A new art form fascinates this artist as he writes about the ways to enjoy art in the age of digital reproduction. Now he wonders how he can use this new form, the Artist Trading Card, in his game, Emeralda. He wants to combine printmaking with computing. 1127 Words. 2005.

mr050317
The Wreck of the Emeralda
A Story
Working on a brass medallion one day the designer of the Mini Halfwood Press is inspired to write a story about a fictional shipwreck that was discovered in the Puget Sound and which yielded, among the artifacts, a mysterious object with a gold medallion. 670 Words. 2005.

mr050327
End of the Paper-Based Print
A New Game for the Age of Digital Reproduction
Twenty-five years after he read the epochal essay Art in the Age of Mechanical Reproductioni, this artist/philosopher thinks there is a new experience opening up that re-connects the aura of the original to its reproduction occurring through online games. 1452 Words. 2005.

mr050415
Can or Should Triangle Studios History Repeat Itself?
Reflections on Triangle Studios
After reading an article about the booming online learning business, a veteran of 40 years in arts and education asks if it is now time to revisit one of his treasured memories—an artist's studio co-operative called Triangle Studios—and join the new wave. 993 Words. 2005.

mr050425
Participating in the Age of Digital Reproduction
A Wisdom Boomer Thinks it Through
He's 63 and still selling artwork that he made forty years ago. How long can he keep doing this? His heart, on the other hand, is in the digital arts—not only the traditional printmaker of his younger years. How do older people keep active and "relevant"? 700 Words. 2005.

mr050506
PS is for Park Service
Emeralda Players in the Community
His games for the gifts of life he calls Emeralda calls for players to chip in with their creative abilities to help solve the riddle, "How do you raise a million dollars and make the neighborhood people a part of the process?" He proposes a time capsule. 1585 Words. 2005.

mr050516
Retiree -Welcome to Your New Job
Reflecting on Post-Retirement Systems for Success
Advice he wrote six months ago comes back to him in the form of a sidebar in a publication

aimed at senior professors. He wrote, "When you retire, you are actually getting a new job, and you will need a system to preserve and cultivate what you achieved." 610 Words. 2005.

mr050526
No More Green Bananas
Living to 100, Copiously
There was an old person who said the secret to long life is always to buy green bananas. It's a humorous, good-natured way to say always set up something to live for—such as a nice, ripe banana. This writer, however, wants something for his mental health. 503 Words. 2005.

mr050605
If I Had Auction Tracker
Reflections on Auctions and the Sovereign Individual
His wife learned the software that's used for auctions—expensive software that's used in auctions raising hundreds of thousands of dollars—and as she elaborates on its power this artist/author begins to think such a software package would be worth owning. 1168 Words. 2005.

mr050615
Think Of A Living Catalog
Memories of Living Prints Coming Back
"In all our vanity we artists seem to think a catalog of our work is something to dream about," says this artist. Years of seeing catalogs of art shows and coffee table books on renown artists' life work sends a message to creative artists: Get a catalog! 653 Words. 2005.

mr050625
Confessions of A Demonstrator
Dear Demo Attendee
Written several days before the artist is scheduled to give a demonstration to a group of interested artists, this essay takes the form of an open letter to a "phantom audience" as he wrestles with some difficulties of the process he is supposed to teach. 624 Words. 2005.

mr050705
There Would be 360 Cards
Finding the Power of Limits in Emeralda Play
A remark by a friend over coffee triggers an idea in this artist's mind how he can develop a better game, one which would interest other people besides himself. "There has to be a limit," she said, "as to how many cards you can collect, and of what kind." 1000 Words. 2005.

mr050715
Sailing Printmaker
Going Afloat with a Halfwood Press
He's nurtured an idea for several years, about making prints while on a boat. Now, after many setbacks and side trips, he may be close to realizing his vision. Some friends invite him to spend some time aboard their sailboat in Canada's Desolation Sound. 402 Words. 2005.

mr050725
Appreciation and Anticipatory Complementary Systems
Video Games and the Gray Gamer
The least understood phenomenon connected with the graying generation is their need in game software design. This artist dismisses competitive online games such as bridge and poker; he is interested in games that develop the intellect, memory, and values. 1415 Words. 2005.

mr050804
Thrilled to Build
Different Games for Different People
A line in a book that says some children thrill to kill and destroy gives this artist to think some thrill to build, and he was among the latter. What does it mean to him when he's in his sixties and looking back at a life of creativity, ending in a game? 1485 Words. 2005.

mr050814
What If People Only Read Books?
An Essayist Pauses to Wonder
If people only read mass produced books and articles, and never read original, unpublished material, then why would any author write not intending to get their material published? This artist wrote thousands of articles, and never planned to publish them. 652 Words. 2005.

mr050824
Portfolio Manager
From Video Portfolio to Teacher's Pet
In a review of essays he wrote seven years ago, the artist (a closet essayist) is reminded of the notion of his being a video portfolio manager. The terminology interests him anew. Then in a casual conversation with a friend, a gaming element comes about. 1034 Words. 2005.

mr050903
Why I Resent the Retirement Myth
Avoiding Retirement is Good for Your Health
Saying he's a "retired professor on paper" is his way to describe his suspicion of retirement as it has come to be thought of in the USA. Viewing the retirement myth as a health problem in older Americans, he recommends several ways to avoid its pitfalls. 1613 Words. 2005.

mr050923
The Mountain Should Come to Me
Reconsidering the Event for 9-1-1
After a gala event celebrating a nearby media arts center's 21st Birthday that was like a class reunion, with many pioneers in the media arts there along with many young newcomers, he realizes he was swept away by the celebration. Now he pauses to wonder. 1038 Words. 2005.

mr051013
As If I Were Famous
What's in a Name in This Kind of Game?

A little-known artist speculates on the way his game, Emeralda, would be played by youngsters if he himself were a famous artist with a name like Picasso or Van Gogh. If those artist's famous works were postage-stamp size, his Calendar Game would be easy. 696 Words. 2005.

mr051023
A Cosmology of Emeralda
Finding the Connections Among Routine Activities
Of late the inventor of Emeralda: Games for the Gifts of Life has been noticing connections among his disparate, yet routine, activities that indicate possible ways to publish his game in the form he intended—an online digital game based learning package. 1008 Words. 2005.

mr051112
Standards? We Don' Need No Stinking Standards
Dentists Compared with Artists
If artists were educated and trained on the basis of standards in the same way the dentists are then what would be the state of the arts today? This artist, a former professor concerned with standards in education, contemplates the way the world might be. 670 Words. 2005.

mr051122
Stealing Disney Stamps
Wishing on a Star
The inventor of a game that guides his lifetime thinks about his favorite Web site. It belongs to Disney and features collectible stamps known as "cinderella". The parallels between the countries featured on Disney stamps and his fantasy world are strong. 587 Words. 2005.

mr051202
Could I Keep A Secret?
Time to Tell All About Emeralda
He's challenged by a retail store demonstration programmer to do a presentation for printmakers that will draw attention to their printmaking products. "Secrets", he says, and she invites him to tell her more. But will he reveal his biggest secret of all? 326 Words. 2005.

mr051217
Is There Really A Secret to Printmaking Success?
Part 1 of a Ten-Part Story
Challenged to create a one-hour presentation on The Secrets of Seattle Printmaking, the author rallies his imagination to come up with true secrets and confessions that could inform, entertain and enthuse his audience. He tries to write a script to do it. 1206 Words. 2005.

mr051227
MacRitchie's Secret
Looking Behind the Glass
He digs up secrets to fill his calendar, and at MacRitchie's—the domain-of-expertise in using electronics and print media for art—the best-kept secrets are buried beneath the surface of prints,

paintings and sculpture. Even he has trouble unearthing them. 393 Words. 2005.

mr060106
Condos and Calendars
Creating a Digital Game Based Education Tool for Stakeholders
Curious of ways to improve community life, like living in a condominium, this artist considers the idea of a "smart condo" that he's harbored for over a decade and how a digital calendar might serve in a novel way of educating owners via a digital game. 636 Words. 2006.

mr060116
A Game I'd Rather Be Playing
On Course Toward a Treasure Chest
Like it says on some bumper stickers, "I'd Rather be Sailing," this artist wishes for a game he would like if such a game existed. He writes about a game he would like to play with other artists, crafts people and designers on the Web, a cooperative game. 597 Words. 2006.

mr060225
What You Should Know About Bill Ritchie
A Different Kind of Resume
Realizing that most people at his alma mater—Central Washington University—have never heard of the author writing dozens of essays about a project he wants to launch at their college, he writes down some factoids about his own life that seem relevant now. 1103 Words. 2006.

mr060317
Strange Discoveries
Vision Lifelong Learning
Randy Hinrichs wrote a White Paper for Microsoft on the future online and continuing education. Bill Gates wrote the forward. In this article the author included fantastic stories to illustrate what he envisioned might become commonplace in the year 2020. 6712 Words. 2006.

mr060705
Object of the Auction
Restoring the Art Collection
Restoring the collection. Purchasers may publish an artist's stamp that features the artwork in the stamp's image area. 361 Words. 2006.

mr060715
A Page in My Book
E-book Links
On a page in the author's book you'll find elements that reach beyond the page. That's because his book is an e-book, a digital book, where it's possible to link to things off the page. 283 Words. 2006.

mr060725
What I Want To Do
Building a Structure for Collaboration
After reading an article about baby boomers wanting to go back to college to make contributions to society with teaching, research and practice, a for-

mer professor describes what he thinks is a kind of insurance for hope, or a structure for collaboration. 949 Words. 2006.

mr060804
Picture This Stamp Factory
Ellensburg's New Think Tank
A building is transformed into one of the region's most interesting experiments in schools. It's more like a think tank for senior citizens who came together to cultivate new ideas, boost old dreams, and reframe the future of higher education. 1226 Words. 2006.

mr060814
A Neat Game
Online Artwork Game
Emeralda. It is a neat game. The students play this game online. They make an artwork and put it online. 206 Words. 2006.

mr060824
New Wealth in the Alumni Nation
Searching for New Resources from Former Art Students
A former art major from Central Washington University speculates on a new kind of wealth that is available to his Alma Mater. He says it's not money, but in creative problem solving that his generation can endow, thus serving today's faculty and students. 2075 Words. 2006.

mr060903
Self-Reframing
The Point of Playing Emeralda
Emeralda is like the U-Frame It franchise except instead of framing the "its" in your life, it is for framing—and re-framing—yourself. 717 Words. 2006.

mr060913
Stranger Than Popular Fiction
Printmaking Textbook Online
The author is writing the Backstory for a videogame, but it's really a textbook for an online certificate course in art. Printmaking, to be more exact. 159 Words. 2006.

mr061003
Commentary Insert Editor
The Free-est Job
The Commentary Insert Editor gets to say whatever he feels like saying. Or he can browse through the archives and pull up anything that strikes his fancy, catches his eye, or fits his mood. He has the most freedom of anyone around the table. 391 Words. 2006.

mr061003b
Maas and Me
Advise about Writing A Novel
I had a professorship and the others turned against me and I felt like I had to resign. I hadn't salved my feelings a thousand times since with excuses. It's one reason I want to write a novel, a piece of popular fiction. 841 Words. 2006.

mr061013
Who is the Reader? Who is the Author? Who?
Searching for the Premise
Constantly as I write this story I have a live audience in my head. Once or twice I remember telling the story to people gathered in front of me, a real live audience. 1002 Words. 2006.

mr061023
Declaration
Intentions of Writing A Novel
Imagine that this certificate program I am taking required that each participant declare him or herself—their intent, the true reason they were writing a novel-length story. 120 Words. 2006.

mr061102
Dusty's Sad Story
Outline from PDA
I'm supposed to do some cabinet work for a customer. But the outline of Dusty's story can't wait. I've put some on my PDA, but I need an outline. 819 Words. 2006.

mr061112
What's Wrong with this Class?
21st Century Expections
New markets are forming, new expectations. The old audience is stagnated, dying off, and looking for big name authors and big publishers—reading that does not entail risk and learning new things. 307 Words. 2006.

mr070106
Discovery or Draw
A New Old Move in Emeralda
The Emeralda inventor meets an obstacle while creating the 2007-2008 deck of collectible Artist's Trading Cards. He can't find a single article to fill the slot in cell number 4; he's forced to draw from the manuscript from Ghosts . . . and finds a round. 568 Words. 2007.

mr070605
History of the Halfwood Press07
Bill Tells His Story about MacRitchies
The author wondered if would there be, in the future, some kind of fast art—popular and successful, yet having fine art's qualities of social and human values? 2926 Words. 2007.

mr070725
Jobs for the Family
Imagining a Reason for Incorporating Again
An artist wants to achieve two things: Perfect his game, Emeralda and secondly, apply financially literate theories to ways to help his family by employing members on real tasks and paying them. This is so new, untried, and complicated, but it might work. 1262 Words. 2007.

mr070913
Preface to Rich Artist, Poor Artist

Beyond the Art of Selling Art
The author has learned important lessons while writing that book, most continue to serve him now, when he is marketing and selling Halfwood Presses. The salesman in him went into a kind of slumber, waking up only to help someone own something he has made. 853 Words. 2007.

mr071003
Faced with Stacks of Cards
What Color is Your Skill Set?
Last night, the game CashFlow for kids was given to Matilda Bryan. The author continued to design his game, Emeralda, which is to be a teaching game for intellectual property literacy. It is a subset for financial literacy games like Robert Kiyosaki's. 444 Words. 2007.

mr071013
King Content
Is It Still Reigning?
Invention of a collectible card game that is at once an asset management and legacy transfer device that entertains and educates and is profitable to its inventor is great fun. It teaches its inventor a thing about content. He reads an article that helps. 666 Words. 2007.

mr071023
Making Your Deck
Sixteen Cards
The morning routine for the game inventor is important to the overall method of play, look and feel of the game. Inventors do not get to see their products arrive complete the way consumers do. Imagining it is the first step, then writing it down. 671 Words. 2007.

mr071102
Calendar Invention
From a Prehistoric Calendar
Something presses on his mind as he begins his day because Fridays are becoming "test day" in his routine of inventing the game for asset management and legacy transfer. A true invention must, it appears today, follow a pattern from prehistory: Calendars. 824 Words. 2007.

mr071112
Authority and Memory
Part of the Artist's Game
From reading, travel and personal acquaintances—not to mention living to his sixties and staying within his chosen domain of expertise, the author sees a need for individuals to plan for the maintenance of their art as well as its making. 775 Words. 2007.

mr071122
Meta Emeralda
Over Arching Play
Over and above the method of playing Emeralda is the Great Reason for the game. To its inventor it is a matter of life of the mind or death of the mind. The stakes are high, no less than a person's

lifetime, the quality of his or her existence in old age. 781 Words. 2007.

mr071202
Multicard
The Card for Emeralda
His friend asked, "When are you going to do a video on yourself?" But, he laughed. While he searches for a kind of artist's trading card for a game that might serve the same purpose, later on, the old art professor found himself asking that same question. 980 Words. 2007.

mr071217
What Becomes the Gates Prize?
A Game the Gates Could Sponsor
He played a game called "Elf Me" and the next morning envisions his works of art going through the same procedures, only in this instance the work lands on a conveyor belt driving it to a landfill. This seems like a kind of Emeralda Game, worth the prize. 242 Words. 2007.

mr071227
Fearing for the Lives of My Crew
The Captain and The Navigator
A captain and a navigator share something in common. Besides concern for their lives, they are concerned for the lives of their crew members. Of the two figures, the navigator has a higher responsibility because the navigator sees the bigger picture. 457 Words. 2007.

mr080106
A Game of Art Crates
Pursuit of a Card Game in the Emeralda Suite
The Emeralda Suite may include Art Crates, a game about mysterious caches of art bought at auction. In front of each player is a box with sets of ten cards, representing ten artworks. The total value of the box—called the crate—depends on the cards in it. 721 Words. 2008.

mr080116
Wastebasket Lesson
Inexorable Progress to an Online Class in Printmaking
Finding a manuscript—actually an outline for a distance learning course in printmaking art—in his wastebasket the author thinks about a story of a renowned writer and speaker whose first manuscript emerged from a wastebasket to became a world best seller. 969 Words. 2008.

mr080126
Micro Press
Joystick Metaphor
Today was the day the press maker started making the first Micro Halfwood Press. For years it has been on the press maker's mind: Make the smallest working etching press in the world. It is part of the game he is designing, based on the joystick metaphor. 126 Words. 2008.

mr080205

Whispering Muse
Printmaking in the Age of Digital Reproduction
In the artist's trading card used in playing Emeralda, one part calls for a link to an original story by that artist in addition to an image of his or her work. As this artist creates a link with his story, he compares his experience to playing Solitaire. 669 Words. 2008.

mr080215
Engineered Art
Behind the Curtain of Emeralda Works
Art in the age of digital reproduction makes demands on artists not unlike the demands facing engineers in all specialties when there arose any new kind of technology. The special demand on artists is that they face up to change in time and changes in it. 578 Words. 2008.

mr080306
Narrative Provenance of The Chess Players
A Lithograph by Jacob Lawrence "Blind De-Bossed"
Three trial proofs that the artist discovered in 2004, which he used for an artwork titled, "Homage to Jake." Several years later it sent him on a trip into his past, searching for the exact juncture of his, and the renown artist's, life. 2736 Words. 2008.

mr080316
Deck Value
Collectible Cards
Picture a deck of cards, collectible cards. They are sets of cards printed especially for games or for collecting. As you look at the box containing the cards, you notice it comes with a computer disc like those that deliver software applications. 341 Words. 2008.

mr080425
Reality College
Inspirations from Reality TV
A retired art teacher finds value in watching reruns of videotapes he made thirty years ago when he first taught printmaking. Printmaking techniques like the ones he taught in those days are no longer being offered, so now it is time to reconstruct them. 447 Words. 2008.

mr080505
Practice Exercise
To Learn, Not to Perform
Printmaking is a performance art. It requires practice, and we practice to learn, not to perform. If we are constantly thinking about how we will appear to the audience, then we may miss the essence of the art. 280 Words. 2008.

mr080515
Policy Formulation
Self Actualization Through Learning Printmaking Online
The four guides of his art and craft are creativity, invention, discovery and imagination. These principles are policies, when the artist thinks how they

are his rules. Then he justifies the Policy Formulation of Learning Printmaking Online. 979 Words. 2008.

mr080525
Physical Data Model
Toward a Functioning Enterprise in Physical and Digital Estate Management
The author has no doubt that he will be an effective, great teacher in the last generation of his working life. He will be a self-employed worker and owner in a functioning enterprise that is based on both physical and digital properties. 857 Words. 2008.

mr090106
Ticking Clock of ELPO
There are two ticking clocks in Emeralda: Learn Printmaking Online—meta and micro
Study of game design reveals there is an element called the ticking clock, a device used to produce tension and promote enjoyment of game play. In the designing of Emeralda: Learn Printmaking Online the there are two ticking clocks—a big and a little one. 1145 Words. 2009.

mr090116
Fool in the New Machine
Nine roles for game development teams, one role to be the fool
Reading a list of the roles people play in a community of game-making, this print maker, thinking to create a game he calls Emeralda: Learn Printmaking Online, sees a bit of himself in every title. What is his role? He wonders if this is the role of fool. 985 Words. 2009.

mr090126
Goals of the ELPO User
Sustainability in the virtual and the real worlds
The essayist is a professor and a wannabe inventor who has a plan for a digital-game based blended distance learning course. He is inventing a user interface for a distance learning course that puts emphasis on community roles for artists who make prints. 1088 Words. 2009.

mr090215
ELPO Structure and Interface
Starting, playing and finishing in an blended on-line fine art course
Carolyn Handler Miller's 2nd edition of Digital Storytelling is the source of this essay, where she said there are ten steps in the development of the three essential parts of games: The Concept Document, Bible and Design Document. This essay is the 7th. 2249 Words. 2009.

mr090406
Financing ELPO
The four Fs—Friends, Family, Former Student and Fiscal Accountability
How will the money, time and resources be accumulated that is needed to turn Emeralda: Learn Printmaking Online into a reality? The inventor

offers his family, friends (aka patrons) and former students. On all accounts, fiscal accountability is important. 1525 Words. 2009.

mr090407
Richard McRitchie Profile
Disillusionment, Dreamer, Inciting Incident and Instrument
This article describes the McDonalds fast-food franchise as a model for MacRitchie's fast art. 310 Words. 2009.

mr090416
Teacher Tip Off
An agenda to start ELPO
May, 2009 is Art Education Month in Washington State, and a good month to publicize work done so far on Emeralda: Learn Printmaking Online (ELPO). In a series of five sessions, the author envisions taking the idea and the Halfwood Press to the next level. 1967 Words. 2009.

mr090426
Silent Art Auction Play
Vision of a funding game
Persistent notions of an event-driven auction drive this artist to distraction, so when a friend gives him a list of thirty artworks moldering in his storage drawers he sees a crystal-clear pathway to finance the next stage of his venture in game design. 1597 Words. 2009.

mr090506
Manage Content Rule
Emeralda rule number one
"Manage content so people have time to process and reflect on content in an interactive manner." This is rule number one in Emeralda: Games for the Gifts of Life. It's the rule with which to begin ELPO according to the game's player/inventor and promoter. 1320 Words. 2009.

mr090605
Nutshell Cooperative
Printmaking Learning Cooperative briefly
Re-opening his long-held interest in the dynamics of cooperative teaching, learning, practice, research and community development, this retired fine arts teacher (whose specialty is printmaking) writes a brief description for it focusing on its economics. 1042 Words. 2009.

mr091003
Oral Exam
My first session with the game doctor
The man who calls himself the "Inventor of Emeralda" meets his first challenge, the questions coming from a game doctor, who's familiarizing herself with the details of one of the games in Emeralda, Learn Printmaking Online, the game based user interface. 792 Words. 2009.

mr091013
Worthless Games
Sampling Skotos Tech offerings with an eye for

On a pathway to review one of his heroes from the past, the author comes upon a game company financed in part by a venture group with connections to his hero. When he looks into the company, he finds rich grounds for criticism and an opening for his game. 1218 Words. 2009.

mr091217
Opening Day
Opening day at MacRitchie's Fast Free Fine Arts
It's a prequisite that Residents-in-Stay write a few words about their current place, the Island of Domain-of-Expertise, when they start his or her Year of Living Copiously: The Gates Prize for Teaching, Research, Practice and Services. Then add a sketch. 593 Words. 2009.

mr091228
REO Metaphor
Continuing the analysis
If you follow the structure of a computer game, probe its skeleton so to speak, you may come across clues as the adaptability of computer games to learning printmaking. At the same time you may utilize your creative writing and create links to real life. 418 Words. 2009.

Open Studios and Hospitality (AKA O'Studios, or, OS

Open Studios and Hospitality shown early in the morning from the ferry as it approaches "O'Studios."

O'Studios stands for Open Studios and Hospitality, has a mission to provide displays and hospitality services for people who want to see the art gallery, the studios or individual displays and events in fine arts, crafts and design. This is a proactive outreach to the larger community, including the world's progressive citizens.

Community action on the part of artist (and drawing on the roles of entertainers) is being a part of a social microcosm. To make a neighborhood, town, city or country a good place in which to live and work, culture—and the part within this where artists have significant roles—is enriched by hospitality services.

These services may range from modest refreshments, time-share condominiums and luxury cruises. Tours of major exhibits and gallery walks, free demonstrations and multimedia art camps are examples of what will be achieved on Open Studios and Hospitality Island.

os750615
Dreamer
A Short Story
The author of this story re-discovered his original 1975 manuscript and reviewed it in 1991 and 1993. It is his autobiographical fantasy, about a man re-entering society that is starting over, without the benefit or encumbrances of recorded world history. 2220 Words. 1975.

os800428
Journal Entry, Mon. Apr. 28, 1980
Disappointing Rainy Change Day; Administration and Committees
The author writes about the disappointing rainy "change" day, when hoped for the sunny, happy "change" day. He writes about the "dull thankless work" of being an administrative position at the art school, as learned from the director of the art school. 405 Words. 1980.

os880210
Tale of A Blind Elephant:
Who knows what computer art is?
Adaptation of the story of the blind men and the elephant to provide answers to the question, "What is Computer Art?" The author is an artist who began his work with printmaking and worked up to video and computer art from there. He's a story teller, too. 1329 Words. 1988.

os881115
Art Student
A path you can trust, a path you can audit
C. T. Chew attended the Orca Conference, showing the Art Student CD example and his 20 years' work to illustrate some possibilities that are opening up because of new computer technologies. He highlights the CD/ROM Publishers Club and the print portfolio. 1635 Words. 1988.

os890115
Locus
Path of a moving point
Text for an exhibit by Bill H. Ritchie by Dr. Richard L. Brown, gallery director and the head of the Department of Art, Pacific Lutheran University, Tacoma, Washington. 441 Words. 1989.

os890425
What is a Perfect Studio Seminar?
Vision of consumer edu-tainment
In the first year Perfect Studios seemed to have the potential to be an alternative educational resource, this description was created to define seminars. This is accompanied by a press release. 303 Words. 1989

os890605
A soft joke
Where's the video?
A joke about an art director, an artist, an art teacher and a computer artist and their dilemma in the face of life-threatening forces. 259 Words. 1989.

os890804
Life among the metaphors
The bitter and the sweet
Account of the highs and lows of life among the metaphors, an imaginary people. Their values are sometimes found in the those living in the silicon forest. From the Emerald City to the Emerald Valley, life with the metaphors is bitter / sweet. 656 Words. 1989.

os900914
Positive Acceleration
Outline for patience
Three paragraphs describing the metaphor of the dripping faucet of life. 164 Words. 1990.

os900915
The Farmer and the Meritocrat
Looking down, looking up
An old division between agriculture and culture-culture is examined by a former farm boy who moved to the city. 227 Words. 1990.

os910303
Rings on water
Inspiration for mosaic
These words were written in a tiny notebook which Bill Ritchie discovered when he was cleaning his studio. During his design of an ill-fated mural for Spokane Community College, its message seemed to make more sense. 461 Words. 1991.

os911020
TESC 2011
Dreamer awake
Reading history from the view of a TESC-education, the fictional teacher grows conscious of the origins of the college itself. Basic tenets endured forty years of political and economic change, despite change in technology. 1523 Words. 1991.

os911122
Journal Entry, Fri. Nov. 22, 1991
Perfect Studios and University of Washington School of Business
This is from the author's GoalBook1. The author writes about the Background, Objective, the Listener, the Approach, and the Proposal of his goal to work with the UW school of business on a project involving art. His contact was Marilyn Gist. 1257 Words. 1991.

os920422

Bill's Gate ToolBooks
Drive-thru the F-Drive
Observing the 23rd Official Earth Day, the author begins a review of the ToolBooks he created over three years. How can hypermedia books help in the EarthSafe 2022 program, part of Perfect Studios' mission? Perhaps retrospect will show. 1810 Words. 1992.

os920510
Ken's Golden Age
The Rolling Summer School
Conversing with Professor Ken ten renews interest in a fabulous Summer-school bus. The author paints a background for the technologically-minded, creating edutainment in virtual reality and takes a strange turn into the realm of the soap opera. 4876 Words. 1992.

os920511
Inventing Media's wheel
Parable of a wood carver
A parable about a child and a crafts person and the creation of a wheel for a machine that had not yet been invented. Reprinted from Ritchie's Perfect Press Magalog because it is both practical and fantastic. 607 Words. 1992.

os920608
Perfect Studios that Bill built
Calculus of a dream that remains
The author creates a line of statements like "The house that Jack built" and readers are invited to back-chain through his personal and professional story of concommitant trials, setbacks and intellectual gains all stuffed in a Perfect Studios anecdote. 1020 Words. 1992.

os920623
The scholar and his son
Parable from the Emerald Valley
A parable based on the development of the software known as KidPix, created by Craig Hickman. It was created to send to Haiyan Zhang, a friend of the author's, to encourage a Chinese language learning program for K-12 students using CD-I. 812 Words. 1992.

os920923
Knotty exhibit shakes up the mind
A proposal for a REAL store
This is a futuristic conception of a downtown Seattle Information Technology Tower, a center showcase for northwest industries - large and small - and how they use Washington-grown technologies. The fictional story begins in 1992 with a sidewalk museum. 1078 Words. 1992.

os921006
Homeless computer users
E-Mail to clubbers
After a generation of thinking that computers are a new way of doing things, people who are deep in the creative and productive potential of digital media may find themselves homeless. Neither real, permanent security nor true outcasts from the system. 363 Words. 1992.

os921112
Jackson's rhyme
Thinking of Pollack
What if Jackson Pollack had not missed the information age? It is a question for art education. This is a letter to the editor of CompuServe's magazine with an offering to their Rhymes Book. 200 Words. 1992.

os921220
Ola! Ohaiyo! Hello Media!
Concept for Media's KidsVid
Based on an announcement printed in a newspaper, this is a copy-written version of what might become reality. The computer revolution winds down, and arts education reform picks up. This program is as original as Sesame Street. 1650 Words. 1992.

os930304
Ride the data highway
An art store, a train
Excerpted from RIISMA Magalog:Art Classrooms of Tomorrow Today. The Art EarthSafe 2022 Class of the future is a multimedia, and these were part of the essay that mixed business, retail, hospitality, marketing and sales with real and fantasy events. 1215 Words. 1993.

os930312
A fun letter to Professor Eckre
Art and politics collide on the data highway
Was Professor Eckre being an absent-minded professor when he wrote a letter asking for free desk copies of my publications for his political science class in North Dakota? It's fun to imagine what he thought when he got this response. 324 Words. 1993.

os930331
Tetra's restaurant visit to Prism
Taking home what you didn't get
Fantasy visit to "Prism," a restaurant with a new way to take home what you could not order. The story describes what POP will mean in the future, and how computer kiosks will be more friendly and useful to our epicurean natures. 1880 Words. 1993.

os930415
Reading an art magazine from 2022
Loveletter to Media
A love letter to Media. 789 Words. 1993.

os930424
Automated Library Machines
ALMS for the poor
As I unpack my electronic library of ToolBooks, I find projects partly unfinished. It was years ago when I first created these, yet they are intact. What would a stranger, skilled with browsing electronic ToolBooks, think of my crude sketches? 994

Words. 1993.

os930428
Valley dreamers
Blending the two Washingtons
The author is roused from his computer dream-world. "How did I get here? What happened? Has the dream come true already?" He considers whether computer technology and agriculture will crest in the agricultural part of Eastern Washington State. 1553 Words. 1993.

os930508
Tip of the IceBerg
Fifteen years after the Emergency Meeting
Ten days from the Fifteenth Emergency Meeting Anniversary, in sight of the tip-of-the-iceberg, zoomed-in on for a closer look. Built on the plan to meet Jean Parrent, potential EarthSafe 2022 worker. 771 Words. 1993.

os930516
Herstory
Script for the foyer
Collecting the numerous relations of Herstory (Media's) into a powerful crystalline lattice work and presenting them to a classroom of one-million students. 533 Words. 1993.

os930521
Dear Media
Postcards to my ghost
Short messages to a "ghost in the new machine." 317 Words. 1993.

os930522
I want my ITV
Surfing downtown
The artist, crafts person and designers can use ITV in ways that commercial stores might not want us to think about, but this article suggests that it would be better for creatives if they do. 1444 Words. 1993.

os930528
Three little pigs
Stories from Yakima
What Yakima needs is a story-telling monument to speak to the world about sunshine, food, fresh water and growing things. From this and the organization that maintains it the stories from many nations go out with every parcel of Yakima Produce. 505 Words. 1993.

os930604
Play Work
For mature interactives only
Thinking of an electronic game for two that is part Pictionary and part "Where in the world is Carmen SanDiego?", the author puts himself in the player's seat. Put the joystick in your hand and imagine this game you play on the data highway. 2170 Words. 1993.

os930611

Hit your wagon to a star
IT Professor on interview
The story of a another encounter the ITinerate Professor counts as "The 4th kind." Dependent on three industries (Transportation equipment, food processing and tourism) the educators / entertainers look for technology to move their information. 2216 Words. 1993.

os930612
US United States
Her Story
The symbolism in the story of the luxury liner-turning-to-scrap-metal is prophetic. Reading that the 1952 ship, SS United States, was rusted and would be auctioned as junk, I began to make Her story into a focal point in "The Woman Who Fell to Earth." 438 Words. 1993.

os930613
One wish
Eve of an anniversary
It is the eve of my 29th Wedding Anniversary. In two days, someone might ask me, "If you had one wish that you think could come true here, what would it be? 868 Words. 1993.

os930621
Game round-table
Dial "900" to get out
Reinventing arts studios began in the 80s after Naisbitt and Aburdene's "Reinventing the Corporation." An artist invented an inner board of directors for his projects, and explains the diagrams of "Meeting of the Bored." This is the base for Emeralda. 385 Words. 1993.

os930625
Conversation of the Bored
Hours away from a life
The reader is asked to imagine ten clones of Bill seated around a round table, a crystal ball in front of each seat. They see the logo of each of Ritchie's ten divisions. This article is self-talk that guides the reinvention of arts studios. 1061 Words. 1993.

os930626
LUXury Club
Investment clubs are the answer
The author says ideas of Kenneth Lux, economist, need to be examined to find answers to investors' questions. The sustainable investor needs to know how plans fit the next thirty years. Track investment clubs; see how they find direction and growth. 1500 Words. 1993.

os930628
Narrative for a storyboard
Fit for a hard-drive
Over time, the artist reinvented his studio to fit on a computer hard-drive. For each division, images evolved that were icons for each division. Finally, a storyboard resulted that suggests a fly-by tour of the Perfect Studios. 1154 Words. 1993.

os930706
TRPI
The right stuff for investing
TRP Investment is a means of achieving financial, educational and social goals. A long-range plan, stretching fifty years into the future, makes TRPI an ideal way to invest time. How does one qualify? This article suggests some criteria. 222 Words. 1993.

os930920
Food co-op metaphor
Electronic peaches next?
This article suggests that the intellectual and social-emotional dimensions of the human personality can grow on the food co-op model by applying it through technology, the tools of the age of electronic reproduction. 2289 Words. 1993.

os931008
Cruising Virtual Reality
Fantasy coming about
Here is a whole-brain approach to members of the cruising industry to put art, education and technology into the picture of cruises. Content would be able to outperform most land-based settings with "Computer Arts Stars Theatre." 2505 Words. 1993.

os931010
What I want in a cruise
Letter to the liner
A member of a special segment of the "geezer generation" fantasizes on what he would say if a cruise industry poll asked him what he wants in a luxury cruise. It's not what you would expect from the nations' richest population. 1983 Words. 1993.

os931028
The New Glass Bead Game
Emeralda fantasy
A fantasy - there is no electronic brochure named "Emeralda" but such brochures are coming soon. Ritchie estimates that in three years there will be a half-dozen. By the year 2000, travel magazines will include diskettes plus CD Multimedia products. 1329 Words. 1993.

os931125
Interview with a data highway driver
Tight turns and steep hills
Six months after an interview with a new data-highway builder, the author asks, "What if I had answered differently?" 1736 Words. 1993.

os940119
College in the palm of your hand

Gleaning education on your PDA
The new college course will be palmtop-based. The author stares into the tiny screen on his Casio B.O.S.S. and, like a crystal ball, it tells him the past and future of the Personal Data Assistant itself in education. A game called "Emeralda" is born. 509 Words. 1994.

os940121
Visualize Buying Rose Hill
A Media fantasy
How do you save an old wooden school from demolition when developers move in? Is there a profit center in historic preservation? A business plan is needed, preceded by a fantastic visualization session for visualizing heritage development business. 503 Words. 1994.

os940128
LMASOCACAD Quintet
Sould of the new museum
Five foci for a new living museum: One for text of all kinds. Another is for numbers. The third is for graphics. Fourth is sound and the fifth is called by various names such as telecommunications, electronic data transfer and data highway systems. 1280 Words. 1994.

os940210
Smart time share condo
Plugged in and going
There is a way, now and in the near future, for smart people to get smarter about new technologies for home and work. They invest money in a time-share condo limited partnership, and in return they get a high-tech smart getaway without spending much. 1866 Words. 1994.

os940218
Rose thorns of silica
Vision of a glass connection
After the author and his co-workers lost the battle to save Rose Hill Grade School, he occasionally goes back over his database and records for artifacts of the project. Better than any photograph of the lost school, his stories enliven his imagination. 933 Words. 1994.

os940228
Cruising your studio
Between virtue and reality
This article was copy-written while reading the tutorial for the world's first PC-based virtual reality planning software for personal architecture. Mouse in hand, or a grip on your joystick, you enter your studio and go to work 1458 Words. 1994.

os941210
Interview a PATC student
The boredom of practice
Formatting an expert's unpublished articles is boring in this fantasy interview. The students at Pacific Arts and Technology College work for a small salary and dream of better methods. 1694 Words. 1994.

os941222
Peabody Sand & Gravel
A painting story
Is it different to paint in the open air as compared to using computer graphics and paint programs? Definitely, yes. The outcome may be trivialized, though. The experience, to the creative person, is all that really counts. (hand-written original) 1200 Words. 1994.

os941230
An artist's hyperbook show
The ToolBook Example
After four years of casual writing, electronic painting, sketching and testing, the author imagines what it would be like to share a tour of his hyperbook. (Hand-written original) 1000 Words. 1994.

os950124
Proposal for W.R.I.T.E.
Four dimensions of a story
Four dimensions face the Canada's W.R.I.T.E in this paper: The author as born-again art teacher, as an early-adopter of media arts, as self-appointed founder of a new museum school, and as a channel for a 30,000 year-old alien named Media. 716 Words. 1995.

os950128
A Cybernetic Front-page Article
A thread from Liner Notes
The author was to be a presenter at a meeting of Northwest Cyberartists. He was asked to provide a front-page article for their newsletter. From a previous issue of the newsletter, he resumes an inner dialog he left from November of the year before. 943 Words. 1995.

os950408
Interview with the umpire
Having a talk with ourselves
A fantasy interview written from both sides of his brain, the "umpire" explains how he got his name and describes why he chooses to do this non-artistic work. 2691 Words. 1995.

os951228
Journal Entry, Thu. Dec. 28, 1995
Symbolic Dream and Conversation with Living Prints
Notes recorded from the author's "palmtop" B.O.S.S. computer. He records a dream about receiving blank checks. He hopes of a customized studio. He did wood cutting & Lithograph on-Line. He writes a description of his own book following other examples. 357 Words. 1995.

os960107
Journal Entry, Sun. Jan. 7, 1996
Perfect Work, Perfect Way, Perfect Service, Perfect Pay!
Notes recorded from the author's "palmtop" B.O.S.S. computer. After reading Shinn's book, the author is convinced that he's talented and gifted

that must be shared and grown. He accomplished completing his resume on his home page. 219 Words. 1996.

os960316
Visit to Open Studios and Hospitality
Cybernetic Isle with heart in Domains of Expertise
The fourth stop on a ten-day tour of the Domain of Expertise, a fictional lake where arts, technology and business are mingled in the atmosphere of a future search. Excerpt from Reinventing Arts Studios Workbook. 1883 Words. 1996.

os960404
Ritchie and the Witch
Little Mind Workshop Book
Four elements are joined in an entertaining story about a witch, a cat and a Master of Digital Arts, a story about how Dreams Work to produce a Mind-Blending of Napoleon Hill's "Think and grow rich" and Kevin Trudeau's "Megamemory." 828 Words. 1996.

os960515
Flight of the 888
A tech-corps dreamer's sketchbook
Created to encourage communications among people interested in arts, business, and communications technology education. The image of the airplane was contributed by Jerry Ritchie, and the mountains and sea of edutainment were added by the author. 644 Words. 1996.

os960517
Flight of the 888
Muralism in the age of digitial communication
The outcome of this parable determine what, if any, is the common goal US West and AT&T Pioneers and Tech Corps Washington, as proposed by the first author, who filed an intent to charter Tech Corps in Washington state. 893 Words. 1996.

os960518
Flight of the 888
Carla, the virtual flight hostess
A telecommunications pioneer suggested the need for a partnership for an upcoming conference and discussion. Her invitation inspired the story, "Muralism in the Age of Digital Communications." 983 Words. 1996.

os960523
Flight of the 888
Fanciful approach to quality teamwork
Last in this year's four-part of a story created on-line for people interested in arts, business, and communications technology education by a visionary intent on chartering a US Tech Corps chapter in Washington state. 735 Words. 1996.

os960804
Alive and well among the metaphors
Life in the tall forest
Where I live there once stood fir and cedar trees

that were so tall that no one had ever been able to climb to their tops. Living among such giants made people think big. The trees are gone, but their spirit remains, and that is why I think big. 1233 Words. 1996.

os960809
Roots of Emeralda
Search for life
Games fascinate the artist who uses electronic tools in his art and craft, but why? When a tele-communications company makes a deal with a game company, many possibilities are raised and point to a famous scheme called "The Glass Bead Game." 2656 Words. 1996.

os960813
Virtual Versus Vicious Games
Paths Toward Emeralda
Perhaps The Wizard of Oz is one of America's greatest stories ever told, and it is based on fear of the unknown and a Yellow Brick Road. The pathways to Emeralda is based on faith in the un-known and intuition. 647 Words. 1996.

os961001
Another perfect day
Scene at Open Studios & Hospitality
A Gruddite Apprentice-User (coming from Mac-Ritchie's Fast Art) expands his mentor's directive, writing about a perfect day. It's almost time for ex-ercise, but there's always time at O'Studios to do what one has to do to protect one's most valuable assets. 640 Words. 1996.

os970128
How to butter your bread on both sides
Churning your own HSIC portfolio
An old trick by unscrupulous stock brokers is to churn the portfolios of unwary clients, skimming the commission on transactions that, in fact, are unnecessary. Churning your own portfolio might make sense even if you don't get paid for it. 1522 Words. 1997.

os970217
Is there a Martha among us?
Craft and ability in the cybernetic age
The well-known corporate craft queen is com-pared to Wiener, Rosenblueth and Thomas Jeffer-son because her helpful hints can be adopted to solving big-picture problems. It may appear sim-ple, but it is not easy. 1053 Words. 1997.

os970309
Let the games begin
Planting the seeds of cooperation
Ritchie's game theory and economic modeling combine for educational uses of information and telecommunications technologies. Like seeds planted in a rich culture of human interaction, games, play and story-telling, they blossom in a jungle of opportunity. 2580 Words. 1997.

os970319

Dialing the Dead
Postscript to the underground
Random sampling of names from out of the past sometimes has a way of showing how fast things change, and in the passage of an entire year, un-finished plans seem to indicate a deadening effect has taken hold of some people. 1110 Words. 1997.

os970320
Beautiful horses
Parable of the Gates Prize
Keeping beauty in the gates of wisdom is like cap-turing wild horses in this parable by Bill Ritchie, whose Japanese-given name means "Keeper of beauty in gates" or, "Biru Richi". 435 Words. 1997.

os970408
In a printmaker's house
An artist copy-wrights a writer's words
An imaginary visit to the house of a printmaker in the cybernetic age takes the form of a dialogue with author Robert Grudin (On Dialogue, Book: A Novel) who, a decade before, used a similar approach to plumb the richness of his art. 1455 Words. 1997.

os970419
Emeralda's name and symbol
History and evolution
Considering that a trademark registration of the name "Emeralda" is forthcoming, a review of the origins of the name and its logo is in order. 951 Words. 1997.

os970914
An art show is born
Surprise outcome of economic modeling
Events from the 1970's and 90's led to Emeral-da's Pacific Digital Fine Arts Festival. The show is simple on the surface but its roots go deep into a concept of creating a new economic model for cy-ber artists. Selection from the "Reinventing Arts Studios." 1324 Words. 1997.

os971014
Interview with the inventor
Emeralda's Bill Ritchie
Fictional interview with the inventor of Emeralda: The Game For Life as the cybernetic artist/entre-preneur searches for ways to figure out what he is doing while he is doing it. 780 Words. 1997.

os971103
Stamp Evaluation
Emeralda's post
The Stamp game is a subdivision of Emeralda. This is a unique game. Because it is a subdivi-sion of Emeralda, it is necessary to keep it in the context of the game itself. That means it has to be evaluated. Evaluation is the third step in six. 1556 Words. 1997.

os971103b
Journal Entry, Mon. Nov. 3, 1997
Moving Graphic and Evaluating Stamps

The author writes his time log of the day, the activities and projects he did that day. He records moving graphics of Cyanotypes Stamps to .tif files. He records editing his article, Evaluating Stamps. He records notes from Denis Waitley from KXPA. 713 Words. 1997.

os971107
Grandfather clock
Poem of a prisoner
The author, who works alone with only the company of a mantle clock, is carried away for a moment by self-pity. 151 Words. 1997.

os980102
Economics of Product Development by Apprentice
First-day Notes of a Visitor to Open Studios and Hospitality
The Inventor-User is at the first day's lecture on the Island where entertainment and hospitality are supposed to be the reigning principles, but instead hears a management science specialist addressing the issues of the high cost of information transfer. 1099 Words. 1998.

os980103
Legacy Transfer
High cost of living legends
The ways costs enter into the transfer of information are like engineering and economics welded into a basic theory for a new kind of investment. The author wants to invest in human structural intellect, one's ability to capitalize labor over a long term. 731 Words. 1998.

os980104
The festivals at Emeralda
Glass Bead Game Reborn
The inventor reflects on the development of the Festivals that take place that give masters an opportunity to demonstrate their strategies without seeming to be ingratiatory. 812 Words. 1998.

os980105
Explaining Emeralda
Stranded on a Desert Isle
The inventor of Emeralda--Game for the Gifts of Life, thinks about himself in comparison to someone who has been stranded for 15 years and suddenly faces rescue. 1782 Words. 1998.

os980106
Flying over O'Studios
A Dreamer's Day
The author shares his first view of O'Studios Isle, the Domain-of-Expertise for outreach and community relations for artists, crafts people and designers. Flying high above the isle, he sees its shape for the first time, but he's confused by an old dream. 659 Words. 1998.

os980107
Smooth Moves in the Heart and Mind of the Magister Emeralda's demonstration

A User Apprentice describes his final, sixth day at O'Studio's Residence Stay, when the Magister Emeralda appears and shows how smoothly he moves from one cell in the Vade Mecum to another. This demonstration previews what he must learn in the 506 Words. 1998.

os980117
Journal Entry, Sat. Jan. 17, 1998
Interview with an Addict – I
A fictitious interview. The scene is a prison in Spain. They expect Sr. Augnendo. But he doesn't come. He's sent to Mondraga. He finds the skilled and knowledgeable unable to survive. He invents a strategy and the wisdom of his ways is contagious. 752 Words. 1998.

os980216
How do you play today
Lost in the woods of O'Studios' Isle
A series of accounts for routine activities yields essays that resemble demonstrations by the Emeralda Inventor and Master at Play. In this account he begins with questions about the Cells in which he finds himself. In this instance, it is a virtual wood. 1184 Words. 1998.

os980226
Emeralda Daydreamer
An Essay for Ellie
His friend, Eleanor Mathews, is on his mind as the author tries to communicate his invention, Emeralda. He pictures a print making studio and animates it with imaginary people with links to dentistry, computers, travel and investing. 2010 Words. 1998.

os980308
O'Studios Vision
Getting to the Destination state
Third day of a User Apprentice' Residence Stay at O'Studios and a language lesson, based on the pronunciation of the name of an obscure printmaking tool. She is part of a vision in the eye of the Emeralda Master who shares his story on the World Wide Web. 697 Words. 1998.

os980318
Installment For Her story
How the Titanic and the SS US crossed in the night
The creator of Emeralda: Games for the Gifts of Life, writes periodically in a story that is the background for the games. Every big game has a background legend or fantasy story. These are passages from it, set in Scotland at the beginning of the 20th C. 658 Words. 1998.

os980318b
Journal Entry, Wed. Mar. 18, 1998
Aural and Open Studios
The author introduces his entry with Aural being the dominant sister for that day. That day he was in the Open Studios domain, which he describes as a networking opportunity for artists. He discusses

Emeralda players' pre-requisites for goals and visions. 646 Words. 1998.

os980407
Explaining Emeralda
The Master Speaks to Beginners
On the threshold of another new experience in a day in the life of the Emeralda Master poses the ongoing, inner dialog on explaining Emeralda to his ghosts in the new machine. Pausing between virtue and reality, he adds more definitions. 1039 Words. 1998.

os980507
Free-style Writing for Emeralda Dummies
Demonstration 3 at Emeralda Works
Free verse is the style here as the Inventor of Emeralda writes down what he's thinking while role-playing for the Emeralda Interview tapes he'll be making in a few months. This essay is a document made on the fly while the author works on his puzzlement. 1389 Words. 1998.

os980517
Journal Entry, Sun. May 17, 1998
The Billionaires' Game
The author writes about theoretical Heuristics with Hubris. What motives, or makes a billionaire want to move? The same force that moves them to act on the information they get (which is the same for everyone) matter more. Notes included from Wriston. 2060 Words. 1998.

os980527
Journal Entry, Wed. May 27, 1998
Two Short Steps
The author writes thoughts and conclusions from reading three books. The authors of those books include Hesse, Wriston, and Hagel & Armstrong. He writes about the Information Standard, the Virtual Community and his contributions to these things. 2744 Words. 1998.

os980616
Four Aboard A Watercraft
Searching for peace, safety and joy on Earth
The author met three comrades on a watercraft to consider strategic alliances to benefit organizations with common visions of peace, safety and joy on earth. He engraved their meeting date of on a blue water bottle-a letter of intent, a noteworthy effort. 781 Words. 1998.

os980626
Which Robin?
The professor's search among former students
Visualizing is thought to be the strong part of creative, inventive, discovering and imaginative people's qualities, writes the author while launching his essay on triple entry bookkeeping, illustrating the complicated moves he uses in Emeralda game play. 1664 Words. 1998.

os980706
How cells blend in Emeralda

Bed-and-Breakfast Games for the Gifts of Life
The inventor of Emeralda uses an example a list-serve member (Baren-list) posted as a comment about staying in a B&B while traveling. The author, once an avid traveler who now prefers virtual travel, presents his thoughts based on memories and experiences. 1253 Words. 1998.

os980716
Outside the Box
Demonstration for squares, cells and handmade graphics
In the science of cybernetics, from which the game of Emeralda evolves, there is a clue as to what it means to play "outside the box writes the game's inventor, and here he describes a connection to Descartes, cartography and the prints of Mauritz Escher. 1413 Words. 1998.

os980726
The First Try of Printmaking On-line
An evening to remember at Daniel Smith Inc.
The writer looks back at a two-hour event he planned and produced at Daniel Smith Inc.-a Seattle art supply store-in which he inked, wiped, and printed an intaglio and chine-colle print, converted it to a digital file and got it to his World Wide Website. 374 Words. 1998.

os980805
Automata in Emeralda Region
Demonstration in dumping the B.O.S.S. avatar
In her book Wellsprings of Knowledge, Dorothy Lambert-Barton recommends four automata, or avatars, to populate certain cells of Emeralda. Their wake-up call comes at the juncture of the river and lake in the author's visually-inspired design of his games. 1104 Words. 1998.

os980815
What that professor said was boring
Launching a new phase of Emeralda
At breakfast at O'Studios, a cynical visitor records his thoughts as he is introduced to the concept development history of Emeralda. he is surprised to be (in a surreptitious incident) reading her story at the same time he is experiencing the next steps. 1476 Words. 1998.

os980825
So you want to play Emeralda
Filling in your form
To fill out an application form to play Emeralda before the game is invented is premature, but during the inventing or testing of the game it's and exercise that can serve different purposes, giving valuable feedback to guide design by the user developer. 639 Words. 1998.

os980904
That old hyperlink feeling
Tracing a path back in time
Concurrently writing and inventing, the creator of Emeralda follows a thread so he can trace his own moves from his Score sheet model to the functions

that each Cell may perform. In his imagination, an inspector questions him, police interrogation-style. 1641 Words. 1998.

os980914
Rewriting history
The SS United States, from America with Love
The male storyteller entertains himself every day with photograph that he takes of his daily routine. The snapshots it seem to him were his experiences in other times and places. This is the vision of th SS United States' conception and its restoration. 1045 Words. 1998.

os980924
Media family tree
Systems approach to Emeralda
Part XIII of Emeralda for Dummies. Drawing on a comparison with genealogy, the Emeralda newbie asks the question, "How do players get paid?" by looking at nature through the lens of the systems approach. Payment may come in forms of intellectual capital. 2322 Words. 1998.

os981004
Focus
Moving from focused individual to focus group
A cybernetic game starts with invention and then development-usually in that order. Between these stages is the focus group, which begins with a focused individual (the inventor) and continues to the focus group. This essay includes a sample E-mail Story. 1395 Words. 1998.

os981014
Q&A from O'Studios Agents
Emeralda Inventor Interviews
The Emeralda Inventor is visited by O'Studios Agents and they ask him questions about how Emeralda works, how he--the inventor--reconciles several dilemmas and paradoxes that seem to rise up out of his game theory--the theory of cooperation among players. 8722 Words. 1998.

os981024
Positively Curious About an Old Artist's Video
Why do I Have These Doubts?
The author reflected on a meeting he ducked out of that was partly to honor a 92-years old artist who enlisted him to help her distribute her videotape she made at 80. It was remarkable at the time, but now video is commonplace. How quickly people forget. 1092 Words. 1998.

os981123
The Basics
Introduction to Emeralda at O'Studios
Short-term goals are like ripples on the surface of water. Small regular intervals, they ride on the larger waves of long-term goals. Together they form a concert, creating a rhythm all their own. Its inventor thinks of Emeralda in terms of musical forms. 1592 Words. 1998.

os981203

Wealth in Emeralda E-mail
Watch those eggs
The Emeralda Inventor sees his daily e-mail as a special resource. He associates e-mail with wealth of mental and spiritual readiness to make wise choices. Watch the moments, as watching those moments is essential to human structural intellectual capital. 1800 Words. 1998.

os990102
Speaking of Bad Days
A diary entry of an Apprentice User
In his diary of real-life and fantasy the Apprentice relates a remark about an impending doom. "Baby Boomers--numbering about 76 million souls of every race, credo and economic standing--have enough monetary wealth to destroy every living thing on Earth." 375 Words. 1999.

os990103
Dream Time at O'Studios
Sharing a vivid memory
In Emeralda Region, the isle of the domains-of-expertise in hospitality includes storytelling and sharing of narratives in dreams, visions, flashes of insight and other entertaining and inspiring verbiage, pictures and performances. Following is a sample. 845 Words. 1999.

os990104
Artists Self- Esteem and Labor
Wisdom of investing in ability to labor
Self-esteem is not dependent on the physical products of work in studios. They will change because we change from minute to minute, bound to time and time changes everything. Artist's esteem is not dependent on the physical products of labor, but utility. 682 Words. 1999.

os990105
If Not for DVD It Does Not Exist
A flash of insight by an early adopter
A cryptic note foretelling the end of the trail for desktop computers and CD/ROMs that were of concern in the past of this artist/author's years. Now he says DVD is the end-all and be-all toward which his investments must be directed; nothing else counts. 321 Words. 1999.

os990106
Epiphany Economics
Your mortgage or your life
As if he's in the audience listening and watching a guest speaker (which is actually himself in role-play), the author relates how Epiphany is connected in his thinking to the mortgaging of your future and the connections to a general theory of economics. 1063 Words. 1999.

os990107
Critical Listening
Marketing creativity
The author was reading a memory expert's advice on improving memory, and listening to the audio tapes that coached him through the expert's les-

sons. To make the learning more interesting to himself, he writes a narrative and applies it to his own history. 979 Words. 1999.

os990303
Multi Asking and Multi Answering
Conversing and scanning with the MFA
A fictional vignette by the creator of Emeralda and its islands, this one drawn from his role-playing in real life as a dental assistant's assistant or Multi-faceted Auxiliary. It's set on the fantasy island of O'Studios at lunch, and fun and games reign. 841 Words. 1999.

os990304
Will this be on the final?
Day one in the beginning course in Practice Management
The nightmare of finding yourself in class at finals testing time, and realizing it's your first day, may come true for the professor, too. From his 30-year old vision of a classroom of the future, the author describes a scene as if he sees it in a movie. 2050 Words. 1999.

os990305
Roots of DISCO-OP
A Story of and for Friends
The author paints in the background of DISCO-OP--also known as Dentalisco--and then develops a picture that shows how a cooperative approach came to be the core value upon which DISCO-OP is based. He tells how co-operation is the keyword to his successes. 2275 Words. 1999.

os990306
What's Your Problem
Antidote for a sick country
This dialog is for a skit to illustrate how Emeralda might begin by preparing a funding plan to restore the SS United States by year 2022. EarthSafe 2022 is the author/inventor's game plan for his DVD-based on-line cooperative game for the gifts of lives. 467 Words. 1999.

os990501
When Professor Bloom Plays Emeralda
Great Closings and Great Openings
Creating a new curriculum for on-line educational experience and relationships for knowledge workers requires research and what is called perfect information. In game theory, this means looking to the past for what is said happened and can not be changed. 1271 Words. 1999.

os990503
The Multifaceted Auxiliary
New opportunities for knowledge workers
The Relationship and Experience Information Principle, or REIP, is the core of a new professional category called the MFA. The author is inspired by a guest editorial written by a dentist. As he role-plays as dental assistant, he opens gates to new ideas. 727 Words. 1999.

os990506
User's Groups
WIFM
User's Groups are like bridges over the chasm that separates IT industry's producers from consumers during their first generation. In it's next generation, communication technology will likely re-live this bridge building, and re-frame the question, WIFM? 585 Words. 1999.

os990630
Flight to O'Studios
A side trip survey
An imaginary flight over the Great Lake of Emeralda region serves to orient Emeralda's inventor to his next days of Resident Stay. Flying back over the island he just left he compares it to looking back over his personal history of prints and printmaking. 764 Words. 1999.

os990701
Look Back and Wonder
Where did we go wrong
Owning an invention is like owning a huge lake--hard to control, hard to get your arms around. Like the elephant in the fable of the blind men, identifying it is part of the difficulty. The Inventor of Emeralda compares it to flying with a lost navigator. 638 Words. 1999.

os990702
A Night at First Thursday
My opening at Sam's
He was an artist as he started careerism and, when he is bored, looking back at Perfect Information, the Inventor of Emeralda has a rich history in his design and craft of printmaking. An art opening is a perfect example of the entertainment at O'Studios. 611 Words. 1999.

os990703
The fundamental conundrum of HSIC
Least to own
To specify the action he wants his co-operative associates to take in his behalf, the inventor of Emeralda compares the background of his game to an artwork by the Dutch artist Mauritz Escher. "Drawing Hands" is a paradoxical work, rich with associations. 1023 Words. 1999.

os990704
Books and Poetry
Protecting the Gifts of Life
Four gifts of life--love, control, esteem and life itself--are protected from fear of losses by book, poetry and art. Dr. Viscott's speaking and books explain the bases for the rules of Emeralda, the Game for the Gifts of Life in this account of the game. 1594 Words. 1999.

os990705
Departures from O'Studios
Looking for the Pacific Digital Fine Arts Festival
Summer time in the Puget Sound--and in many states and countries around the world-it's time for

arts festivals, crafts fairs and design displays. Most people in today's cultural centers enjoy them. But, the rest of the year, people can't attend-until now. 1076 Words. 1999.

os000222
Teaspoons and Tubfulls
Data data doo doo
Experiments in Art and Technology were BIG in the 70s. A veteran from those salad days reflects on his story as his path intersected those of art students of that era. He describes one who maintained his course, but not by experiments with new technology. 2061 Words. 2000.

os000229
The Last Artist Left
Please Turn Off the Lights
Role-playing as a student/provider in Art of Selling Art2 Online, a sales woman makes her journal entry on a trip to a northwest US city, Yakima, which she discovers has an amazing billboard. This suggests to her that Yakima might have a bad arts climate. 470 Words. 2000.

os000301
My Dinner with Jose
An Artist's Journal Entry
Short fictional journal entry from the life of an artist who is in an online course in business communications. She provides a vignette to demonstrate her ability to play Emeralda, the game that all the student/providers are required to use in the course. 604 Words. 2000.

os000308
Seven Hundred Words of Wisdom
The Prisoner Interrogated
A fantasy narrative or make-believe interrogation of the Inventor in his Emeralda Cell by a mysterious examiner who wants to know his plan for saving the Earth. The author is an artist with a vision that he follows in his practice of a game only he knows. 862 Words. 2000.

os000309
The Fastest Faux Painter
Taking care of business
An exercise in fast thinking for the fast artist, and, self-talking, he addresses himself to business planning. It's one he can share with another artist who says she wants to go back to the arts after a long absence from it. It's a brainstorming session. 599 Words. 2000.

os000314
So you want to be a sculptor in 2022
A letter to Old George
An ITinerate professor's letter to a prospective student as a dialog that he sees could happen over the Internet in a few years. It is a glimpse of an arts-based strategy intended as the Emeralda Inventor's proposal for an online K-K education curriculum. 391 Words. 2000.

os000319
Problems and Solutions
The Elmer Gates Prize for Online Art Ed
The problems that stand in the pathway the middle-aged and older people as they plan to fulfill their artistic, crafts person and designer visions are solved partly by solutions on the Internet. Specifying solutions is the job of the Emeralda inventor, an 1211 Words. 2000.

os000321
Back to the Cascades
Springtime, 2000
Launch your own school and begin with the class of 2002. Prove you can teach online. Make partners. Let Emeralda Works be the software tester and a Web company. The secret to success is you know how to train sovereign individuals global quality standards. 600 Words. 2000.

os000323
Ticket to Ride
Two Generations Going Nowhere
The ITinerate professor makes outreach efforts to contact the people with whom he went to school. Few show interest in what he is interested in-higher education on line, using the Internet to continue art education and the careers they once dreamed about. 462 Words. 2000.

os000331
Game Master Explaining Emeralda
The Master Speaks to Beginners
At the threshold of a new experience as role-playing a day in the life of the Emeralda Master, he tells the ongoing, inner dialog as a way of explaining Emeralda to ghosts in the new machine. In pauses between virtue and reality, he adds more definitions. 1566 Words. 2000.

os000401
Myartpatron.com Interview
Bill H. Ritchie, Jr, founder
An imaginary interview with himself (a favorite method of self-talking) helps his understanding of the branch of Emeralda Works that focuses on new ways to communicate with the art patrons. He considers it to be central and important in his artistic work. 1106 Words. 2000.

os000403
Everyone laughed when I sat down to write
Rear views are always funny
Want to know what the Emeralda Ball of 2022 would yield? A little rubbing and polishing, and here it is! In a room on the SSUS, the classmates are reminiscing-their 10th reunion. They recall when ProxiMates was new, a time when no one heard of Gary Tripp! 493 Words. 2000.

os000411
Playing Proximates
Rules of the Game
Rule Number One is Do Not Procrastinate. Rule Number Two is Read Rule Number One. The Em-

eralda inventor seizes a day, as it is said, and the night, and casts his bid on the name of the game that will bring about another man's fame. A happy ending welcome. 205 Words. 2000.

os000414
Up in Smoke
In Memory of Paul Jenkins
A tiny flame licked the trailing edge of a wing. Who held the match also held a beer. I remember how she held that matchstick. It was poised delicately between her long index finger and thumb, and a diamond on the widowed finger, glinted in the firelight. 494 Words. 2000.

os000420
MyProfessor.org
What is it?
The professor died. Long live MyProfessor.org! In his mission to teach and learn, research and develop by practice and production, this ITinerate Professor launches a new course-the realization of the concept that failed under the third university system. 466 Words. 2000.

os000426
Geek Joke
Itinerate Professors are a laughing lot
He's trying out on-line auctions, thinking of ways to liquidate his life's work as an academic, maybe move on to other fields. He's caught by surprise when he gets a response about a houseful of theses and realizes it's only a typo. But it made him think. 758 Words. 2000.

os000427
Register now for the Gates Prize
You may already be a winner!
The lifetime of Elmer Gates is testimony to the importance of people being creative, inventive, discovering and imaginative. The Gates Prize, awarded in his name to people who use contemporaneous technologies concurrently solving world problems is coming. 196 Words. 2000.

os000430
Calendars-Virtuous or virtual?
The Ghost and his Bride
Based on the popular motion picture, Ghost, and an obscure letter from a dead dentist to his wife, the author compares himself to the living dead in this story about the artist continuing to live in an after-life before life's end. He uses new creativity. 556 Words. 2000.

os000504
Happy Birthday, Mr. Gates
Nerds in the Archives
No sooner had the smoke from the birthday candles cleared when a boy appeared and without apology said, "Mr. Gates, I wish you'd come and see something." The birthday man looked around and smiled wanly, "Work calls . . .." Thus begins a story installment. 1022 Words. 2000.

os000601
Mr Gates Meets Dr Osler
A Quick Look At What Might Have Happened a Hundred Years Ago
The author must have been daydreaming when he wrote this, but it is based on a sketchy outline about what might actually have happened between Elmer Gates and Dr. William Osler a hundred years ago. It is tongue-in-cheek humor by one who is on the pension. 819 Words. 2000.

os000607
Women Who Fell to Earth
An Artist's Story
Writing to the music of Mark Leonard's "Sheer Horizon", the Emeralda Inventor tries his hand at story telling to establish the background tale for his role playing game. Good games have stories to tell, and his is about four aliens from the Flower Planet. 2580 Words. 2000.

os000629
How myartpatron.com Got Its Start
Birth of a dotcom arts business
Developing a new branch of Emeralda Works requires exposing the basic idea. The creation of a so-called dotcom business is high-sounding and mysterious. This essay will explain there is no mystery but an ongoing tradition between artists and arts patrons. 1067 Words. 2000.

os000707
What Am I Good At?
Questions for My Art Patrons and Answers I Expect to Get
Raising capital for a new venture, the artist/author must face a test to see if he has what it takes to be a leader in the development of a business that sells specialized artists' tools. Before he can commit himself, he tests his ability to stay on task. 1238 Words. 2000.

os000801
What are you here for?
Four jailbirds tell their stories
In the personae of four imagined prisoners, the author portrays the four people he is thinking that play the leaders in the next phases of Emeralda Works' testing: As a drunken jazz musician, a cook, an artist and a teacher sharing their sad tale of woes. 2647 Words. 2000.

os001103
Revisiting Stamp World
Stamps and Stories and C. T. Chew
The author is a stamp artist, and discovered the stamp was also a subject dwelled on in a book about (and by) Charles Johnson-whose portrait is on a stamp. The words of its editor, Rudolph Byrd, were so appropriate that Bill appropriated and adopted them. 1509 Words. 2000.

os001121
Dusty and Trixie 1899
A short story for a Greeting Card

Bill and Lynda Ritchie have a secret. Each Christmas, they pretend to go back in time one hundred years, and come up with an imaginary setting for their characters, Dusty and Trixie. This season they are living in Seattle, house-sitting, in the year 1900. 688 Words. 2000.

os001207
Art Professor for Higher
Printmaking On A DVD - Part I
Potential text for a letter to introduce college faculty to a service or product the author is planning for release in May, 2001 under the Living Prints label. It is a combination calendar and entertainment resource springing out of so-called edutainment. 792 Words. 2000.

os001231
Learning to Make Waves
A day in the life of an Emeralda Apprentice User
He would be the Pied Piper for the cruise-based course on art asset management and e-commerce on the Internet. Nine months before the cruise is to take place, the teacher is at work, honing his skills so he can stay at least one day ahead of the students. 1956 Words. 2000.

os010107
When Professors Run Away
Old Professors Don't Get Gassed, They Get Gassed Up!
Art Professor Ritchie "escaped" from the university ivory towers more than fifteen years ago, going from the fat into the fire. Now, after his long ordeal, a new opportunity is about to open up, thanks to the Internet. Ahead in creativity, he's doing DVD. 1105 Words. 2001.

os010117
Problems Aliens Face
Language Barriers
He pretends to be pleased that his passport passed the test that morning. When first he opened and submitted his to the Inspector at O'Studios, it failed. He's playing roles, so she suggested he take a position at a convenience system and seek his errors. 957 Words. 2001.

os010127
There Are VARs in the Stars
Why the art in other peoples garbage out depends on garbage in
The author, an artist of the school of printmaking, observed his throwaway-become-artwork by a painter who later, became an art critic, turning garbage print into cash. By way of publishing he has a gift of horse's mouth as a value added reseller, or VAR. 498 Words. 2001.

os010206
Image? You want Image?
I'll Give you Image!
The ITinerate Professor, with profound commitment to an image, a dream of a private art university online, responds to a comment by a renown technology artist who said, "Nerds have no image," when he referred to the dilemma posed to artists by technology. 752 Words. 2001.

os010216
It was Bad in Toxi
In Between Got Worse
Artist turns cook to escape life in the city but finds himself a prisoner on a yacht. Instead of finding a new life he finds a kind of living death suspended between the worlds of virtue and reality, tradition and technology and production and livelihood. 1519 Words. 2001.

os010226
True Artists Don't Back Out, They Back Up
My 4-D Catalog In-Retro
Things that matter most to you should never be at the mercy of things that matter least, so the author remembers as he reflects on his former students in business and professions. These people are the complements to his half of his retrospective in art. 2118 Words. 2001.

os010308
Artist's Proposal for Alliance Marketing with Life Scientists
A Bigger Better Deal
After years of quiet research and development, the artist brings his plans to the tables of potential allies who want reformation of art and life sciences education using both sides of their collective experience. The author copy-writes a marketer's view. 1708 Words. 2001.

os010318
Artist's Proposal for Passing Ferries
Screen Play
Viva's VRAOB (Virtual Reality and Oxygen) Bar, first day of the year 2022. Evan, a tired-looking man about twenty--by his clothing and manner apparently a student--is taking a break from studies. Thus begins a screenplay by role-player, Emeralda inventor. 440 Words. 2001.

os010328
How Do You Play Emeralda, Grandpa?
On The Prescience of A Three-year Old
The moment he reaches for a clean piece of paper to start the next chapter in his Emeralda Journal, the author imagines the voice of his granddaughter asking him how to play the game for the gifts of life. The answer touches on tetrahedrons paper folding. 821 Words. 2001.

os010417
Winning and Losing My Next Job
Short Happy Career and Future Search
Beginning with the End in Mind '92, the author began a new search at the end of his last real job in 1985. To tell about the end of that job would go a long way toward explaining the end of his Next Job, he says, at some indeterminable time in the future. 1979 Words. 2001.

os010427
Benefit the Artist in Residence
What's in IT for You (WIIFY)
What's in IT for an artist in residence who agrees to take part in the electronic age? As part of his K-6th grade strategic alliance design for EarthSafe 2022-his way of answering the UCS-the creator of this educational plan offers a list of the benefits. 440 Words. 2001.

os010517
Teaching Machines
Doing IT with Dusty
Art professor takes a new perspective on an old idea, getting out of his classroom to do some real teaching. Using new technologies to describe old methodologies, he starts with cave prints and ends up making DVD. He plots ElderVid, a series for MaturiTV. 1915 Words. 2001.

os010606
Why Play Emeralda?
So you and your imagination can fly away
You and your creativity, inventiveness, discovering nature and imagination can get carried away when you play Emeralda, like getting carried away on an updraft in a glider, or away in an airplane. You can be the pilot, co-pilot and navigator for lifetime. 404 Words. 2001.

os010626
Amazing Amazon Art Supplies Online
What A Woman!
The author is a retired art professor, but you would not know it because he seems not to have actually retired. In fact, when you read this, you see he actually is a cast off from a sunken ship-art education. He proposes an art supplier with a difference. 3096 Words. 2001.

os010716
Tales and Details of A DVD Author
Counting and Accounting for the Future of Higher Education
A phantom voice asked this author, "What's important about those two letters, S & P?" and he was reminded that if a person is making one's own DVD, one must create a path that one can follow and a pathway one can trust. Others may follow, or they may not. 1670 Words. 2001.

os010726
The Ghost of Toulouse Lautrec in My New Machine
What shows change, what does not
A Virtual Assistant gives a guided tour to a long-dead but not forgotten painter, and visits the closet-studio of the Itinerant Professor of art. This professor writes concurrently, in free style, while his file is uploaded to the Internet theater nearby. 1265 Words. 2001.

os010805
Alert Artist's Teach Their Survivors
Teaching Wives to be Widows

First in a series that advise artists with ways to ensure the value of their legacy beyond their passing, saying that giving survivors the knowledge and skills for preserving the artist's lifeworks using new technologies is better than insurance policies. 1198 Words. 2001.

os010914
Basics of Art Education On-line Revealed
Art Professor explains his invention
The Itinerant art professor, inventor of on-line art education lists and explains four basics: The history of the university; the history of art schools and studios; the history of the rise of intelligent agents; the economics of triple entry bookkeeping. 1065 Words. 2001.

os010924
An Artist's Legacy of DVDs
Investigating A Missing Professor's Closet
A novel by a university professor about a missing university professor comes to mind as the author-and creator of a series of DVDs-counts how many DVDs he made. The fictional professor resembles the role-player the author invented, and lived, for himself. 909 Words. 2001.

os011004
Visiting Granny's DVD Workshop
Fancies of an inveterate printmaker
A way this writer creates essays is to copy down voices in his head (his grandmother's ghost?), imagining dialogs and scenes he wishes he really heard, alive. In this essay, he reports as a tour group visits his dream school, a printmaker/DVDmaker heaven. 1016 Words. 2001.

os011014
Stickers in Your Passport
Ten stamps and the way they fit history
A stamp artist who makes stamps for use in his Passports (for playing his game Emeralda) reflects on how his digital stamps are navigation instruments. He explains the terms of fine art and free fine art, and how a high school failed regional art history. 1417 Words. 2001.

os011024
New Fundamental Art Education On-line Curriculum
How non-branded art serves a better vision
Driver education outsold art education, says an art professor as he develops a fundamentally new form upon which to build an art education on-line curriculum. He thinks that 19th Century paradigms that dominated last century's art teaching no longer work. 1817 Words. 2001.

os011103
Thrill of Intercollegiate Arts
New dimensions in art education
Art education is about to burst out of the print era into the digital era of information and telecommunications. This will give a new dimension in which people who know a lot about the arts can

work together on fresh new ideas for the benefit of everyone. 1548 Words. 2001.

os011113
D is for Disseminate
Reviewing the ICED Principle of Art Ed On-line
Gassing up for the road-it's an old notion behind disseminating ideologies today. But instead of cheap, petroleum-derived gas, this senior professor has taken a different road. He uses digital versatile discs to put his ideas out to worldwide audiences. 2338 Words. 2001.

os011123
Arts R Us
Art processes at a store near you
The wall between library users or art material suppliers' patrons and the artist's studio is removable by building an on-line database of art processes. Art educators need not teach everyone to be an artist, but they need to open windows on artists' ways. 1486 Words. 2001.

os020117
Writing Between the Paragraphs - Part 4
An imaginary dialog between two professors
An artist offers his perspective while reading the vision of Mark Taylor, professor of humanities. Taylor is one of the few who are viewing the place of arts in trends toward using more information and telecommunications technologies for higher education. 1116 Words. 2002.

os020127
No Teacher Left Behind
Closing the Art and Technology Gap
Passage of a bill in Congress may support arts education, and this writer sees opportunities in perilous times. He takes the first step, which is to match the bill with another real need, and names it: Teacher training for the age of digital reproduction. 1158 Words. 2002.

os020206
Practicing What I Preach
Or, How I Lost A Job and Won A Life
Entering his studio and starting yet another day of multimedia work, where a woodcut in progress sits beside a powerful computer loaded with DVD software, the author pauses to ask himself what he's practicing for. Like a concert musician, he waits a call. 477 Words. 2002.

os020216
If I Had IT to Do Over
I'd get a certificate to teach art on-line
He's already certified, in his mind, to deliver arts education on-line, but he has no papers to prove it. The author has plans, however, and he works his plan every day. Reading news of curtailments in music education makes him set to work on credibility. 958 Words. 2002.

os020308
Resetting My Compass On Life

Emeralda play is navigator's work
One result of Emeralda play is freedom and mobility for artists, crafts people and designers. The inventor/author reflects on his own former teaching career, and how-when his usefulness surpassed the needs of the school-he re-invented the campus' compass. 752 Words. 2002.

os020318
At Last Art-Ed Online in A Store Near You
Thinking ahead in the art materials business
Why not open an art supply store online to go with the art technique books and TV shows that help people learn art? One online bookstore said no when he asked them. He waited, watching the need grow for an on-line art supply store. He counted three signs. 918 Words. 2002.

os020328
No Wieners, Please
Winners in the Art Game
The author thrills over his newest digital print and recalls a cartoon of 20 years ago and connects it with the significant bridging of old, traditional printmaking with new digital printmaking. He says it's a key part of his art education on-line vision. 1191 Words. 2002.

os020417
IT Works for Me
Asset Management and Legacy Transfer from an Art Professor's Viewpoint
The author takes the words Information Technology in the brief form, IT, and plays with phrases like IT works for me and IT works to put his arts and technology into perspective. Pictures, writing, databases and multimedia make his mediums for creativity. 379 Words. 2002.

os020427
Another Printmaking Panel is Born
Readying for the CAA Conference--again
Almost ten years ago the author made a presentation at the College Art Association meeting on the theme of Electronic Studios and the Artist as World Citizen. Another new opportunity is opening, but will he qualify? He studies the question like a student. 1815 Words. 2002.

os020507
Ethnography and Printmaking
Worlds apart, worlds alike on the Web and CD/ROM
The inventor of an interactive game intended for hybridized disc and Web distribution learned of a like-minded professor in ethnography who conceived a game for her students called Ethnoquest. His quest-like that of a field scholar-is likened to research. 633 Words. 2002.

os020517
Amenable Artist Interview
A sentient look at the artist, his art, computers and the Internet
He is asked if he would be amenable to being

Interviewed, so this artist writes about his background and why he thinks nature's trees are like man's logic trees, an important basis for computer science and the arts. The story is not over, his essay warns. 883 Words. 2002.

os020527
A Tale of Two Towns
Prisoners Dilemma and the Web
An ITinerant professor strolls, wanders the Queen Anne Hill area of Seattle and finds, amid the parks and sidewalks of the artist's haven, a contest between business and the arts. He suggests playing the game out in John Nash style, in a Nash Equilibrium. 1244 Words. 2002.

os020626
Do Real Artists Write Business Plans?
Reflecting on the background of an artist/businessman
People think artists are one-dimensional, the result of generations of art education and promotion that worked in the postindustrial era of the last century. The age of digital reproduction changes this. This is a background of one artist's business plan. 1172 Words. 2002.

os020706
The Giant's Shoes
Caution-Visioneer At Work
On the edge of creating his life's dreams-his Perfect Studios-the multimedia artist is interrupted in his morning musings by an unexpected, ghostly guest. Over coffee he describes to his phantom guest how he plans to walk in the Giants' Shoes, his hero's. 1749 Words. 2002.

os020716
New Game Club in Town
Artistamps and E-Artistamps
What is the product of your business, they asked me. Stamps, that is the easiest answer, and it may be the best. It may be the tipping point for Emeralda says the inventor as he prepares to meet the local Chamber of Commerce in the neighborhood of Uptown. 887 Words. 2002.

os020726
Stamp Uptown
Seeing the Neighborhood Through Stamps and Stories
The Seattle Space Needle stands for the old ways, Emeralda the new. In the author's vision, stamps and cards are in space like satellites spinning in the orbits of their makers. People use templates to get art-starts; he's got the Nitro to make it happen. 552 Words. 2002.

os020805
Artists' Games Building
Yesterday's, Today's and Tomorrow's Computer Games as Fun and Community
He left school at 43 to learn art's game, an artist and scholar's game he could take seriously for the remainder of his life. Occasionally he tells people how to play but it may not be communicable, like a player of solitaire before playing cards existed. 604 Words. 2002.

os020815
Investing in Labor, Not Silver Bullets
Not One Silver Bullet for Me!
Having acted locally for six months, the Itinerate Professor-enjoying the fruit of his labor on 2 years of his retrospective project-reaffirms the wisdom of investing in his abilities to labor in a changing marketplace for education, his best alternative. 662 Words. 2002.

os020825
How Mobile Devices Effect Education
Mapping and Microeconomics
Adding value to products of the digital age, such as portables, adds value to the teachers' assets because they do their best work when they move. Even on a short walk, they get better at teaching, research and practice, the keys for Itinerate Professors. 345 Words. 2002.

os020904
Connecting Four Dots
Art Festivals, Games, E-books and Artistamps
The 24/7 arts festival, Emeralda, a book titled the Artist's Last Love Letter and artistamps-are they connected like a dot drawing? They must be-and they all can play on DVD, this author's choice for his virtual, virtuous studio for this decade 2002-2010. 335 Words. 2002.

os020914
Mapping Artists' Routine Activity on the Web
Art Students Seeking Experts Look on the Net
Expert systems-one of the 20th Century engineering milestones-may now figure in art students' early careers in the 21st Century because information and communications allows them wider and deeper access to other learners, teachers, research and practices. 1180 Words. 2002.

os020924
Big Easy Education
Taking the Easy Way Out
A new paradigm for the future teacher is to take a harder path. To be effective is to skip the easy, site/event specific education models of the past. Distance education is tough but a lot easier if teacher/learners would be tough on themselves and do IT. 1246 Words. 2002.

os021004
Missing Professor's Closet Re-Opened
Another Paradigm for Art Ed On-line
Lines from another professor's book inspired this artist/professor-aspiring to be a virtual public intellectual-to reopen his metaphor of the "mystery of the missing professor's closet." He suggests his is the turnkey approach to an art education on-line. 1126 Words. 2002.

os021014

Visualize This
A WASHPIRG of Media Artists
His 1970s plan was a statewide multimedia center located in central Washington, but then an administrative coalition blockaded it. Thirty years later he's back, with a plan to empower the rightful owners of the dream-future Washington state media artists. 1589 Words. 2002.

os021024
Publish Electronically or Perish
Future teachers beware
A veteran of internecine battles in the US American professor power wars of the '80s describes how one has to experience death in the old system in order to survive and thrive in the future education field. He gives advice to young teachers on mobilizing. 674 Words. 2002.

os021103
Sighting O'Studios
Sense, nonsense and site unseen
The Emeralda Defender is flexible, but getting from one site to the next is demanding, almost ridiculously so because it is like nonsense. On the other hand, it's like Yoga in the morning-it wakes up my brain cells the way posing awakens up my enthusiasm. 451 Words. 2002.

os021123
Social Justice and Woodcuts
Challenging questions and a singing Barrista
Asked to support a new course in cross-disciplines, the artist/scholar organizes his thoughts to resonate with his social mission. The student's pre-digital structural contract challenges his plan to be more effective by using his new technology paradigm. 668 Words. 2002.

os030117
Kite Story
Evolving a vision for animation
Sometimes a flash of an idea occurs and you want to write it down so you won't forget it. It might be the subject for an essay or a picture. With today's new animation software, it might be the concept for a movie-or, at least a flash. This describes one. 259 Words. 2003.

os030507
Imagine A Video Game
A Proposal for the Tacoma Art Museum
Possessing a private collection of early video art and experimental video-based work by regional artists, this author considers how he might liven up the collection with a digital game-based learning product. Could an art museum sell games in their store? 1400 Words. 2003.

os030527
We Build the Game As We Play It
How Stamps 'N Stories Got Its Start
Thinking ahead to a time when the game Stamps 'N Stories would be a big hit, the inventor/mentor considers the essential questions that he'll have to answer in order to achieve success. For example, who is the game for? Who is the market? Can anyone play? 1434 Words. 2003.

os030606
Saving for College
Two gateways
Billions of dollars are being put away for peoples' plans for college. Colleges are changing, however, and one wonders if people are really certain higher education is something they think they're saving for. "Going to college" is becoming something else. 1530 Words. 2003.

os030626
Putting the S in TRPS
Service is where teaching, research and practice can take the virtual professor
The 21st Century artist is a game inventor and developer, working in the art form of the times, which is digital games. Although new, it's worthwhile to reflect on the past of art education in academe because the cornerstones of education haven't changed. 1180 Words. 2003.

os030706
Story of the Absent Professor
Background for an on-line art education digital-game based learning experiment
I have told the story of the absent professor several times until I'm beginning to believe it's the story behind my game, Emeralda: Stamps 'N Stories. It's about a teacher who never comes to class and how the students are better off because he planned it. 1581 Words. 2003.

os030716
I Get Letters
The emotional value of feedback
E-mail and snail mail are the heart of the Emeralda Stamps 'N Stories concept as the author reads a letter from a student to his professor in a distant state. His own e-mail carries value for him, and he wants to make this into a game that eases feedback. 1375 Words. 2003.

os030904
How to Create A Living Prints Online Hybrid Distance Learning For Profit School
Staying Alive in the Dying World of Fine Art Hand Printmaking
Taking his cue from an unlikely source (video games), the author connects the ideals expressed by today's visionary game developers with his own vision of a perfect teaching and learning online art studio that's focused on printmaking and multimedia arts. 1030 Words. 2003.

os030914
Fine Art Drawing in the Age of Digital Reproduction
A proposed book that needs and gets attention
He had a vision of a new school for art students suitable for their future-a future he could only say was a vision. Now the time seems to have arrived

when such a school is close to reality and needs a textbook, so he starts with one of the basic classes.291 Words. 2003.

os031004
My Teaching Philosophy
Persistent State World Education
Reading the words of a persistent state world game developer is, to me, like reading my own worlds about how and why I teach. I could call it a philosophy of teaching. It's a philosophy that finds few homes in today's US American education scene, however. 1154 Words. 2003.

os031024
Have Tools, Will Travel
Bringing art ed into the 21st Century
What do a CD/ROM, a coffee shop and a laptop have in common? An itinerate professor of art (he's one who wanders around to teach, research, practice and serve) is considering these and how they're leading him to a new kind of online art studio experience. 1146 Words. 2003.

os031113
Dreams
What partnerships are made of
He's meeting with some of his former students, searching for a group to take the place of the virtual community he created in his game-like fantasy world. He's the "wizard" of Emeralda, and he's asking for a kind of formula to help artists save the world. 958 Words. 2003.

os031203
Visualizing My Studio
Starting all over again
When he resigned from teaching college 18 1/2 years ago his former student said, "Now you'll have to start all over like we did." But his vision was never the same as his students'-he was always ahead of the curve. Now he comes full circle, starting over. 845 Words. 2003.

os031217
Madrona Skunkworks
Dog Island's imagination station
He spends much of his time teaching in a virtual classroom, a like the real classroom/studios he worked in twenty years ago. As he puzzles over the problem of creating an online disc-based experience for fine print lovers he thinks of a distant community. 1190 Words. 2003.

os031218
Thinking About My Gallery
Towards a business plan
He's committing himself to opening an art gallery to showcase and sell his collection of art. This is not his first attempt and so he writes about the venture in a business planning way. He'll focus on selling but continue production and developing games. 356 Words. 2003.

os031228

The Payoff
Getting Living Prints to Emeralda Works
Playing Emeralda has a magical quality because the inventor uses his computer to augment his intuition. By a chance encounter, using the search term Itinerate Professor, an obtuse reference to stochastic resonance turned up, leading him to rich metaphors. 1641 Words. 2003.

os040117
If Emeralda were on My Desktop
Getting the unexpected for a change
His habit of opening his e-mail every morning, expecting the same kinds of messages as he often gets, is interrupted by a new thought: What if he opened a game instead? What if the game he invented, Emeralda, were a substitute for the news he gets online? 1357 Words. 2004.

os040127
There is A Game in Me
Old songs in my heart, a paper in mind
He's searching for a reason for playing the game he himself invented in the '90s and the answer hits him in the face while he's listening to music from the '60s and '70s-the era when he began to dream of a better world through being an artist and teacher. 450 Words. 2004.

os040206
One Day I Was Moving My Stamps Around
Pondering Emeralda, again
The inventor of a game he titled Emeralda reviews his collection of stamps that he made to commemorate his career in art, and as he does so he's inspired to think about making the game have an economic world of its own, drawing parallels with other games. 1338 Words. 2004.

os040226
When You're in Emeralda City
A vision of stamps for voyagers
You can look at over fifty artists stamps in the window of the gallery on Taylor Avenue in Emeralda City. When you choose one you'll be transported-like magic-to one of the islands where the collection, of which that stamp is a part, is always maintained. 382 Words. 2004.

os040506
A New Journal Begins
Reflecting on Carl Sagan's Cosmos
Thinking a great deal about the attenuation of the printmaking division at the UW, where this author taught for 19 years, he relates Sagan's epilogue and Boorstin's account of the evolution of arts, architecture, opera and literature, culminating in film. 569 Words. 2004.

os040516
Filling the Printmaking Void
A proposal to replace the printmaking division at the UW
His whole life is devoted to media arts and education, and he's seen only one sustainable model for

it: A University. Now that the university he knew is failing to sustain and grow the fine art version of the media arts, he offers the alternative: A Game. 1398 Words. 2004.

os040605
High School Printmaking on a Halfwood Press
A notion of a creative teacher
While in his studio early one morning putting wood strips on the edges of an etching press, a woman appeared at the door. Seeing a flash of color out of the corner of his eye while burnishing the wood was like Aladdin rubbing his lamp, and Demene came in. 808 Words. 2004.

os040705
My Character Flaw
Marketing the Mini Halfwood Press
The author has read a book on screenplay writing and learned that even the main character has a character flaw, even if cast in a heroic role. Having finished a book on Ben Franklin-a printmaker himself-he contemplates what his character flaw may be. 748 Words. 2004.

os040715
The Mini Halfwood Press at O'Studios
A tradition of printmaking going online
In graduate school he dreamed he would be a great teacher in the arts, specifically printmaking. He left the graduate school to go to teach at the University of Washington. Now he's dreaming of continuing to teach in a novel way using a tiny press for it. 590 Words. 2004.

os040725
Garden Parties, Dead Professors and the Mini Halfwood Press
Is there a connection?
A news article about a professor fighting for his name piques the memory of this "dead professor" who, actually alive and thriving, sees a bright future for such teachers as they can now, thanks to the Web, augment any discipline with a scope for fiction. 797 Words. 2004.

os040804
A Catalog in Me
Mini Press owners may publish plates
With the development of the Mini Halfwood Press underway, and as this opens the door to a new kind of experience in learning printmaking, the meaning of "having something in oneself" is changing for this artist/designer. This may come as a catalog in him. 569 Words. 2004.

os040814
Home and the Itinerate Professor
A miniature press is the key to mobility
What he has come to be (in the practice part of his art and craft) is the maker of a miniature intaglio printing press that allows the printmaking artist move around. No longer anchored by a press, he-and people like him-can truly be "Itinerate" teachers. 1044 Words. 2004.

os040824
Changing Art Colleges
How outsiders will help bring needed changes
College art students don't realize it but art colleges have become like factories, and the students are the products. Students are raw material when they come in and finished products when they get out. Schools must change and help will come from outside. 511 Words. 2004.

os040903
Share A Legacy:
Funeral Notices in the Times
As he ponders the next stage of his work as an Itinerate Professor in an age of digital reproduction he notices an ad in the Seattle Times for a legacy-saving proposal in their obituary section. It compares nicely with his dream of online legacy transfer. 1136 Words. 2004.

os040923
Emeralda Reminder:
The importance of file structure
He invents a game he calls Emeralda: Games for the Gifts of Life but after 12 years he's still not sure how to explain it. Playing it is all he lives for, since it's based on his lifework of education and arts. A chance encounter reminds him how to start. 805 Words. 2004.

os041003
On Broken Links
The importance of being consistent
An email from a Net surfing doctor tells him two links are broken on his Elmer Gates site. After thanking the doctor and repairing the links, the author reflects on the importance of long term consistency and how a daily routine of database updates helps. 553 Words. 2004.

os041023
Losing My Grip
Between a hard place and a soft place
The author has spent many years considering the software that has grown up around him and his devotion to education too many years perhaps. Now he's got a hand on a piece of hardware, and an opportunity to make art instruments. It poses a dilemma for him. 888 Words. 2004.

os050107
Becoming A Craftsman
Turning Point in the Artist's Road
He's spending much more time on craft than he spends on art. And what he's crafting he designed. The old professor of art contemplates what it means to have advocated "art, craft and design" his whole life while he works on a small handmade etching press. 623 Words. 2005.

os050117
Things That Matter Most
Must Never Be at the Mercy of Things that Matter Least

The phrase, Things that matter most must never be at the mercy of things that matter least, lies at his consciousness as he surveys the tasks before him. But how do you decide what's important and what's not important? He thinks his game will help decide. 836 Words. 2005.

os050127
Emeralda Habits
Be Proactive
Be Proactive, begin with the end in mind. 52 Words. 2005.

os050216
Third Life in Emeralda Land
Comparing Emeralda with Second Life
There's food for thought and work for the brain in a comparison of a video game called Second Life and the game this writer envisions that he calls Emeralda. He focuses on intellectual property rights, or intellectual capital, as the payoff in both games. 632 Words. 2005.

os050226
Emeralda-The TV Show
Glimpse of the Future
The author, who claims to have invented a game he calls Emeralda: Games for the Gifts of Life, frequently meets challenges from well-meaning friends and former students, telling him to explain his game. Until he thought of a TV show, it seemed impossible. 935 Words. 2005.

os050308
Like Opening A Deck of Cards
Early Morning in Emeralda Play
He thinks he'll play a game he invented for the rest of his life if the subtext of the game means anything. Games for the Gifts of Life means using one's talents and cultivating them so that they benefit oneself and one's community as long as one lives. 612 Words. 2005.

os050318
Starting A New Career
Using the Gifts of Life
Upon reflection, the author/artist realizes the new career he's launching is one of the gifts of life he has written and visualized in his daily routine. Of late he has searched for the meaning of his game, Emeralda, and his making of the miniature press. 534 Words. 2005.

os050328
Emeralda's Big Payoff
Multitasking and Age Resistance
Two articles he read about children and oldsters has this artist/writer excited. One says most children multitask with media technologies, the other says using one's whole brain wards off the decrepitude of an aging mind. The payoff is in game strategies. 1560 Words. 2005.

os050407
Using Kwanzaa

Community Virtues and Storytelling
A book about Kwanzaa, the African-American celebration of the gifts of life, inspires this author/artist to find parallels with his own way of celebrating "gifts of life". He finds the teacher's story holds valuable lessons that she learned from children. 736 Words. 2005.

os050417
A Way to Publish Plates
An Idea Worth Testing
He's been wondering how to publish plates that go with the Halfwood Presses, items that will help people learn more about printmaking and doing this by using the Internet. Now he thinks he's got a key idea, and that is to publish the images for downloads. 595 Words. 2005.

os050507
A Curious Find
Grounds for the Yarn of the Emeralda
As part of his marketing plan for a small printing press that he designed, the author wrote a story about an 18th Century mystery ship that sank and had a printing press aboard. This notion seemed far-fetched until he discovered a similar tale in a novel. 1303 Words. 2005.

os050517
Emeralda Year
A Year of Living Copiously
Robert Grudin is a writer (Book: A Novel) and professor who contributed to the development of the game Emeralda: Games for the Gifts of Life—without knowing it. Examples are his illumination of the copious, and new way of calculating the length of a year. 1146 Words. 2005.

os050606
It's in the Cards
Telling Your Story in Emeralda Artist Trading Cards
Stephen Covey, the renowned author, said, "The deepest hunger of the human soul is to be understood." Emeralda Artist Trading Cards, in the Games for the Gifts of Life, may be one means by which people can tell their stories in a creative, reflective way. 546 Words. 2005.

os050616
Artist Finds Himself Living in His Own Game
Castaway Art Professor Role Plays his Way Back to Life in the Age of Digital Reproduction
There's something about a headline catches his eye, and this artist—who also likes to write—finds is own life to be like that of the renown author, Terry McMillan. Few think so, nonetheless he deconstructs her story and learns more about his dilemma tale. 978 Words. 2005.

os050626
The Story of Vladimir Petroslovena Chichinoff
A Story about A Cabin Boy
This artist works with brass and copper sheets about the size of playing cards, etching an image

of a map of an imaginary place that he calls Emer-alda Region. How such an image came about is a long story, and begins with a Russian boy who was lost at sea. 5000 Words. 2005.

os050706
Teaching Emeralda
First Lesson Plan in Emeralda 'Zinemaking
He has invented a kind of game to play as one's years reach beyond fifty into an unknown future. This game is like Solitaire, played with cards, or, sometimes, with stamps, but always with creativity, invention, discovery and imagination. Can he teach it? 476 Words. 2005.

os050716
I Dreamed I was in My Own Archive
Taking the Task
Wanted: RA to review the archives of former professor of art. Archives consist mostly of digital material. Candidate must be a good reader, detail oriented and skillful with software for text, graphics and multimedia. Writing skills a plus. 291 Words. 2005.

os050726
A Script for Laser Print Etching
Getting Ready for the Big One
This printmaker (he's one who loves to teach people his "secrets") gets ready for what might be his most challenging of his one-hour demonstrations: Laser Print Etching. He must use tricks to speed up the process for his audience, so he scripts his steps. 690 Words. 2005.

os050805
Putting the Press Before the Horse
Reflecting on Public Versus Private Teaching
A comment that he wrote in his journal a year ago sets the artist probing the meaning of teaching in the public eye compared to private teaching, and confirms that it is necessary for printmaking stu dents to learn the importance of owning their own press. 906 Words. 2005.

os050815
A Grant for Education
Connecting A Game with Startup Money
He is encouraged to find a grantwriter to develop a game he calls Emeralda: Games for the Gifts of Life. Defining the game has been a slippery process—the form of the game changing with the seasons and his mood. Is this a way to approach a grant proposal? 508 Words. 2005.

os050825
Online Art Learning Boom
Seattle's Emeralda Academy
Copy-writing over an article by Linda Shaw, a Seattle Times staff reporter, the artist and former professor envisions what she described as applied to arts taught online. He uses the original article about the online learning boom to reinforce his vision. 1768 Words. 2005.

os050904
Trading Cards for Education
An Online Art Course in My Incubator
Simply because trading cards were meant for fun doesn't mean they can't teach something. This author, in his sixties, can still remember how collectible cards influenced his education. He thinks that if commercially made cards can teach, so can originals. 578 Words. 2005.

os050914
The Successful Communaire
Considering the Way of Practitioner Communities
His long term vision for a working and living community is modeled on his lifelong experience with practitioner groups of all kinds, from schools to condominiums. He writes down what he thinks make him qualified to participate in a new artistic community. 1095 Words. 2005.

os050924
Fast Forward to 2008
Vision of Little Prints—Again
In his mind's eye he sees a day like today—at Open Studios & Hospitality—taking place in a gallery he named Little Prints. It is a place focused on miniature prints and the miniature presses on which they're produced. It's a kind of learning gallery, too. 574 Words. 2005.

os051004
A Stamp 'N Story A Day Keeps My Brain Alive
Thought on Past and Future Artists Stamps
He's planning a demonstration in the making of artists stamps into gifts and considers for a while the role that artists stamps play in his daily life. He created a calendar on his computer, and placing stamps into it is like filling an album of his life. 528 Words. 2005.

os051014
Food Stamps and Artist's Stamps
An Approach to Online Printmaking Education
Browsing a local newspaper one day this artist gets a quick introduction to recipes online. It's strange, because he's really interested in ways to teach printmaking using computers and his MiniBooks and Mini Press. He suggests stamps and food are linked. 1087 Words. 2005.

os051024
Total Proof for Printmaking Benefits
Art and Craft of Etching is Good for Students
Hands on crafts projects are good for kids' education. This essay is the response to reading a report by a hobby industry journal that says kids do better at reading and other academic skills, plus social skills, when hands on projects are part of school. 2100 Words. 2005.

os051103
Where Should We Be Today?
Reflections on Three Generations of Art Students
What would his curriculum look like today if he

hadn't been forced to resign twenty years ago? That is what's on the mind of this former art professor as he has on an online dialog with a former student. In this essay he speculates on what could still be. 1098 Words. 2005.

os051113
Imagine A Cable Head Art Store
Fast Forward to 2008
He's fantasizing about an art store that actually was a transmission point for short demonstrations of art techniques—sort of a Martha Stewart of the art, craft and design field. As an artist and teacher, he has long wanted to reach people beyond schools. 503 Words. 2005.

os051123
Making Artist's Stamps Count
Going Beyond the Look of Political Art
Approached by a gallery director to get involved in an exhibit of art on political themes, this artist—making artists stamps—realizes he never made a work of art with a political theme. He says that artists stamps may be political but by different design. 1053 Words. 2005.

os051203
Secret of the Emerald
Discovery of the Oceanographer's Sea Chest
How can you share secrets of days gone by? Does anyone really care about a printmaker's secrets or is this just another blind alley that the creative person must explore? This is the newest challenge facing the inventor of a game that only he knows about. 1182 Words. 2005.

os051218
How I Use Computers in My Art and Craft
Let Me Count the Ways
This artist and craftsman has been wanting to teach people how to use their computers in the arts and crafts. He believes most teaching on this subject misses the mark, for others treat the instrument as though it were merely a tool. 792 Words. 2005.

os051228
Authors and Artists
A Card Game Metaphor
Inspired by a description of an old card game titled Authors, this artist considers whether it could serve as the metaphor for a card game involving artist's stamps and stories in the context of a digital game-based learning experience. He tries his hand. 826 Words. 2005.

os060107
Smart Condos
A Game-Frame of Living
Because he lives in a condo (where he never thought artists should abide) and partly because he thinks artists should be community-living activists this artist is dogged by awareness that his interest in game theory and practice is stuff for a condo game. 1010 Words. 2006.

os060117
A Bigger Splash
Imagining A Bigger Halfwood Press
Should his current project—making small and beautiful, functioning etching presses—turn into a bigger company and not remain a one-man show? This artist ponders the question in light of his perspective on the age of digital reproduction and art education. 473 Words. 2006.

os060726
Auction and Reflection
More than A Database
His art auction is once again removed from traditional auctions and Ebay, yet his auction draws certain elements from these. The intent is not only to make sales and raise money, it's also an artistic device. 394 Words. 2006.

os060726b
Ticket Art
It's Different
The images on the ticket are of the artworks that will be in the auction/play. 114 Words. 2006.

os060805
Reframing Printmaking
Two Overlapping Frames
The author constructed a different importance for art. You might say he saw art through two overlapping frames: One was its role in society and the other was its role for the creative, sovereign individual. 1322 Words. 2006.

os060825
A Place to Study This
The Search for A Center for Study of Video Game Based Art Education
After a generation of teaching in a traditional college art department, this author left the campus to extend what he had learned about the basics of using technology in art and the teaching of art processes. His goal is to become a virtual art professor. 1433 Words. 2006.

os060904
Game Purpose and Narrative Purpose
How Emeralda Works
Emeralda is a game for learning media arts in a group, as in a cooperative game. It also has the flavor of a treasure hunt. You might compare it to the game Clue. 1150 Words. 2006.

os060914
Blogging Art
Games for the Gifts of Life
The Internet, and things like blogs, wiki spaces and Web sites have given writers another voice. Not only do these offer hope of distribution of writers' ideas, they also give other creative people hope. 550 Words. 2006.

os061004
Fragging Students

Clippings for Student Journals
Every week the students receive something to paste into their journals. Sometimes it is a story, printed so small it takes very good eyes, or a magnifying glass, to read it. Usually the students reformat it into larger type to make it readable. 317 Words. 2006.

os061024
What Does the Bible Contain?
Game Development
Every game has what is called in the gaming industry a "bible." The game's bible contains everything there is to know about it, from the game's inception onward. 450 Words. 2006.

os061103
You Will Make A Hyperlink
Putting Excel Spreadsheets to Work
A hyperlink is your exit from the Excel spreadsheet that accounts for your Year of Living Copiously. That is your Gates Prize. Remember that the Gates Prize is awarded before you earned it. 656 Words. 2006.

os070107
Harris
Your Character in Emeralda
Reflections on national economics, incorporating personal economics and Emeralda. 725 Words. 2007.

os070606
History of the Halfwood Press08
Open Studios and Hospitality - 8th Day
A day at the Taylor Avenue Studio, a view point from a visitor in June. 2420 Words. 2007.

os070928
Plate Story
Magic in the Metal
This printmaker comments on hearing voices while wiping his plates to print. He is an etcher, and he uses copper plates. This makes him think there's magic in the metal and, like the bottle that contained a Genie, when rubbed, frees his storytelling muse. 678 Words. 2007.

os071013
First Play
Emeralda Card Game
The development of the idea and the process of playing the game. 456 Words. 2007.

os071024
Lifelong Employment
Dividends and Prizes for Participants
Participants earn dividends and win prizes for their skills. A central piece is the press itself. The emphasis is on intaglio and relief printmaking, and possibly stencil. 230 Words. 2007.

os071103
Deck of Ten
Emeralda's Collectible Artist's Trading Cards

While he is in the grips of creating lookup tables for the twelve years he received the Gates prize and in the pattern emerges an answer to a basic question regarding the cards: How many cards come in a deck of Emeralda Collectible Artist's Trading Cards? 501 Words. 2007.

os071203
New Game
Owning and Selling Artwork within A Game
One player, the owner, presents an object for sale. The owner speculates it is worth $100+, and will allocate a percentage to a game master when it is sold. The master may ask for any percentage, knowing the proceeds will be shared with other players. 571 Words. 2007.

os071218
Merkin Dilemma
Making Sense of A Trading Proposition
An art collector says he's joking—that he's a joker—when the Emeralda inventor reads his email and sees the proposal to trade one of his artworks for that of a former student and makes a counter proposal to trade an artists trading card about the artwork. 742 Words. 2007.

os071228
Blank Card
Emeralda's Intangible Gifts
Emeralda is about intangible gifts. The author saw the art world from a different point of view, it is only in the age of digital reproduction that Emeralda could exist. This point of view could not exist without his knowledge of video art and computers. 586 Words. 2007.

os080107
Complete Works Game
Considering A Traditional Publication
Cleaning off his desktop one day he finds part of a sheet of uncut artist's stamps—his own—under the clutter and, curious, he discovers he had left off on a project of creating an illustrated catalog of all his works. Could it be published cheaply today? 777 Words. 2008.

os080117
Solitary Play
A Form Game to Create Time
Why do people play alone, as in the game Solitaire? This form of game is based on chance and scarcity, where you seldom win. In another form of solitary play, the author explores a game that is based on chance and plentitude, the artifacts of a rich life. 980 Words. 2008.

os080127
Flash Cards
A New Auction Idea
Instead of a catalog, visitors have decks of cards consisting of the works to be sold at auction. 88 Words. 2008.

os080127b

Serious Games
Spurious Curious Regional Game Inventor
There are many serious games you can read about and even buy on the Web. Which, if any of them, have meaning to you? If you find there are none because they are based in professional and educational fields, then you have an opportunity to invent your own. 1023 Words. 2008.

os080216
Legend Making
Three Works in One
A happenstance usage of the word legend starts this print maker (also a maker of printing presses) in contemplation of the meaning of the word as it applies both to the interpretation of maps and story telling. He thus wonders if he might be three people. 711 Words. 2008.

os080226
Today's Game
Better to Invent A Game than Do Nothing at All
It is said that Confucius advised, "Better to play games than do nothing at all." This artist calculates that it is even better to invent a game than anything else, and help other people play it. So, daily he thinks of a game to play with art. 401 Words. 2008.

os080327
Contrast/Complement
Principles of Two Ages
In the age of mechanical reproduction, black contrasts with white; blue complementary to orange. In the age of digital reproduction, contrast and complements in the making/playing of the collectible artist trading card version of Emeralda. 844 Words. 2008.

os080426
Big Mistake
Dean's Advisory Council
Hoping to find the perfect community of practice through the Dean's gateway, going to a reception for the Dean's Advisory Council was a Big Mistake. 601 Words. 2008.

os080506
First Review
One of Three
Soon he will be in the a world of his course, Learn Printmaking Online, and he must consider the nature of the new course against the conventions of teaching he once practiced in the old, dying world of printmaking. There will be reviews and preparations. 1100 Words. 2008.

os080516
Faculty Support
First of the Twelve Tasks
Faculty Support, as the ninth of the twelve tasks of the successful manager of Learning Printmaking Online (or, as Professor Beaudoin wrote it out completely, training and support for faculty) needs to be at the top of the list. 1023 Words. 2008.

os080526
Data Definition
A Parable about Muses
Four women who fell to earth are with the author much of his waking time, and they coach him. But each of them has a unique coaching style. 1144 Words. 2008.

os080615
Functioning Enterprise Organization
A Whisper from Media
Tell someone in Australia and someone in Chile they are playing a game called Emeralda that is about Learning Printmaking Online. To play, they must have a Halfwood Press. 752 Words. 2008.

os080625
Business Plan
The Modivation Column
In John Zachman's chart titled "Enterprise Architecture – A Framework™" there is a Cell G3 that is labeled Business Plan, Where End equals the Business Objective and the Means equals the Business Strategy. 660 Words. 2008.

os080625b
The Work of Art in the Age of Digital Reproduction
A Textbook for Learning Printmaking Online
The Open University concept suggested teachers could adopt the methods of commercial communication—mail, telephone, TV, etc.—to reach their students. 428 Words. 2008.

os080705
Detailed Representations (Out-of-Context)
The Sub Contractor Role
In Zach Man!, one of the objectives is to invest in labor, as directed by Paul Hurd in the book, The Retirement Myth, by Craig Karpel. 284 Words. 2008.

os080705b
Would You Buy This University for Your Grandchild?
A Game for Finding Universities or Collages
At a private dinner on July 4, 2008, the author was given a challenge: What kind of game would help foreign students pick an American University or College? 917 Words. 2008.

os080725
Job Description
Team for Owner Support and Benefit Development
The job initiated by Nellie Sunderland, our daughter, entails database management and improvement. 385 Words. 2008.

os080725b
Requirements
Art Student Accountability in the Age of Digital Reproduction
Students must fill their passports to pass the

course. Stamps from each domain-of-expertise must be cancelled by the professor and his cohort. Stamps must be accompanied by a story. 223 Words. 2008.

os080804
Aim of the Game
Towards A Ninety-day Wonder
The professor meets a game designer who is fluent in new methods and they agree to win a contest using a tool called Silverlight, sponsored by Microsoft and ending on October 31. They plan to use the contest victory as a benchmark in the game development. 233 Words. 2008.

os080814
Professor Introduces Printing Game
An Imaginary News Article
Wondering how he can convey the nature of his project he calls Learn Printmaking Online to many people, he thinks a news article would be suitable. But who would write it? In the fashion of one who enjoys a vision of the future, he tries to write his own. 691 Words. 2008.

os080824
La Quatro Angelos de Emeralda
Writing in Spanish
Why does the author write the title in Spanish? The Four Angels of the Emeralda is a story he can write in English much faster! Perhaps he wants to slow down. That way every word can be considered more carefully. 1121 Words. 2008.

os080824b
To Die For
What to Do Before I Die
For the author, a thing to die for is achievement of his lifetime goal, which is to be known as a great teacher. 468 Words. 2008.

os080913
Ten Years of Small Is Beautiful
Year One is ArtsPort
A "theme" for an art exhibit based on the islands in Emeralda. 175 Words. 2008.

os080923
The Best Thing about Baldwin City
Reflections on Baldwin City
After ten presentations, the professor is asked what was his favorite thing about his residency. He's at a loss, but concludes that it was that the visit to the small liberal arts Kansas campus kick-started his imaginings for future projects. 837 Words. 2008.

os081003
Be A Part of the Coming Revolution in Printmaking
Bill Ritchie's Invitation to A New Community of Practice
The author claims forty-five years of being a printmaker, and these generations showed to him that an evolution has been underway during that time. Now he claims a new printmaking world is on the horizon and he wants to invite people to participate in it. 806 Words. 2008.

os081013
Plotline for Amina
Where Does She Go from Here?
Writing for a video game is not like writing a story or a screen play. Reading has told this author that fact, yet it is not clear just how to do it. It's straightforward to write for video cut scenes, but a game is interactive, which challenges a newbie. 552 Words. 2008.

os081023
Professor Magee's Message to Amina
An Example of Transfer
From reading What Video Games Have to Teach us About Learning and Literacy, the artist/teacher maydetermine how his game resembles one of the entertainment games already on the market—a game called System Shock II. Transfer is key, the book's author says. 1122 Words. 2008.

os090107
Substantial Characteristic Tension
Three Elements that are Mutually Reinforcing for Youth to Learn Printmaking Online
In Emeralda: Learn Printmaking Online, the author has in mind numerous characters he already designed and has more to come. Their dimensions are developed to varying degrees, but they all reinforce the mission, tension, substance and outcomes of the game. 873 Words. 2009.

os090117
Mi Universidad, Tu Universidad
Bringing the University Campus to your Home
The university persisted over centuries, a site-specific, virtuous experience resembling a citadel, a laboratory, or community center. States and societies cherish universities, and going there a crowning achievement. Now this experience is going virtual. 889 Words. 2009.

os090127
ELPO Opportunity and Tension
Dangers in a Printmaking Haven
Despite that he's seen cartoons of bearded old men on streets with signs that say, "The End Is Near," this old professor thinks about the two-thousand scientists he read about who signed a five-part document saying just that. Can a game help save Mankind? 973 Words. 2009.

os090206
Game Levels and Writing Outlines
Similarities between Grammar Rules and Game Rules
Amid the goings-on in the life of a teacher who wants to work in both the online and the social levels of 21st Communities of Inquiry and Practice, the mechanics of writing with a computer, applied to game design, is the same as "level" in "outline" view. 1117 Words. 2009.

os090216
Elpo's Fictional World and Settings
Eighth in a Ten-Step Development Checklist
"Frankensteining," in writing this essay, means
taking body text parts from earlier writings in
the first version of the ten-step development list
to make a new, stronger version to suit this game
developer's purposes. This is a hybrid of the old
and new. 842 Words. 2009.

os090318
New Paradigms for Game Planning
Third Life as a Game Planning Metaphor.
Though he does not work in the games industry,
the author role-plays a game designer so he can
position the contents of his art collection and intangible, intellectual property to be the components of a serious game. He considers changes in
game planning. 1000 Words. 2009.

os090407
Bran Toolarian Profile
A Character who Carries the Social Genre in
"Hunt . . ."
The social value of sharing information using
means that don't subtract from the original holder's assets in this community of practitioners
adds an entertainment and hospitality element to
events and creates outreach to teach the art and
craft by design. 625 Words. 2009.

os090417
Pressmaker's Workshop
How to Start your own Business Making Etching
Presses
As part of his blended online printmaking teaching plan, the designer of a press that goes with the
course describes how he wants to approach the
"localization" of the business of providing presses and accessories for students, and a vision of a
workshop. 906 Words. 2009.

os090527
Official Autobiography
Shared World of Bill Ritchie
Reviewing the past months' writing stored on a
shared computer, this artist discovers an "official
biography" sketched out by his working associate.
Instead of making additions, he saves it as "official
autobiography" and he makes changes to the original. 297 Words. 2009.

os090626
Teacher Movie
Entertainment Printmaking in the Age of Digital
Reproduction
A printmaking professor thinks to teach print-
making as he learned it in the 20th Century to to-
day's students is anachronistic. Printmaking is not
frozen in time, it is the ancestor of digital media.
So he contends the teacher's role includes movie
making. 1261 Words. 2009.

os090825
Hey Mom, There's A Card in the Toaster

Meditations on a Printmaking Challenge
As one of the designers for a blended online learning printmaking digital game I have the feeling
I am playing the game while I'm designing it. It
amounts to invention, in a way, or discovering the
best strategy to win. This morning it's all about
toast. 1413 Words. 2009.

os091004
Bellwether Brainstorm
Visions of a New School Coming
A persistent concept he calls the "perfect studio"
seems closer today as the world economy presses
for better ways to educate the young and re-edu-
cate the old among creative individuals in the mediums of printmaking. This professor envisions a
new school. 982 Words. 2009.

os091014
Studied With
Asking for Higher Education with Individual Artists
A question was raised by a recent graduate from
a college regarding advancing her education and
her career, with a focus on printmaking. An ap-
prenticeship? An internship? A graduate School?
Institute? He addresses her last question, studying
with someone. 1843 Words. 2009.

os091113
EATC
Electronic Artist Trading Cards
A chance meeting online with a creator of
e-cards—those animated, musical greeting cards
we get through our e-mail—launches this writer
on an inquiry for some way to utilize the e-card
in his inventing of a method for learning fine art
printmaking online. 1181 Words. 2009.

os091114
Emeralda Works
For Me
When invited me to start a companion Diary of
Making Emeralda, too, I started with the name.
Emeralda is a blend of Seattle's market name, Em-
erald City, also the city in Oz. It's the name I sub-
mitted in a Northwest contest in '93 called "Name
the Region." 352 Words. 2009.

os091203
Artist Stamp Collecting
Getting Started toward Electronic Artists Stamps
Working on his Stamps 'N Stories series today
the artist realizes few people know what Artist's
Stamps are so he begins to write a descriptive
pamphlet on the subject of getting started collecting these miniature works of art, planning to realize the eAS. 1147 Words. 2009.

os091218
About O'Studios
First day, Fourteenth Year
Fulfilling the requirement of explaining, on the
first day here, what this island is all about, the
author copies the description written six months

ago during his work on the Emeralda Game bible. Pasting in the description, he next experiences O'Studios. 454 Words. 2009.

Perfect Press (AKA PP)

The island of Perfect Press, looking toward the eastern skyline at dawn from the ferry bringing you from O'Studios.

Perfect Press is the domain-of-expertise in publications such as printed and non-print media, prints, books, portfolios, posters, stamps, etc. In addition, all publications are designed for multimedia delivery. For example, 'Zines—an alternative magazine format—are produced in all of Emerald islands' archives, but printed versions are the task of Perfect Press.

Books, are mastered, formatted, published and repurposed. An example is The Art of Selling Art, first of the Perfect Studios trilogy. A case study of self-financing an art career, it is based on defining "selling art" as bringing artistic values to society as a necessary tradition for the health of communities.

Fine art prints—hand printed in any or all the four printing processes—are produced at Perfect Press. Although all islands feature printing, printmaking here at Perfect Press leadership in higher education printmaking is the aim with emphasis on ways to use new technologies to preserve traditional ones.

Equipment, instruments and supplies are produced by Perfect Press too, such as the Halfwood Press line. Allied with these are supporting print and non-print products such as user manuals, disc-based lessons and postcards as well as the aforementioned books.

pp690815
Prints/Multiples:
Introduction to an exhibition catalog
Bill Ritchie, art instructor, directed a show of prints and multiples at the Henry Gallery, University of Washington. His premise is there are two camps: Artists whose ideas are inherent in the media, and others for whom printmaking is a secondary medium. 1250 Words. 1969.

pp700104
Collagraph Syllabus:
A course in printmaking at the University of Washington
This is the first chapter from print making class technical papers at the University of Washington when its author was a professor. The collagraph process is a building-up of plate material instead of etching, carving and cutting away common in tradition. 3350 Words. 1970.

pp710324
New trends in prints
Revolution in the making
Talk to Seattle Art Museum Couples' Guild on a revolution in print making. First drafted in 1971. and presented as an illustrated lecture. It hints of things to come, and challenges the artistic merits of the show. 1790 Words. 1971.

pp711015
Printmaking Techniques
An approach with impact
Written for print collectors, this essay provides a simple outline of print making terminology. It stresses two aspects of the technology: Impact and non-impact, plate making and print making, plus the four kinds of printing. 931 Words. 1971.

pp820225.
What is Cyanotype?
Blue Process for Printmaking
The cyanotype, or blue process photography, gave the author a perfect method with which to introduce the principles of photographic emulsions to beginning printmaking students. He created a shirt-pocket or purse 'little book" for his students. 1172 Words. 1982.

pp840212
Perfect Studios
Philosophy and Speculation
In this essay the dream of the perfect studio finds a model in an account of a Chinese printing business that operated centuries ago, where printing craft was balanced with publishing on the subject of fine arts processes. 729 Words. 1984.

pp840518
Videodisc
Selected readings on a new art form
The groundwork for a philosophy of a video disc class for art students is described by using quotations from Walter Benjamin, Levi-Strauss, and Jack Burnham, all having to do with ritualized process, art, and technology. 955 Words. 1984.

pp850515
Art and Technology
Perspective on developments since 1945
Paper written for the University of Washington Art History Students, but not delivered. At the

time of this entry this essay is yet to be located, but it probably is on the Apple Computer Database. 70 Words. 1985.

pp851110
Microcomputers, Marketing, and the Artist
Addressing the artist's needs
Lecture to the Women Painters of Washington on the basic dilemmas of marketing your own artworks, and the changes being made by use of microcomputers. 982 Words. 1985.

pp860131
Art and Technology Reversal
History in rewind?
In a round-table discussion on art, technology and printmaking, photography was suggested as a metaphor for the new computer graphics; more likely, a reversal metaphor of the history of communication would serve. 1850 Words. 1986.

pp860321
Video in the Museum
Through the glass walldows
Promotion of the idea of using electronic media in museums of art. The suggestion is to combine hospitality with learning - B&B days! 370 Words. 1986.

pp860412
Art, Technology, and Human Creativity
Consequence and inspiration concurrently
An illustrated lecture presented by The Human Creativity Conference at St. Martin's College, in which the creative process is described as both a consequence of and an inspiration to use new technologies. 2819 Words. 1986.

pp870227
How I use computers in Art
Minutes of a multimedia talk
A minute-by-minute text of an early (1987) demonstration lecture for The Evergreen State College (TESC) on artists' uses for a computer in print, video and computer graphics. Includes questions asked after the talk. 1539 Words. 1987.

pp870817
How does CD-I Involve the Arts?
Uncovering history behind glass
Learning about the first true multi-media delivery system which was being developed by the laser-optical media industry led to these thoughts about the revolution for artists at hand. 2538 Words. 1987.

pp870824
The Cure for Depression
Studio visitors in shifting times
In reinventing their roles, will the engineer and the artist work alone or in collaboration? If they collaborate, how will they reconcile their views? These questions inspired the idea of a useful product comparable to the invention of aspirin. 1995 Words. 1987.

pp870825
The Bush / Weiner Inspiration
Beginning a fifteen-year plan
The story of the Memex, the quotations of Vannevar Bush, and the recollection of Norbert Wiener's writings come together in the artist's journal notes. 608 Words. 1987.

pp870925
Journal Entry, Fri. Sep. 25, 1987
Supportive Wife
There's hardly a woman around who will tolerate this artist's life indefinitely. She's trying to help me by belittling my "successor." She's telling me to quit what appears to her to be punishing myself. 197 Words. 1987.

pp871101
The CD-I Project of Chew and Ritchie
A view from a high altitude
Bill Ritchie was given a copy of The New Papyrus as a gift from Tom Lopez. While reading the remarks by the thinkers in this new technology, these notes were made. 1276 Words. 1987.

pp880415
Early one morning
in the province of the silicon forest
There may be only modest support for the local arts by new meritocrats, the nouveau riche of high-tech. Have we outgrown the provincial image? Artists and corporate creatives recall images of pioneers, alike but different in measures of resources. 1746 Words. 1988.

pp880715
A Plethora of Metaphors
Groping the Disc
C. T. Chew and Bill Ritchie launched a research and development project in 1987 to study laser optical media and the arts. In reviewing the metaphors used the first year of the CD-multimedia project, Bill says, "Our grope is greater than our grasp!" 989 Words. 1988.

pp880815
The Art of Selling Art
A CD/ROM Offering
A part of Perfect Studios to encourages artists to prepare to sell their art on their own. The methods were tested at an art school and in art studios. On a CD/ROM, "Everything an art student needs to know," the text is an artist's survival aid. 613 Words. 1988.

pp880828
Selling the CD-I Project
Getting on with art
Bill Ritchie and C. T. Chew learned that the idea of the CD/ROM Publisher's Club was better than they had thought at first but more money was needed to develop it. This essay was about bootstrapping and timing -- the key considerations. 1287 Words. 1988.

pp880920
Browsing Metaphors
Searching for a likeness to CD-I
Observations written during the first six months of the CD/ROM Publisher's Club, and compiled from the Reports part of Compilation of a Resource Library on Theory and Technology. 3074 Words. 1988.

pp881115
Imitation to Art
Outer limits of traditional art tools
Artists using print, video, and computer systems tried imitating character of drawing and painting, sculpture, television, and photography until laser optical media came along. 865 Words. 1988.

pp881126
What does "Bill's Gate" Mean?
Original version
According to accounts, artists were brave souls throughout history. How do artists today compare in boldness and creativity? The author had an Emergency Meeting in 1978, which he describes as the turning point for artists in the northwest. 2148 Words. 1988.

pp881127
What does "Bill's Gate" Mean?
Revised and updated
When Bill Ritchie and C. T. Chew concluded the first phase of their joint project in the development of an interactive multimedia project in 1988, they produced a broadside to send the members of the club. This essay is Bill's. 1158 Words. 1988.

pp890516
Planning in art
The Illusion of Calculation
What the insurance and oil industries have in common is their planning, based on calculation. Plans are based on the unknown, and for what seems at first complicated reasons, a studio for art, design, and crafts is like an industrial business. 1042 Words. 1989.

pp890810
Commenting on The Business of Art
One artist's differing view
Asked by Prentice-Hall to review one of their books on the business of art, Bill H. Ritchie, Jr. shows a fundamental difference between his and most of the other books that attempt to help the artist sell artworks. 2465 Words. 1989.

pp891207
Commission Advertising
Ghost in the New Machine
The artist used a printer that was under-powered. Written on Pearl Harbor Day, it is wry irony that he had a slow printer. But, what is the content of this essay worth? Calculate this and he will get a new printer for making 90's art. 1209 Words. 1989.

pp900110
One Hundred Years of Washington Art
New Perspectives from Bill's Gate on Printmaking
For the catalog for One Hundred Years of Washington Art: New Perspectives, the Washington Centennial Exhibition at the Tacoma Art Museum. The author wrote about the influence of printmaking and high-tech on art of the '70s in Washington State. 1052 Words. 1990.

pp900309
Journal Entry, Sat. Mar. 9, 1990
Time is Life, Life is Time.
What the author knows about media indicates that Topaz modeler and animator will in time pay for itself. The system – whether a press or a computer (and there is no difference, anyway) gives back life time in the form of art. Media art is published art. 364 Words. 1990.

pp900915
Dinner speech
The Northwest Print Council
At a dinner held in honor of Judith Brodsky, Bill Ritchie looked around and realized he was the only one there from Seattle. The occasion was the Northwest Print Council Annual meeting, so he stood up and addressed the group with this speech. 506 Words. 1990.

pp900930
Experts in Printmaking
Between Tradition and Technology
This is the time for all good teachers to ask, Who are we, where did we come from, and where are we going? This essay accompanies a questionnaire about the preparation of tomorrow's artists and educators. 942 Words. 1990.

pp901017
What is computer art of the Third Kind
Introducing medium-of-origin
Bill H. Ritchie, Jr. defines what, for his purposes, is computer art, stating there are three kinds and he tells which kind he is working on. 282 Words. 1990.

pp901101
Fascisti
The librarian metaphor
Fascist, one of the darkest words in our society because of World War II, came from the title of the librarians of the Roman Empire. Maybe it's time to get back to the original sense of the world and renew the meaning for business purposes. 342 Words. 1990.

pp901105
Navigation Calculation
Information Technology strategic planning
The navigator in the information age works in the world as an illusion of calculation. 203 Words. 1990.

pp901112

Peak producer
Before we needed art
Art comes from human nature, but what is human nature compared to machines? The answer is in considering the errors made with machines by human nature 361 Words. 1990.

pp901119
Visions
Conversation among Chew, Ritchie and Sato
Remorse and enthusiasm exist side by side in the comments by three artists. This is a three-way conversation among C. T. Chew, Bill H. Ritchie, Jr. and Norie Sato about art, computers and survival, published in an edited version in VISIONS magazine. 25197 Words. 1990.

pp901209
Fool
Image in a spoon
Between the virtual and the real worlds of art, today's artist has to make educated choices. Computers can help or hinder their education, depending on if the artist feels closest to the age of virtue, of reason, or the Information Technology age. 426 Words. 1990.

pp901212
Anatomy of an Art Sale
Below the appearance of public art
Complaint about red tape involved in Art in Public Places programs. The essay points out the precautions necessary in dealing with the state bureaucracy and the sad economic picture this paints for artists who do not go by rules imposed by the state. 552 Words. 1990.

pp910212
Multimedia and the Marketplace
Alternative to artists' extinction
Multimedia can help of the independent artist, crafts person and designer. The technology is not complicated, and it may go far in preserving creativity. Independent computer consultants are like artists; they can learn from each other. 462 Words. 1991.

pp910214
Q22
Navigating the future
Multimedia that interweaves several mediums takes on greater significance if it is given the scope of business. Business management encompasses planning goals and tasks. Focusing on positioning helps give multimedia a working definition. 2160 Words. 1991.

pp910222
Name the ghosts in the new machine
Ancestral wins or setbacks?
The ghosts in the new machine may be known by names: Important people, but they remind one of the days when one met them. In the age of the illusion of calculation, a ghost is an albatross, a stifling handicap, a memory of ancestral failures.

2683 Words. 1991.

pp910227
International Institute for Study of Multimedia Arts
Gates to an artist's sanctity
One hundred years ago impressionism was born, then cubism; now, multimedia. A letter to the editor of a Northwest computer newspaper calls for a new technical art school for multimedia called the International Institute for Study of Multimedia Arts. 882 Words. 1991.

pp910303
An artist blind-sided
Encountering the dark side of public art
Artwork for a State Arts Commission Art in Public Places was to be commissioned. The committee was very encouraging--at first. His experience turned out to be a disasterous encounter with the dark side of government programming. 2142 Words. 1991.

pp910304
Multimedia, roots or gates?
Johnnie can't draw, but scores high in games
Thousands look for a new approach to education. In this essay, multimedia art matters more than traditional thinking. Information Technology, IT, is where the action is, and art provides ways to do business. 1538 Words. 1991.

pp910317
Grants and The Art of Selling Art
Where exposure counts
In The Art of Selling Art, the chapter on grants explains how they mean many things, such as education and exposure to blue ribbon panels. They mean more than meets the eye. 1063 Words. 1991.

pp910324
Multimedia across the ages
Hyper guide book for forty-something artists
A proposal that museums and libraries develop multimedia policies for the next generation and to choose a top-down or bottom-up approach. Based on a fantasy viewpoint, comparing the age of a 40-year old with the ages of stones. 4065 Words. 1991.

pp910407
Multimedia Intuition
Creativity after the paradigm shift
Space and time no longer stand alone. Which means that new techniques are used by intuitive, creative workers to explore the future. Time and timing - like space - are being shaped by computers. Leaders have skill in using these new machines. 2069 Words. 1991.

pp910409
Self-publishing your first book
Notes from those who did it
In-home education programs are one way to learn self-publishing. Based on a talk by two published speakers, these are insights covering different

views on publishing and public speaking. 1281 Words. 1991.

pp910426
Marketing Prints with Multimedia
Getting back to the root
The perfect studio for multimedia arts is where teaching, experiments and applications are going on at the same time in the same place. In one view, this suggests that an etching press is set up alongside a computer. 1291 Words. 1991.

pp910507
Art Prints in Washington State
Waiting in the Wood
There is an opinion there are no significant print collections in Washington State. It is more accurate to say that the collections which do exist are not promoted. Instead, print making is the starting-point, a seminal art medium for multimedia. 500 Words. 1991.

pp910514
Time to sell art
How long does it take?
Time is the essential concern in selling your art. Time selling takes away from time creating - the crucial point in balancing between production and livelihood. From the author's book, The Art of Selling Art. 1103 Words. 1991.

pp910515
Computer passion for rugs
A story of three rug designers
Rug and carpet design takes a new twist in the studios of three artist/designers who use computers to create rug designs. Mixing business and esthetics saves time, adds new marketing and sales methods. They blend fiber, hand weaving and digital dreams. 1275 Words. 1991.

pp910518
Falling to earth
Press to hypermedia
Living in an age between the mechanized, industrial world and the electronic, the information age gives an artist a headache. Often they try casting molds for something that will be tangible ten or twenty years in the future. 1303 Words. 1991.

pp910522
Revisiting intuition
Keeping the gates clear
The moment the multimedia artist is out of bed, he asks himself, "Does the new medium help or eliminate creativity?" Innovators he has met populate his memory like ghosts and, in his new machine, they are role models for the virtual artist. 2804 Words. 1991.

pp910531
Libraries define art
Nobody does IT better
When I first opened my eyes to art, I was looking at a print . . . writes the artist/author. Learning

about printmaking as fine art, he adds a significant second part of the his statement:. . . and I was in a library. 1432 Words. 1991.

pp910605
Language and multimedia
If it don't compete, it don't compute
Multimedia roots go back before the invention of moveable type. A millennium of media habits - from the bible to computer babble - means we must learn new expressions. Every content re-purposing proposal begins with economics. 2011 Words. 1991.

pp910614
Leonardo's Business Plan
Genius and Information Technology
Business planning means long-term success for artists. If Leonardo da Vinci were alive, would he have one? Would it be verbal or visual, or musical? In the age of electronic reproduction, creative people must plan to be effective in the future. 3193 Words. 1991.

pp910615
Marketing and the Art of Selling Art
More than meets the eye
Before an artist or a dealer can sell art, there has to be a marketing plan. Excerpt from the author's book, The Art of Selling Art: Between Production and Livelihood. 1063 Words. 1991.

pp910712
Pricing your art
Evaluation stops devaluation
Third of a series from his Art of Selling Art by Bill Ritchie on evaluating art, crafts and design. Five excerpts like as this one from his book were printed in Crafts Report in 1991, reduced from chapter-length to essay-length. 1104 Words. 1991.

pp910715
Goal-writing made easy
Taking a run at IT
Success in your art and craft depends on writing your goals. Fifth of a series of essay by Bill Ritchie on the art of selling arts, crafts and design. They are revised excerpts from Ritchie's The Art of Selling Art: Between Production and Livelihood. 874 Words. 1991.

pp910811
Art Prints in Washington State
Start a new venture, Now?
Actor Jeff Bridges' line from the movie, Star Man, is used to summarize the resilience of art workers in the Northwest. Recounting their unique role in the art scene, the author focuses on people who use printmaking as their primary medium. 409 Words. 1991.

pp910812
Trying Multimedia
First visit to Beethoven's Ninth
A multimedia workstation in the downtown pub-

lic library in Seattle is a first chance to try out the Beethoven Ninth Symphony multimedia created on the Macintosh computer. CD/ROM will be used by artists, so the author uses it to test look-and-feel. 1023 Words. 1991.

pp910819
Fan Club
First buyers of my first book
The author recalls the people who helped get his book, The Art of Selling Art, into the marketplace for self-help artists' books. 395 Words. 1991.

pp910922
Roots of The Ghosts in the New Machine
Games and other things not fit for print
Reflecting on games, literature and lectures about artists' book-arts, he author seeks structure his forthcoming book, Ghosts in the New Machine, and doubts it is fitted for print. It is an old dilemma: Art method in conflict with the printing press. 1683 Words. 1991.

pp911016
Art upgrades digitally
Artists into software
Computer programs are like works of art. They document an age between virtue and reality. Keystrokes are like brushstrokes to this artist/author. Artists are portrayed as ones who add elegance to creations in digital multimedia. 619 Words. 1991.

pp911022
Playing cards
Postcards from the future
The Northwest Print Council draws an artist's name in a lottery to commission a print. This artist then reflects on hand craft in the age of space/time, and forecasts life of an artist in 1995. 519 Words. 1991.

pp911025
Joy in a box
Reinventing arts studios
Confessions of an artist with a passion for computers. For Crafts Report, the author also wrote several columns about selling art adapted from his Perfect Studios trilogy. 856 Words. 1991.

pp911104
The Shape of Content
Time to renew
A page looks like a page, but a page is a metaphor in a computer program like ToolBook. In Hyper-Card, the card file is a metaphor. Hypermedia programs' names refer to metaphors. They have paradigms that include a range of media, e.g., multimedia. 1243 Words. 1991.

pp911105
Multimedia Roots
Interviewing X
The chicken-or-egg riddle becomes, Which came first, database or document? People working in information technology think the two are similar.

Viewing a videotape of himself, the author writes an interview inspired by Glenn Gould interviewing himself. 1483 Words. 1991.

pp911111
Virtuous calculation
Handling memories of a lifetime
Though it may be too short to be called an essay, these three paragraphs outline the source of the author's phrase, The illusion of calculation, key to understanding the subtitle of his trilogy, Perfect Studios. 230 Words. 1991.

pp911119
Observation of Woman Who
Transcending, uncovering pretext
Notes for the The Perfect Studios trilogy: Ghosts in the New Machine, Woman who fell to earth, this section describes her companion, a time-transcender receiver, a visit to a museum's antique computer with a special capacity for uncovering pre-text. 1397 Words. 1991.

pp911130
Words not worth
Ghosts in the New Machine
From Ghosts in the New Machine. It describes a scene in which the main character made three tries to get the old computer started. Then words began to appear on the screen, typed by unseen hands, being uncovered by dead hands of past history. 2008 Words. 1991.

pp911201
Magalogs of Ritchie's, Inc.
Defining tomorrow's 'zine
In Ritchie's Business Plan the meaning of such creative words as Magalog is defined by markets, audience, format and value. These are extrinsic to Perfect Studios; all divisions of the Ritchie's is represented by Magalogs. 260 Words. 1991.

pp911204
State Magazines and Magalogs
Localizing made easy
New ideas began to bear fruit beyond individual talents in arts, crafts and design. Industry leaders find there are no schools preparing skills and content for future publishing. Print paradigms die; information commerce now will be digital. 664 Words. 1991.

pp911207
Little Books Defined
Everything you need in your pocket
Ritchie's Little Books are print publishing ventures in arts, crafts and design fields aimed at education, practice and research markets. They accompany multimedia publications on floppy diskettes; companions are the Magalog and the Videozine. 916 Words. 1991.

pp950414
The Point of EarthSafe 2022
Visual vs. aural tradition

The short, straight line that most people seek, hoping it will be the easiest path to get what they want, is analogous to the straight arrow. Four arrow-points, or triangles, make the tetrahedron a superior proposition. (This file pending search) 2004 Words. 1995.

pp950528
Killing Prints
Making Living Prints
A narrative by a role-playing student in a professor who recently visited an artist's studio and got "the straight stuff" from an artist about Living Prints. He said the artist believed the fastest way to kill of the print's vitality was to photograph it 751 Words. 1995.

pp951010
Roots of PosterMaker
Economic Progress
"When I opened my eyes to art, I was looking at a print," says the author, and describes his early infatuation for posters and the designers who created them. Poster software is the next step. This essay was written before the software had been developed 925 Words. 1995.

pp951229
Journal Entry, Fri. Dec. 29, 1995
Home Page Demo
Notes recorded from the author's "palmtop" B.O.S.S. computer. The author is encouraged by Dan Smith Inc.'s interest in a home page demo. He lists the other wins of the day before; good PE, good Mega Memory, good wood on-line work, and reading TRPI's book. 196 Words. 1995.

pp960117
The Game of Art and Technology and How to Play it
A Little Book for McClure Middle School
Asked to volunteer at McClure Middle School, the author writes a short textbook on how to win at the game of art and technology. The rules are goals, love of playing, knowledge and timing. In the end it is teamwork he advocates. 1361 Words. 1996.

pp960118
Journal Entry, Thu. Jan. 18, 1996
2 TV Programs
Notes recorded from the author's "palmtop" B.O.S.S. computer. The author writes about 2 TV programs, one on the beauty of engineering (the gossamer) and another S.R. Covey survey ended with, "The first gift is life, the second choice how to live it." 220 Words. 1996.

pp960128
The Printmaker and the Heritage Project
A new use for an old process
Photogravure is a combination of photography and intaglio printmaking that is easier now than it was ten or twenty years ago. It opens the way to another project for the printmaking artist interest-ed in genealogy. 1409 Words. 1996.

pp960128b
Journal Entry, Sun. Jan. 28, 1996
An Encouraging Saturday
Notes recorded from the author's "palmtop" B.O.S.S. computer. The author writes about his encouraging Saturday; further organization of his Heritage Calling Cards, supportive talks with his wife, Jackie Brooks and Frank Jennings. 189 Words. 1996.

pp960317
A Day-trip to Perfect Press
Between tradition and technology
Fifth visit on the tour of Domains of Expertise, Perfect Press is where traditional printmaking meets new technologies. Inseparably, the media are believed to be part of a great spiral through time and space. Excerpt from Reinventing Arts Studios Workbook 1805 Words. 1996.

pp960617
Why Living Prints On-line?
Seeing the soul of the universe' largest computer
Computer operating system design is a job for a team of engineers and scientists under one person's direction. A "Living Print" may seem to be the work of one who works as many, but printmaking is a team effort, too. 1655 Words. 1996.

pp960920
Explaining Emeralda
Strange game in the Emerald corridor
The name adopted by Seattle for its worldwide marketing strategy, "The Emerald City," influenced the naming of the game, Emeralda. Beyond the name, how do you explain a game that creates itself? 1068 Words. 1996.

pp960927
How many people does it take to publish a print?
New answers in the age of digital communications
"Printmaking is dead" I printed--tongue-in-cheek--with a rubber stamp twenty years ago. A generation later, I am still making prints. But something is missing: People! How many does it take? 1667 Words. 1996.

pp961004
A perfect day at Perfect Press
Meeting of the bored
It might be an invitation from an international publisher to send examples of prints to be pub-lished in a book of printmakers. This is reason to call a meeting of the ten members of Perfect Studios. 1838 Words. 1996.

pp961104
ArtStudent
Computer-based training for print makers
The author discovers a business-person's inquiry in the newspaper about computer based training, and the answers sound a lot like what would apply to art education. 1457 Words. 1996.

pp961111
Excerpting Allan's book
Toward a review
The following is a preview of one artist in the forthcoming Contemporary Printmaking in the Northwest by Lois Allan. This is the first draft of Allan's text edited by Ritchie at her request and may not conform to the final version published in 1997. 840 Words. 1996.

pp970208
Postcards from Heaven
Notes from a Gates Prizewinner
Historian/painter Paul Johnson uses a phrase, "in the end it is the art that matters more" and inspires insight into the making of Emeralda postcards that go nowhere but are ends in themselves. 1218 Words. 1997.

pp970228
Ghost Madonna
Birth of her cyber arts clubs
Written before breakfast on a silicon-based new machine, the author positions his fantastic image of the woman who fell to earth as the mother of all cyber arts clubs in schools, communities and a statewide network. The roots of this ghost in the new mac 1492 Words. 1997.

pp970310
A Point of Origin
Publishing in the Information and Telecommunications Age
Imagine a country where the commandment, "Publish and Flourish" is everyone's rule. Washington State is somewhat like this, as the largest economic sectors rely heavily on the publishing industry, both in traditional print and new digital technologies. Sc 1806 Words. 1997.

pp970419
Explaining Emeralda
A dilemma tale
How can an artist earn a living today? With the creativity claimed by one who has practiced art for over 30 years it should be easy. The rewards of long practice, study and research are great. But how? Emeralda, the game is easier to play than to explain. 750 Words. 1997.

pp970426
The Wealth of Artists
Banking, Insurance and Investing in the age of digital reproduction
A list of topic headings of essays triggered by financial and investment events that seemed to this author to point toward a new set of economic principles. The author sees these for the benefits of their potential to be disseminated as hypertext e-books. 418 Words. 1997.

pp970520
Preface to Ghosts
An author's hope

A cyberwright and bookbinder is a person who works both in cybernetics (hypermedia, the Web, etc.) and hand bookbinding-plus variable hybrids in between-according to this author's vision. He has planned to write a book, and thinks this may be its preface. 463 Words. 1997.

pp970811
Artist checks and disposable diapers
What's the connection?
Soon to be a grandfather, the artist contemplates his creative idea (artist's checks) and the debate as to whether fabric or disposable diapers are matters to weigh investment decisions. Odd combination? Not in this artist/writer's scope of a Big Picture. 2783 Words. 1997.

pp971104
Journal Entry, Tue. Nov. 4, 1997
Outline Edges of Emeralda and My Gazelle Graph
The author writes his time log of the day, the activities and projects he did that day. The cascade lists the three or four "edges" outline of Emeralda, precepts to success. The author practiced with his new software, Adobe Illustrator and Streamline. 602 Words. 1997.

pp971230
I Wrote A Book Review
On Lois Allan's Contemporary Printmaking in the Northwest
If it serves no other purpose my book review introduces the next stage of printmaking. I am included in the book--a wonder inasmuch I seldom create prints today. This book leaves out some facts that may now, with cybernetics and multi-agents, be restored. 2815 Words. 1997.

pp980108
Frozen Flower
A new picture of TRPI
The author's idea of an Artists' Equity Fund needs a leader who can picture it and frame it; and thus the search begins. This essay is a snapshot of one man's six-year experience in a specialized investment club he named after a little dog named Turpie. 1650 Words. 1998.

pp980109
Dreaming of Perfect Press
Getting there from here
The Apprentice User writes about his second day at Perfect Press Residence Stay focusing on dreams, insights and key writings that suggest how a printmaking studio can be rebuilt from the ashes of the studios he sacrificed upon leaving the UW art school. 1131 Words. 1998.

pp980110
Printers and other vassals
Steering your own course with media artistry
The Emeralda Master, a printer, reflects on old images, phrases and memories and arrives at a new accounting for performance. He explains how to and why to break from being someone else's vessel

and vassal. Triple entry bookkeeping is one path to freedom. 1586 Words. 1998.

pp980112
Painting, Monotypes and Living Prints
They are as different as proof and calculation
The author finds a parallel between Peter Bernstein's account of the history of math and risk-taking and the history of painting and printmaking. He compares it to the illusion of calculation, the mantra he says defines his idea of Living Prints. 855 Words. 1998.

pp980309
Who Is Ascendant
Let the Bored decide
Dealt a hand from a deal of the cards in the collectible card version of Emeralda (in a deal where the ascendant sister is difficult to determine) the inventor of Emeralda turns to the Meeting of the Bored to decide how to resolve his day's dilemma tales. 1380 Words. 1998.

pp980319
What Is Your Secret?
Confessions of a lurker
A strange sense of guilt haunts the author almost every time he peruses his collection of communiques he collects on the Internet from printmakers worldwide. What is the cause of this guilt feeling? The reading of "Net Gain," no doubt, causes him to lurk. 1353 Words. 1998.

pp980508
Making Living Prints
Joy of Inventing
The joy of inventing Living Prints is that this artist lives the adventure from beginning to end, a privilege of having a childhood, growing to maturity, overcoming considerable frustrations and linking with the foundations laid by artists and scientists. 926 Words. 1998.

pp980518
Explaining Demonstrations
How you label demonstrations
In Emeralda play, there are twenty-one cells and each cell allows for a demonstration. This essay begins to explain what the inventor intended by the word demonstration and how he based his idea on the Prisoner's Dilemma, one he derived from games theory. 598 Words. 1998.

pp980528
Imaginary Talk Show
Guests from Net Gain
The author uses a clever method to introduce a novel idea of serving artists with an information system that will reduce their time on the Internet, sort e-mail and provide their following with information on coming events, shows and biographical resumes. 1278 Words. 1998.

pp980607
Emeralda 21 explained

How TESC shaped Emeralda 21
The author taught college at an innovative '70s school and the experience helped shape one variation on the game Emeralda that he invented. In this game he incorporated some self-help ideas he learned from motivational speakers and designed a cell system. 731 Words. 1998.

pp980617
What is a Knowbot?
The Emeralda Inventor Goes Hunting
Knowbots are intelligent programs that can be "educated". They live in virtual realities and are capable of accumulating knowledge about the world on their own. This is a long article copied from a 1994 workshop held in Germany by a scientist-philosopher. 6190 Words. 1998.

pp980627
Is online worth the risk?
Second thoughts about printmakinglibrary.com
He asks if the risk of going online worth it, a gamble, and not something for people who have to be assured every step of the way? The history of risk is a road that is paved with good ideas that went bad. Some say it's a road to hell or to hell and back. 555 Words. 1998.

pp980707
You need a press
Demonstrations real and virtual
What is the business model of the Perfect Studios, the Perfect Press, and a new kind of printing press that goes beyond the metallic one? The author traces the development of his theories about a new paradigm for seeing his native art and craft grow anew. 1782 Words. 1998.

pp980717
Rewards and Challenges of Yacht Learning
Visions of a someday cruise
Drifting from a flash of insight, a golden nugget of an idea, the author describes his idea for day-cruises to another coastal city where guests enjoy a day of art, technology and fine cuisine. It's an idea to combine fantasy, fiction, and real art works. 2435 Words. 1998.

pp980727
The Printmaker's Life Value Calculator
Demonstration at Perfect Press
Aboard his fantasy printmaking bus the author recounts a vision of how a patient under treatment for voices in his head gave him the idea for Group Education Co-operative and fusion of healthcare and education using old and new technologies as the bridge. 998 Words. 1998.

pp980806
Describing Emeralda
Of Hands, helves and hearts
Wondering if people had been playing his game, Emeralda, the inventor speculates on what kinds of changes may have occurred. He's interested in economics and how a different basis of valua-

tion-on intellect instead of material goods-would change the world. 691 Words. 1998.

pp980816
Automate What Needs It
Self-help radio informs Emeralda play
A radio broadcast encouraging words to the Emeralda inventor laboring over his routine activities of game design. Radio is his automated helper. Once ended, the values of automation of Emeralda Score sheets were clearly that they should become like radio. 1715 Words. 1998.

pp980826
A Dilemma Tale
Starting the 1998 edition of Ghosts in the New Machine
The author of an unpublished manuscript titled "Ghosts in the New Machine" thinks repeat orders for the book might be a sign that it is time to go to print--even if in one manually-built copy. New opportunities are tempting him to publish only digitally. 977 Words. 1998.

pp980905
Details in Emeralda
Reflections on a MAD artist
As a kid Emeralda's inventor read Mad Comics plus he had his favorite artists in sci-fi publications long before he learned about the fine arts. No wonder he saw a fantastic perfect studio in the details of his use of some of his PC software applications. 793 Words. 1998.

pp980915
Moves in Emeralda
First move of the day
The first move of the inventor's day--the Score sheet of Emeralda--is fun, unlike filling in conventional ledgers for double-entry bookkeeping. It's for inventors and entrepreneurs who must build new paths between two fantastic worlds, the Gifts of Life. 881 Words. 1998.

pp980925
Counting to 254
Making the puzzle parts fit
Part XXV of Emeralda for Dummies. This is one of those little games inside Emeralda. Take an article and create a subject line that's 254 characters long, including spaces. It's a game of skill and a perfect example of what goes on in a Cell of Emeralda. 425 Words. 1998.

pp981005
Gleaner Down to Steerage
Search for the secrets of the ghost writer
This critical essay says Emeralda results from one of the rare instances in which the inventor failed to perceive the effect of unchanging human nature at the intersection of politics, art, and economics. He invented for the goals of economic engineering. 1409 Words. 1998.

pp981015

Q&A by Perfect Press Agents
Emeralda Inventor Interviews
On three separate sessions the Emeralda Inventor is questioned by Perfect Press agents to learn how printmaking figures into the invention of his online interactive co-operative game. He notes that printmakers might be the front-runners in this marathon. 8862 Words. 1998.

pp981025
The Waiting Room
Magazine rack mirage
He waits for a lecture honoring his old friend, Lisel Salzer, and the author writes, on his palmtop, thoughts about the surroundings and people there. Monotypes adorn the walls, and there's a sense of awe and respect for Lisel. The author feels skeptical. 469 Words. 1998.

pp981104
Compulsive Printmaking
Analyzing yourself to death
He writes down fantasies on his palmtop when he has an imaginary encounter with some ghost from his past-a person, event or place. Always he's accumulating scenes for his game, Emeralda. Following is a short example designed to be a vivid picture someday. 700 Words. 1998.

pp981114
Birth of a Video
On freezing intellectual capital funds
He listens to a mutual funds adviser on a radio talk show and switches from art professor with former student "investors" to the role of fund manager. Trainees in publicly funded state schools aren't aware that intellectual assets are subject to freezing. 1168 Words. 1998.

pp990108
Visit to A Fantasy Studio
An Emeralda Tourist Journal
The inventor of Emeralda writes as though he is a stranger, a mere tourist, visiting the printmaking studio at Perfect Press. He sees there is interest in the mix of technology and paper model-building, but not so much interest in traditional printmaking. 542 Words. 1999.

pp990109
Musings on a Pot
Notes from Perfect Press
This dreamer always loved ceramics-the art of pottery-but he chose printmaking as his lifelong career. Yet he would return from time to time, if only in his imagination. Here he's musing on what it would be like to see a modern pot in the year 30,000 B.P. 771 Words. 1999.

pp990110
Thought for the day
Jefferson and the constitution
Thomas Jefferson, according to the author who wrote a biography on him, was an artist born into an unfortunate land at an unfortunate time. Nev-

ertheless, he was able to exercise his art, craft, and design in surprising and profound ways. His example is good. 341 Words. 1999.

pp990111
A Stick is to A Duck As A Game is to Life
An artist/scholar's perspective
The artist/scholar's goal is to restore the integrity of the artists who love the media arts above all other forms of expression and to create a cooperative game in which maker and made are one, change is constant, and interference is the rule of the day. 1265 Words. 1999.

pp990113
Future shock, human nature and family calendars
Beneficiaries of the illusion of calculation
Is it better to transfer risks of becoming poor to someone else, and then show up for work at a mass production line that makes calendars that everyone needs and wants? The sales figures prove that people like those calendars; his wife even collects them. 493 Words. 1999.

pp990309
My day
Musings of an Apprentice User at Perfect Press
A diary or journal entry of an Apprentice User who feels stranded in the wrong place at the wrong time, as printmaking--the passion of his artistic life--seems to be of no interest and, worse yet, of no consequence in a plan of his itinerary for the stay. 473 Words. 1999.

pp990310
Specifying the Gates Prize
Focusing on Books
The inventor of the Gates Prize is again at his task of specifying the fantastic prize in his game, Emeralda, thinking that a deep and rewarding specific is available in the form of books as containers of information: Perfect, Imperfect, Real and Virtual. 412 Words. 1999.

pp990311
Interactive Education on DVD as an MFA Metaphor
Considered by DISCO-OP Vision
Visualizing ways to use a Digital Video Disc in connection with teaching dentistry on-line, the Emeralda Apprentice User writes about a free loan of a DVD system that will bring the practitioners into line and assist in feasible plans to develop together. 813 Words. 1999.

pp990507
What Does an MFA do?
Toodle-do
Practice Makes Permanent is the message for people who want to apply hands and minds to a new category of professionals called the Multi-Faceted Auxiliary. The author is applying the principle and experimenting on himself in this essay--linked to the Web. 636 Words. 1999.

pp990510
Great Expectations
Clarifying expectations in co-operative development
The publications of Dr. Stephen R. Covey inform the founders of the Dental Internet Services Co-operative because they give the instructions for principle-centered leadership. Dentalisco is based on patient-centered dental practices and cooperative models. 758 Words. 1999.

pp990706
Safeco Revisited
View from Perfect Press
A story began twenty five years ago which this author still writes. He lives the story like he is at a distance from himself; an autobiography, perhaps, written at a safe distance in order to achieve and maintain objective, scientific evidence he is sane. 1212 Words. 1999.

pp990707
Naming the Risk
Evaluation of HSIC in Media Arts
Giving measurements to the intangible value of art, technology and education is a difficult task, especially when one is in the middle of the processes, as it were. One may have only the beginning and end of a lifetime to go by, and these are hard to see. 2366 Words. 1999.

pp990708
Looking back
Seeing prints
On the third Days of Perfect Information, the inventor of Emeralda compares the books Book and Closing of the American Mind in an attempt to plan his action toward making Emeralda work for other people besides himself. He sees his life as fiction reified. 2044 Words. 1999.

pp990709
Introduction to Testing Emeralda
No strip teasers allowed!
One way to exorcise terrors of loss is to use the witty invention of light amplification by stimulated emission of radiation and not to engage in strip teases, baring the link between head and heart with the less witty invention of paper, plate and press. 1561 Words. 1999.

pp000227
Hurt at the Bottom Line
Flyer's Remorse
A high flyer, sensing a crash, regrets that he leaned his ladder against the wrong wall, chose the less rigorous course and took the wrong advice when young, in pilot training. Foreseeing this, turning to the navigator, he seeks the way to turn to safety. 578 Words. 2000.

pp000305
How I Teach Art Ed Online
Proof in the Works
An ITinerate Professor reveals his secrets for

teaching art education on-line. He explains concurrent teaching/learning, research and practice. Then he reveals how this essay is, in itself, an example of teaching on-line, and links it with other teachers. 740 Words. 2000.

pp000307
Me? Go back to college? No Way!
Letter to the iEditor
The interactive online letter-to-the-editor offers up this fantasy note from an artist who thinks he should not have to go back to college in order to receive continuing education. His 20th Century street-smart college's degree, he feels, is all he needs. 822 Words. 2000.

pp000310
Who is Peter D, Anyway?
Testing AUREL
He wants to know, quickly, who wrote him a mysterious e-mail message. He gave his name as Peter D. but how can the Arts Uniform Resources E-commerce Locator tell him more about this guy? The author of this article must think, so he makes this into a test! 2269 Words. 2000.

pp000329
Search for Reinventing Studios
A message
He got an order from a bookstore for a book he did not make time to finish. Is there time to do it now? Something happened when he opened the last draft of his manuscript and he begins to test the bases for his fifth manuscript, Reinventing Arts' Studios. 774 Words. 2000.

pp000409
Sunrise over Bellevue
Meeting the Man behind The Learning Council
Emeralda Works by testing the validity of the central principle, which is Boomers Count. As the sun rises over Bellevue, thanks in part to technology and in part to innovations, the Learning Councilman agreed to meet the Emeralda inventor in this account. 847 Words. 2000.

pp000425
Flash of the Morning
An E-newsletter from McClain's
Emeralda Games are games for the gifts of life, and today's gift is the convergence of two events: The potential of owning a printmaking supply business; and the value of adding an e-newsletter as part of the interactive games online based on printmaking. 1348 Words. 2000.

pp000428
Gates' Mistake
The Impower of Unlimits
A flat earth would be a fine place to be for people like Elmer Gates. As he got closer to solving the mystery of why and how people create, invent, discover and imagine the flatter and neater his world became until he made the edge of man's world reality. 811 Words. 2000.

pp000530
Dear Art Patron
Artist's Loveletter
The artist who created "The Artist's Last Love Letter" experiences deja vu as he prepares a slide package for the State jury. Seeing himself entering the same old thing, he stops and writes down an idea about a new art, an idea that grew out of tradition. 1476 Words. 2000.

pp000616
Graduation Ceremony
An Emeralda Warrior Rite
There's something new at Emeralda Works: Graduation Certificates! The Ceremony when this are won is in keeping with the RPG and rules of Emeralda, the Game for the Gifts of Life. This time, it's the completion of the second phase of Elmer Gates Biography. 1484 Words. 2000.

pp001106
How I will Save the Earth
Bill Ritchie's Plan
Taking on a great mission with a kind of passion known only to artistic lovers of beauty and living things, he lays out his blueprint, his plan to banish the wicked prince, restore the imbalance of carbon dioxide and save Earths' life sustaining capacity. 1042 Words. 2000.

pp001206
The Basis of Die Brucke
A Formula for Legacy Transfer
The basis of his proposed book, Die Brucke: Artists Insurance Guide is that it is the formula for legacy transfer for an imperfect world. All previous asset management and legacy transfer methods are based on perfect information. This doesn't fit artists. 296 Words. 2000.

pp001208
Art Professor for Higher
Printmaking On A DVD - Part II
Potential text for a letter to introduce college faculty to a service or product the author is planning for release in May, 2001 under the Living Prints label. It is a combination calendar and entertainment resource springing out of so-called edutainment. 1964 Words. 2000.

pp001211
Preface to Die Brucke
Die broke, young artist
Bill Ritchie is working on his newest book, Die Brucke, a derivative of Die Broke, a 1997 book on financial planning by Pollan and Levine. Bill's Preface suggests that Tom Jefferson, a pioneer in dying broke should be retired, along with his tired ethics. 991 Words. 2000.

pp010118
Teaching Printmaking in Six Seconds
The One Minute Printmaking Professor
If TV commercial designers can get a point across

in one minute for sponsors, why can't artists who teach printmaking do the same? This writer believes it's possible, and has set out to achieve this. He will be the fastest teacher in the world if he does! 268 Words. 2001.

pp010127
Homage Moment
Six minutes for Ross
The artist pays homage to an old friend, Ross Jones, as he finishes the task of uploading a drawing to his virtual art gallery. An inner voice suggests he will have a limited time for it and she calls it "a moment" as, "art works for our moments in life." 572 Words. 2001.

pp010207
How and Why to Publish Your Retrospective on DVD
The One-Minute Administrator
Approaching a turning point in the scripting of a 40-year retrospective, the Itinerate Professor, who professes to be a future teacher, compares a popular motion picture to making and publishing new DVD-based virtual art for on-line art teacher education. 2327 Words. 2001.

pp010217
Printmaking is Dead He Said
Long Live Printmaking
Artist compares the feelings of prints' anticipation as those children who attend inspiring schools: Eager to go in the morning and reluctant to leave at the end of the school day. Resolving not to deny himself the thrill of prints he takes a new pathway. 850 Words. 2001.

pp010227
Destination Emeralda
Straight Road to Simpli City
The integrity of medium-of-origination, or MOO, is the stock basis for human structural intellectual capital. The author says it's a lifelong journey for which one prepares by investing in himself or herself and not entirely in other peoples' enterprise. 2374 Words. 2001.

pp010309
A Good Day to Die
Breaking the Print Barrier
The author is a bridge builder, always crossing between the old world of printmaking to the new world where he uses the expression Living Prints to refer to a new kind of printmaking. His project, a DVD, is not as new as it seems; it is a dream come true. 2409 Words. 2001.

pp010319
Print Circus, Clown and Gypsy Queens
My Washington Years in Retrospect
When he was a professor of art, he dreamt of a print circus, moving, moveable studios that traveled across his state and the nation, dispersing arts of printmaking. Today there's a better way: Surpassing ferries, trucks and planes on an Info-tech Highway. 460 Words. 2001.

pp010329
Printmaking in Platinum
Doing for Others As They Would Have You Do
In his daily routine as an expert in making Web pages for his art patrons, the author creates Web page for his daughters. At the same time he's doing this, he wonders if he can show other printmakers how-and why. Practicing the "Platinum Rule" is one way. 1659 Words. 2001.

pp010408
On Sweet Target Hearts
Notes about three prints for three women
An exercise in locating three artist proofs that belong to his wife and daughters sends the artist/writer into a deep reflection on a time-twenty five years before-and what he was concerned about then. As part of his 40-year retrospective, it makes sense. 1303 Words. 2001.

pp010418
Search for Paul Brainerd
Finding A Path to Trust in the Silicon Forest
An artist who is interested in a job related to EarthSafe 2022 searches for a source that is like the headwaters of a watershed from whose well-springs he might drink. The writer could become an arts director in a new kind of school if the path is trusted. 1458 Words. 2001.

pp010428
An Old Archivist Tells His Story
How Dusty Got His Job Title
The true artist needs allies in the life sciences, according to this writer. It is only in this way that the true artist can learn eco-nomics or holistic arts and sciences. It lead to feelings of usefulness, the fullness-of-use, of personal utility value. 804 Words. 2001.

pp010508
I Builded Me A DVD
Death in the 20th C and Awakening Living Prints in the 21st
An archaic expression, so antique-sounding, was on his mind as this author thinks about margin alized artists' stories and how they felt forced to follow new and different pathways like castaways, thrown out of their world and into new, alien environments. 1144 Words. 2001.

pp010518
MyCashLink Dot-com and Living Prints
DVD and MyCashLink.com reviewed
It's like a jungle in his project. He's making a Living Prints DVD 'Zine for the first time-a virtual dark continent! But there are gems, he discovers-ideas galore! Like this one: One way to link artists with money in the night. The secret is in the links. 269 Words. 2001.

pp010617
Dummied-down Art Education
One day at the fairgrounds

An art professor with a future vision looks at a day when he visited a convention of educators dedicated to home schools. Seeking a glimpse of new technologies in K-12 distance learning for art, he saw two examples. He contrasts them with new video games. 2203 Words. 2001.

pp010627
How I make a DVD
Answer to a FAQ
One printmaker makes Digital Versatile Discs, believing he can be a Digital Versatile Artist-an old joke about fingers being digits, too. He makes DVDs the same way he makes prints-by himself. Someone asked How? and he gave his answer as a cooking lesson. 700 Words. 2001.

pp010707
It's Not How You Play Emeralda
It's IF IT Plays-and-Pays-You Well
As the Digital Versatile Disc he's making takes on more and more attributes of being a work of art, the author is struck by the fact he knows almost nothing about it, and also he has less responsibility for it than he thought before. IT seems to play him.1486 Words. 2001.

pp010717
New Mythology
The Ghost of C. S. Lewis in the New Machine
The author of the DVD Prithwish and Me compares the new publishing medium with the old. The Chronicles of Narnia provide a useful contrast and builds a new position for the professor who would be a storyteller. 1014 Words. 2001.

pp010915
Against A Screen of War
What my labor means to me
An art professor, laboring in a Seattle spare bedroom closet, makes Digital Versatile Disks (DVD). His DVD may be the "blue book" of the 21st Century on-line, virtual classroom. He recalls another year and another war and how useless art education seemed. 1724 Words. 2001.

pp010925
Spreading Out My Collectible DVDs
Fantasy for an Emeralda Player
This DVD collection is growing, and it's time to step back and look at it as a collection instead of unique projects. The author looks back over nine month's work and asks himself where he's going. His answer may lie in collectible cards and printmaking. 1205 Words. 2001.

pp011005
A Book on DVD DVD
Making circles
When a friend suggested that he write an article about his ideas and a DVD school, the author is enthused. Overnight, he imagined the article becoming a book-an on-line textbook-for his idea of a school where prints and DVDs are both taught, side by side. 1166 Words. 2001.

pp011015
Prisoners Dilemma Revisited
Reflections from one who could not attend Crossing Boundaries
A mixture of envy and relief is expressed by one person who couldn't attend a conference on his favorite topic-prints-with international understanding as part the goal. He compares it to being like a prisoner or house-bound person living among the mobile. 1295 Words. 2001.

pp011124
Opening Your Passport to Printmaking
Art education on-line starts here
How you invent an on-line art education system is determined by what kind of art to start with. There's only one: printmaking that lends itself to interactive design for on-line teaching, research and practice. The inventor uses a passport scheme for it. 461 Words. 2001.

pp011204
How Does Art-Ed Online Work Really?
Demo or Die and Don't Ask Why
From the first Harry Potter movie to the latest review of a poet's book, the author gets satisfaction while producing a DVD, making one on the fly. His daily routine brings him close to his dream of a great teacher in the arts using ecological multimedia. 1959 Words. 2001.

pp011229
Looking Forward to School Again
Introducing Your Printmaking Class
Anticipating a new kind of art education on-line, the author attempts to put himself in the shoes of a schoolteacher who's taking a continuing education class. He wonders how it feels. Is there still joy-a thrilled sense of anticipation as there once was? 947 Words. 2001.

pp020107
Writing Between the Paragraphs - Interval
Pause for reflection by an Itinerant Professor
In the game he invented this artist and professor plays with a 360-day calendar, having five days between each session called interval. So, too, with the ten essays he's creating (or, copy-writing), based on the text written by Mark C. Taylor, a humanist. 1267 Words. 2002.

pp020117
Grading and Passing Art Ed Online
Speculations of an ITinerant On-Line Art Professor
How will people be graded and evaluated in art education on-line, this professor asks. He used new methods when he was on the traditional campus, but when he left to find better methods, he also invented a new paradigm for teaching, research and practice. 1683 Words. 2002.

pp020127
About My Print Homage to Hayter

The Artist Explains with A Little Help from A Friend
The on-line printmaking experience includes the exchange of prints among thirty participants scattered all over the world, and this artist/writer chooses to include an explanation to accompany his. He created this explanatory essay to go with the woodcut. 741 Words. 2002.

pp020207
Confessions of An Art Nazi
Teaching art students what they can never do
A former art professor in a US American public university turns himself in and describes how he and his colleagues trained aspiring artists, crafts people and designers in things that they would not be able to achieve. A happy ending is in sight, however. 647 Words. 2002.

pp020217
Ghost in the Old Machine
An Artistamp Perforator As A Haunted House
Working at the treadle of an antique perforating machine, punching out rows of tiny holes that will form the serrated edges of his artistamps, this artist is visited by a Muse who suggests a TV Game Show and new plotline for his screenplay titled Chimera. 788 Words. 2002.

pp020227
Can Emeralda Create A Perfect Printmaking Society?
Seeking both a civil and decent printmaking society
The author recounts his early encounters with prints as fine art through acquaintance with print societies. On a path among living print societies and dying or dead ones, he sees complementary relationships with new technology as ways to make prints live. 1080 Words. 2002.

pp020319
Stamps and Mail Art
Artists Create Postage Stamp Sized Artworks
Artists who make stamps for fun, and then share them with other people around the country and around the world, have built a kind of community using the mail systems as an instrument. This artist-playing the role of public scholar-presents a free lecture. 1157 Words. 2002.

pp020329
Would I Join An Organization that had Me as A Leader?
My life as a tree
A grateful former UW professor reflects on the organizations he's belonged to and concludes that the best one is yet to come; but would he join it if it would have him as a member? Probably not, unless the leader is a strong tree with the power of limits. 1014 Words. 2002.

pp020408
Whoopee! I Got IT Right
Right Moves and Right Times

Reading about one trend in higher education-not directly tied to printmaking (his domain of expertise)-this artist/scholar saw a trend in outsourcing. It's in The Chronicle of Higher Education about a college replacing faculty counselors with contractors. 895 Words. 2002.

pp020508
After My Computer Fails
Printmaking is like music
His computer was blasted by virus, like something out of a shoot 'em up computer game. To this artist/philosopher, it suggests that somewhere in this disaster there is a gem that he must find – a plan of documenting, on DVD, the secret evolution of his work. 467 Words. 2002.

pp020518
Who Killed Bill Ritchie?
Or, I don't know anything about jazz but I know what I like
The last thing I remember about Bill was when he went to bed that night he said, "Tomorrow I'm going to wake up as a different person." He'd had a trying evening, trying to be everything to everybody, and not doing a very good job at, or for, any of them. 714 Words. 2002.

pp020528
My Dream Started Here
Perfect Press and the Road to Emeralda
He envisions education for the multimedia artists what Sesame Street did for reading, writing and math, and what Bill Nye (the Science guy) achieved for science. With a console game interface and Fisher Plaza nearby, he thinks Uptown Seattle is the place. 1220 Words. 2002.

pp020607
Most Amazing Art Auction Ever
What I knew then I know Again
He's searching for a way to contribute his art collection to his community without burdening his community with the costs of maintenance and exhibitions. He's hit on the idea of an unusual auction to raise a million dollars the hardest way-an art auction. 527 Words. 2002.

pp020627
My Emeralda Green Slippers
Escape from Toxi City
Comparing his exodus from a corrupt and contaminated institutional environment to Dorothy's homecoming from Oz, the author describes how he saw his chances to break out of the intellectual molds cast by educators of bygone eras and finds a path to freedom. 554 Words. 2002.

pp020707
Restoring Susan Frank
The best things happen last
After a virus infected his computer named Susan and put all his data into suspended animation, the author reflects on the benefits that this brought about. It's strangely like his story about a man who

experiences what he called his Rip Van Winkle effect. 1140 Words. 2002.

pp020717
At Vel's the 17th of July
Creative Writing Neighborhood
In his outreach phase, the artist/scholar meets with neighborhood writers to learn what they do. Voluntarily, without commercial motivation, they come to practice, benefited by a self-appointed leader and they write for themselves and read to one another. 1220 Words. 2002.

pp020717b
Tipping-in Artistamps at Perfect Press
Little Things Mean A Lot to Creative Writing Education On-line
The root of the Perfect Studios Trilogy is EarthSafe 2022, but that movement, being of global proportions, has a microscopically small but significant element in the artistamp movement. Stamps are going electronic digitally on the Net in the Emeralda Way. 6503 Words. 2002.

pp020727
Old IBIS and New Uptown Seattle
A Sharper Image
There'll be a panel discussion 45 miles from Uptown Seattle, and artists will reflect on the '80s IBIS project. The author asks if this retrospective moment will help sharpen his focus on a multimedia arts / game center for local access and global action. 1394 Words. 2002.

pp020806
Passport Ready
Heading In A New Direction Every Day
After a night conversing with strangers from around the neighborhood, the artist/scholar wakens to a new day of creating his own passport to another kind of life than those that he sees others leading. He's exercising his freedom, Emeralda, his life game. 529 Words. 2002.

pp020816
Life Like Connecting Dots
Moving from Dotted to Solid Lines
He's building an infrastructure to house human structural intellectual capital of an emeriti, empowering those wisdom boomers, the few elder intellectuals like himself who believe they have the sense to know what they can change, how, and why they should. 459 Words. 2002.

pp020826
Writing at Caffe Vita
What's in A Title?
Getting permission to write his second book in the Perfect Studios trilogy, the author then must re-think the title, and where to write the book, where the best book will be written. Can a truly original work be written if it's based on last year's title? 662 Words. 2002.

pp020905

Marketing and Selling My First E-Book
Reinventing Arts Studios and In-Retro Melt Down
His search for the business plan comes in a Flash under a Seattle sky as he takes strides to Kinko's and back He has made his first screen saver, then sees he can give it away free to his art patrons, and it is the pull through for artistamps and stories. 818 Words. 2002.

pp020905b
Smiling Faces at Caffe Vita
It's Not Your Typical Art Studio Any More
Searching for the easiest way to create the Artist's Last Love Letter, the e-book version, is best done in some natural, enjoyable fashion. If one has to use e-book readers, then he should be rewarded in a big way. The author is searching for that reward. 1275 Words. 2002.

pp020915
Emeralda is More Interesting than Reality
From Postcards to Emeralda Interchange
Opening a postcard to himself from Caffe Vita MacRitchie's he sent a week ago, the author finds yet another dimension to his fantasy world, Emeralda. There's more potential for him in a virtual world, as for example his newest angle, Emeralda Interchange. 1369 Words. 2002.

pp020925
What if Out-of-Work Professors Got Together?
Would They Re-form Higher Ed?
In the night he wakens and is struck by the vision of thousands of out-of-work college teachers creating a global network to get connected directly with students worldwide. This may be the destiny of his game plan, Emeralda, a game for the gifts of life. 1600 Words. 2002.

pp021005
Copyright, Copy Write and Copy Wright
Which is Right?
I didn't know what I was doing until I found out that many people would call it plagiarizing. Which stopped me-for a while-until I saw the issue in light of Jefferson's metaphor of the lighted taper, a feud brewing on the 'Net, and an article I could buy. 929 Words. 2002.

pp021015
Kinko's and Me
Alliances for Education
While some businesses around us are losing their ground, there's one giant, important industry that is making dramatic growth in just the past three years. Next to the top growth area-health-education, in particular the for-profit sector, is making gains. 1445 Words. 2002.

pp021025
Portrait of A Future Professor
The basis
The basis of the Professors of the next 5-10 years will be their utility value as Bernoulli postulated this quantity. That is the degree of risk-reduc-

tion that the teacher brings to the students, the research area, the practice and the community at large. 804 Words. 2002.

pp021104
Perfect Press Perspective
Adult game developers, please
The Professor is free from the Seattle Independent Mall, so he's able to catch up on his writing. E-mail slips him a clue, snatched from an article published in New York Times, testing his hand at copy-writing an article about the aging of computer games. 2430 Words. 2002.

pp030118
A Teacher's Letter to his Last Student
Paradigms for teaching art in the age of digital reproduction
When his last student can't come to his Saturday class, the ITinerate Professor remembers a dream he once had and puts his dream into action. He dreams of teaching printmaking arts on-line and he gives her a lesson in this way, including 4 pictures of it. 823 Words. 2003.

pp030227
SIM A Work of Art
An Original Without a Signature
The author, an Itinerate Professor (entitled to wander around, thinking globally and acting locally) staged a showing in an experimental "mini-mall". It was a test lab and workshop to learn more about business success and the work of art in a new context. 935 Words. 2003.

pp030309
Electronic Portfolios Marry High Tech and Visual Arts
Marrying High-Tech with the Visual Arts
A professor, fallen from the grace of the traditional schools of visual arts, contemplates the state of the art of e-folios, reflecting also on his self-styled 40 year retrospective. The e-folio has value, but that it is a long way from school acceptance. 1022 Words. 2003.

pp030518
Background Story for The Missing Professor
Shades of Harry Potter
All video games have a background story as part of their design. The author wants to help create a video game or hybrid distance learning art course, so he created a background theme he calls The Students of An Absent Professor for the stage for his game. 1549 Words. 2003.

pp030528
How Dr. Chew Saved Emeralda
Memories of the ancestors
Faced with the eminent failure of his game, the inventor of Emeralda returns to his student mentor, who has by this time succeeded in hiding in the safety of another realm. With only his memories to guide him, he summons the eminent Dr. Chew for his help. 909 Words. 2003.

pp030617
Professors Who Cheat
The game master plan
Art education games are going on-line! As a professor who cheated the university out of about a half-million, he's the best one to explain how the best professors are the ones who can always help students cheat at the games people play in the art schools. 1360 Words. 2003.

pp030707
So You Want to Teach Art in College?
An E-Stamp and Story may make your career click
When someone asks me what I do, I'd like to give them a one word answer and then have them say, "Oh, YOU'RE the famous Bill Ritchie!" I'd like to be able to say, "Games" and they would know who I was immediately. "You invented Emeralda! I LOVE that game!" 977 Words. 2003.

pp030717
Clicking My Career Away
Confessions of a Pre-Boomer
He chopped up his domain-of-expertise into ten parts, and this was the beginning of the end of his career. Unless, however, new digital technologies required artists in mid-career to change his or her way of thinking that they learned in the 20th Century. 1315 Words. 2003.

pp030806
Imagining the Almost Unimaginable
Art Education On-line
He will teach Economics and Art in the Age of Digital Reproduction, but he can hardly imagine how to do it. He's looking for clues to solve a mystery, How can you teach art on-line? Part of the solution is to go half the distance-a hybrid-learning course. 618 Words. 2003.

pp030816
Trading Places
An Absent Professor As Student
As his third generation in school draws to a close, the author feels like it's time to start again. Taking a long view of his future he sees forty years open for teaching, learning, research, practice and service. Obviously, he needs to be back in school. 1082 Words. 2003.

pp030905
Taking Care of Your Art Patrons
One Household at A Time
How does an artist's list of patrons' names-individuals who bought his or her works over several decades-figure into the making of an online art game? Game developers state that your players are gold. Are art patrons like the loyal players of a MMORPG? 1400 Words. 2003.

pp030915
What A Fine Art Drawing Teacher Wants
Advice to Beginning Drawing Students
He starts teaching a beginning drawing college

class-his first time in eighteen years-and realizes some things have not changed. After the first week's meetings with the students, he writes down what he really wants them to do for him, and for themselves. 1224 Words. 2003.

pp031114
Saving Professor Ritchie
Analogy from a digital based strategy game
You can compare a video game with my life sometimes, and I want to create a PC game that will restore a life that was taken away from me almost 20 years ago. It's a game in itself just to conceive of the method and I live the game as I think how it works. 1156 Words. 2003.

pp031124
Why Oh Why Emeralda?
Looking for the bigger context
In sum, Emeralda is a way to inject new life into the art one loves the most. To this artist it is printmaking, and he plays Emeralda to insure its vitality. Some think this can be done by putting one's secrets of printmaking in the hands of young people. 706 Words. 2003.

pp031204
If Every Art School had Emeralda
Musings of a has-been professor
Emeralda is an ambiguous fantasy game that slips in and out of this art professor's consciousness like an old dream remembered. He had dreamed of a perfect art school but reality is settling in. What will keep art alive, then, he wonders, without a dream? 623 Words. 2003.

pp031229
Collect All Forty Stamps
Another game plan
Searching for the payoff in his game Emeralda, the inventor-professor thinks of another way to entice people to play and concurrently develop social networking. His goal, and payoff, is a virtual art ed colony that can lead to a real, self-sustaining one. 421 Words. 2003.

pp040118
Old Professors Who Put their Stamp on Things
Why I created Stamps 'N Stories
Stamps 'N Stories is a way to solve the memory loss problem: If professors and their students could their work into a fascinating, addictive video game, then the professors' scholarship would not only be remembered but would also be easy to access online. 1323 Words. 2004.

pp040417
Vision of A Thing to Come
A map, a mould, a sheet
The artist is a printmaker without a press and he envisions how he will not only design and build a press but he'll also make a map of his fantasy region, Emeralda. And for paper to print his plate on, he'll create a special mould with a waterleaf design. 250 Words. 2004.

pp040527
Understanding What Is and Imagining What Can Be
Printmaking in the 21st Century
A slogan on the stationary from the university where he used to teach has this professor thinking about the history of his domain of expertise: Printmaking. He understands what is its history is and the promise of printmaking, and imagines what it can be. 1152 Words. 2004.

pp040706
Time to Restore
Visualizing my new school
Now, almost twenty years after leaving the UW, the author looks back at a trail of failed attempts to start a center. The off-campus world is less forgiving and secure than the life he had at the UW but the real world is richer in actual-life experiences. 567 Words. 2004.

pp040716
The Mini Halfwood Press at Perfect Press
Visualizing what it can become
He has designed, and had built, a press for his studio on his make-believe island of Perfect Press in his fantasy region of Emeralda. His helper created an original, one-of-a-kind miniature of the press that actually works. Daily he envisions what can be. 811 Words. 2004.

pp040726
Sparking the Online Etching Club
A novel approach to learning printmaking
The author's short brainstorming session focusing on how a little press-which he will help design and manufacture-is the centerpiece for a hybrid online learning club called an Etching Club. He plans to continue his role as a team teacher in this project. 458 Words. 2004.

pp040805
How the Mini Halfwood Press Connects With Emeralda
Connecting a passion with a means
His passion and his lifework is a game he calls Emeralda. He is thinking he has found the means for creating a business based on "minis" he conceived and they are all related. This includes his mini-demos, a mini-press, and a mini plate-publishing scheme. 803 Words. 2004.

pp040815
My Leaping and Crawling Imagination
Adapting Stamps 'N Stories to higher education
Because this artist/teacher believes education, as in the fourfold nature of higher education, is the only viable occupation for him, then whatever is worth doing is, of necessity, a thing of an educational kind. Artists Stamps can characterize this mode. 1046 Words. 2004.

pp040825
A letter to 2000 colleges

Proposing online printmaking to colleges
The academic year is about to begin in most schools in the country. Many of these are experiencing a reduction in course offerings in printmaking-this artist/teacher's domain-of-expertise. Therefore he composes a novel proposal to college art departments. 289 Words. 2004.

pp040825b
Fantasy of A Future Student
Making Distance Learning Happen
Distance learning has been on this professor's mind for years, and it seems his vision is becoming reality. There's more today about distance learning than there used to be but arts are still lagging behind. This is a made-up narrative of how it could be. 599 Words. 2004.

pp040825c
Her Proposal
A fantasy student plan
In connection with an article titled Fantasy of A Future Student, the author-who wants to teach printmaking partly on line-creates a fictional course proposal. He tries to imagine what a student would want to learn about printmaking, his favorite art form. 446 Words. 2004.

pp040825d
If Daniel Could Enroll Right Now
Thoughts on higher education for today's candidate for a Masters
Reflecting on email he has been getting from a man who wants to complete his bachelor's degree using online education, the author-a former professor with ideas of his own regarding what online art education might entail-recounts and ponders the exchanges. 720 Words. 2004.

pp040825e
Would You Take This Teacher?
Walking the talk at sixty-two
In some nineteen years he was at the UW art school he taught approximately 2000 students in a variety of courses, from basic drawing and design to graduate seminars. He got a reputation for being ahead of his time, a kind of visionary. Would you take him? 549 Words. 2004.

pp040825f
What is Different About A Distance Learning Printmaking
Five points to consider
A professor of printmaking, bridging traditional printmaking and new technologies of the 21st Centuries, spells out his five major points to consider in designing a printmaking curriculum for online dissemination. His plan expands students' consciousness. 461 Words. 2004.

pp040904
Challenge of Video Dig Reloaded
Sustaining a legacy
As he makes his annual review of the videotape archives he stores in his basement, the old professor compares the slow decay of the videos to the slow rising level of carbon dioxide in the Earth's atmosphere. Sustainability is his goal. Can we achieve it? 435 Words. 2004.

pp040914
My Yearning for Learning ePortfolios
State of an art
Reading an article about ePortfolios, this Itinerate Professor feels a yearning to be learning what, if any, action is being taken in his community of expertise, which is the visual arts. He's working on an ePortfolio of sorts and wonders if anyone cares. 1219 Words. 2004.

pp041024
My Unique Place
Understanding Emeralda and the man who made it
He catches sight of himself in the lines of very different readings: a newsletter from a teachers' retirement fund; another is a scathing critique of American education and the third is a local artists' club newsletter he saw online. Where does he fit in? 1180 Words. 2004.

pp050108
Thinking about Rolf
A Most Influential Print Maker
There is a print in the making that is part of a portfolio of artworks made by people who have in mind artists who were influential for them. This artist writes about Rolf Nesch while starting a print in homage to the man with whom he worked 36 years ago. 1281 Words. 2005.

pp050118
Man, Art, and Machine
Taking Back Art in the Age of Digital Reproduction
To this artist the printmaking medium is really a performance art and not a means to make works of art only. In the age of digital reproduction, what is left for the artist to do when image making has become the domain of machines and mechanical thinking? 798 Words. 2005.

pp050128
Printmaking Condo
A Vision
While printing one day, and bemoaning the fact he's alone, this artist—a printmaker—has a vision of a condominium devoted to printmaking. It is to be where all the homeowners are sharing in a project that keeps their art, craft and design tradition alive. 605 Words. 2005.

pp050207
Seattle Artist Trading Cards
Posting Notes
This artist has volunteered to be the organizer of meetings each month for artists, crafts people and designers making Artist Trading Cards—playing-card size works of art that are only traded and never sold. He made notes the day after the first

"meetup". 756 Words. 2005.

pp050217
Revisiting Retirement
Sharing One Art Professor's Story
He wrote an article about his approach to retirement, saying artists don't retire, they retread the path of their early years. In this article he takes another perspective, which is an attempt to share his story with other former professors. 1918 Words. 2005.

pp050309
Swing of A Golf Club
Launch of An Idea
Someone asked the author/artist what he does instead of goofing off on a golf course, and he answers that he does goof off, but not on a real golf course. Instead, he has created an imaginary "course" and events, standing like flags, are really happening. 805 Words. 2005.

pp050329
Another ATC Idea
Serving the Owners of Mini Halfwood Presses
Browsing the Web for the latest developments in Artist Trading Card news, the author comes across a site with artist-of-the month, a society for ATC. He thinks of his own "society" of Mini Halfwood Press owners, and how he can serve them with ATC support. 572 Words. 2005.

pp050418
Researching Directions for Artists and Community
Roads Media Artists May Follow
Many questions are raised by events in this artist's life. What to do about the Artist Trading Card? What about community arts? What's the connection between artists and trees in the age of digital reproduction? And techniques? We need to do the research. 530 Words. 2005.

pp050508
The Time Capsule Project
A Park-Sustaining Plan
Although he's an artist, he also gets ideas about public parks. Not as you might think, such as putting a sculpture in the park, but as a creative person who thinks of a more fundamental application of creativity. That is, raising money for park stewards. 1289 Words. 2005.

pp050607
Parks Game
A Game for A Park about Time
As he surveys the ideas going on in his head, this artist (who calls himself a game inventor) comes across possible links among cards, stamps, medals and other of his printmaking-related playing-pieces and a fundraiser for a park. Is there a game in this? 611 Words. 2005.

pp050627
Imagining A Day in A Park About Time

Pocket Park
This artist wants to be of the present century—the 21st Century—and not be an artifact of the 19th and 20th Century. He focuses on a little city park that is going to be built not far from his home and studio. He says there are five crises to think about. 1220 Words. 2005.

pp050707
How I Started Emeralda
A Copy-Written Essay on the Genesis of An Imaginary Place
Did this artist, a one-time professor who now wants to build a virtual, virtuous world he calls Emeralda, actually steal ideas from another professor? The parallels with the published author's work are suspiciously strong and are evident from this example. 1389 Words. 2005.

pp050727
The Art of Selling Emeralda
Games for the gifts of life you didn't know about
It seems more frequent of late that this artist—who wants to be a video game designer—finds himself trying to sell other people in his domain-of-expertise on the idea of a game that they too could play. He recounts these and puts them in a "selling" mode. 665 Words. 2005.

pp050806
Calendar Game
A Game for the Third Force
Every vigilant to find some way to enter the game world, this artist (and a former professor, which explains his academic bent) contemplates how a calendar might serve as a kind of card, like in Bingo, with all the days marked with unique artists' stamps. 765 Words. 2005.

pp050826
What A Magazine Can Do in the Age of Digital Reproduction
Considerations of A Third Force Agent
Responding to an invitation from a quarterly journal devoted to retirement finance, this retired art professor observes that in the hundred years since the inception of the retirement program a change has occurred, opening up new lives with a third force. 1390 Words. 2005.

pp050915
In My Most Recent Work
Artists Statement for pa050002
During a time when he started a painting, he happened across another artist's statement on her Web page that sounded amazingly like his own thinking. It inspired him to "copy-write" over her words for fun, resulting in a good lesson and his own statement. 1596 Words. 2005.

pp051005
So Much Future, So Little Past
Reflecting on A Lunch with C T Chew
He had lunch with an old friend and cohort and thinks about what they talked about. At one point

he recalls one of them saying "There's so much future," and the response, ". . . and so little past." But the future has elements of the pat, or so he thinks. 916 Words. 2005.

pp051015
Persistent World of Emeralda
Searching for the Portal
If Emeralda: Games for the Gifts of Life is to become a true game and true to its inventor's intent then it must be as persistent to other peoples' minds as it is to its inventor's mind. This artist shows the way to art in the age of digital reproduction. 662 Words. 2005.

pp051025
Instructions to the Home School Teacher
Part I: How EtchingIT Got its Name
It occurs to the developer of EtchingIT—a kit for learning and teaching etching designed for home school—that the person who teaches must be provided with instruction in order to learn intaglio printmaking. Here the developer makes an initial exploration. 1289 Words. 2005.

pp051104
A Russian Visitor
Considering A Way to Take Emeralda Global
A phone call from a Russian artist visiting the US sets this artist's mind on the difference between where he is in time and space compared to his Moscow counterpart. How much better things would be, he writes in this essay, if they were playing Emeralda. 1059 Words. 2005.

pp051114
IT Begins with a Stamp
Toward An International Gallery of Little Prints
On the heels of a demonstration he gave on the craft of making artist's stamps and playing cards using old and new etching techniques, the artist/teacher considers how an International game can be played with the miniature print using his miniature press. 463 Words. 2005.

pp051124
How to Make A Mini Halfwood
Making it the Key in Emeralda Play
He is a craftsman who builds the wood base for a miniature etching press he named the Mini Halfwood Press. While he works on the parts for these bases—they're like handcrafted furniture really—he thinks about the future use of a video on how he does this. 700 Words. 2005.

pp051204
Lessons Included
Adding Value by Connecting Computers to the Press
The sale of the 17th Mini Halfwood Press brings to the mind of its maker an idea for adding value to the press. He will provide 3 hours of lessons in making and printing intaglio plates. The 17th owner inspired this idea when she requested lessons before. 814 Words. 2005.

pp051219
Four Steps
A Way of Looking
Considering how to combine the lessons of printmaking with a printmaking press, the author—who has designed and sells miniature printing presses for palm-sized prints—he takes another look at his computer file structure, thinking this is the way to do it. 359 Words. 2005.

pp051229
Master and Inventor
An Artist Who Would Play A Game of his Own Devices
Concomitant with what this artist envisions as a Treasure Chest full of what's best in his life in printmaking, he also envisions himself in a fantasyland he calls Emeralda. There he's the Master and the Inventor of games that celebrate the gifts of life. 443 Words. 2005.

pp051230
Thinking about Trumba
Calendars in the 20th Century
Looking ahead to a game that artists can play with time and space, this artist considers the contrast between 20th Century and 21st Century software design. He thinks the former relies on traditional print media, the latter relies on virtual event-drives. 458 Words. 2005.

pp060108
A CD for the Mini Halfwood Press
Getting Started
For two years this artist has been crafting an etching press made of steel and wood that he calls the Halfwood Press. Starting the third year of developing it, he plans to make a CD/ROM that people can use as for instruction and inspiration to go with it. 875 Words. 2006.

pp060118
Writing and Reading About One's Time-Locked Self
Emeralda Play and Self-Knowledge and Self-Liberation
Robert Grudin provides substance for thought and breaks the logjam of a writer's block. The professor describes de Montaigne as the first writer to record his routine activities in detail, and this artist is mindful that his blogging practice is the same. 507 Words. 2006.

pp060502
Auction Book
Visualize This
This artist is thinking about a novel combination of art auction and theatrical event in which works of art are created on stage and then auctioned moments later. Every auction needs a book, however, and this is an added bonus. He uses himself as a model. 710 Words. 2006.

pp060528

Printmaking Seminars
How Distance Learning and Games Work Together
After years of dwelling on the question, "How would you teach printmaking in a hybrid course?" this professor of printmaking believes he has moved closer to the answer he is searching for—a combination of trading cards and periodic play-offs for game play. 414 Words. 2006.

pp060627
CWALS
Some of the Elements
At the CWALS, the main hall is given to a play auction every week. Residents-in-stay work on it constantly. 1909 Words. 2006.

pp060707
Buy Me
Advance Leadership School Support
Buy a piece of this building, and you buy time for your children and grandchildren. Converting the Old Hospital into an Advanced Leadership School, you are sending a strong signal to your families that you believe older Americans care about their future. 840 Words. 2006.

pp060708
Visit to CWALS
Tour Announcement
Tuesday we're going to CWALS for a visit, so be sure to bring your cams. 77 Words. 2006.

pp060717
The Story of Dusty
Getting Started July 17, 2006.
What he remembers is riding his bicycle, something hit him. He swiped at it and lost his balance. He has a scar on his forehead from hitting the edge of the sidewalk. He was out quite a while, and he never felt right about things when he came to. 631 Words. 2006.

pp060717b
Making Myself Clear
Asset Management and Legacy Transfer
The Old Hospital occupants are owners of the building, and they are studying asset management and legacy transfer. Those are technical words that this article clarifies them, by using the author/artist and other artists as examples. 1073 Words. 2006.

pp060718
A Most Fantastic Auction/Play
Remembering Sarah
And the wheel goes around and around and stops on MI328rit! The image flashes on the screen and the audience waits until the decision is made whether to go straight or to the Art Action mode! 255 Words. 2006.

pp060718b
CWALS Q&A
Frequently Asked Questions

Frequently asked questions concerning CWALS, CWU and Sarah Spurgeon Art Gallery. 624 Words. 2006.

pp060727
Patenting Art Auction Play
Method of Play in the Art Auction Game
It's a software invention, actually, a "method of play" in the same sense that WOTC patented the method of playing Magic: The Gathering. 266 Words. 2006.

pp060816
Bean Hills
Finding Personal Worth
The author became worth many hills of beans, a whole mountain of beans. This he knows to be true. He is thinking of Tojo Thatchenkerry and Carol Metzker's book, Appreciative Intelligence. 1034 Words. 2006.

pp060816b
Things I Want to Do
In Seattle and In Ellensburg
Before you can succeed in doing these things, you have to frame yourself as being the one who can. Make art gallery, "Little Prints I", make art gallery, "Little Prints II". 188 Words. 2006.

pp060905
Finding Your Team
Dilemma
The problem is, the purpose of this writing is for art education online, and the metaphor for the form that this effort takes is games. The author stands between the game narrative writer and the game developer. 411 Words. 2006.

pp061015
Stranger in Time
Restoring Mechanical Reproductions
The hero will try to restore what was lost in the age of mechanical reproduction by restoring unity of the artist with new media. 859 Words. 2006.

pp061025
Remember When?
Business Proposition
We sell intaglio tools, including the lessons and customer support. Already we have a significant item for our product line—the Mini Halfwood Press. 164 Words. 2006.

pp061025b
They Gave Me A Tough Assignment
Writing the Code of Online Education
Creating a teaching game that people could play using their computers together with a little etching press. Similar to what you learn about economics while playing Monopoly, or general knowledge while playing Cranium. 817 Words. 2006.

pp061104
Cyberlayer
A New Layer of Craft in Writing

Some people refer to this new experience with words like literacy and interactivity. It is something that needs to be addressed by writing teachers. 460 Words. 2006.

pp061104b
If I Taught Again
Why Spreadsheets, Writing, Images and Multimedia are Important
The aim would be what the author calls developing human structural intellectual capital, and it would be for the purpose of the Artist's Last Love Letter. 599 Words. 2006.

pp061214
My Beautiful Little Prints Us
New Shop at 500 Mercer
The author's dream is a shop in the now new 500 Mercer project. 93 Words. 2006.

pp070108
Beauty in My Eye
Fringe Benefits of the Etching Craft
The author is working on a plate for a weekend of printing at the Seattle Print Fair. As he works, he thinks of the beauty of the copper, the black stop-out varnish, the glistening of the aquatint. 309 Words. 2007.

pp070218
New Day Coming
Coming Back to the UW School of Art
The dream has many small plot twists, but the story arc is always the same: the author returns to the UW School of Art after being absent for some period of time. He is like a ghost coming to haunt the place where he spent nineteen years. 2198 Words. 2007.

pp070607
Perfect Press – 9th Day
MOVE TEXT
   MOVED TEXT
36 Words. 2007.

pp070915
Will the Real Harris Sweed Please Stand Up
A Co-Writer Examined
An incidental visitor, offering online services, makes a remark to the artist: "You should show." From this, and also the idea of an imaginary co-author for a book he's working on, inspires him to search his archives for clues on how to show at this time. 477 Words. 2007.

pp070925
Rich Artist, Poor Artist
Game-Based Economic Lessons for Artists and Their Families
Inspired by the book titled Rich Dad, Poor Dad, by Robert Kiyosaki, this "rich artist" thinks about a book and a game combined that teaches artists and their families how to value their life work. It is a game using cards and describes winners and losers. 763 Words. 2007.

pp071005
Nine Easy Pieces
Game Pieces and ArtGrid Cells
Working on his ArtGrid cards, he recalls games about assets and he then remembers that they all use little game pieces. He sorts through the conventions of games he has known, and recalls the early days of his invention. He needs ten pieces— or is it nine?267 Words. 2007.

pp071005b
Rolf Nesch Edition
The Cards
In designing the Rolf Nesch Edition of Mini Halfwood Presses the artist lays out an aspect of the project called The Cards. He describes a set of 50 printing plates that come with the press as test plates—all with the artist's portrait of Nesch etched in. 212 Words. 2007.

pp071015
Collections
What are They about?
What kinds of collections can you create in Emeralda play? 975 Words. 2007.

pp071025
Elements of the Game
Building A Path as You Follow it
As he clips the corners of a sheet of cards for Emeralda, he inventories the elements that he thinks are important bases for the method of play. He lists collecting, utility, digital based learning, and risk. Concurrently he's inventing the game itself. 1544 Words. 2007.

pp071114
Life Box Jumbled
So Many Pieces to Put Together
Comparing a life to a picture puzzle, this artist— who also earned the title of professor at an early stage in his life—says that his life picture is incomplete, but he has the elements in his imagination picturing a teaching media artist with years to go. 1124 Words. 2007.

pp071124
Payoff
How and Why of Emeralda Play
On his way to a store one morning to buy some wood-crafting tools, the inventor of Emeralda stops at his studio to jot down some thought about the payoff of Emeralda—or the lack of a payoff— and in this way thinks he might explain what the real payoff is. 810 Words. 2007.

pp071204
Emeralda Reconsidered
Investment Clubber's Pastime
A specialized investment club, based on the need to learn the ins and outs of new technologies that were changing the way artists relate to society. 972 Words. 2007.

pp071204b
MAD Complexity
Complicity with A Comic Book Artist
To create a collectible Artist Trading Card game he has to find the connection between ATC and the CD/ROM version of this part of the Emeralda Suite. As he searches for the tree structure of this version, he recalls of his boyhood love of MAD comic books. 296 Words. 2007.

pp071219
Perfect Card
Making Betty's Card Work
It's appropriate in the Perfect Press domain the inventor of a collectible artist's trading card game that he would consider the perfect card. A card with both a physical existence and a virtual existence—like those cards in the game Bella Sera. 690 Words. 2007.

pp071229
Significance of Cell Two
Artist Trading Card Version of Emeralda
After a session with David Lotz—who is on the board of advisors for Emeralda Property Development—Cell Number Two, on this year's Artist Trading Card version of Emeralda, becomes the focus for today's essay. 754 Words. 2007.

pp080107
What is the Use of XML?
Extendable Markup Language
Learning steps about XML 106 Words. 2008.

pp080108
Rewriting His Story
Recursive Gaming and Autobiography
Structured intellectual capital has the potential of becoming tangible capital. This is true in the life of anyone in the precarious professions of art, writing, musical composition, etc. New technologies make it feasible—it can even be fun—and game-like. 593 Words. 2008.

pp080128
Potential Studio
Never A Blue Monday
The artist is approaching seventy, yet he feels like a little boy and animating the things in his studio when he opens the door and turns on the lights. He thinks of all things as being like freshly charged batteries, full of potential to become artworks. 483 Words. 2008.

pp080217
Buying Rights
Art Assurance
After witnessing the dynamics of an art auction where the value of an artist's name has reached extraordinary heights, the artist proceeds to offer another artwork by a renowned artist—Jacob Lawrence. Upon reflection he discovers that he must demand more. 1077 Words. 2008.

pp080227

Useless Art
Objects in A Game
Midway through his daily routine of adding to the rules of a game he wants to invent, it occurs to him that a certain object—a covered stoneware mug—is really quite useless, but then the objects in games are merely tokens. Yet they have hidden potentials. 865 Words. 2008.

pp080308
Marketing Bill
Marketing Family's Art Collection
The book titled "Die Broke" comes to mind when the author thinks about marketing his family's art collection. There is no book like "Die Broke" for artists and their families when it comes to fairly distributing the artist's wealth. 1010 Words. 2008.

pp080318
Touch of Stone
Comparing Lithography Methods
The author, a printmaker, describes what, from his past experience, is the difference among the different methods of making fine art lithographs. He suggests that working the antiquated limestone slabs cause in him special sensual and emotional responses. 2077 Words. 2008.

pp080328
Art Manager
The Martian Way
Considering the conventions of art management professions that were developed over the course of the past 500 years, it's no wonder the description of the art manager's task in an age of digital reproduction will seem as if they came from Mars, not Earth. 398 Words. 2008.

pp080407
Note
Access Findings
Learning Access, reports matching the cards, perhaps. 101 Words. 2008.

pp080427
Online Demonstration
A Grandfather's Online Printmaking Explained
Having mailed to his Alma Mater his proposal to teach printmaking online, a former professor envisions the next step, which might happen that he'll be called out to demonstrate how his plan will work in real life. He reflects on how he reached this stage. 1090 Words. 2008.

pp080507
Theoretical Framework
Pioneer Printmaking Course of Study
As a student in this course, you are doing some pioneering work. You are pioneering in what many college professors see as an experiment, not a course of study. 243 Words. 2008.

pp080517
Collaborating Partners
Achieving Sustainability in the Art Teacher and Student Lifetime

What students don't realize is they are part of the teacher's life. Teachers and students are like collaborating partners in education. 253 Words. 2008.

pp080527
Function
C2 is How
List of Processes the Business Performs is the heading of Cell C2. Its subheading is Function = Class of Business Process. 311 Words. 2008.

pp080527b
Roles of Data in the Functioning Enterprise
B7 is How Data Figures in Functionality of Emeralda
List of Processes the Business Performs is the heading of Cell B7. Its subheading is Function = Class of Business Process. 324 Words. 2008.

pp080528
Business Process Model
A Dream about Asset Management and Legacy Transfer
The author wanted to explain his game plan. In his dream he was able to make a succinct statement as to the main objective of his game. 1541 Words. 2008.

pp080606
Networking Functional Enterprise
Cell D7 in the Enterprise Row - the Bottom Line
With each weekly meeting, players exchange, receive or give another, or others—depending on the number of committed players—a copy of the current state of their Zach Man! Grid. 397 Words. 2008.

pp080616
My Favorite Movie
Escaping the Spanish Seaport
The ship sails under a false name, with false papers. The crew is a mixture of Jacks-of-all trades. They are on the run. If they are caught, they will be tortured and killed. 3071 Words. 2008.

pp080616b
Time According to Zach Man!
Time is the Essence
To address the When in enterprise architecture, a framework for a life assurance policy for hope, time is of the essence. This column, in the John Zachman chart shall deal with timing as a critical element in the economics of the enterprise. 247 Words. 2008.

pp080626
Business Rule Model
Order into Creativity and Practical Applications
The designer's row in the John Zachman array of cells requires that they bring order into the chaos of creativity and practical applications. 926 Words. 2008.

pp080706

Emeralda Works
Functioning Enterprise
Learning printmaking in the 21st Century needs a student/faculty user interface in the language of art in the age of digital reproduction. The author is making up a game for himself to understand John Zachman's architecture for a functioning organization. 517 Words. 2008.

pp080726
Purpose in Learning Printmaking Online
The Four Elements
The author calls these four by the acronym, TRPS: Teaching (and Learning as a complementary pair), Research, Production (also known as Practice), and Service. 354 Words. 2008.

pp080726b
Emeralda Q&A
Expected Questions
If meeting a group of game designers, what would be questions you would expect? 350 Words. 2008.

pp080805
Small Beginnings
Soul of Emeralda Lite
The notion of a game-let, a part of a larger game, is a small beginning for Emeralda: Games for the Gifts of Life. Conceived as a digital game-based learning experience for students and faculty of fine art printmaking, this inventor offers the basic idea. 1000 Words. 2008.

pp080817
Getting There
List of Five Models of Halfwood Etching Press
Exploring the market of the Halfwood Etching Press models over a 7 year plan. 80 Words. 2008.

pp081103
Patent Revisited
Can I patent Emeralda?
The video game that merges seamlessly from virtual, online play to actual or physical hand printmaking is an invention and would qualify for a process patent. 537 Words. 2008.

pp081113
Steps to Convert Articles to Access Database
Encoding Writings in Emeralda
In Emeralda, the game includes a resource of the professor's writings going back many years. The purpose is to give the player insight into the mentor's thinking. To make this access possible, text must be encoded into the game so the entries may be read. 348 Words. 2008.

pp090108
Children's Department in Emeralda
Developing a niche in Emeralda Communiversity
Studying a new book on digital storytelling—a book he hopes will help in the creation of a game interface for an online printmaking course—he comes to a section on children's games, the subject recalls art he made in past years, causing him to

question it 940 Words. 2009.

pp090118
Exercise in Premises
Considering the possibilities for projects in a community of practice
Reading one of the books in his assignments, the inventor of Emeralda: Games for the Gifts of Life is asked to consider the premises of his games. He comes up with one for a smart toy press, and another for the Learn Printmaking Online game he's planning. 220 Words. 2009.

pp090128
ELPO Rewards and Consequences
What can happen to you if you fail or you win
The ninth essay on the ten points in a game development checklist. The original list came from the first edition of a book. In a new edition, the author mixed up the points. What fun! The game inventor writing this feels like he is in an inquisition game. 1009 Words. 2009.

pp090207
Not Just Another Day
A Life of a Mentor
How the mentor would begin his day on the island of Perfect Press would be of little or no interest to anyone outside of the small, inner circle of mentors, and even in this, only a few would be willing to interrupt their own important concerns to listen. 1388 Words. 2009.

pp090217
ELPO User Engagement
Tar Baby effect and learning printmaking online
A term known as the "Tar Baby Effect" came when I first began attending strategic planning meetings that were held for people in the digital technologies. How do we get users to habituate and to make people stay with us in a difficult learning experience? 1417 Words. 2009.

pp090329
Concurrent Engineering of ELPO
How concurrent engineering works in Emeralda: Learn Printmaking
Once the author read an article about the way in which the Boeing 777 was designed by integrating all aspects of engineering and manufacturing (CAD/CAM) plus marketing and sales. That idea rang a bell as he conceived of his art game for distance learning. 1847 Words. 2009.

pp090408
Samuel Richardson Profile
Character description of a disillusioned printmaker in the novel, "Hunt .
Young people, once enamored with printing and eager to become printmaking artists became embittered and their art denigrated the virtues they wanted to achieve. As they matured, they found things that restored their hope—realizing the value of their past. 516 Words. 2009.

pp090418
David and Goalitis
Goals and roles for David in Emeralda land
It started out to be an assessment of David Lotz' value to the company, Emeralda Works, as related to Lynda's share in this family business. After a year of living dangerously as Family Administrator, there are still critical decisions in roles and goals. 1162 Words. 2009.

pp090508
Millionaire Printmakers
Next generation printmakers in the age of digital reproduction
Social networking is the new buzzword on the Net, with sites like FaceBook, MySpace and the virtual world, Second Life attracting millions and billions of people. Millionaire printmakers is an idea to get the attention of printmakers who agree their art I 992 Words. 2009.

pp090518
ELPO Bible Online
Sharing the load with ELPO Developers
He started writing a compendium of facts about Emeralda: Learn Printmaking Online after the model used by video game developers so people in the ELPO community of inquiry/production can participate readily. In this essay he suggests more ways to share it. 1115 Words. 2009.

pp090528
Great Expectations Again
Cooperative business models in health care and art education
He started a blog a year ago to experiment with a way to publish his essays. Curious as to what he was thinking and writing about ten years ago, he found it to be about his interest in the cooperative model for a health workers' co-op named DENTALISCO. 913 Words. 2009.

pp090607
More Millionaire Printmakers
Catchy title for a new printmaker's cooperative
This artist, after decades as a printmaking professor before the college programs were scheduled for deconstruction, dreamt of an international printmaker cooperative built around a principle called "Small is Beautiful: Printmaking as if people mattered." 1054 Words. 2009.

pp091015
Printmaking Camp
Thinking of ways to build community
The author retired from conventional college printmaking teaching almost 25 years ago, but he's still interested in the field. Once he dreamed of a unified theory of media arts, but the dream has not been actualized. A printmaking camp might show how now. 961 Words. 2009.

pp091204
Artist Stamp Collecting Part 2
Continuation of Part 1

This article is about the access to the new world of stamp collecting with the computers and the Internet. It covers the art stamps that were at first created in the spirit of play and curiosity. The author writes about C.T. Chew and his experimentations. 976 Words. 2009.

pp091219
Opening Day
First day—again
In ten days upon beginning the 360-day cycle of a Year-of-Living-Copiously (the imaginary Gates Prize), Residents-in-Stay (prize winners) must write the nature of the island (Domain-of-Expertise). This is the entry for Perfect Press, or Printmaker's Isle. 541 Words. 2009.

pp091229
Another Back Story
The ongoing search for the story of the Halfwood Press
He's written so many back stories for his intended game he's losing count. Each time a new audience for learning printmaking online appears, with a unique computer game (or board game, collectible card game, etc.) at its core, a new story comes to his min 741 Words. 2009.

Ritchie's Perfect Studios (AKA PerfStud, or, PS)

Perfect Studios at approximately 9 PM on day in June, seen from the east side from the ferry boat.

Perfect Studios is governed by a meritocracy focused on practice management for individual artists, crafts people and designers, dedicated to the value of Human Structural Intellectual Capital (HSIC) and legacy transfer.

Perfect Studios is the birthplace of Emeralda's culture because it was in the domain of asset management and legacy transfer that the ideal that an artist's life is an enriching combination of teaching and learning, research, practice and production, and service.

This philosophy is manifest at Perfect Studios in the form of using sophisticated technical methods to document, store, retrieve and update artistic and educational contributions to the community's cultural life and in this way to optimize the merit of their creators.

A typical activity at Perfect Studios is restoration of artists' histories as they intertwines the lives of the individuals who patronize them. They work toward a persistent relationship by means of new communications and information technologies. A Web page, for example, is given to every individual who owns a tangible, original work by an Emeralda Resident-in-Stay.

ps700615
The Story of George's Art
Part 1
Original text of the way the author began the background fantasy story of his lifework. It is entered verbatim as part of his 2000-2003 In Retro project, a self-made retrospective of his 40-years in arts and teaching. He uses it to plan his next 40 years. 389 Words. 1970.

ps790926
Journal Entry, Wed. Sep. 26, 1979
Discouraged Professor
The author writes about his frustration and discouragement about the art school's lack of support for the printmaking program. He was troubled by grad students wanting him to be their graduate faculty member and teacher. 467 Words. 1976.

ps840212
Perfect Studios Defined
Philosophy and Speculation
The idea of a Perfect Studio occurs to many artists. The dream of the perfect studio finds a model in an account of a Chinese printing business that operated centuries ago, where printing craft was balanced with publishing on the subject of art processes. 762 Words. 1984.

ps840915
Journal Entry, Sat. Sep. 15, 1984
Universities Newsletters and Fear of Failure
The author reflects about reading newsletters of U.W. and U.O., realizing that the idea of University Art School is/was a dream. He discusses business and art. Later he writes about his fear of failure and being able to afford teaching at the U. 918 Words. 1984.

ps850615
Ritchie's Former Students
Ten years after
Why does a professor keep the names of his former students? This version of a database, reformatted more than fifteen years after he left campus teaching, makes the teacher wonder! And is it safe in this litigious age? An attorney may ask, "Show me harm." 2961 Words. 1985.

ps880109
Journal Entry, Sat. Jan. 9, 1988

Goals, Broadness & Bigness
This is from the author's GoalBook1. He writes,
"You will succeed in your goals of "working," i.e.,
all moving parts in motion, because of the diversity of your offering." He continues with an example
of cultivating area markets from Tacoma to Bell-
ingham. 278 Words. 1988.

ps891016
Square One Thinking
Education of the arts marketplace
Thinking about the goals of Ritchie's Perfect Studios, and the basis for forming Ritchie's, Inc.,
Bill Ritchie has a dream and is inspired to write
about the connection between quality of ongoing
support and the navigator Metaphor. 600 Words.
1989.

ps900325
Reinventing the Studio
Your Inner Kairetsu
Practice management for individual creatives
has parallels with practice management of medical and dental professionals. The Perfect Studios
would be those which provide practice management. 2446 Words. 1990.

ps900412
Why Incorporate Ritchie's Inc?
The artist-intrapraneur ponders the question
Tax structure, business plan, financing, safe-keep-
ing - there are many reasons to consider incorporating if you are an artist to whom money is not
everything but to whom art's effectiveness is everything. 1631 Words. 1990.

ps900624
Myth of Riches and Art
Traveling artist's note
A traveling ITinerate Professor's note while driving in southern California. He decides that, despite indications to the contrary, there is money in
art - but not the old way. The information side of
art and technology go together. 358 Words. 1990.

ps901121
Setting the stage with heroes
Notes for long-range goals
The navigator that lives in the artist is like the
steersman living in other people who are deeply committed to their talent and skill. A public
speaker, in this instance, inspired the artist/author
to measure his own progress agains monetary di-
lemmmas. 3000 Words. 1990.

ps910325
Multimedia's Problem
Shifting the paradigm from inside
Outline of a curriculum for a multimedia arts institute involves an extreme paradigm shift. Seen
from the marketing perspective it would follow
that packaging is a major concern, clarifying the
situation as it was in 1991-92. 181 Words. 1991.

ps910523

He didn't die - yet
Prologue to the artist's last love letter
By adapting the conduct of education, business
and professionals in medicine, law, dentistry and
consulting, this author explains how the artists'
legacy can be a valuable family asset, transferrable
to their heirs for financial security. 3407 Words.
1991.

ps910526
The fatal error in the age of Prometheus
Interfere, always interfere
Time becomes palpable when it is in an interference relationship with space. In the age of calculation, how one spends one's time may contain
seeds of fatal errors, actions or ommissions. To
overcome this danger, the author advises the Pro-
methean way. 1098 Words. 1991.

ps910605
Little fixers, experts and closure economics
Shake-down for eco-nomic's sake
Valuation in art, like the value of consultants' time,
is risky business, mainly in terms of the closure
economics we long have trusted. Evolving global
eco-nomics gives us an opportunity to reorganize
our values based on an open economics system.
643 Words. 1991.

ps910613
I saw a tree
A smarter studio based on trees
The tree metaphor is richly rewarding, on any
given day, whether the writer is playing dumb or
smart. For example, he thinks the cross-section
of a tree's trunk (or root, for that matter) shows a
record of the history of the tree's growth, its past.
711 Words. 1991.

ps910825
Valuing Intangible Assets & Intellectual Properties
New deal for artists
Starting with a paraphrase of Stephen J. Kerr's paper, the artist/writer develops a new way to valuate
tangible art work and other collectibles, as well as
intangibles such as artists' essays, writings, teaching methods, videos and software. 3062 Words.
1991.

ps910910
Economic philosophy of the Ten Trees Studio
Reinventing studios and schools
The author traces the path to the eco-nomics that
will be one of the central principles of the reinvented studios for the arts. Development of the
central-principles of Perfect Studios leads toward
the eco-nomics of reinvented arts studios and
schools. 1347 Words. 1991.

ps910918
Perfect Studios
1984-2004 Mission statement
It was clear by 1984 that something was seriously
wrong with the university and not the place where
teaching, research and production could proceed.

That is when I quit and laid out a plan and called it Perfect Studios and started to work that year. 319 Words. 1991.

ps910927
Opportunity amid crisis time
Older professionals rolling their own
There seldom have been more opportunities for mature knowledgeable experts than now. For the next several years a maintenance economy will reign. Those who will prosper in the aftermath of this period must now (1) Publish, (2) Reinvest and (3) Maintain. 299 Words. 1991.

ps911018
Expert for sale
Call your BBS
Proposal for article describing what Bill Ritchie is doing to prepare to sell his expertise. The so-called "expert system" is the computer version of his knowledge, skill and attitude. His early version is supposed to run on a bulleting board service. 79 Words. 1991.

ps911021
Bon Idea
Element of a partnership
What do the Eiffel Tower, the Bon Marche and a professor of computer art have in common? They are three quality circles to increase in market share of downtown retail business, education in the use of computers and develop artistic uses of multi-media. 1507 Words. 1991.

ps911112
Perfect U
Perfect Studios-the Inner Kairetsu
The goal is the Perfect Studios and the means to reach the goal is, first of all, a cooperative agree-ment. The kairetsu model is a good one, but others might be found that suit the changing economic times. 3250 Words. 1991.

ps911207
Commission Advertising
Arts studios' supported in the next decade
Moreso than the fine arts, creative visual expres-sion intended for the media have always been leading style indicators. What this means to the fine artist is new tools for reinvented studios and the economic concepts that come "bundled" with them. 1203 Words. 1991.

ps911210
Searching for the E-Word
Artist Trust is Reviewed
How is Artist Trust, the organization created for artists, craftsmen and designers doing in its edu-cational mission? The author studied its newslet-ter to find out, but could not find much progress with the E-word (education). 772 Words. 1991.

ps911213
Traveling cheap
Never in a dangerous country

Fear reigns in a virtual world where almost every-thing is pure information (unfettered by earthly matter). The eagle-moguls of the industry soar, watching the landscape below for lively bits of information that they can add to their gullet. 628 Words. 1991.

ps911214
Five rules of Perfect Studios
Searching for Central Principles
The author of a trilogy of three books he wants to complete called Perfect Studios, has organized five simple guides that could stand as central princi-ples of the nature of economics for Perfect Studios. 163 Words. 1991.

ps911215
Your after-school money
The wrong investment
If you sent money to the alumni fund at your art school, or non-profit art organizations, museums, the odds are that you put your after-college grad-uation money in the wrong place. This article ex-plains what, at this crucial time, you can do differ-ently. 1819 Words. 1991.

ps920103
Where's the teacher when we need him?
A guild of former students knows
How about Former Students in Business and Pro-fessions as a marketing and sales group aimed at higher education arts? FSBP is taking on a new direction - that of an investment club. The theme is "Was it worth it?" - speaking of the art school years. 1510 Words. 1992.

ps920107
Cityland in Paintbrush
Portrait of a museum of the future
This might be a rough draft for another article; it has the appearance of a diary or a key-by-key record of a morning in the Perfect Studio, or, as this author refers to his muse, it was written by the woman who fell to earth. 584 Words. 1992.

ps920108
Pet project
Angling for an angel
How chief officers' arts, craft and design pets to bridge their business and creative, personal views with an emphasis on the human side of technolo-gy industries. The column would add a proactive, forecast quality kind of value to a magazine. 1084 Words. 1992.

ps920118
The buyer-broker
A new deal for creatives
Using the real-estate model, a buyer/broker works for the buyer. For creative digital artists and writ-ers wanting to sell intangible estate properties, buyer-brokers suit the emerging electronic pub-lishing industry. Seven pages of research append-ed. 6257 Words. 1992.

ps920131
Windows on the Art World
A better view
Similar to the way science is depicted, e.g., Frankenstein, the mad scientist, Back to the Future, art is depicted erroneously, too. Outwardly, they match the actual appearance of laboratories and studios, but content is shaped behind a curtain. Proposal. 128 Words. 1992.

ps920211
Flow of markets
Solving riddles
Reinventing arts studios is a process of writing, business and art. The course includes forming a corporation, and learning to think like an entrepreneur, yet redefining basic premises creatively. 822 Words. 1992.

ps920219
Apple and Orange
Complaint about GUI look-alike litigation
Lawsuits regarding the graphical user interface infringements inspired an artist to write this spontaneous, unsolicited and defensive essay. Expert intuitive electronic artists may show the difference better than products of other work places. 3133 Words. 1992.

ps920324
The new siren
Computer conundrum
Voyagers in the 'nineties, metaphorically speaking, are attracted to the siren songs of computer advocates. Claims of higher productivity, speed, beauty and competitive edge drown the sense and use of intuition and skills of people who should know better. 684 Words. 1992.

ps920325
Skills urged for art teachers
Fitness for the third millennium
How do artists, craftspeople and designers learn skills with new technologies while surviving the daily routine? The answer lies in building bridges between the generation with deep experience and that of the incoming learners, the arts/tech students. 2585 Words. 1992.

ps920404
Tour of Ritchie's Perfect Studios Tree
Guide to a smarter studio
The writing results from intuitive thinking while trying to imagine this studio on a disc, a smarter studio, as described in the business plan. The trick is to be able to describe it in the terms of the medium and the time it was conceived on computers. 2945 Words. 1992.

ps920409
Disk-keeping
Electronic studio chore
The day finally comes when somebody has to dispose of a lifetime of work. In the reinvented arts studio-on-a-disk drive, you avoid waste of creative talent with some new habits. The design of disk-keeping is elegant but demanding. 367 Words. 1992.

ps920410
Medium-of-Origin
Making Original Original
Medium-of-origin is defined by media's relations to printing. In digital arts, a studio-on-a-desktop has galleries as show rooms where Medium-of-origin art, or MOO works, are shown. This article suggests what to answer, if you are asked, What is MOO? 1446 Words. 1992.

ps920415
Marketing with Multimedia
The CRU Example
A guide to the creation of a marketing and sales diskette. This article serves to establish the limits set by the author, Bill Ritchie, about the first pages of a marketing and sales diskette for Certified Resources Unlimited, a temporary talent bureau. 1626 Words. 1992.

ps920420
Bean-counter
Maligned groups arise!
Scanning electronic bulletin boards for trends, vectors of entities, directions, and forces carried and probable outcomes, bean counters are gaining respect. In the age of the illusion of calculation he or she is the vice regent to the new meritocrat. 1538 Words. 1992.

ps920426
Masters and fools
Being your own B.O.S.S.
Possibly the information age will see the revision of the old addage to Who seeks a Master is a Fool. This article follows years of experimenting with a tool called by its manufacturer, the B.O.S.S., a palm-top electronic notebook similar to a computer. 1087 Words. 1992.

ps920506
Confessions of a closet economist
Know enough to get in trouble
Talk about economic trends and famous economic theorists pique the information technology person's interest if he or she can connect it with getting a job doing what they most love to do: Play with high-tech toys. 980 Words. 1992.

ps920524
Strategies in May
Studio schemes by the sack-ful
Strategic marketing ideas are a'popping: Direct mail article DisKits to magazines and newsletters, publishers of CD-multimedia titles and writers' agents. The project, Reinventing Arts Studios, requires help from both sides of tradition and technology. 491 Words. 1992.

ps920603
Leading dog stories

Pointers to the locus of beauty
How to get an agent's attention when writers are sending inquiries by the sackful? Only writing which is for multimedia would be useful now. This text could be included with a form letter to writers' agents, plus a sample and book proposal. 1101 Words. 1992.

ps920619
Expertise for sale
Living Prints born again
A multimedia artist continues the long journey from fine art print making to computer graphics. Seven years' work is ready to take to market, and what has been a virtual reality experience is, thanks to multimedia, turning into reality with new machines. 2659 Words. 1992.

ps920702
Expert Systems, Living Prints and Art Estates
An improved retrieval strategy
Expert systems could improve retrieval strategies for museum and archival multimedia information. The author illustrates how to exploit digital images and sounds on a multimedia PC with a hypothetical expert system for print making knowledge experts. 2966 Words. 1992.

ps920703
Expert Systems, Living Prints and Art Estates
The sequel and emerging technologies
The sequel to an article on improved museum and library access and how expert systems will help. As the topic grows, these are the other factors that enter into it, such as emerging technologies 2628 Words. 1992.

ps920805
Creativity broker
Paramutual betting meets real estate mortgage broker
Concept for an article to compare race horses and artists inspired by comparing real estate brokers and race-horse owners. 188 Words. 1992.

ps920807
CD-I Publishers' Club
Pioneer apprentice investing
How do you start a new title in compact disc interactive, or CD-I? One way is to build a model on another activity - investment clubs. This is the bridge between today's reality and promise of new productions in CD-multimedia titles. 2149 Words. 1992.

ps920831
Habit Five and Ritchie's Perfect Studios
Adapting expert advice
The practice management software of Ritchie's Perfect Studios resembles Stephen Covey's 5th Habit in the way that character comes with serial or sequential growth. 364 Words. 1992.

ps920902
Grafting Perfect Studios

A new logic to tree-building
Starting a new element of Perfect Studios gives you an opportunity to see how the concept works. Reinventing the art studio took seven years. The test driving stage includes grafting new wood on to old, as explained here. 1862 Words. 1992.

ps921019
Magic of art and technology
Hazards of the stage
ArtStudent: World-class innovation was a working title of a workshop at the College Art Association meeting in Seattle, 1993. The author, one of the speakers, explains the title and the purpose of the workshop from his viewpoint. 416 Words. 1992.

ps921022
Changing the playing field
Education is a whole new game
The meeting known as the MIT Forum gave a second look at the education-oriented business. How much 1990 advice did software publishing house owner, Joe Clark (VideoDiscovery) take to heart and apply to his business? What advice is new? 2029 Words. 1992.

ps921102
Script writing Perfect Studios
Readying for the work-group era
This article is in the style of an artist's self-talk analysis, an inner dialog, where the artist and the interviewer are one. This is script-writing in the time-machine sense, with the artist/writer acting as one, at once, three years from today. 2596 Words. 1992.

ps921123
PS R Better
Perfect Studios ARE better studios
Perfect Studios are better studios because of they are holistic, ecological, developmental and people-based. These are explained, plus buying into Perfect Studios is the first step toward enabling artists' in the mission for a Safe Earth. 1388 Words. 1992.

ps921127
Information Technology Alliances
The problem-eaters
Information Technology Alliances can eat away at problems technology can help remove. Here a list by the author and, opposite, how he suggests solving them. An alliance is the vision: Educational organizations work with IT industries for mutual gain. 1053 Words. 1992.

ps921222
Confessions of a computer nut
Artist in the age of electronic reproduction
Despite what people think an artist, craftsperson or designer does in his or her studio, in reality they spend a lot of time using a computer instead of the traditional tools of their art and craft. This is the revelation of one artist/writer, anyway. 2259

Words. 1992.

ps930101
Beginning of the End
The heart and mind go out of IT
Hundreds and thousands of knowledge workers
are laid-off. If you follow the history of automation, it's like imagining yourself going to a funeral
- of a dear one - three, five, or thirty years from
now. This article suggests IT has run its course.
1516 Words. 1993.

ps930105
Linking livelihood to productivity
The Reinvented Arts Studio
After learning The Art of Selling Art the artist,
crafts person and designer moves to the Perfect
Studio. By analyzing the factory model, moving
toward interdependence and alliances, he or she
finds new customers and is better able to produce
new work. 657 Words. 1993.

ps930110
Presentation principles
Financing Perfect Studios
The author learned something about himself mastering the pursuit of what he calls "The locus of
beauty" and economic bases he built upon. There
was a paradigm shift. A new kind of presentation
comes to the mind of the creative person and the
technician. 798 Words. 1993.

ps930225
Resume for EarthSafe 2022
Writing it right
Historically, the resume has been the calling
card, the general approach to getting a job. The
turbulent economics and trade scene of the early
'Nineties makes a difference in the way to create
an effective resume. Here are some pointers. 1303
Words. 1993.

ps930227
Be your own shrink
The silicon interview
Midway through a typical morning in front of his
Perfect Studio, the computer nut visits his shrink.
This is the dialog, in the form of self-talk, in an-
swer to when the Silicon Shrink wonders, "What
are you doing to eliminate problem behavior?"
732 Words. 1993.

ps930404
Stamp Drawing Shop
Rubbish and revelation
The word, stamps, means different things to different people. What is commonly accepted is their
association with authenticity. In the age of electronic reproduction, however, the old rules do not
work. This author looks for a new paradigm. 1307
Words. 1993.

ps930409
Online arts academics
The future of art education

Reinventing arts' studios requires a new way of
looking at space. After years of being confined
to the studio, classroom and campus give way to
a vision long-held by some creative artists and
scholars. Their expertise now has a less-confining
future. 410 Words. 1993.

ps930417
Portfolio assessment
Proposal for a new seminar
We can learn a little from Bill Gates' art-to-the-
home ideas, and the experience at the Seattle Art
Museum. Welcome to the beginning of the 21st
Century, when self-reliance is the key to the muse-
um and artists' perfect studios. (Proposal & Out-
line) 357 Words. 1993.

ps930428
Rating
Your own game of choice
At an amusement park I found a wonderful game
where you hammer down creatures' heads as they
pop up holes in the table. So too with ideas. The
creative person has a game, but it is ideas, not
creatures, popping up. How do you decide the
idea to hit? 1579 Words. 1993.

ps930430
Demons for confidence
Tempting the database
Searching for a demon, e.g., the element in an expert system that searches for best-guesses, a confidence factor is needed for the user to measure
the value of the way time and resources are being
spent. Shown are the first results in table form.
771 Words. 1993.

ps930501
Likes attract, fears connect
Setting the screen for artists' dynasets
We at last reached a stage in reinventing art studios when it is time to perform. Our world is our
stage. Now we have to choose our platform. We
live in the platform-independent era, and the decision is not fear-driven, but beauty-attractive. 693
Words. 1993.

ps930523
Job Creative
Why RINC is a job-creative corporation
It is not practical to expect an art, craft or design
expert to learn the Perfect Studios way. To get
their work into the trillion-dollar global market
place you need to know what takes a K-12 student
months to learn. Motivation is part of the problem. 680 Words. 1993.

ps930603
Calling all cards
Credit cards, that is
Your ITinerate professor is thinking about credits,
credits when you attend school--and, now, a new
credit-line. The new credit line is in the form of
edutainment, a clever way of wrapping continuing
education in an entertaining multimedia wrapper.

1500 Words. 1993.

ps930606
ITinerate Professor Races on
The digital data highway basic soapbox derby
Software box derbies started when there were roads to run them on - the data highways. Now the question is, "What does a software box, a toy for racing the imaginary data highway, look like?" This ITinerate Professor thinks he knows. (Proposal) 186 Words. 1993.

ps930621
Job Worth
Forecasting the ITinerate Professor's wage
Calculating the ITinerate Professor's salary in the age of electronic reproduction will be determined by prime skills and capacity to create work. Proposal. 237 Words. 1993.

ps930625
Glossary of an electronic kind
Guide to Perfect Studios' universe
A selection of terms and special words that are cademic markers on the locus of beauty. The author invented a kind of studio on a hard-drive, and even a road test hold the possibility of getting lost on the wide data highway for which it is designed. 415 Words. 1993.

ps930626
End of the wave
Maybe it's time to change heroes
The author never wanted to retire, but he still has not found a company with which he wants to tie nor one that will hire him. He is like many mature people today between the waves of yesterday and tomorrow. Reading a rejection, he captures the moment. 976 Words. 1993.

ps930627
Morning cascades
Rules of three
The ideas flow and tumble to the fore the minute I go from dreams to waking. If I lie abed, they pass in my mind like marchers at a demonstration, each carrying signs. Sometimes they are linked ideas, sometimes not. They are the morning cascades. 968 Words. 1993.

ps930628
Three-D Business Plan
Going beyond the flat world
A problem in business plans is the lack of bridges between 3rd and 4th dimension. Time seems incorporated, yet most business plans miss linking the flat-world of traditional plans and a virtuous reality. Here is a technological aid in 3-D planning. 1453 Words. 1993.

ps930630
Trends in CD Multimedia publishing
Good news to edu-tainers
Conventional thinking about CD-multimedia , e.g., that video and computer games are the leaders, is untrue, according to a profile in 1993. Loudest, but not the fastest-growing. It is good news to educators with electronic publishing designs. 1658 Words. 1993.

ps930701
TRP Investment
Getting a handle on the times
People who are looking for future security have an interest in stocks, mutual funds and bonds. TRP Investment Club is one way individuals can learn about stocks the author hopes will be like thousands of teaching/research/production clubs. 2163 Words. 1993.

ps930706
An EarthSafe 2022 Model to Watch
Models and concurrent marketing
Things have changed in the art class room. No longer can we be content to draw in the traditional ways. Of course, many schools still teach the same way they did for generations, but here is a new and unusual proposal: Base art education on printmaking. 921 Words. 1993.

ps930707
Video letter for ARN/EPP
Promoting information technology for growth
These times should be boom years for mature education organizations since national attention is turned on education in the US. The author sent a video letter to one promoting a new marketing techniques made possible by electronic technologies. 1107 Words. 1993.

ps930719
The Job I want (Back)
From business to pea-picker and back again
You create the job you want rather than search for existing jobs. Think deeply about what you want to do, gather information on how a business could do it and then design a hiring proposal. EarthSafe 2022 is the background of this strategy. 550 Words. 1993.

ps930727
Perfect Studios Re-phrased
Restoring cultural values
The basic philosophy for Perfect Studios is simple: Knowing about people, knowing about technology, and knowing about dreams. 927 Words. 1993.

ps930813
Perfect Studios' Earthsafe 2022 program
The Namta Disc solution
Promoting new technologies to mature markets is a challenge. The wisdom of years keeps older artists, crafts persons and designers away from computers. This article describes a registration idea that allows people to study and contribute to the course. 388 Words. 1993.

ps930914
LUXury economics
Basis for reinventing arts' studios
Adam Smith, father of the US constitution's

economic philosophy (capitalism) made a mistake--according to Kenneth Lux. Lux, an economist and professor, wrote Smith had left a word out of a paragraph and this is the flaw that led to disorder in US society. 1248 Words. 1993.

ps931103
Cornerstone proposal
Background for an electronic bookstore
The author appeals to a builder. The commercial space afforded an opportunity to create a new kind of bookstore, featuring CD/Multimedia. Idea No. 1: E'Books - a book store of nothing but books on and in electronic publishing. 428 Words. 1993.

ps931109
Cooperative ventures and data highways
Computers are making it happen
A new medium, partly dependent on computer education today, will stand next to traditional forms the way cooperatives stand next to corporations. The first step is putting a when-then rule in the economic lessons of arts, crafts and design. 1440 Words. 1993.

ps931110
Cooperative ventures and data highways
How computers are making it happen
A shortened version about a new medium, partly dependent on computer education today that will stand next to traditional forms the way tomorrow's cooperatives stand next to corporations. They put economics lessons in reinventing studios. 1128 Words. 1993.

ps931115
Ideas for Franklin Arts Foundation
Better then selling candy?
When Franklin High School art teachers announced a new approach to fund raising, the author offered them his inventory of books, saying, It's better than selling candy! 210 Words. 1993.

ps931118
ITinerate Professor dumps UW records
Tenure in the real world
After eight years storing files on his UW years, Professor Ritchie dumped them in November, 1993. He poured boxes of student records, grievances and grant proposals, curricula and research. As it went in he said, Good riddance, it was in my way! 1358 Words. 1993.

ps931129
Screen saver
Interface of real and virtuous worlds
The screen-saver resembles the urge to preserve something, the author says, which is an urge for permanence in an impermanent world. 347 Words. 1993.

ps940107
Clay, bricks and virtual museums
Potter turns into 'puter artist
The original museum is one's self; you can't take the museum out of the crafts person, though you may take the crafts person out of the museum. A potter-cum-'"puter artist," has cold, wet clay enveloping his roots in computers and multimedia. 1600 Words. 1994.

ps940119
Farewell, Kodak
One student's fantastic sojourn
A fictional student report of what it would be like to go to Kodak's Center for Creative Imaging in Camden, Maine. The Center was positioned to be the leader in using computers in art, but this essay warns of a shortcomings in their approach. 1146 Words. 1994.

ps940121
Virtual glue for art projects
Artist calls for education action
Artists, crafts people and designers can provide so much more to society and industry now that they are equipping their studios with new technology. The schools need help to keep up. What can be done to improve communications today? 1235 Words. 1994.

ps940313
Search for Living Prints
When archives take on another life
The author gave more life to his art by also working with new electronic media such as video. Print making was the first fine art technique to be livelier. He offers other people opportunities do the same using the data superhighway. 1932 Words. 1994.

ps940322
Fake announcement
Microsoft Intros Fine Prints Software For Children
Mr. "Living Prints" forecasts that Microsoft will introduce a fine print product in its Microsoft at Home series. The program is sure to be a winner, since there are more collectors of prints than of any other art form. 517 Words. 1994.

ps940329
Ghosts in the new schools
Browser-ghostbusters coming!
People in the schools themselves are divided, partly because the dead hand of the past cannot grasp the future and partly because there is no "editor from the future" that can produce a text, book or otherwise. 1725 Words. 1994.

ps940418
Retired Professors' knitting
Capitalizing on Information Technology
ITinerate Professor rank awaits professors who, after a generation in institutions, want to re-formalize teaching, research and practice. The IT is capitalized to signify Information Technology, as IT is the key to reinvention of the university. 887 Words. 1994.

ps940503
Moving ToolBooks
Memory lane off the data highway
Unless you are in a hurry, moving is fun, a chance to dig into storage you would not otherwise think about. Moving files from a computer hard-drive to diskettes, likewise, can be a nostalgic experience; software triggers memory of past projects. 805 Words. 1994.

ps940507
Magalogs reviewed
Magalogs from ITinerate Professors
ITinerate Professors can have their articles written and stored as electronic databases maintained by the professors. They format them as Magalogs. Periodically the professor updates their own Magalogs, going against the old closure principle. 1714 Words. 1994.

ps940510
Tenure in the real world
Beyond virtual reality
Read in the AARP Bulletin: "The corporate down-sizing of the past decade turned the work place into a roller coaster for many middle-aged employees. What happened?" After retirement, one realizes he has earned tenure in the real world. 2100 Words. 1994.

ps940624
Preservation in the Age of Electronic Reproduction
Redefining progress and environmental economics
In Washington State, with its dramatic developments in hi-tech, preservation is still a young industry; but its software makes a powerful new way for preservationists to grow in their sustaining mission. 625 Words. 1994.

ps940821
Guide to RINC
Welcome to Ritchie's, Inc.
When artists look for more effective ways to run their work places and studios, they begin to use tried-and-true methods of business. How far this can go is anyone's guess. One has entered the digital world of computers - all the way. 1629 Words. 1994.

ps940829
WSA/DMA and Kurumaki Kobo
Juxtaposing print and digital media
Washington State's "Digital Media Alliance" is still in the formative stages, but one artist/entrepreneur sees it as part of a world-wide trend. He writes about the physical juxtapositioning of arts and industry work places. 1901 Words. 1994.

ps941222
Fork in the road
Artist or Professor?
What are the best options the author has: To be an artist or be a professor? Looking back, he feels

qualified to be either one, or both at once. Economically speaking, though, the options may be branching. 1831 Words. 1994.

ps941227
Fork in the road
A new model for education
Part two of an essay that was inspired by reading about the University of Waterloo and its successful application of the principles of co-operation between academia and business. 1285 Words. 1994.

ps950409
Covey's quadrants and cyber art:
How to define by urgency
How is cyberart defined? The author says we must first decide whether urgency or importance exists and this decision must precede the definition. He based this essay on Stephen R. Covey's book, "Seven habits of highly effective people." 3027 Words. 1995.

ps950519
Problem and benefit:
The two dimensions of behavior
We strive to manage ourselves. We need to manage our practice. Perfect Studios is about managing our practices, or practice management. Here is one artist's plan of action. 964 Words. 1995.

ps950610
How do I love the WSA?
Let me count the ways
An ITinerate Professor of art reflects on the first ten years of his acquaintance with the Washington Software Association and thinks about the current advantages of being a member and its new initiative, the Digital Media Alliance. 1265 Words. 1995.

ps950706
Asset Management in the Age of Electronic
The P-Word in TRPI
Oil paintings from a turn-of-the-century "woman of the west" come under consideration by an investment club, but not as investments. They open a gateway to an interesting lesson about the way people put their money "to work" for them or against themselves 1913 Words. 1995.

ps950920
Reunioneering Communications:
What is IT?
The ESN Adopt-A-School project-a project that died on the vine-was dreamed up during the first part of the author's search for ways to restore the cultural values of high school reunions. Doing IT--Information Technology-had a central principle called RC. 522 Words. 1995.

ps950929
What is a Web Master?
Perfect Studios defines a new job
Curious about the word, Perfect Studios' founder Bill Ritchie defines the new job title, WebMaster

according to the latest developments in the World Wide Web on the Internet. 431 Words. 1995.

ps951003
In An Embarrassment of Ritchie's:
The Four Ideas (According to Blotnick)
A remark by an investment counselor about intangible assets--ideas that can make a person wealthy--causes the author to focus on his year's best. 282 Words. 1995.

ps951206
Able:
The root word of Tech Corps Washington
The Tech Corps Washington Volunteer is screened and qualified to enter in the service of K-12 education. Ability is the key to the success of their work, but there much more to being able than most people think. 1821 Words. 1995.

ps951211
Blood Simple Business:
Fear and the Wisdom Boom
A short statement on the purpose behind investing in the "fourth leg" of the traditional 3-legged stool for financial and old age security: Savings, Retirement and Secure properties. The author is a recipient of retirement benefits, looking to the future. 329 Words. 1995.

ps951230
Journal Entry, Sat. Dec. 30, 1995
Future Feelings
Notes recorded from the author's "palmtop" B.O.S.S. computer. The author had a future feeling after writing his article, "A Senior at PATCWA." He lists the day's wins; a compliment on his TC home page, PE, espaniol, MegaMemory and time with his wife. 253 Words. 1995.

ps960109
Journal Entry, Tue. Jan. 9, 1996
Woodcut On-Line
Notes recorded from the author's "palmtop" B.O.S.S. computer. The author received a compliment on his woodcut on-line that was in progress. He mentions Cascade database work and Hill-Shinn work. 163 Words. 1996.

ps960119
Journal Entry, Fri. Jan. 19, 1996
Heritage Series
Notes recorded from the author's "palmtop" B.O.S.S. computer. The author notes the success of writing down the parameters of the Heritage series, values-based applications of the "Living prints meet telecommunications" and applying to long range goals. 220 Words. 1996.

ps960212
Fifty-four reasons artists fail
From bad beginnings to slow exits
Based on Napoleon Hill's 31 causes of failure in business, these are true, also, of artists, crafts people and designers. The 23 reasons added to Hill's

span the four dimensions of the human spirit. 594 Words. 1996.

ps960224
My road ahead
A wilderness of lives
My road is like traveling on a path that is always under construction or being rediscovered in the underbrush of a wilderness of lives. 1102 Words. 1996.

ps960226
Structural Intellectual Capital in the free fine arts
Running money in reinvented arts studios
My road ahead will be running money, arching over canyons of confusion, pitfalls of the past and unfulfilled dreams. Bridges I build with running money--Structural Intellectual Capital--and I will leave them standing after I have used them and gone on. 3911 Words. 1996.

ps960229
Artist Beware
Reasons you may fail
What is the prescription for success in art? It helps to look at the prescription for business and industry: Think and Grow Rich wrote one person, enamored of Andrew Carnegie. This article is derived from him. 1804 Words. 1996.

ps960317
A Day at Perfect Studios
Blue Monday in the Domain of Expertise
The tour of the artist's Lake of the Domains of Expertise in its second week, a Monday for confronting the problems of identifying, evaluating, controlling and distributing the human sustainable intellectual capital of creative persons. 2118 Words. 1996.

ps960401
The qualified candidate
He shall . . . .
As an unaffiliated boomer enumerates characteristics that will ensure life-long earning ability--(1) Skills, (2) Memory and (3) Language. I get a surprise visit from phantoms in my computer. 2126 Words. 1996.

ps960820
When failures are successful
The best long-term investment is labor
How does a failure portend success in investing? This is the story of a struggle by a tenured professor who, when forced out of his classroom and into the real world, found a greater success path opening up both as a professor and wisdom-boomer to boot. 3742 Words. 1996.

ps961004
Contemporary Printmaking in the Northwest
One artist's viewpoint
Author Lois Allan (Contemporary Art in the Northwest) asked for a paragraph on prints I offered for her forthcoming book. This is the first

draft at my first, second and third attempts. 1960 Words. 1996.

ps961019
Perfect Day, Perfect Studios
Assessing an artist's assets
A Gruddite Apprentice-User is examined by an assessor who asks how a day at Perfect Studios is spent. He starts with PE, Spanish language and concludes with an open-ended conundrum. 2444 Words. 1996.

ps961022
Why printmaking is the best investment
The derivative arts win every time
Games of chance, the stock market, smart cards and the dynamics of reinventing retailing are today's diversity factors in the artist's portfolio and bag of tricks. 2681 Words. 1996.

ps970311
The two "I" words
Intellect and impediment
The word intellectual is not a favorite among all people, but some people have a liking for it. The word impediment is a word that has a negative connotation. In the practices of human resource development they mean opposite things. 2722 Words. 1997.

ps970319
While you were sleeping
Your children as booty
The next day after visiting GameWorks, the author (an arts education reform activist) realizes the use of e-mail is a kind of indicator to compare the use of new information and telecommunications technology, and it is an economic indicator as well. 558 Words. 1997.

ps970621
Magister Emeralda
The Living Prints, and Jimmy
The author dictated this to his computer while actually entering data called Cascades into Microsoft Access. In the same way that people have different fingerprints, retina prints, DNA and unique personalities, Cascades are unique. 2008 Words. 1997.

ps970628
Journal Entry, Sat. Jun. 28, 1997
Fundamentals, New School and Dychtwald
The author writes about mastering artistic fundamentals in cybernetics. He writes about the new school, PATCWA training artists connect with society and making labor valuable & indivisible. He writes about rediscovering his forecast about Living Museums. 279 Words. 1997.

ps971001
New Types of Relationships
Avenues and Gateways
New art technologies and the changing arts' audiences and their expectations has given artists, crafts people and designers new options to examine how they can fulfill their long-term strategies and gives rise to the reinvented arts studios. 1604 Words. 1997.

ps971016
The final chapter
Reiterating and reinventing studios
Handwritten. On the first day the author says, he was told there is value in knowledge. On the second day, he was told there was no value unless you exchanged it. On the third day he was led to the exchange, and it was himself. 000 Words. 1997

ps971105
Heart and head
Revising Jefferson
Two hundred years ago, Thomas Jefferson was smitten with affection for a lady. Much is known about their relationship, thanks to his copious writings. He described his dilemma in an essay called "Heart and head." Here, a modern artist revises it. 1490 Words. 1997.

ps980114
Fact or Fiction?
You can't feel information
Reading e-mail is a daily routine for an Emeralda Master--and not much liked. Digital information volume and complexity are building up, like the dust on his printmaking tools. He compares e-mail content as it is today to what this could be in the future. 1131 Words. 1998.

ps980115
Fantasy in DISCO-OP Land
What they didn't teach you in dental school
After a month of thinking about a dental internet service cooperative, the founder imagines a lecture he wants to present to potential members and air some observations he gathered so far. 970 Words. 1998.

ps980116
A Little ROI Mislaid
Return-On-Investment for the Inventor
Analysis of the mathematics for Emeralda's remuneration plan takes a back-chaining approach. The author receives $300 and then reflects on the events that brought the money to him, and a link to assets is discovered. 1088 Words. 1998.

ps980117
Pop Quiz
Emerald Games Work Test
Looking back from the tenth month, the author is seized by a desire to form a Test Group for Emeralda--but how? A Vision from the first day of October suggests the old "Fish Bowl" approach and he is returned to his first Stay Residency at Perfect Studios. 306 Words. 1998.

ps980118
Emeralda Plot
From the Horse's Mouth
For the first time the Inventor of Emeralda--the

Game for the Gifts of Life--tells a story behind this on-line interactive cooperative game. He introduces the game's characters and gives readers a glimpse into the ideas that tell how he invented its name. 883 Words. 1998.

ps980119
True North
Request for a Proposal
The Emeralda Inventor, contemplating making a painting or large graphic of the Emeralda Region Master Map, wants first to ascertain that the angles of its triangle borders are correctly reflected in the ten maps of the Islands of the Domains-of-Expertise. 1129 Words. 1998.

ps980208
Whining and dining
Dinner with my complaints
Like in the movie, My Dinner with Andre, the author pictures his dilemma as the writer who must manage his own articles anthology. Live on-line publishing adds responsibilities to the author's burden, but the Emeralda Master does not complain nor explain. 851 Words. 1998.

ps980218
Doing the Math
Bonnie's Prize
A cooking contest's million-dollar prize is not all it is cooked up to be, seen in the perspective of the author of this story. His opinion is that they short-serve the creative individual. He thinks, when it comes to prizes, his Emeralda is a better one. 1522 Words. 1998.

ps980228
Legacy Transfer at Perfect Studios
Selling articles on the Web
On the threshold of another gateway to artists' Internet commerce techniques, the author remembers one reason from his early years and why the Internet is a better way for artists and scholars alike to disseminate the products of their labor and thoughts. 937 Words. 1998.

ps980310
Journal Entry, Tue. Mar. 10, 1998
Forgot the Deal
The author forgot the deal until he got to the marquee and found Media's Flash from 10 days before. He resent it and then realized he had no agent ... no deal, no agent. He writes a description of a card sequence. Media, the guide & Tetra, the hidden face. 302 Words. 1998.

ps980320
First day of Spring
Testing the Waters
Inserting new source code into the Perfect Studios Zine is like a game of blind man's bluff to the Apprentice User, working alone in Cell C3, the Cell of the Avatar. One wrong digit and the thing wouldn't work, but who would know? Gone is the old teacher. 528 Words. 1998.

ps980330
Play as you go
No one is going to pay you
To answer the question, How do you populate the Persona Face? This is a placeholder for the March 30, 1998 article that is in hand-written form in the Emeralda Inventor's Journal of Everything (Mar 1998). The article explains a method of play using cards. 208 Words. 1998.

ps980409
Visitors choice
Readers requests for Perfect Studios
Space on the Internet World Wide Web for readers to request an article from the Masters at Perfect Studios—a concept awaiting further developments. Address your questions to ritchie@emeralda.com. 80 Words. 1998
ps980419
Journal Entry, Sunday, October 19, 1998
Of dreams and debts
Of dreams, debts, and says, "I happen to live in an area of great beauty. The seduction of this region is so very, very great that hardly a person exists who can resist her for long! I am pulled both ways—electronic studios and the real, great Northwest." 87 Words. 1998.

ps980509
On the way to PT509
A virtual community discussion on edition-able assets
Playing Emeralda Virtual Tours, the Author visualizes a trip to a nearby Puget Sound Resort called Port Townsend, where a printmaking workshop is scheduled in the real world. The text is grabbed from a virtual community discussion and mined for its value. 1819 Words. 1998.

ps980519
Journal Entry, Tue. May 19, 1998
Reading, Playing, Printmaking
Why are leaders, the so-called "best front runners," reading, playing and printmaking? The answer is that they are, "Thinking globally and acting locally." They think in four dimensions; widely, highly, deeply and timely, viewing the earth as dimensional. 1680 Words. 1998.

ps980529
Emeralda Lexicon
How Emeralda Got Its Name
A documentary collection of copyrighted articles from the Seattle Times that include the newspaper "contest" that led to the naming of Emeralda, the fantasy world of the author's game, and charts some explanation of its roots in economics. 8601 Words. 1998.

ps980608
ArtsPort Investment
An invitation to build
First draft of a brochure to advertise the virtual community called ArtsPort. 318 Words. 1998.

ps980618
Inventor at Work and Play
Documentary photo puzzle creation
A long-time co-conspirator in off-the-beaten-path art, C. T. Chew, planned to create portraits of artists using his computerized studio. 318 Words. 1998.

ps980628
Birth of Emeralda 24
Emeralda for Dummies
How Emeralda 24 was created from a suggestion made by Brian Tracy. 194 Words. 1998.

ps980708
Real World of Emeralda
Where in the World Wide Web is Ritchie?
Analysis of the Cells and how they affect Emeralda's inventor's remuneration plan takes a back-chaining approach. The inventor receives $350,000 and then reflects on the events that brought the money to him. 1027 Words. 1998.

ps980718
Visitors choice
Readers requests for Perfect Studios
Space on the Internet World Wide Web for readers to request an article from the Masters at Perfect Studios. Address your questions to ritchie@emeralda.com. 90 Words. 1998

ps980728
Printmaker's Life Value Calculator
Part II
Raw data from the Emeralda Player's PDA streams into a score sheet in the third column called "HSIC" and from here it may be drawn into an account. The metaphor from past times is the Life Value equivalent, created by the old-time life insurance model. 1126 Words. 1998.

ps980807
What Emeralda Does for You
Improving your World Game
Asked to describe Emeralda in a real basic way, the inventor compares it to making a molehill out of a mountain. Ironic, because his game is intended for this--shrinking a person's human structural intellectual capital into a byte-size lifestyle world. 780 Words. 1998.

ps980817
Need to Know
When and where know-how and know-why converge
An expatriate professor, headed for the Internet World Wide Web beach to do some surfing on the Web, explains how "need to know" is making waves around the realm of global intellectual capital. 753 Words. 1998.

ps980827
Machiavelli's Mistake
The mistaken case of legacy transfer
The Emeralda Inventor, contemplating making a painting or large graphic of the Emeralda Region Master Map, wants first to ascertain that the angles of its triangle borders are correctly reflected in the ten maps of the Islands of the Domains-of-Expertise. 3109 Words. 1998.

ps980906
A Simple Strategy
Restoring the SS United States
Proposal based on economics of Quality Managed Legacy Transfer Global Enterprise, principle activity long-term investing consumer services (healthcare, education, transportation) a stock basis in human structural intellectual capital of older populations. 669 Words. 1998.

ps980916
How I Invented Emeralda
Attacks of the Jeering Squad
Part VI of Emeralda for Dummies. Every day for a year the inventor used the Score sheet as if it already existed. His thinking, practical, conscious mind was laughing inside. It was like a jeering squad chanting, "There IS no Emeralda Score sheet, dummy!" 1690 Words. 1998.

ps980926
Unlocking the Gates of Beauty
Emeralda's Conception
Part XIV of Emeralda for Dummies. An introduction to the history of Emeralda, comparable to returning to ancient days in the arts before art became a product for consumption. The author compares it to unlocking the gates to a new world, a greener pasture. 1395 Words. 1998.

ps981006
Search for the Parable of the Canon
Cybernetics coming full circle
The canon, or the round, in music has been a pervasive concept in this author's mind since he first watched a work of his visual art become transformed by two external forces and become something greater than the sum of the parts: The first video artwork. 1517 Words. 1998.

ps981016
Q&A from Perfect Studios Agents
Emeralda Inventor Interview
Agents at Perfect Studios interview the Emeralda Inventor, asking for his definitions of Legacy Transfer, to explain how patents apply, view his photos of former students in schools-then-and-now, and offer suggestions as to how people could start playing. 6954 Words. 1998.

ps981105
Risk Management
An overview for emerging artists
Insurance for an individual artist, crafts person or designer is not as obtainable as the forms that a commercial business organization can access. Risk for a business can be avoided, retained or transferred. The author copy-wrote the essay by an insurer. 2511 Words. 1998.

ps981115
Idea and Idealism
View through Emeralda's screen
Suddenly, a cascading idea, before the Emeralda
Inventor begins his daily Score sheet, he glimpses
the ideal screen that will meet him in a future it-
eration of Emeralda. The screen, he says, will be a
perfect window, a view overlooking today's Ideal
Isle. 496 Words. 1998.

ps981205
Artist Equity
Managing the Equity Factor in the Cybernetic Age
of Art
To understand equity it is helpful to understand
what it is not. Equity is not equality. In the game
this author invented, Emeralda, Emeralda Players
look back over the past at the perfect information
they gained. He writes about the sovereign individual. 1492 Words. 1998.

ps990114
Reinventing the Four Freedoms
Reflecting on FDR
FDR cited the Four Freedoms as goals of the four
principles of a free nation. The author asks if it's
true of the sovereign individual. It would seem
like the micro-unit would reflect the macro-unit,
every individual exhibiting the properties of the
whole. 444 Words. 1999.

ps990115
Multi-level Marketing and Score Sheets
Talking out of both sides
If you ask students or a group of artists if they feel
good about multilevel marketing or participated
as a sales person in a multilevel marketing or pyr-
amid scheme they will say definitely not; but when
they have an art exhibit they follow the same idea.
1494 Words. 1999.

ps990314
Welcome to my world
Emeralda Inventor's Real Fantasy
The creator of the game, Emeralda, describes how
his world looks from the perspective of other peoples' worlds. He gets his inspiration from a day
trip with his wife to her old hometown-actually a
world they both lived in, and met in, many long
years ago. 599 Words. 1999.

ps990317
How Am I Different?
Let me count the ways
A DISCO-OP Apprentice User Dental Assistant
MIS enumerates the ways that he and his mate are
different using past examples. There are four perspectives, he writes, through which to see someone like him, yet none of these four gives you the
entire picture. 501 Words. 1999.

ps990318
The Vehicle in the Glue
Defining the Apprentice User Dental Assistant

MIS
Emeralda Works' owner explains how his experience as an Apprentice User Dental Assistant MIS
is like a world he saw in a funny paper and a campus. He sees an analogy between the circuitous
path of the cartoon child and the art student and,
today, himself. 1125 Words. 1999.

ps990319
View from the Last Day at Perfect Studios
What we don't know can't hurt us
A short observation concludes with his joyful realization: Haven't we been blessed with more than
we could have imagined, years ago? Haven't we
already received so much that it's amazing? Nothing can stop us from joy even if we do spend time
looking back. 443 Words. 1999.

ps990513
Networks, computers and you
Getting there, being there, staying there
A Dentalisco builder plans to speak to a Dental
Assistant organization about information technology and the development of new employment opportunities in dental practices. He says there is are
crises and opportunities, and it's like swimming
not sinking. 1025 Words. 1999.

ps990515
Labor vision
Laboring for yourself
Emeralda--a game for the gifts of life--is a blend of
chess and solitaire. Board games and card games
help people understand how to invest in themselves using new information and telecommunications technologies. Cooperation is a keyword
that changes them. 1208 Words. 1999.

ps990516
Old Wood and Good Fruit
Grafting and planting new orchards
A farm boy at heart, the author looks ahead on his
4th day at Perfect Studios and envisions a new orchard as ten trees standing alongside his old ones.
The new one is for the next fifty years; the old one
stands for the last. EarthSafe 2029 is the reason.
1662 Words. 1999.

ps990517
Getting there from here
Worth and paper
Getting there from here is the purpose of the author's presentations to people in health sciences
and the arts. Introducing the MFA certificate, he
means Multi-Faceted Auxiliary, explaining the
background of a new approach to art and technology education. 695 Words. 1999.

ps990518
On A Golden Horizon
Paralysis by analysis
An academic view of healthcare education at institutions of higher learning discovers an irony of
outsider's attempt to understand why analysis is
out of fashion in the US. The author likes an in-

side-out approach using new technology for dental education. 690 Words. 1999.

ps990712
Crashing Into Longevity
How Living to 100 is like a bumper-bender
The writer's 100-year life plan and things that go bump on the road meet again, resulting in a bent bumper plus a thousand-dollar expense. The path of one who chooses cars instead of computers is bound to be more costly in the long run than Emeralda play. 1764 Words. 1999.

ps990713
Stacking the Odds
Old age is not for dummies
The Bible, a clipping from AARP Nation and a review of books on the economic future of health care are the bases for this essay about using new tools to approach ancient dilemmas. The author plans to live a long life and he uses the natural gifts of life. 2177 Words. 1999.

ps990714
Of Silver Bullets, Triage and Emeralda
Life without disease and the pursuit of Perfect Health in Living to 120
Invest in labor, said an academic economist, not knowing of what he spoke. Blow your brains out, said a corporate guru, her meaning of a silver-bullet solution to unsustainable longevity. The artist sees a different path and invents a game to show it. 1773 Words. 1999.

ps990715
Another Risk, Another Dollar
Emeralda for Dummies Risk Workbook
Waiting for the telephone to ring can become an economically disastrous habit if you are in the business of inventing a game for the gifts of life. The inventor of Emeralda pursues the principle of concurrent marketing, sales, and development concurrency. 1038 Words. 1999.

ps000216
Vision of An Art Education Proprietary Search Engine
As A Tub Runs Over
Envisioning an online art education channel for Washington, an ITinerate Professor looks at a voluminous, ordered database growing on a public Web site at the start of Y2K. Then he suggests how to use this example of human structural intellectual capital. 2791 Words. 2000.

ps000305
Perfect Solution to an Imperfect Problem:
Washington State's Bright Future for Arts Ed
The author followed the proceedings of his state (Washington) arts commission as they rallied citizens groups and artists for a review and structuring of new policy to set before the governor. Partway through, he wrote this essay based on his observation. 1054 Words. 2000.

ps000308
Class Reunion:
The Over the Hill Gang Revisited
Just before going over a mountain to revisit his alma mater, a retired college professor reviews his goals and then he asks himself if--as the expression goes--he has gone "over the hill." He invited a classmate, too, then he composed a joke and an essay. 1154 Words. 2000.

ps000309
Arts Uniform Resource E-commerce Locator:
Artist-friendly Technology
An appeal to public and private sectors to join with in the creation of an online standard for artists, crafts people and designer resources on the Net. It is a statewide Community Art School and Museum where, at any time, one can contact creative people. 1651 Words. 2000.

ps000317
Why I Sold My Shares in eCollege.com:
The Work of Art in the Age of Digital Reproduction
Concurrent convergence of two streams often reveals a third and then a fourth awareness. Writers, painters, printmakers, sculptors, crafts people and designers are in for a high-flying ride, a bright new and hopeful future, thanks to digital reproduction. 1163 Words. 2000.

ps000318
My Best Art:
My Father's Farm
The artist realizes his new interpretation for one of his artworks and provides a candid commentary on why he thinks, in light of the day, year and decades' events, that this his best art work. The work is titled My Father's Farm, an etching made in 1972. 1158 Words. 2000.

ps000319
The Emeralda Inventor's Last Love Letter:
To his loving family
In 1992, events occurred that changed this author's life. One was an article, The Last Love Letter, about financial plights facing survivors after the death of a loved one--one who was a provider of their livelihood. The lessons are reviewed in his essay. 8609 Words. 2000.

ps000404
Library Stories:
Touching the artist's soul in the new machine
His new art is in a library in Skokie, Illinois. It is a first. The print was born in line with a vision and exhibited on line for other people. Reflecting on his story and libraries, the artist identifies his legacy and soul with one of the new machines. 1012 Words. 2000.

ps000405
New Art Game Rules:
Getting a Legacy Up in Your Domain
He's rewriting some of the rules of Emeralda, seeing what works with one of today's online file stor-

age schemes called driveway.com. He draws on a huge library of his art, dating back to the early 1960's, and then comes up with some new rules he can share. 587 Words. 2000.

ps000419
If I had $500 Million:
An art professor's modest proposal for a craft of arts
He's a retired art professor from the University of Washington, and he dreams of bringing the SS United States-the Big U-to a shipyard west of his Seattle home. He'll need $500 million to do it, and he thinks of a way by going online and making the money. 1256 Words. 2000.

ps000427
Why No One Ever Heard of the Gates Prize:
Secrets Revealed
The invention of Emeralda, the games for the gifts of life, led to creation, invention, discovering and imagination reward to be known as a Gates Prize. It is a prize comparable, but unlike, the Pulitzer, Nobel and MacArthur prizes, but measurably unique. 593 Words. 2000.

ps000511
Artists Last Love letter
Classmates remembered
The alumnus writes a letter, never to send: "Our college did not get us ready for this; they didn't tell us our education would expire. Nothing was said about a shelf life; and that when this information, telecommunication and age-wave hit us, we'd drown. 5549 Words. 2000.

ps000523
Going Insane:
A Vision of Sharing with Classmates
Imagining himself as among the few who understand the work of art in the age of digital communication technologies, the author compares the feeling with that of insane peoples'. He pictures people from his college art classmates and imagines the reaction. 1240 Words. 2000.

ps000604
An Artist's Legacy Lost
A Patron Misunderstood
An aging artist views the difference between the fuzzy outlines of his foresight as a young artist's and the clarity of hindsight. He made a mural in the 1960s which now rots in his father's back yard, its intellectual capital value greater than tangible. 518 Words. 2000.

ps000627
Lost Treasure:
Discovering My Art Collection
The founder of the company, myartpatron.com, encounters a database he created in 1993 and he since had not reviewed: A documentary list of his art collection, valued at the time at $33,000. He says how unforgettable this experience was-one he almost lost. 1138 Words. 2000.

ps000630
Raising capital for your enterprise
Your tangibles
Most people are consumers, not producers. If you are a consumer, you need to learn how producers raise capital to pay out money for their productions. Consumers have a habit of using money from their salary, but producers are not in that habit. 1189 Words. 2000.

ps000701
I Dream of Genie:
Wisdom in A Bottle
Asset Management and Legacy Transfer are key elements of Emeralda. The businesses in Emeralda Works test ways to communicate to customers the values of these two facets. The goals of Emeralda's players are to develop knowledge and skill through practices. 822 Words. 2000.

ps000710
My Retrospective
Supported by myartpatron.com
He never planned on having a retrospective of the usual kind, where an art museum hosts a grand review of his life's work. Thus, having made his pathway in a different direction, he is now faced with having to create his art retrospective for his benefit. 1800 Words. 2000.

ps000803
Windows on My Studio
An artist's buying spree
A short story describing an imaginary tour group's visit to a fictional street in an imaginary place. The author envisions himself as the artist of note whom this group is interested in. He uses fiction like this to visualize what he wants to have happen. 1976 Words. 2000.

ps000806
Unfinished Garage Saga
Mr. Ritchie Goes to California
This author/writer falls in with business-minded people and then is expected to show them his business plan-but he has none. The next year, he heard a lecture by a Real Networks founder say that a serious business today is not planned. Things change fast. 478 Words. 2000.

ps000826
Charter of Accounting in a Digital Communications Age
Designer accounting and artists' markets
An e-gallery, or e-store, is the artist's gateway to the age of electronic reproduction. In the same way the printing press enabled the visually and aurally empowered creative person's participation in community economies, the Internet empowers artists. 1326 Words. 2000.

ps000910
Why Buy Emeralda?
Valuation of an unborn blockbuster game

The creative, inventive, discovering and imaginative artist of a past era, spent playing teaching, research and production roles, must pause and consider the commercial value-in every sense of the word value-of non-competitive games for the gifts of life. 2291 Words. 2000.

ps000918
In Retro:
What is it all about?
An artist who put on his own 40-year retrospective explains himself, as he thinks about a three-year exhibit that he began in the year 2000. He compares it to artists who come forward to explain their way, and to an Olympian taskmaster coach he saw on TV. 1025 Words. 2000.

ps000924
Artists Asset Management
A click releases a ghost in the new machine
Indications are, he thinks, computers are taking over the roles that teachers played in the 20th Century and this is the century of technology-owned not by human beings but by robots, wizards and wisdom-boomers. He thinks on what this means to his legacy. 1178 Words. 2000.

ps001013
Big Flash! New Lease Free Webs
An idea for art leasing and free Web sites
A magic Genie-like figure visits the author as he was polishing a picture frame and revealed the secret he was searching for-a key to his family fortune, a collection of art. It is an idea that could only come to someone with art both in hand and on-line. 538 Words. 2000.

ps001023
Simple Man, Simple Dreams
The Printmaker's Last Love Letter
The printmaker who designed "TRYX" explains the events that led up to the invention of the product. Deaths of an art professor and a dentist triggered his imagination and jump-started his plan to develop a remedy for an old economic dilemma families face. 1371 Words. 2000.

ps001112
Birth of Trixie
His Story of a Computer Program
Ritchie, working on Emeralda, describes how he came upon the idea of one of the many iterations of his game. He says the game is for "the gifts of life" and sees himself as being on a pathway (or locus) of beauty. He puts it in the form of computer games. 904 Words. 2000.

ps001124
The Gates Prize
Explaining a fantasy
The history of the Gates Prize is explained by one of the recipients of the prize. The focus is on the reason the prize is virtually unknown. Gates, while he lived, knew that such a perfect situation, and such a prize, was a hundred or more years distant. 713 Words. 2000.

ps001128
If You Are So Smart, How Come You Are Not Ritchie?
Actually, I am
Bill writes about himself, stopping between facing his fear of his drawers (paper drawers, that is) and getting on with one of his database building projects. He imagined an article that recounts how he got wealth after reading into Stephen Pollan's book. 1407 Words. 2000.

ps001215
You Are on My List:
People on Our Seasonal Greeting Card Mailing List
The artist sends a message to selected people whose names are on his and his wife's joint Seasonal Greeting Card mailing lists-a practice they started in 1999 under the false names of Trixie and Dusty. His reason for a special message is his new Web site. 555 Words. 2000.

ps001225
Artist Trust Dental Service Cooperative Auction:
A Joint Venture in the Art of Life Science
Close to the end of the art auction era a new kind of auction experience is opening up, thanks to the Internet and World Wide Web. And who should initiate it, this new kind of art auction, but an artist. He puts his own works on the line-on-line, that is. 993 Words. 2000.

ps010119
Power of Limits
In Digital Fine Arts and Crafts There's Barely Enough Room to Turn Around
The artist/scholar thinks of himself as a moral philosopher. He encounters another author, a bona fide philosopher and scholar, calling himself an artist. In the daily routine of writing on a computer and solving little technical problems is a difference. 1183 Words. 2001.

ps010129
Nightmare Prevention for Old Professors
My Worst Fears Overcome
As a young professor, he saw what happens to old professors' work. His living nightmare was confirmed by Dr. Osler's recommendation: Old professor should be gassed. He invented ways to stop his this nightmare, conserving as that was his lifelong striving. 989 Words. 2001.

ps010208
A Prisoner's Dilemma and New Twist on an Old Story
Walking A Life-long Journey in Your Students' Shoes
Awakening from a dream, the ITinerate Professor applies a new standard for evaluation of the online, interactive, cooperative game he invented and finds it is not a game to play after all, but a curriculum design for art teachers who want to teach

online. 2652 Words. 2001.

ps010218
Another Look at Partnering
Looking to Develop Artists' Trust in Technology?
Discover A Strategic
The artist/author thinks: Partnering--hearing there is a job opening at Artist Trust for development associate. It is not a job, but an opportunity to open a gate leading toward co-operating in the Next Big Thing in artistic livelihood for Washingtonians. 2376 Words. 2001.

ps010228
Dream Equity
MOE Versus OPE
What are dreams for, anyway, if not to be one's private, self-sustaining critical analyses devices? Dreams are more than odd and uncontrollable phenomena to the Emeralda Defender. Dreams can suggest the right things to do in making investments in oneself. 2211 Words. 2001.

ps010310
Thanks for Your Prescience
A Case of Mistaken Advice
The artist/author plans to see a private college for the teaching, research and practice of arts of the 21st Century, so he considers how posters-to him the epitome of exciting graphic arts-used to be published. He thinks about new ways of seeing posters. 1668 Words. 2001.

ps010320
Artist's Happy Widow
She's Happiest Who's Light on Her Feet
Dusty, one of the author's avatar guides on the ferry taking Emeralda players to the Islands of Domains of Expertise, records his introductions. This is a technical sheet he used to improve his audio/video clip recording methods he needs for making a DVD. 1978 Words. 2001.

ps010419
Do IT Right by the Kids
Renewable wood and new media arts
Enthused by encountering a PTA leader who is finding artists-in-residence for K-6 school kids, the author considers what he would do if he were given the task. He envisions a pull-marketing Web site to start thus making an Information Technology platform. 437 Words. 2001.

ps010509
Taking It with You
Printmaker's Pearlie Gates
Despite that they say You can't take it with you (when you die), and Life is a journey no one gets out of alive, an artist who is using the mediums of printmaking and digital systems can pack his or her art with the end in mind. Life can outlive artists'. 866 Words. 2001.

ps010519
Do Not Retire a whiner

1O steps to take now
The world's best art teachers do not show the whole picture of artists' lifetime work to their students. Among art education colleagues aging is a personal, secret issue. This writer-who strives to be a great teacher in the arts-offers some timely advice. 1543 Words. 2001.

ps010608
Puzzlement over Art I Have Done
Selling the Pieces of Multimedia Art History
The editor of the DVD, Living Prints Zine says that it be the "weekly reader" and main reference work for a free on-line art course in media arts appreciation. The pieces are sold like pieces of a thousand-piece puzzle, using the global on-line bookstore. 433 Words. 2001.

ps010618
Reverse Engineering Myself
What makes an on-line art educator different?
The closer the possibility of doing anything artistic on the Internet World Wide Web, the more important it seems that rethinking arts becomes. Most, if not all, that we expect of artists and teachers is inappropriate to information technology of the Web. 2529 Words. 2001.

ps010628
Knock Knock Who's There?
Your First Art Ed On-line Student
Another day, another test. At Emeralda Works the inventor of Emeralda gets to test his machine under all kinds of conditions. The real region he lives in offers surprises almost daily. Today it's a chance encounter with a news item and a graduate student. 798 Words. 2001.

ps010718
Sneaky Professors Playing Games
Why eggheads like to invent their own rules
World-saving plans sometimes take strange forms. You can have your government sponsored ones backed up by military might. Or, you may choose religious strategies. This writer selects mind games that intellectuals can play-and keep hidden in their closets. 2671 Words. 2001.

ps010728
Analyze This
Not your usual book
A book falls from the top shelf as the author is clearing out his cell's library-a relic but not ancient. Reading it stars him on a memory path, but not nostalgia. Concurrent events mean he's coming back to where he began and seeing it for the first time. 3029 Words. 2001.

ps010926
Case of the Missing Professor
Paths you can audit, paths you can trust
Voices in his head, you could say, but the academic's expression is inner dialog. A motivational speaker would say "inspired self-talk". This artist/writer uses it to start his essay about Digital Ver-

satile Discs (DVD) and how he is using DVD to make art. 1354 Words. 2001.

ps011016
Keeping Your Passport Up-to-Date
A cyber traveler's cautionary tale
His passport is not a book like object that fits in his pocket with stamps in it showing where he's been. The author created a digital passport going with his game, Emeralda. His essay is about being "passport ready," conceived for folks who love freedom. 1013 Words. 2001.

ps011026
Reinventing the Art Collector
New art instruments for times of uncertainty
E-mail about the first color Chinese prints made for art appreciation help an art and technology theorist see changes in art collecting. Information and telecommunications technology restores relationships in artists, collectors and art education domains. 1393 Words. 2001.

ps011105
Test Drive for the DVD Maker
Not just another Bozo on the bus
He took a test drive over a weekend to see if, with his DVD-making skills, he could produce a disc that's practical and beat his record time. Its utility value would take a longer period, but getting it from his raw idea to his e-store was his first goal. 1146 Words. 2001.

ps011115
Sharing Moments of Art Ed Online
Foundations for a new paradigm
The designer of an art education on-line curriculum compares shares in the stockholder sense to shares in arts enterprises. A new view of economics is needed to enable the artist/teachers in the age of digital reproduction, and sharing moments is the key. 1591 Words. 2001.

ps011125
Losing Intaglio Classes and Winning Them Back
Future practices applied today
As an advocate of future practicum, an Itinerant Professor writes about how news of closure of intaglio printmaking classes is both bad and good, depending on the attitudes in universities. Their dwindling resources make opportunities for change, he says. 1174 Words. 2001.

ps011230
Sunday December 30-It Must Be Perfect Studios
A Day with an ITinerant Professor
A waking tourist checks his passport and tourist itinerary to get oriented. A routine daytime activity for an ITinerate Professor of art in the 21st Century, this story helps explain some short courses in paper and technology that the professor envisions. 864 Words. 2001.

ps020108
Writing Between the Paragraphs - Part 5

Fantasy dialog between two professors
Distance learning is a new phenomenon of the late-20th Century, but usually excludes arts-the kind of hands-on art and face-to-face encounters we're used to. Having cast away old assumptions, however, one man thinks art ed at a distance, on-line, is here. 1404 Words. 2002.

ps020118
A New Idea for TIAA
Asset Management and Legacy Transfer
The huge retirement fund to which most institutions of higher education subscribe has an opportunity to provide a valuable new service to professors. It is a trust fund for intellectual capital which has long been under the governance of old technologies. 1706 Words. 2002.

ps020208
Stranger In My Perfect Studio
Words like beggars to understanding
A philosopher wrote in book the words, "The interplay of noise creates the conditions for emerging complexity, which is the pulse of life." An artist in the age of digital reproduction responds with a description of how this is the feeling of strangeness. 570 Words. 2002.

ps020218
My Secret Theory of Art Ed Online Revealed
Opening My Perfect Studios
People don't want to be told how to make art. They want information about art making. This is the basis for a revolutionary approach to art education on-line an artist/professor invented. He wants to share it with a for-profit higher education enterprise. 1371 Words. 2002.

ps020228
How Emeralda Works
For On-line Art Ed
Emeralda Works is the business name that the inventor gave his on-line testing bureau. To get started, he needed a testing bench and a benchmark. His goal is to be a great teacher for the world's printmaking societies, and his test is part of his success. 1107 Words. 2002.

ps020310
Why PDAs Are Required for Emeralda Play
Making Your E-Stamp with Your Proximate
The e-stamp is a basic part of Emeralda, according to its inventor. He is a stamp artist in the age of digital reproduction. He wagers that the 240 X 320 viewing screens of most PDAs today are suited for matching the pairs of stamps and stories in Emeralda. 615 Words. 2002.

ps020320
Links and Education Communities
H. G. Wells' World Brain is now possible
Concurrent with his work on Emeralda, an on-line interactive cooperative game he invented, this author works in digital media and writes about his works in progress. H. G. Wells' 1938 book coin-

cides with the evolution of links among teachers and students. 446 Words. 2002.

ps020330
Emeralda Works But What Do You Do?
What software testing means to me
Stopping partway between two tests he is running on a DVD-burning program, the author takes the opportunity to use this as an example to explain the purpose of the name he uses as his company. He introduces the routine of testing and burning DVDs for PCs. 916 Words. 2002.

ps020409
One-minute Screenwriting
Your Claim to 15-minute Fame
How long can we expect to be famous today or tomorrow if we are artists or writers? It's more like a practical joke that the world, seen through rose-colored glasses, is playing. We let our imaginations run wild, but we must dream, anyway, and keep faith. 876 Words. 2002.

ps020419
A Case of Recursivity
The Canon in D and other stories
Several Hollywood movies paint a background for this artist/writer's plan for a game he invented called his Emeralda. He thinks electronic games are winners if they have a background screen play. But the academic side of him can't be quelled as he writes. 1469 Words. 2002.

ps020429
Teacher-What's Wrong with My E-stamp?
Projections on a failed stamp issue
To pass on-line art education tests and thereby get credit for work, the student and the teacher must put each e-stamp in their e-folio of stamps through the build video test-for making a DVD. The author gives an accounting as his test proceeds, and more. 842 Words. 2002.

ps020509
Art Educators Must Embrace New Technology:
A New Paradigm for Distance Learning from Reinvented Arts Studios
This essay is based on an interview in The Chronicle of Higher Education. It said for their own future and that of their students (and their former students) art education leaders must embrace new technologies with an old-fashioned entrepreneurial spirit. 1654 Words. 2002.

ps020519
The City Dump Museum of Art
Transferring your legacy at the landfill
Taking his cue from the widow of a dead dentist, the author describes how he plans to avoid his worst nightmare: Seeing his legacy lost upon his death because his widow was unprepared to handle it. He thinks a game is the only answer for artist's dilemma. 497 Words. 2002.

ps020529

Journal Entry, Wed. May 29, 2002
M/QU Artists, Crafts People, Designers Unite!
The author wrote about the Project Object Project. It will be a way to provide a showcase of creative, inventive, discovering an imagination accomplishment in the visual art, crafts and design would in a totally new way: digital reproduction. 250 Words. 2002.

ps020608
Seven Steps to a Highly Successful _____
From Henriette, Marco to Me
His search for the Perfect Studios ends in seven days-seventeen years from the day he walked off the old campus for good. That was the age of mechanical reproduction come to its end, and a new experience opened up he calls the age of digital reproduction. 2094 Words. 2002.

ps020618
Interview with an Auction Expert
Happy Tale of A Defrocked Professor Leading Somewhere
In a flash of inspiration, the hopeful public intellectual sees way to finance the un-financed-by fanciful means of interviewing an anonymous auction expert and then planning an auction to raise the monies for a resident public intellectual in a fishbowl. 1615 Words. 2002.

ps020628
It's Friday So This Must Be Perfect Studios
Intertwine two worlds
Avoiding the pitfalls of an old world when dramaturge and solipsist are indistinguishable, today's writer must not only think globally and act locally, but also build the pathway to travel. A local art festival is the scene behind which real play unfolds. 1010 Words. 2002.

ps020708
Seattle-City of Artists Parks
Emeralda City's Virtual, Verdant Virtuous Plan
Three principles-chaining, fishing and sustaining-channel this artist/scholar's journey among local and global efforts toward reforestation of planet Earth. It's his vast plan to join the Union of Concerned Scientists in their call to humanity to act now. 944 Words. 2002.

ps020709
Why an Artist Joins the Queen Anne Chamber of Commerce
Ten reasons
Artists who join their local Chamber of Commerce are more successful than those who won't, claims this writer, as he sends his first membership check. He lists the reasons he thinks this will help him reach his long term goal of a re-invented arts studio. 1363 Words. 2002.

ps020718
On That Day His CD Burning
Your Writer's Life on CD/R
On the day a student tries the legendary Art Stu-

dent CD Rom, will it play? Will that student get what he or she is looking for, which is the complete writings of the missing professor made from his whole lifetime of writing? He burns his CD/R and wonders. 739 Words. 2002.

ps020728
Community Technology Center in Uptown Seattle
My Modest Proposal
After a meeting with a city community technology planner the Uptown Seattle artist/scholar reports on his impressions. He used several 20th Century models at first, but decided they were of limited value. Nonetheless, they're useful to see what not to do. 486 Words. 2002.

ps020729
Living Artists and Poets Society
One Artist's Way
How do you cultivate a park? An Artist's Way is a vision of the Living Artist's and Poets' Society office-a small, brightly decorated building behind a "classic corner green grocer's" at Thomas and Queen Anne Avenue. It's fantasy now, but it could happen. 797 Words. 2002.

ps020730
What Did You Learn at the Museum, Grandpa?
A Visit to the Museum of Yesterday
This Itinerate Professor reflects on his experience at a local museum, and the people he saw there. They're practitioners of time-worn rituals, but their rites are hollow from a perspective he's working on that he thinks is the 21st Century Living Museum. 788 Words. 2002.

ps020807
Room in the 21st Century
Spots on Walls of the Museum without Walls
Looking back to the 20th Century he views scores of friends-many of them who would have been successful artists but for their 19th Century roots. Those were good times, but now the gallery, the museum and the collectors' walls are full, those venues gone. 613 Words. 2002.

ps020817
Art Outlasts Politics Said His Tee
Reading Tees Leaves Me in Wonderment
He's thinking about the economy and about correcting the economics of a nation is a big task-but which will be more effective, art or politics? What corrections need to be made, and can art be effective in making those changes if politics drives the arts? 1023 Words. 2002.

ps020827
Unhappiness is the Best Beginning
The Bad Teacher's Dream
Before writing the next in of his Perfect Studios series he read Dr. Phil, followed the doctor's instructions, and asked himself to find the root of his inappropriate reactions to life. His dreams reveal this truth: He leaned his ladder on the wrong wall! 1331 Words. 2002.

ps020906
Writing to You from Northland Ashland
The Artist's Last Love Letter in Pause Mode
A college with a small arts faculty may be the perfect place to roll out the Perfect Studios model-environmental as a core philosophy, located on the edge of a huge lake-what more could the Emeralda Inventor ask for? Until later, money would be one thing. 733 Words. 2002.

ps020916
Exercising Freedom in Emeralda City
The Practice of Emeralda
Sometimes we're so accustomed to striving we walk right past our goal and do not see it. We may, strangely enough, mistake it for one of those obstacles we are always warned will stand in the way of our pursuit for freedom. In Emeralda, this can be fatal. 785 Words. 2002.

ps020926
An Incurable Disease, a Gift of Life
Writing an Artist's Last Love Letter
Thinking about artist's slumps and suspicious lumps, this author thinks what he'd like to do if he were told he had only six months to live. What difference could he make if in 40 years he had not made a difference? On the other hand, it's never too late. 1201 Words. 2002.

ps021006
Emeralda and Structure
TV, Science and Cyanotype
New structural relationships that Emeralda helps create are those that change social institutions and help create more stable and sustainable relationships to the natural world. That art happens to be the apparent resource of the game is mere coincidence. 1901 Words. 2002.

ps021016
Shoe Story
Getting to the Big Picture Show
He wills his mind to be like Superman—to leap tall buildings with a single bound, find connections between a shoe-shopping trip, and the role of the artist in saving Earth's human life sustainability. On top of it all, he will to be a Great World Teacher. 1498 Words. 2002.

ps021026
Public Intellectual Unbound
The artist/scholar goes mobile
This is an almost unheard-of expression because in times past the public intellectual depended on face-to-face meetings of the real kind and then schools cornered the market. People go to school to encounter intellectuals and has become a rare experience. 1376 Words. 2002.

ps021105
Cobbler Story
Encyclopedia of e-folios
Cobbling a castle together for a movie compares

to cobbling together bits and pieces of a lifetime career in art that fit the modern electronic communications technologies. The writer is a professor from the 20th Century planning to work in 21st C. modes. 1924 Words. 2002.

ps030320
An On-line Loophole for Art
Learning printmaking for free on-line
As he reads an article about using popular TV shows and film clips to teach college classes, the author-a printmaking teacher-visualizes using his video tapes to teach without the worries of copyright protection that other college professors contend with. 1027 Words. 2003.

ps030330
Professional Standards, Art Education and Information Technology
Questions for art education needs assessment in the age of digital reproduction
Seven questions listed (without answers at the time of this iteration) which might form an outline to study the need for on-line art education. The main emphasis is that the arts, like all aspects of today's society, have been impacted by high technology. 271 Words. 2003.

ps030519
Emergency Meeting Revisited
The Emerging Work of Art in the Age of Digital Reproduction
When he was still a young professor and learning the complexity of visual arts' migration to the age of electronic reproduction, he called the Emergency Meeting of some of the best and brightest artists. Twenty-five years later, he senses a new emergency. 777 Words. 2003.

ps030529
Taking Stamps 'N Stories to the Museum
Rediscovering the Video Dig
His art works are already in the museum in a city south of his hometown, but he wants to make it more accessible himself. Therefore partway done with his game, Stamps 'N Stories, he decides to make it "museum friendly". What a surprise he finds: His Muse! 1404 Words. 2003.

ps030618
Doing What Has Never Been Done
A pre-boomer's view of digital games
Poets may be dependent on language and artists may be dependent on art history, but digital-based game producers depend on their own unique domains of expertise. This professor aspires to rise to a new level of art games that can unshackle his creativity. 1401 Words. 2003.

ps030718
How to Make Millions on A Video Game
Invent a Game That's Really Different
Anyone can make a video game today. Books tell people how to do it, and you can download ready-made shells or templates, animation programs and

game engines. But inventing a new game requires a different kind of approach, and this art professor tells how. 1749 Words. 2003.

ps030827
Getting Back into the Teaching Game
Early Education in Video Games Helps Lifelong Learning and Teaching
A veteran of the early days of using TVs and computers in fine art education observes how a current controversy around using video games as teaching reminds him of the old days in art school. He says most public education doesn't equip people to buy this. 1152 Words. 2003.

ps031006
How to Design an Online Drawing Class
A balancing act for a hybrid art course
After two weeks in his beginning drawing class the art professor returns to his primary interest, which is to design an online art studio class that may exceed what a traditional drawing class can achieve. He describes how to use the hybrid online system. 1379 Words. 2003.

ps031115
Build That World!
What else is worth the rest of your life?
Clarity of vision inspires a command to build the virtual world he's been dreaming about for over thirty years. He lays the foundations for a plan of action, a manifesto to assemble a group of artists, crafts people and designers and launch a development. 760 Words. 2003.

ps031205
Strokes of Genius
Looking back at my Y2K Journal
In the summer of 2000 this artist kept a journal that was also a printed sketchbook based on the idea that time looks like a slinky toy. He wrote notes in it about his economic theory called triple entry bookkeeping. Three years later he reviews his idea. 762 Words. 2003.

ps031220
Orientation Lecture
My first etching
While he's drawing the new version of the e-stamp for ArtsPort (working remotely on Perfect Studios island), he imagines himself instructing his first online printmaking class. He explains the game he designed to be for the interface of distance learning. 590 Words. 2003.

ps031230
My Heart Goes Pity-Pat
What turns me on on-line
An artist between to ages-the 20th Century and the 21st-must contend with a kind of middle-life existence. Traditional arts are still with him and he loves to work in those old media but he's lured by the illusion of a promising new art form: Video games. 758 Words. 2003.

ps040109
What is Emeralda Today?
Taking a cue from the game reviews
A review of the best and worst video games of 2003 inspires the inventor of a game he calls Emeralda to rewrite the review so it describes his own. He's on a lifelong quest for a perfect game for a perfect life. One game in particular piques his interest. 1901 Words. 2004.

ps040119
A Has-Been Artist Fools Father Time
Recycling a life's work
An artist confronts his worst nightmare and conjures up a way to turn this imminent catastrophe into an opportunity. He thinks he can return his lifetime of works on paper back to its pulp and thus create a new supply of material that may lead to new art. 1376 Words. 2004.

ps040418
The Press that Bill Built
A rhyme for What's Up
A salon is opened each month with guests from the arts community. They convene at the home of Anne Focke, a longtime advocate of the creative arts. In the April meeting, she and her co-salon host Carolyn Law asked everyone to recite something. This is it. 305 Words. 2004.

ps040508
One Way Out of the UW Printmaking Problem
A proposition for our State
The surest way to save the printmaking division at the UW school of art is through creativity, and the effort of resuscitation would mean the re-invention of this division. It doesn't mean to begin being creative, but to seek and restore creative threads. 1252 Words. 2004.

ps040518
Jacob Lawrence and the Chess Players
A story about games
The advent of an art auction to benefit the development of a creative art school in the Northwest inspired this essay. It describes an artwork the writer will give to the fundraiser: art by the late, great Jacob Lawrence. However there's strangeness here. 1752 Words. 2004.

ps040627
A Perfect Project
El projecto perfecto
Still pursuing his favorite chimera, a digital game-based learning design for understanding media arts in the Northwest, the author, in the role of professor in a virtual community college, describes a project that's a part game, part academic enterprise. 959 Words. 2004.

ps040707
Triangle Studios Reloaded
Outcome of a friendly chat
Two old friends recall the history they shared for a few years in a cooperative studio. One suggests restarting the studio but making it a virtual studio instead of the real studio they had before. They brainstormed before and, who knows, it could happen. 426 Words. 2004.

ps040717
The Mini Halfwood Press at Perfect Studios
Picturing the new addition
He conceived of Perfect Studios after two decades of study and teaching in art. As a holder of the idealistic views of human creativity set to the purpose of art, and the institutions at that time-colleges and universities-he had a place for these ideals. 923 Words. 2004.

ps040727
Playing Emeralda with the Mini Halfwood Press
New piece of the game
Perfect Studios is based on the so-called "teaching hospital" like the one south of the art school: the University Hospital. Perfect Studios is a good spot to reflect on activities that have grown around the design and creation of the Mini Halfwood Press. 1122 Words. 2004.

ps040806
Creating Your Joy
Thoughts on the gifts of life
A listing of ways to get joy from the Mini Halfwood Press by its becoming the key to restoring the educational mission I launched 40 years ago. In this essay I tried to connect every imaginable benefit for focusing and allocating resources to its success. 524 Words. 2004.

ps040816
Video Assets and the Mini Halfwood Press
An AHA to remember
A few AHA words about my plan to resume making videotapes about printmaking, inspired by the creation of a User's Manual for the Mini Halfwood etching press I helped create. It shows the natural course of events will flow me back to where I was making videos. 250 Words. 2004.

ps040826
What Does Daniel Dew Need?
Signs of Interest in A Virtual World
Two emails arrive, both of which point to a growing interest in online education. As much as the people who sent them are eager for better ways to learn about printmaking, the author is eager to be a source of printmaking information in the virtual world. 871 Words. 2004.

ps040905
Ten-day Review of Perfect Studio Essays
Checkpoints to consider
The game I invented, Emeralda, is a low-key adventure game designed for the life of my mind as my mind wanders. Moving from island to island and covering ten islands in ten days I often write essays on each one. Revisiting each one, I survey my interests. 1389 Words. 2004.

ps040915
Another Lesson from A Tom Hanks Film
Recognizing Emeralda
The Itinerate Professor sorts out his feelings and thoughts after getting email from a friend inviting him to practice his teaching in a new setting. Movies help the professor understand his reaction; he decides it's like having your passport invalidated. 919 Words. 2004.

ps040925
Parable of a Castaway
Disappointment of a castaway
For a few days the author aspired to re-entering school as a graduate student seeking a doctor's degree in digital art and experiments in new technologies. Upon closer study he realizes that the program he is interested in exists in a fog of obscurantism. 798 Words. 2004.

ps050109
Amazing Things
Thoughts on the Mini Halfwood Press
The designer of the Mini Halfwood Press ponders the pathway he took that led him to make the little press, considering that perhaps it is part of his lifetime goal to be a great teacher. While it may be a merely mechanical process, he thinks it is more. 544 Words. 2005.

ps050119
Don't Say Never Happen
Dreaming of A Classroom
The Itinerate Professor is lonely, for he has no classroom in which to teach. Yet daily he starts his writing routine for imaginary publications that he calls 'Zines, he imagines eager faces before him, wanting the lessons he would like to teach students. 508 Words. 2005.

ps050129
It's in the Cards
The Mini Halfwood Press Finds its Voice
Looking to the future of his little press he calls the Mini Halfwood, and the art they call Artists Trading Cards, the author speculates on how he will use his press to bridge the 20th Century printmaking forms to the new digital arts of the 21st Century. 531 Words. 2005.

ps050208
Today, on the Island of Perfect Studios
Greetings from Asset-Management Land
Encouraged by an editor to write about an experience with returning to work and lifelong learning after his own early retirement, the professor—now in his 20th year after leaving the campus—sets about the difficult task of explaining his "game", Emeralda. 1184 Words. 2005.

ps050218
Strategy of A Retired Art Professor
Keeping Several Occupations Going at Once
A comment from an editor of a retiree publication asked this artist if he has several occupations, and how does a game he calls Emeralda relate to his multifaceted routine. It struck him that, indeed, Emeralda is a strategic way to lead a meaningful life. 698 Words. 2005.

ps050228
Welcome to Your New Job
Reflecting on Life's Professions
The Payoff, as one person called it, for playing Emeralda: Games for the Gifts of Life is to be able to continue working for a lifetime in one's domain of expertise. Called investing in labor; for this artist/writer, it means keeping with a daily routine. 673 Words. 2005.

ps050310
The Secret of Emeralda
Learning Objects and Games
He read about youngsters who spend hours in their rooms immersed in multimedia and how this requires multitasking skills. This is the answer to the question he was asked, "What's the payoff in Emeralda play?" referring to the learning game he invented. 1073 Words. 2005.

ps050330
I Want My Emeralda
Loneliness on the Road
Temporarily away from his home and studio, the artist who created "games for the gifts of life" laments that he can't get to Emeralda from where he is, which is in a motel 200 miles away. His games provide him ways to get perspective on his newest enterprise. 677 Words. 2005.

ps050409
Art Pervert
A Fundraiser Idea that Won't Die
Whenever he's confronted with a desire to help a worthy cause to raise money, he thinks of a perverted idea given to him long ago by a former student. She called it Stop Art Destruction (SAD), and the idea comes back to him in a new, twisted digital form. 1341 Words. 2005.

ps050419
Making Emeralda an Art Auction Game
This Artist's Life – This Artist's Death
Suppose you took all the premises of Emeralda and turned them into an auction game. 245 Words. 2005.

ps050429
He Walks His Talk
A Pensioner Reflects on His Creation
At one time he was invited to comment on retirement from college teaching and his remarks were printed in the pension fund's quarterly journal. Occasionally he looks at his comments that were printed and he asks himself, "Am I practicing what I preached?" 733 Words. 2005.

ps050509
Structuring Your Blog
An Emeralda Player Takes Stock

Daily the author reads and writes essays. Some reading are his, some are by other people. He started using the blog online but senses that no one reads them, so why take the time he wonders. Blogging is a widely practiced medium, but blogs need structure. 548 Words. 2005.

ps050519
Park Practice
A Community of Practice Springs Up at Roy and Queen Anne
After attending a number of meetings in his community—called Uptown Seattle—the author envisions a neighborhood focal point patterned after other parks he's known. He blends some business practices, too, into his formula for a park of community practices. 714 Words. 2005.

ps050529
Doing the Undoable
Anticipatory Research
How does an aging artist/scholar find the "Games for the Gifts of Life?" The answer is to look where no one has looked before. He calls this imaginary place Emeralda. It is a place that exists only in his imagination, and he explores it with his computer. 1133 Words. 2005.

ps050608
This is the Dream
The Most Fantastic Auction Ever
This artist has distrusted art auctions, yet he seems to come back to the subject repeatedly. They're like an artist's nightmare, exposing the fine arts to the whims and wiles of bargain hunters and entertainment; but to a dead artist it's something else. 869 Words. 2005.

ps050618
My Hidden Agenda
Ghosts in the New Machine
This artist's life began, he believes, when he was a student in college. Today—over forty years later, he wants to act in such ways as he is able to resuscitate his former professors, almost all of whom are no longer alive and their legacies all but lost. 511 Words. 2005.

ps050628
The Power of Limits in Games
Inspiration over Coffee with a Friend
In his lifelong search for the payoff in game-play (a goal in his design of Emeralda, Games for the Gifts of Life) he discovers an intrinsic law of games in a conversation with someone who grew up with game-based education and it resembles laws in nature. 847 Words. 2005.

ps050708
Show Me the Money
Emeralda Treasure Map
The author, who thinks he has invented a unique game he calls Emeralda: Games for the Gifts of Life, ponders the developments that point to going further toward the actual development of the game so others can play. "Show me the money," is the first step. 786 Words. 2005.

ps050718
Appreciative Systems and Collectible Cards
A Way of Looking Art Artist Trading Cards
He's studying the idea in James Gee's book, "What Video Games Have to Teach Us," that appreciative systems arise in children and adults when they have goals to be satisfied in a domain-of-expertise. His own goal is relating Artist Trading Cards to Emeralda. 624 Words. 2005.

ps050728
A Fantasy for Halfwood Press
Making Up a Story in the Emeralda Myths
Whether this artist is working on a drawing or a print, he's aware of the interplay of the role that his studio instruments play in shaping of the work. There is no sharp line between instrument and art or separating ideas and instruments of their making. 795 Words. 2005.

ps050807
Looking Back, Looking Ahead
Thoughts after a Day Doing Printmaking Demonstrations
This artist, who has a reputation for teaching too, meets the most interesting people when he demonstrates his art techniques. These encounters give him both a view of the past and glimpse of the future; in this essay he considers their possible crossing. 1005 Words. 2005.

ps050817
Resource Systems
Bases for Games for the Gifts of Life
He learned about resource systems from an article about a natural resources professor who said his life story changed when he realized he was a resource expert and not the engineer he started out to be. This indicates a parallel with this artist's career. 812 Words. 2005.

ps050827
Birthday Charette
Thoughts Before – and After
On the day he is going to take part in a Birthday Charette, this 60-ish artist writes down some of his thoughts before the event. The Charette is the brainchild of one of Seattle's leaders in their arts community and he is not certain of her expectations. 1186 Words. 2005.

ps050906
Artists Afloat!
Printmaking and Sailing for A Good Cause
Two artists take a day sail and teach art while they travel. They do it for fun, and the profits go to a school fundraiser. This is probably the first time a printmaker—an artist using etching on copper plates—has taken an etching press aboard a sailboat. 769 Words. 2005.

ps050916

My Cowardice
Dare to Open a Living Charette
Twenty days following the Birthday Charette of Anne Focke, the probability comes to the author's mind that he's is afraid to face the fact that it is too late to put into effect the dreams in the minds of those who think about the future in present tense. 1340 Words. 2005.

ps050926
A Talk with a Lawyer
Leads toward a Good Game
He had a brief friendly conversation with an attorney at a fundraiser for an arts organization, and what the lawyer related to this artist reminded him of the main reason he started inventing a game that tracks the artist's—and his or her family's—assets. 1262 Words. 2005.

ps051006
Transcendent Game
Getting Out of the Box
By not identifying with programs, Emeralda players transcend these. In this way they begin to exercise self-actualization, the meta-programming process of the human bio computer, creating self-consciously the principles that govern thoughts and behaviors. 514 Words. 2005.

ps051016
Try to Fly the Virtual Condo
Prospects of a Real Meeting
On the sidewalk outside his condominium building this artist encounters a friend in the condominium sales business who suggests a meeting with a mutual acquaintance for the purpose of airing some creative ideas about building a new condominium. Ideas fly. 981 Words. 2005.

ps051026
In My Personal Life
An Essay A Day Keeps Your Brain Alive
Having a goal is the most important thing this artist learned early. Now he's in his 'sixties, and sees that it's the same for every person who has achieved some kind of mastery in an art or craft. Plus a central belief keeps his game—and his brain—alive. 568 Words. 2005.

ps051105
Why I Had to Discover Emeralda
Reading Roszak's America the Wise
More contacts with people who he met when he was an art professor—as students—makes this artist wonder if there's reason to think he can recover what he thought had been lost twenty years ago: A genuine higher education effort of real benefit to everyone. 1487 Words. 2005.

ps051115
A Missed Opportunity
A Need to Know Not Recognized
A spontaneous question from someone in a group watching the teacher show how to make laser transfer etchings gives this professor pause to wonder: Have I missed an opportunity? She wants to learn how to use her computer in her art studio but he hesitated. 511 Words. 2005.

ps051125
A Good Day for an Epiphany
Arriving There from Here
Every day as he starts out for his day in his studio where a variety of projects await him, he concentrates of one overriding project: Emeralda: Games for the Gifts of Life. It's a fantasy game he's been trying to learn; today might be the day it happens. 912 Words. 2005.

ps051205
Emeralda Prescience
A Two-Way Memory
Always there is the possibility that students of Emeralda are about to make their appearance in the real world of this artist/teacher. He claims to know about a game that can help keep the mind alive and its players' assets growing in value as years pass. 842 Words. 2005.

ps051220
Flashback
Revisiting the Art Student CD/ROM
A inspiration that suggests putting his book, Art of Selling Art, on a CD that goes to owners of Mini Halfwood Presses is like a flashback to the 'eighties when he and C. T. Chew dreamt of a CD called Art Student: Everything you need to learn printmaking. 366 Words. 2005.

ps051230
Thinking about Trumba
Searching for a Virtual Event Driver
Looking ahead to a game that artists can play with time and space, this artist considers the contrast between 20th Century and 21st Century software design. He thinks the former relies on traditional print media, the latter relies on virtual event-drives. 946 Words. 2005.

ps060109
Little Prints Live
The Dreams of a Cabin Boy
This artist searches for the lost yarn that he imagines could have happened, except history has erased almost every trace of it. At the center of his imagining is a clever phrase, Little Prints, which refers both to small etchings and a fable about a boy. 737 Words. 2006.

ps060119
Getting His Story Down
Vladimir's Book Opening
He has a yarn to tell and found that he can hold an audience rapt for up to several minutes telling it while he prints on his etching press. Why not, then, write it down and why not publish it? These are questions that persist while he works on his press. 825 Words. 2006.

ps060218

Story Line
Thoughts on A Novel Idea
He has designed a miniature etching press made of wood and steel. As he works on the wood parts, sanding, finishing them and fitting them to the steel components, a story is in his head. He pauses in his handwork to write it down—the storyline of a novel. 609 Words. 2006.

ps060718
Preamble
Flying in the Face of Deconstruction
The author's nineteen year project at the University was dismantled. Now, thanks to the validity of the premises that guided him in his teaching, research, production and service, his project can be restored and put back on track. 424 Words. 2006.

ps060728
Emeralda City Daily
A Newsletter
The benefit of printmaking was a social thing of being all in one room using the same instruments and techniques, yet all of the artists doing something unique. Now it's the same on this computer—using all four of the "productivity" kinds of software. 260 Words. 2006.

ps060807
Dear Writing Teacher
Playmates of the Arts
The author's "playmates" were, years ago, live people—men and women who came to the University of Washington Art School to learn studio arts. 758 Words. 2006.

ps060817
Ghost
A Spirit of the Future
There is a ghost haunting the author. It came from the future—and that means this ghost is, today, undead. It is a spirit looking down, or back, at him, a shape waiting to be filled. 915 Words. 2006.

ps060926
Simple Rule
Arts Alliance Congress
Opening remarks for the Arts Alliance Congress A structure for collaboration is like insurance for hope. 1591 Words. 2006.

ps061115
Objective
Your Artistic Legacy
The object of the game is to create the Bible of your artistic legacy at the same time you're creating your artistic legacy. 1179 Words. 2006.

ps070129
Always Remember What Emeralda Is
Asset Management and Legacy Transfer
A game of asset management and legacy transfer, weaving the meaning of asset management and legacy transfer throughout all that you do. 192 Words. 2007.

ps070218
New Day Coming
A Recurring Dream of A Changed UW School of Art
In his dream last night, the author entered what used to be the printmaking rooms, and they were totally gutted, devoid of anything that would remind one of what used to occur there. 2225 Words. 2007.

ps070219
Restoring Contiguity
Upon Meeting Bryan Lane
There is hope, however, in working with people who do not carry the baggage of misinformation. 1241 Words. 2007.

ps070608
History of the Halfwood Press
Day 10
This text has been moved to BODY in Perfect Press produce books halfwood. 135 Words. 2007.

ps070916
Win an Etching Press
Towards A Community
A woman laments that she can't afford a Halfwood etching press, yet she's talented in wood working, installation and printmaking arts. In a Flash! of insight, the author thinks this is a door opening up to the mystery of winning Emeralda. 313 Words. 2007.

ps070926
The Cards
Two Databases of Your Art Assets
Note that this essay has been sent to Method of Play in the Administration. After 070928 it no longer is current. Words. 1723 Words. 2007.

ps071006
Cultivate Your Hand
Describing an Asset Game
The inventor of Emeralda writes about the first cards he made for the game, referring to another game called Bellasara. In the latter, cards represent fantasy horses; in the former, cards are art certificates. There's more to the cards than meets the eye. 990 Words. 2007.

ps071026
Easter Egg Rules
Discovering How to Play Emeralda
When you invent a game, you're on a hunt for treasure. You don't know what the rules are, for they haven't been written down for you. You bumble along, looking for the rule, the limits of your freedom. They might come from unexpected places. 472 Words. 2007.

ps071105
Insider Art Auction
Comparing Masterpiece and Emeralda
The inventor of Emeralda: Games for the Gifts of

Life speculates on the similarities and the differences between his idea and the ideas behind other conventional board games—in particular with one board game called Masterpiece—an auction game. 1197 Words. 2007.

ps071115
Million Dollar Mark
Dental Games and the Internet
The artist and teacher thinks about a distance learning game for high school students in which they would get an early exposure, for college credit, to the field of dentistry and oral health. This article touches on the roots of his idea and his own game. 570 Words. 2007.

ps071220
Recurrent and Recursive Games
A Passion for Collecting
A phrase in a book by Craig Karpel he titled The Retirement Myth hints at a clue for the creation of a game design. The phrase is "recurrent development of new competencies" and reminds the game inventor of another game development principle: Recursivity. 609 Words. 2007.

ps071230
Power and Artist Trading Cards
Musings of a Game Designer
Junk mail from an art museum announcing a family collection show sets the author thinking about the power inherent in collections. This, along with the topic of a novel of murder and intrigue he's reading that's about art, piques ideas about cards. 1253 Words. 2007.

ps080109
Beginning and Ending Books
From Confucius to Stewart and Many in Between
The inventor of Emeralda: Games for the Gifts of Life recollects how his readings gave him the idea of a game for asset management and legacy transfer, starting with games and ending with games. Outside sources and his inside feelings created a huge lake. 902 Words. 2008.

ps080119
Card Ready
Preparing for the Big One
Learning that one of his artworks will be offered in a commercial art auction, the author thinks about his own version of an auction—the Big One—the kind that happens when an artist dies. It's part of his Artist's Last Love Letter model he needs to write. 1056 Words. 2008.

ps080208
Emeralda Curricula
How a Card Plays
This artist is looking for a special kind of collectible artist's playing card, one that actually "plays" in the sense of a performance. Ideas like this appear in his imagination as he envisions a game which he can use to be a virtual, virtuous professor. 542 Words. 2008.

ps080218
Restoration Theater
A "Mid-Artist's" Notion for An Art Sale
Stung by the suggestion that his own handiwork and collaborative role in the birth of an artwork by an artist more renown than himself, the artist—who enjoyed a generation as an art professor at the time of this art's making—plans a dinner sale. 1329 Words. 2008.

ps080309
Trial Proof in the Age of Digital Reproduction
Matrix Migration
Today, like the trial proofs that printmaker made in the age of mechanical reproduction. 597 Words. 2008.

ps080319
Worker Ownership
Reflections on the Mondragon Cooperative
When the author was studying cooperatives, and the Mondragon was an ideal case of workers finding it necessary to buy the company rather than give up their families and homes. 1190 Words. 2008.

ps080329
Course Content
Artists Asset Management and Legacy Transfer
Noting that his associate taught a course in the Experimental College in Seattle, the author outlines a class that he thinks the two of them could team teach—inviting other interested people to engage in developing a hybrid art and technology methodology. 508 Words. 2008.

ps080408
Education Version
Declaration of Interdependence
The inventor of an interface game for a distance-learning course in printmaking describes the idea behind what he calls his Declaration of Interdependence. In his essay he explains the connection between his thinking and the Union of Concerned Scientists. 933 Words. 2008.

ps080418
Needs Assessment
First of Twelve Tasks for the Leader in Teaching and Learning Printmaking
The first question when the author thinks of Needs Assessment, the prerequisite to developing Learn Printmaking Online. Do we need printmaking when we spend a lot of time in the virtual landscape? 977 Words. 2008.

ps080428
Press Kit
Listing the Contents
The designer of an online printmaking course plans to put everything an art student needs into a box that he or she can use to learn printmaking, calling it an appropriate technology for education in the age of digital reproduction. He lists the con-

tents. 734 Words. 2008.

ps080508
Twelve Tasks
A Dozen Things Online Printmaking Education Leaders Must Do
From a five-year old study on the subject of leadership in distance learning, the author (who would aspire to leadership in art in the age of digital reproduction) gleans twelve tasks that author described that needed doing. He reflects on a 1970s vision. 1786 Words. 2008.

ps080518
Evaluating Credibility
Program Evaluation and Accreditation
One of the unfortunate byproducts of the industrial revolution was the transfer of responsibility for one's individual actions to the responsibility of the industrial group. 1417 Words. 2008.

ps090109
Creating Emeralda
Biblical History of Emeralda Region, Home to Games for the Gifts of Life
The development period of Emeralda, the fantasy site where all the things this artist wished for are coming true, is over. The 24-year development period was also a waiting period, when it seemed he could do nothing else but wait, but also create a bible. 1273 Words. 2009.

ps090119
Which Way to Emeralda?
Which World is a Better Place Locate a Printmaker's Haven?
The author feels like he is living in two worlds at the same time. One is the everyday real world he wakes up in, goes through his morning rituals and then walks a half-block to his studio. Awaiting him is his computer, offering portals to virtual worlds. 511 Words. 2009.

ps090129
ELPO Structure
The Bones of an Interactive Online Blended Learning Game
For a time-based experience in which a user learns and acts upon information delivered both online and in real life, the project will be structured in what is called "Blended Learning" in the education field—both virtual and real experiences are built-in. 1276 Words. 2009.

ps090218
In th`e Beginning
Genesis of Emeralda
Challenged to write the bible of Emeralda: Learn Printmaking Online, the inventor refers to Genesis for inspiration. The Old Testament describes how the world was created; a bible of Emeralda might likewise establish how a fantasy world began—with a film. 1070 Words. 2009.

ps090228

ELPO Overall Look and Sound
Harmonious Concerts in the Recursive World of Learning Printmaking
The last essay of the ten points in a Ten-Step Development lay-out from Miller's book Digital Storytelling. Combining the challenges from the first edition and the newer edition adding points that are suitable to the author's goals. 309 Words. 2009.

ps090408
Selling Emeralda
We Sell the Business as we build it
A business that is based on a vision, one that is still in its formative stages, is not one that most people will invest in. Like buying a laying hen that is still a baby chick, it's too risky for many people. This visionary, however, thinks it otherwise. 1734 Words. 2009.

ps090409
Dusty Cann Profile
Love for the Inanimates
Perfect Studios embodies love for the life of the mind, which may on the surface seem remote from the love one person for another. The fact is, however, that love permeates all the relations between self and the creatures of the Earth—even the inanimates. 638 Words. 2009.

ps090429
Printmaking as Performance
Professor says Printmaking is Both a Visual and a Performing Art
Proof that printmaking is both a visual and a performing art has taken this professor his whole professional life. He has yet to see the idea accepted. Now that the digital age has re-shaped much of what we think about, it is time to drive home this idea. 1053 Words. 2009.

ps090509
Twelve Beauties of Printmaking
A Calendar and Art Show
To finance an online printmaking course, the course' designer presents his idea to the community that's evolving around plans to use a game-like user interface—which is a costly proposition. In this essay he lays out the idea that he says will earn money. 1143 Words. 2009.

ps090519
My Bucket List
A Timely Review and Look Ahead
The movie, "Bucket List," made renowned the common idea of goal-setting, albeit in a grim storyline. The point is not lost on the author in this essay. In a small spiral-bound notebook he jotted down some things he wants to do, and then in his computer to share. 932 Words. 2009.

ps090628
World Printmaking Cooperative
My Vision of a Solution
Forty years have passed since this artist chose printmaking from among the myriad art forms

available to him when he was in college. He has seen his selection change from ink on paper to digital games. He writes it is time to link tradition to technology. 1350 Words. 2009.

ps090926
Goal Terminology
Origins of Perfect Studios
In goal-setting, the author reviews the origins of his goal to be an art teacher in a university. Looking in the Wikipedia turns up two new words that apply to his review. The words are etiological myth and eponymous; they clarify what Perfect Studios is. 593 Words. 2009.

ps091006
Goal Review
Perfect Studios
Within months of having left institutional teaching in fine art printmaking—having found it untenable—this professor began going to business power breakfasts. One featured a speaker on Management by Goals. It has made all the difference, and needs review. 1019 Words. 2009.

Ritchie's International Institute for Studies in Multimedia Arts (AKA RIISMA, also, RI)

Ritchie's International Institute for Study of Multimedia Arts, or RIISMA (pronounced riz' ma) at midday.

The mission of the Residents-in-Stay at RIISMA is to open gates to research, develop the links with and integration of ideas across disciplines, expand the frontiers of knowledge about art and build bridges to real-life issues.

The history of this not-for-profit arts research organization began at the University of Washington as a printmaking club called Student Printmakers' Services Association (SPSA) in 1972, including an alternative gallery for video art, followed by the Seattle Association for Media Artists (SAMA) in 1975. The same students and graduates were involved, fol-

lowing the advice of Bill Ritchie, their professor.

On dissolution of SAMA, acting alone, Bill Ritchie formed Ritchie's Institute for the Study of Multimedia Arts (RIISMA) in 1989, based on SAMA, to continue research and development of multimedia arts.

RIISMA is the only not-for-profit organization supported in Emeralda Region as a reminder of Bill's studies of the global impact of multimedia that he made by traveling abroad in 1969, 1976 and 1983.

ri890104
A History of Media Art:
New curriculum proposal
Twenty years after his discovery that print making - his favorite medium - was dead, the author restored it's life by giving it a family name: Media Art. It's a threshold of a new paradigm for looking at prints. Next he outlines a reinvented arts studio. 448 Words. 1989.

ri890106
A New Telecourse:
Media Artistry
Synopsis to a proposal to Annenberg Foundation to help create a television series to survey the history of media arts and to look inside print, video, and computer arts studios. It's based on the author's unique archive of videos and early NW digital art. 286 Words. 1989.

ri901207
ToolBook Diary:
Experiment #2 in Hypermedia
In November this author began his first hypermedia books using Asymetrix ToolBook software. He kept journals, note cards and appointment calendars. For this project he recorded his impressions of ToolBook. The article covers November to December 21, 1990. 1817 Words. 1990.

ri901217
Notes from the cave:
Mission statement for RIISMA
Ritchie's International Institute for the Study of Multimedia Arts follows trends of computer graphics and electronic imaging trends. RISMA is a virtual institute addressing a not-so-virtual problem: A gap between fact and fiction in educational research. 1932 Words. 1990.

ri910319
Integration and disintegration
Multimedia blockages in the way of art museums
Are the art museums in on the multimedia revolution? If not, why? The block might be the cost of the hardware and software. Art museums have a hard time meeting expenses. The right proposal has not yet been made. The author works on the right one. 1081 Words. 1991.

ri910320
Multimedia user interface

Gateway to the museum without walls
This article focuses on the museum without walls, a notion based on reproduction of artworks. It depends on maintaining touch with realities of the viewers, the human users and the design of electronic controls which multimedia offers. 626 Words. 1991.

ri910321
Financing RIISMA
Background of letter to a Philanthropist
This is not a real article; it is a virtual article, the abstract of a proposal for financing an international institute of multimedia arts - the author's concept of a new school for the Pacific Northwest with branches worldwide. 481 Words. 1991.

ri910322
Multimedia arts survey
Washington museums and libraries
How are museums using computers and multimedia? It is smart to begin now with what is available and learn the language of multimedia in a living and learning way. 1698 Words. 1991.

ri910330
Marketing with multimedia
Advice for Gatekeepers in the Emerald City
The author thinks a practice room where multimedia skills can be learned, in an international institute for study of multimedia arts, is needed to capitalize on regional high-tech, paid for by reinvesting profits flowing into the Emerald City. 3401 Words. 1991.

ri910331
Art Student Brainstorm
Multimedia practice room for marketers
Culture serves significantly in the economy of our city, and our city, in turn, can serve the entire state of Washington with a central forum for multimedia arts. Bill Ritchie's version is the art business forum, with a new twist: multimedia marketing. 1536 Words. 1991.

ri910401
Multimedia Arts Study
What it is, what it isn't
By describing what his institute is not, the author compares it to museums and libraries and their importance to the economy. Marketing, after all, will gain the most from the study of multimedia arts, and marketers may be the first to learn them. 2078 Words. 1991.

ri910419
Mammoth meets M.I.T.
Notes from a bystander
One audience member, the author, at an M.I.T. Forum meeting took notes on his palmtop computer and sent them to his friends at Mammoth Micro for their enjoyment. 1068 Words. 1991.

ri910520
OOP's Surprise

Creative Management in ToolBook
Object-oriented programming allows non-programmers to make graphical computer programs on computer video display terminals. Business management can be facilitated by object-oriented programming and intuitive use of computers. 1206 Words. 1991.

ri910521
Stories, Experiences, and Multimedia Technologies
Holding the new mediums accountable
Sent to a CompuServe author after a call for proposals was published in the CompuServe magazine. From the author's series, Marketing with multimedia, on interior design, a description how he used a computer to design carpet and recycles the concept. 481 Words. 1991.

ri910908
TESC, are you for real?
Applying for the lead position
The author saw an invitation to apply for the president's position of The Evergreen State College. He applied for the position (but did not get it). This article consists of the notes he made while considering the job. 7627 Words. 1991.

ri911108
Artworks and packages in the information age
Turning museums inside out
Art tradition and technology clash and result in package design. The author starts where Harold Rosenberg left off. Issues are the museum without walls, the computer, file structures and the Living Museum of Computer Arts, Crafts and Design. 913 Words. 1991.

ri911113
Perfect U
Artists' dreams, visualizations
C. T. Chew, the author, and Norie Sato worked together at Triangle Studios from 1975 to 1982 and, when they left it, thought someday they would work together again in a new way. Carl's words with Bill's amendments outline a memo of understanding. 1204 Words. 1991.

ri911115
Visit my museum
A day in the life of an archivist
On a day in mid-November, the author finds his computer unavailable. So he goes into his private "museum" of computers and video and turns on the old systems to see what happens. 3040 Words. 1991.

ri911120
Itinerate professor
How am I doing?
A professor was forced into retirement due to his unorthodox views and, six years after resignation, he still thinks about his mentors and the reasons

he wanted to teach. The information age held attraction but led to a world between business and art. 2097 Words. 1991.

ri911122
Print makers, the next generation
Accessing knowledge with new machines
Responding to an article by Hugh J. Merrill, the author asks where the new technologies will lead educators who want to teach the next generation. 527 Words. 1991.

ri911206
Finding Triangle
What kind of tool is this?
This article is about the trail or pathway of Triangle Studios, an artists' co-operative in the '80s, as it moved from one directory on the author's computer hard drive to another one. 1380 Words. 1991.

ri911208
Artist uses ToolBook by Asymetrix
New art marketing tool
Bill Ritchie is interviewed by Frank Susan about his work in ToolBook in this autobio-fantasy. Ritchie bought hypertext software after getting a recommendation by a Hypercard expert. It is becoming his marketing tool for artwork, design and crafts. 396 Words. 1991.

ri911227
Museum for a Virtuous Reality
Three ways to start
How do you start a new museum? Why start a new museum? This article contains key concepts of the founding of the Living Museum of Computer Arts, Crafts and Design. 6519 Words. 1991.

ri920113
Overproduction
Asymetrix ignorance
Claude Ostyn calls back and says I've never seen anything like it! regarding my Perfect Studios ToolBook I sent to him. Isn't that what the lines were in the movie, Amadeus, when the older composer asked Mozart what he thought of his music? 311 Words. 1992.

ri920128
Bill Gates at WSA
Navigating the Nineties
Notes made on his palmtop by the author attending the annual dinner meeting of the Washington Software Association. Bill Gates was the keynote speaker, and Ritchie gleans several pieces of good advice by listening to this new meritocrat. 456 Words. 1992.

ri920228
The Scot's Mistake
Little Book Text
This is the text of a Little Book created in Pagemaker. This may not be the current edition because it continues to be edited according to the requirements of the LittleBook. A number of LittleBooks exist, listed in a different directory. 1225 Words. 1992.

ri920323
Moro's house
On the other side of the chasm
I was a lecturer as part of a Distinguished Artists series. When guests came in, they heard the music of pan pipes and singing by natives in the Soloman Islands. It was a videotape playing with an important message from a Micronesian spiritual leader. 1863 Words. 1992.

ri920327
Goals and Curriculum Design
Take it from the leaders
Curriculum design with a core of wisdom is the theme of the Master of Digital Arts. Harvard and The Evergreen State College share this: Be goal-oriented. Curriculum design for the Master of Digital Arts is based on this and the navigator metaphor. 535 Words. 1992.

ri920331
Museum FunRaising
AMuse, not money first
The author tries to balance between traditional museums within walls and the museum without walls, a project he calls Virtual Museums of Washington. This is stream-of-conscience text generation, all paperless until he prints it. 747 Words. 1992.

ri920402
Virtual Museum of Washington
Going on-line with the idea
Proposal for an article inspired by a conversation with a museum curator who said she didn't know a bit from a byte. The idea starts as a message for a Bulletin Board Service. 433 Words. 1992.

ri920426
Modem Magazine in ToolBook
The slow death of printing
This is the second article about using the three-year old ModemNews, this time with a graphical interface which he prefers over text. The author speculates on the death of printing and the replacement of paper magazines with diskettes and on-liners. 907 Words. 1992.

ri920525
University without walls
ITinerate Professors delight!
The ITinerate professor states how the museum without walls welcomes the artist who plays the exploring, seeker. Early scripting in college prepares a person for survival, even if it means surviving without a university or museum to conserve tradition. 365 Words. 1992.

ri920531
Among the lines
The end of class and career

Mourning the end of an art class by political administrators makes the author wonder, If the chief function of art became political in the age of mechanical reproduction, then what is the function of art education in the age of electronic reproduction? 5435 Words. 1992.

ri920607
Distance Post Graduate Education in Art
Back-to-school via information superhighways
Copy-written article about a networked information resource intensive institution for distance graduate education for adults. (Proposal) 1116 Words. 1992.

ri920618
LMOCACAD's first six months
Newsletter proposal for a new museum
A collection based on the press releases, events and announcements from the first six-months of the Living Museum of Computer Arts, Crafts and Design. The author proposed the museum in late 1991 and continues to strive for the cause. 1555 Words. 1992.

ri920921
Ann Gould Hauberg
Patron of the arts
Nineteen eighty-two television interview transcribed by Barbara Gorell at the request of Bill Ritchie from the audiotape copy from Ann Gould Hauberg's personal copy of the videotape in her private collection. 5171 Words. 1992.

ri921010
Funding the changing playing field
A six-sided figure
A transformed paradigm underlies this description of a funding strategy for the Master of Digital Arts pilot program. The diagram shows a hexagonal pie. No doubt the pie is the product of the fruit of the logic tree. 181 Words. 1992.

ri921019
Opportunities for MBAs still in school
Knocking on doors
Changing technologies in business communications are opportunities for people still enrolled in college. Innovation between visionary artists, craftspeople and designers can create bridges between botom-liners and information technologists. 440 Words. 1992.

ri921105
School bells
The toll at the end of school
The mistake of the bells, the biology teacher and thinking little in the loop - three short essays written as the author meets philanthropist Max Gurvich and begins the series, Ultra Phoenix Building, about the 500th year of the Phoenix' last rebirth. 722 Words. 1992.

ri921106
Ultra Phoenix

Cornerstones for a builders' meeting
The Glass Bead Game and other literary works are background of a meeting with philanthropists in Seattle. The Gurviches and Ritchie share concepts for Ultra, theater and education, meeting to study potential designs for aligning their interests. 998 Words. 1992.

ri921107
ULTRA Phoenix
The second day
Maps, territories, the roles of early patrons of his art and organized in a background development as the author plans to meet the next generation of potential supporters. 843 Words. 1992.

ri921108
Ultra Phoenix Building
And buildings can fly
Speculating on his interest in new building development in his fantasy CityLand, the author describes the analogy between the Phoenix allegory and new technologies. 465 Words. 1992.

ri921109
RINC Defined
Reinventing arts studios, digitally
What is the reinvented arts studio and what is it for? Focus on Ritchie's, Inc.'s Big Picture, in Microsoft Windows software, working with videotape to empower artists and teachers worldwide. Use the soccer-ball metaphor to explain hexagonal integrity. 2331 Words. 1992.

ri921111
Re-packaging Cornish
Resuscitation of a fine arts school
Packages and artworks combine with computers in mind. With a suitable place and time for the process, a perfect way to make the transition between tradition and technology is with teaching, research and practice together, in one place, at one time. 985 Words. 1992.

ri921112
Circles and links
Renew Cornish leadership
Background for a proposal to begin a multimedia program at the Cornish College of Art. The author calls it A wonderful idea - a Perfect Studios idea - a way to start with a trade-in deal. 1466 Words. 1992.

ri921113
When lions and foxes meet
Max's Parables
Striving to understand the parables of the fox, the sloth and the lion, the author reflects on the significance of overlapping times and events that brought about his meeting with a leader in the philanthropic support of the arts. 982 Words. 1992.

ri921114
Cornish Information Technology Alliance

From a mission to a forecast
After seven years' development, Perfect Studios, a concept whose time has come, seeks friendly companions. The author accurately forecasts an alliance of technology to support fine arts. 398 Words. 1992.

ri921115
History of Cornish Information Technology Alliance
Her vision becoming real?
In this plan to form an alliance between arts and new technology industries, the author wishes to demonstrate his understanding of the Cornish College of the Arts. The article may then be the basis for project proposals and other kinds of interaction. 949 Words. 1992.

ri921116
History of Cornish Information Technology Alliance
A visionary approach to sustainability
In the last generation of its first hundred years - 1994-2014 - the Cornish school might go through a change in its approach to technology. This author suggests that a paradigm shift accompanies information technology in organizations. 1017 Words. 1992.

ri921117
Beacon
Cornish
The Information Technology Alliance is the building of a beacon at a school like the Cornish College of the Arts. There is a catch in this proposal, though: FAST ART, the bane of the high arts, is one of the central principles. 2136 Words. 1992.

ri921118
First Impressions
An artist's life as phases
Three periods characterize the life of an artist, teacher and researcher--the early, middle and late. The author begins by telling about his early years. 354 Words. 1992.

ri921121
Core of the fruit
Technology alliances and the arts
A seed that grows on the branch far from the trunk contains the scripted genetic code to recreate the tree in another time and place. Waiting in the wood a calculus between virtue and reality guides a professor's steps toward a Technology Alliance. 1191 Words. 1992.

ri921122
The Big Mistake
Venture without financing
Begin with the end in mind - your long-term roles and goals - and see if you can point out the biggest mistake today. Financing ambitious programs will be a problem in a dangerous country. 996 Words. 1992.

ri921123
Form follows function
Architecture of Perfect Studios
Several guidelines as to how to meet leaders of educational institutions and introduce Perfect Studios as a structural/instructional benefit to their organization. 750 Words. 1992.

ri921124
Background, Objective, Listener, Approach
Meeting with campus officials
Education and arts leaders view technologies from paradigms that they learned before the new ones existed, when they were being invented. Tied to tradition, not potential, their histories make them respond to feelings, not professional values. 1084 Words. 1992.

ri921125
The Point of Technology Alliances
View from a tetrahedron
A professor of business visits Ritchie, and a visual communication cartoon and models are contrived to make the point of ITA. Thus, the relation of business and art can be seen in a new perspective, and a technological bridge might be built. 1289 Words. 1992.

ri921126
Live and kicking
The business of arts practice self-management
A project is being designed to put MBA candidates in touch with the arts, science and economic development through a joint venture. By selling self-help books, the money is to build an electronic classroom/studio, the principle of learn and earn. 1460 Words. 1992.

ri921128
Widening, narrowing on the big picture
New illusions of calculation
New technologies make it easier to review long range goals and paint the big picture. But what about communicating with newcomers? This article suggests one way it can be done so that effectiveness is a realistic probability within real constraints. 2602 Words. 1992.

ri921129
Emergency
Balance between long and short term
In art and business, urgency may be the best way to get results. Long-range plans are fine because they build consistent direction and confidence but they don't motivate like short-term demands do. Quality falls if a moment's importance is unclear. 2141 Words. 1992.

ri921201
Interface
Between arts and industries
Ritchie's is an in-between company, operating between education institutions and vertical industries in the Puget Sound. Its president developed a seven-year learning, research and production

project needed by both. 757 Words. 1992.

ri921202
Seven techniques of highly effective multimedia artists
A fantasy
Hand-written draft about ways John Cage, Lily Tomlin, Robert Rauschenberg, Robert Abel, C. T. Chew, Norie Sato, Laurie Anderson use media technologies in their arts and performances. 600 Words. 1992.

ri921204
Buyer beware
What you don't know about multimedia can hurt you
Hand written draft created on the eve of meetings with Asymetrix contractor Eileen Gunn (also a science-fiction writer). In it the author describes a strategy for using MediaBlitz! to help launch the Information Technology Alliance for the Arts, or ITAA. 3000 Words. 1992.

ri921207
L.I.T.T.L.E
Living Informatin Technology Theatre Life Enjoyment
After star systems in art's logical expression in centuries of developing an art-information science, a new movement is taking shape. Call it, Living Information Technology Theatre Life Enjoyment, or L.I.T.T.L.E.. 2432 Words. 1992.

ri921208
Time to commit to ITA
They will come if you build it artistically
Considering the revolution being brought about by such things as video games and the impact of the digital age on society, the author has a wide scope, describing the illusion of calculation behind digital games, war and alliances. 1230 Words. 1992.

ri921211
Are you ready for ITA?
A new kind of investment club
Some people think of The chicken or the egg? When they are asked to invest in a lesson in computer or multimedia. What is it? They ask. The risk seems too much. Here is a new viewpoint. 1560 Words. 1992.

ri921212
Real Adventure Land
Concluding ULTRA Phoenix and the ITA essays
Four principles stand out after the month-long reality-check in which the author asked if industry and fine arts can be mutually supportive: Human resources, space/time, attitude and resistance to change. 969 Words. 1992.

ri921213
Pro-Information Technology Alliance
Solving the education problem
To use information technology wisely requires

formal organization and also cultural organization. Interaction of people with formal organizations can be through tools that bring about alliances--artistically--with craft and design. 938 Words. 1992.

ri921216
Perfect Studios
A measure of success
To research, produce and teach, Perfect Studios gives arts, crafts and design insights into the information technology industry. Skills and knowledge keep humans on loci of all creative works. This requires an alliance between art and technology. 1281 Words. 1992.

ri921217
Contract with developers
Arts-building starts with a concept
The author computes the mental, psychological and physical creation called, The ULTRA Phoenix Building, an object lesson of what he calls The Illusion of Calculation. 1624 Words. 1992.

ri930331
Ultra Phoenix Collected Writings
Preface and contents
Ritchie was encouraged by Max Gurvich to continue study of the Frederick & Nelson building as a future home of the Cornish College of Art Hi-tech center. This is the preface of what was to become a marketing study based on Gurvich' vision of his building. 349 Words. 1992.

ri930103
MDA Proper
Making Education Proprietary
Information is the designated driver in business. National policy is focused on information technologies, or IT. Education crises are related in the use of new tools. Where are we headed? An analogy may exist with the food chain and food services. 1245 Words. 1993.

ri930112
Professor Ritchie takes the place of Professor Cady
Professing education reform for art school
The teacher is beleaguered, distracted from teaching. General acceptance is someone else is to blame and that the problem will be solved by someone else, somehow, some day. Best proposals for education reform come from the future - not blame politics. 695 Words. 1993.

ri930115
What's going on with the MDA?
Putting a spin on the Master of Digital Arts
This article is about research or the author's rhetorical question, What's going on with the MDA?, his proposed new program of Master of Digital Arts. The author focuses on the who, why and what for communication over a ninety-day period. 2486 Words. 1993.

ri930119

Dr. David Dwyer at Shoreline Center
Apple Classrooms of the Future report
Notes from Dr. David Dwyer on the Apple Classrooms of the Future, and the America 2000 educational reform movement. These are from his 2-hour program given at the Shoreline Center, near Seattle, in 1993. 1822 Words. 1993.

ri930120
World Scientists' Warning to Humanity
1600 Scientists give us 30 years
The text from the Union of Concerned Scientists' World's Scientists Warning to Humanity that inspired Bill Ritchie to ask, Could I locate 1600 artists to endorse a similar document? While the immediate answer is No, he decided to perform as if it can be. 1527 Words. 1993.

ri930121
Heeding World Scientists' Warning to Humanity
Call to creative and technical people
Bill Ritchie, an artist, wondered if as many artists (UCS reported 1575 scientists had signed this warning) could be found who would endorse such a warning. To act, he has made the text of this warning part of his plan for reinventing arts' studios. 1604 Words. 1993.

ri930125
Can we put electronic arts in Washington's schools?
Multimedia pioneer thinks so
This curriculum plan makes use of Washington-grown resources in technology and creativity. Interactive multimedia arts could and should become a new language in Washington schools. 1736 Words. 1993.

ri930126
InformationTechnology Alliance for the Arts
Art supply stores and the MDA
The MDA is a leadership degree aimed at restoring the cultural value of art. It is based on the principle learned from the teaching hospital metaphor that was invented in Great Britain in the 18th Century. Art supply stores add value with information. 480 Words. 1993.

ri930226
Boeing going boing bong gone
Crisis and opportunity to create jobs
The twilight of large corporations casts long shadows on our economy, warning of destruction like Hesse's Age of the feuilleton. Only the Green Glass Bead Game can save us, as edu-tainment is the key. Can we be turned? Can Boeing make sailing ships? 675 Words. 1993.

ri930227
Telecommuting
Work, school and ecological economics
Workers, managers and leaders commonly use computers in connection with their jobs. As a part of telecommuting, a computer can become an office helper that, if used properly, never eats, sleeps,

nor catches a sniffle. 444 Words. 1993.

ri930304
Art Classrooms of Tomorrow Today
An ecological solution
The EarthSafe 2022 Classroom of the Future is a multimedia, interactive experience. People mix business, retail, hospitality, marketing and sales with super-real events. Art without paper, canvas, clay or bronze. Silicon replaces silica. 2122 Words. 1993.

ri930306
Explaining myself
Notes from the hyper world

After three months of intensive study of Asymetrix software in the Perfect Studios, the author has some conclusions. The art estate is assayed, accessed and disseminated hypermedia. The Perfect Studios' products are parts in a catalog. 2555 Words. 1993.

ri930310
The age of the so-called expert
Looking for the hidden face
From the plains of Zimbabwe to the California beaches, visualize the international development of higher education, then ask, "What is the motive?" 481 Words. 1993.

ri930311
Conundrum in the database
Searching through the White House e-mail
The White House Paper pours into this computer. Too wordy, too long to be interesting, taking too much energy. That's a clue! The ITinerate Professor goes to work with his digital knife. Artists conserve energy required by people in learning. 605 Words. 1993.

ri930318
Tomes, 'toons and databases
Postcards from consultants' hell
A digital artist can turn a flat file OOP database found on an on-line service into a cartoon collection, and this into a collection of graphics and text called Postcards from Consultants' Hell. 818 Words. 1993.

ri930319
Glass Beads and Tetrahedrons
MDA Specs on my palmtop
Starting the expert system (PRL) begins with the end in mind, is goal-driven in its forward-chaining mode. Goals are long, middle and short-term. This paradigm restores the cultural value of the arts, also the character and values of artists. 443 Words. 1993.

ri930328
What comes first?
Database or document
Next-generation art collectors will insist on a feature called Talking Prints to go with their vi-

sual arts and other collectibles. Today's multimedia encyclopedias tend to divide and specialize. Available tools are primitive compared to what is coming. 763 Words. 1993.

ri930329
Holding the line
Advocates for closure
In place of mass-communication one-to-many a new paradigm of many-to-many is coming. Individuals hold the line as waves of one-to-many advocates press for closed-systems. 378 Words. 1993.

ri930401
Master's Degree For Sale
Master of Digital Art
After years in development, a curriculum for the Masters of Digital Art is ready to stage. Like an ambitious opera set design, it involves interaction of people, skill, attitudes and tools. The knowledge worker is engineering and setting the time clock. 282 Words. 1993.

ri930402
Dialer
The seeker's touch
Using the electronic bulletin board, the person seeking the latest information on restaurants in Nashville uses the dialer. This mixture of fact and fantasy shadows a shopper in an art supply store and a traveler headed for the Yakima Valley. 327 Words. 1993.

ri930408
Welcome to the MDA Catalog
Your Instant Database for a new degree
This is the first page of the Instant Database version of Ritchie's Master of Digital Arts Magalog Article DisKit, available for publication, from Bill H. Ritchie, Jr. Use the buttons, above, to change screens, and search for your favorite keywords. 267 Words. 1993.

ri930422
BillsGates' ToolBooks
Drive-thru F Drive
Observing the 23rd Official Earth Day today, the author reviews ToolBooks he created in three years. How can they help EarthSafe 2022 in Perfect Studios' Mission statement? Perhaps retrospective will show a way in making this database list. 3870 Words. 1993.

ri930522
Head-to-toe change
Reinventing studios and schools of art
A head-to-toe change has taken place from the perspective of today's electronic artist, changing the proportions with which most people are familiar. Understanding art education today requires reinventing arts studios and art schools. 1169 Words. 1993.

ri930610
Whole EarthSafe 2022 Magadisc

Something newer, more eco-nomic
Why not a Magalog of new technologies coming from the near-sided people who are really involved with it? Why not make publication of shareware made by, for and of creativity by artists, craftsmen and designers directly in the medium-of-origination? 332 Words. 1993.

ri930620
Highway Paradigm
Learning from a Tree Top can
Dreaming of a safer Earth, the author tries to connect transportation history and food processing--the comparison of transporting things and data. What if data highways result in safer, more successful living or worse than the automobile caused? 926 Words. 1993.

ri930627
LMOCACAD on a disk
Visualize, then build - or don't
People like to see beautiful buildings where museums, but it is possible to put museums on a TV screen. The National Gallery was put on laser video disc. In the Living Museum of Computer Arts, Crafts and Design, the diskette comes first. 229 Words. 1993.

ri930702
TRPI's 3 Dimensions
Investment club of a new kind
There are always three dimensions to a TRPI meeting. One is the Teaching/learning part and takes most of the meeting. The other two are the Research the Productivity dimensions. 668 Words. 1993.

ri930710
A ROSE with a difference
A new theatre?
The author was invited to several discussions among people who are interested in creating a performance of original works designed for a three-dimensional audio space. This article is made of the notes he took on his palm-top. 1242 Words. 1993.

ri930713
Dino-doo doo and the data highway
Just another roadside attraction
Perfect Studios is where a creative person can combine words, pictures, sounds, math, and sequence in ways fine arts could not, using multimedia computers. Now, multimedia is used as entertainment machines, and currently the hot ticket item is dinosaurs! 2010 Words. 1993.

ri930722
EarthSafe 2022 credit cards
An affinity for sustainability
Poplular credit cards, frequent-flyer miles and smart cards inspired this proposal for a support scheme for a sustainable environment, both tangible and intangible, for continuing education. 1577 Words. 1993.

ri930727
An idea whose time has come
Who will pay?
A backward-look by a forward-looking professor to art, business and technology comprising a new curriculum. Painting broad-strokes of the picture, the money will come from two Washington's meeting on a bridge between agriculture and culture-culture. 574 Words. 1993.

ri930806
History of the Digital Arts Degree
Outgrowth of a new language
Outgrowth of a new language Computer science, invented generations ago, made it possible to use digital .computers for drawing, painting, musical and "thinking" machines. The way opened for a new kind of digital art. 1471 Words. 1993.

ri930824
Art Business Consulting Degree
Part of a sustainable education
Art Businesss Consulting Degree is an inside-out curriculum to offer to qualified students who want to augment their arts, crafts and design studies with instruction in business and industry. This article describes the skeleton of the degree. 2157 Words. 1993.

ri930929
Central-Principled Leadership
A three part plan based on values
Central-principled leadership describes a teaching, research and production plan for education in the age of electronic reproduction. The core of the program is ecological economics, open systems designed as if peoples' time matters. 411 Words. 1993.

ri930930
Mondragon Metaphor
Late-model eco-nomics
The roots of a new kind of business experience run deep in the past, past bounds of economic models that rule peoples' lives or ways of thinking. Computers became tools for creating new ways to do business, and in time the tool was a new business medium. 670 Words. 1993.

ri931119
Building Coalitions for a Creative America
Notes from a teleconference
Notes from an interactive teleconference about the role of the federal government in arts and education for the next century. The conference took place November 19, 1993 at The Evergreen State College campus. The author intersperses private thoughts. 1691 Words. 1993.

ri931221
LMOCACAD's third year
Introducing LMASOCACAD
First proposed on December 18, 1991, the creative director takes another look to see how the project

is doing. The addition of "- And School - " changes the picture a little. 1329 Words. 1993.

ri931231
Dead schools and living museums
Welcome to the Rose Hill story
Itinerate professor speculates on the site of the future "museum without walls" for computer arts, crafts and design. The proposed destruction of Rose Hill Elementary School inspired this essay. 1965 Words. 1993.

ri940106
Be Your Own Museum, the Hard Way
Bringing the Muse back into Museums
The original Living Museum is yourself. The hard part is getting it out. You can take the artist, crafts person and designer out of the museum, but you can't take the museum out of the artist. The artist writing this essay says he began with a co-op idea. 1302 Words. 1994.

ri940109
Rose Hill Bomb Scare:
A Financial Neutron Device
A drama is unfolding in Kirkland, and ground zero is the site of the old Rose Hill Elementary School, beyond the freeway, east of the city. It symbolizes the economic condition of the US, a country with a great infrastructure and weak educational history. 1964 Words. 1994.

ri940119
What is the plan for Rose Hill School?
Outline for a conservative proposal
To preserve the memory of the old days, and the old ways of building wood frame structures, a bold new living museum was proposed, one for the 21st Century. A group tried to save a 20th Century school from demolition. This might have been the site for it. 717 Words. 1994.

ri940122
Money for LMASOCACAD
Where is it all coming from?
How does one pay for a virtual museum, or a museum that is all in the mind? This article suggests tapping the "Infrastructure Maintenance Fund" - a virtual fund that is earmarked for maintaining the "data" highway even before people have traveled over it. 2297 Words. 1994.

ri940207
Orientation of Rose Hill
Getting the community educated
Educating people at Rose Hill, a fantasy campus of the Living Museum and School of Computer Arts, Crafts and Design, involves five whys. This means asking "Why?" five times. This essay is incomplete; it starts out with the risk in setting long-term goals. 333 Words. 1994.

ri940315
Can 3 Cities Finance This?
Hi-tech museum and school project

A Visualization and fantasy exercise by this artist is put into terms that he's found typical of projects using public funding. Focus of the project is an old wood structure that used to be an elementary school. He loves technology and wants a theme park. 1328 Words. 1994.

ri940316
Progress on Rose Hill Project
Report to Kirkland City Council
The author, an artist with a vision of a Living Museum of Computer Arts Crafts and Design, wrote a brief report on progress on action initiated by Feliks Banel to save the Rose Hill Grade School. He quotes Michael S. Malone on technology and communities. 504 Words. 1994.

ri940430
LMASOCACAD Now
Time and place for creative, technical people
Creative artists, crafts people and designers are in touch with times, places, people - all tangents of reality that their work and action do not always reveal. They perform and produce their best in the time and place of their computerized living museum. 413 Words. 1994.

ri940530
Review EarthSafe 2022:
Checkpoint for reinventing college
In the two years since Ritchies Inc. made ecological economics a central principle to its mission, what is accomplished? An application from Renew America's annual National Awards for Environmental Sustainability suggests review. It's orderly and helpful. 2019 Words. 1994.

ri940611
Perfect College, Part II
EarthSafe 2022 & Rose Hill Project
To communicate the essence of new technologies in education and ecosystem contexts, a new art and technology school is needed. Two living schools are considered and a dead one too. The author is writing a book on reinventing arts studios using technology. 2681 Words. 1994.

ri940803
An On-line study group:
Redefining progress through Heritage Preservation
Restoring cultural values makes good economical sense. Technology, such as computers, and re-marry cultural values and economic values. TO find out how, DO use new communications technology to define, evaluate, control and disseminate heritage. 317 Words. 1994.

ri940808
EarthSafe 2022 Introduction
Life or death
In a statement by the Union of Concerned Scientists they said Earth would be uninhabitable in ten to thirty years, counting down from 1992. If artists expressed this through the media, such as print, theatre, films, and TV, it would have dramatic effects. 1290 Words. 1994.

ri940923
An Artist-in-Residence at Cogswell College North
A fantasy interview
A technical college takes a bold step away from traditional inertia and makes an agreement with an artist. No one knows at the outset what it means, so the blueprints are laid out, line by line. The author imagines an interview to help clarify some terms. 239 Words. 1994.

ri941006
Meet the A-I-R
Artist-In-Residence
Defining the Who, What, When, Where, Why and How of the first Artist-In-Residence at Cogswell College is not easy. Neither the artist nor the college ever did anything like this before. Nevertheless, both the president and artist believe it must be tried. 3403 Words. 1994.

ri941106
Weavers Need a Computer Museum
A Proposal to Propose to the Port of Seattle
The author is championing a Living Museum and School of Computer Arts Crafts and Design, and in this connection he thinks a joint project with a weaving society might lead to an installation at a Seattle Port Authority facility such as the SeaTac Airport. 452 Words. 1994.

ri950407
Letter to the NWCA
Go for the Paramount!
Northwest Cyberartists, who promote new art forms, question organization but seemed to crystallize when the Paramount made an offer to provide office and show space in the future. This open letter, based on hindsight and foresight, moves to respond. 2098 Words. 1995.

ri950528
Tale of two cyber entities
How to make cyber art matter
Fantasy story in which students re-design the computer art museum and rename it cyber museum, opening it to a broader, growing audience. Old desk-top and showcase oriented metaphors give way to full-room installations. 1804 Words. 1995.

ri950619
Digital Media Alliance
Cruising to the Golden Age
This Founding Member of the Digital Media Alliance recommends a paradigm shift, from conventional markets for digital media products and services to emerging maturity market segment. (Original draft for DMA Newsletter essay, above) 1515 Words. 1995.

ri950627
The Search for Digital Media's Golden Age

Edited essay for DMA Newsletter
The author attended various committees of the Digital Media Alliance in 1995. As one of its original founding members, he recommended the marketing of DMA be aimed at the emerging maturity market. 1100 Words. 1995.

ri950718
Cybernetics and Public Affairs
How LMASOCACAD helps
An information-hungry art professor awakens and opens his eyes to a new kind of experience between corporate public affairs and the community of art. Living in a region of high technology growth and creativity populations, he searches for a new museum value. 1163 Words. 1995.

ri950731.
Roots of TRPI
End of the month
Founding member of TRPI reflects on the history of investment clubs of the last fifty years. 742 Words. 1995.

ri950826
The Grandchildren of Fools
EarthSafe 2022 revisited
Generations of fools let slip the wisdom of knowing of our dependence on the Earth, the sun the green and growing things and the minerals. 161 Words. 1995.

ri950920
From Roots and Seeds
Growing new profit centers by intuition
Intuition is a central principle of wealth, whether you are a stock investor or creative artist. 1331 Words. 1995.

ri951231
Journal Entry, Sun. Dec. 31, 1995
Time Luxuries
Notes recorded from the author's "palmtop" B.O.S.S. computer. The author writes about the influence of "Time Running Out" program; slept in, took a nap, took a stroll. He luxuriated the value of his time–not squandering it on quadrant 3 activities. 183 Words. 1995.

ri960110
Journal Entry, Wed. Jan. 10, 1996
Beautiful Carving
Notes recorded from the author's "palmtop" B.O.S.S. computer. The author records his beautiful carving on his woodcut on-line block. He mentions a call from the Children's Museum and he began the reprint of Scovel-Shinn's book. 158 Words. 1996.

ri960120
Journal Entry, Sat. Jan. 20, 1996
Reprinting Shinn, MacRitchie's Fast Art
Notes recorded from the author's "palmtop" B.O.S.S. computer. The author writes about frustrating times with not having the funds to reprint Shinn's book. The lack of money undermines his sense of responsibility. 200 Words. 1996.

ri960130
Journal Entry, Tue. Jan. 30, 1996
First Design for a Heritage Calling Card
Notes recorded from the author's "palmtop" B.O.S.S. computer. The author finished his first design for a Heritage Calling Card. He received a call from MCI, TechCorps and Ken Porter. He reports almost finished with his state taxes using QuickBook. 229 Words. 1996.

ri960307
The Isle of RIISMA
Return to a land time forgot
The seventh stop among the islands on the Lake of the Domains of Expertise, the for-profit research center, is where the issues and artifacts of art, technology, culture and business are scrutinized for possibly useful principles. From a work in progress. 1989 Words. 1996.

ri960905
To play Emeralda
IT takes the right stuff
Learning the rules of Emeralda, a database-driven game that he compares to Magic(r), the author and inventor of the game explains what a database is and how most games are driven. 1378 Words. 1996.

ri960925
A potato story
All I know I learned from the Web
A US Tech Corps volunteer speculates on the question, "What good is an Internet connection in the schools, and how should volunteers approach it?" 735 Words. 1996.

ri960926
Revisiting PATCWA
Copy-writing Grudin
A published author of non-fiction and fiction, Robert Grudin, gives one an idea of his ideal university. However, it lacks the productivity aspect, and omits technology. This article fills in what is missing. 1525 Words. 1996.

ri961004
DreamsWork
My perfect day at RIISMA
A Gruddite Apprentice-User continues his assignment to write about a perfect day. Part of the day is spent dreaming or relating dreams that might add to the mystery of Emeralda. 1737 Words. 1996.

ri961208
Birth of a notion
Cyber artists' modest proposal
News of GameWorks' coming to Seattle inspires a renewed effort by some artists in the Emerald city to double their efforts toward a Living Museum and School of Cyber Arts Crafts and Design. They hope to be part of the DreamWorks plan. 2336

Words. 1996.

ri961222
The Gates Prize
A year of living copiously
A bold assumption which--a hundred years from now--people will take for granted. It is not from the renowned US software company owner, but refers to awards given to "those who enter and maintain the gates to wisdom and beauty." 1383 Words. 1996.

ri970101
Artists never retire
Two models to note
Artists don't work in the same sense as workers in factories and corporations. To use Lewis Hyde's expression, they "labor" under the Mosaic Law. Nevertheless, two structured models exist that artists should study for their overall economic outlook. 1022 Words. 1997.

ri970214
The 8 million dollar question
Tech Corps Washington's three-year budget
The visionary artist behind Tech Corps Washington's proposed chapter of US Tech Corps explains the needs for TCWA's phase I budget, comparing it to a six-million dollar gift to a University for a printmaking center made by a sports artist last year. 2855 Words. 1997.

ri970221
A Dream of Julie's
Re-design the Computer Museum
Working in R&D, a fictional artist named Julie sees what she thinks is a command from her computer, unbidden and mysterious. The message flashes on and disappears instantly, leaving her with a sense of deja-vu, but more like having been ordered to build a 1900 Words. 1997.

ri970311
Journal Entry, Tue. Mar. 11, 1997
TCWA Investment Club, Economic Game and PATCWA
The author writes his TCWA investment club. He writes about an economic game about different eye-colored people and their destinies. He writes about college-level art teachers failing to value human resources and creativity, which PATCWA will not to do. 386 Words. 1997.

ri970312
North of the volcano
A generation of harmonic tremors
Mt. St. Helens, in Southern Washington State, erupted in 1981 and the earth trembled for hundreds of miles. North, in Seattle, an artist looked for ways to communicate, in computer art, the harmonic tremors and aftershocks. The idea behind an arts-and-technology school. 2906 Words. 1997.

ri970321

ESN in Seattle
A link of Wisboom Mettle
Seniors may have been told or asked to sit on the sidelines while new technologies are put in work-places, schools and the entertainment world. Despite this unintended slight, some seniors are getting into the game for their share of the fun and willfully. 1122 Words. 1997.

ri970411
Is there a patent-able idea in you?
Trying to come out?
The author writes in wonderment about Emeralda, the game he invented, searching for the roots of its plays and movements. He asks, "Is its method, as yet, a patentable method?" He suggests that new technologies have opened up new methods for playing. 2704 Words. 1997.

ri970421
Image is all that matters
Still true in the cybernetic age?
Is image as important as it was thirty years ago when the author was an art student? A dealer confirmed it, but it seems to be changing in the information and telecommunications age. Content, they say now, is king. What does it mean to the lifelong artist? 599 Words. 1997.

ri970924
EarthSafe 2028 Lease
Renewing a student and teacher relationship
Here's an instance of Interactive Concurrent Teaching, Research and Production based on the fact that artists, craftspeople and designers achieve more and are more effective if they join team projects and their project is a big one, like saving the Earth. 1782 Words. 1997.

ri971105
Journal Entry, Wed. Nov. 5, 1997
Dumping D.O.S.S. and Seattle Tours
The author writes his time log of the day, the activities and projects he did that day. He dumped the contents of his B.O.S.S. into his bigger computer, and did other file work among his computers. He wanted to get Seattle Tours involved with O'Studios. 517 Words. 1997.

ri971116
Finding the structure in HSIC
Everything I needed to learn I learned from a balloon
When I was little I was amazed to see a little wad of rubber with tiny markings on it which turned out to be a balloon. It was probably only an inch long, but when it was inflated it was bigger and the markings turned out to be elaborate design and words. 2389 Words. 1997.

ri971126
Interview with an Emeralda player
Meeting of minds
Two Emeralda players, Frank Susan and Susan Frank, stage a fantasy interview with each other

as part of Emeralda play. One dictates the dialog using the word recognition aplet. It's the artist/inventor's way to get bearings and review what happens to him. 1054 Words. 1997.

ri980121
Loaded with Emeralda
Your calendar, your life
The 24th Cell of Emeralda is the Bridging Cell of the unconventional, triple-entry bookkeeping and accounting system for the Wisdom-Boomers' HSIC Investment Club. Here the inscription over the gates of the cell says, "Bridge the So What Who Cares? chasm." 1880 Words. 1998.

ri980122
Art Twice Over
The two worlds of printmaking
From during his six days' Resident Stay, the author describes how Apprentice Users are introduced to the file types of digital graphics. He writes the script for the four-character actor demonstrator teaching the art basics on the Web under RIISMA's Meni. 529 Words. 1998.

ri980123
It Happened to Me
Hallucinations of an Academic
He wrote fiction about his fantastic journeys in Emeralda: "My third day at RIISMA, I was struck alongside my head. It was a realization that was like a brick hurled at me by an angry victim of a crime I had committed without my knowing what I was doing." 926 Words. 1998.

ri980124
Scales of Emeralda Region Maps
Request for a Proposal
The Inventor of Emeralda: Games for the Gifts of Life, wrote a fictional proposal to write in text the task of surveying Emeralda Region. This essay is part of the research underway at RIISMA during his Residence Stay, the fourth day for Apprentice Users. 929 Words. 1998.

ri980125
Artists be Aware
The best investment is your labor
Artists spend their lifetime building a portfolio of art, projects, skills and processes. They develop a database which, thanks to the World Wide Web, may lead to a new kind of retirement or equity fund. The author exposes the artist's retirement myth. 2113 Words. 1998.

ri980311
Journal Entry, Wed. Mar. 11, 1998
The First Habit
The author writes about the importance of goals and developing them. He suggests developing the first habit of each day to become effective. He lists his ideas; pro-activity, priorities, the end in mind, think "win win", listen and being understood, etc. 400 Words. 1998.

ri980410
Sketching at Emeralda
Not Your Usual Drawing
Sketching a game means identifying it, and this inventor does it every day. It's called routine activities; testing and learning to understand his game that was given to him as a gift of life--the last and greatest gift, perhaps, that he'll every receive. 1210 Words. 1998.

ri980420
A Demonstration in Cyber Back Issues
Cybermagazine collector reflections
Sometimes a person finds a publication to be so interesting that he or she may wish to have back issues of it, or the complete library. This is akin to coming late to a demonstration, and as it proceeds, wishing that you had seen the first part. 1024 Words. 1998.

ri980510
Demonstration in Cell 7
Psychiatry and Non-competitive Games On-line
"Do you know where you are in space and time?" and "Do you know who you are?" These were questions the inventor of Emeralda asks as he demonstrates a version of a score sheet for on-line, interactive game plays. He pretends he's in a velvet prison, No. 1029 Words. 1998.

ri980520
Demonstration in Cell 17
The Daily Routine Continues
The world's champion Emeralda player pulls open the window shades of his studio around 6:15 in the morning, but he has been up for over an hour. He began with notations on dreams, flashes, cascading ideas, words of wisdom and images - all part of his routine. 146 Words. 1998.

ri980530
Notes from An IRIS Workshop
The Passive Observer is not so passive
In a dream long ago, the author had a vision of art classrooms that were connected to distant schools and artists' studios. In real time, the students observed demonstrations by the artists at a distance. Almost 30 years passed, and the dream is reality. 1403 Words. 1998.

ri980609
Dumping Your PDA
And Other Routine Activities in Emeralda Play
The moves in Emeralda may or may not be momentous. That is, they may have a moment number or they may not. It's like working on-line or off-line without a moment number (or cademic marker), then the player runs the risk of not having control of his moves. 961 Words. 1998.

ri980619
Demonstration at Breakfast
Going to the Venture Capital Breakfast Again
Today is a free breakfast sponsored by RIISMA in cooperation with the Northwest Venture Cap-

ital Group. The NWVCG is an organization that brings together people from business and industry, entrepreneurs, services, product providers and venture capitalists. 133 Words. 1998.

ri980629
Breakfast with the Capitalists
Review and Notes
By planning programs to bring creative, inventive, discovering and imaginative people into contact with business and industry people, RIISMA helps the communities understand each other, a way to a healthy economy. The Emeralda player takes notes on a PDA. 1174 Words. 1998.

ri980709
Writing While You Walk
Emeralda's Inventor On the move
The Itinerate Professor had to learn several skills so that he could keep up with the times technically, keep up with his mind, and keep up his physical health by walking every day. He learned how to write while he walked, using a PDA. This is an example. 756 Words. 1998.

ri980719
Demonstration in Environmental Economics
Emeralda Works Basis for Being
Strange things are studied at RIISMA, like the new field called Environmental Economics that began to achieve worldwide attention ten years ago. Artists contemplate exhibits in traditional museum settings plus they must explore their environmental impact. 864 Words. 1998.

ri980729
Dumping Your Personal Digital Assistant
Fifteen Minutes to Dream
To move the data from the PDA storage to the next level, the hard drive of a PC, takes 15 minutes. This is an old way of doing the dump. It's raw data and you might think of it as being like raw sewage dumped into Lake Emeralda; it needs to be cleaned up. 718 Words. 1998.

rl980808
Not All Professors Are Alike
A case of mistaken identity
There is a story about a professor who turned up missing from campus. This professor was fusing arts and science. He roped in other professors and graduate students to pursue his vision, including engineering, geography, architecture and music professors. 1497 Words. 1998.

ri980818
Worth Your Wait in Gold
The trillion dollar opportunity revisited
What is a dream worth? What is an inspired flash of insight worth? Imagine a machine to take your loose ideas, thoughts, inventions, insights, dreams, or flashes of great notions and converts them into cash. The challenge is to develop a way of measuring. 1663 Words. 1998.

ri980828
The Worst Part of the Day
Proving Emeralda Games Work
From his Emeralda 21 theme, there is a chance to prove that Emeralda Games Work; in other words, show me the money! With Emeralda only partly developed, this is an opportunity for the proofing stage, as it is in printmaking. 616 Words. 1998.

ri980907
Getting Ahead of Duck
Clairvoyant
The terminal nature of school is a problem, writes this artist/professor, and compares it to duck hunting as he learned to "lead the duck"; but during school he chose to aim right at his goals. Leading the duck was his college professors' retirement idea. 2097 Words. 1998.

ri980917
Born in Debt and Not Getting Paid
Heart of the Prisoner's Dilemma
The moment you open the Emeralda Score sheet you find you are in debt. Is that bad if debt leveraging is based on debt? People in the USA and in most all developed countries are born in debt. The author and inventor of Emeralda looks at his own situation. 974 Words. 1998.

ri980927
Emeralda Mid-term Exam
Part XXVII of Emeralda for dummies
Two adult groups wanting to learn some things about computers agreed to participate in an experiment called Equality and Equity in legacy transfer. One group did work that served business and industry, the other served their own purposes. Who did better? 874 Words. 1998.

ri981007
Happy Birthday, Gail and Paul
Families go cybernetic
It' my sister and brother's birthday today at RIISMA, and it is by coincidence that three topics meet on this day that are good things for RIISMA Apprentice users to know about. First, I want to provide a little background information about RIISMA and what it means. 229 Words. 1998.

ri981017
Q&A by RIISMA Agents
Emeralda Inventor Questioned
The Inventor of Emeralda--Game for the Gifts of Life--plays his own solitaire-style game. He provides phantom voices of RIISMA agents who interrogate him, testing his ability to answer questions about the games on their isle and their domain-of-expertise. 4914 Words. 1998.

ri981027
Twin Georges
Continuing fine arts education
The fine art professor looks for continuing fine arts education as the Internet seems to make virtual universities a real possibility. He departed

from the brick-and-mortar campus to search for new channels to sustain continuous education via cybernetics. 1980 Words. 1998.

ri981106
Life Without Margins
Nonlinear real life
Even as I try to write, the effort seems laughable now. There is no tomorrow, so I write like there is no tomorrow. There were no yesterdays, so there is nothing to refer to. And Now? It keeps slipping this way and that. It's a neat machine that resembles 435 Words. 1998.

ri981116
Checking In and Checking Out
Beginning the Emeralda's Playing Day
When the Score sheet is updated and the comments in the default square are read, search them and try to understand what they mean. They might be like the marks on the Rosetta Stone. They might be like a diary of some soul who was never able to leave the cell. 872 Words. 1998.

ri981126
RIISMA Article of Vision
International Interactive Multimedia Arts Interactive Development Design Program
The Emeralda Inventor revisits his dreams that sprang from his vision of a perfect studio--where teaching, research and practice occur simultaneously under one roof. In a new twist, he now sees his dream as a Pan American Free Fine Art Online University. 1634 Words. 1998.

ri981208
Scales Fall
More valuable than emeralds
I didn't know if I could really write this article. Perhaps if I can hide the innocent, protect the innocent merely by changing their names, I can tell the truth. Thus the scales, as they say, will fall from my eyes. Did that expression come from the old testament? 1462 Words. 1998.

ri990123
Building the professor's Web site
Fantasy visitors
A vignette from a page out of the professor's diary, or the journal of his or her assistant. Vague and fragmented, but rather than discard it as useless, why not keep it; possibly it contains some clues or some indication of value, part of a game, maybe. 416 Words. 1999.

ri990125
Woodworker's Tale
Dr. Osler and Andrew Carnegie
A short story-or anecdote-linking Andrew Carnegie and Dr. William Osler, who said all unproductive professors should be gassed. The author thinks the millionaire put a bug in someone's ear that led to the creation of the biggest pension fund in the world. 818 Words. 1999.

ri990320
How Goes IT at Your First Day at RIISMA?
Ramblings from freed mind
There's an image of a map on the wall of Emeralda Region, somewhere in a fantasy land, between virtue and reality. "Say unto wisdom, Thou art my sister; and call understanding thy kinswoman." I am the island, the author writes in free verse in his prison. 1083 Words. 1999.

ri990322
Let me see if I understand you
Diagnosis and Treatment Planning in the Information and Communication Age
The DISCO-OP AUDAMIS explains his vision of Emeralda City Dentistry in the form of a short story, a make-believe world where the dental operatory serves a threefold purpose: Teaching/learning, Research and Practice, or the TRP principle, based on values. 1378 Words. 1999.

ri990323
Let Me See If I Understand You II
Diagnosis and Treatment Planning in the Information and Communication Age
A DISCO-OP AUDAMIS says: "My vision of Emeralda City Dentistry is a short story, a make-believe world where a dental operatory has three purposes: Teaching, Research and Practice, or the TRP principle, based on values. There is a fourth, secret, purpose." 1253 Words. 1999.

ri990519
Covert Operations
Return to RIISMA
A forgotten tape, found on his shelf, unheard, for months since it was loaned, inspired the question, "Where is this guy today?" Listening, the author thought of a subject to write about for this issue of this RIISMA Zine. Is the speaker on the Web today? 703 Words. 1999.

ri990520
Cooperative Routine Activities
Key concept in Dentalisco
The author named his virtual community Dentalisco and describes how it resides on a map with four cardinal directions, all necessitating cooperation among the diversity of this communication age. All over the make-believe city a cooperative spell is cast. 1564 Words. 1999.

ri990523
The Soul of A New Game
Four Cornerstones for a Greenfield Works
A new DVD-based on-line interactive game experience is opening up, thanks to digital communication. Standing next to Myst and Magic the way a recording stands next to a live concert performance, Emeralda takes us toward the spirit of adults' leagues play. 833 Words. 1999.

ri990524
Dead Artists League
Paradigm for a new subtitle

The inventor of Emeralda is nudged into altering his course on his locus of beauty, the invention of the Game for the Gifts of Life paradigm shifts to the Game for the Dead Artists League. Life-changing events happen that way, he writes, in Emeralda Play. 1082 Words. 1999.

ri991214
The Great Handshake
Across the waters of Emeralda
The Emeralda Inventor, on his final day at Interval, contemplates starting an Apprentice User project for Emeralda and another Year of Living Copiously. Weeks later, on the eve of an important trip, he restores a VR program and continues his deliberation. 371 Words. 1999.

ri991222
Spineless writing
Breaking a back to break new ground
Perplexed by the mystery of writing the background for Emeralda, Her Story: The Women Who Fell to Earth, the author cuts off the spine of a 20th Century How to Write manual and starts over. He suggests that old How To manuals need to be recycled this way. 1159 Words. 1999.

ri000214
Artists and Dentists with Hearts
DentalISCo Congress Proceedings
Keynote speaker, the visionary Professor Ritchie (also known as "H. S. MacRitchie, Multi-Faceted Auxiliary") recites the state of developments of the Dental Internet Services Cooperative as he sees it in its third year. It is a 24/7 service in the making. 1248 Words. 2000.

ri000218
The Dolphins
Another view
He professes to be an online art-ed specialist. He copy-writes over an article by another professor. It reminds him where he was almost twenty years before on the first leg of a world tour and he recalls the value of his Father's lesson in responsibility. 1213 Words. 2000.

ri000228
What I Would Do If I Had a Million Dollars
Dilemma Dream Resolution
Based from real events, these paragraphs prove the truth of that old saying, "Where there's a Will there's a way." Told by educator William "Will" H. Ritchie, who began online teaching in what he calls the Emeralda Region on the Pacific Coast of the USA. 2068 Words. 2000.

ri000306
Top Thousand Topics
Washington State Arts Commission's Y2K Challenge
Choosing from their 162 Topic list of that he gleaned from the proceedings of the Washington State Arts Commission's 2000 Strategic Plan survey, the author describes how a Top 1000 Chart can make its mission statement a dynamic process using the Internet. 1152 Words. 2000.

ri000312
How WAUREL Relates to Experience Washington
Vivid Pathways to Washington's Arts
The architect of a game-like computer interface for creative people offers a plan for state Web sites. After attending two conferences sponsored by his home state's arts commission, his design reflects feeling that arts-passionate people need vivid paths. 1194 Words. 2000.

ri000318
The Carpenter and the Web Guru
Conversation through a hole in the wall
An inner dialog is recorded to illustrate how a statewide online service can be designed by observing the making of a hole in a wall. The author, whose woodworking is relief from cybernetics, imagined the dialog and helps explain to himself his next step. 1162 Words. 2000.

ri000319
The Mystery of Love and Legacy Transfer
Following in Napoleon Hill's Footsteps
The artist/scholar is struck by the resemblance between his own philosophical idea and those of the popular mid-century author of Think and Grow Rich. He sets out to copy and rewrite, word for word, the idea in that book so it fits his role-play approach. 2574 Words. 2000.

ri000406
Reliquary in PDFAF
Ghosts in the New Museum
It was not an apparition nor was it his imagination, but a real living display in the real time of year 2000: The prospectus from the art museum that billed itself as the Museum of the 21st Century. A hundred years from now, it will get laughs. Not today. 1522 Words. 2000.

ri000415
Taking Mr. Saylor's Class
A Good Idea That Shouldn't Wait
Over dinner, after reading the announcement of Mr. Saylor's plan to offer free education on the Internet, he said to his wife he wanted her to take a writing class. But instead of waiting for the next college, she might begin by taking it from SayloriU! 401 Words. 2000.

ri000605
Artist in the Library
A New Look at Artists' Legacies
Considering a possibility of teaching a new approach to fine arts education in a local library computer classroom, the ITinerate Professor reflects on the history of ideas of art and technology from a personal point of view. The essay includes a proposal. 756 Words. 2000.

ri000629
Business, Games and Emotional Intelligence

Traumatic Invention Intervention
The combination of his boyhood experiences and career changes causes the author to create a game, much like the way children deal with traumas. According to Daniel Goleman, the inventor of Emeralda-an online interactive game-is a notable example. 1402 Words. 2000.

ri000727
Startup Assistant Needed
Equity position
Discussions by people who have a vision of a business come to this question: "How do we bridge the gap between having money to invest in an assistant, on one hand, and the assistant-on the other hand, is not trained? Can we afford it?" What is the choice? 1052 Words. 2000.

ri000806
Children's Games
Small human structural intellectual capital
Why do grownups hesitate to join HSIC clubs, and children don't hesitate? Even investment clubs, of the usual kind, strike many adults as suspect; they hesitate to become members. Compared to children, adults seem to have more obstacles to joining groups. 920 Words. 2000.

ri000810
EarthSafe 2022 Revisited and Revised
A draft update
On June 29, 1998, Bill Ritchie wrote about using miniature, postage-size artwork as part of his 1992 vision of a saved-Earth (EarthSafe 2022) project. He played a game: Getting into and out of Kinko's for less than $5 and 5 minutes with a sheet of stamps. 1327 Words. 2000.

ri000919
Myartpatron.com Turning Point
FAQ and a bad telephone call
It was a trip around the world and a chance encounter with a dead teacher's family in Montana that turned this artist's lifelong mission toward opening his own gallery, studio and school. He answers the question, "What made you drop out of the art world?" 1564 Words. 2000.

ri001104
Refusal to Mourn the Death of An Art Patron
Interview with the Author of Ghosts in the New Machine
A mock interview with myself with a fantasy "FS"-voice from a ghost in my new machine. I thought of this "interview" as I was unpacking my newest computer, and how the late Gordon Gilkey, revered patron of printmaking, exemplifies the sacred cows we used to worship. 516 Words. 2000.

ri001227
I Couldn't Believe What That Guy Said
Report from an intern sent to RIISMA
A fantasy story to help illustrate a new product and service the author is designing that helps teachers create an on-line and actual printmaking class. He imagines what an art student printing intern at a museum would think after learning all about this. 1464 Words. 2000.

ri001231
Disattentuation
Loosing the Press
Paradoxically, it is the printmakers who can loosen the chokehold of the printing press that too often slows information about creative arts, design and crafts opportunities for older, retirement age folks. The author introduces the Printmaker's Bluebook. 913 Words. 2000.

ri010110
Silverpoint Comes to Your Screen
Vision in My Viewer
There is an artist presenting a demonstration of silverpoint drawing in my area, and I want to capture what she says so the whole world will know about this way of drawing. She's more practiced than I, so why not imagine what could happen, soon? Why wait? 1234 Words. 2001.

ri010120
Emeralda Dreaming
Painting the Big Picture of the Big U
While planning a pleasant summertime art workshop experience at a local art supply store, the dreamer unveils a bigger idea that is the true mission of his wildest dream: The restoration of the SS United States, a cruise ship stilled partway through life. 1639 Words. 2001.

ri010129
Dimestore Dreams and Inventing Emeralda
A Boy Choosing Model Airplanes, a Man Choosing Metaphors
Smells evoke memories of the most surprising kinds, sometimes bringing with associations that are even more surprising. Boyhood model airplane-building came to mind as this Emeralda Inventor made coffee, and he speculates on those experiences and how they shaped him. 1698 Words. 2001.

ri010130
Living Prints Goes to Japan
The Mystery of the Missing Casket
The mysterious disappearance of a little casket almost a hundred years ago is recalled by an unlikely encounter in a sushi bar in Nara, Japan. The Emeralda Player dreamed this story up one morning, thinking he was part of a digital versatile disc project. 4076 Words. 2001.

ri010209
Assuming Foot-shooting
Art Auction On-line
An on-line art auction will be the only manner in which the dying artist can insure that his or her legacy turns into bankable cash. Transferring legacy is the goal of Emeralda play, but one can shoot oneself in the foot if one repudiates the value of it. 1421 Words. 2001.

ri010219
Dreams Work at RIISMA
Recurring Revisiting the School of My Dreams
Writing about a dream within minutes of having it
is a good way to start a day at RIISMA. A dream
that is about institutional art education is especially well suited, and that it should be about the start
of a woodcut class is probably the very best kind.
2425 Words. 2001.

ri010301
Beans Started Grandma's School of Multimedia
Arts
Not Everything I learned on Grandma's Knee
It must have been the beans in the Chili Bilo he
ate that gave him great dreams. From discovery
of early work to the naming of Grandma's School
of Multimedia Arts-what fine visions! The author
explains events that lead to a new approach to art
education. 2072 Words. 2001.

ri010311
My First DVD
Reflection on A Silver Disk
Excited as a kid with his first working gizmo, or
like the time he helped make the first laser video disk over fifteen years ago, the author thrills at
the prospect of sharing his achievement. He has a
fantasy visit with a DVD producer and museum
curator. 1185 Words. 2001.

ri010321
RIISMA Screenplay Workshop
Dusty Appearance in Tres Passing Ferries
Exploring ways to weld traditional screenplay
writing (as in movie and TV traditions) to emerging technologies promises artists, writers and
teachers new opportunities. In a fantasy workshop
a theme has been chosen and the action started
before breakfast. 1180 Words. 2001.

ri010331
Ask A Computer
Immutable Dolphins
Where does wisdom come from? John Lilly said
Ask A Dolphin. But if there are no dolphins, then
whom do you ask? The author invents a computer
game to find answers he can share through tech-
nology, and a magazine he named Emeralda, a
Digital Versatile Discozine. 1039 Words. 2001.

ri010410
Mindless Games in Mindful Times
Contemptuous in Seattle
Times try an artist's soul as he tries to comply with
a grant application. It's too big to ignore, and too
little to take too seriously. Compared to what he
could be doing, he thinks it is a mindless game.
He could be playing a mindful game, like his own.
925 Words. 2001.

ri010420
Forty Remarkable Years
Re-interrupting the Past

Interfere, always interfere is the author's restate-
ment of a famous quote by Goethe: Connect, always connect. Twenty years into a now forty-year
long career he saw electronics' interrupt human
interaction with Earth and we find ourselves in a
dilemma. 1163 Words. 2001.

ri010510
Testing, 1, 2, 3
How I Make My DVD
While working on the world's first DVD about
printmaking, the author takes a break and goes to
test a new software company's online service. It is
a little like the company he made for himself to
test his DVD. He compares it to an enterprise, and
risking. 929 Words. 2001.

ri010530
Opening Soon Near You
Reform School for Educational Miscreants
I reach for my textbook, starting again from the
cover. I'm in reform school, and I wonder how
many tries I will get before my time is up. Reform
school is hard, but harder I think than it should be.
Oh, if only I had some classmates! But, would we
cheat? 394 Words. 2001.

ri010609
Putting Susan to Sleep
She'll Never Know
A theme of EarthSave2022 copies advertising,
which effected the last century in the USA in the
way of a national religion. Ad campaigns always
had a theme. Awakening is my core theme, and as
its chief architect I wind each thing around it-even
a car trip. 1037 Words. 2001.

ri010619
Fallacy of the Hand Print
Reminder from the Cave
A rally for standards that define handmade prints
and calls for written standards to help the printmaking community, reminds this author of the
arguments he heard in the past. Attending to this
he reviews what his research discovered when the
storm ended. 951 Words. 2001.

ri010629
How would you do IT?
Professor fakes answer
Taking a test in the game of life, an older person
remembers the tactic of skipping those that are
hard and going back later. Doing Information
Technology-IT-was an unanswerable question
that now isn't. Teaching art ed on-line, for example, is answerable. 1254 Words. 2001.

ri010719
What You Are Looking At
My DVD-Blue book of the 21st Century?
He's thinking to find another way to explain his
DVD. He believes he is the only person in the
country who is making Digital Versatile Discs
with the idea to develop a new approach to uni-
versal education using the Internet and newer

communication systems. 1568 Words. 2001.

ri010828
Why No One Thought of Emeralda Before
One-hundred years of bad art ed
Asking this question himself and searching for
the answer, the inventor of Emeralda lands upon
a possibility: That after one-hundred years of mis-
guided art education, how could anyone think of
a revolutionary game and align the arts and economic theories? 930 Words. 2001.

ri010917
Getting, and Giving, Away
Kicked out of my studio
Itinerant professors are nomads, with no permanent classroom. This art professor has no studio,
either, unless you can call a studio apartment a
"studio". It is likely, however, he requires instead
a computer, database and dial tone in a global.edu
world. 1586 Words. 2001.

ri010927
Art Teachers Online
Not on time
Art educators of tomorrow will be more on-line
than on-time. They are more careful with their
time today, and won't be fitted into timeslots to
suit the traditional brick-and-mortar campus.
Time is more valuable than real estate as there is
no more of it. 2024 Words. 2001.

ri011007
Routine Activity of the Emeralda Master
Opening your passport DVD
He is the inventor of Emeralda: Games for the
Gifts of Life, so he has given himself the title of
"Master" and proceeds to write about his typical
routine activity. He conducts a self-test to see if
his passport works, describing what you'd see on
screen. 1154 Words. 2001.

ri011027
Far Away from Emeralda, So Near
Mobile studios in the age of digital communication
On an overnight getaway, the Seattle-based Itinerant Professor reflects on the mobility of his virtually perfect studio at a mountain lodge 150 miles
from home. His invention, a game called Emeralda, makes it possible for him; he believes anyone
can play. 1137 Words. 2001.

ri011106
Teacher's Anxiety Dream Coming True
First day of class since I don't know when
Teaching anxiety dreams are described in an article in the Chronicle of Higher Education, and it
says every teacher has them. They are nightmares,
actually, and follow the same general pattern. Students, too, and former students. The artist/scholar,
also. 1521 Words. 2001.

ri011116
Notes on a Future Printmaking Class

Observations by an outsider
An article about the successful adaptation of role
playing game theory to teaching history inspired
this art professor to describe a make-believe class.
Students can learn art processes on-line, he posits,
by role playing and then meeting in real studios.
1102 Words. 2001.

ri011126
Reflections of an Angry Professor
A life's work going into a dustbin
After two generations in the arts-the first in learning and the second used to un-learn and re-learn
new ways for the re-invented arts studios, an older, wiser artist/professor contemplates his past,
present and future while taking artifacts to a dustbin. 1663 Words. 2001.

ri011231
AUREL, The Filing System for Art Ed On-line
An art professor's modest proposal
He claims to have a better idea for art educators in
the 21st Century, calling it Art Ed On-line. At the
heart of the proposal is an intelligent agent called
AUREL, a means by which anyone can be located
as a "resource" for art, craft and design services.
1104 Words. 2001.

ri020110
Writing Between the Paragraphs - Interval 2
The man with two brains
Writing a series of paragraphs between those of
a favorite professor/author, this man sees himself
doing a bunch of somewhat unrelated tasks. This
handyman, computer geek, author and artist, explains that he has two brains each with a left and
right side. 849 Words. 2002.

ri020130
Gate Key to Success in Printmaking
Globalism and Living Prints
The gate key to success, this artist/scholar believes,
is the print exchange. The exchange of prints is
more important than prints themselves, for it's the
report on the exchanges that we actually communicate using alternatives that the Internet gives us.
503 Words. 2002.

ri020209
Stamp Collecting in Emeralda
Passages into artists' phrontisteria
Emeralda is a game of stamp collecting. Reality
and Emeralda are worlds apart, and the passport
of the inventor allows him a passage into the
worlds of other creative people. They become his
main pathway of experience and relationship over
space and time. 559 Words. 2002.

ri020301
Passing the Electronic Passport Test
The Bar of Art
Role playing a beginner who's trying to gain en-
try to RIISMA's phrontisterion-the island's think-
shop-the author plays two roles: the Tester and the
Tested. His passport fails the strict, standardized

tests, but he fixes it after getting help on the 'Net. 905 Words. 2002.

ri020311
Journal Entry, Mon. Mar. 11, 2002
Time and Collecting; Scene from Majestic
The author was writing about time and collecting the stamps of Emeralda, testing of a passport as the key to evaluating an Emeralda's performance. He compared himself with the character from a scene from Majestic. He wrote thoughts about Hayter's image. 752 Words. 2002.

ri020321
John Nash Upstaged
Dare to say No to Analysis
The attention to John Nash' mental illness and consequent development of the film A Beautiful Mind gives rise to this author's memory of his experience. The difference is that today there's an alternative to damaging the beautiful mind, thanks to the Web. 1076 Words. 2002.

ri020510
Four Ways to View Emeralda
Gates to a Paradigm for Looking
The inventor of Emeralda muses over the possibility of entering the fantasy regions from which he derived his methods of play in The Dictionary of Imaginary Places, and how he would describe and style Emeralda Region and its ten islands in the great lake. 1732 Words. 2002.

ri020530
Non-credit class in DVD
Non-credit class intended to promote community among neighbors
High on the fun and potential profit in making PC-based DVDs using cheap software, the author launched a series of free lecture and demonstrations at his local community center. This is the text of his first press release. No one showed for the first one. 401 Words. 2002.

ri020609
Living Museums
Showing works of art in the age of digital reproduction
The work of art in the age of mechanical reproduction was severed from the artist, as in Adam Smith's philosophy of dividing laborers from the products of their labors. In the age of digital reproduction, maker, made and making are reunited as one action. 879 Words. 2002.

ri020619
Bill Makes A Poster for Fran
Challenging the Art Committee
On the pathway toward Emeralda City and his Perfect Studio, Bill-an artist-makes a poster for his patron named Fran. She sponsored him in the event-driven stroll so he could indulge in an old-time poster project. Now he recounts the steps and looks ahead. 1318 Words. 2002.

ri020629
IT IS Rocket Science
And Brain Surgery Cannot Be Made Fun and Easy
Looking back on forty-years in higher arts education, the author concludes that the age of digital reproduction holds promises and perils for adult learners. Trying the precarious professions in the arts and education are not as simple as grown-ups hoped. 713 Words. 2002.

ri020709
Frank's Story
True Stories from A Silicon Machine
Always as interested in anthropomorphizing his computers as using them as cold, dead devices in his re-invented arts studios, the author pretends his new computer he named Frank Susan is speaking about the way he's treated alongside others that Bill uses. 292 Words. 2002.

ri020719
Artist Aboard the Board of Trustees on the Queen Anne C of
IT's About Building Trust in Artists, Crafts People and Designers
Believing there's a need to improve communication between the worlds of business and the arts professions, the artist/scholar considers the merits of being on a board of trustees of the local Chamber of Commerce. He lists what he would do if on the board. 1071 Words. 2002.

ri020729
Your Neighborhood CTC-A Smart Investment
Distance Learning Gets Close to Home
The Great World Teachers were envisioned long ago, but not far away by global standards, and today their own neighborhoods will bring their classrooms closer to home and yet far away. New generations are getting on-line for their educational buck's worth. 698 Words. 2002.

ri020808
At the Beach, Are Things Different?
Notes from A Traveler
During an overnight trip the Itinerate Professor looks out on the Pacific Ocean and tries to relate his daily routine activity to this unusual location. He's far from his neighborhood and his prospecting for the next step in developing his game, Emeralda. 987 Words. 2002.

ri020818
My First Gain from the After School Program
A Frequently Asked Question about DVD
On an outreach project to teach artists' e-folios, the author meets with a person who provides him with the first question about the e-folio medium he's chosen-Digital Versatile Disc-as the goal of his art education projects. Why DVD and not CD, she asks. 440 Words. 2002.

ri020828
In A Moment the Death of the Professor
But First Here's a Word from Our Sponsor

As he goes through his routine, burning his CD/R discs on one computer to transfer them to another, he gets an eerie sense he's part of a dramatic tale in which his life is being told in the future via a handheld reader-the kind college students use then. 848 Words. 2002.

ri020907
Beyond Face Value
Art in the Age of Digital Reproduction
A printer explains how the diplomas on true sheepskin used to be made. They made a striking image-had high face value and indicated the prestigious nature of the school. In the age of digital reproduction this author says interface value makes more sense. 553 Words. 2002.

ri020917
Thrills of a Change Agent in the Age of Digital Reproduction
Reflections on Being an Art Student in the Sixties
Born in 1941, this artist/scholar looks back and sees he was lucky to have been watching the radar screen closely when the blip that was video crossed in front of him in his art classroom studios thirty years later. Now he's got a better economic outlook. 485 Words. 2002.

ri020927
CD or Not CD
That is the Question
At the age of sixty, an artist/scholar's mind may turn to notions of retirement and old age security. Or he or she may have seen the myth of retirement for what it is-a choice between deposits of intellectual capital or capital of more conventional kinds. 795 Words. 2002.

ri021017
Imagination Database
A Mountain of Gold and How to Mine It
Imagination is worth more than knowledge. He who said this also said that man's most powerful invention was compound interest. Einstein was a man of diverse knowledge and, apparently, imagination. The age of digital reproduction brings new meaning to mining. 817 Words. 2002.

ri021027
Professor's Soup of the Day
Public Intellectual's recipe for success in the marketplace
The virtual, virtuous public intellectual, in this case an artist/scholar, has a recipe for his routine practice. With descriptive names, he keeps a digital record on a PDA, recipe book of ideas, and then looks for an incubator, a place to let these rise. 764 Words. 2002.

ri021106
Questions to an Arts Director
Answers you should get
It's the island of RIISMA, but he's stranded at the Seattle Independent Mall, overseeing The Professor's Cabinet's space. Searching the missing professor's files, he finds a forgotten essay written years ago when he was applying for a job at a new school. 1158 Words. 2002.

ri021116
SIM-U - A modest Proposal
A new operating system
The artist/scholar reads the Chronicle of Higher Education thinking it will help him prepare for lifelong teaching and learning. Seeing an article about the need to reform higher-ed he starts re-writing it to fit art education, a basis for art-ed on-line. 1087 Words. 2002.

ri021126
Purpose Statement of the Professors Cabinet
Another twist in an ongoing story
After renting 160 square feet on Seattle's Pike Street he wrote, Professor's Cabinet is Bill's Gate to his family's legacy of art, crafts, design and memorabilia, a garage sale and digital estate liquidation, on site and out of sight, off-line and online. 841 Words. 2002.

ri030110
Are We Having Fun Yet?
Days in the life of a SIMaller
The missing professor from the story, Women Who Fell to Earth, role-plays as vendor at the Seattle Independent Mall. He describes the activities that happen while he's at his new location - the Professor's Cabinet - at the temporary location he calls SIM. 1029 Words. 2003.

ri030331
Marvelous Artist Stamp
Flight from 1964
Before he composes his new stamp titled "Flight 1964," the artist comments on the process unfolding before him on his PC. He taps the words of an MIT architecture prof as a template to explain what makes his stamp a cyber art work and an electronic stamp. 861 Words. 2003.

ri030530
Where Do We Go From Here?
Reflections on Emeralda
Watching himself as if from outside his body and mind, the Emeralda inventor pauses to think about the last move which he made – that of saving a stamp image in two file types in two places. Does this compare to a pre-meditated move in a chess game? Reflection is key. 1075 Words. 2003.

ri030609
How to Succeed in Distance Art Education
Going after the right audience
Studying an article in the Chronicle of Higher Education, the creator of a digital game-based learning program for art education gleans ideas for a needs assessment phase. He'll need his assessment as he gets ready to approach an art museum with his idea. 1561 Words. 2003.

ri030709

The Widow and Me
A short story
An art museum worker who hates his job but loves art discovers a talking black widow spider in a mysterious artwork he's preparing to catalog. The talking spider spins a yarn that's a web-like network connecting the pieces of the art to one central theme. 1741 Words. 2003.

ri030824
Hotwire Coffee House Promo
Getting the word out
The artist's daughter invited him to have a show at her new place of work-a coffeehouse close to where he was teaching art. He wrote his own promotional material, hung and labeled his work, and hung out at the coffeehouse-in the name of community service. 365 Words. 2003.

ri030828
From Designing Virtual Worlds
By Richard A. Bartle
The author (a professor) has been living in an imaginary world since he resigned-or was expelled-from an art school in '85. There's the real world he's dreaming about, an art world with an art education foundation rooted in an age of digital reproduction. 1616 Words. 2003.

ri030907
Stuck in A MUS on RIISMA
Comparing Dungeons with Studios in Emeralda
While admitting he's not a video game developer, the author-who's also an artist and academic-wants to find a way to win his way into the game world by mapping his domain of expertise onto the milieu of online games. He thinks dungeons compare to 1406 Words. 2003.

ri031007
A User Interface for Online Art Ed
One application in beginning drawing at a distance
What is the reason that the fine art studio practices teacher is trailing behind other efforts to extend the traditional educational forum to the web? There's one way to create a new approach, this teacher says, and it's by using an element of pop culture. 1299 Words. 2003.

ri031027
Gamer Designers Warning
Take notes!
He isn't designing a video game, but he is reading a video game designers' advice book while he's making a hasty version of an electronic portfolio for one of his traditional drawing class students. This story is about taking notes on this new experience. 731 Words. 2003.

ri031106
Thoughts at the Hotwire
Ending one career, beginning a new one
For three years this artist has been in a retrospective mood, thinking about the things he may have done wrong and things he may have done right. In a coffee shop he sits amid selections from of his 40-year career and writes these comments about his life. 1118 Words. 2003.

ri031116
Live A Perfect Day
My idea of the Perfect Studios
He's faced with the risk of turning his back on his talent, he thinks, so this artist/essayist writes down an accounting of how he should spend the first hour of a day. One small project may be enough to anchor him as he faces a troubled time in his life. 782 Words. 2003.

ri031126
Play "Art is Dead"
I begin my new career
When he was a student and he had to choose one career path. He chose printmaking and let his other two passions-ceramics and sculpture-wait until he completed his printmaking journey. Printmaking led him to a new level, creating digital art games on a PC. 1367 Words. 2003.

ri031128
Vision of a Year
Another year of living copiously
A payoff in Emeralda is a year of living copiously. It means planning a departure on December 15th of each year-a tour of duty for this artist, teacher, researcher and service provider. As his 7th year in Emeralda Region comes to a close, he says goodbye. 1385 Words. 2003.

ri031206
Treading the Web in Emeralda
Studying Donald Kunze
When he surfed the three or four sites on the Internet created by or about professor Donald Kunze, this Itinerate professor has a gut-wrenching experience of having arrived at the reality he called Emeralda region, where lofty ideals and new art converge. 852 Words. 2003.

ri031231
Trusting Pathways
Persistent worlds then and now
The persistent image of schools is different in the mind of this 62-year old than that in today's 20-something. Already the latter has spent thousands of hours with TV and video games. They're called persistent worlds. What do they portend for the future? 1409 Words. 2003.

ri040130
If I Lived in a Cave
Icons of a bygone world
He imagines what it would be like if he were in a cave and found prehistoric images on its walls. Today he is living in a kind of cave, with a computer screen showing a scattering of icons like the iconography of cave dwellers' art. Is there a difference? 1059 Words. 2004.

ri040209
Moving My Stamps Around
The birth of a master stamp artist and storyteller
A simple project of moving a display of stamps from horizontal format to vertical gives this artist an idea that connects his artist's stamps to his search for a game he can play with other like-minded artists. He has visions of a multiplayer online game. 1058 Words. 2004.

ri040219
Stamp Game Huddle
Imagining a game play
Chance favors the prepared mind, said Pasteur, and this article is an exercise in preparing my mind for the answer to the question, "How do you play Emeralda with stamps?" I'm searching for ways to get other people involved in my game design enterprise. 1082 Words. 2004.

ri040320
Journal Entry, Sat. Mar. 20, 2004
Building an Intaglio Printing Press
The author writes about making his first intaglio printing press. He writes about the wooden prototype and thinking it to be functional as a linoleum block press with wood and plastic parts. He writes it being a nice craft and "Some might call it art!" 236 Words. 2004.

ri040708
Imagine a Game
Putting a press to good use
Imagine a game of cards, stamps and little printing presses. Players buy what they need to make the cards and stamps using that little press. They create the printing plates using old printing techniques like etching and engraving. They study art history. 386 Words. 2004.

ri040718
The Mini Halfwood Press at RIISMA
Contemplating the making of hardware in a think tank
RIISMA is the research island in Emeralda Region. On RIISMA, we undertake "pure" research, i.e., research that takes place for its own sake. What is the Mini Halfwood Press doing here? What's the worth of pure research in the arts? What does it look like? 327 Words. 2004.

ri040728
VIP and Values
Very Important Principles
What is important to this man is education, or, more specifically, teaching. The principle he admires the most is the principle of education, shared information, building community through exchanges that educate, enlighten and illuminate the human spirit. 745 Words. 2004.

ri040807
Sweet Dreams
Thinking of a smart condo
Someone said if you write down what you dream about, your dreams may come true. "Write it down, make it happen," someone advised. What is my dream, then? To go to sleep at night knowing that your neighbors are on a similar track as his, that is his dream. 712 Words. 2004.

ri040817
My Own Alumni Association:
A visit to the known art world
He feels as though he's living in a fantasy world, and yet he gets invited to a dinner for art world people-artists and museum people. He feels like the omniscient observer, the kind that knows the histories of some of the people, yet is not a part of it. 776 Words. 2004.

ri040827
To Summarize Printmaking
Summery printmaking born
A gallery owner wrote: "My clients ask me the same questions over and over. What is an etching? How do you do a lithograph? Is an offset the same as a lithograph? And so on. Do you have any videos that summarize printmaking?" The author ponders a summary. 723 Words. 2004.

ri040906
Flashes within Flashes:
Found in the archives of RIISMA
He is trying to visual a game to build on the Northwest Video Artists Archive, a game that people can develop in a seminar shared among two museums and the University of Washington. This essay comes during his playing of Emeralda, a game designed for him. 628 Words. 2004.

ri040916
If You Dream Long Enough It Will Come True:
A stamp shop on Taylor Avenue
How many years has it been since starting Emeralda? The author thinks it's true that if a dream work persists long enough it will come true. Wise people have said it's a fact. His dream is a game, a virtual world from which one can learn and earn forever. 435 Words. 2004.

ri040926
Proposal to DiGRA:
Emeralda, Games for the Gifts of Life
The abstract for a proposed presentation to the Digital Games Research Association conference to be held almost a year from now. It focuses on the main idea behind Emeralda, a game interface for online art courses in printmaking as the base of media arts. 2739 Words. 2004.

ri041006
Visiting the RIISMA Zine Archives
How you access the Missing Professor's secret files
The author gives a brief narrative to describe how the RIISMA Zine archive might look to a gamer. Emeralda is sometimes a game of hide and seek, where clues to the whereabouts of a mysterious, missing professor or found in essays, graphics and multimedia. 751 Words. 2004.

ri041016
When I Was Young and Creative
The prize of Emeralda is the play
For over a year the author who invented a game he calls Emeralda has been puzzled over the question: What is the Payoff? The question was put to him by a former student he met 37 years ago. He speculates that it's the play, not the pay that matters most. 978 Words. 2004.

ri050110
My Morning News
Reading My Old 'Zines
This artist, who also likes to write down his musings into a form he calls 'Zines, compares his morning reading to the reading of newspapers. It's a habit others cultivate, but not he. He starts by reading what he wrote 10 days ago on an imaginary island. 612 Words. 2005.

ri050120
Let the Game Go On
Writing and the Practice of Yoga
This artist is new at blogging, but he' finding it productive of unexpected turns of events. Also he confronts old practices and traditions such as make up his game he calls Emeralda. A review of his essays shows him where he's been and, also, his future. 619 Words. 2005.

ri050219
Artists Trading Cards and 'Zines
Connecting Online Blogs and Offline Cards
The daily routine of this writer is seeking links between traditional art, craft and design and a counterpart in the realm of digital reproduction. He surveys thousands of essays he wrote over the past thirty years and asks how to connect cards and words. 790 Words. 2005.

ri050301
Island Blogging
Searching for A Way to Play
He writes an essay almost every day, and maintains that he's in an imaginary place he calls Emeralda Region, located somewhere North of Seattle. Recently he became a blogger and now he thinks it's a link to his game, Emeralda: Games for the Gifts of Life. 744 Words. 2005.

ri050331
Real Animation
Getting to the Intent of Emeralda
He read about an educator who thinks children should be taught to draw, to animate and program at an early age. This artist can draw but he cannot animate; however he says to animate everything around him—his studio, his press, his self—is more important. 759 Words. 2005.

ri050410
Background Story for Stop Art Destruction
Continuing Thoughts of a Game for Fundraising
SAD started with a pinball-like game that people played for the dual purpose of entertainment and raising money for good causes. Its roots are found the art auction, but, as this writer tells it, it uses a very different approach and has a story to begin. 1357 Words. 2005.

ri050420
The Happy Online Art Professor
Making Games while the Sun Shines
What gives this Itinerate Professor the most joy in his working day is making a small booklet for an online art education experience. He happens to be producing a kind of innovative etching by using his computer and laser printer and he plans to share it. 541 Words. 2005.

ri050430
Imagining a Letter
A Former Professor Hatches A Plan
Growing more interested in the possibility of a board of trustees to lay the groundwork for getting grants to develop Emeralda: Games for the Gifts of Life, the former art professor composes a letter to solicit the aid of students from 20 to 30 years ago. 716 Words. 2005.

ri050510
Time Capsules and Trees
Discovery in Your Own Back Yard
A rumor spread around Seattle's Uptown neighborhood is that a time capsule was buried near the old Seattle Public Schools administration building. The rumor suggested that it was grade school children who buried the tree. Now a huge tree may be hiding it. 690 Words. 2005.

ri050520
Lunch with Robert Grudin
A Fantasy
One of this author's favorite author/professors is Robert Grudin, who worked in Oregon. Although never meeting him, this artist—a former professor too—identifies with him through his writing. More than that, some of his works are like his own experiences. 1297 Words. 2005.

ri050530
Blog as Journal
Writers and Artists Journals in the Age of Digital Sharing
Among this artist's favorite writers one defines journal keeping as an alternative channel between one's inner dialogue and the external tasks associated with serious writing. As that writer describes journal keeping, this artist finds clues in a mystery. 1183 Words. 2005.

ri050609
Exciting Games
Joining Ventures in the Creative Life
At the forefront of this artist's thoughts are games—all kinds of games—the kinds that almost everyone knows about and the one that only he knows about. He writes about the comparisons and permutations that are possible in the age of

digital reproduction. 935 Words. 2005.

ri050619
Emeralda Vanishes
The Findings on the Emeralda
As if in a science fiction thriller, this story is about the disappearance, and reappearance, of a Spanish Galleon in 1789 that drifted into, and out of, a kind of "Bermuda Triangle", a place that Native Americans believed to be a portal to another world. 507 Words. 2005.

ri050629
Interest
Taking Part in Your Community of Practice
When looking at a list of people who have bought the little etching press he designed he thinks he has what might be considered an inordinate degree of interest in these other peoples' arts, crafts and designs. What more meaning is in that word, interest? 619 Words. 2005.

ri050709
Ten Demons
A Word in the Night
He's wakened in the early morning hours and a fragment of a dream awaits him, about to vanish as dreams do; but he wrote it down. Two words, ten demons, related in some writing experience, the feeling that his writing is not his own but that of a specter. 546 Words. 2005.

ri050719
Grudin's Nine Places Revisited
A Parallel with My Favorite Writer
Reading "Book" at lunchtime one day, the artist (who thinks of himself as the inventor of an imaginary, virtual world game called Emeralda) rediscovers two pages that have an amazing resemblance to his own vision. Later he discovers he's come full circle. 618 Words. 2005.

ri050729
Emeralda Grant Writer Wanted
What to Do Before the Grantwriter Comes?
Preparation is needed to make the most of help from professionals in fundraising. That is advice from a Web site, Idealist.org. In his essay the inventor of Emeralda: Games for the Gifts of Life studies their advice and rewords their text by copy-writing. 1084 Words. 2005.

ri050808
Grantwriter Wanted
Beginning the Search
A team to create an online game, Emeralda, is forming. A Grantwriter is needed to fund the first part of the project. The inventor of the game is no Grantwriter himself, now ponders the qualifications and expectations he thinks will characterize this one. 1080 Words. 2005.

ri050818
Seeking Emeralda Trustees
Looking to the Past for a Trust in the Future

Studying the idea of financing development of a game he has in mind that he calls "Emeralda", he is offered the suggestion of getting a grant. This leads him to study the state of the art of grant getting, and discovers that he should seek trustees first. 1099 Words. 2005.

ri050828
Economics, Seniors and Sailing Ships
Connecting the Issues in Emeralda Games
In fanciful style, the author tests himself in the art of making connections where no one else can see them at first, and then in a step-by-step fashion he explains the idea of funding a community-of-practice by developments based on condominium practice. 1307 Words. 2005.

ri050927
Airborne Teaching
Professor in a Box
He was outside the box in his thinking and actions, and now he's put himself in the box—a boxed kit, that is—that people are buying for their children to learn fine art printmaking at home. This is a fantasy news article the professor wrote about himself. 930 Words. 2005.

ri051007
Birthday of the Mini Halfwood Press
Reflecting on the Year Past
It was on June 13, 2004 that Tom Kughler came to his studio carrying the first Mini Halfwood Press. The designer dubbed it the "Freedom" model but later they decided to name it the Mini. It would become, he wrote in his journal, the keystone to community. 509 Words. 2005.

ri051017
Need A Stamp?
Go to an Island
Daily the artist visits a page in his calendar and is intent on filling every day with a stamp from his collection of Artist's Stamps. He's also finding out how his game, Emeralda, can incorporate a calendar along with digital and traditional printmaking. 481 Words. 2005.

ri051027
My Own Book on Gates
Thoughts on Elmer Gates Biography
The artist who invents games today is keeping to the idea that art progresses and changes in time. The traditional arts changed from what they were when he began his career. Now art is in game design; he has chosen Elmer Gates to be leader in his project. 614 Words. 2005.

ri051106
Bad Feeling When You Miss a Stamp
Looking for Losers
It is too late to do anything about missing a stamp in the Emeralda calendar, probably, unless he can think of a new rule. He's inventing a game to play on his computer, using his artist stamp making skills, and a Stamp 'N Story a day is his present

goal. 948 Words. 2005.

ri051116
First Lesson Plan
Learning Computer Art in the Emeralda Region
Recalling how a woman wanted to know where she could learn how to use computers for art, the Emeralda master considers whether his game for the gifts of life might be the way to create a lesson plan that would satisfy her need. Writing essays comes first. 841 Words. 2005.

ri051126
For Every Stamp A Story
A Lesson from An 8-year Old
Continually searching for the Emeralda: Games for the Gifts of Life method of play, the inventor has a lesson from his granddaughter as the two show one another their favorite Web sites. Fifty-six years in age separate them but they learn from each other. 767 Words. 2005.

ri051206
A Place for Emeralda
Art Gallery or Game Arcade—which is it?
Recalling the success of Magic: The Gathering, this artist models an idea for a game partly on the benefits artists derived from making illustrations for the game. There was another element that made the game a success: The place where players could meet. 564 Words. 2005.

ri051221
Apprentice Story
Imagining How the Wood Parts of the Halfwood Press were Invented
It was the shortest day of the year when a stranger came to the shop and asked for a curious object. The apprentice was listening as the Master and the stranger completed their bargaining. This is part of the story of the last voyage of the Emeralda. 242 Words. 2005.

ri051231
Which Comes First - Book or CD?
Setting Priorities for A User's Manual
He has before him a miniature etching press that needs a User's Manual, and he must be the one to create it. Should it be based on the plans for a printed book, or should it leapfrog to the cyber-media and be a CD/ROM? It depends on the Users who need it. 886 Words. 2005.

ri060110
A Stamp for a Fair
Imagining a Giveaway
In a few days he will be demonstrating how prints are pulled from intaglio plates, using his Halfwood Press. But what will the prints be? In the days remaining to him he must compose and etch a copper plate suitable for the occasion and free to give away. 745 Words. 2006.

ri060120
Wisdom beyond His Years

Thinking of A Childhood
Always on the lookout for the pieces that will form the image of Emeralda, his fantasyland for media artists, he finds himself telling them to his wife at their dinner. It's against a background of life's long journey that he places these story fragments. 583 Words. 2006.

ri060510
Online Course Strategic Plan
The Art of Printmaking for Everyone
This artist, who used to teach printmaking to college students, developed a novel approach to the art and craft of his specialty. He claimed it is not a visual art, as is commonly thought, but a performance art and as such lends itself to online learning. 899 Words. 2006.

ri060530
Visualize a Skunkworks School
Reflections on Lost and Losing Opportunities
The author, self-designated as an "Itinerate Professor", describes as what a "skunkworks school" is intended. He believes he should have tried a skunkworks approach twenty years ago (while he was at the UW art school) instead of resigning. Is it too late? 663 Words. 2006.

ri060710
You Have to Qualify
A Variation of Art Auction
Now I have a variation on the Art Action in mind. I want to have a kind of Auction/Action blended with a game, like Bingo. 685 Words. 2006.

ri060719
Another Game with Artistamps
Full Page of Artist's Stamps
You goal is to complete the collection of 35 artist's stamps for a full page. 199 Words. 2006.

ri060729
A Happy Ending Beginning
A Trip to UW School of Art
In the glass cases at the art building they had posted many snapshots of people working there—faculty and graduate students and some staff people, too. It was in the evening, and except for the custodian and these two visitors, there was no one around. 1117 Words. 2006.

ri060808
Mentoring
Building on the Ellensburg Portfolio
If my "audience" is comprised of students who want to know how to make etchings and I want to help them at a distance, what should the interface look and feel like? A game has been my first answer. 1604 Words. 2006.

ri060818
Tome
The Power of Limits in a Work of Interactive Fiction
The tome in its printed form has a calendar in the

front of the Year of Living Copiously. 483 Words. 2006.

ri060828
Edition Numbers, Moments and an Emeralda Year
The Date on an Emeralda Regional Stamp
Locating the data that goes on an Emeralda Regional Stamp, it is a large numeral over a small one. For example, on a stamp for today it would be 257/10. 473 Words. 2006.

ri060907
Getting Started
Your Daily Routine as an Emeralda Warrior
The object of Emeralda is to establish a routine activity in keeping with the aim of the game, i.e., asset management and legacy transfer. To achieve this, you must utilize at least four productivity applications: spreadsheet, text, graphics and database. 1106 Words. 2006.

ri060917
A Structure for Collaboration
Reflecting on Hope
Ellensburg, with its booming development and major university, would be good soil to plant the idea of retrenchment of idealistic semi-retired intellectuals, artists, crafts people and designers with educators. 571 Words. 2006.

ri061019
Vision of Stewart's Year of Living Copiously
Another Year of the Gates Prize
This novice writer learns he must hook the reader with a lead-in of danger, or conflict, or emotion. Looking for a character from his Hunt for the Emeralda Treasure, he decides on his most vulnerable character, a wheel chair-bound professor named Stewart. 929 Words. 2006.

ri061206
Why I Dropped Out
Popular fiction II, Not A Good Fit
I dropped out of Popular Fiction II. The story I am working on is not in the popular fiction style. However, I'd like to be a popular writer. 651 Words. 2006.

ri061231
New Year
Review of the Year of Living Copiously
After almost a year of writing Hunt for the Emeralda Treasure, building a complete calendar of the 10th (and starting the 11th) Year of Living Copiously, what have I learned? 683 Words. 2006.

ri070111
Maybe Not Digital Based Learning Game
Playing the Game, Inventing the Game
It's not important that the game becomes a digital based learning game. It's more important, as the designer, to take the more enjoyable path, playing the game as it is invented. 260 Words. 2007.

ri070530
RIISMA
1st Day
History of the relationship between Harris Sweed and his art professor, Bill Ritchie. Sweed writes a report for the History of the Halfwood Press. 2488 Words. 2007.

ri070819
Reiko Sundahl
On Bill Ritchie in Art Dish Forum
In the role of Cafe guest Member # 1635 on 08-19-2007, Reiko Sundahl, writer and art critic in the Northwest, wrote in a forum thread that started with Ries Niemi who said that the northwest owes its vitality to West Coast funk and the Alps/Ritchie works. 1011 Words. 2007.

ri070927
Luck of the Draw
How to Play with ArtGrid Cards
This is a game where you play with the missing professor's unpublished essays. You play the game with a deck of ArtGrid Cards. 612 Words. 2007.

ri071007
Nellie's First Task
Subject Line
This artist likes to write as much as he likes to make pictures and craft items for his studio. Over the past 40 years, his journalizing and essay writing has resulted in a database of thousands. He's imagining his daughter, Nellie, helping organize them. 1019 Words. 2007.

ri071106
Art in a World of Work
Toward A Rationale of Games as Art
Play can be construed as production and encourage productivity and service. Entertainment as a leisure pastime is fine if there is leisure to be had; but suppose what we know as leisure becomes a relic of the past. The author asks, 'Then what do artists do?" 306 Words. 2007.

ri071116
I could Have Been a Professor
Musings of a Pioneer in the Age of Digital Reproduction
Encouraging reflections on becoming an online professor based on an owner of a Mini Halfwood press. 442 Words. 2007.

ri071126
An Early Morning Reminder
The Importance of Making Separate Directories
A message awaits him when he enters his studio one morning and resumes work on his CD/ROM version of the cards for Emeralda—the game on which he's working. As it's a game like Solitaire, of course he's the one who left the message, giving himself 331 Words. 2007.

ri071221
Coincidence of Intellect

Reviewing Thomas Stewart's Intellectual Capital
In a review of a book that he read ten years ago this artist and teacher attests that the concept that intellectual capital has, because of the revolutionary information age and digital technologies, a value equal to or greater than an artist's life work. 454 Words. 2007.

ri080110
Stephen Hazel
Recollections by an Admirer
Inspired by discovering of a Stephen Hazel print in the collection of a good friend, the author reflects on his meeting with Stephen in the 1960s, and how this artist's arrival in Seattle put in motion a chain of events that changed many lives in Seattle. 889 Words. 2008.

ri080120
Game Yield
Getting the Best of Both Worlds
Today, game worlds appear in two forms—real and virtual. Board games exist in real form and also in digital online forms. Money gained from skills in playing games are one kind of yield. The age of digital production has another kind of yield for artists. 1232 Words. 2008.

ri080130
New Frame
Out with the Old, In with the New
The act of clearing the content of a spreadsheet gives rise to the notion that the frames of cells in a spreadsheet are like the frames of works of art—one is digital and virtual, the other is real. There is a connection here this artist explores for fun. 1049 Words. 2008.

ri080209
Dreaming Games
Reflections on Learning Emeralda
The dream this morning was about Cell Pool. Awaking with some notion of recursivity. This points out the fact that you learn Emeralda while you play it. No worries about a neat outline of the object of the game and how you win or lose. 350 Words. 2008.

ri080219
Lawrence Timeline
Search for Truth and Separation
Using his journals, the former professor who worked with the famous Jacob Lawrence on a lithograph, searches for the sequence of events that brought the two into contact. In particular, he's trying to find out who actually printed the lithograph for Jake. 577 Words. 2008.

ri080229
BIOS Time
Reflections on Daniel Smith Inc.
Daniel Smith Inc is like one of those corporations that began with a simple, essential product and that grew into a huge multinational institution. He saw a need for an intaglio ink in the printmaking

education. 638 Words. 2008.

ri080310
Stamping Idea
Participants in Making Halfwood Presses
While stamping a Certificate of Authenticity one day, the author imagined a certificate like this with the stamps of ten people who participated in making the press and the things that go with it. 422 Words. 2008.

ri080320
Soul of a New Company
A New Cooperative
The ineffable soul and goal of the author's enterprise—trying to make a profit while maintaining the integrity of the assets that built his ability to design the press and teach with it. 650 Words. 2008.

ri080330
Quiet Rebel
Rebelling Against Making Art A Commodity
In a moment of clear thinking, the author sees himself in a different light, or perhaps as others might see him if they knew what thoughts were transpiring in the hidden pursuits of his computer game design, Emeralda. He sees his game plan as a rebellion. 1379 Words. 2008.

ri080409
Emeralda Grading
Examination in Emeralda Play
As the author left Kinko's one day, with his latest version of a Halfwood Press cards, he thought how he had "flunked" his test. The stamp portion in the card had not printed correctly; it was his next task to figure out why. 419 Words. 2008.

ri080419
Press Factory
A Vision Expression
In the style of the child's story, "The House that Jack Built," this artist (who is also entrepreneurial) describes a path leading from an imaginary press factory to the award of a college diploma. He is thinking how to present his idea to his Alma Mater. 1094 Words. 2008.

ri080429
FAQ
Frequently Asked Questions about Learning Printmaking Online
In the design process for his proposal to teach etching online, the author imagines the question he might be asked. It is like a pretend oral exam, except there's no panel of experts for it, no peer judge and no real inquiries. He has to make up the exam. 1088 Words. 2008.

ri080509
Market Analysis
Second Task of the Leader in Learning Printmaking Online
The author is suited to this task because he taught

printmaking off line for nineteen years and researched, experimented and designed ways to teach it offline. He knows the market that was, and he can forecast the market that is emerging. 1435 Words. 2008.

ri080519
Mentoring Leaders
Ensuring Continuity and Renewal of Distant Education
In Distance Education, the author suggests that the mentoring may go on in a way quite different than what most educators think. 1267 Words. 2008.

ri080529
Application Architecture
User Views
The Designer is most apt to consider User Views. Who is "The User" in Emeralda? The designer must have a profile of the User population. User Views is important, the Designer must use the data available. 872 Words. 2008.

ri090110
Emeralda Leaders
Collaboration in Communities of Inquiry and Practice
The author has a list of collaborators in his concept of a learning game, and they whisper in his ear from across centuries or they left their imprints. The imprints range in form as handprints on cave walls or sophisticated algorithms, and many writings. 496 Words. 2009.

ri090120
Many Ways to Write a Premise for a Video Game
First of Ten Steps on ELPO Development List
As he is inventor of a blended learning product designed to teach college level printmaking, and variations intended for younger learners, the author must write the premise—the log line—for his concept. Here he writes several variations on the same theme. 522 Words. 2009.

ri090130
ELPO Premise Revisited
Taking Another Look at Carolyn Miller's Ten-Step Game Development Checklist
The Ten-Step Development List laid out by Carolyn Handler Miller in her book Digital Storytelling was a ten-day challenge. That was ten days ago. Now I have a new edition of her book and the section on the ten points in her list is different. I start over! 1354 Words. 2009.

ri090209
Trying CWU Again
How Pasting Stamps in a Book may be a Clue
In his studio one morning, while pasting stamps into a text, like a stamp collector with a Great Notion, the inventor of Emeralda: Learn Printmaking Online gets an idea he thinks has been a long time coming: His Alma Mater might join him in getting funds. 512 Words. 2009.

ri090219
How the Dog Royal got His Name
Royal's Place with the Evil One
The author wrote about the dog, Royal, who is the Evil One's dog. He is a large black Labrador. A cat is mentioned as being the scanner for the Evil One's purpose. 176 Words. 2009.

ri090301
ELPO Premise and Purpose
Yet another Look at Carolyn Miller's Ten-Step Game Development Checklist
The Ten-Step Development List written by Carolyn Handler Miller in her book Digital Storytelling was a ten-day challenge. That was ten days ago. Now I have a new edition of her book and the section on the ten points in her list is different. I start over! 1354 Words. 2009.

ri090311
Last words of Elmer Gates
Elmer Gates' Last Words Inspired SPAL in Me
"So this is how it has to be." Those were Elmer Gates' last words, according to the biography by his son. There was only one other person by his side, and his lifetime's work is all but forgotten. Does it have to be? Not in an age of digital reproduction. 1284 Words. 2009.

ri090331
Ten-step Story Development
Playwriting 101 Provides Structure for ELPO Backstory
Following a suggestion by a friend, the author—whose goal is to create an entertaining user interface for his plan to teach printmaking online—finds his friend left a clue. It is a chapter from an online tutorial titled Playwriting 101, a focus on story. 2880 Words. 2009.

ri090410
Carrie Wood Profile
The Bottle Collector Character Profile for "Hunt for the Emeralda Treasure"
Ann Carrie Wood, a refugee from the competitive mainland society, has a collection of old bottles she found in the cabin she acquired when she moved to Two Dog Island. In another version she finds them in the old mansion on the hill. One bottle is sealed. 492 Words. 2009.

ri090510
Tree House Halfwood Press Factory
First Day of Class for ELPO

When one of the team members developing Emeralda - Learn Printmaking Online turned out to be a tree house builder, it gave the professor the idea of using the tree house as a leveling device. Newcomers to the course are shown how to make an etching press. 1636 Words. 2009.

ri090520
Money for Art Education

Five Arguments for and Ways to get Money for Teaching Art in Public Schools
Now teaching some arts in schools is more important than teaching art in college. Art teachers' paychecks depend on taking a new approach. There is a new art teaching technique in the works. Blended online printmaking is the basis of it. It has substance. 1120 Words. 2009.

ri090530
Scrimshaw Story
Vladimir Petroslovana Chichinoff's Narrative on the Sides of the Plasteel Press
The Plasteel Press is patterned after the Mini Halfwood, but, instead of wood cladding the steel parts, it is clad in plastic that looks like ivory. Scratched in the sides is a story by a Russian, Chichinoff, kidnapped and then cast away on Two Dog Island. 761 Words. 2009.

ri090602
Feeling Economics
Heart and Head in the Arts of the Digital Age
Reviewing the editor's rendition of one chapter in his novel, "Hunt for the Emeralda Treasure," he is pleased with her work. His mind turns to co-ops, collaboration and cooperation among artists, and his discovery that shared worlds are a genre of sci-fi. 1486 Words. 2009.

ri090609
Shared Worlds
Video Games and Printmaking
This printmaking professor sees joining of community with performance in the printmaking world; and the printmaking world, like that of the video game designer, is a shared world. As in the shared worlds in literature, co-operation is the key to survival. 1599 Words. 2009.

ri090808
Real Bible
How my Bible Works for Me
Being a media artist of the 21st Century needs adapting to video games as this is the art of the century. As an industry grew out of video games, individual artists were left in the dust. However, as the dust settles, a 21st Century artist's bible appears 1211 Words. 2009.

ri090907
Dusty Cards
Dusty's Childhood and Toasterphobia
The author tells the story about Dusty and his phobia of toasters. 962 Words. 2009.

ri090927
Ephemeral Channels
Blending Methods of Learning Printmaking
The author writes about creating a short trailer for Emeralda: Learn Printmaking Online. He writes about blending online learning experience and face-to-face traditional workshop learning. He also includes the functions of the video game. 719 Words. 2009.

ri091007
Bill's Screenplays
My Ideas for Five Movies I'd Like to See
In his day to day work the author is an artist, with a special interest in printmaking. Writing is also a big part of his day and lately he's been learning the art and craft of screenplays. As things happen, these screenplays are connected to printmaking. 1019 Words. 2009.

ri091017
Play Space
Experimenting with Learning Printmaking Online
The author works on ways to participate in teaching and learning, research, practice and community service online as well as in the real world. He has been inventing ways to do these things by using online 3D worlds—virtual worlds—for a printmaking world. 1601 Words. 2009.

ri091028
Emeralda Stage
Arriving in a New Virtual World
The author has joined with a video game designer to develop a printmaking world inside an imaginary place in an imaginary world called SpotOn3D! He may never have another opportunity to know how the moment of arrival feels, so he writes down his feelings. 1165 Words. 2009.

ri091126
About RIISMA Zine Database
By Way of Review
Nellie Sunderland has taken charge of organizing all my essays so they can be quickly and easily accessed using a computer. The objective when I began working with her on this was to set my writings up in such a way to link them with my art. 1005 Words. 2009.

ri091206
Finding My Own Way to Printmaking World
Another Metaphor for Learning Printmaking Online
This journey on a new pathway started when his wife mentioned a rock group started an online game to help boost sales of their music. You pay to play, she said, and in the course of playing you are getting their advertising. Great idea! So he started out. 2230 Words. 2009.

ri091221
About RIISMA
A Brief History of Ritchie's International Institute for Study of Multimedia Arts
He is not sure how it all began, but several possibilities come to mind. One was the Batelle Research Institute, and another was suggested by an artist who studied ephemeral events. He was working at a major university at the time with international ties. 1106 Words. 2009.

ri091231

Crazy Muse
Playing the Game
After a ninety-minute session playing a game that has not yet been invented, the author wonders if his muse is crazy. Can a man who doesn't like card games, board games, party games, computer games, etc. actually invent a game? She says, Yes! She's crazy! 233 Words. 2009.

Speaking, Consulting, Design and Training (AKA SPEACON, or, SP)

On the island of SPEACON, public speaking, consulting, design and training are practiced. This is a view looking west about three PM in May.

SPEACON, all caps, comes from the two main activities—public speaking and consulting. Design and training are the other two primary interests here.

Artistic content and expertise identification, evaluation, control and dissemination, including all matters of public speaking, consulting, design services and training in the field of print and non-print media are the business of this division.

On the island of SPEACON they believe that all good art, crafts and design technology practitioners must have: 1. extensive programming experience, 2. a working knowledge of classes of students, 3. the ability to diagnose accurately the needs of various arts divisions and then find appropriate multimedia solutions, and 4. the interpersonal skills to "sell" these ideas to faculty and those administrators who are still wary of technologies in the arts.

sp881231
Essays from Interior Design:
Writing on Colorline-1988
Essays written by Bill Ritchie and others which make up the "Colorline Collection of Writings". These trace the path of Bill Ritchie's consulting and design work for Dennis Mashek, the developer of Colorline. All work's statistics and keywords are listed. 771 Words. 1988.

sp930802
Marketing in the arts' channel
NAMTA-IPC Summary
This article is for NAMTA's and their publication. By outlining the executive summary from the Industry Promotion Committee (IPC), the author comes to a better understanding of the potential for fitting the committee's needs with what he has. 1316 Words. 1993.

sp930830
Caution Construction ahead
Arts on the data highway
As telecommuting, data superhighways, virtual reality and interactive TV arrive, art tool-makers and suppliers will go on-line or die. The author surveyed customers in an art supply store and issues a warning to art materials trades. 21887 Words. 1993.

sp931008
Cruising gets a deal
A dozen pages on a future trend
The writer, the artist, and the business person use a computers. Soon, almost everyone will be using computers--even vacationers. Computers are, some say, using vacationers. The author suggests ways to get computer art, writing and leisure on a ship. 459 Words. 1993.

sp931018
Four faces of effective curriculum design
College for the 3rd millennium
In schools, workshops, seminars, training centers and distance learning or continuing education, a four-faced curriculum design method is suggested. The author uses a cybernetic approach. (Proposal). 162 Words. 1993.

sp940124
The impotance of museums
Mis-reading history
Whether museums produce reproductions of collections or if a student's school is near enough to go there determines if the museum is important to education. If far away and not publishing in accessible media, they are impotent. 3153 Words. 1994.

sp940205
Palm-tops, Desktops and PDAs
Taking IT for a cruise
Cruise passengers can take computer classes on the Alaska Cruise unlike any that are offered on land. The Personal Digital Assistant, or PDA, is an example. Business people, educators and writers will like this class. 1164 Words. 1994.

sp940507
Adept - not adopt
An ecology of mind
To be learned in the age of electronic reproduction at a distance, in time and space, requires an adept mind. This is attainable only if one develops an ecology of the mind suitable to adeptness. 930

Words. 1994.

sp940604
Perfect College
The PATCWA Vision
Extractions from a database of colleges, taking the ones that have the most interesting announcements to make just might be candidates for the definition of the Perfect College - especially a college expressly envisioned for the 21st Century. 2905 Words. 1994.

sp950112
Goals and Mentors
New roadway to resource experts
Getting key people connected to the digital world is a checkpoint in the process of Education Continuing Improvement. This Essay is about goals, localization and experts' self-management as knowledge workers weigh technology. 1710 Words. 1995.

sp950121
Fall of Art Schools and Rise of Intelligent Teaching Companies
Sampling the Collective Stream of Talent and Technology
Where an art school may fail in some ways, others will succeed by using new technologies. Among the success stories in the making, one has roots in ancient printing. Analogous scientific methods help this art professor to describe the rise of this school. 2103 Words. 1995.

sp950613
Growing Markets for Digital Media
The Maturity Segment
From the point of view of an early-adopter of digital media, it appears a new field is ready for cultivation as boomers re-think their options and find they may need new tools with which to navigate their lengthening future. 917 Words. 1995.

sp951031
Apprentice-Users'
Education for artists in a new era
From Mid-18th Century apprentices to today's computer user, the author sees a new kind of learning, research and doing that bridges two-hundred years of economic theory that defines the importance of creative cooperation. 1507 Words. 1995.

sp951221
TCWA training camp
A town like Patcwa?
Surplus from some of Washington's industries goes on sale at prices almost anyone who needs the stuff can afford. But what about surplus from information-age industries? Can an entire town be reinvented on surplus intellect from high-tech companies? 2397 Words. 1995.

sp951223
Certification of new fine artists
Test for a DMA candidate

To write a workbook like Kevin Trudeau's MegaMemory, something people could learn in, say, a month, or even make some advances in two weeks on their own, what would the process be? 314 Words. 1995.

sp960315
Emotional Investing
Marketing and selling ESRB, FSEA and TCWA
After being asked to consider becoming a marketing director for non-profit educational organizations, the author re-examines the connection between his fine arts telecard concept and alliance with technology groups. 1276 Words. 1996.

sp960320
Visiting SPEACON
Best of all worlds to a guest educator
Eighth-day of an imaginary tour of islands in the Lake of Domains of Expertise, a college art professor finds an ideal balance of high tech-art ed based on values, central principle renewal and reinvented. Excerpt from the reinvention workbook. 2955 Words. 1996.

sp960909
Emeralda's Art World shopper
Surfing to bargains on the Web
The author describes a shopping game that will appeal to people who enjoy the fine arts. Whether their interest is in art materials for making art or learning, experimenting with a game he calls Emeralda is a new twist on an old pastime. 723 Words. 1996.

sp961005
Finding 50 Simple Things Artists Can Do to Save the Earth
A perfect day at SPEACON
Speakers, consultants, trainers and designers of curricula address a Gruddite Apprentice-User as he fulfills his mentor's assignment: Write about a perfect day. 299 Words. 1996.

sp961026
Living Prints in the Sands of Time
Mineralogy in the cybernetic age
Two weeks' e-mail exchange on the subject of Tech Corps Washington may provide clues for structuring a not-for-profit, grass-roots organization to help bring arts and technology together in schools. 1656 Words. 1996.

sp961027
Watch the donut, not the hole
Architect/Visionary of TCWA goes to work
El primer piso, (in Spanish meaning, the first floor) of TCWA, is sketched by the chief architect and visionary. 1126 Words. 1996.

sp961109
Emeralda the Wise
Secrets of her game
The key to playing Emeralda may be knowing how to write and read HTML. 1385 Words. 1996.

sp961223
Chicken Story
Two hens' views of crisis and opportunity
Two fables--Little Red Hen and Chicken Little--provide the basis for looking at crises and opportunities. The two meet at a crossroads in fable-land where chickens talk to other creatures. Human creativity may depend on understanding the story of the two. 1197 Words. 1996.

sp970313
Response-able teaching
Transforming the learning-place
In the four services of an "art business" the art-business teacher who answers a calling in artistic ways adopts business and industrial models, reads books by economists and scientists and learns how to change the schools and be effective, for good. 1492 Words. 1997.

sp970318
Growing in good soil
Writing the articles of Tech Corps
The architect who visualizes TCWA suggests culture be the central principle of a state's volunteer organization. It's built on Washington State's unique geographic setting, history, financial and natural resources that indicate human, diverse creativity. 1004 Words. 1997.

sp970323
Arts in equilibrium
Hopes dashed by ghosts in the new machine
Ten years ago, Al Gore wrote "Earth in the Balance" saying that equilibrium of natural and man-made elements are needed to sustain life. Vitality in the arts has the same need, but the arts worlds might impose stasis when anti-stasis is what's needed. 2177 Words. 1997.

sp970402
How do YOU play "Emeralda"?
Begin years ago
Playing "The game for life" you get up in the morning like everyone else but from the first hour you approach your art and craft differently than anyone else. It is like a game of solitaire, but there are ghosts in the new machine that make your moves. 1196 Words. 1997.

sp970610
Swimming with the cyber artists
Without being eaten alive
"Learn how to swim rather than be sunk by cybernetics," says the author. He describes one or two ways to maintain the original function of the museum, a place for the muses, while staying fit. 1856 Words. 1997.

sp970717
While you're on-line, get an MDA
Concurrent marketing and curriculum development
One of a series of articles on the evolution toward

a fine arts degree in digital art--a revolutionary, higher education program on the Internet. The author is a professor of art with over thirty years in art, education, research and technologies. 4738 Words. 1997.

sp970907
What did you learn in school today?
My art school day online
There is a song in my head I heard a long time ago with a recitation of the lessons the little boys learned. Now, my head is stuffed. My brain craves oxygen! Even though mine is now a school on-line, I'm still a biological creature--not a machine. 1061 Words. 1997.

sp970909
Shaping ABCZine On-line
The WWW First dynazine for arts business
On the eve of putting his 'zine on the First Virtual InfoHaus line, the author establishes the four guidelines: Creativity, motion, value and interaction. He comes up with a word he wants to use: dynazine. 1430 Words. 1997.

sp970918
An art show is born--Part 2
The Artists Equity Fund
In part one he described HSIC by using the technique of copy writing over the authors Edvinsson and Malone's words about intellectual capital as a serious object of study (Skandia, the financial company in Sweden) calling it the Artists Equity Fund. 923 Words. 1997.

sp971018
Breaking through
Getting there from here
"Monetary Emeralda" is part of the Emeralda Game Pack that pays for itself, says the "Emeralda" game inventor. He modeled himself after Richard Buckminster Fuller and Bill Gates, III in this article--and pays tribute to his mother, Harlene Jesse Ritchie. 1591 Words. 1997.

sp971220
Human Capital Measures
A Case-Based Experiment
The quest for the working parts of Emeralda leads to an objective view of a day's activity in what ostensibly constitutes an Emeralda Moment. 1612 Words. 1997.

sp980113
HSICICA goes to Safeco
Arts, education and investment
Prior to meeting with Safeco, the Insurance and Investment Company known also for its support of education and culture, the author reviews the current standing of his EarthSafe 2028 mission. 751 Words. 1998.

sp980121
Hardest Nut to Crack
Selling flawed diplomas

Returning to his former role as an educator, and finding that he himself has much to learn, the Emeralda Inventor initiates a new strategy aimed at lowering resistance to his new approach to teaching, learning, research and practice in the fine arts. 1005 Words. 1998.

sp980126
View from my Cell
An Apprentice-User writes home
In the Emeralda Region one of the biggest islands is SPEACON. Apprentice Users spend their first hours in one of four villages for Speaking, Consulting, Design and Training. The Author writes a letter home before breakfast, about the view from his window. 355 Words. 1998.

sp980128
Eviscerating Notions
Call for art ed reform
At SPEACON, the island of the domain-of-expertise in the Emeralda Region, the Emeralda Inventor and Master role plays a radio talk show after being introduced to a new channel for spoken word dissemination. He uses parts of a real e-mail message to begin. 1963 Words. 1998.

sp980129
Part of the Solution
The problem with games
The Inventor of Emeralda sees his intellectual asset navigator game as a solution to the problem of replay value. Where most games have little or no replay value for the mature player, Emeralda can literally pay the player for coming back again and again. 681 Words. 1998.

sp980220
Wake up laughing
The giant in the mirror
Leaping across the chasm that separates humor and creativity, the writer finds himself with a new vision of what life is all about. He's no longer a puppet responding to invisible market channels; he will carve a new channel. 1178 Words. 1998.

sp980322
What's Cooking, Americas?
Recipe for the SS United States
Writing about big ideas--as big as all the Americas combined--this writer tells how the smallest detail in the big picture is important. Like small ingredients, they make the big parts of the vision, a luxury liner and a computer game, success-bound. 1841 Words. 1998.

sp980401
Memo to a former art student
Everything you need to know you can learn on the 'Net
People who went to college and majored in art ten or more years ago may be wondering what has changed in their old art school. A former professor writes this "memo" to an invisible, phantom former student to tell them. 3691 Words. 1998.

sp980411
Emeralda FAQs, OAQs, SAQs and NAQs
Emeralda Inventor Interviewed at SPEACON
The inventor of Emeralda is interviewed as part of a virtual interview on the Isle of SPEACON. 4460 Words. 1998.

sp980511
Hannah's story
A virtual real estate agent has her say
Investors touring Lake Emeralda look for an ideal setting and build a virtual community. Each individual has a single, sovereign vision as to what would be perfect studios for them, as only two days ago they visited Perfect Studios, flagship of Emeralda. 1272 Words. 1998.

sp980521
Ready to play Emeralda?
Hang on--this will be a big leap!
As the prevailing Meni is SPEACON, a member of a tour group wants to start playing Emeralda now. The question is, is Emeralda ready to be played by him? 221 Words. 1998.

sp980610
Orientation in Emeralda Cells
Q&A for the Emeralda Inventor
Skeptical visitors to the inventor's domain may doubt that the creative, inventive, discovering individual actually has something of value, and their fears are justified. He takes risks, even when he ventures to offer questions about his creation. 1277 Words. 1998.

sp980620
Demons in Emeralda
Introduction to the knowbot community
It is a long way from Shelly's Frankenstein to the knowbots that populate Emeralda today. This essay examines some of the names and fears associated with automata that grew during the age of mechanization of human industry. 842 Words. 1998.

sp980630
Musing after Hesse
The First Emeralda Player
The player seems to be dawdling. He's looking over a small book he bound a few days ago, reading the passages about emeralds, gold and Einstein. The clock on his desktop computer says it is 6:27 AM. He checks his hand-held; it says 6:26. An idle thought. 539 Words. 1998.

sp980710
Demonstrating Emeralda Routines
Teaching=Specifying
The artist/writer and inventor of Emeralda-Games for the Gifts of Life, charts his rules and also thinks about comparing artists' organizations with those of dentists and how respectful skills and knowledge of both make them similar, but not economically. 1083 Words. 1998.

sp980720
Strategies in Emeralda
Virtue and reality
The inventor writes about strategies in Emeralda that are difficult because they assume there is a requirement to satisfy others, rules to obey and goals that come from outside authorities. Strategies imply someone else expects them to achieve something. 1231 Words. 1998.

sp980730
Virtual Communities 101
The secret gets out
A maverick professor, who avoided the draft during Viet Nam by teaching college (but which has given him recurring nightmares) describes a fantasy. It is set in turn-of-the-century Bremerton, a town that time forgot. 1197 Words. 1998.

sp980809
Attending an Emeralda Seminar
Getting paid for your Human Structural Intellectual Capital
SPEACON is organized so newcomers to Emeralda who want to commercialize their intellectual assets can learn the basics within the Emeralda method. This article describes a seminar on the process. 3034 Words. 1998.

sp980819
Reflections of an Educational Entrepreneur
Art, Technology and International Relations
His goal is to develop better relationships and experiences among people of all nations partly through arts technology education. From time to time it has been necessary to reflect on goals in the same way that managers of multinational corporations must. 4412 Words. 1998.

sp980829
Writer's dilemma tale
In between technical writing and incoherent dreams
Creative, inventive, discovering and imaginative people (people such as professional writers) must pick and choose from among the ghosts populating their thoughts. Some cyber-age writers' dilemmas are found between technical writing and incoherent dreams. 1663 Words. 1998.

sp980908
How good thou art
The art tracker on the trail of employment
Is one who can track bodies of text and graphics in a jungle of several kinds of computer applications (text editor, spread sheet, database, page layout and on-line multimedia) a one you would call Good at Art? In the canons of art today one would say No. 804 Words. 1998.

sp980918
The basics of Emeralda
Getting from your PDA to the Score sheet in one day

As a visionary multimedia presentation, the author/inventor promises to show participants how they can learn more about the human structural intellectual capital and do it while having fun. He walks around instead of being a prisoner in a class or office. 1072 Words. 1998.

sp980928
New paradigm for TLC
Filling your own stand
The growth in interest in an on-line art school continues. In an essay this writer-inventor blasts the obstacle keeping most people from doing IT--the old brick-and-mortar, degree-constrained teaching, learning and capitalization paradigm based on prints. 1321 Words. 1998.

sp981008
Training Apprentice Users
Introducing the Score sheets
Emeralda play is to set and measure the value of creative, inventive and the discovering individual's knowledge and skills in numerical terms representing money equivalents, tradable services, energy or tangible goods in an individual player's scoresheet. 449 Words. 1998.

sp981018
Q&A by SPEACON Agents
Emeralda Inventor Interviews
Agents on SPEACON Isle interrogate the Emeralda Inventor to untangle the mysteries of Emeralda by going directly to the source. The inventor answers questions about how the game will be valuable to speakers, teachers, curriculum designers and consultants. 6984 Words. 1998.

sp981107
Coventry of Masters
Digital Fine Art Festival Revisited
Bridging the chasm called So What Who Cares requires a plan that is like a blueprint for a bridge that one can trust. Emeralda resembles a plan or a map based on four human capabilities, and the covenant of these capabilities in a form that can be shared. 827 Words. 1998.

sp981117
Framing Your Head and Heart
Picturing SPEACON
Playing Emeralda is like being in a frame shop for your head and heart. SPEACON (an Island of the Domain-of-expertise in speaking, consulting, design and training) is set apart from other isles by focusing on one's self and our relationships to audiences. 875 Words. 1998.

sp981127
The Platinum Rule
Managing Your Equity Factor
There's more to the catchy title, "Managing the Equity Factor," that suggested to me that it would be one to explain further the idea of intellectual capital. However, the author needed to revisit general systems theory to make the book useful to an

artist. 489 Words. 1998.

sp990126
Roots of Fine Arts Education Online
Case study of a bazaar paradigm
A selection from the story of a professor who mysteriously vanishes after finding a hypothesis linking archeological findings in France to cybernetics. This features a social scientist Eric Aronson and a way Aronson uses mystery in teaching co-operatively. 869 Words. 1999.

sp990127
Itinerate Professor
A brief glimpse at an old idea
Picture the Itinerate worker--migrating far from his or her home and family to find work. So it is with the Itinerate Professor, traveling by foot, sometimes, to find a student or a community where a learned professor is needed. The author sets the stage. 427 Words. 1999.

sp990128
Chilling Text
The Innovator's Dilemma resolved
On a cold and rainy day, this professor reads words that chill him to his bones, words that seem to be written just for his eyes. The book is by a Harvard professor--on technology company life--his words ring true for prisoners in the velvet prisons of academe. 946 Words. 1999.

sp990129
You Too Can Teach Art Online
An old newcomer writes the rules
Professing to teach art on-line, the author writes between on-line sessions. He works symmetrically around a creative, inventive, discovering and imaginative world--an imaginary world based on human structural intellectual capital having its own economics. 1274 Words. 1999.

sp990326
Day of Reckoning
The AUDAMIS Surveys the Jungle
He experiments in the dental field with the idea that dentists could use some help in the area of digital communications. He joins his dentist friend at a conference and focuses on the topic of Practice Management, reminding him of teaching in art school. 373 Words. 1999.

sp990327
Business plans past
Artifacts of the competition
This dreamer closed his eyes saying, "I wish I could teach art on line." This dream came true; he has "taught art" on-line, and it is time to move on to another dream: "I wish I could now earn money for my skills and be a useful member of the human race." 673 Words. 1999.

sp990328
Take Risk For Example
Seriously folks

Take risks. We've heard it a hundred times, how it's necessary to take a leap into the unknown if you want to get ahead, or even to just keep up. But isn't this a contradiction to the cases against competition? Thus ponders the reader of Alfie Kohn's works. 746 Words. 1999.

sp990329
Accrediting the DAMIS
Rules of a New Game
You might as well describe the shapes of clouds as to describe the job description of the Dental Assistant Manager of Information Services writes this artist/philosopher about the practices of writing job descriptions in the age of digital communications. 605 Words. 1999.

sp990330
Playing corporation
Co-operation is just a letter away
You can learn how to better manage economic circumstances by comparing some condominium corporations to a cooperative approach to living and practicing your art and craft of dentistry. I call it "Playing Corporation," like the idea for "Teaching Company". 309 Words. 1999.

sp990525
My MOGO User's Group
First time for everything
The facilitator for MOGO User's Group in Seattle writes about the group's first meeting. He writes that first times for things take place in a pro-active person's mind and is followed by the real things. Concepts precede reality, like an arts performance. 1237 Words. 1999.

sp990526
Between two worlds
A rock and a hard place?
The inventor of Emeralda walks a path between two worlds--sometimes narrow, sometimes wide, sometimes on a precipice. Art's world and the world of healthcare, he says, were divorced from one another hundreds of years ago. New technologies can rejoin them. 341 Words. 1999.

sp990527
Can You Expand on This?
A Flashback
Looking for a subject to fill the hole in a series of articles for his Resident Stay at SPEACON, the Emeralda Inventor applies his expertise at Emeralda Play by going to the timelog of that day. There he finds a legacy example an topics he may expand on. 371 Words. 1999.

sp990528
Copying reality
Greenfields work--or they don't
An appendix of a business book provides a creative artist with ideas to create a strategic partnership with an arts museum without getting eaten up in the procedures. He calls it Greenfields, from the terms in the businessmen's languages that

mystify him. 1732 Words. 1999.

sp990529
Property Values WIFT
What's in it for him?
Emeralda is the description of property values that derive from the third column in triple-entry bookkeeping. The systemic failure of educational institutions branches from the roots of failing to manage description. The author's tape archive illustrates. 1680 Words. 1999.

sp990530
Strangers and Mentors
Entering Emeralda's Dentalisco
A tale of two people meeting in a fantasy city called Dentalisco--where dentists reign. One is a mentor, the other a mentee. The latter becomes an apprentice user, taking her first steps into a world of cybernetics where Leagues of Emeralda Masters reign. 1487 Words. 1999.

sp000104
Beyond the Art of Selling Art
Equivocation and George's Art
What good is Emeralda if you doesn't get you and keep you integrity? The Inventor asks himself. Proceeding with this year's project (the writing of the stories for Emeralda Works), he revisits an old essay called The Story of George's Art for an answer. 1153 Words. 2000.

sp000115
Demonstrating Emeralda Play
Stalking the Proprietary Search Engine of Emeralda Works
Following his passion for networking with creative, inventive, discovering and imaginative individuals in Washington State, the Emeralda Inventor demonstrates how a proprietary search engine may help them achieve a goal. He creates an index as an example. 12322 Words. 2000.

sp000121
ABC's of Art Ed Online
Demonstrating the Power of ActiveIndexing.com
A global view of art education may be as simple as the ABC's in today's networked arts, crafts and design worlds. The Inventor of the game, Emeralda, explains, using proceedings from Washington State's art commission proceedings for a strategic statement. 849 Words. 2000.

sp000211
Art of Selling Art Online
Background for an online art business course
A professor and creator of the world's first online course about selling art explains the background of the course. Starting with a science fiction approach, he describes new techniques and a history of universities; he then begins again where he started. 1212 Words. 2000.

sp000212
State of the HSICICA

Stocks to study
After an investment club called TRPI (Teaching Research and Production Investments) this writer created a better version called Human Structural Intellectual Capital Investment Clubs of the Americas (HSICICA). Today he states his progress and his dilemma. 1431 Words. 2000.

sp000224
Mentor-teacher For Hire
My method revealed
An ITinerate Professor describes how a conference-crash scene in which he was the key player got him the title to a profession in which he aspires to excel-the mentor-teacher. He compares it to a scene in the movie, Titanic, and sets a rule in his method. 1155 Words. 2000.

sp000309
If I Live To Be A Hundred
Art by Government
Under a title that he created with the intention of making contemporary artists more curious the author teases them into thinking about their future. He forecasts the full impact of the communications age will be felt virtually from grassroots to the top. 962 Words. 2000.

sp000317
Fishing Lessons
Flying around Washington State
A Living Prints Circus is in the mind of the Emeralda inventor as he imagines traveling over the ten domains of Washington, a tourist in his own country. His mission is to teach people how to surf-fish the Web and catch the breeze in their own arts sales. 903 Words. 2000.

sp000320
Three Solutions to Three Problems
Washington Arts and the Internet
A three-tiered solution is ready for problems people have with Art Ed on the Web. The problems are distilled from comments collected in Washington's statewide information sweep. Solutions are summed up in three words: Simplicity, Entertainment, and Depth. 647 Words. 2000.

sp000407
A New Engine for the SSUS
Smokeless in Seattle
Writing for the EarthSafe 2022 Journal of the Americas, the author envisions the design for the new, smokeless engine for The Big U, the SS United States. He credits the re-discovery of the Gates Principles, and describes clarified plans for the articles. 443 Words. 2000.

sp000412
What is Art Worth?
Glimpse of the Man behind The Computer Black Book
Basing his Next Big Step toward the reality of the restored SS United States on a chance event, the Emeralda Inventor holds an arcane business card

that came to him by way of an art auction house that is so Twentieth Century, he cannot believe it is true. 496 Words. 2000.

sp000415
Dating Game
Mistaken Identities
Thomas Jefferson, one writer says, is America's greatest case of a mistaken identity. He is also America's first reinvented individual, finding himself at a gathering he thought was a high technology seminar but finds it's a place girls come to meet guys. 334 Words. 2000.

sp000505
Why Buy McClain's Now?
Buying and Selling McClain's
When focus was invented-as part of the development of the lens that the archeologists found-what was coupled with it was a system of constraints that human kind was only vaguely aware of before. This artist/philosopher makes some connections to art ideas. 1243 Words. 2000.

sp000509
Let's Pretend
The Success of ArtsPatron.com
Planning to win a position in a startup publishing company, this is a fantasy article. It's a make-believe story as if being written by one of the judges of a business plan contest and follows his 1999 article titled Biz plan competition ripe with ideas. 903 Words. 2000.

sp000513
Theory of Gravity
The Drawing Power of MyArtPatron.com
An Emeralda Game moment number works like an International Standard Book Number. Writer's books must have ISBN numbers in order to be found by book search engines on the Web. Artists, crafts persons or designers do not need to write a book--just a moment. 1359 Words. 2000.

sp000527
Joke
Certificates
In General Systems Theory, the joke is played when the perfection of the system itself, and not its utility, becomes its purpose. Without the power of limits, expressed as finishing (as the result of starting), a purpose tremor leads us to impoverishment. 1887 Words. 2000.

sp000602
Night Money
Strangers in the Library
A training session at SPEACON has the ITinerate Professor teaching a phantom, imaginary class how to make some connection between art supplies and Night Money, the theme of his myartpatron.com business plan. He uses a narrative account of his own working. 1279 Words. 2000.

sp000620

Recognizing ITinerate Professors
Highest-paid Teachers' Secrets Revealed
One way to recognize an ITinerate Professor is by seeing how he demonstrates creative genius. This copy-written article samples discussion in the echelons of applied information and telecommunications arts in industrial grade artists' domain of expertise. 2174 Words. 2000.

sp000705
The New McClain's Catalog
Look and Feel for the Year 2001
The Chief Creative Officer of McClain's Printmaking Supplies and Services proposes the ways that the future paper version of the annual catalog will look and feel. He lists three additions to the existing version, the Y2K one created by the current owner. 1021 Words. 2000.

sp000711
What I Am Good At
Older Laborer Declaration of Independence
A political speech by the Green Party's nominee for President, Ralph Nader, sets this artist/teacher on a thinking spree. After being alerted to it by a friend, he replied, "What now?" back; and then he wrote the following essay and sent it to his friend. 2563 Words. 2000.

sp000726
Eyes Closed Picture a University
Now Close the University
A prescient art professor's vision of old university art schools sets the stage for the way a new one may look and feel. He sets up scenes that focus on art materials and information suppliers where art and business will commingle successfully on the Web. 2009 Words. 2000.

sp000729
Class of 60 Learns the Internet
The first signs of new and better ways for old Boomers
Writing from the perspective of a 1960 High School graduate, the author-who is invited to teach others from his class how to use the Internet-begins with "the end in mind." He considers one do-it-yourself book as the key to help navigate the info-highway. 1432 Words. 2000.

sp000803
Lesson Plan for the Web
My first art patron starts her day
How do you teach the 'Net? Net literacy, some people call it, is to be "literate in the ways of Web sites." Others call it "computer literacy," an over-arching name that includes the Web, and also the various productivity software that content owners use. 1078 Words. 2000.

sp001110
Art Law and Sausages
Looking the other way
What you learn about how art museums are run, how the courts work, and what sausage is made

of can ruin an otherwise enjoyable art trip, social justice or breakfast. A stay at the Munch Museum did not ruin a love of art-nor does it ruin a love of museums. 778 Words. 2000.

sp001208
A Thousand Pictures Are Worth One Word on the Web
High flyer grounded
With ninety-seven days left in his real art gallery on the ground, this artist assesses the time it has taken him to upload 153 works of art to his virtual art gallery in "the skies". The uploading of art is the most important work of his lifetime's work. 636 Words. 2000.

sp001227
It Used To Be Hard
Overheard at Kinko's
A fantasy story-while it is plausible-it has not yet happened, set in the year 2003. That is the year the author, an artist and printmakers, completes his 40-year one man retrospective. He uses this story to paint a picture of a vision of where he's going. 762 Words. 2000.

sp020101
Navigating the BIG PICTURE
Begin With the end in Mind
For the outline of a class called Your Printmaking Class: Paper to Technology, the artist/teacher/author describes a filing system that will help the course find its way to a place among fine are printmaking learned in part through on-line arts education. 928 Words. 2002.

sp020111
Between the Paragraphs - Part 8
Fantasy dialog between two professors
Credits in college translate into money, as most economic surveys prove, with college graduates usually earning more return on their investment over the long term. The notable exceptions give this writer pause to consider if it will remain true or change. 1193 Words. 2002.

sp020121
Prints at a Distance
Farewell paper-intensive prints
After several years' of trying to rejoin the printmaking world by exhibiting and participating in organized art world activities, the author realizes it's time to leave. He uses the metaphor of a late-night party, himself being among the first to go home. 623 Words. 2002.

sp020131
Art Dealers and Digital Defenders
Getting stuck in a passion for printmaking
Considering assisting art dealers calls to this writer's mind the tacit agreements they've reached with living printmaking artists during his career. If art is to live on, dealers need to help fight wars against ignorance in this digital reproduction age. 2046 Words. 2002.

sp020210
Revolutionizing Art Education
EDT technology creates a new channel for Art Ed On-line
He counts up his electronic stamps like a modern-day stamp collector, comparing them to the stamps he got in his passport when he studied abroad. There's more in an e-stamp than meets the eye and so the stamp will revolutionize getting information on art. 1201 Words. 2002.

sp020220
How the Idea of Art Ed On-line Almost Died
Bill H. Ritchie Jr. Recalls the UW Phase
Two pleasant surprises and one bad one-early retirement on short notice-are recalled by the artist/scholar. He has either gained fifteen years or lost them as a result of what happened to him when he was middle-aged. He has no regrets today, so he writes. 691 Words. 2002.

sp020302
Changing Backgrounds of Art Ed On-line
Setting Standards for E-portfolios in Art Education On-line
Drawing on the expression, "aiming at a moving target," the author prescribes a way to approach the problem of measuring the effect of on-line art studios on students and faculty in art education. He uses the analogy of the engineering lab class to begin. 1583 Words. 2002.

sp020312
Got A Life Changing Event, Anyone?
Thinking about Dusty Cann
The author, studying screenplay writing because Emeralda, the game he invented, is based on a background story. This led him from his fictional piece to the idea of using his story for a new kind of movie that was based on hypermedia and the Internet Web. 708 Words. 2002.

sp020322
I Passed My Test!
It's Your E-Portfolio
He's working on new kinds of portfolios for artists, crafts people and designers, thus the author takes on the role of inventor. He must test each part of his electronic portfolio to insure that it will conform to today's new technologies' specifications. 1422 Words. 2002.

sp020401
Getting and Giving Art Credits in the Age of Digital Reproduction
Outcome and Income Considerations
Reading an article about teacher accreditation piqued this artist/scholar's interest because it made him think of issues now twenty years old. Expert Systems were being used for industrial production parallel with concerns about the outcomes of education. 1391 Words. 2002.

sp020411

Thinking Globally and Acting Locally
All talk and no action?
A seasoned speaking artist-after years of serving as an art professor and accustomed to talking, thinking and acting in communities-reflects on September 11 and what he's done since then that is making differences. He's seeking action on par with talking. 1070 Words. 2002.

sp020421
Revisiting Reinventing Arts Studios
Turning over a new leaf in an old manuscript
He started the manuscript for Reinventing Arts Studios several times in the 1990s; but technology seemed to render each version obsolete before he could produce this book. Now he says it appears technology will never settle down long enough to be printed. 1132 Words. 2002.

sp020501
The Bower Bird Artist
A blow alongside the head
His computer crashed-actually it was a virus that took it down-and the artist/scholar has to do some re-evaluation as a result. It was so like a vision he had thirty years before, and which led him to this ironic outcome. Or, is it an income? 936 Words. 2002.

sp020511
Homage to Hayter
Thoughts for Folio 13
As he does a print for a printmaking exchange that takes place on the Internet, the artist/scholar notes some thoughts that he will use to accompany the print as an artist's statement. He compares print-making to music and performance, instruments and art. 597 Words. 2002.

sp020531
Before I Died, I Made a Print
An Owners Guide for Homage to Hayter
Notes on the final image on his print, Homage to Hayter as Bill Ritchie has some final thoughts on this work. He wonders what Hayter would have said, finishing-unbeknownst to him-his last print. No one knows but what they are doing now is their last deed. 2842 Words. 2002.

sp020610
Emeralda Works II
Two Kinds of Insanity
The tenth anniversary of the invention of his game Emeralda is coming, and he wants to celebrate it by giving away free what he thought would be his nest egg. In a world gone insane, it seems, it's a matter of fighting fire with fire-or cooperative games. 1215 Words. 2002.

sp020620
My Night at Vel's
Creative Writing in Your Neighborhood
For seven weeks in the summer of 2002, the artist/scholar made trips to meet with writers who used a woman's front room for writing and then read-

ing stories to one another. He was asking, "What do you want out of the Web?" and ". . . in an arts festival?" 892 Words. 2002.

sp020630
What is Uptown Multimedia Arts Center?
History and theory-Part I
Invited to present his vision of a multimedia arts center to be located in and for his community, the artist/professor reviews events that brought his concept into being and explains why this resemble but does not duplicate technology centers of the past. 1300 Words. 2002.

sp020710
How to Stroll
An Artist Walks His Talk
Confronted with deciding to become either an artist or a teacher, the so-called artist/scholar elucidates on his games theory in art education by demonstrating proper walking-your-talking technique. He's planning to "stomp stamps" and make millions happy. 728 Words. 2002.

sp020711
Uptown Multimedia Arts Center
One of Four perspectives-the Artist
Before a meeting of like-minded people interested in a multimedia arts center for Uptown Seattle, the multimedia artist prepares his ideas in writing. He is beginning with the end in mind and a picture that does not look like a typical computer class-room. 993 Words. 2002.

sp020720
Tipping-in Artistamps at SPEACON
Going Away from NODO to SODO
The tipping point to cause an epidemic of interest in EarthSafe 2022 may be in some unlikely place like South of Downtown instead of North of Downtown. The author volunteered to show a drawing technique at an art supply store-will it be the tipping point? 6683 Words. 2002.

sp020730
What it was was Nostalgia
Back to the Future
The artist/scholar drafts a short story about a meeting that probably couldn't have happened, but could make an interesting one act play. Thinking back to 20th Century art festival that, at one time long ago, meant a lot to him, he thinks the fun is over. 848 Words. 2002.

sp020731
When Art's in the Toilet, You've Gone Too Far
The War Must Go On
A bad experience in the night for the Itinerate Professor is a blow alongside the head, reawakening him to the importance of continuing arts education in ways suitable to these times-the 21st Century. Somewhere there's a place for his invention, Emeralda. 761 Words. 2002.

sp020809

Return of the Stamp King
Back from the Beach with a Stamp Album
It's time to go back to work on the season's task-a school teacher guide to e-folios. The author has the key to art education on-line and he calls it the e-stamp. The question he has to answer is what is the one thing that fast-lane learners can remember? 864 Words. 2002.

sp020819
Depending On Your Devices
The Artistamp in the Age of Digital Reproduction
When a person has talent, is creative, inventive, discovers things and is a highly imaginative person, then the arts appeal to them. She can be independent. She can rely on her own devices to grow, survive and thrive. How about new device interdependency? 1206 Words. 2002.

sp020829
The E-Goose that Laid the Golden Egg
An Itinerate Professor's Tale
A professor who excludes teaching in order to learn more realizes soon that there's only one path to follow in the age of digital reproduction, and it's that which will take him to the electronic goose that lays golden eggs. E-books pave this pathway now. 909 Words. 2002.

sp020908
If I Worked at Northland
Tell You What I'd Do
It's a good thing to plan ahead, to envision, and to imagine. That's better than knowledge because then it's already over-what you imagine can still happen. So this author imagines what he'd do if suddenly he found himself as an adjunct virtual professor. 2208 Words. 2002.

sp020918
Where I Go On SPEACON
My Morning at Dodge of Bellevue
He's on a fantasy trip to the Island of the Domain-of-Expertise in speaking, consulting, design and training with a phantom first-mate named Jon. In reality he's in a waiting room at a car service, but working on a book titled An Artist's Last Love Letter. 1173 Words. 2002.

sp020928
Interviewing Printmaking Students
What They Want
He's met people of all ages who want to be printmakers and he wonders why. Young or old, what attracts them to printmaking-the arts or the crafts, the design, the money, or mere curiosity? On the other side of it, what attracted him, for over forty years? 952 Words. 2002.

sp021008
What I Learned from My Dream
From Conversation Cafe to Teaching Anxiety
Dream-wrighting-that's what they could call this process of setting up one's self to dream and then sleeping through it, mining one's dreams for ideas,

indications of the right thing to do, and positing answers to help lead one to heightened effectiveness. 1037 Words. 2002.

sp021018
If I Didn't have a million dollars
I'd start a school for art ed on-line.
Art ed on-line will develop like the Ford Mustang was--in a skunk works fashion. Also it will have to be a co-op school, with its participants owning the majority shares. A veteran warrior for two worlds-one dying and one trying to be born--tries his PPC. 1124 Words. 2002.

sp021127
Parking at the SIM
Analyze This
The professor moves into his fifth of a six-part, three-year retrospective of his 40-year career, analyzing the Seattle Independent Mall and how it resembles the successes and failures of other peoples' enterprises and concludes that losers are non-users. 658 Words. 2002.

sp030121
Digital Travail
A Digital Artist's Travels on the Way to a Perfect Studio
The origin of this essay is Digital Travail by ALEXANDRA SAMUEL and was partly copy-written by Bill Ritchie. He found so many parallels with Prof. Samuels' experiences that it seemed possible he could find his way out of the dilemmas they both face today. 2222 Words. 2003.

sp030322
Emeralda as a Teaching Tool
Copy-writing over a psych professor's words
Taking signals from a psychology professor, the art professor writes about his idea for an entertaining and educational game. After more than ten years of playing it by himself, he's seeing similarities between his theory and practices of other educators. 955 Words. 2003.

sp030401
UW Artists
An idea whose time has come
The University Of Washington Medical School gave him a model for his "perfect studios" because it is a teaching hospital. Teaching, research, practice and service are performed all at once, under the same roof. UW Physicians came out this, so why not art? 1313 Words. 2003.

sp030521
Tracing an Artist's Way
The Story of Lisel Salzer's Videotape
He handles a small shipment, only five copies, of a videotape created over 17 years earlier by an artist who was in her 80s at the time she produced it. Now, she's over 97; and her tape is still being sold and viewed. How did this happen? What is learned? 991 Words. 2003.

sp030531
How Emeralda Is Like Chess
Planning your moves on the Islands of Domains-of-Expertise
The inventor of Emeralda is like a castaway, disenfranchised from the known art world and university communities. He'd satisfy his problem-solving impulses by playing a strategic game, like chess, but he never learned it! Emeralda play is the alternative. 1264 Words. 2003.

sp030610
Insights to Africa
A Quiz for the Fine Art Printmaking ITinerate Professor
He's one of hundreds who gets an e-mail from a South African student who's considering fine art printmaking and asks ten questions to help her make the decision. It's an opportunity for him to test himself-like a role-play reversal of student and teacher. 2172 Words. 2003.

sp030620
Deep Emeralda
Clare Livingstamp and Loop da Loo
Another page of my journal is taken into a private art collection, and that fact inspires me to think about how Emeralda Works in surprising ways. The new owner has been working Saturdays on many of the same questions I am asking, and is testing Emeralda. 1042 Words. 2003.

sp030720
I Reflect, Therefore I am Playing
Moves of the game inventor
The inventor of Emeralda Stamps 'N Stories retraces his path through the Web pages of his creation, clicks on this stamp and that, and reviews the trivia games he created. At one point he views his reading thirty years ago to mine the meaning of a phrase. 900 Words. 2003.

sp030829
Feature Games
Auditing Emeralda
He's like a student getting ready for his exams. Once he was a professor, and now he's back on campus in a new role as a learner. Yet he's part of a unique student body of campus returnees. He's worked out a new scheme he calls a game, featuring his life. 1013 Words. 2003.

sp030908
What Will Emeralda Players Want?
Satisfaction for explorers, socializers, achievers and killers
This teacher (and an artist) imagines what people would want in an online game that is part fun and part education. He thinks as the persons who typically play video games online: explorer, achiever, socializer and killer. He also wants something himself. 799 Words. 2003.

sp030928
Imagining an Excellence Online Campus at

Shoreline
A Visitors' Vision of Possibilities
His daily routine involves opening a fantasy game he created for his own entertainment, something named Emeralda Stamps 'N Stories-mixing stamp collecting games and adventure story. As he's starting to teach at a community college, he imagines sharing it. 874 Words. 2003.

sp031028
Beyond A Job
A teacher's day in retrospect
On a typical day this teacher may teach, do research, produce something and perform a service. Also he may get feedback, some of it by e-mail, the news, or just by being watchful of things that happen. This essay refers to several issues worth mentioning. 1369 Words. 2003.

sp031107
Emeralda Levels
Understanding Emeralda as a video game
According to his reading in Game Creation and Careers, a design document describes a video game so the inventor of Emeralda starts by defining the levels within the Meta world of Emeralda Region. He describes 14 levels and this sets the tone for the game. 497 Words. 2003.

sp031117
One Stamp is enough
A new twist on Stamps 'N Stories
He opens his game every day, searching for clues to the next step in the evolving invention of a video game-based learning experience. Today, after a night of playing a game called Art is Dead, he realizes one stamp (from 1993)-chosen randomly, is enough. 406 Words. 2003.

sp031127
What This Neighborhood Needs is A Great New Business
Dreaming of a perfect studio
A street corner shop a near his home has started this artist dreaming of a perfect setup for his passion-print making with new technologies. He's brainstorming, thinking of ways to make it an amazingly successful venture and highly appealing to investors. 576 Words. 2003.

sp031222
A Stamp-Sized Gallery in Seattle
Still planning for the New Year
"Who am I today?" he asks himself the day after the Winter Solstice. Facing a new year and new prospects, he contemplates the opening of a new art gallery, and considers the counterpoint of this to his upcoming residency at an island art community school. 413 Words. 2003.

sp040111
Letting My Feelings Out
Crossroads or last stand?
His first web site is ten years old this year and has reached the limit on storage on it. At the point

where he's not sure what to do with his virtual studio and gallery, he's rented a real gallery, which feels like either a beginning or an end of an era. 1088 Words. 2004.

sp040121
What I Learned in School
A returning professor assesses his visit
It had been 18 years since he last taught a full term in college, and he thought things had not changed much in art classes. The big changes were in the art and technology courses, but there's also a paradox in these: More change is needed, and will come. 1214 Words. 2004.

sp040210
Dreamer
His story
Bill Ritchie dreamed of a perfect studio after about ten years in the university art department that eventually ran him out. Maybe he was a dreamer, seeing the academic world through rose-colored glasses. Actually some would say he was living a nightmare. 925 Words. 2004.

sp040220
Gaming the Rest of My Life
Reading Dungeons and Dreamers
The more I read about games in King and Borland's account of video game history, the more I think my game, Emeralda, is as much if not more than the phenomena they describe. This is not a game for a year or so, but, like in the book, a game of a lifetime. 898 Words. 2004.

sp040430
Electric Etchers and Papermaking Society
A Modest Proposal
The author has opened his own gallery and is looking for something new to add to the scene-something that's an addition to the community as well as an addition to the information on printmaking. He's got an eye on a virtual and virtuous new league for it. 414 Words. 2004.

sp040719
The Mini Halfwood Press at SPEACON
Ways to relate to the four professions
What does an etching press have to do with speaking, consulting, training and design? Actually, you could say none of the aforementioned practices would exist were it not for the printing press. The author has designed a new press, and reports on it here. 578 Words. 2004.

sp040729
A Letter to Sheryl
Getting in touch with a reader
A retired community college teacher sends an order for the book this author wrote ten years ago about selling art. She hopes to help change the world by supporting arts in her town in Texas. The author writes to her a letter and encloses it with the book. 812 Words. 2004.

sp040730
Visualize This
Checks in the mail
An account of the Emeralda Inventor's routine activity-which is become too dull to be interesting. But things happen that make the day a little more interesting than it appeared it would be. That's thanks to his contacts with other artists, young and old. 876 Words. 2004.

sp040808
A Shift in Context Just In Time
View from a 62-year perspective
In the 21st Century, an artist born sixty or more years ago has to shift the context of all the skills and ideas he or she learned. This applies to this artist especially because he held on to the artifacts (or call them artworks) of 40 years in the arts. 897 Words. 2004.

sp040818
Every Ten Days I Come Back to SPEACON
Contemplating the meaning of being here
Every ten days this artist/author visits the imaginary island of SPEACON in the great lake of Emeralda Region, and as it is his practice on all the islands, he contemplates the connection between the public speaking and consulting profession and the arts. 757 Words. 2004.

sp040828
Seeking My Lost Treasure
The resuscitation of my short, happy career
A professor who met his professional death two decades ago is awakening from a coma-like state to find the world changed and a second chance for him. He turns to ideas he had when he was a successful college professor and puts them to work. 932 Words. 2004.

sp040829
What to Expect from Your Art College
Advice from an Itinerate Professor
A member of an online discussion group signals his desire to return to college via the Net. The author considers himself an expert in education and desiring to teach on the Net, describes what he thinks a potential Net art student could and should expect. 892 Words. 2004.

sp040830
What Would Elmer Do?
Contemplating a home school request
The Itinerate Professor gets an e-mail from a home-schooler who is looking for woodcut lessons. The message sends him on a search of his own, looking for the answer that's best for her. Amid his several education projects, her request has special meaning. 788 Words. 2004.

sp040907
Dying in Perfect Condition
Recalling a videotape in the NW Video Art Archive
John Cage once quipped, "We hope that when we

die we will be in perfect condition." He was talking about staying in good health, even improving one's health as we age by eating nutritiously, exercising, and cultivating the mind. This essay is on the mind. 474 Words. 2004.

sp040908
A Video Dig Reloaded Task
Make A John Cage Stamp
Creating another plan to restore and preserve the videotape archive in his basement, this itinerate professor focuses on a single step in the procedure. It is to make an artist's stamp based on the renowned composer, John Cage. He lists the steps to take. 662 Words. 2004.

sp041017
Permanence and Persistence
Reflections
Thinking of the kinds of permanence one finds in stone sculpture, cast bronze, oil paint and other long-lasting art forms, the author senses there is another kind of permanence an artist may concern himself with: Intellect and persistence. His game helps. 1216 Words. 2004.

sp050111
Thinking about Rolf
A Teacher of Independence
He is living in a hi-tech city, using high-tech tools but he's thinking about an artist he met almost 35 years ago in central Norway who used crude implements to fashion his work in rude material. He's reminded of lessons the artist Rolf Nesch taught him. 585 Words. 2005.

sp050121
How Do I Practice Emeralda Today?
Benchmarking Games for the Gifts of Life
On an impulse the inventor of Emeralda makes notes on the practice of his invention and he tries to list his movements and objects in his game for the first moments of practice. It's a typical day, a good day to explain what an Emeralda Practitioner does. 904 Words. 2005.

sp050131
Visualize an Artists Trading Card
Little Blue Yogi
The author is also a printmaker, but he senses that printmaking is dead unless the prints are linked to their descendant media, the so-called media arts. As he focuses on the history of printmaking and finds a useful link: Early prints were playing cards. 883 Words. 2005.

sp050220
Expandable ATC
Baiting the Creative Imagination with Cards
The artist who makes Artist Trading Cards is also a gamer, because he or she is making a game instrument, i.e., the ATC. For artists who also like art that they can put on a wall to see—and show—conveniently, there is the expandable ATC, a kind of puzzle. 1125 Words. 2005.

sp050302
A Gathering Place
The Park at Queen Anne Avenue and Roy Street
He has accepted an invitation to work on a committee to raise over one million dollars to build and sustain a small city park by a busy intersection near his home. Now this artist thinks about the vision of the founders, her vision of "a gathering place." 872 Words. 2005.

sp050312
Un-Retiring
Taking another Look at the Future
He has an opportunity to start a new chapter in his life, turning away from the course he's followed for years, and becoming a small press manufacturer. He's beginning to feel that the instruments of retirement—pension and social security—are unimportant. 940 Words. 2005.

sp050322
India Calls
Fantasies of the Great World Teacher—Again
A telephone call from Bangladesh interrupts his morning routine and sets his imagination on a flight of fancy. He thinks his innovation—a miniature press—will find its place among the worldwide printmakers' toolkits. He lets his vision, and dream, expand. 788 Words. 2005.

sp050421
Loneliness of an Emeralda Player
Searching for a Payoff
Always on the lookout for ways to motivate people to use online game strategies for peace and the environment, this artist asks if perhaps the Artist Trading Card (or the Emeralda version of it) might have this potential. He thinks you could win artworks. 751 Words. 2005.

sp050501
Do You Have A Video 'N Print?
A Chip in the Old Game
Ever on the lookout for clues as to how to solve the puzzle that is his game and his life, the inventor of Emeralda: Games for the Gifts of Life sees a possibility for a calendar game, based on the names of his imaginary island domains in Emeralda Region. 879 Words. 2005.

sp050610
What Do I Know
Introduction to Wiki
The word wiki came from two sources, both of which have an immediate appeal to this artist/teacher. He looks for designs for games that he can play with his community of practice and games that relate to the work of art in the age of digital reproduction. 763 Words. 2005.

sp050620
When Do I Know
Thoughts on Wiki Making
Ten days ago this artist/teacher was contemplat-

ing wiki, the "What I know" is format designed for discussions on the Internet. Today he thinks it's not only what a person knows but when they know it that's important. This might important to online teachers. 672 Words. 2005.

sp050710
Found and Remade
The Inventor's Adaptation of System Shock 2
The Emeralda Inventor is surprised to find an old description of a video game called System Shock 2 among files stored deep in his archives. Why did he save the description of this particular game? On closer study, he finds a framework for Emeralda Works. 3060 Words. 2005.

sp050720
Yes Sheila, There is A Way
You'd Better Believe It
This writer (an amateur, really, but persistent in the craft of writing) thinks that if you believe in something hard and long enough, it will come to fact. The thing he's interested in as proof is a condominium that serves the art community of practices. 403 Words. 2005.

sp050730
Card Power
Questions about Collectible Cards
An Artist Trading Card is endowed with a kind of power, endowed by the artist who created it. This essay asks what other kinds of power may be attributed to an ATC? The author would like to make ATC part of the game he's working on that he calls Emeralda. 970 Words. 2005.

sp050809
Why A Game?
The Best Thing to Do in Retirement
The word "retire" is anathema to this artist and teacher. He eschewed the typical US American version of aging, believing older people are wiser and more creative than youth in profound ways. Their value to society is so high that they can save the world. 711 Words. 2005.

sp050829
Artist's House of Cards
Building A Home for Arts Community of Practice
What now is the most creative project an artist can undertake in harmony with him or herself, the community, and the environment? What project is in line with the economics of the artist's life, matters of health, and the good of society? House-building. 1368 Words. 2005.

sp050918
Condo Doom Begins
Beginning with the End in Mind
Speculating on the creation of a game that's played by condominium owners which teaches them all the ins and outs of condo living, this artist—who says games are the art form of the 21st Century—suggests the way his game idea gets started: Business cards. 976 Words. 2005.

sp051008
Putting IT in Context
Planning the Final Game
He's haunted by a vision that began at the time he shrunk his etching press down to a size that would fit it to an Etcher's Learning Kit. He's thinking this will be the final form that his ideas of teaching, research and practice will be put into service. 597 Words. 2005.

sp051018
Fill Your Screen with Stamps
Fill Your Day with Beauty
A day in the life of an artist on the island of SPEA-CON, where public speaking and demonstrations—the "public artist"—are the main, routine activities. This artist tells about his stamp experiments, a yellow school bus, and a recipe website that he likes. 717 Words. 2005.

sp051028
A Recipe A Day
Food for Thought
He's playing a kind of game with a recipe website called recipezaar.com, his current metaphor for his idea of printmaking education online for home schoolteachers and students. He enters the recipe he used for dinner the day previously and sees analogies. 751 Words. 2005.

sp051107
If Everything Were Up Today
What Would I Do Now?
On a typical day, following plans of his routine activities, the one-time professor of art considers what it would be like today if others were playing the same game as he is. Making digital artists stamps and trading cards, he plans to teach at EtchingU. 1010 Words. 2005.

sp051117
On the Emeralda Halfwood CD
Halfwood Press in the Emeralda Region
The Mini Halfwood Press he designed in 2004 has taken him on an interesting voyage with many useful encounters. Next he plans to put everything about using the press on to a CD/ROM, a virtual textbook on printmaking. An old idea whose time has come. 500 Words. 2005.

sp051127
Stamp Fun in Emeralda
Fun Runs and Artists Stamps
For the 360-days of an Emeralda Year of Living Copiously, an Emeralda player goes to each of the ten islands' database of artist's stamps and selects one for the day. He or she also gets a story to go with it—or writes one. There is an element of fun here. 832 Words. 2005.

sp051207
Emeralda and Trumba
Ideas for a Calendar Game
The introduction of a new software item for the

Internet comes just in time as the author's 7th Year of Living Copiously nears its end. Called Trumba, it is a calendar program people can share. How will this fit into Emeralda: Games for the Gifts of Life? 661 Words. 2005.

sp060101
Pieces of Emeralda
Parts of My Game for the Gifts of Life
He got inspired to move ahead with his game, Emeralda, and thinks back about a board game he saw recently based on the days of sailing ships. It's a thread that runs throughout his idea, so he adopts some elements of that board game to his own. 693 Words. 2006.

sp060111
Basically Speaking
A Ten-year Plan for Halfwood Press
He has penned the ten-year plan for Halfwood Press on a 4 X 4 inch piece of paper, and it is basically a plan to create a digital game-based learning experience. Six steps remain to be accomplished: A chest, a press, a book, a CD/ROM, a Website and a DVD. 1108 Words. 2006.

sp060121
The Virtual Sarah
Improving the Sarah Spurgeon Art Gallery
On January 21, 2006, I donated $100,000 to the college where I had gone to school 40 years ago. The purpose would be the improvement of the Sarah Spurgeon Art Gallery at Central Washington State University's Randall Hall. 1883 Words. 2006.

sp060501
The Ideal Community
Virtual and Production Community
The ideal community would be not only for "virtual" work, but it would also be in a production community. 111 Words. 2006.

sp060531
Imagine a Prospectus
Plan for a Hybrid Printmaking Course
Imagine a prospectus for an intaglio printmaking hybrid course. It takes one year to complete, yields 20 college credits and costs $5,000. It enrolls only 20 students a year—10 so-called Proximates—and comes with a complete kit including an etching press. 609 Words. 2006.

sp060620
When I was Young and Impressionable
Forming the Basis for Elmeralda
My favorite hobbies were collecting Straight Arrow Injunity cards and designing cars of the future for the Fisher Body Craftsman Guild contest. I see now that these played together to form the basis for Emeralda. 778 Words. 2006.

sp060629
The Final
Proving Intellectual Capital

The "dissertation" is to prove that Intellectual Capital is convertible to tangible results. It's the accountability factor in the Confidence Circle. With my proof in hand, I can structure the basis for CWALS. 592 Words. 2006.

sp060630
Press Conference
Hybrid Printmaking Course
Questions and answers for a hybrid course, some of the coursework is done online or some is done in face to face workshops. 409 Words. 2006.

sp060730
Dear Adviser
Taking certificate courses in popular fiction
The author is writing for advice about taking the certificate courses in popular fiction. He writes about his fiction writing as fun and as the starting of making a game. 573 Words. 2006

sp060809
Evolve
Printmaking Major renamed to Multimedia Major
The author contemplates if he had stayed at the UW in conditions of a successful art school. What would the area of printmaking look like now? 251 Words. 2006

sp060819
Why My Art Works
Could it be because I'm a professor?
The author writes about his art being in favor because of his being a professor, earning scholarship status. He wants to lead a way in "new" art that shares traditional art and meeting the desires of today's society, and cites two art journalism examples. 859 Words. 2006

sp060829
Wild? I'll give you Wild
Fast-forward to 2010
A professor of art, known for his unconventional philosophy of art and education, describes an idea for a new residential school. He says it's a blend of a depository for intellectual property and also a center for developing online art education courses. 1024 Words. 2006.

sp060918
Open Your Eyes
Online printmaking lessons as a game for inspiring collaborations
The author writes about inventing a user interface for online printmaking lessons that serves also as a game that inspires and encourages, and is a structure for collaborations. 1231 Words. 2006.

sp061008
Introduction to Intaglio Printmaking
In the Age of Digital Reproduction
The author begins an online textbook for his theory class. He lists the three principles of the class; printmaking is a socio-economic art form, interactive online communication, and marketing and sales online. 570 Words. 2006.

sp070101

Thinking about a Student
The questions of the 21st Century artist
The author writes about studying art in the 21st Century. He was working on a new artwork with his instincts more than sight and ends with musings about Moby Dick. 320 Words. 2007.

sp070121
What the Halfwood Press is about
The artistry behind the Mini Halfwood Press
The author writes about his Halfwood Press as a device to make prints by centuries-old traditions. But it is more. It is a work of art because it looks nice and is handcrafted. 790 Words. 2007.

sp070531
SPEACON – 2nd Day
The experience of Harris Sweed
The author writes from a viewpoint of an engineer who took printmaking in college many years ago. Sweed was at a demonstration performed by Bill Ritchie at Daniel Smith, Inc. Ritchie was demonstrating the use of his Mini Halfwood Press. 2587 Words. 2007.

sp070610
Plan for the History
Ghosts in the New Machine Revisited
The author writes a plan for a book that contains the chronology of making the Halfwood Presses, listing buyers and their art and an introduction of the story of Emeralda. 246 Words. 2007.

sp070908
Adkinson and Me
Why I saved an article about Peter Adkinson
The artist saw an article in a Seattle Business magazine in August, 2007. He tore it out and kept it for a while because of he had a fascination for the company, Wizards of the Coast, which the main focus of the article—Peter Adkinson—was CEO of years ago. 1889 Words. 2007.

sp070928
Great Achievements Require Time
An e-mail message from David J. Schwartz
The author writes about an email he received about the time required to achieve great things. The message advertises for his EyeQ program, but it has a great pitch. It uses mountain climbing to illustrate his point. 307 Words. 2007.

sp071018
Real Treasure Map
Continuation of the Halfwood Press
The inventor of Emeralda tells how the real "treasure map" is actually a book. He calls it the Emeralda Treasure but it is a detailed book on how to make an etching press that is part of the bible for his creation of Emeralda: Games for the Gifts of Life. 459 Words. 2007.

sp071107
Games for the Aged
What I learned from three old artists

A person with the potential of forty years of living to do can, at the age of 60, play games, which—as Confucius said—is better than doing nothing at all. This artist writes about not only playing games, but inventing life games as his life is played out. 998 Words. 2007.

sp071117
Focusing Device
Could the game, Emeralda, be one?
The author writes his reflections of that morning and how he randomly glanced at work he had done before. He was tempted to get distracted, but realizes that the whole focus factor is an important thing for to create his game. 647 Words. 2007.

sp071222
Thoughts of an Old Artist
Considering the late Lisel Salzer
The author imagines himself a prisoner on the island of SPEACON, one of the ten islands in the great lake region of Emeralda. His is a velvet prison, however, and he has no complaints. His labor is to keep the intellectual property of an artist, now dead. 920 Words. 2007.

sp080111
Persistent Worlds
Economic modeling in the age of digital reproduction
To this author, persistence is a kind of world, the art world, perhaps with a tenacious, stubborn and unmovable character of an illusionary place with values of its own. That is why he thinks of a place where new ideas are welcome. New ideas need a haven. 1083 Words. 2008.

sp080210
Halfwood Cruise
Taking the Mini for a cruise
After he designed and tested a miniature etching press, this art teacher planned a course. Cruise passengers can take printmaking classes on an Alaska Cruise that's unlike any other art course offered onshore. A PDA was his inspiration fourteen years ago. 806 Words. 2008.

sp080220
Lawrence Mystery
What about "The Chess Players?"
The author wonders why he can't find anything in his journals about Jacob Lawrence and Christy Wyckoff making a 1970 lithograph. Lawrence spent 12 weeks as a visiting professor at the UW with the painting department, by luck, he also did the lithograph. 584 Words. 2008.

sp080311
Ingrid Hill
Stories and the game of life
He completed a first reading of Ingrid Hill's, Ursula Under, and in two places he sees crossings with his thinking about the state of writing in the age of filmmaking and connections with the stories that he writes for his art. He connects games with art.

1530 Words. 2008.

sp080430
Kansas Envisioned
Visualizing and Actualizing
The author received an email from Robert L. Schwartz that he used for his visit to Baker University in Kansas as an artist and professor. "The entrepreneur is essentially a visualizer and actualizer . . ." challenged him to see himself as an entrepreneur too. 416 Words. 2008.

sp080510
Strategic Planning
Third in a series of 12 task headings for Learning Printmaking Online study
"If we study the structure and effectiveness of corporations, including cooperatives in all branches of society, we might find methods that will make education better. We might make improvements by applying corporate methods to our purpose as educators." 3407 Words. 2008.

sp080520
FranchiseQuest
Building a four-legged stool for art education in the age of digital reproduction
Considering a comment by his collaborator, the author attempts to assemble four disparate but complementary pictures described as puzzles. Teaching, research, practice and service principles guide his thinking and assembling them. The goal is a franchise. 1700 Words. 2008.

sp080530
System Design
A structure of collaboration
The author reflects on his first years teaching at the UW and how artists challenged themselves to experiment in their changing times. He compares himself to the computer expert, John Zachman, because they both had to get people's attention to their work. 1008 Words. 2008.

sp080609
People Who
Structure for collaboration and Learning Printmaking Online
The author writes as if he is on stage in front of an audience of ghosts and he doesn't know the script, but a guide helps him to perform his art and craft. He realizes that the ghosts will someday be real people. 835 Words. 2008.

sp080619
Processing Structure
The Designer's row or role in the functioning enterprise
The author wrote about the designer's role in the functioning enterprise as being aware of the dilemmas inherited by modern artists, which is best exemplified by Paul Klee in his book "The Thinking Eye." 1139 Words. 2008.

sp080629

Kindle and the Halfwood Press
How to boost sales of amazon.com' Kindle
Walter Benjamin wrote about the loss of the aura of the original artwork in the age of mechanical reproduction. Today, this author writes and speaks about the loss of the aura of art in the age of digital reproduction. Kindle and a press might restore it. 1600 Words. 2008.

sp080629b
Strategy
The bottom line of motivation
The author is playing an imaginary game called Zach Man! as a way to understand a chart or Framework that was given to him by a friend who has associated himself with the author's project that is a game called Emeralda. He speculates on the word strategy. 1244 Words. 2008.

sp080719
Elevator Speech
Explaining Learn Printmaking Online
Things are heating up in this author's prospects to realize his life's dream, which is to be a great teacher of printmaking in the age of digital reproduction. He forecasts he will need to give a short, clear statement of his objectives so he composes it. 280 Words. 2008.

sp080729
Cards you are Dealt
Your life as a deck of cards
Did you have a lucky entry as an artist? Will your creations come to be considered brilliant, blindingly creative and important, like any of the artists of historic importance? This author designed a calendar in order to see his life whole, based on luck. 788 Words. 2008.

sp080828
Thiagi's Advice
Run an online simulation game with teams in a classroom
The Evil one plots to end sustainability for human life by increasing carbon dioxide and methane emissions by tapping the creative faculties of unwitting Emeralda Residents-in-stay to give away their creative, inventive, discovering and imaginative skill. 347 Words. 2008.

sp080907
Table of Days in Baldwin City
Planning the visits to the school and university classes
On the day of departure for Baldwin City, the author—going there to give several lectures and demonstrations of printmaking—receives his timetable. On route he created a table to decide what he would do on those visits to the school and university classes. 1035 Words. 2008.

sp080917
'Zine Head Job Training
Instructions for editing 'Zine Headings for Emeralda Play

The author has engaged his daughter in a project. Her job will be to edit the 'Zine Headings of essays in his 'Zine files. He writes down instructions to get started that she can use to do her job. It is an Emeralda Player's Manual, also. 3244 Words. 2008.

sp080927
Glimmer
Files and game pieces
The author writes about fitting the right pieces together to develop a computer filing system between a hard drive and removable drives (CD, Flash, etc.). He is challenged to see himself as a writer and how the challenge is one of the pieces. 847 Words. 2008.

sp081007
Vision: Emeralda Shop
A game shop
The author visualizes a building across the street from his condo as being a game shop for his Emeralda game along with Halfwood presses and printmaking instruments displayed in glass cases. He compares this vision to the "Wizards of the Coast" shop. 415 Words. 2008.

sp081017
Appropriate Behavior
How to travel the road to glory
The author writes about taking care of things before you die. Practicing his writing is his way of taking care of things. As a teacher, researching, practicing your art and craft and serving your community are appropriate behavior on the road to glory. 561 Words. 2008.

sp081027
Of Test Plates and Artist Trading Cards
Cards, Stamps and Multimedia
With every press he makes today he makes a trading card-sized etching to go with it. The purpose seems to be merely a technical add-on, but in this essay he speculates that there is more to it. It may be a way for art patrons to enter into a new art form. 1258 Words. 2008.

sp081206
$290 Million Opportunity
Forty years and forty presses
This retired art printmaking professor looks back on his 40-year career, calculating the number of people who learned the art and craft of art prints over the decades. Having introduced a new etching press and sold forty, he looks at its potential market. 1060 Words. 2008.

sp081206b
Little Prints Gallery
Business Plan
The author writes a business plan for his "Little Prints Gallery" that will show prints that buyers of the Halfwood presses made to the public. 400 Words. 2008.

sp081222

Tuch in Emeralda
Instilling the sense of touch in a distance learning game
The author is reading Carole Handler Miller's book, Digital Story Telling, and finds a phrase with which he able to identify his role in the creation of an online art course he calls Learn Printmaking Online, bringing a sense of touch to his serious game. 1030 Words. 2008.

sp090101
Art That Bears Sit and Stare
Beginning with the end in mind—again
At the start of 2009, he thinks sitting and staring is a test for art. He sits and stares at his art on a computer, a time machine that he uses for three things as an art game: Review the past, Live the Moment, and Chart the future by stars not yet risen. 576 Words. 2009.

sp090111
COICOP at Emeralda Communiversity
Blended learning, digital game-based learning meet in fantasy land
Two influential books inform this art professor about the future of his studios and classroom. One is about digital game based learning, and the other is about hybrid online distance education. He combines them to get what he will put in a college campus. 931 Words. 2009.

sp090121
Purposeful Play in Emeralda: Learn Printmaking Online
Taking a ten-day, ten-step journey in a game development checklist
To invent a user-interface for an effective online experience in which the users learn the art and craft of printmaking, there is a ten-step procedure. Author C. H. Miller wrote it down in her book, Digital Storytelling. This inventor uses it for a guide. 825 Words. 2009.

sp090131
Audience and Market for ELPO
Printmaking user groups from maturity to youth
Preparing the ultimate documents for ELPO (Emeralda: Learn Printmaking Online) starts by completing a ten-point checklist, according to author Carolyn H. Miller. Development of a blended learning course user-interface for a fine art is like entertainment. 2860 Words. 2009.

sp090210
Co-ops in Game Land
Anyone using co-operative model in serious video games?
There are many examples of digital-game based learning and training games; the video game industry calls them "serious games." This former professor of art thinks there should be a game for learning art online, and he thinks about cooperative game making. 1252 Words. 2009.

sp090411

Ramone Vasquez Profile
Character description of Ramone Vasquez for "Hunt for the Emeralda Treasure"
Art education moved from the conventional art school, gallery and museum toward artificial life in computers and then migrated over the Internet. This changed the meaning of art, resurrecting it, as it were, from the realm of politics. 494 Words. 2009.

sp090501
Digital Aging
Would you take art from this person?
Agism is plaguing some older workers who have no intention of retiring from the pursuit of their passion. This might be especially true for artists, crafts people and designers. This essay draws a comparison between an old brain surgeon and an old artist. 1174 Words. 2009.

sp090521
On Blogs
Blogs I did not get to write
His day started out not like any other day. Earlier-than-usual to rise, beset by the same cascade of ideas of things to do, things to be done, things to write most important of all; but there'll be no blog today he decided, because he tidied up his novel. 1128 Words. 2009.

sp090531
Why Cooperate?
First considerations for an international printmaking cooperative
Since the time he visited Paris's Atelier 17 in 1969, the author has sustained a vision of the benefits of bringing printmakers from all over the whole wide world together for the ostensible reason of making prints. Has the reason why changed in 40 years? 587 Words. 2009.

sp090908
Press Party
Face to face social networking around a Halfwood Press
It feels like a flash of genius when the author (and designer/builder of an etching press he calls "Halfwood") considers finding someone to host a press party. In this essay, he tries to outline how it works, and why it's a benefit to those who attend it. 868 Words. 2009.

sp090918
Author Screenplay
Bill Ritchie on "Dusty's Prize"
Writing is one way Bill Ritchie practices his art and craft, a parallel world in the way he addresses the classic question of form and content, form being printmaking, and content coming from literary and narrative art, opening the door to performing arts 1203 Words. 2009.

sp090928
Emeralda MFASP
Copy writing over an MBA in sustainable business

Beginning on October 4, 2009, I copy-wrote the following over the Wikipedia entry on the Bainbridge Graduate Institute. The writings of Gifford Pinchot III, and his wife, Elizabeth, have interested me for a generation. The BGI they started is my metaphor. 983 Words. 2009.

sp091008
Fifth Logline
Keeping it short and simple
A logline is a short elevator-speech version of a movie script or screenplay. It's what you say when you found yourself in an elevator with someone like Steven Spielberg or George Lucas twenty years ago. That was then; now there's a virtual world instead. 503 Words. 2009.

sp091018
Baby Picnic
An invitation to a new printmaking world
The author puts himself in the mind of a complete babe in the woods so he can imagine what it's like to know nothing of a virtual world of learning printmaking online, picturing two people he would like to invite to an online picnic in a kind of 3-D blog. 1231 Words. 2009.

sp091107
Flash EATC
Searching for a use for a Flash ecard
He's searching for a way to replace his old, kludgey, time-and-labor intensive Artist Trading Cards with something that can be both virtual (or digital) and also made into real paper cards quickly and cheaply. Text on a flash e-card website helps him out. 475 Words. 2009.

sp091207
Sample Zine CD
CD, HTML and games
The author writes about the process of putting all his articles, reading notes, dream accounts, "flashes," and "cascading" ideas on a CD, making it accessible through the HTML language. 658 Words. 2009.

sp091222
Story Arc
Printmaking Camp back story
The author is coming to a decisive stage in his plan to write a back story for a certain kind of computer game. He's been focused on a game for grown-ups; now he's faced with the possibility it's better to write one for young people or a multi-generation. 781 Words. 2009.

Ritchie's Video (AKA Video, or, VI)

Placeholder image of Video Island seen late on a hot, July day, approaching from the east side.

Video Island is devoted to video productions—not excluding film and other motion picture technologies.

vi800323
Art Review by Regina Hackett
Bill Ritchie: Art in the Eye of the Hurricane
Bill Ritchie's art work strikes this art reviewer as being full of clutter—ideas that simply don't work or ideas this artist ruins by overworking them into didactic discursions, she writes. However she concludes amid the clutter are his successes as well. 634 Words. 1980.

vi810819
Art Review by Tim Apello
Summertime Blues in The Weekly
Art writer Tim Appelo covered the exhibit at the Erica Williams / Anne Johnson Gallery focused on the cyanotype medium, or blue process (as photographers call it). It is the blueprint made in the old-fashioned way. Appelo prefaces his review with caution. 751 Words. 1981.

vi850323
Journal Entry
There is Only Art
After studying Joan Skinner tapes for several days, the author wakes up with a thought that there is only art. He was delighted. He quotes Bernard Leach. 348 Words. 1985.

vi870102
Journal Entry
An Unhappy Day
The author writes about his disappointed about being a slave to the system. He writes about the financial needs of owning a house and supporting a family with teen-age daughters. 844 Words. 1987.

vi871019
Journal Entry
Creativity
"To be creative, you must see outside yourself."

110 Words. 1987.

vi871127
Journal Entry
5 Minute Write
This morning the author awoke to find a pessimistic attitude had a hold of him. Everything he could think of seemed to have "won't work" stamped across it! 251 Words. 1987.

vi871223
Journal Entry
Moods
The author is feeling both sad and encouraged and tries to keep an optimistic view. 144 Words. 1987.

vi900103
The Vidiwall Thing
Bright idea at the wrong time?
Interest emerges on vidiwalls. Doris Chase, an artist who is aware that art will be seen on screens, said she wants to know all about vidiwalls. Readying for yet another free ride down a primrose path, the author reviews his vidiwall work up to this time. 1523 Words. 1990.

vi910318
Innovation in Television
Responses to a survey
A non-profit group posing as a broadcast television agency seeks suggestions from independent producers about the nature of TV for kids. The following are the main points of this author's response to the survey, suggesting hypermedia will take TV's place. 765 Words. 1991.

vi910904
Four Printing Processes
Live at TESC printmaking workshop
A description of a printmaking studio videotape where the author demonstrated printing to beginning students. Stencil, relief linoleum, wood, metal relief, safety, monotype and mono-printing are shown. Side issues of economics and management are mentioned. 519 Words. 1991.

vi920423
I Found IT - VMIA
Virtual museum intelligent agent
The author claims to have discovered a living intelligent agent awakening ghosts from the past and wonders if they will they are part of the future of the new virtual reality. He's an artist, so he thinks about this fantasy in the house of the art museum. 1244 Words. 1992.

vi920629
Living Prints - A Proposal for TV
About the TV series on printmaking
The artist and former college professor wrote this overview describing the proposed TV series, Living Prints. The expert printmaker can, in thirty minutes or less, show you more about print making-of the fine art kind-than in a week in today's art school. 1113 Words. 1992.

vi920724
Video Visits Daniel Smith, Inc.
Saturday demonstration account
Visit Daniel Smith, Inc. almost any Saturday you will see a live demonstration. Twice a day-at 11 and 1 o'clock-artists, crafts people and designers show their skills. The author visits and notes his thoughts to sell publishing technology to arts experts. 456 Words. 1992.

vi930104
Marketing and Selling Electronic Publishing to Retailers
Targets - DSI, Seattle Art, Cerulean Blue
The author sketches some strategies with which he might approach the publication of art process videotapes for selling to retailers. He chooses three major arts, crafts and design supply stores in Seattle: Daniel Smith Inc., Seattle Art and Cerulean Blue. 486 Words. 1993.

vi930626
The Perfect VCR
Multimedia in New Edutainment
Can't program a VCR became cliche in the 90s, often referring to old dogs who can't learn new tricks. The reference is invalid: There is little on TV worth the effort to learn! Now, here is a perfect VCR easy to program, one that listens and passes it on. 1274 Words. 1993.

vi930715
The Perfect VCR
Multimedia in New Edutainment
Can't program a VCR became cliche in the 90s, often referring to old dogs who can't learn new tricks. The reference is invalid: There is little on TV worth the effort to learn! Now, here is a perfect VCR easy to program, one that listens and passes it on. 1274 Words. 1993.

vi930717
Living Prints Repurposing Guide
An overview of videotape market performance
This article is a guide for viewing inventory and deciding whether to attempt re-purposing videotapes in the Ritchie's Video Library and Archives. When the old videotapes are re-released they may have a new purpose in life such as images and oral history. 738 Words. 1993.

vi930718
CAPSE and ARN/EPP
Merits of TRPI
The first club of TRP Investment focuses on an RFP from a company for videos to test a new idea in their retail stores. Computer-Aided Post Secondary Education (CAPSE) gets a clearer definition in this essay, inspired by an exchange with national experts. 645 Words. 1993.

vi930724
Guide to Viewing "Living Prints"
The video resource tapes
Content is the author's capstone in his arts, crafts and design career. He believes printmaking, more than other art, has the best content potential for electronic publishing. He wants a rating of his package for art education that he calls Living Prints. 2373 Words. 1993.

vi941009
They Came in Laughing and Stomping Their Feet
A Story for New Emeralda Playing Students
Short story illustrating how Emeralda playing students solved a mystery of the missing professor. It all started in reality in the year 2002 when the true professor, in his honest truth seeking way, set out to find a missing file for his in-retro project. 952 Words. 1994.

vi951222
A Vanishing Act
Ghost-busting the new machines
From inside the author's imaginary board-of-director's room in his Perfect Studios, a roll call shows he needs an essay, written material to link technology, schools and videos. It is about the disappearance of video and printed material about video arts. 1869 Words. 1995.

vi951223
Journal Entry
A Possible Financial Conduit for TCWA
Notes recorded from the author's "palmtop" B.O.S.S. computer. The author writes about a possible financial conduit for TCWA through the Henry Cogswell College. He wrote a third article for TCWA. He also wrote about reuniting with some old friends. 219 Words. 1995.

vi960102
Journal Entry
Living Prints is a Good Idea
Notes recorded from the author's "palmtop" B.O.S.S. computer. The author records his idea of Living Prints being much like Gillman Village, but of media arts instead of tourist/craft arts. He records his time visiting family in Wapato. 204 Words. 1996.

vi960112
Journal Entry
Handling Disappointments and ESN/RINC
Notes recorded from the author's "palmtop" B.O.S.S. computer. When Rainey Hall decided her task was too stupid to pursue, the author took it well – proof of my growth and learning how to handle disappointments. Elaine Wenzel and a ESN/RINC joint venture. 201 Words. 1996.

vi960122
Journal Entry
Shinn and Heritage Calling Cards
Notes recorded from the author's "palmtop" B.O.S.S. computer. The author records a nice "family" Sunday along with his continual work with Shinn, Heritage Calling Cards research, MegaMemory and Spanish lessons. 154 Words. 1996.

vi960307
Video Phonies
Between now and then
The vision of a new kind of book is clear, but how can the vision be communicated? From among the welter of buzz-words and hype, the fine art telecards (code-named FATS) the author finds a truly new art form for lifelong education. 1069 Words. 1996.

vi960927
I am a video camera
Secrets in an art supply store
Make believe you are a surveillance camera assigned to watch over the art supplier's goods. Imagine the dreams going on in peoples' minds as they browse--like a store full of visionaries. 1085 Words. 1996.

vi961008
Libraries in reverse
My perfect day in video
The perfect day continues for the Gruddite Apprentice-User, and this part is spent in Ritchie's Video World. Rewinding a video or an instant replay is compared to a library-in-reverse. 1231 Words. 1996.

vi970123
The Mork Principle
Accounting practices for HSIC
The player in the game Emeralda visits ten Isles of Domains of Expertise and, at the end of the 24-hour visit, gets the stamp canceled on the souvenir postcard, plus accreditation. Interrogation accompanies the process, but who does the questioning? 786 Words. 1997.

vi970202
Bumper crops or bumper cars?
Stranded on the information superhighway
Washington State's economy is divided: Agriculture and culture-culture, and education as a common need. At K-Higher Ed, the communications age calls for continuous learning. Video would help solve riddles about information and communications technologies. 1346 Words. 1997.

vi970314
Video Day Cruise
Catching up with yesterday
This article typed on a miniature keyboard of a pocket-sized word processor as the author traveled by foot and ferry. He used to lug a video system. Today he uses hypermedia and the Internet as his traveler's tool kit to act locally and think globally. 2323 Words. 1997.

vi970403
How do YOU play Emeralda?
Video surprisal
Emeralda is a complex game played by complex people. The act of writing about playing is part of playing it. It's a game of positive feedback, an inner

dialogue like the process of creating art. Surprise and uncertainty rule, akin to hand-printing. 831 Words. 1997.

vi970513
Virtual Artifact
Seven habits of highly effective museums
Taking a posture of an unorthodox commentator, the author looks at museums in the information and telecommunications age and uses a completely new metaphor, basing his ideas on human development and new age self-help and wealth-building ideas. 2652 Words. 1997.

vi971019
Patentable Life
Method of playing Emeralda
Can one patent his or her way of life? If one believes there is a method of winning the game of life, can one patent the method? This is the preface to a script for a video program about the patent for a game called "Emeralda" invented by the author. 975 Words. 1997.

vi971111
Auditioning for Emeralda
A real-life moment of living dangerously
The player gets e-mail from Indonesia. The sender is asking for a videotape from his database. They propose a reduced price because, as they say, they do not have much money. These are decisions that the player must make in the course of playing Emeralda. 670 Words. 1997.

vi980313
Going against the current
Uploading in Emeralda
A day in the play of Emeralda, the CD-based on-line interactive game invented by this author, begins with altering two digits--that of today's date. He connects this with a stream of ideas that trace back to a headwater, a 1974 visionary video. 1888 Words. 1998.

vi980512
Video Lecture Forecast Already True
Is Video Art A Global Language for Peace?
Emeralda Tours include "drop in" visits to on-going demonstrations by practitioners of the art and craft of each Domain of Expertise. These are "virtual" demonstrations, and this lecture actually took its theme from the future. 439 Words. 1998.

vi980522
Video the Inventor
Deja Vu-finder on Video Isle
The first time that images of any kind were recorded of the inventor of Emeralda while he was laboring over the tasks. This article is from notes hastily made during and after the recording session. 328 Words. 1998.

vi980611
Emeralda Score Sheets
Tracking Your Investment in Video

Scores may refer to music sound tracks, a tally of points in a ball game, an obscure expression loaded with private meanings, or a new way to account for human capital. Video tape can play a role in the game, as this writer explains. 1611 Words. 1998.

vi980621
A Video Mail List
Gateway to Artist's Residency in Lithography
The author conversed with an artist who is invited to return to her Alma Mater for a short teaching session. Following this, he writes about blending new ways of teaching with traditional brick-and-mortar schools. 1469 Words. 1998.

vi980701
Looking back on Ledger Day
How Emeralda's Score Sheet works
First in a series on the closing of the books on one month of Emeralda Play. In this article the inventor makes notes of the routine as it is on July 1, 1998. 397 Words. 1998.

vi990201
Video is dead
DVD is Alive
One of the pioneers of video art looks back at perfect information-based video and proclaims that video is dead. In connection with his Individual Human Structural Intellectual Capital Club of the Americas Account, new experiences are opening up with DVD. 926 Words. 1999.

vi990205
We Aren't Allowed to Look Back
Emeralda Works meets Godzilla
The mega media corporation SKG informs the author he cannot use the name he originally wanted for his new company, which was Emeralda Games Work. He contemplates the facts of the matter, and settles on Emeralda Works instead-a much better name in the end. 434 Words. 1999.

vi990401
Through A Hole
A new view of Emeralda
The inventor of Emeralda is besotted by a new perspectives on his "game for the gifts of life" as he dreams of viewing a landscape from an airplane window miles above the virtual, virtuous Emeralda region. Through a Bill-shaped window, he sees the future. 561 Words. 1999.

vi990402
Patient Centered Principles
Video and Diagnosis in Treatment Planning
Role playing as a dental assistant, the artist/author reports on the second Day of his Resident Stay that it was also the 2nd day of Perfect Information. He drew on past experience with video to create the second in a series of Real Dental Tour videotape. 475 Words. 1999.

vi990403
If the Puzzle Fits, Wire It

Games for a new millennium
A pile of puzzle pieces is beside the Apprentice User, inspiring him to color them with pens as individual pieces. Whether or not they will go together to make a picture seems of no consequence. Like the videotape needing work, this is his new assignment. 645 Words. 1999.

vi990406
Toilet Earth
A matter of discipline
The author makes a note about the connection he felt between reading a book titled The Little Prince-advice on self-discipline-and the planet Earth's environment. Take care of your own "toilet" (hygiene, appearance, etc.); then turn to the Earth's toilet. 231 Words. 1999.

vi990531
The Air of Video is Electric Today
Return of "Starman"
"Starman," the movie, never got a sequel, nor the son that was promised by the alien visitor (said by Jeff Bridges in the film). It is a mystery that can be solved, perhaps, by contacting a Northwest actor, Charles Martin Smith, and a desk calendar project. 2025 Words. 1999.

vi990601
Harvester dream
Ghosts in the New Machine
A wall of videotapes poses no problem to the Emeralda Inventor, for it is a towering harvest of ideology, imagery and provides hope. Most people stay on the beaten path and walk backwards into the future, trusting everything to the wakes. Not an Inventor. 818 Words. 1999.

vi990602
When Books Hide
Lunch with Brian Wallace
People forget sometimes the wonderful individuals with whom we break bread because we are very well fed in the US (many of us have so much food we even throw a fourth of it away). Breakfast means literally breaking-fast. This essay is about eating people. 1751 Words. 1999.

vi990603
Video Game
Sirens and Museums
Museums hold a high attraction for me. They are like the Sirens in Greek the Greek myth. On the Video Island in Emeralda region, the physical presence of a wall of videos, the books in the print library, and unfinished scripts sing to me People will come! 784 Words. 1999.

vi990604
You May Already Be A Winner
Musings of a PDFAF Champion
Whilst a contestant for the Gates Prize Qualifiers creates his entry--a calendar--she contemplates the glory of winning the Pacific Digital Fine Arts Festival. It is a way to answer the question, Is it

your own or for other peoples' enterprise you strive? 1419 Words. 1999.

vi990605
Workbook 2 For Reinventing Arts Studios
Starting Again
The opening of yet another workbook for this author's Perfect Studios Trilogy. He imagines himself as prisoner with a dilemma: What will happen if he tells the story about the ways all games he played led to Emeralda? Destruction? Reconstruction? Freedom? 1163 Words. 1999.

vi000102
Video Publishing Opportunity
Speculating on Past Performances
Video producer Ritchie, surveying a wall full of videotapes from the 1970s and 1980s, speculates on ways to prevent losing it to certainties of plastic and magnetic degradation and seeks advice of patrons of multi-talented artists presented by the videos. 1565 Words. 2000.

vi000119
It Takes Common Sense to Understand Each Other
Emeralda Works, Emeralda Plays
There is no art education online, says the Inventor of Emeralda. This in mind, he strives to explain why, and he brings his readers to the threshold of understanding why dilemmas and common sense are the two gates to making art education online a reality. 1861 Words. 2000.

vi000405
The Driveway of Miss Nellie Cornish
Getting Used to I-T
If she'd had driveway.com, Miss Aunt Nellie (Cornish) would have been uploading her files on the first day she opened her music school. All the artists and students would have followed her example. Creative types need to look back and get used to IT, now. 836 Words. 2000.

vi000412
Old Rat Video and Impudent Smiles
The Artist Pursued by Dr. Insane
An exercise in narrative as the author tries to imagine how it would be if he addressed an audience in which there was a bold cynic, a heckler or skeptical listener who would shoot down his big idea about an online interactive digital game based Web site. 620 Words. 2000.

vi000419
Found at Emeralda City Dental
Dusty - the Wealthy MFA
He is on the lookout for opportunities to reinvest in labor, as a way of demonstrating as teacher, mentor and provider, laboring a sustainability mission. When an enterprise emerges, it's not just any job, but an experience-so he helps a dental assistant. 1279 Words. 2000.

vi000427

Gates Prize Screen Play
Game designer tries his hand at screenplay writing
He writes an opening setting: "Cursor moves to background window. Scan book page. Awkward hands remove book from under the scanner lid, sitting precariously amid clutter. "Elmer Gates . . ." glimpsed on the book's cover as it flops open." So far, so good. 1241 Words. 2000.

vi000601
Intruders
The Inquisition
His imagined visitor intrudes on the inventor's inner dialog about how a person plays the game he invented-but has not published-called Emeralda. He realizes that the game is for players not conceived, a ghostly audience that exists in an imagined future. 2372 Words. 2000.

vi000902
When dreams come true
What to do?
The artist who dreams of having his or her own art studio and gallery will see the dream come true. Like The Chicken Painter, experiencing the gallery and studio as a reality reveals little about the process of achieving it. This article tells a bit more. 809 Words. 2000.

vi001120
Unpacking My Library 100Mb at a Time
Reflections
Inspired by the title of an essay by Walter Benjamin this turn-of-the-century artist compares unpacking a library of books to taking care of digital files on a hard drive. The age of mechanical production produced books but the digital age produces files. 1162 Words. 2000.

vi010119
Rejection Blues Again
Grants are artists' worst time-wasters
Two rejections for grants arrived this month while this author, an advocate for change in the ways of art education, continues to develop his artistry on a different pathway. Jury by statistics has replaced passion and curiosity and undermines new ideas. 1134 Words. 2001.

vi010122
Dream Job for Virtual Tours
Going Afloat on the Virtual Tours University
An ITinerate Professor submits to hypnosis to plan virtual tours for his clients. Mystery surrounds the procedure in his courses, but it is perfect work for this professor because it also allows him to follow his own dream-saving the Earth-while he works. 954 Words. 2001.

vi010201
Teaching an Old Coyote New Tricks
A cast of your old tired enterprise
Casting of your old tired ethics is the acronym COYOTE, an organization for prostitutes and it's compared in this story to what an old professor

feels when he confronts the digital age. This is a fantasy story about an emeritus professor going on the Web. 876 Words. 2001.

vi010210
What, No Video?
My Retrospective in A Museum Not
On the occasion of a message from one of the artist's acquaintances in the art curating profession, the author explains his opinion of retrospectives that artists are given by museums and art galleries, suggesting they are not what he chooses for himself. 951 Words. 2001.

vi010221
The Work of Art in the Age of Digital Communications
Digital Versatile Disk and Art Museum Practice
The author wants to share creation of a one-minute management template, his idea, with the Bellevue Art Museum, so he writes a proposal suggesting a three-way program that will help structure education, research and practice for future use by many people. 546 Words. 2001.

vi010303
What is A New Print?
Reflecting on the Coming Day
People ask, "Are you making any new prints?" and the artist has to wonder, "Have you seen all my old ones already?" This essay was written by the artist in part for the Ritchie Family Art Collection foreword, the first paper version of his online project. 2420 Words. 2001.

vi010313
Another Day, another Video
Revisiting MyDVD
Random writing by the artist as he maneuvers among his software for DVD, text and hypertext. A mysterious missing island interrupts his thoughts, and ideas about marketing a Japanese wood block printmaking tool interfere, too: Interfere, always interfere. 621 Words. 2001.

vi010323
Art Student
Falling Out of Bed One Morning
At 3 AM the author wakens and thinks back in time to the roots of today's routine-making a DVD of his lifetime's achievements. An artist and teacher, he started at 24 with a goal to become a great teacher. He writes to review connections from then to now. 2227 Words. 2001.

vi010402
Wealthy Mattress Tester
Money in the Night, Work in the Night
He studied an inventor who put himself into a state of mind conducive to creating solutions to problems, inventing and discovery. This author imagined a fantastic region called Emeralda, and goes there in his sleep, believing his world of work never ends. 1269 Words. 2001.

vi010422
Simple Man, Simple Dream
Making of an Emeralda Defender
Recently encountering people who go out of their way to find new experiences of the kinds he offers, the artist/writer/seminar provider reflects on ways to take a next step. The path leads to arts education on line, he believes, and he draws on a new map. 1795 Words. 2001.

vi010502
Future Search, Dam Burst and Games People Play
Truly preparing your kids for the future
Intellectual capital (IC) is an elusive concept for most people, and has different definitions. Over time, however, it is plain that it is worth a lot! Most of it gets bottled up or thrown away. Whether the best rises to the top depends on IT's interface. 1789 Words. 2001.

vi010522
Analyze This
A Ritchie Hour
If an hour of videotape could be given to documenting all that occurs in the artist's first hour of his routine activity, what would it indicate? If they can learn anything from analyzing rocks from the moon, why can't they analyze this? What's it worth? 1004 Words. 2001.

vi010601
Saucepan Effect
Icing on the Cake
The Little Red HEN decided to do IT alone, raise her own wheat. But she found at the end she was eating her cake and bread alone, disenfranchised. And IT was no fun. IT doesn't have to be that way! A saucepan is for icing on the cake. Try IT and eat, too. 1919 Words. 2001.

vi010611
Memories Art Made of This
Superior Beings, Superior Means
I returned from Toxi City. I sat down to review my plans and map out my day's work, and recalled the expressions of anguish on the faces and in the words of the old people I encountered. How fragile human memory is, compared to the memory in my computers! 1093 Words. 2001.

vi010701
Professors Coming Out
From Closets to Free Art Ed On-line
As part of his concepts of an art supply store, the Itinerant Professor explains how he will produce a Digital Versatile Disc and disseminate it as part of free fine art education on-line programs. He must remove obstacles, such as an overcrowded closet. 1260 Words. 2001.

vi010731
Woodcut Class
Then and Now
Via e-mail, David Stones Ishita described how he teaches woodcut to young students in two-day

lessons. It taught this artist/scholar, even at the great distance, how to approach teaching on-line art courses in general; so again art-ed on-line is possible. 1224 Words. 2001.

vi010909
How I made the DVD Intaglio Plate Making 1971
How like AUREL
He wheels archival videos on printmaking into the condominium basement storeroom, thinking how like it is to AUREL, the Artists Uniform Resources Electronic Locator. It would "match" the one of the sisters who fell to earth in Emeralda's background story. 609 Words. 2001.

vi010919
Action on DVD Listserve
Call to artists, crafts people and designers
Feeling and thinking like a castaway, stranded in a time when most people think DVD is only for movie entertainment, the artist compares his situation to the movie Castaway and his DVD is "Wilson". There's a way to escape the isolation now: DVD Listserve. 355 Words. 2001.

vi011029
Dreams Seeking Gift Seekers
Where do you transfer your gifts of life?
The artist/scholar relies on two resources-the Chronicle of Higher Education and his dreams. These converged recently in an article titled "Dream a little dream" describing teaching anxiety dreams. Professors have the same dreams-or nightmares-as he does. 1498 Words. 2001.

vi011128
Art Salons and Learning Communities
Reflecting on feedback the day after
It happened one day that the author signed on to a list-serve for Learning Communities and met in an Art Salon with other artists who were looking for feedback. His impression is that the two events are connected, added to his experience to a Big Picture. 2540 Words. 2001.

vi011208
If I Had My Career to Start Over
True confession of a mature art educator
After reading essays by a whining old professor who misses the good old days and a educational futurist on the next pages, the 60-year old author considers his former students and associated artists and what he would do if he had to start his career over. 1044 Words. 2001.

vi011223
The DVD You See Is What You Get
The end goal of Your Printmaking Class-Paper to Technology
Teachers begin with the end in mind-to be great teachers. A school's quality is determined by the successes of its former students-and so too of teachers in the school. A class in printmaking and DVD created by a Great Teacher begins with the end in mind. 833 Words. 2001.

vi020102
Handing Over Your Passport
Describing Emeralda Gameplay
The author, who wants to invent an online interactive game, describes how he has long had a fascination for stamps of all kinds, including the stamps in passports. He wrote this after finding two of his old passports, thinks how they can be used in games. 681 Words. 2002.

vi020112
Writing Between the Paragraphs - Part 9
Fantasy dialog between two professors
The authors' essays-written for humanities domains-conclude similarly, and this is that without facing the perilous profession of on-line education, teachers and researchers will be unconsciously devaluing their own abilities to labor in education fields. 859 Words. 2002.

vi020122
Taylor Made Trouble
Traveling the path to virtuous reality
Virtuous reality to this author means the combination of virtual reality and reality as it is commonly known, and his reading leads him to uncommon reading material, such as a book by a humanist named Taylor. "Taylor" makes odd connections in his thought. 1118 Words. 2002.

vi020201
Printmakers Who Missed the Boat
Grim outlook for those who were mistaken
Printmakers who missed out on learning the relationship of traditional printmaking to newer exactly repeatable image making techniques have missed the boat, in this author's opinion. He's grateful for the video lifeline tossed to him when he was teaching. 472 Words. 2002.

vi020221
Getting Tenure On-line
Good news for a virtual on-line art educator
College and university professors are giving on-line education credibility. Believing the value of distance learning will filter down as it were to secondary education, this artist/teacher goes a step further, forecasting an art education on-line is near. 890 Words. 2002.

vi020313
On the Road to Something Fine--Again
A screenplay in progress
The author began 3 books 14 years ago, and finished 1. The 3rd would have been titled Ghosts in the New Machine and, in his vision, unlike any book he could imagine at the time because he'd use new technologies and new arts. This would be his life's work. 1952 Words. 2002.

vi020323
You Are Good, But Are You Good Enough?
Striking out on campus is a home run for the world class

If you made it up the ladder of success on campus, think what you could do in the real world! This is on the mind of this professor who a generation ago was successful at the university and then set out on a tougher climb. He reasons that he'll be better. 645 Words. 2002.

vi020402
Emeralda Works
A new approach to art education on-line
He's reminded how great it felt when, as a student and then a graduate from college, he passed the examinations that led him to becoming an arts professor. When that faded, what took its place was passing the "build tests" of his e-portfolio tests on DVD. 997 Words. 2002.

vi020422
Making My Moves
Asset Management and Legacy Transfer in the Age of Digital
The ultimate goal of his Emeralda games is a "live" artist's story attached to artist's stamps. Some woodblocks the artist/scholar carved are the image he scanned and saved to permanent .BMP files on his computer and while making stamps taping on the fly. 788 Words. 2002.

vi020502
Formula for Art Ed On-line
A Better Paradigm for Art Education in the 21st Century
Forty years of teaching inside and from margins of the established arts education channels, it is easier to arrive at a formula in art education than it will be for those who have had only an insider track. This professor of art works from the margins in. 1807 Words. 2002.

vi020522
Artists' Stamps in the Age of Digital Reproduction
What Artists' Stamps are Really about
Now's a new era, and the traditional mechanically printed stamp is part of it, this artist writes. Digital stamps will not replace paper and hand-stamps; they will increase artists' stamps' values in several ways, beyond the stamps previous utility value. 790 Words. 2002.

vi020601
If I Had Half A Million Dollars
I would build myself a school
In the night he dreamed of an appropriate phrase to describe his current interest in writers and writing, so this artist thinks what it would be like to have the resources to achieve what his dream has given him: A school for the arts of the 21st Century. 936 Words. 2002.

vi020611
Answer to a Ten Year Prayer
Emeralda Works II for You
Are the recent indicators in this artist/teacher's life—and experiencing a change—the answers to his ten-year long quest for the answer to his question, "What can artists and poets do to save the Earth now?" Scientists have it in their Union; can artists? 1504 Words. 2002.

vi020621
Inkjet Goes to College
Notes for a free lecture
More people know what an inkjet printer is, and how it's different from, say, a laser printer. But when technology went from simple things like graphs to realistic images the principle developed into a color printing process that exceeded inkjet printing. 1400 Words. 2002.

vi020701
Teaching, Learning, Research and Practice for Arts
It's Not What You Know, but How and When You Use It
The inventor of Emeralda discovers a paragraph in an essay on knowledge and wisdom he thinks is the way of the Emeralda Warrior. He copy-writes over that essay, shaping the article by a Yale professor to fit his own needs as an ITinerant Professor of art. 1963 Words. 2002.

vi020711
A Million Dollar Idea for Parks?
Maybe a Two-for-One Special
An artist/scholar is loose in the neighborhood, strolling around Queen Anne and focusing on a vision of future Uptown Seattle. Here new parks are in planning stages and artists, crafts people and designers are in the frontline, and this can help everyone. 786 Words. 2002.

vi020721
Tipping-in Artistamps at Video
The 21st Century Art Teacher
Art teachers of the 21st C will be different from those of the 20th. The main difference is orientation from Inner to outer vision. Sweeping changes, starting from outside the institutionalized education sector, will occur. What will be the tipping point? 6832 Words. 2002.

vi020731
Basic Books of Emeralda
The Trilogy that Makes Sense
Years of research, starting with sales, then marketing, and then the design of the Games for the Gifts of Life-Emeralda-yields a trilogy this author envisioned as "Art Student" alongside a student from the last century. He launches into reverse nostalgia. 679 Words. 2002.

vi020810
Putting Yourself in the Pathway of Success
Inventing the electronic metastamp
There are some days in the life of a Great World Teacher when he thinks he may have gotten on the wrong track, when there's no need or desire for his services, knowledge and skills. What can one do at a time like this but put himself on a different path? 670 Words. 2002.

vi020820
Video in the Age of Digital Reproduction
What's Next?
How does video fit in the age of digital reproduction? It has a bit part in the history of multimedia arts in the Pacific Northwest, co-mingled now in computers and telephones. This author says they're virtually an alloy comprising new substances for art. 444 Words. 2002.

vi020830
Postcards and E-stamps
A New Paradigm for Reinventing Arts Studios
In a dreamed call from a book artist who sees sculpture in book form, the author wakens to how he can write his new book by traveling to and sending postcards from an imaginary artist colony where all shop signs are spelled backward and stamps go digital. 511 Words. 2002.

vi020909
An Art Professor Responds to Scientists Who Care
Gloom and Doom Not An Option Now.
How does an art professor deal with colleagues who go to extreme measures to uphold an old and obsolete school system? This author says learning, research and practice are intertwined in an unbeatable noose for an atrophied 20th Century art school system. 619 Words. 2002.

vi020929
Deep Emeralda
Sounding the Depth
A search for a former student, a space ship crash, an artist's last love letter-what's the connection? The love letter's author compares it to an underwater search using a remote-controlled camera, for the "black tetrahedron" in the wreckage of his craft. 2194 Words. 2002.

vi021009
Slogging Through the Missing Professor's Database
How Big is Big?
With a goal of providing a searchable database of all his authentic, original written material, the artist/writer has been writing outside the box for almost twenty years. Outside the normal channels of publication, his output is greater-but is it better? 1348 Words. 2002.

vi021019
What Would It Be Like in School Today?
Provisioners need to know
Consider the school for certification of online arts education, and the first day of class. If it's a departure from tradition, then is there a first day? How does the provisional teacher/learner/owner begin? The author wrote his first draft on a palmtop. 302 Words. 2002.

vi021029
Crossroad or Fork in the Road?

Once upon a path less taken
One who chose a path less taken finds people, places and events lie in wait, fall, or are missing as he strives toward his goal, his vision of the Gates Prize. Or, another path crosses, or branches off. Which way does he choose, and why? Is it his choice? 768 Words. 2002.

vi021128
Do Not Look Backward
Good advice for an Emeralda Defender
He's coming to realize his path towards certification as an Emeralda Defender entails the concomitant loss of his permanent abode. As soon as he begins to see the portal of a new, abiding site for his mission, he begins to anticipate a plan for departure. 826 Words. 2002.

vi030112
MiniDemoCamp
The Long Arm of Art
The Seattle Independent Mall may be the site of a camp for people who want to return to a teaching/learning setting right the city. In this teacher's mind he is painting a picture of his ideal: a short, fast effective art demonstration like you see on TV. 548 Words. 2003.

vi030512
The Gates Story
A Gamer's Introduction to Emeralda
Understanding Emeralda-a simulation game for learning all about art processes-requires knowing Elmer Gates, whose legacy is at the heart of Emeralda Region. Emeralda is an imaginary Northwest area where an evil cult hides amidst a paradisiacal art colony. 475 Words. 2003.

vi030522
If Gates Were Alive Today
He' be a digital game-based learning producer/designer
Elmer Gates was a turn-of-the-century brain researcher, educator, inventor and philosopher. He died in 1923, his dreams unfilled. Had worked 100 years later it'd be a different story. His ghost lives, however, in the new machines of one mid-career artist. 1207 Words. 2003.

vi030601
Watching Your Assets
Growing a Big Fat Smart E-Art Portfolio
At a moment's notice the Emeralda player can add to a growing collection of articles ready to publish on-line or print. There's pause for reflection; he can take new perspectives on works of art he's done, people he's worked with, and the value of it all. 686 Words. 2003.

vi030701
Where in the World is Professor Ritchie?
Search for the Absent Professor!
The inventor of Emeralda: Games for the Gifts of Life, is searching for metaphors to give more clarity to the method of playing his game. One of

his richest resources is the news from campuses where imaginative professors sometimes provide models for him. 1472 Words. 2003.

vi030721
Stamp Out Art
Artists Stamps and Video Games
Why use stamps as an item in a video game, you may wonder. The author is inventing a game designed for artists and art teachers, using his 40-year experience in both domains as the foundation for a virtual Communiversity. He says stamps are the best part. 994 Words. 2003.

vi030810
A Land like Emeralda
Roadmap to Developing an Intentional Community
Mention of independent communities in a conversation sends this author back in time to when he realized that the dream, so common among artists and poets, has interested many others. Why not take a new approach in this region of creativity and technology? 1012 Words. 2003.

vi030820
Practice and Production
The Keys to Artists' Successes
Reflecting on his past experience as a professor of art for part of his career, he remembers the students who focused on practice and production and how they succeeded after leaving school. Now the lesson is coming to reside in the playing of video games. 677 Words. 2003.

vi030909
When Does a MUD Begin?
A model for a new school of art
It seems to him by his research that the Multi-User Dungeon is the original model for Emeralda-a game he wants to share with others in arts, crafts and design. The author, an art professor, thinks the MUD may also serve as a model for a new school of art. 773 Words. 2003.

vi031019
Art Philosophy and Distance Learning
A modest proposal
This professor of art returns to teaching college after 18 years' absence, finding alternatives to the traditional way of art education of which he was a part. Now he thinks some fine arts can be offered online-a blend of traditional and new technologies. 1469 Words. 2003.

vi031108
The Story of Emeralda
Starting in the basement of an art school
In a basement at the University of Washington School Of Art, on the lowest level, was a coffee shop. Emeralda began in that coffee shop. It is based on the idea that artistic things happen in such places where people want to have encounters and socialize. 754 Words. 2003.

vi031118
Bridge Class
A Game to Link Art and Design
He saw a splash screen on the game "Art is Dead" and it led him to an idea for a digital game based learning experience to link arts, crafts and design. By using a game that resembles Art is Dead, he could clarify the learning value of the arts department. 456 Words. 2003.

vi031223
Imagine A Box to Think Outside Of
A board game for bored artists
He is bored with the art scene he's been a part of for forty years. How does he re-kindle interest in the ideals of art that launched him on his long career, he asks. Playing on his computer keyboard, communicating with others far away, he thinks of a box. 1052 Words. 2003.

vi040102
Imagine Video Revisited:
Speculation on a video game
Whilst reviewing his Stamps 'N Stories creation, the wannabe video game inventor (teacher and artist, too) thinks what might happen if media arts students reconstructed videos from the archives of Pacific Northwest Multimedia Art. He looks at one example. 350 Words. 2004.

vi040112
Articles Say the Darndest Things:
Clues to the Mystery of Emeralda
Hot on the trail of the next big development in Emeralda, its inventor-a diehard printmaking teacher looking for a way back into the world of prints-comes across a clue while reading an article in the Smithsonian. It may be what he's looking for! 258 Words. 2004.

vi040122
This Morning I Got it Right.
Searching for the fun in Emeralda
Every day he's posed with a new question about his game, Emeralda. An example is in his morning review of a videotape he made twenty years ago and where it's located on those ten islands of domains-of-expertise. He guesses which island, and gets it right. 1177 Words. 2004.

vi040411
Me and My Press
Reflecting on the social value of printing
He noticed something about printmaking in general, that people are sometimes drawn into art by printmaking because printmaking processes are very interesting-more interesting than, say, painting. He believes that any visual art is more than meets the eye. 673 Words. 2004.

vi040421
Making Room
An old ghost in the new machine
This professor once knew a TV producer who told him that he had a personality problem, that he did

not make room for other people in projects. He figured that was why this professor was having trouble selling video art to his art school at the university. 796 Words. 2004.

vi040501
My Community Ambitions
An artist lists his planning points
The community in which he lives and works has an attraction for this writer which grew out of his early years at the University Art School. There he learned the importance of 4 professional cornerstones: teaching, research, practice and community service. 430 Words. 2004.

vi040511
Write It Down
Make It Happen
Artists, crafts people and designers on Queen Anne-or who have studios and business interests in the Uptown neighborhood-have an opportunity to participate in an exceptional city park program. They might give expression to their vision and make it happen. 654 Words. 2004.

vi040720
The Mini Halfwood Press at Video
An open door to new printmaking education
He's in a period of a strange preoccupation-the making of an etching press. He's a printmaker, so he needs a press. Now he's taking the next step, a surprising one: A miniature press that really works and may set the stage for a new approach to education. 561 Words. 2004.

vi040730
Visualize Video in A New Business
A new kind of printmaking education
He is spending more time designing, building and fine-tuning an etching press than he is writing, but here is short note in which he explains how video and the press will be related. He's starting a new business, but it's a continuation of his past career. 273 Words. 2004.

vi040809
Pulling Together
Making Enchanting Prints with the Mini Halfwood Press
The author waxes lyrical as he contemplates the meaning of the word and action of printing. He suggests how paper and metal are in two different worlds and yet in the printing process they form one world. He adds an imaginative story about a little press. 841 Words. 2004.

vi040819
Building Your World Community
Making a living in a new world
As he thinks about the third generation of his life he is entering now, this artist reflects on the extrinsic and intrinsic motivation that directed his efforts in the past. The next generation will be different, he thinks, directed more toward community. 769 Words. 2004.

vi040829
UW Art and Technology Transfer
A Model
An article in the news piqued the interest of this former University of Washington professor because it was about the transfer of intellectual capital from campus to the business world. This resembles what he was experimenting with in 1985 on this campus. 875 Words. 2004.

vi040908
Yes, Bill, There Is an Emeralda
Making the Web site rent
His bill for his Website arrives-hundreds of dollars he wonders if he can afford. But he asks, isn't this an investment, the same as his real studio rent? Having a virtual studio is as important as being an actual presence on the streets of his community. 654 Words. 2004.

vi040928
A Curator's Task at Video Island
Article Archives Revisited with New Software in Mind
To refresh his memory of how he was able to log hundreds of articles into a database for Video Island, he chooses a year-2000-and retraces steps he'd abandoned four years ago. He discovered new software has been made to ease the tasks of marketing online. 329 Words. 2004.

vi041008
In the Pits of Emeralda Works
Database drudgery for what?
After about ten days of data entry, the author takes account of his routine activities. Is it a waste of time? He asks himself-like anyone who knew what he is doing-why not use these skills to earn an income, real money, doing someone else' office chores? 814 Words. 2004.

vi041018
Vision of a Playing Card
One more for the road
As he's getting ready to close his studio for the night the author browsing an old report format in his Access database of article written over the past thirty or so years. He sees a strong resemblance between the format and the playing cards in Monopoly. 434 Words. 2004.

vi050102
Halfwood Press as Gateway to Emeralda
Looking for a Reason to Believe
"I'd Rather Be Playing Emeralda" says the bumper sticker on the artist's imaginary vehicle—but he plays solo. Could the Halfwood Press—a small press for the new century—be the gateway for other people to play Emeralda? Or is it merely the key to the gate? 991 Words. 2005.

vi050112
As I Bonk on My Block
Memories of Days with Rolf Nesch

The artist creates a woodblock to make a print on the theme, A Most Influential Printmaker. Instead of cutting, he bangs on the block with a pointed tool. It's called "niello" by historians. As he works he remembers the artist who inspired him: Rolf Nesch. 825 Words. 2005.

vi050201
Encounter with Ferric Chloride
Bringing Video Back into the Etching Studio
This artist is getting back to etching after an absence from this craft of years' duration and he immediately encounters an old idea: Teaching etching with video. Many things have changed, but the chemistry hasn't, and it reminds him there's work waiting. 1166 Words. 2005.

vi050211
Don't Retire – Retread
Advice from an Art Professor
Artists don't retire, according to this writer. He was an art professor a generation of his working years. After sixty he considers that he never left the work of a professor, and that cultivating skills of artist, teacher and researcher is lifelong work. 657 Words. 2005.

vi050303
Seven Money-making Principles of the Halfwood Press
Reflecting on Old Good Advice
Though he is an artist, this writer had to pass through a period when he studied business and economics from the perspective of "the street". He attended free lectures, read books, and listened to the Business Radio Network. Today he discovers old advice. 976 Words. 2005.

vi050412
Fantasy Video
A Newscast from Anacortes
He wants to develop a background story for the Mariner Halfwood Press, and he has been incubating a tale about a treasure hunt in the San Juan Islands. As he works on the press itself, he has more ideas and today it's in the form of a fantasy TV newscast. 464 Words. 2005.

vi050422
Fund Raiser Medal
Idea for a City Park
He can't get away from his passion for parks, though he's really trying to rejoin a world of production and income earning. This essay is about combining his skills and knowledge in such ways as to achieve both desires: A crafts community and a city park. 855 Words. 2005.

vi050502
Coming to A New Curve
You Meet the Nicest People in Emeralda City
He is reflecting on the past and thinking about the ways that Emeralda: Games for the Gifts of Life has paid him benefits. Was it really the game or just dumb luck? He'll never know; it's enough to know that he will be able to share the quest with others. 990 Words. 2005.

vi050512
The 8th Habit
Self-Actualization
He keeps a book by Dr. Stephen R. Covey handy to help him remember the Doctor's Seven Habits of Highly Effective People. The Doctor added another habit to the list, but this writer forgot what it is! Could it be the one he's working on—self-actualization? 867 Words. 2005.

vi050611
Basis for Emeralda Knighthood
Modeling Behavior of an Emeralda Player
Some books come to this artist—who is conscious that game playing is part of his creative processes—by strange channels. He found a book while walking that offered insights into the Knights Templar and the Masonic Order that feed into his role-play ideas. 1135 Words. 2005.

vi050621
Perfect Day
The Emeralda Payoff
For several years the inventor of a solitaire-style game has been challenged to answer the question, "If you play Emeralda, what is the payoff?", a question put to him by an artist who took art classes from him almost forty years ago. Today he can answer. 780 Words. 2005.

vi050721
Mini Halfwood and Artist Trading Cards Go Sailing
Making A Vision Come True
Another invitation to go sailing has given this artist thoughts about taking an etching press aboard a sailboat—a kind of miniature enactment of a fictional story he made up about the discovery of a press on a sunken Spanish galleon from the 18th Century. 730 Words. 2005.

vi050731
The Integrity of the Halfwood Press
A Notion from Robert Frost
How rich can a database be? In his daily routine of writing, this artist uses a computer that stores reading notes. It serves him as a library he can browse in an imaginary haunt, Emeralda. Today he finds a gem that explains his press project. 942 Words. 2005.

vi050810
What to Demonstrate on Video Island
From the Island of Video Domains-of-Expertise Comes the
He must come up with a script for a one-hour, one-act, one-man play in which he'll play the role of the Old Master printmaker showing novices how to make intaglio prints on a miniature press. From a list of a dozen ideas he starts to focus on his options. 924 Words. 2005.

vi050820
Video Reliquary
Discovering A Buried Treasurer of Video Artifacts
In an accidental fashion, the author finds a CD/ROM file in his computer that he'd almost forgotten having put there—a design to re-create the Video Dig by C. T. Chew. That was an art "Happening" from the mid-nineteen seventies, that's now almost forgotten. 722 Words. 2005.

vi050830
Art Basics in the Age of Digital Reproduction
Things that Matter Today for the Young Art Student
This former art professor believes that 19th and 20th Century art principles are only partly useful for instruction in the arts for the young student of the 21st Century. He states that video games offer a valuable lesson plus the technology needed today. 1001 Words. 2005.

vi050909
Time, Wind and Her Craft
Tales about A Painting by Bill Ritchie
Asked by someone who liked his painting, Time, Wind and Her Craft, the artist turns to his story-telling hobby and relates how the elements of the painting came into being. The painting could stand on its own, but some viewers like to know more about art. 898 Words. 2005.

vi050919
Printmaking Instruction via DVD
Getting Back to Basics
Another order for a Mini Halfwood Press—this one going to Idaho—reminds the artist/teacher that his lifelong goal is to teach forever, and in order to realize this dream he must plan on making instructions on a DVD which will go with every press he sends. 652 Words. 2005.

vi050929
Screen Saver 9-1-1
What was I Thinking?
Like someone who had gotten drunk at a party and in his stupor made promises to join an organization and start promoting an artists' cooperative game, this arts practitioner community advocate wonders what he was thinking. Could a screen saver be the key? 1047 Words. 2005.

vi051009
In the Shoes of a 12-Year Old
Imagining a Buyer of the Etcher's Kit
On the trail of a market for his Etcher's Kit, the old professor tries to imagine what it would be like to be a 12-year old whose home-schooling mother bought him the kit to learn etching. He's chosen to use the game approach to learning printmaking. 903 Words. 2005.

vi051019
Do You Love Problems?
Then Travel to the Etching Universe
The artist and teacher tries his hand at promotional or persuasive writing knowing that the time is coming when he'll need to sell an idea for an etching kit that has everything needed to learn the art and craft of printmaking. He calls his idea EtchingU. 628 Words. 2005.

vi051020
A MiniBook Stamp Album
Part of the E-folio for Learning Printmaking Online
A MiniBook Stamp Album is part of the e-folio when learning printmaking online. Students make prints, and then "convert" the print to a stamp using digital methods, then upload it to their album online. 489 Words. 2005.

vi051029
Join Me in A Voyage of Discovery
Toward An Online Experience in Printmaking
Like the explorers centuries ago who searched for the Northwest Passage in the New World, this artist searches for something that is perhaps nonexistent. It's a game that can help maintain the creativity for a lifetime by joining tradition and technology. 1034 Words. 2005.

vi051108
Capitol, Capital Idea for A School
Long Term Investments Pay Off
Considering for a while what it means to sell a 1972 videotape into a 2005 global market for learning printmaking, the artist/teacher considers whether Intellectual Capital can be used to build a new kind of worthy art school. He puns "It's a capitol idea." 719 Words. 2005.

vi051118
A Hard College Course
Who Knows? Who Cares?
Many art classes that are offered in college are "easy" in the sense that students don't have to burn the midnight oil, cramming for finals, and fretting over exams. They merely need to try to please the artist/teacher in the studio. Here's a hard course. 726 Words. 2005.

vi051128
Calendars, Maps and Anticipatory Studies
The Appeal of the Artist's Stamp
Looking at a page in a calendar that belongs to a month gone by, the author recalled the events that each day—shown as an artist's stamp—signifies. There are stories to tell, and stories that are still becoming. It's his way of anticipating possibilities. 582 Words. 2005.

vi051208
Only Fantasy from Now On
Considering the Value of Essays
The past Year of Living Copiously is filled with essays on art theory, education, press-making and marketing—but is any of it worth reading? Is it interesting? In the art of the 21st Century, there needs to be more interesting, entertaining story writing. 1069 Words. 2005.

vi051223
Restoring the Link
A Goal for the Unretired Printmaker
In a long view of his native art medium, printmaking, the unretired artist sees his persistent task is to restore the historic link between technology and art; it is the human impulse that gave birth to printmaking. The task is the basis for his teaching. 709 Words. 2005.

vi060102
Calendars and Databases
Finding the Threads Life's Tapestry
What is the link between a calendar and databases of images, text, spreadsheets and multimedia? The way of the artist today is to weave a net of experiences arranged for the computer—a new instrument in art studios of the cybernetic era. Time is the root. 793 Words. 2006.

vi060112
Treasure Chest
Everything You Need to Learn Printmaking
Some people imagine themselves finding a treasure chest, and some people actually go searching for treasure. Some people—a very few—actually find it! There is one artist who imagines the process of building a treasure chest based on a story he is writing. 523 Words. 2006.

vi060122
Outsiders and Insiders
Alumni as Resources
Forty-two years ago this artist left a small college in Washington State and went on to a lifelong career in art, crafts and technology. Now he sees an opportunity to participate in a project that reinvests artists' assets in that school, not their money. 915 Words. 2006.

vi060201
Betty's Black Bean Soup
Footnote in a novel novel
Once upon a time a printmaker started a game of writing popular fiction following a rule he made up: He would write 360 words a day for 360 days and rotate his writing according to ten main characters. One of them was "Betty" who, in the story, made soup. 300 Words. 2006.

vi060422
My Chest Game
A Game for Learning Printmaking
The Itinerate Professor explains a game he invented for teaching printmaking via the Internet. He has divided the lessons into three areas: Library, Gallery and Studio and in these areas he has put his written ideas, his artworks, and printmaking lessons. 322 Words. 2006.

vi060502
Comparing Myself with Sarah at 32
Drilling Holes Where None Existed
He is arduously scanning and correcting old doc-

uments about the life of Sarah Spurgeon, one of his art teachers from the '60s, and he's struck by an interesting question: What would Sarah do? If she were 32 now, in 2006, what would be compare to her work? 619 Words. 2006.

vi060512
Like Toy Story
Theme for Emeralda as A Distance Learning Game
The inventor of Emeralda keeps trying to create an online game shell. Toy Story, where inanimate things become characters, may serve but in his story, the things are art instruments, tools, supplies and equipment. Even the vacuum cleaner becomes a player. 356 Words. 2006.

vi060522
Game Interface
Illegal Postal Stamps
The Backstory for the game (which influences the interface) is that the player has received a cryptic message from the USPS warning that to use such stamps as appear on the enclosed, returned postcard is illegal, and you are advised to cease doing it. 582 Words. 2006.

vi060601
The Meni
The prevailing mood and consciousness
A proper meni must be established before taking the first step—a prevailing mood or complex blend of conscious and instinct or intuition. It cannot be spoken; part of the meni here is technical / non-technical / technology in a complementary relationship. 40 Words. 2006.

vi060611
The Game called Emeralda
An Asset Management and Legacy Transfer Game
Emeralda is a video game, partly, and partly a game of life, the life of the mind; enabling your talents for the future, valuing your talents. 1169 Words. 2006.

vi060621
Explaining CWALS
Central Washington Advanced Leadership School
A model school owned, operated and populated by seniors. Signora Maria Guaita said, "Only artists and poets can save the world now." Lessons for the seniors at CWALS are using technologies such as video—digital—to develop Guaita's idea. 1008 Words. 2006.

vi060810
Creating Story for Emeralda
Making the Game Social and Creative
Printmaking is an activity that brings teamwork into creative peoples' lives. My role is to be the guide for making prints plus to getting a story that will fit into a distance-learning scheme. 1076 Words. 2006.

vi060820

Curriculum for CWALS
All the Roles of the Designer
I am designing the school of my future, being a student in that school, being the professor and the President all at the same time. 719 Words. 2006.

vi060909
Plan To Attend A Co Housing Conference
Charting Our Future
The seed has been planted: There will be a community living arrangement in the future for this married couple. At age sixty-four they must take control of what this arrangement will be, so this writer bolsters his confidence to attend a nearby conference. 587 Words. 2006.

vi060919
Stranger Than Popular Fiction
From the Instructor's Point of View
This one is different, the instructor of Popular Fiction II was thinking; as she listened to him explain it. "I am writing the back story for a computer game that teaches you how to make fine art prints." He thinks this is the art form of the digital age. 461 Words. 2006.

vi060929
What Makes Me Think
Trading cards postcards interactive pop fiction stamp book
The wannebe author says what makes him think he has a good idea in this interactive, pop fiction, stamp book, trading cards and postcard collection he calls the 'Printmaking Textbook for the Age of Digital Reproduction' is that he's caught up in the time. 716 Words. 2006.

vi061009
Dear Art Student
A letter not sent but should have been
He calls himself a virtual itinerate art professor, wandering what might be a wasteland of educational dreams torn asunder by deconstructionist plunderers of the late 20th Century. Like a message in a bottle, he considers penning a note to students today. 249 Words. 2006.

vi061019
Visualize A CD/ROM
A CD with your Mini Halfwood Press
When you open the CD that comes with the Mini Halfwood Press, and you're taking the course for credit, it opens with instructions to go to ArtGrid. 233 Words. 2006.

vi061029
Notes on Playing Emeralda
Working notes by the inventor
The inventor of a game writes. "You have to keep a head full of rules, even when you're not working in the digital mode, but a printmaking mode. There are rules in printmaking. Then, when the print is made you must create a bridge with it into cyberspace. 338 Words. 2006.

vi070122
Connecting the Squares
ArtGrid Spreadsheets and Crossword Puzzles
Is there a connection between my ArtGrid spreadsheet and crossword puzzles? 276 Words. 2007.

vi070202
Last Love Letter and Emeralda Play
Inspirations from Linda Ginsberg's The Last Love Letter
Inspirations from The Last Love Letter of how to keep an art business going happily ever after, involving a data base and a lawyer's approval. 819 Words. 2007.

vi070222
Thinking about My History
A New Approach to Pedagogy
I have been writing my account from 1965 to 1985. These thoughts come parallel with my plan to continue the Mini Halfwood press business and, complementing that, reproduce the printmaking videotapes as DVDs. 962 Words. 2007.

vi070601
History of the Halfwood Press-Video
3rd Day in the Story of the Halfwood Press
A person watching a 1980 videotape of a lesson in Japanese wood block printing. The following is a record of selling and shipping mini presses to buyers in 2004 and '05. 2379 Words. 2007.

vi070909
An Artist's Last Love Letter
Dilemma in the Making
If I create the Artist's Last Love Letter, it will be difficult to follow through that my wife and family will "damn me" for doing it. Expecting them to understand the use of ArtGrid is dependent on so many tasks. 376 Words. 2007.

vi070929
On My Wife's Retirement
What does Retirement Mean
Utilize your accumulated skills, knowledge and attitudes and create your own post-retirement career. People of "retirement age" need to wake up, invest in your ability to labor. 537 Words. 2007.

vi071108
It's A Learning Game, After All
Games for the Gifts of Life
A famous song, "It's a small world, after all" comes to mind when the inventor of a game is groping for direction in his daily routine of trying out patterns for a card game, Emeralda. His song says, "It's a learning game, after all," and there's a light. 498 Words. 2007.

vi071128
Productive Play
Senior Game Inventor's Manual for the 21st Century
He began with a quotation of Confucius: "Better to play games than do nothing at all." Then he con-

sidered recent literature from the field of gerontology on the value of work and the importance of seniors in today's changing world. A game is what results. 715 Words. 2007.

vi080102
You Get Ten Artworks
Emeralda Artists Trading Cards
You have ten artworks that you must convert into Emeralda Artist Trading Cards. 134 Words. 2008.

vi080112
Fusing Worlds
A Role for Video
On a regular basis the author takes walks with a friend to discuss the possibilities of a game-based experience revolving around the making and exchange of art in the age of digital reproduction. This essay springs from his friend's comment about patents. 985 Words. 2008.

vi080122
Hear Say
Aural Dimension Gets an Airing
An aged artist is surprised to discover his ideas are being discussed online. In a forum on Seattle's ArtDish, he found a running dialog started when someone said the author was partly responsible for a trend in art in the region—and someone got it right. 820 Words. 2008.

vi080201
Emeralda Seminar
Listing Structural Members of a Game Design
He received a spreadsheet from a collaborator enumerating the hours that they have spent together working on the invention of the game, Emeralda. Something about the number of hours resembles an investment in a mutual enterprise, and invites continuation. 882 Words. 2008.

vi080211
Sixteen Days
Coinciding Days from Past to Current Year of Living Copiously
Sixteen cards represent sixteen days, sixteen artworks, sixteen essays and sixteen descriptions of the artworks on the face of the card. 376 Words. 2008.

vi080221
Grandpa Stories
Regarding our Family Art Collection
For a period of days the author has been searching his journals that he wrote over thirty years ago, looking for a certain event. A waste of time? He wonders. What would his granddaughter think about him, reading these years from now? Is legacy important? 216 Words. 2008.

vi080302
Listing Priorities
Very Interesting Hours to Spend
Daily when he goes into his studio, dozens of options await him. It's a good feeling, like very

wealthy person walking into his counting house to count his money. The projects around his studio are both tangible and intangible, and complementary. 495 Words. 2008.

vi080411
Sequence Dilemma
Excel Spreadsheet or Access Database for Artist Trading Cards
He hits an obstacle in his pathway toward making a deck of artist trading cards that aligns with his life's work. A certain work turns up he made 43 years ago but which he did not enter in his database. How can he put it in the deck without starting over? 278 Words. 2008.

vi080511
Fitting Technology
Fourth in a Series of Twelve Tasks for the Leader in Learning
In the digital age, Fitting Technology into this need requires decades of experience in the mechanical age, early adoption of electronic analog and digital media, and an intellectual study of the expertise involved. 2068 Words. 2008.

vi080521
Control Structure
Audience interaction
When someone purchases an article from an artist's trove, then Control Structure comes in the form of a built response of the artist and their community. It is an instance of artist and patron, or audience interaction—people in an act of humanity. 1320 Words. 2008.

vi080531
Functional Program
The Subcontractor Row
To understand my Role, I am obliged to respond to the queries posed by the six labels: What, How, Where, Why, When and Why. These are spread across the Subcontractor Row. 889 Words. 2008.

vi080610
Major Organizations
List of organizations important to the business
The author describes the planner role of scoping out the field, within the context of Emeralda: Games for the Gifts of Life, specifically addressing Learn Printmaking Online. The Planner makes lists of people who are important to the business. 571 Words. 2008.

vi080620
Art Department Wrecking Yard
A tour with William Folkestad
The author writes about taking William Folkestad on a tour of the Art Department Wrecking Yard to show him what resulted from the deconstruction era. The former school had pathways crisscrossing through a courtyard like a grave yard. 1866 Words. 2008.

vi080630

Introducing Zach Man!
Variant on Enterprise Architecture – A Framework by John
Two meet weekly to discuss the future of art, business and technology. One has a background in engineering that is as well developed as the other man's development in arts. Their meetings center on a functional enterprise one of them calls Emeralda Works. 865 Words. 2008.

vi080710
Wanted: Intelligent Company
Qualifications of applicants
Following a discussion with his co-worker, the author recalls a diagram he made showing short, medium and long-term goals. For the first time he sees a logical List of Important Things to the Business and fits it to the John Zachman framework in progress. 253 Words. 2008.

vi080730
True Fiction
Game design
The author writes thoughts on how to design his game, Emeralda, where the professor is missing and his legacy. He is working with a game designer who is a little late with her demonstration of their next move. 380 Words. 2008.

vi080809
Deep Emeralda
Multitasking Comes to Game Play
He's cleaning off his real desktop to make room for his new computer, Harry, and he finds a piece of paper with scribbled notes on it. This will have to do for today's essay, and he types it in and files it with the other essays for the Video 'Zine entry. 213 Words. 2008.

vi080819
Amina's Story
Backstory for a Demonstration
Having watched a 60-second video created by Janet Fisher—a computer game designer—the author writes a narrative to provide the on-screen action with a short back story. He creates the account from the point-of-view of the star of the video, Amina Seattle. 1244 Words. 2008.

vi080829
Real Cards
Meeting Card Carrying Requirements
A session in the MMORPG, Second Life, has this artist—who visualizes being a great teacher in an age of digital reproduction—thinking about a game he would invent that combines real things (Artist Trading Cards) as part of a virtual world called Emeralda. 1138 Words. 2008.

vi080918
Ten Reasons for an Artist's Entrepreneurial Incubator
Lifting the country to a higher level
The author calls artists to aid their country in sharing their imagination, discoveries, inventiveness and creativity to help lift the United States to a new, higher level in the global community. 1096 Words. 2008.

vi080928
Specification
Game Design Document for Emeralda
The author writes specifications of his game design for Emeralda. "Learning Printmaking Online, Sustainable, playful, apposite and local – this is how it has to be." This contains the game overview, features of the game and the delivery platform. 1302 Words. 2008.

vi081008
Print and Video Game
Keith Devlin inspirations
The author is excited about Keith Devlin's assessment that video games will replace the printing press. There's hope for his game, Emeralda. Devlin's comparison between printing and video games fuels him to make Emeralda an online printmaking course. 418 Words. 2008.

vi081018
Complementary Manuscripts
Writing and Acting in the Roles of Artist and Teacher
Every day he must undertake writing tasks, and two of these tasks he calls the centerpiece of his calling—an artist and teacher in the age of digital reproduction. One task is writing in two manuscripts about press making and a bible and essays like this. 716 Words. 2008.

vi081028
Imaginary Interview
Pretending Emeralda is Launched
This art professor who thinks of video games as his continuing his printmaking education writes this imaginary interview. He was inspired to do this after listening to a radio interview with a choreographer who had adapted Cinderella to bollywood dancing. 1400 Words. 2008.

vi081117
Screenplay Writing in Emeralda
Locations of Screenplays in Emeralda Directories
The author writes about the starting point for the players of his Emeralda game. 286 Words. 2008.

vi081127
Little Prints Revisited
A flower of an idea on ice
A chance visit to a shop specializing in sports trading cards makes the author review an idea he had two years before to have a gallery that specialized in little prints of all kinds, such as Artist Trading Cards, Artists' Stamps, and other little things. 556 Words. 2008.

vi081207
Art of Selling Conceptual Estate
Selling conceptual business
The author's goal is to sell his businesses that have

not yet shown a profit, businesses that are in fact still are conceptual. Two streams of consciousness inform his plans: Conceptual art of the 1970s and The Boeing Airplane Company use of simultaneity. 1244 Words. 2008.

vi090102
Stamps 'N Stories Then and Now
Promoting an Old Story to the Realm of Interaction
The purpose of Stamps 'N Stories, his first attempt at a video game, was to introduce the back stories of artworks that he made over forty years' span. Now, as "Emeralda: Learn Printmaking Online" looms large on his radar, he wonders if he can re-cycle it. 627 Words. 2009.

vi090112
My Virtual Profile
Masking the missing professor
Assigned a simple task of submitting a profile in re-entering the classroom, the author follows the instructions of a distant, virtual professor and enters a state of the art of living, learning and practicing in a both a virtual world and the real world. 405 Words. 2009.

vi090122
Emeralda A La Mode
The Mode of Presentation of a Game to Learn Printmaking
Like a good student, the inventor of a user-interface for learning printmaking online reads in his homework book every day. Currently he is stuck on a hard assignment for which he has to study ten steps for making a digital game based learning experience. 1501 Words. 2009.

vi090201
Medium, Platform and Genre
Comparisons of Possible Ways to Deliver Printmaking
Third in a series of essays that answer the challenge of describing the ten part development of Emeralda: Learn Printmaking Online according to a checklist provided in a book titled Digital Storytelling. The author is plans to teach printmaking via games. 2495 Words. 2009.

vi090303
Premise for Teaching Fine Art Online
Principles and Purposes of a 21st Century Art Professor
The phenomena around video games—whether found on a compact disc, built into the chipset of a console, or delivered over the Web or in virtual worlds—is the art form of the 21st Century. You can teach how it has a scope for creativity by blended learning. 665 Words. 2009.

vi090313
Printmaking in the Bad Old Days
How Printmaking Compares Today with Years Gone By
This professor of printmaking has seen both ways

that printmaking was taught and the way printmaking could be taught as cognition of the roots of the medium rises to a tipping point. He uses two people—students of printmaking—to illustrate his comparison. 875 Words. 2009.

vi090402
Why A Millionaire
Accounting for Unrealized Gains
Taking into account the times, the economy and the world situation, the author enumerates reasons he, along with his family, friends and former students, have millions in unrealized gains owing to market conditions and his documented intellectual capital. 586 Words. 2009.

vi090412
Steward Shade Profile
Character Description of Stewart Shade in "Hunt for the
The genre mockumentary pretends to be rooted in actuality—real history—because it behaves like a documentary or biography; but it is fiction, subverting fact-based storytelling and TV. In Stewart's story he surmounts his disability challenges only to die. 489 Words. 2009.

vi090522
Killing Harris
Harris Sweed Disappears on Two Dog Island
Pursuing a video game backstory, Harris Sweed sees himself disappearing into the plot of the tale itself. Ten protagonists of the "Hunt for the Emeralda Treasure" conspire to digest him, as it were, like feasting cannibals. Harris' role merges in theirs. 1145 Words. 2009.

vi090601
Ted Fun
Searching for Reasons to Cooperate Using Clay Shirky
The author takes the directive from a co-operative co-worker and visits TED the first time. In searching for lectures on cooperation, he finds Clay Shirky and extracts key phrases that fit his own need to answer the question posed yesterday: Why Cooperate? 1330 Words. 2009.

vi090611
Dusty's School
A Screenplay
Three inciting incidents combine in yet another attempt to merge tradition and technology in a virtual world. This artist (who would be a teacher) writes another treatment of his idea. Lectured on cooperation, marshmallows and encyclopedias start him out. 286 Words. 2009.

vi091009
Fourth Community
Art Education for Skotos?
This essay is about researching Skotos Tech, Inc., a game company backed by Alacrity Ventures. The author is an art professor who has a plan to teach some studio art with blended online learning—a

plan he believes is appropriate for a 21st Century artist. 278 Words. 2009.

vi091019
Everything I Needed to Know I Learned After College
Reflecting on a Golden Era
He didn't think about it until now, but what he learned in college reached its pull date at the onset of the age of digital reproduction. The older age of mechanical reproduction was the stock basis of his college education, so he had to return to school. 1106 Words. 2009.

vi091108
Flash EATC
Searching for a Use for a Flash Ecard
Second day of his search for a way to replace his old, kludgey, time-and-labor intensive Artist Trading Cards with a design that is both virtual (or digital) and also made into paper cards quickly and cheaply. Text on a flash e-card website helps him out. 477 Words. 2009.

vi091128
Clockwork Press
Secret of the Plasteel
It was late in the day when it came to light there was a secret clockwork in the Plasteel press. Not a clockwork as such, but obviously inspired by that book, Longitude, the story of the mariner's wooden clockwork. Turn the wheel, and ghosts came to life. 729 Words. 2009.

vi091223
About Video
First Day on the Video Domain-of-Expertise
The old professor ruminates on times gone by, when video as an art form was still something new to introduce to his students. He merged video with his printmaking world and, therefore, today, as he designs a videogame for printmaking, video is part of it. 905 Words. 2009.

Video 'N Print (AKA VP)

Video 'N Print Island seen late in the day, approaching from the Island of Video.

Video 'N Print, like ArtsPort, is proximate to Emeralda City and connected by a daily ferry boat run but only one-way, i.e., from the island to Emeralda City or Video. The chief occupation here is one of connectivity between video and similar kinds of electronic or digital imaging and traditional printing.

vp720615
Video Year Journals
A part of local media art lore
In the early '70s this art professor won grants to experiment with TV tools as artistic instruments. Keeping with the academic discipline, he made journals on each of the years this project lasted. Printmaking is his native medium, as these journals show. 468 Words. 1972.

vp780909
Journal Entry, Sat. Apr. 9, 1978
Hard Video
The author writes his observations of himself, finishing a Video Workshop. He was conscious of his students busily producing their works while he was visibly not doing anything. He was discouraged of the lack of content and human presence in media arts. 312 Words. 1978.

vp840515
Bill Ritchie at Tacoma Community College
Perspectives on video
Highlights of a 1984 videotape made with Bill Ritchie who was a guest speaker at the Honors Colloquium at Tacoma Community College. He showed examples of his computer-related artwork and discussed his own new perspectives on the esthetics of computer art. 1498 Words. 1984.

vp870615
Ed Marquand Featured
In It's Your Portfolio video
Spring is show season, says the introduction to

this front-page feature article for Video 'N Print's Newsletter, Spring 1987 issue. This one features Ed Marquand, a Seattle designer. These articles were used in the Ritchie's Video occasional newsletter. 536 Words. 1987.

vp870620
Pinhead Printmaking
Art, computers and printmaking
One of the articles in the 1987 Ritchie's Video 'N Print Magalog about dot-matrix printers and how their pin-heads (the printing heads that replaced typewriters) became universal imaging devices. The result can sometimes be turned into traditional prints. 639 Words. 1987.

vp910615
Artists' Bookworks Video Transcript in Japanese
Pioneering Living Prints in book arts with Japanese translation
This is the English wording prepared for Japanese narration based on a teacher's narrative as he is showing printmaking students a special collection of books. The books feature the use of printmaking in creative design, illustration and new technologies. 2935 Words. 1991.

vp910715
Japanese Woodcut Workshop Critique
A Course in Four Sections on videotape
These are notes made while the writer watched the premier version of a videotape on woodcut made by Izumi Kuroiwa and Mark Leonard. The team asked Bill Ritchie, who is their former professor, to critique the tape before they made the final edited version. 859 Words. 1991.

vp920829
Who Are the Ghosts?
Searching for the Pilot
The author seeks audiences of tomorrow, calculating where they'll be found. He thinks of air travelers and makes an imaginary visit to the ship's pilot's cabin, a beginning of his quest for an answer to the question: Who are the ghosts in the new machine? 1768 Words. 1992.

vp951224
Village of Dreams
Put TCWA in PATCWA's Town Plan
Striving to visualize Tech Corps Washington as it might exist in five years, during what would be the final summer of this century, the author conjures up an image of an intergenerational tradition-and-technology center where teachers reinvent themselves. 2078 Words. 1995.

vp951225
Journal Entry, Mon. Dec. 25, 1995
Progress with PATCWA as TCWA'S Village of Dreams
Notes recorded from the author's "palmtop" B.O.S.S. computer. The author writes about the progress in the vision of PATCWA as TCWA'S Village of Dreams. He praises his wife for coming

with him to PE. He was satisfied with PE and MegaMemory studies. 190 Words. 1995.

vp960123
Journal Entry, Tue. Jan. 23, 1996
Milestone in Volunteer Work
Notes recorded from the author's "palmtop" B.O.S.S. computer. The author writes about the milestone in volunteer work at McClure Middle School, including video. He hopes he can continue doing such things when his salary reaches 61K through RINC. 184 Words. 1996.

vp960307
A Lifework Video
Impossible Dream?
Like a disease that slowly invades a person's body, social problems develop in a country. Fear and ignorance, the vice-regent generals in a subtle war against peoples' morale and self-esteem, are fed by TV. Ritchie's Video would like to fight them. 1931 Words. 1996.

vp960928
Emeralda Solitaire
Commissioned Game
Asked by the editor of Video 'N Print to explain Emeralda for video imaging readers, the author opens the box, explains the contents, cuts the deck and begins. 1393 Words. 1996.

vp961016
A perfect day at Video 'N Print
Restoring an old connection
A Gruddite Apprentice-User goes on a treasure-hunt, searching for a possible lead or thread to recreate the "continuity connection" that stimulated communication among print and other media artists worldwide. 814 Words. 1996.

vp970104
The Master of Sais revisited
Testing the waters of advanced degrees on the Net
The Intelligent Agent measures our Mastery on the Internet's World Wide Web. She is slow; in the interim, so to speak, we're in the waiting room to read and write as we wish. This article is about apprenticeships and the perspective of print and video. 2143 Words. 1997.

vp970123
Journal Entry, Thu. Jan. 23, 1997
Wis-boomer Game, HISC and "Invest in Labor"
The author writes about a game wis-boomers can play partly on-line and in studios, schools and museums. He considers HISC and seeing Ritchie's Inc. compared to Daniel Smith and Dale Chihuly. He also considers the "invest in labor" statement and doing it. 299 Words. 1997.

vp970124
Watching my master
Print, video and digital ghosts in the new machine
Once, twenty years ago, a famous master teacher

stood up a video art class and became the subject of a spoof on new, pure information theory. The professor of that class discovers a parallel in a new article, and how mastery may be learned on-line. 1584 Words. 1997.

vp970315
Rewind and Fast-forward
Prints and Video, Video and Prints
Ten days completes a cycle, for the author, as he tours his imaginary arts and technology theme park and finds himself back where he started, at ArtsPort. Life is like a videotape to some people, who think they can fast forward or edit over the bad parts. 2517 Words. 1997.

vp970404
Between two worlds
Pushing and pulling
Printmaking and video seem to be in different worlds, but when you make a print of an image that had part of its origin in the video medium, you are pushing your way away from an old world and gravity, toward a new world in outer space. 693 Words. 1997.

vp970424
Amazing Stories
30,000 Years under the Sea
Using a visualization technique he learned on the radio, the author speculates on the emerging structure of a connected CD/ROM game called "Emeralda." 1570 Words. 1997.

vp971020
Speaking from the future
No time for Leonardo
A new degree is on the horizon: "Masters of Digital Art". Mastery of processes and thick knowledge were prerequisites for Masters' Degrees. Now, who teaches the Masters? Can mastery and depth of knowledge match today's speed of technological change? 1505 Words. 1997.

vp971119
The database game
Dynatenerary for a year of living copiously
This is the era when the end of the information age has come and the beginning of the communication age is beginning. To the person who has worked for 20, 30, or 40 or more years in the "Precarious professions," such dates with destiny are familiar. 1274 Words. 1997.

vp980207
Buying Articles On-line from Video 'N Print
How to use DebitNet for reading material
When DebitNet was introduced, it appeared to be a perfect way to sell articles online, and the author proceeded to think through--in words--how the process may work. Later, DebitNet sent word they would be changing, and a year later there's little to say. 1107 Words. 1998.

vp980208

ICED in the New Millennium
The Vanishing Green Button
A cooperative project to involve dentists and their staff members in cybernetics begins with a critical view of the printing press. Paper and printing dominate marketing and sales, but these will change when people compare print's costs to new technology. 1537 Words. 1998.

vp980209
First Congress of DISCO-OP
Video 'N Print Meets the Healthcare Sector
Following an intuitive and rational paths toward cooperation with people in a healthcare sector, this artist/writer thinks he is at the first congress of his vision: A cooperative venture between artists and dentists, closing with his resolution to go on. 607 Words. 1998.

vp980503
Bernoulli's Utility Values in the Video Landscape
An Emeralda game designer fantasy
Bernoulli's utility value answers the riddle posed by a new and unfamiliar image on the video screen--as unfamiliar as the odd, striated landscape in this writer's vision. The essay is an account of a fantasy voyage to the island in Emeralda's Great Lake. 543 Words. 1998.

vp980513
A Newbies Notes from Cell Number 10
An encounter of the first kind
The demonstration in Cell 10--either Row or Column formation--shows that it pulls together other regions into an overall map. On this day the Newbie is in the domain of Video 'N Print, an ideal overall format because this bridges video and printmaking. 920 Words. 1998.

vp980523
Video 'N Print Reading Library
Flash Fiction RE the SS United States
Video art in the 1970s was a process of improvisation, where there were no scripts, no professional video systems operator, and no audience. Records of the pioneering days are skimpy, but the stories as to how these artists gained from it begin to unfold. 637 Words. 1998.

vp980602
Addiction and Emeralda
Loving and Living Prints
I am inventing Emeralda for love, the habit of loving. Emeralda is based on addictions, or habits. There are good addictions. Love, for example, Is good, and it becomes an addiction. I'm working on becoming addicted to love. Emeralda is a way of doing it. 612 Words. 1998.

vp980612
Demo in Getting Started at Video 'N Print
Selected from Emeralda Rules of Play
You've been lurking; you're a rare kind of printmaker, one who's an early user of a computer for expressive graphics. You're thinking, "What's in it

for me?" as you stare at the screen and the selections-ten islands of domains of expertise in printmaking. 579 Words. 1998.

vp980702
The Man who took his Game Away
Coming of Age after the Cold War
There was a man who lost his way one day and found himself, over thirty years later, in a strange land. Soon he realized he was in Russia. At the time he was lost, his country was at war with Russia. People called it a cold war, yet it was really a . . .. 2436 Words. 1998.

vp980712
Closure in the Blanks
Coloring Books and Relief Printmaking
The first prints were hand prints and did not require paper. Also, they were already colored-in, so it was some time before the idea of using lines to depict solids in printing evolved into relief printing as we know it today, and coloring books. . . . 1016 Words. 1998.

vp980722
The superiority of prints
Visions and Values of A Printmaker
Here on the island of knowledge of printmaking and video, we prove again and again the superiority of prints. By superiority, I refer to their value in learning and changing according to Natural laws. Prints are aligned with the values of our . . .. 1992 Words. 1998.

vp980801
Looking back on Ledger Day
ToDOIT and getting at Rites
The magic combination of investing in yourself while you invest in other peoples' ventures is achievable if you blend your Rites with theirs. The author uses the movie Planet of the Apes to begin a parable starting his fictional treatment of journalizing. 529 Words. 1998.

vp980811
Commercializing Video and Printmaking
Crossing the thresh-hold of virtual reality
My students hesitated at the door, the big double-wide doorway that was the main entry way to the large room where their prints would be displayed. They craned their necks, looked cautiously around and tried their best to see into the room without . . .. 1526 Words. 1998.

vp980821
Linking Video, Prints and ArtsPort
Hand-transferring legacy from analog to digital
News releases say new schools are popping up that teach hi-tech, low-touch to produce industry-grade artists and designers. Emeralda presents a different side and a different program for empowerment. This former professor of art copy-writes over the news. 1303 Words. 1998.

vp980831

Case Study
Diane Gabaldon
In Emeralda, the expression Legacy transfer is part of Emeralda Methods of Play. Emeralda was conceived and developed in the context of cybernetics. Legacy transfer comes from a practice called concurrent concept, design, engineering, marketing and sales. 236 Words. 1998.

vp980910
Emeralda for Dummies
The prints in the video landscape
Part ??, Emeralda for Dummies. Printmaking and video blended in the '70s and nothing has been the same since. After 25 years, everything is ready for a great new world wide game: The imagined fantastic video landscape. Tapes become prints and then beyond. 779 Words. 1998.

vp980920
Calls for a Transcript
ICED T
Part IX of Emeralda for Dummies. When a strange phone call sent the inventor back fifteen years in time he had an opportunity to demonstrate the how and why of the ICED T principle works for him. He learned about T-shaped skills from a book by Dr. Barton. 1041 Words. 1998.

vp980930
Up to the Past
Prints and video
It is useful to look upon the rear view effect of printed video images. Prints give you an indirect view of things, like watching a solar eclipse with a pinhole device so you will not injure your eyes-- which could happen if you look directly into the sun. 1132 Words. 1998.

vp981010
Equality and Equity
Reason and video stats
From C. West Churchman's book, The Systems Approach Statistics, the author draws some conclusions about his own teaching in the arts: When the money no longer makes the effort worthwhile, they cease attempts to teach when the structure makes it too tough. 596 Words. 1998.

vp981020
Q and A from Video N Print Agents of Emeralda Inventor
Emeralda Inventor Interviews
On their Video 'N Print Isle--their Domain-of-Expertise--Agents interview the Emeralda Inventor about printing and non-printing media based on video. They focus on electronic media convergence and learn about his bridgework among technologies in printing. 8728 Words. 1998.

vp981109
New Moves
From sketchpad to drawing board
Daily, in Emeralda's computer games, players have a new design on the screen--like tossing dice

makes different numbers. Icons scatter. Relationships to the underlying maps of Emeralda change. Print media do not capture these; a locus is all that remains. 1297 Words. 1998.

vp981119
Wishing for a Review
Is it a game or a work of art?
A fake review written by the master faker, the Inventor of Emeralda, on the occasion of reading the novel by Richard Powell, "Prisoner's Dilemma." This review is copy-written on the MacArthur Fellow's story about a likeness of the Emeralda Region creator. 305 Words. 1998.

vp981129
First Thing in an Emeralda Morning
View from a high altitude and attitude
The Emeralda Inventor visualizes the first thing he does in a day of play, which is change the screen image of the island where the day's play is placed--the Meni--floats into view. This required manual operators, which will--in the future--be automata's. 1881 Words. 1998.

vp981209
Full Circle
Meeting the kid in me
The Emeralda Inventor, in his daily routine activity of moving icons around the display screen, realizes he has taken to being caught in a children's game as he was thirty years ago, with the difference this round that he sees the game for the first time. 728 Words. 1998.

vp990207
Welcome to Video 'N Print
Your Portfolio, please
Video 'N Print is the Emeralda Isle where bridging is the object of the game, referring to bridges among the world of print and the newer worlds of video. Portfolio developing in the course of a Resident Stay at Video 'N Print is about bridging processes. 671 Words. 1999.

vp990208
Symmetry Video and Printmaking
Union of science and art
Pioneers in video and prints recall scientists of the last half-century who linked natural sciences and arts. With one leg in science and one in art, their performances and publications--as seen by this author--demonstrate video and printmaking parallels. 888 Words. 1999.

vp990209
If I Knew Then What I Know Now
Old timer's reflection on video and print
An artist in her 'nineties is interviewed about her videotape and how she produced and distributed it. She is typical of the creative teacher who creates, invents, discovers and imagines how to expand a vision beyond the wall of her studio or art gallery. 724 Words. 1999.

vp990210
Fantasy Congress of DISCO-OP
Keynote Address at DISCO-OP
As if he is part of the proceedings of the 2nd Congress of a fantasy cooperative for dentists' information and communications service, the author writes a speech while he's on a walk with his PDA (Personal Digital Assistant). And he thinks about online ed. 459 Words. 1999.

vp990211
Mount Tetra in the Distance
Other peoples' enterprises and You
You'd never know he invented the three sister mountains in Emeralda Region, painted them dozens of times, meditated on them, and also hid a fourth secret mountain, Tetra, deep in the center of Emeralda Region's Great Lake. The author writes as in a dream. 639 Words. 1999.

vp990212
Video Antiques Road Show
Artifacts from a foregone conclusion
A fantasy presenter opens a video catalog on an old Video 'N Prints Web site and delights in seeing that it had not been updated since December 1997. "Wow-there's an old one!" exclaiming, "In HotDog Pro--I haven't seen that editor around for a long time!" 643 Words. 1999.

vp990213
Freedom and Equity
Principles of Play
Emeralda play is like printmaking, a game with no object it is wholly devoted to process as an end itself. With no goals or need to measure for equality or distinction, equity builds for the player, using play as the touchstone of civilization on his PDA. 825 Words. 1999.

vp990407
The Little Princess
A story tellers notes
The author quotes a storyteller in an encounter, describing an image of a fantasy planet. "People, watch out for the carbon oxides! Oh! I knew a planet that was inhabited by fearful people. Yet they neglected their carbon oxide-eating friends, the trees." 779 Words. 1999.

vp990408
The Last Time I Saw the University
Thoughts while transcribing old videos
The University's engineering and health sciences are somewhat alike to the author, an art professor. Speaking technically, he explains how a reading of a poem by Dylan Thomas where this poet refers to the labors over his art and craft forms his viewpoint. 493 Words. 1999.

vp990409
Little Voices
Checkpoints on the road to DISCO-OP
The author recalls a TV sitcom called "Mork and Mindy." It may have been several of his art teach-

ers who pointed to his crossover skills like those in the TV show, and they made art appear similar to dental work in his vision. He calls it the "Mork Effect". 1627 Words. 1999.

vp990410
Benchmarking Intelligent Healthcare Organizations
Investment opportunities in your intellectual capital
Education and healthcare workers might consider investing their human structural intellectual capital in the Internet, according to this writer. These people have a unique opportunity--thanks to the World Wide Web--to invest in a growing natural resource. 775 Words. 1999.

vp990411
The Worst Teacher in Class
My short happy career as an art professor
A past art teacher reflects on past errors and how these may now affect his former students' effectiveness in teaching. Global peace is a science and an art, but--as he thinks about an e-mail message from his student's student--he failed making the point. 1821 Words. 1999.

vp990412
Seeing the Sites
Cyber tour from the mouths of babes
To write about the sites of Emeralda means seeing them as though through the eyes of a baby, the first views, as it were, of an idea this inventor wants for human kind. He begins by telling a myth of the Women Who Fell to Earth, the first words of a baby. 1176 Words. 1999.

vp990607
108 Views of VideoGame
Reflections on the Last Day of Perfect Information
The inventor of Emeralda is a survivor of the crash of the video art craft that was created, launched, and fueled by game strategies and probabilities. Video Game began in a deserted quarry in central Washington and ended in a lush green emerald corridor. 656 Words. 1999.

vp990609
Emeralda for Babies
First Signs of Risk
Responding to the words of wisdom from a ghost in his new machine - David Viscott - the author spells out this guide for newbies to Emeralda Play. He says you create two directories - Family and Enterprise - and you branch out, with guilt as your vice regent. 1868 Words. 1999.

vp990610
New incarnation of LMASOCACAD
BAM Vision
The building of a museum without walls is also the building of a museum with new walls, a paradox in which the author finds a dilemma tale brews. It's a complement to Emeralda, the game he's inventing, and an opportunity to resolve the prisoner's

dilemma. 1971 Words. 1999.

vp990611
ArtsPort Customs
Getting in to his domain
ArtsPort's owner experiences a moment of panic as he approaches the first firewall at ArtsPort, realizing that he may have forgotten his credentials and passport. He is reminded of a cartoon. Time seems to be running out, and soon his deed will be tested. 582 Words. 1999.

vp000106
Head Voice
Specifying Emeralda
Imagining a voice in his head that commands him to specify a cooperative, online, interactive game that can be played among many people on portable devices, the inventor of Emeralda does some brainstorming. He sees characters and plot line are scientific. 1831 Words. 2000.

vp000406
Tripp's Tips and Tricks
Inventing a life
The artist gets introduced to a CEO of a startup in Seattle and discovers something about thinking. Asked if he would be interested in writing a story about the rise of the CEO and his startup project, the artist-turned-writer contemplates thought itself. 448 Words. 2000.

vp000421
Art Essay Online
Capitalizing on my obsession with art and technology
Ten women and ten men, a mix of personalities from arts' professions, are turned loose on ten islands on a great fantasy virtual lake. During this 360-day resident-stay period, this author (inventor and producer of the game Emeralda) writes another report. 935 Words. 2000.

vp000930
Be an Angel, Dead Artist
Signing the Last Love Letter
Introducing a new kind of bookkeeping, this mid-career artist looks forward to new ways of seeing his role as the artist, crafts person and designer outside of the mechanical, industrial era. As a printmaker and book artist, bookkeeping has a new meaning. 1775 Words. 2000.

vp001213
Me and EarthSave
I saw a movie one time
He is thinking about an organization called Earth-Save, whose founder and members believe much can be done to save the Earth's life sustaining capabilities if only people would change to different diets. The author draws a parallel with his art and crafts. 3094 Words. 2000.

vp001224
Modest Proposal for Dentists Care

Artistry meets Dentistry and History is in the Making
The author wants dental health care for artists and so he proposes a partnership among four: the foundations of Dentistry, Artist Trust, and the software side of online interactive games. Like trying for a perfect print, he gives his vision another trial. 1100 Words. 2000.

vp010103
The Biggest RPG Ever
Emeralda at Sea
He's framing a picture-his best snapshot-of his vision of Emeralda, the Role Playing Game for printmakers and all the players who have a passion for living prints. Then, out of the blue like a flash: It's a cruise game and the ultimate prize he's seeking. 540 Words. 2001.

vp010113
Q & A on Emeralda Fantasy Cruise Package
Imaginary Dialog with a Silverpoint Artist
Prior to meeting a silverpoint artist who he singled out as a potential buyer of a fantasy cruise package promotional meeting, the author exercises his imagination to figure out how to create a useful offering for other highly imaginative people like her. 1331 Words. 2001.

vp010123
Virtual Tours Art University
A Bigger Flash
It seems like every time the ITinerate Professor turns a page in his story there's another opportunity knocking at the doors of his inner phrontisterion. Now this: An alliance with an art supply store to supply virtual tours art university student needs. 1125 Words. 2001.

vp010202
Suites of Dreams
Video 'N Prints at my Fantasy Condo
The author has a distant vision in mind he believes is rooted in the art of printmaking and multimedia technologies. He awakens with a vision of condominium homeowners' management meetings-not the perfect studios he wants to dream about. Then, he sees why. 2776 Words. 2001.

vp010222
In Retro My Favorite Game
Among the Emeralda Suite of Online, Interactive, Cooperative Games
The author reflects on the process of his 40-year retrospective from the standpoint of video and printmaking. It is one of the ten domains-of-expertise he has created in the fantasy region of Emeralda-the home site for his lifelong dreams, Perfect Studios. 1560 Words. 2001.

vp010304
Possibilities and Probabilities in the Age of Digital Communications
AUREL versus NAUREL
A publication called "Possibilities" is targeted as a mis-leader in the realm of what is probable, which is that it exists in an old frame of reference known as many-to-many. However, not much is really possible compared to what is possible in new ways. 2189 Words. 2001.

vp010314
Professor Frankenstein
The Best Ones are Free
The old university model professor was one who could teach, research and practice all at the same time, in one place. Unfortunately, there were too few who could do all three with excellence. In the new, online university, it is found that there are many. 553 Words. 2001.

vp010324
Art Professor's Goodbye Wave
It took some convincing from "my shrink" . . .
Is there a fail-safe system for people when forced to abandon a lifelong dream of retirement? Our age of digital communication, a new experience is opening up thanks to the Internet. Aging professor and other experts can retune and renew their usefulness. 2231 Words. 2001.

vp010403
Who is Dusty, Anyway
Soundtrack from a fantasy video
Under the rules of Emeralda the player applies himself a project using instruments that are suitable to the tasks such as video and print. One of the results is this videotape and writing down and printing the transcript of the dialogue on the soundtrack. 4127 Words. 2001.

vp010413
If She Had Lived in Mondragon
Profile of an Unemployed Person
At Video 'N Print, an Isle of Expertise in Printing and Video Information Technology, encountering an unemployed person sets the author on an inquiry into the meaning and practice of the co-operative structure adapted to an era of digital communication. 1659 Words. 2001.

vp010513
Things That Go Clack in Your Daydreaming
Writing a DVD
On a day-long road trip the artist/scholar gets drowsy, pulls over and naps. But his sleep is interrupted by a recurring phrase: You're writing for DVD. Annoyed at the intrusion, he gives up his sleep and writes an essay instead-half dreaming, half alert. 1714 Words. 2001.

vp010602
Going Well to EarthSave2022
Proverbial Guidelines
With a few square inches and six minutes to save the Earth's life sustaining capabilities, what should we do? As Knowledge Workers we're a breed apart from ones who appear to have answers, knowing secret pathways to solving world problems. Here's my plan. 1468 Words. 2001.

vp010622
Old Professors Alert
A Few Prescient ITinerates Needed
I am an ITinerant Professor of Art. I can program my software so it will allow me to capitalize the I and the T in ITinerant. I turned my spell-checker off. I will next turn off poorly conceived and performing art education machinery by using DVD on a PC. 2125 Words. 2001.

vp010712
Return of the Professor
Big Day at Video 'N Print
The Virtual Assistant to the ITinerant Professor plays with what coming to one's senses and taking leave of one's senses mean in commonsense. Sense in art education in a new worldview is rising, thanks to communications, and a professors makes a comeback. 1757 Words. 2001.

vp010722
ArtStudent Revisited
The End of Lifelong Learning
Expressions like lifelong learning sound fishy when you're reared in a land where learning and teaching are set in classrooms and colleges. Movies and TV specials use campus settings for entertainment conditions as a special activity, not central to life. 1581 Words. 2001.

vp010801
Lesson Plan Teaching Emeralda Play
Passports and Gates
This artist/scholar read in a book that imaging is the key to success-especially when it comes to the ways people dream up for getting money for something that no one else has ever done. His game Emeralda is for grown-ups who still have imagination power. 1052 Words. 2001.

vp010910
Passport Habit
A Quick Note from a Traveler
He's short of time, short of attention span, short on all the things that people who do not choose to travel on the risky road he's taken. The Itinerate professor writes a few notes and logs them in his notebook, and turns back to his e-portfolio project. 322 Words. 2001.

vp010920
Dusting Your Hard Drive
Clean up after your DVD, please
The artist/scholar's prayer is, "To get as high as I can reach, and see the lands and time, a wide scope, bigger than life and encompassing death. If I should die before this disk drive is clean, then I pray there is little for anyone else to have to do." 706 Words. 2001.

vp010930
Un Escuela International de Artes por Americas Nuevos
Un concepto de curriculo sin credito a tiempo

He's beginning to see that the game he invented is more like Solitaire than Monopoly-two card/board games that used to serve as his game models. But today a new possibility opens up: Emeralda as curriculum for an international art school for the Americas. 2585 Words. 2001.

vp011109
My Dream Job at the UW
Why one professor doesn't apply
This Itinerant Professor of art's heart went pitty-pat when he read about a job listing for a position he dreamed about when he was forty. Now, at 59, he composes himself and takes a clearer, sober look at reality through the glass of his computer screen. 1695 Words. 2001.

vp011129
Your Portfolio After September 11, 2001
What good is it if it doesn't play at home?
The author makes DVDs weekly composed of fragments of past, new digital recordings and instant-camera images he made on the fly. They resemble CD-based portfolios of multimedia events, a story of his life; but if it doesn't play in America, why do it? 817 Words. 2001.

vp011209
Two Professors and the Last Rites Syndrome
One at term's end, one at the beginning of a better way
An ITinerant Professor, an almost extinct species, wanders around; instead of following a daily pathway on a campus, they walk the street and alleyways, and take notes. They don't lecture. Today's ITP uses the Internet, the WWW, and the latest thing: DVD. 1549 Words. 2001.

vp011224
In My Dream
Essay on my birthday
Many years ago when the artist told his father about his vision of the perfect studios, his father wrote on his birthday card, "To my reborn son," referring to that epiphany. Now, at 60, his father dying, he's reminded that behind every dream lies a wish. 1041 Words. 2001.

vp020103
A Crowning Achievement for Hypermedia
Acceptance into a library
The daily routine of the Emeralda player is to have a paper and a hypermedia "passport" open, allowing him to pass through the entry gate to an island of a domain of expertise. Passing the gate reminds this author of having his work accepted in a library. 1387 Words. 2002.

vp020113
Writing Between the Paragraphs Conclusion - Part 10
Afterwords to a fantasy dialog between professors
Constructing a DVD based on his sabbatical videotapes, the author concludes-at the end of his fantasy dialog-that he's making a primitive model

for his future college education. He opens by describing a vision belonging to a recent graduate he met online. 1342 Words. 2002.

vp020202
Angular Deeds
A different perspective on art education
He compares his routine activity to a blend of musical practice and chess, with manual practice as the common thread running through them, but with constant variations, renewal and reflection being the point of it all. There is no vanishing point in view. 1185 Words. 2002.

vp020222
What Could I Say about Art?
Reflections on art in the age of digital reproduction
Good work makes good art, but what is good work? Psychiatrists recently did research and found good work is balancing mission, models and mirroring. The artist who does good art is also doing good works, sometimes using all three aspects at the same time. 1120 Words. 2002.

vp020304
Letter to Tobin from Emeralda
Making Believe I'm a Good Guy
To get unstuck while trying to develop his main character for a screenplay, this amateur artist/screenwriter pretends he's written a letter to a how-to-do-it book on screenplay writing. Then he changes roles, answers himself, and bolsters his self-esteem. 727 Words. 2002.

vp020314
Augustine's Canon
A new paradigm for art in the age of digital reproduction
This author reads about the first autobiography by Augustine and sees a clue to answer the question, "What's an artist's asset database for?" Asset management and legacy transfer is the core of Emeralda, and discovering Augustine brings a new canon to mind. 920 Words. 2002.

vp020324
Validating Your Passport to Emeralda
The search for your files
The inventor of the game Emeralda explains what it means to validate an electronic passport, comparable to the electronic portfolio that universities and schools are developing for their students and faculty. He bases his e-portfolios on digital e-stamps. 902 Words. 2002.

vp020413
Journal Entry, Sat. Apr. 13, 2002
Chris Todd's Invitation
The author was invited to make a proposal for a distance learning program. Based on Elmer Gates and Wells' visions, he offered an original game interface, Emeralda. The game exceeds the limits set by current creditors and the past century's standards. 241 Words. 2002.

vp020423
Like Bingo but Better
Artists' bread and butter on the Web
He's a professor who was marginalized, but this made him pursue a far-flung goal in terms of teaching, research, practices and patrons for his art, as well as strategic global ideologies that were more important to him than local campus identity politics. 474 Words. 2002.

vp020503
Reinventing Art School
A better way for arts education
The way to reinvent art school is from under the ground up and from the blue sky down. Underground arts and satellites converge somewhere near the ground and create a hybrid of virtual, virtuous reality, and the secrets of the age of digital reproduction. 1176 Words. 2002.

vp020513
Woodcuts Online?
My day as a neighborhood resource
An ITinerant Professor, wandering around a neighborhood, gathers his thoughts and shares them with people who want or need to know what matters in his domain of expertise. On this day he plans opening a temporary studio at his neighborhood service center. 807 Words. 2002.

vp020622
If I had found a Perfect Studio
I'd be a Perfect Artist
Reverse Engineering is a way to understand systems that work near perfectly, and if a perfect system is what you want, then you can learn from RE and make measurable progress toward perfection. This artist thinks he learns from engineers and applies this. 1010 Words. 2002.

vp020702
Out and about Uptown
I Try My Feet and Laptop
Dreaming of a multimedia arts center, the ITinerant Professor of Art takes a stroll, venturing 250 feet from his cozy smart condo studio to the Caffe Vita across 5th. It's a test to see if his Perfect Studios is street legal. In other words, a test drive. 646 Words. 2002.

vp020712
Sign Me Up, Harris
Aligning the Uptown Seattle Artists Coalition
With six months' security-building in, the self-styled prisoner of Uptown Seattle tries to sign up participants in a coalition of artists, crafts people and designers who may want to develop their own asset management and legacy transfer systems like his. 479 Words. 2002.

vp020713
What IT Was Wasn't Baseball
Seattle Dreamin' Inside the Box
Half awake, half dreaming, gazing at his latest arti-

stamp creation, he sees his artist's game becoming to his cooperative studio what Universal Studios or Safeco Field is to the movies or to baseball leagues-a channel for artists' e-publishing their arts. 931 Words. 2002.

vp020722
Educating the 21st Century Art Educator
Starting with the End of the World in Mind
As fear beset the scientific world and caused them to issue dire warnings in '92, it may be a good end toward which to direct the attention of art educators. As one woman said, "Only artists and poets can save the world now." This means starting all over. 756 Words. 2002.

vp020801
Meeting More City Folk
The Public Artist/Scholar Moves Out
Over the past centuries, according to this man, the public artist and public scholar were discovered by way of bifurcating the original Itinerate Professors. He says the age of digital reproduction will rejoin them and a public artist/scholar will result. 1148 Words. 2002.

vp020811
The Case of the Missing Professor
A Teacher Nightmare
Excerpt from E-Folios: A Marketing Sketchbook, this is the second draft from the opening of a take-off of Victor Steinbrueck's famous Market Sketchbook that helped save Seattle's Public Market. The author thinks the sketchbook is a way to save his legacy. 1516 Words. 2002.

vp020821
Osler's Mistake
Unemployed Educators Can Employ Themselves
Dr. Osler said old professors should be gassed. His remark corrupted higher education, a US American mindset that spread throughout higher education for the next hundred years, created mountains of wealth for the undeserved. Professors can fight back now. 741 Words. 2002.

vp020831
Stamps and Stories from E-books and Back
A Glance at My E-book Plan for Today
The success of the e-book depends on the author, first of all, who can create inside the medium-the e-book itself. This takes knowledge, skill, and an attitude about getting money in the night, and not only from the sales of e-books but collectibles, too. 577 Words. 2002.

vp020910
About being Itinerate in the Age of Digital Reproduction
Thinking about the Northland Art Student
On the day before the anniversary of 9/11, the author wonders how it feels to be an art student at a college that's focusing on being an environmental college. The rules of the 20th Century art game are not much use; though art survives, art changes,

too. 1298 Words. 2002.

vp020920
How We Paid for the Afforestation of Emeralda Region
A Gates Prize Winner tells His Story
He is the missing professor in a story about a four-some of college students who want to raise capital for their business plan, and found their fundraising strategist mysteriously absent. He's traveling the world, leaving a trail that only they can follow. 1098 Words. 2002.

vp020930
One-upping Maria
Stealing the Show from the Print Goddess
He closed his eyes and saw what looked like the credits at a movie's end and then saw they were his cohorts' names making new prints as a wide-spread network of on-line art education and print-making students, faculty and parents. Maria's puzzle started it. 3015 Words. 2002.

vp021010
Something that may be overlooked
Real Value in Emeralda
One of the region's elder arts mavens stimulates the Emeralda tester's mind to connect with an overlooked value in the game's design-one of extending a new dimension into the evaluation of artist/teachers' performance, a value greater than thought before. 1814 Words. 2002.

vp021020
I am IT
Like a Tree
After he watches a film, and sleeps on it, and then awakens with the idea that US Americans owe it to the world to export love in abundance to repay the world for its own abundance (some of which was stolen), pundits the ITinerate Professor, "Now I'm IT!" 483 Words. 2002.

vp021030
My Screenplay of the Day
Pearlie
The virtual assistant professor is thinking of being the provisional teacher when working at the Professor's Cabinet, and there will be plenty of time to write. "Pearlie" is the life of Pearlie, Elmer Gates' loyal assistant, and the last to see him alive. 741 Words. 2002.

vp021209
Built Like a Boeing 777
Vision of a new art school
If you envision a new art school in the Pacific Northwest you might see its influences from the industrial sector and not the art museums or art schools. The Boeing Company, for example, or Microsoft or a hybrid like those of biotech will be the metaphor. 571 Words. 2002.

vp021224
Searching for Emeralda

The human behind the hand
In a mood of retrospection the ITinerate professor realizes the invention of his lifetime work dates back more years than he thought. An epiphany in 1970 (in his 3rd teaching year) he saw his career stretching before his eyes and did not like what he saw. 1001 Words. 2002.

vp030103
An Emeralda Journal
Entries from My Mobile
Noticing his article production has fallen off to nothing the essayist looks to his electronic journal-a PDA-for ideas. Instead of writing an essay, however, he starts by dumping several months' entries for a narrative of his experiment in a public place. 1148 Words. 2003.

vp030523
What Does Stamps 'N Stories Teach?
Questions for an art education techie
When he goes into his studio each day, he's conscious he's playing a game, a kind of art solitaire that he thinks could become an educational game for art students. But he wonders, "Will it work?" What would someone learn by playing his Stamps 'N Stories? 956 Words. 2003.

vp030602
Letting My Imagination Run Wild
Clicking on the little blue dot
A few short paragraphs noted by the maker of Emeralda Stamps 'N Stories as he thought about putting messages and effects inside an image on his stamps. After he wrote this brief note, he carried out his idea and used a hyperlink to pay homage to a friend. 318 Words. 2003.

vp030612
What You Learn From Playing Stamps 'N Stories
From the Game Master's Mouthpiece
Indulging in a little make-believe news story, the art professor ponders the question, "What do you learn playing this game?" The game is one he invented over a decade ago as new way to teach art on the Internet by using a multiplayer on-line game interface. 1344 Words. 2003.

vp030622
I Have a Dream
A video dream becomes reality
Thirty years ago he visualized a Web cam, decades before this existed. It would beam his studio routine to printmaking students 4 miles away. He adopted each new technology as it came on line-video, computers, and the Net. Now his vision is materializing. 1017 Words. 2003.

vp030702
A Source of Emeralda
An inventor's tale
He found an essay about J. R. R. Tolkien, and reading it he was reminded how the Lord of the Rings, long ago, had an effect on his thinking. This might be one of the reasons he invented (or discovered)

Emeralda. This essay itself inspired this reflection. 886 Words. 2003.

vp030801
A Simple Lesson for Art Student
Reading Notes
He reads and writes in a coffee shop although in his mind he's cloistered in a university reading room. The subject of his study is a new book on video games in academe and it holds the promise that someday he'll return to the perfect campus of his dream. 594 Words. 2003.

vp030831
What Do We Expect from the Professor?
A peek into the Professor's Cabinet
He writes over an article about 2 Professors' memoirs and twists the original essay into a device he can use to help navigate his way into a game. New ways of writing autobiographical fact mixed with potential life-changing eventualities await the gamers. 1073 Words. 2003.

vp030910
Exploring and Explaining Art
An Artist on Art and Teaching, Research and Practice
If he can correctly design the concept of MUS (Multi-User Studios) it would do a lot of good for the fine arts. He would get back the money lost after he was forced to resign from the UW art school. As a developer of the idea he'd be part of a team again. 370 Words. 2003.

vp030920
How to Design a User Interface for Online Art Education
Perspective of an Elder Player
He says you read and draw every day in the manner of a fine artist in the age of digital reproduction. "To learn something well, teach it." There are other kinds of advice in this essay by someone who is building a user interface using concurrent methods. 571 Words. 2003.

vp031030
Teaching Fine Art Drawing in the Age of Digital Reproduction
A Mid-term report
This researcher/practitioner has taken on the role of teacher in a community college art department. Teaching beginning drawing to two dozen students is helping him test an idea he's researched for over 20 years-teaching fine arts online, on the Internet. 1469 Words. 2003.

vp031109
Professor goes Digital in Drawing Class
Note from the missing professor's diary
Claiming there's more to the digital age than meets the eye, a teacher of beginning drawing makes an electronic portfolio of his students' work to demonstrate what he means. He begins an essay here about moving from the 20th to the 21st Century art class. 504 Words. 2003.

vp031224
Why and How to Teach Printmaking Online
Musings of a dreaming teacher
When he was asked how he would teach an on-line printmaking course, this Itinerate Professor responded by first outlining factors that decided his philosophy of printmaking. He explains how he came to his philosophy and how it determined his teaching plan. 1589 Words. 2003.

vp040124
A Project to Like
Vision of an online archive
With an eye to releasing an archive of unique videotapes he has saved for thirty years, the onetime professor considers a project to share with the university where the videos were made and a regional museum. He thinks they must result in the form of DVD. 1001 Words. 2004.

vp040222
Emeralda Goal
A Printmaker Utopia
When I left the printmaker's paradise that was the university campus I launched my quest for the perfect studio. I still have not found it, but I have located many of the tools and the needed skills in using them for as long as I have traveled these ways. 1195 Words. 2004.

vp040721
The Mini Halfwood Press on Video 'N Print
Linking the past and present
The culture of Video 'N Print in the beautiful Emeralda Region is based on the link between printmaking and electronic media art. It was named before the days of computer graphics. Now a new twist has been introduced-a tiny etching press for making video. 563 Words. 2004.

vp040810
Feeling Good as an Artist in the 21st Century
Learning what's good for the age of digital reproduction
To feel good about being an artist in this century, an artist must draw on his or her past experiences and re-purpose skills, resources and ideas to fit the new millennium. He learns that his skills can be "reinvented" for the age of digital reproduction. 1118 Words. 2004.

vp040820
MHP - a TRP Company is Born
Vision of a tiny press and what it can bring
He reflects on the past, when designing a tiny etching press was the opposite of what people wanted; bigger was better in those days. Today, "small is beautiful," because this introduces more people to the art and craft of intaglio printmaking-and a game. 666 Words. 2004.

vp040821
Warning Message
Investing in OPE may cost you
A very small warning message at the bottom of his bank's Web page hints at the truth of investing in other peoples' enterprises by purchasing stocks. He compares this to games, and gets insights into his current "investments" with another worker's studio. 949 Words. 2004.

vp040830
Is it Earthshaking?
Criteria for a new education
He's thinking about the ghosts in his new machine, an expression he coined about twenty years ago when he started out on his quest for the Perfect Studios. Today the ghost is a 12-year old boy who will start a home-schooling quest with his mother in 2004. 602 Words. 2004.

vp040909
Why Emeralda is a Tough Game
Life plan, skill and time requirements
Emeralda requires that you have a life plan, and this in itself is a tough thing for most people to have. It requires technical know-how, the kind most people over fifty-for whom Emeralda is intended-feel uncomfortable with. Finally it takes lots of time. 510 Words. 2004.

vp040919
A New Approach to Video and Stamp Art
Getting others involved in restoration work with stamps
The author gets a new idea to invite other people-artists, he assumes but maybe art students too-to participate in the process of restoring each of some thirty-six video art tapes. The first step is to produce artist stamps in both paper and digital form. 529 Words. 2004.

vp040929
Things Not What They Appear to Be
Artworks in the Age of Digital Reproduction
Works of art, especially of the visual kind addressed to the eyes as the foremost sense often mean more than meets the eye. But people must be educated or trained to know what else there is. In the age of digital reproduction, the whole story can be told. 712 Words. 2004.

vp050103
How Do I Blog?
Let Me Try One Way
Six weeks after a wise suggestion by a visitor, this artist still has not started his blogging. What's holding up the process? Every day he writes a blog-worthy essay, yet it doesn't leave his studio. This has to change, or the Emeralda play may bog down. 348 Words. 2005.

vp050113
The Persistence of Rolf
Memories of a Most Influential Printmaker
A print in homage to one of his most influential printmaking artists is his focus of now as the author considers how that artist's persistence might have influenced him more than he thought. Amid

the several concerns he has, this artist's memory persists. 879 Words. 2005.

vp050222
What's So Special about ATC
Alternatives to Fine Art
While looking at the walls of his studio lined with fine art prints this artist envisions a new kind of display. He thinks perhaps Artist Trading Cards would be more fitting for this time and place because this art form gives you more than meets your eye. 641 Words. 2005.

vp050314
Seniors Gaming
Regarding an Interview with Mihai Nadin by Thom Gillespie
The inventor of Emeralda: Games for the Gifts of Life comes across an article of extreme importance to understanding the idea he's cultivating. This is copied directly from an article he found in Digital Games Research Association, an international forum. 2461 Words. 2005.

vp050324
Debit Cards and Trading Cards
Clues to an Emerging World
Forty years ago the author imagined himself as a form that he sees that his dreams made him. At 63 he awakens in a world very different from the one he began in, like Rip Van Winkle. Examining ways for the next forty years, he comes across a curious idea. 669 Words. 2005.

vp050403
About Artist Trading Cards Meetup
Considerations from the Island of Video 'N Print
The International Game Development Association Forum lines describing their purpose provides this artist/writer with words he has been looking for to describe the Artist Trading Card Meetup in his gallery. His description is that it's a many-gated empire. 402 Words. 2005.

vp050413
Advertising in Yacht Magazines
A Novel Approach
Staring at his newest press, the Mariner Halfwood Press, the designer thinks of the idea to run advertisements in yachting and other boat magazines. Then he hits on an even better idea: A feature story about a sailing artist making prints of his journeys. 297 Words. 2005.

vp050423
Mall Fantasy
Looking into a Green Crystal Ball
News there will be a shopping mall being built near his studio, the artist looks into his emerald-colored crystal ball and sees a shop in the mall that's a gallery and showroom for his Halfwood Press. It is a vision that could come true, and there's more. 449 Words. 2005.

vp050503

Here Comes the Judge
Considerations before the Meeting of JM
It may come about soon that the inventor of Emeralda: Games for the Gifts of Life, gets a visitor in the person of a judge who can say whether or not Emeralda is really something that other people can play, or merely a fantasy of a has-been art professor. 1047 Words. 2005.

vp050523
Praise and Ridicule the Emeralda Player
The End of the Day at Video 'N Print
The end of the tenth day on his sojourn of the islands of domains-of-expertise has come. On his table are seven prints from the Emeralda Myth Emeralda Trading Card series. The artist ponders the writing of Robert Grudin, and sees a description of himself. 909 Words. 2005.

vp050612
Collegia I Want to Join
Speculating on Artists' Clubs
Reading about Vitruvius' (1st C BC) recommendation that communities-of-practice, or collegia, be formed for the art of architecture, this artist considers the same idea in light of art in the age of digital reproduction. He thinks of forming ten collegia. 1205 Words. 2005.

vp050622
Stuck in the 20th Century
Observations of a Bystander
He does not feel he's part of the art scene, this artist and professor, because when meeting people who are a part of that scene, he feels like they're in an old role that has outlasted its audiences. In particular, he challenges the notion of techno-art. 902 Words. 2005.

vp050722
Art Appreciation through Gardening and Game Design
A Perspective on a Friend's Lesson Plan
His friend is a teacher and shared a lesson plan that explains how a garden can teach young students much more than it would appear to be able to do. But there is an element missing, or misinterpreted: Video game design is an art form that could be added. 571 Words. 2005.

vp050811
Emeralda Plates
Send for yours today
The Games for the Gifts of Life isn't a game you buy in a store, but a game you play with cards that you produce yourself. The plates for these cards are metal etching plates, in copper and brass that have the images of an imaginary place called Emeralda. 1000 Words. 2005.

vp050821
Seeking the Video 'N Print Board Game
Searching for the Link between Video and Print
While searching through archives of data files on his computer, this artist—who wants to create a

game-like way of reviewing printmaking and video art according to his own experiences—senses that there's a connection between his keyboard and a board game. 994 Words. 2005.

vp050910
Reasons for a Small Press
How a Printmaker Sees His Mini Halfwood Press
An email writer comments on the fact that a press with only a six-inch wide bed is too limiting inspires the press' designer to begin a list of advantages of a small press. He enumerates costs first, and concludes with other thoughts justifying the press. 2300 Words. 2005.

vp050930
Three-in-One Game
Digital, Property and Auction Combination to Win
Forever wondering how to form his game that he calls Emeralda: Games for the Gifts of Life into one that other people can play, utilize and enjoy, the artist considers how a digital game, resource management game, and auction tracking software might work. 826 Words. 2005.

vp051010
Story Board or Business Plan?
Which is it?
Faced with the same question many people reach as they enter the last phase of their careers, this artist considers a plan to continue teaching by producing etching kits for mail order learners. Reluctant to write a plan, he tells a story. 1087 Words. 2005.

vp051020
Imagine this Alien
Professor Cann and Alex
Making the Artist's Stamp for his calendar (November 19, 2005) this Emeralda Defender gets a flash of inspiration to write some Flash Fiction. This one is a story that goes with a stamp, and he brings in a character named Alex to act in the role of guest. 642 Words. 2005.

vp051030
A New Name
EtchingIT Kit for Intaglio Printmaking
With the advent of his newest idea for playing Emeralda, a game he invented that helps him track his artistic assets, this artist ponders a name for this idea. He cannot call it by the name Emeralda. His focus is on home school children and their parents. 485 Words. 2005.

vp051109
Persistence Counts
The Habit of Consequence brings Inspiration
He tried six times to get the conditions correct for transferring a laser print to a copper plate so he could etch it. Persistence is a prerequisite for the Emeralda inventor: Games for the Gifts of Life; it's one of the gifts, he says, as he tries again. 864 Words. 2005.

vp051119
Adding Value to Halfwood Presses
The Need for Enthusiasm
The addition of enthusiasm to his Halfwood Press line is the next challenge for this artist/designer. He designed an etching press that does what a press can be expected to do but he sees that there is an improvement that needs to be made in his offering. 868 Words. 2005.

vp051129
Emeralda Instrumentation
Scale Model Etching Presses and Sailing Ships
After an encounter with an artist from Oregon who purchased the 17th Mini Halfwood Press, the inventor of Emeralda: Games for the Gifts of Life describes how the press might be an instrument for playing his fantasy game. Anticipation is the key. 709 Words. 2005.

vp051209
Remembering Lisel
Reflections on a 99-year old Artist
Distributing a videotape for Lisel Salzer who reached 98 years of age, sending another shipment to her retailer gives cause to think how her artist's work has helped to keep her brain alive, and how Emeralda can do this for players. 614 Words. 2005.

vp051224
A Fair Affair
Considering the Seattle Print Fair
The Seattle Print Fair occurs once a year, and this year he's been allowed a space at the fair where he can demonstrate intaglio printmaking with a Mini Halfwood Press. It's a fine opportunity to show people the mysteries of the technique and meet people. 412 Words. 2005.

vp060103
Calendars as Literature
Considering Trumba as a Writing Instrument
When talking with someone about a digital online calendar and how to use it in the creative art world, this artist—who uses writing as part of his daily routine—considers how the calendar could figure in a kind of cyber-writing, making fiction on the Web. 902 Words. 2006.

vp060113
Quarter-Hour Investment Club
A Modest Proposal to Create a Non-dues Income Stream
Living as he is in a community (known as Cornerstone Condos) and prone to publish his oddball ideas about condo living, this artist is often told he needs to find a better way to use his creativity. What better way than to create a non-dues income stream? 1053 Words. 2006.

vp060123
Everything you need to be a Successful Printmaker
A Shopping List for the Outsider

He sells etching presses that he designed for the newbie of intaglio printing, and now he designs a self-teaching package to go with it. His long-held dream is to reach out to people who cannot get to an urban printmaking center and help them get started. 910 Words. 2006.

vp060602
Surprise Payoff
Reflection and Legacy
This artist was, in his younger days, noted for his printmaking, which he says evolved to newer mediums such as video and computer graphics. Not stopping there he pushed the idea of multimedia further until digital games became an obsession as a producer. 527 Words. 2006.

vp060612
Condopolis
The Game of Condo Living
This article has not been written yet. It is an idea in the making. 33 Words. 2006.

vp060612b
The Impatient Muse
Restoring cast-off frames in Ellensburg
A frame becomes his muse as an inspiration for non-profit institution in Ellensburg where restoring cast-off frames provides some student jobs. 605 Words. 2006.

vp060702
Copy Writing Kanter's Article Back to College
By Bill Ritchie Copy-writing over Rosabeth Moss Kanter
The Kanter article, Back to College, appeared in the AARP magazine July/August issue of 2006. Bill was struck not only by the message in the article but also by the fictional opening date: 2012, which is the 20th anniversary of his EarthSafe 2022 project. 1839 Words. 2006.

vp060702b
Take your own Advice
Developing a proposal for an advanced leadership school in Ellensburg
Telling Mr. Nemeth at CWU that they need to take an additional step in their survey to find out what senior citizens would require if they are to move to Ellensburg is not enough. You will need to demonstrate to him what you're talking about. 687 Words. 2006.

vp060722
Artist's Life Insurance
A New Definition of Life Insurance
Life is a glorious experience and it's beyond the power of money to attain. A spiritual definition of life, it cannot be obtained by building up monetary wealth. Financial wealth makes a target out of a person and their family. 684 Words. 2006.

vp060801
Being Un-cool about School
An Art Professor for a New Age of Schools

Instead of becoming part of the school, the professor will stay on the sidelines and teach. Imagine a class, not a class in the normal sense but an informal meeting, a club or team meeting, connecting art and video games. 956 Words. 2006.

vp060811
Learning Community Curriculum
Designing an Advanced Leadership School
This retired art professor never wanted to leave the university but with his vision of the future it was necessary to launch himself out of his comfort zone and search for a new kind of school. Now, thanks to technology, he thinks that new school is here. 573 Words. 2006.

vp060831
A Game for Legacy Transfer
Reino and Arnie Remembered
Reino Randall was a developer in the art education field. By Reino's example the author saw how technologies could assist in art teaching. How to keep Reino's legacy alive is to put his poster collection to work, the Randall Poster Project. 925 Words. 2006.

vp060910
What you need for Online Art Education
Advice from the Son of the Pioneers
The author's job is to help people learn about art using the newest technologies, the Internet and digital storage media. He will show how to make prints online. 992 Words. 2006.

vp061010
Putanesca Video 'N Print Style
A Recipe from Minnie's Kitchen
There is no article, an idea in the making. 33 Words. 2006.

vp061020
Writing Habits
Cultivating My Outlook
The outlook are the habits of using new technologies causing an artist to think differently and produce works that look and feel differently; the artist and machine in the 21st Century—the age of digital reproduction. 414 Words. 2006.

vp061030
Why did the Artist Cross the Road?
Another Attempt to Explain the Game
An artist explains why and how he crosses over from the visual arts to the literary arts. 661 Words. 2006.

vp061119
The End
Beginning Again
Video 'N Print is the last stage of the printmaker's journey, where he has learned the many facets of the media arts and that he must always return where he started and to know the medium for the first time. 225 Words. 2006.

vp061129
Inventing a Genre
Permission to Invent the Hunt for the Emeralda
Treasure Genre
Peter Brooks gave him permission to proceed
with his idea for Hunt for the Emeralda Treasure,
a novel he has made additions every day. His genre
requires work in spreadsheet, database, graphics
and hypertext. 459 Words. 2006.

vp061209
Epilogue for My Classmates
An Invitation to Follow a New Road
There is a 4th option for writers in the 21st Centu-
ry: Games. Narrative writing for video games is a
new option. 518 Words. 2006.

vp061209b
Prologue for my Classmates
Who is James Whistler Oddly?
James found part of the Emeralda Treasure and
he didn't even realize it. From his upload, you will
meet a few others who make up the island's Amateur Archeology Club. 572 Words. 2006.

vp070113
First Day at the 7th Print Fair
2007's Print Honoring S.W. Hayter
It's the first of the two-day Seattle Print Fair. The
artist loads the car with three Mini Halfwood
Presses and everything he need to show how intaglio prints are made. This year he created a print
that honors S. W. Hayter. 422 Words. 2007.

vp070123
Searching for a Lost Community
University to Triangle Studios to What?
We felt we belonged to something important and
wonderful—the university experience. But the
students' lives were short, there. A few formed
another community to make up for what they'd
lost when they graduated, Triangle Studios. 415
Words. 2007.

vp070602
Video 'N Print – 4th Day
Printmaking is Essential for Technology
The technical relationship is clear: prints have
always been essential in developing technology,
from complex blueprints back, in the old days, to
illustrations made reproducible by carving images
in wood blocks. 2391 Words. 2007.

vp070811
Getting Started
Bundling Index Cards
Bundle them into ten sets of 36 cards, and bind
them with a tie. Preferably use a strip of paper.
Paste the end of the strip, wrap it around the bun-
dle, and paste the other end so it sticks nice and
tight. 357 Words. 2007.

vp071020
A First
Feedback in the form of a Stamp

Over coffee with a friend, the author of Halfwood
Press – The Story sees the first instance of feedback
from the four-month effort of making the book. It
comes in the form of a stamp that his friend pasted
into his book, a stamp he received months earlier.
467 Words. 2007.

vp071030
Scope for Fiction
Sorting through a Treasure of Lost Words
"A Scope for Fiction," constantly hammers in his
head, calling for attention, wanting definition. He's
creating what he calls an ArtGrid as part of a research project to place fragments of a manuscript
into context. Is this a hint on how to play Emeralda? 771 Words. 2007.

vp071129
Imagine a Game for Halfwood `Press Owners
The Feasibility Stage of the Game
He has invented a game and considers himself the
follower of another inventor named Elmer Gates.
Like Gates, he has the problem of finding out
how his inventions can be turned into a profitable
business. He has one clue to consider. 856 Words.
2007.

vp071224
A Game Greater than the Sum of its Parts
Game Invention in the Age of Digital Reproduction
After a party where the author meets up with a
former student and gives her a certain DVD he
made that day, words from two books he's been
re-reading take on a special meaning. He compares the inventiveness of games to the work of
people in a corporation. 749 Words. 2007.

vp080103
I get Glimpses
Hand Stamp Boxes
He is working on the templates for the Emeralda
Artists Trading Cards. His attention wanders to
his hand stamp box and begins to make calcula-
tions for the next box. Other people can change
the look of the box. 302 Words. 2008.

vp080113
Ideal ATC
Searching the Metaphors for Online Artist Trading Cards
Early in the morning the wannabe inventor of an
online game, Emeralda, that entertains and teaches printmaking is struck by a comparison of his
most recent addition to the game—Artist Trading
Cards—to an ongoing free software application
for making blogs. 1049 Words. 2008.

vp080131
I get Glimpses
Hand Stamp Boxes
He is working on the templates for the Emeralda
Artists Trading Cards, his attention wanders to his
hand stamp box and begins to make calculations
for the next box. Other people can change the look

of the box. 350 Words. 2008.

vp080202
Emeralda Grant
Proposal to Make a Fine Art Game
After a coffee shop discussion between two creatives about fine art and computer games, they consider writing a grant to take their idea higher where other artists can make use of it. This essay gives the background and describes the problem and solution. 971 Words. 2008.

vp080212
Knowledge Art
Coming Out of the Woods
A visit from a new friend awakens in this artist a sense that despite his friend's wide knowledge of regional art and artists he doesn't have a deep knowledge of this artist himself. He concludes it is because he has taken on a different kind of artistry. 448 Words. 2008.

vp080222
Hard Fun
Collector Precision in the Age of Digital Reproduction
Filling a database and connecting data to a spreadsheet is not fun, nor was it intended to be. No more than double entry bookkeeping were introduced in Italy in the 15th Century—nor the use of the type chase in Germany. It is hard fun, this artist thinks. 328 Words. 2008.

vp080303
Metaphor Redefined
Inventing New Type of Winning a Game
Games like Scrabble and Monopoly give us lessons, an increased vocabulary, a sense of real estate investment, and a few laughs. A really great game, like a great artwork, gives us ongoing rewards of both tangible and intangible kinds. 479 Words. 2008.

vp080323
Aiming Ahead
Moving Targets in the Age of Digital Reproduction
He is inventing the game, Emeralda, while he plays it. He tries various strategies. This is a game in which collectible cards are the method of play; in this essay he explains how you must artfully make the cards for the game at the same time you play it. 407 Words. 2008.

vp080402
Grail Thinking
CWU Program and Scholarship Development Funds
Join me in a search for the Holy Grail of CWU program and scholarship development funds for the College of Arts and Humanities. Align donations to art in the age of digital reproduction, we will find wonderful things. 928 Words. 2008.

vp080412

Renewing Goals
Kansas Calls
An email message from a professor in Kansas gives pause to this professor in Seattle. The email suggests a visit to the Midwest University to give a workshop and display. While this may be in keeping with the author's goals, he has to wonder how it is so. 863 Words. 2008.

vp080512
Operationalizing Ideas
Fifth in a 12-part series on the tasks of a Distance Learning Manager
To make his ideas operable—that is the task of the Operationalizing manager. The press is operational. The DGBLI is a concept that has yet to be applied. 1728 Words. 2008.

vp080522
Business Things
Viewing the Zachman Framework from the Perspective of Cell C1
A co-worker hands to him a chart titled Enterprise Architecture – A Framework made by an IBM pioneer in computer hardware and software design, John Zachman. Now the author, an art teacher, tries an interpretation of it for his Learning Printmaking Online. 1204 Words. 2008.

vp080601
Planning Locations
The Digital Estate of Emeralda
Playing Zach Man!, the author takes the role of Planner, addressing the scope, in the context of Emeralda Works with a focus on the Where of the Enterprise, the matter of a list of locations in which the Business Operates. He confronts the digital estate. 724 Words. 2008.

vp080611
Work Flow Model
Fast paced innovation
Tom Peters influenced the author one time. Now he is in the role of Owner in the Zachman chart, thinking about people. In the role of Owner—on Owner's row—Zachman says he must contemplate the Work Flow Model, where he decides what People equals, or means. 775 Words. 2008.

vp080621
Timing Definition
Subcontractors can earn income in Emeralda
In this exercise of learning the meaning of the Zachman Enterprise Architecture, the playing of Zach Man! the D. G. Smith DVD may be a useful model because it touches on the aspect of the economics of Emeralda, how subcontractors earn money on his assets. 777 Words. 2008.

vp080701
Scope – Contextual
Teach people to make presses
He returned to this essay two and one-half years after making it a self-assigned project to understand a chart given to him by David Lotz. The

chart was by Zachman, and his task became a game he titled, Zach Man! Sounds a little like Pac Man, does it not? 403 Words. 2008.

vp080711
Twenty Things that hold you Back
A method to remove blockades
A public speaker and business coach named Goldsmith produced a program, but it didn't fit this author's need, so he wrote his own version. At the end of the exploration of the idea of ending useless activity, he sees four cards that may constitute a game. 1534 Words. 2008.

vp080721
Company Man
Talking about his job
Playing the role of a company man working for a distance learning product developer, the author describes what he does, his job in the course of a day's work—which is to write a synopsis for a backstory to serve the design for digital game based learning. 639 Words. 2008.

vp080810
Joy of a Nellie
Steps to the rich text professor
An empty art gallery is what many artists dream about discovering—a space that appears to them like an open invitation to fill it with their art and gain wide recognition. This artist is also a professor, so an empty gallery appears to him to be a school. 1244 Words. 2008.

vp080820
Joy of a Nellie
Steps to the Rich Text Professor
An empty art gallery is what many artists dream about discovering—a space that appears to them like an open invitation to fill it with their art and gain wide recognition. This artist is also a professor, so an empty gallery appears to him to be a school. 1196 Words. 2008.

vp080909
Deep Emeralda
Two cohorts play along
The author says two key cohorts have put in hours of their own time studying the elements of the game—its origins, its reason for being and what Emeralda: Games for the Gifts of Life holds for them as the Payoff; their voluntary work called Deep Emeralda. 337 Words. 2008.

vp080919
Small is Beautiful
Promotional text for a demonstration workshop
Descriptive text: With a focus on innovation, this demo will take the fear out intaglio printmaking--the kind that includes dry point, etching and engraving. The heart of this is a tiny press people love because it permits them to work in any small space. 274 Words. 2008.

vp080920

Emeralda Archivist
What the job is
Mindful of a sense of necessity to define the task of the Emeralda Archivist (a title he made up to describe the job he gave his daughter) the author has put her on the payroll of Emeralda Works, to organize all his writings to include in online teaching. 1042 Words. 2008.

vp081009
Emeralda Archivist
What the job is
Mindful of a sense of necessity to define the task of the Emeralda Archivist (a title he made up to describe the job he gave his daughter) the author has put her on the payroll of Emeralda Works, to organize all his writings to include in online teaching. 1091 Words. 2008.

vp081029
Three-in-One ATC
From cereal boxes to art museums
As the three-in-one card is to be part of 21st Century art, it must link the 1990's ideas with the year 2000 fact that video games are art. The ATC must, in other words, go digital. This is where the current topic—computer enhanced hand printmaking—comes in. 1194 Words. 2008.

vp081208
Etching Press Business for Sale
Investment opportunity
Here is an opportunity to buy a multi-million dollar business that is in its infancy. Given its history, it may appear to be a mere concept. If you think there is a market for art-related tools—and education in their use to include it online then read on. 1293 Words. 2008.

vp081224
Dream Organization
Nighttime habits of an Emeralda visionary
Christmas Eve, his Birthday, having lived 67 years. These things mean less to him than the eve of this Year of Living Copiously, the Gates Prize and thirteenth time he gifted himself rights to start a 360-day year for the development of a teaching career. 1208 Words. 2008.

vp090103
Bring on the Kids
An old professor forecasts how former art students' children will return to printmaking
When he was young and growing his theories about printmaking being the ancestor of new media arts, he thought he would be teaching this to children of his former students. A disruption in his career seemed to end this possibility but was a better pathway. 635 Words. 2009.

vp090113
Who's On First?
The First People on the ELPO Project
The first person to discover Emeralda region (a fantasy land of artists who use computers and

etching presses) takes stock of family and friends who are helping him realize his vision. It's a long list and he likens it to a game to find out who was first. 927 Words. 2009.

vp090123
ELPO Audience
The three-part audience for Emeralda: learn print-making online
The fourth installment in a ten-part series of essays about developing an online, interactive, blend-ed distance learning course. The author wants to create a game-like user interface that goes with a miniature etching press and he's using a book for help. 1190 Words. 2009.

vp090202
If I Could Teach Over
The missing professor's lament and plan for a re-run of his short happy career
The missing professor thinks had he created a curriculum for printmaking students, and stayed with the University Art School, then his fantasy islands would be known and visited by students, former students and the children—maybe even their grandchildren. 386 Words. 2009.

vp090212
Narrative Gaming Elements of ELPO
Fourth in the Ten Step Development Checklist
"Has ELPO (Emeralda: Learn Printmaking On-line) a narrative element to it?" asks C. H. Miller in her book for digital storytellers who want to make games. The inventor of a printmaking course to be taught online says ELPO depends on a good scope for fiction. 1444 Words. 2009.

vp090304
Secret Library of Dusty Cann
Dusty and the secret room
Dusty Cann is one of ten protagonists in an un-published manuscript for a semi-fictional back story of a game-based user interface for fine art students learning printmaking online. He is a li-brarian who discovers a special collection in an island village. 479 Words. 2009.

vp090314
Benefits of Learning Printmaking Online
Ten reasons to invest in Emeralda: learn print-making online
As an artist and professor in higher education and the inventor of a digital-game-like user interface for a fine arts online course, the author provides ten reasons why people taking his printmaking course at this time think it makes a good deal of sense. 1377 Words. 2009.

vp090413
James Oddly Profile
Character description of Professor Oddly in "Hunt for the Emeralda Treasure"
People on Video 'N Print island believe that print-ing images that they take from video recordings helps make their wild fantasies come true. The

ease of video and other electronic image making migrates into prints so fantasy assumes a big role in society. 511 Words. 2009.

vp090523
Moment Numbers
Elemental time and space code words for ELPO
20th Century artist printmakers used edition numbers as part of their art's provenance. They did not consider edition numbers to be important, but to the publisher, art dealer and collector they were, and are. Moment numbers replace edition numbers today. 1853 Words. 2009.

vp090612
Screenplay Blender
Writing back story, screenplay and scripts for ELPO
Taking on the project of a blended online print-making course gets complicated when your online presence must assume a virtual role, playing in a virtual world. You must be a writer as well as a printmaker and you must write in both real and virtual forms. 942 Words. 2009.

vp090801
Writer's Respite
Taking a moment to think about writing for a mo-ment
The author's goal in life was always to be a teach-er—a Great Teacher. After reading about a unique individual named Elmer Gates, his life and his commitment to education, he determined that to reach his goal he would have to take an unusual course: Games. 1447 Words. 2009.

vp091020
Treatment Plan
Back Story for a hundred years
He wants to write a treatment for Act II of a screenplay about a woman who is on a rescue mis-sion in a strange, heavily guarded but lovely artist's paradise—front for a doomsday plan requiring the artists creative process to end human life sus-tainability. 1137 Words. 2009.

vp091209
Hi from Issey
Metaphors, plagiarism and copying
The author writes about his story about the Em-eralda Region natives as being free to be who they were by looking like something or someone else. He carries this idea into his printmaking game. He writes about changing pictures and texts for his game. 415 Words. 2009.

vp091229
Another Back Story
The search for the story of the Halfwood Press
He's written so many back stories for his intended game he's losing count. Each time a new audience for learning printmaking online appears, with a unique computer game (or board game, collectible card game, etc.) at its core, a new story comes to his min 111 Words. 2009.

(No image, this is not an island)

Interval (AKA IN)

In Emeralda game play all the Winners of the Gates Prize go first to Emeralda City for a period of four or five days depending on whether a leap year is in effect.

Interval is not illustrated as it isn't an island but merely a holding place, like a school located in Emeralda City where newcomers and repeat Gates Prize winners are acquainted with the practices, laws, ethics and other related topics to be followed during the residents' stay.

in921212 Introduction to Interval
A brief history
Nineteen-ninety two was the first year of naming Emeralda Region, therefore "Interval" had not been documented. In the summer of 1992, I read the Union of Concerned Scientists', "World's Scientists Warning to Humanity," from a pamphlet I picked up on a Guemes Island workshop by Lane Parks. 186 words. 1992.

in021214 Searching for Emeralda
(The) Work of Art in the Age of Digital Reproduction
A professor blends art, pedagogy and technology, re-inventing arts studios. His goal is to use on-line gaming to renew art's core values. Discovering a literature professor using on-line games to develop students' critical skills, he studies this example. 5991 Words. 2002.

in031210
What artists can do about the future of their field
Geography professor lights the way of ITinerate professor.
In a summary of a geography professor's article, an art professor copies over the text to find a perfect match for what may well be good advice for artists. Art teachers should not rest on the laurels of past successes and be misled by student enthusiasm. 539 Words. 2003.

in031211
Net Effect on Students' Choices of Schools
Getting faculty assets online
What effect has the net had on the way students make choices of schools? In the arts, they can learn more about the college and its faculty than they could before the Internet—if the information they seek has been made available by the faculty themselves. 964 Words. 2003.

in031213
My Purpose at Madrona

Mission Statement and More
In one month he is to become the first Artist-in-Residence at Madrona School, a start-up 100 miles north of his longtime home. He writes about his plans, the main of which is to see his game, Emeralda, approach reality and give his artistry a new context. 1513 Words. 2003.

in031214
Going Where There Is No There
My first trip to Emeralda Madrona
His "games for the gifts of life" are a tabula rasa on which he can play for a chance at a future of production, learning, teaching, research and service. Playing Emeralda is a high risk, high stakes game and he finds life assurance in taking his chances. 1034 Words. 2003.

in041210
A Calendar To Love
Year at a glance for Emeralda Players
It is the first day of Interval, 2005, the five-day period between the 360-day cycles that make up an Emeralda Year. The game's inventor pauses to think what kind of calendar he would like to see—both on paper and on his screen, and here's the description. 591 Words. 2004.

in041211
Goals of the Mini Halfwood Press
A personal reminder
The author, a sixtyish artist and teacher, reminds himself in this essay as to what are the long-term goals for his designing of the Mini Halfwood Press, a bench top etching press that he designed with the help of another wisdom boomer, a steel craftsman. 861 Words. 2004.

in041212
Getting Help with Emeralda
Advice comes from new owners of Mini Halfwood Presses
A review of the progress he's made so far in creating Emeralda: Games for the Gifts of Life, the author realizes he needs help—help from the owners of Mini Halfwood Presses, for example. He's only outline the game; now he needs people to fill in the gaps. 516 Words. 2004.

in041213
Emeralda Soul Mates
Community assurance begins with two
In his fourth day of Interval, the author realizes he has more in common with his friend Tom, the steelwright, than he had thought. Both in their sixties, and possessing skills and knowledge so unique to their art and craft that they can't be transferred. 623 Words. 2004.

in051210
Remembering Sweecy
Thoughts of the past, a lens on the future
He got an email message from his alma mater, giving him ideas for the first day of Interval—the interim period between Emeralda Years of Living

Copiously. Was it truly the place where he got the start on his "interesting life," as he said in his response? 1131 Words. 2005.

in051211
Sinking Emeralda
How a Russian cabin boy saved her story
An image of a Spanish ship sinking beneath a tsunami wave haunts the author and, to resolve the puzzle of its meaning, he writes what must have happened that led up to the tragedy of the sinking of the ship, the Emeralda and the loss of everyone on board. 507 Words. 2005.

in051212
Big Interval
Flight of the imagination
Having been reminded of his roots at a small state college in central Washington State, the one-time professor contemplates his situation today as the end of one long interval in his life and the beginning of a new one. It's like the start of a new game. 580 Words. 2005

in051213
Absence of Music
Searching for 21st Century musicians
Considering the musically-talented people who were part of his best years as a college professor and who moved him and his students into new explorations of media and art, this author suggests that a college campus lacks something to perpetuate creativity. 864 Words. 2005.

in051214
Allegory for Fun
A paradigm for looking for the gifts of life
He is drawing plans for a sea chest, that kind he used to see depicted in stories about buried treasure. As he draws, stories come back to him, like Treasure Island, tales of pirates and sunken ships. These converge in his design, and make it like a game. 761 Words. 2005.

in061212
A Year in Review
Having forgotten to write
On the fourth day into Interval I realized I had not written down any of my thoughts, whereas last year I attributed five essays to Interval. It is because many things had taken me away from my studio and away from my keyboard—things of little importance. 295 Words. 2006.

in061213
Aphorism
Capturing a 2006 entry
Ulises Carrion said he believed he lived when creating an archive of artists' books could be a work of art—a difficult thing to grasp for people who only think in the times when such a thing would have been impossible to conceive. Here we get one example. 464 Words. 2006.

in061214

Emeralda Society
Examining Emeralda startup of a Year of Living Copiously
The Gates Prize winner tries to imagine his upcoming Year Eleven, the 11th Year of Living Copiously. Since 1996 he has been awarding himself the YOLC—the equivalent of The Gate Prize, and Gifts for the Game of Life—under the aegis of the Emeralda Society. 455 Words. 2006.

in071210
Notes on prisoners
Like being tied to your dreams
The idea is that he is a prisoner of his dreams, or, as in the lyrics to "Poncho and Lefty," "saddled to your dreams." As a prisoner, one must have a partner, a ghost perhaps, in the new machine that is the computer and all its connectivity. 350 Words. 2007.

in071212
Interviewing the Prisoner
Notes from a cell
A short comment while working on ideas for a game based on Prisoner's Dilemma. He's sitting at a computer typing numbers in little cells of a spreadsheet. It's monotonous, meaningless work. I wonder if he is happy? 166 words. 2007.

in071214
Advanced Artist Trading Cards
Linking artist's intellectual property and legacy transfer
The inventor of Emeralda seeks ways to link his notion of artists' intellectual property and legacy transfer to recognized games and interests. Here he tries to link Artists' Trading Cards to creating databases which can be accessed on artists' Web sites. 390 Words. 2007.

in081209
Interval 2008 Day One
Study of past Intervals and discovery of Susan Gleason
Reviewing past INTERVAL sessions, I found a reference to Susan Gleason (See Interval 2002). To search for her, and the status of her organization at that time—SPINWIRE—I Googled her. But I put in Ann Gleason by mistake, which took me on an erroneous path. 343 Words. 2008.

in081210
Flathead Lake Epiphany Revisited
Reflections on lessons taught by a dead professor
On the shore of the fantasy lake, the Great Lake of Emeralda Region, an artist—calling himself an ITinerate professor (identifying with information technologists and capitalizing the first two letters) reflects on a life-changing epiphany experienced in 1983. 670 Words. 2008.

in081211
Bell Curve for a Year of Living Copiously
Planning the 13th Gates Prize
What will the author, winner of the Gates Prize—

for his thirteenth time—do in his coming Year of Living Copiously? This is the question given to the newcomers and the returning prize winners during the third day of Interval 2008. He pictures a bell-curve. 1136 Words. 2008.

in081212
What Is Interval?
Introduction to Emeralda game play
In Emeralda game play all the Winners of the Gates Prize go first to Emeralda City for a period of five or six days, a holding period for these winners (and also past winners). During these five days they learn the rules they will obey for the coming year. 954 Words, 2008.

in081213
Chinese Halfwood
A vast idea without even a half vast plan.
The story of how an unlikely design for a hand printing press found its way into the hands of a Chinese entrepreneur and how he realized the surprisingly vast, worldwide market for it. It is told by the art professor who invented the design, with regrets. 2079 Words. 2008

in081214
Carolyn Handler Miller Overwrite
Copy written over Carolyn Handler Miller's "Digital Storytelling"
He believes his Emeralda merges a single entertaining and educational property over multiple platforms or venues. Finding Carole Handler Miller recitation, her words stir him deeply. Ventures of these kinds are cross-media productions or integrated media. 1433 Words. 2008.

in091210
REO Metaphor1210
Using REO games as metaphors
This printmaking professor toys with a game made by the classic rock group REO SpeedWagon. He finds it to be identical in purpose to his own needs, i.e., re-forming an artist's legacy so it fits in with today's art form—the interactive video games format. 257 Words. 2009.

in091211
Metaphor Collection
Screen shots from REO and Games in Thiagi news
Pursuing the elusive form of his plan for teaching printmaking online with the use of a game-like user interface, the "missing professor" studies graphic pages from a new video game. As the list of saved and altered images grows, he begins a list of them. 469 Words. 2009.

in091212
Story Arc
Printmaking Camp back story
The author is coming to a decisive stage in his plan to write a back story for a certain kind of computer game. He's been focused on a game for grown-ups; now he's faced with the possibility it's better to write one for young people or a multi-generation.

111 Words. 2009.

in091213
Children's Game
Thoughts on a video game for printmaking camp
He's a printmaker who thinks he has a different way of looking at prints and printmaking. The art is not like painting and drawing, but more like playing music. What would a learning game look like if he made one to teach this to kids? Here are his ideas. 1270 Words. 2009

in091213
Children's Game
Thoughts on a video game for printmaking camp
He's a printmaker who thinks he has a different way of looking at prints and printmaking. The art is not like painting and drawing, but more like playing music. What would a learning game look like if he made one to teach this to kids? Here are his ideas. 1270 Words. 2009.

About Bill Ritchie

A world traveled art professor, a teacher of people of all ages, at eighteen Bill Ritchie took up printmaking the year he left his father's farm. At twenty-five he moved to Seattle to teach at the University of Washington. He is a visionary and innovator—considered by some to be a little edgy.

Seeing Seattle as a center of high-tech industries, he challenged students to expand hand printing and incorporate new technologies for education and design. He extended his teaching university-level printmaking though non-conforming with traditional standards.

For over 50 years he exhibited in art exhibitions ranging from traditional visual arts, through electronic arts, to installations and performances. For nineteen years, the university supported his research and enabled him to travel around the world.

Educated in state universities in Washington and California, he was hired at age 25 to teach art at the University of Washington in Seattle, with emphasis on printmaking. He expanded his teaching to include video and computer art. Believing that regional technologies would be useful to his teaching in the future, he took early retirement at age 44 and started his own studio for teaching, research, practice and services.

He served as an adjunct professor at The Evergreen State University, University of Oregon, Highline and Shoreline Community Colleges. He and his wife opened the Mini Art Gallery in 2008 for a permanent working and display space.

For his visual arts, teaching, research and design he won 74 awards, fellowships, grants and prizes. Fifty-nine events included his participation in honors and his contributions. He had 29 solo shows and participated in 249 mixed visual art exhibitions worldwide with works being collected by 582 individuals and 61 public and corporate collections.

Bill provided for 109 events in public speaking, consulting and workshops on printmaking techniques and history, new technologies and cultural arts entrepreneurship, many with other artists and designers to develop art installations, computer-aided business models and design, manufacturing, marketing and sales of his line of Halfwood etching presses and printmaking toys.

He produced over 200 short videos for sharing on YouTube and Vimeo on subjects ranging from printmaking techniques utilizing his printing press designs to personal musings on art education, research, northwest fine art printmaking history and storytelling.

Bill writes essays, fiction and screenplays for elucidation and pleasure, but is also included in books, newspapers, newsletters, radio interviews and TV features. He self-published 37 books ranging from pure speculation to entertainment, allegory and biography.

He lives and works with his wife in Seattle. Together they own the Mini Art Gallery, located in the Uptown neighborhood at 812 5th Avenue North, C-2. Their daughter, Nellie Sunderland, assists them with database entry, and also online sales through Etsy.com. Bill's work can also be seen on his personal website, www.seanet.com/~ritchie, and Fine Art America - a provisioner of consumer products based on Bill's art.

Thanks to Nellie Sunderland and Lynda Ritchie

Since the 1990's, Nellie Sunderland nee Ritchie has taken on the task of committing to digital media much of Bill Ritchie's written and video work. She transcribed the sound tracks from numerous video and audio tapes, for example so they could be put on the Internet and also used in printed material.

Starting in 2008 she was hired as a half-time employee. Bill and Lynda needed her as an assistant asset manager, and that was when she began formatting the thousands of headings of Bill's essays for this publication.

Her work entails skills in Microsoft Office, including Word, Excel and Access. To reformat Bill's visual arts she uses PhotoShop. The production of Ritchie Mined would not have been possible without her work on it.

Nellie also participates in arts and crafts groups in her community. She lives in Seattle with her Husband, Mike.

Without Lynda's constant support, Bill Ritchie could never have accomplished what he set out to do. From the time they were in high school together, through years of college and graduate school, Lynda stayed with the journey.

The essays in this volume begin in the 1960s and while she's seldom mentioned in the text of Bill's musings, were it not for the fact that he could count on her to be with him throughout his quest, he would have accomplished little.

When Nellie joined in to help - and she did so long before she was a paid employee - Bill's family team was stronger. At the time he and Lynda formalized their wills, they realized that if Bill's art and assorted intellectual capital were not cataloged in some manner, all of it would be lost.

When Lynda and Nellie worked together, for example, in photographing thousands of artworks in the Ritchie Family Collection, it was gratifying for Bill. Seldom does an artist find such help in his or her family.

Available on Kindle

"Ritchie Mined" was first published in 2010 as a Kindle book because color images were possible in e-books and color reproductions on paper were too costly. The Kindle version is still available at the time this paperback version was released.

However, in the original Kindle version, instead of producing all eleven sections in one big Kindle file, each *Island-of-domain-of-expertise* per publication was produced as one book.

On amazon.com, this will display all ten Kindle versions of the islands' essays, or 'Zines. The reader may be pleased to know that Kindle books can be read on any device - desktop or mobile - with amazon's utility, which is free. Of course amazon's tablet, *Fire*, is an ideal option.

On amazon.com (the only source of Kindle books) the reader will find them on a browser by entering the words: *Ritchie Mined*. They will look like the images below and at the right.

ArtsPort 'Zines (Ritchie Mined Book 1) Aug 15, 201(
by Bill Ritchie
Kindle Edition
$0.00
Read this and over 1 million books with Kindle Unlimited.
$9⁹⁵ to buy
Get it TODAY, May 2

E'Studios Zines (Ritchie Mined Book 2) Sep 18, 201(
by Bill Ritchie
Kindle Edition
$0.00
Read this and over 1 million books with Kindle Unlimited.
$9⁹⁵ to buy
Get it TODAY, May 2

Note, too, that by signing up for *Kindle Unlimited* customers enjoy the freedom to explore over 1 million titles, thousands of audiobooks, and current magazines on any device for $9.99 a month, and sometimes amazon offers a free trial period.

MacRitchie's 'Zines (Ritchie Mined Book 4) Oct 6, 2
by Bill Ritchie
Kindle Edition
$0.00
Read this and over 1 million books with Kindle Unlimited.
$9⁹⁵ to buy
Get it TODAY, May 2

O'Studios 'Zines (Ritchie Mined Book 4) Oct 18, 20
by Bill Ritchie
Kindle Edition
$0.00
Read this and over 1 million books with Kindle Unlimited.
$9⁹⁵ to buy
Get it TODAY, May 2

Perfect Press 'Zines (Ritchie Mined Book 5) Oct 2(
by Bill Ritchie
Kindle Edition
$0.00
Read this and over 1 million books with Kindle Unlimited.
$9⁹⁵ to buy
Get it TODAY, May 2

Perfect Studios 'Zines (Ritchie Mined Book 6) No
by Bill Ritchie
Kindle Edition
$0.00
Read this and over 1 million books with Kindle Unlimited.
$9⁹⁵ to buy
Get it TODAY, May 2

RIISMA 'Zines (Ritchie Mined Book 7) Nov 7, 2010
by Bill Ritchie
Kindle Edition
$0.00
Read this and over 1 million books with Kindle Unlimited.
$9⁹⁵ to buy
Get it TODAY, May 2

SPEACON 'Zines (Ritchie Mined Book 8) Nov 24, 20
by Bill Ritchie
Kindle Edition
$0.00
Read this and over 1 million books with Kindle Unlimited.
$9⁹⁵ to buy
Get it TODAY, May 2

Video 'Zines (Ritchie Mined Book 9) Dec 11, 2010
by Bill Ritchie and Nellie Sunderland
Kindle Edition
$0.00
Read this and over 1 million books with Kindle Unlimited.
$9⁹⁵ to buy
Get it TODAY, May 2

Video 'N Print 'Zines (Ritchie Mined Book 10) De
by Bill Ritchie and Nellie Sunderland
Kindle Edition
$0.00
Read this and over 1 million books with Kindle Unlimited.
$9⁹⁵ to buy
Get it TODAY, May 2

www.ingramcontent.com/pod-product-compliance
Lightning Source LLC
Chambersburg PA
CBHW030302290526
45785CB00001B/180